DICTIONARY
OF
PSYCHOLOGY

Second Revised Edition

J. P. Chaplin, Ph.D.

A LAUREL BOOK
Published by
Dell Publishing Co., Inc.
1 Dag Hammarskjold Plaza
New York, New York 10017

Laurel ® TM 674623, Dell Publishing Co., Inc.

ISBN: 0-440-31925-0

Printed in the United States of America
Second Revised Edition
First printing—October 1985

Contents

Introduction

This dictionary of psychological terms has been designed to explain the meanings of technical terms in psychology. Terms from the related disciplines of psychoanalysis, psychiatry, and biology have been freely included where these have found wide usage in the literature of psychology. A number of semipopular terms and terms from the literature of pseudopsychology and spiritualism have been included for the convenience of those who may find these terms discussed in psychological or popular writing. Because many of the more specialized terms have been deliberately coined by writers who wish to convey special meanings, the names of responsible individuals or schools have been included in many instances.

Every attempt has been made to render accurate, concise, and meaningful definitions. Technical jargon has been avoided as far as it is possible to do so without loss of accuracy. Pronunciation has not been included, since readers rarely consult a technical dictionary for this purpose and because most technical terms are derived from easily pronounced Latin and Greek word elements. Occasionally variant spellings have been indicated where these are commonly found in the literature. In general, the use of hyphenated forms and old spellings has been eliminated, consistent with the parallel tendency to eliminate such forms in general English usage. No attempt has been made to suggest guidelines for usage among different definitions of the same term. It would certainly be desirable if all psychologists could agree on the meaning of such terms as *reinforcement* or *emotion*, but until such agreement has been reached, the user's theoretical or systematic position will have to serve as his guide.

In the case of the more central concepts of psychology, such as memory, perception, the schools of psychology and theories of learning, and of the discussion under *psychology*, the entries have been made encyclopedic rather than lexicographical, on the assumption that these entries will be consulted primarily by student readers or laymen in search of somewhat extended discussions of these topics. For much the same reason, short biographies of famous men of the prescientific period who contributed to psychology, founders of schools, and prominent contemporary theorists have been included. A listing of special topics follows this introduction.

Every effort has been made to make this dictionary comprehensive without including rarely used or highly specialized terms. A thorough search of the recent literature in the field, especially that published during the past six years, was carried out in order to include many new terms not found in earlier dictionaries and glossaries, particularly in the areas of physiological psychology, personality theory, social psychology, and information processing theory. However, it is acknowledged that there will be inadvertent omissions in a work of this scope. For these the editor bears sole responsibility and asks that such omissions be called to his attention by readers.

The editor wishes to express his thanks to his professional colleagues at the University of Vermont and at St. Michael's College. Their unflagging interest and encouragement during the entire course of the project is deeply appreciated. Particular thanks are due to Dr. Robert Lavallee, Dr. Barry Krikstone, Dr. Vincent Naramore, and to Dr. H. L. Ansbacher, whose comprehensive knowledge of the field is matched only by his unlimited patience in assisting with numerous difficult concepts. Thanks are also due Dr. Eugene Hartley, who read portions of the manuscript for the first edition and made numerous helpful suggestions.

J. P. CHAPLIN

Burlington, Vermont

SPECIAL NAMES AND TOPICS IN PSYCHOLOGY FOR WHICH EXTENDED ARTICLES WILL BE FOUND IN THIS DICTIONARY.

Appendix A

ABBREVIATIONS COMMONLY USED IN PSYCHOLOGY

A: 1. amplitude. 2. age. 3. the albedo. 4. (*Murray*) ambitendency.

AA: 1. achievement age. 2. Alcoholics Anonymous.

ACE: American Council on Education.

ACH: acetylcholine.

ACHE: Acetylcholinesterase.

ACTH: adrenocorticotropic hormone.

AD: average deviation.

ADH: antidiuretic hormone.

AGCT: Army General Classification Test.

AI: anxiety index.

AL: 1. adaptation level. 2. absolute limen or threshold.

ANS: autonomic nervous system.

AQ: achievement quotient.

ARAS: ascending reticular activating system.

BMR: basal metabolic rate.

C: 1. a constant. 2. a controlled variable. 3. Centigrade. 4. Celsius.

c: a statistical correction.

CA: chronological or life age.

CAVD: completion, arithmetic, vocabulary and directions (test).

CE: constant error.

CER: conditioned emotional response.

CFF: critical flicker frequency.

CNS: central nervous system.

CR: 1. critical ratio. 2. conditioned response.

CS: conditioned stimulus.

Cs: conscious.

CVC: trigram nonsense syllable—consonant, vowel, consonant.

d: 1. a deviation from the mean. 2. a difference in rank between two sets of values.

DA: dopamine.

dB: decibel.

df: degrees of freedom.

DL: difference limen or threshold.

DNA: deoxyribonucleic acid.

DR: an increment of response.

DSM III: *Diagnostic and Statistical Manual of Mental Disorders*, 3rd ed.

E: 1. the experimenter; *pl*. Es. 2. environment. 3. excitatory tendency.

e: the base of the natural logarithms: 2.7182. 2. an error.

EA: educational age.

EEG: electroencephalogram.

EKG: electrocardiogram.

EMG: electromyogram.

EQ: educational quotient.

ERG: electroretinogram.

ESP: extrasensory perception.

ESPS: excitatory postsynaptic potential.

EST: electroshock therapy.

ETS: Educational Testing Service.

F: Fahrenheit.

f: 1. frequency. 2. fluency, a factor ability. 3. function.

F_1, (F_2, F_3, . . . F_n): the first (second, third, . . . *n*th) generation

FFF: flicker-fusion frequency.

FSH: follicle stimulating hormone.

G: 1. goal. 2. a general intellectual factor or ability.

GABA: gamma-aminobutyric acid.

GAS: general adaptation syndrome.

GG: goal gradient.

Gp: group.

GPS: general problem solver.

GRE: Graduate Record Examination.

GSR: galvanic skin response.

H: the harmonic mean.

Hz: Herz.

I: induction, a primary mental ability.

i: a class interval in a frequency distribution.

IQ: intelligence quotient.

IU: interval of uncertainty.

j.n.d.: just-noticeable difference.

j.n.n.d.: just-not-noticeable difference.

k: 1. the coefficient of alienation. 2. a constant.

L: the limen, or theshold.

l: the lower limit of a class interval.

LH: leutinizing hormone.

LTM: long-term memory.

M: 1. the arithmetic mean. 2. memory ability.

M: a guessed average or mean.

m: a meter.

MA: mental age.

MAT: Miller Analogies Test.

Md: the median.

Mdn: the median.

M_G: the geometric mean.

Mg: a milligram, or 1/1000 gram.

mm: millimeter.

mμ: millimicron.

MMPI: Minnesota Multiphasic Personality Inventory.

Mo: the mode.

ms: millisecond, or 1/1000 second.

msec: millisecond, or 1/1000 second.

MU: (*Heins*) mental units of growth.

mv: mean variation.

M_w: a weighted mean.

N: 1. number of cases. 2 number factor or numerical ability. 3. a symbol for need.

n: 1. number of cases in a subcategory. 2. number of variables. 3. need. 4. nucleus.

NE: norepinephrine.

nm, *nu*: nanometer.

NS: nervous system.

O: 1. observer. 2. organism. 3. oscillation or fluctuation in behavior.

OT: occupational therapy.

P: 1. perceptual speed, a factor ability. 2. probability ratio. 3. a symbol for psychometrist. 4. (*Eysenck*) a symbol for personality organization and stability.

P–: (*Eysenck*) a poorly organized, unstable personality.

p: 1. proportion. 2. probability. 3. a percentile. 4. a symbol for the difficulty of a test item. 5. percentage.

Pcs: the preconscious.

PE: probable error.

PGR: psychogalvanic response (reflex).

PH: a symbol of hydrogen-ion concentration. Distilled water = PH of 7; values higher than 7 indicate alkalinity; values below 7, acidity.

PI: proactive inhibition.

PK: psychokinesis.

PKU: phenylketonuria.

PR: percentile rank.

PSE: point of subjective equality.

Q: quartile deviation.

Q_1, Q_2, Q_3: the first, second, and third quartiles, respectively.

q: the proportion of anything present in a sample.

R: 1. a stimulus (from the German, *Reiz*). 2. a response 3. a multiple correlation coefficient. 4. an abbreviation for Spearman's footrule correlation. 5. reasoning factor or ability.

r: product-moment correlation coefficient.

r$_{bis}$: biserial correlation coefficient.

r$_{12,34}$: partial correlation.

RAS: reticular activating system.

REM: rapid eye movement.

RI: retroactive inhibition.

RL: the absolute threshold (from the German, *Reiz Limen*).

RNA: ribonucleic acid.

RQ: recovery quotient.

RS: the reinforcing stimulus.

RT: reaction time.

R$_t$: tetrachoric correlation.

r$_t$: tetrachoric correlation.

S: 1. a subject in an experiment (*pl.* Ss.). 2. a stimulus. 3. sensation or sensory intensity when R (*Reiz*) is used for stimulus. 4. spatial ability.

s: 1. sensation. 2. in psychophysics, a variable stimulus. 3. (*Spearman*) a specific or specialized ability. 4. standard deviation for sample data.

s^2: variance for sample data.

S$_D$: a drive stimulus.

s$_{\bar{x}}$: standard error of the mean.

s$_{\bar{x}_1-\bar{x}_2}$: standard error of the difference between two sample means.

SAT: Scholastic Aptitude Test.

SD: the standard deviation.

SE: the standard error.

S-O-R: stimulus-organism-response.

SQ34: a symbolic representation of Robinson's formula for efficient learning: *study, question, read, recite, review.*

S-R or **S → R:** stimulus and response; stimulus elicits response.

STM: short-term memory.

SU: sensation unit, a logarithmic unit of loudness corresponding to the decibel.

T: 1. temperature. 2. in psychophysics, a transition point.

t: 1. a ratio of any statistic to the standard error of that statistic. 2. time.

TAT: Thematic Apperception Test.

TE: 1. trial and error learning. 2. time error in psychophysical judgments.

TR: terminal stimulus (from German: *terminalischer Reiz*).

U: upper, in psychophysics.

Ucs: the unconscious.

UR; UCR: unconditioned response.

US; UCS: unconditioned stimulus.

V: 1. verbal ability or verbal factor. 2. variable stimulus.

v: 1. volt. 2. volume. 3. variable. 4. coefficient of variation.

VTE: vicarious trial and error.

W: 1. the Weber fraction. 2. a weight.

w: 1. will factor. 2. a weight.

WAIS: Wechsler Adult Intelligence Scale.

WF: word fluency.

WISC: Wechsler Intelligence Scale for Children.

X: 1. a raw score. 2. a dependent variable.

X̄: the arithmetic mean.

x: a deviation of a class interval from a mean.

x′: a deviation from an assumed mean.

Y: 1. the dependent variable. 2. a raw score of a y distribution.

y: 1. the value of an ordinate or the vertical axis. 2. a derivation from the ordinate value.

z: a standard score.

Appendix B

COMMON RORSCHACH SCORING SYMBOLS

A: animal response.

Ad: animal detail.

Adx: part of an animal where most would see the entire animal.

At: anatomy response.

C: pure color responses.

C': responses determined by black, white, or gray.

c: responses determined by shading that which is seen as a flat surface.

CF: responses determined by color with form secondary.

D: responses involving large detail.

d: responses involving small detail.

dd: responses involving minute detail.

di: a category for inside detail.

Do: impoverished responses indicative of low intelligence.

Ds: responses primarily dependent upon white space.

Dw: responses dominated by interpretations based on figures that are part of blots.

F: responses determined by form.

F–: poor form responses.

F+: good form responses.

FC: form responses influenced by color.

Fc: responses where form is primary, color secondary.

FK: responses where shading is taken to indicate depth.

FM: responses involving animal movement.

FV: see FK.

FY: responses where form is determined by flat gray.

G: responses involving the entire blot.

H: responses involving human figures.

Hd: responses involving human detail.

K: diffusion responses; shading without form, such as clouds.

k: toned-down diffusion.

M: human movement.

m: movement involving inanimate objects.

O: original responses.

P: popular responses.

Q: qualified or reserved responses.

S: responses based on white space.

V: vista responses or those involving depth.

W: whole responses or those involving the entire blot.

Y: responses determined by flat gray.

Z: responses inputing organizations to the blot.

Appendix C

GREEK LETTER SYMBOLS COMMONLY USED IN PSYCHOLOGY

β 12.3, β 12.34, etc. Beta coefficients.

χ Chi-square.

η a correlation ration.

ϕ mean square contingency.

ρ correlation coefficient calculated from rank differences.

Σ sum of.

σ standard deviation.

σ_x standard deviation of scores on x.

σ_y standard deviation of scores on y.

$\sigma_{x.y}$ standard error of estimate of x from y.

$\sigma_{y.x}$ standard error of estimate of y from x.

θ any statistic.

ζ test for linearity of regression.

Appendix D

PREFIXES, SUFFIXES, AND COMBINING FORMS COMMONLY USED IN PSYCHOLOGICAL TERMINOLOGY

P. S OR C F
MEANING   EXAMPLE

a-
  (See AB-; AD-; AN-; ANA-.)

ab- (a-; abs-)
  from; away from   *ab*normal; *a*version; *ab*straction

acro-
  extremity; height   *acro*megaly; *acro*phobia

ad-(a-; ac-; af-; ag-; al-; an-; ap-; ar-; as-; at-) to; toward   *ad*ient; *a*spiration; *af*fect; *ag*gressive; *al*leviate; *an*nihilate; *ap*parent; *ar*rest; *as*sertive; *at*tention

-ad
  to, toward   dors*ad*

-al
  pertaining to; like   genit*al*; saggit*al*

ambi-
  both   *ambi*dextrous; *ambi*valent

an- (a-)
  not; without   *an*osmia; *a*moral

ana- (an-)
  upward; backward; again; excessively   *ana*lysis; *ana*phylaxis; *an*ode

ante-
  before; prior to   *ante*cedent; *ante*natal

antero-
  before; in front of   *antero*grade amnesia

anthropo-
  man   *anthropo*logy

anti-
  opposed to; against   *anti*pathy; *anti*dromic

audio-
  hearing   *audio*meter

P. S OR C F
MEANING   EXAMPLE

auri-
   ear   *auri*cle, *auri*cular
auto-
   self   *auto*nomic, *auto*matic
bi-
   two, double   *bi*sexual
bio-
   life   *bio*logy, *bio*psy
cata-
   downward, low   *cata*bolism
centi-
   hundred, hundredth   *centi*meter, *Centi*grade
cephalo-
   brain, head   *cephalo*caudal index
cerebro-
   brain   *cerebro*tonia
chrom(o)-, chromat(o)-
   color   *chromo*some, *chromat*opthometer
-cide
   destroy, kill   geno*cide*, sui*cide*
contra-
   against, opposite   *contra*indicate
di-
   two   *di*chromatism
dia-
   through, across   *dia*tonic, *dia*gnosis
dis-
   apart, separate   *dis*junctive, *dis*placement
dynamo-
   power, force   *dynamo*meter
dys-
   imperfect, impaired, morbid   *dys*lexia, *dys*genic
ecto-
   outer, outside   *ecto*derm, *ecto*morphy
endo-
   in   *endo*derm
epi-
   upon, above   *epi*dermis
-esthesia
   feeling, sensitivity kin*esthesia*, syn*esthesia*
eu-
   good, normal, agreeable   *eu*genic, *eu*phoria
ex-
   from, out of   *ex*cise, *ex*tirpate

P. S OR C F

MEANING | EXAMPLE

extero-
from outside | *extero*ceptor

-genetic
pertaining to origins | phylo*genetic*

-graph
pertaining to writing | kymo*graph*, electroencephalo*graph*

gyn-, gyno-
woman | *gyn*androus, *gyn*ecology

hebe-
youth | *hebe*phrenia

hema-, hemat(o)-, hemo-
blood | *hemo*stat

hemi-
half | *hemi*sphere, *hemi*section

hetero-
other, different | *hetero*sexual, *hetero*geneity

homo-
similar, alike | *homo*sexual, *homo*zygous

hyper-
excess, above, over | *hyper*tension, *hyper*opia

hypno-
sleep | *hypno*sis, *hypno*therapy

hypo-
under, below, deficient | *hypo*thalamus, *hypo*mania

-ia
quality, condition, illness | apha*sia*, phob*ia*

-iatric, -iatry
medicine, healing | geri*atric*, psychi*atry*

-ic, -ical
pertaining to | hypothalam*ic*, son*ic*, psycholog*ical*

ideo-
thought | *ideo*motor, *ideo*logy

-il, -ile
pertaining to | percent*ile*, sen*ile*

infra-
below | *infra*human

inter-
between | *inter*action, *inter*quartile

intero-
from the inside | *intero*ceptor

intro-
directed inward | *intro*vert, *intro*spection

iso-
equal | *iso*metric

P. S OR C F

MEANING | EXAMPLE

-itis
inflammation — encephal*itis*, myel*itis*

kilo-
thousand — *kilo*gram, *kilo*meter

kine-, kines(i)-, kinet(o)-
movement — *kines*thesis; *kinesi*meter; *kineto*genetic

-lalia
speech — echo*lalia*, a*lalia*

-lepsy
a seizure or trance — epi*lepsy*, narco*lepsy*

-logy
a science, body of knowledge — psycho*logy*, zoo*logy*

macro-
large, enlarged — *macro*cephaly

mal-
defect, disorder — *mal*adjustment

meso-
middle position — *meso*derm, *meso*morphy

meta-
between, by means of, beyond — *meta*bolism, *meta*psychology

-meter
measure, measurement — milli*meter*

micro-
small — *micro*cephaly

mono-
single, one — *mono*tone, *mono*tony

-morph; morpho-
form, shape — meso*morph*, *morpho*logy

multi-
many — *multi*phasic, *multi*polar

myo-
muscle — *myo*tatic, *myo*genic

neo-
new — *neo*-Freudian

non-
not — *non*parametric, *non*adjustive

nyct-, nycto-
night — *nycto*phobia

oculo-
eye — *oculo*motor

-oid
resembling, like in form — elipt*oid*, paran*oid*

-oma
a growth, tumor — sarc*oma*, neur*oma*

P. S OR C F
MEANING   EXAMPLE

omni-
   all
   *omni*potent

onto-
   being, existence, individual
   *onto*logy, *onto*genesis

-opia
   vision, eye
   my*opia*

ortho-
   correct, normal, direct
   *ortho*dox, *ortho*gonal

-osis
   disease, a pathological condition
   neur*osis*, psych*osis*

-osmia
   smell, olfaction
   an*osmia*

oto-
   ear
   *oto*logy, *oto*lith

pan-
   all
   *pan*ophobia, *pan*sexualism

para-
   distorted, abnormal
   *para*geusia, *para*mnesia

ped-
   child, boy
   *ped*iatrician

peri-
   around
   *peri*metry, *peri*pheral

-phobia
   fear
   agora*phobia*, claustro*phobia*

phren, phreno-
   mind
   *phren*ology

phylo-
   race, species
   *phylo*genetic

post-
   behind, after
   *post*natal, *post*hypnotic

pre-
   before
   *pre*natal

pseudo-
   false
   *pseudo*scientific

psycho-
   mind, mental
   *psycho*logy, *psycho*pathy

retro-
   behind
   *retro*active

-scope
   a device for viewing
   strobo*scope*

scoto-
   darkness
   *scoto*pic

semi-
   half
   *semi*conscious, *semi*tone

P. S OR C F
MEANING   EXAMPLE

socio-
  to join, be a companion   *socio*logy
somno-
  sleep   *somno*lence
stereo-
  solid   *stereo*scope
sub-
  below, lower order   *sub*normal
super-
  above, higher   *super*sonic, *super*normal
supra-
  above, on top of   *supra*optic
syn-
  together   *syn*thesis
tachy-
  rapid, quick   *tachy*cardia
tele-
  distant   *tele*pathy
-tomy
  cutting, surgery   lobo*tomy*
trans-
  across   *trans*verse, *trans*fer
ultra-
  beyond   *ultra*violet
un-
  not   *un*pleasant, *un*real
uni-
  single, one   *uni*modal
-vert
  turn   intro*vert*

Appendix E

LIST OF COMMONLY USED STATISTICAL FORMULAS IN PSYCHOLOGY

1. Mean: $\overline{X} = \dfrac{\Sigma X}{N}$ for ungrouped data.

2. Mean: $\overline{X} = \dfrac{\Sigma fX}{N}$ for grouped data.

3. $Mdn = L + \left(\dfrac{\frac{N}{2} - f_B}{f} \right) h$

4. $AD = \dfrac{\Sigma |X - \overline{X}|}{N}$ Average deviation.

5. SD or $\sigma = \sqrt{\dfrac{\Sigma x^2}{N}}$ for ungrouped data.

6. SD or $\sigma = \sqrt{\dfrac{\Sigma fx^2}{N}}$ for grouped data.

7. $\sigma_p = \sqrt{\dfrac{pq}{N}}$ The standard deviation of a proportion.

8. P. E. $= .6745\sigma$ The probable error.

9. $Q = \dfrac{Q_3 - Q_1}{2}$ The quartile deviation or semi-interquartile range.

10. $P = L + \left(\dfrac{pN - f_B}{f} \right) h$ a centile or percentile.

11. $Z = \dfrac{X - \overline{X}}{\sigma}$ The standard score.

12. $T = 50 + 10\left(\dfrac{X - \overline{X}}{s}\right)$ The T score.

13. $Y = \dfrac{N}{\sigma\sqrt{2\pi}} \ \omega - X^2/2\sigma^2$ Normal probability curve.

14. $C = \dfrac{100 \ s}{M}$ The coefficient of variation.

15. $k = \sqrt{1 - r^2}$ Coefficient of alienation.

16. $r = \dfrac{\Sigma Z_x Z_y}{N - 1}$ Pearson product-moment coefficient of correlation.

17. $\sigma_r = \sqrt{\dfrac{1}{N - 1}}$ Standard error of Pearson correlation.

18. $byx = r\dfrac{\sigma_y}{\sigma_x}$, $bxy = r\dfrac{\sigma_x}{\sigma_y}$ Regression coefficients.

19. $axy = \bar{x} - \bar{y} \ (b_{xy})$ The y intercept.

20. $\rho = 1 - \dfrac{6 \ \Sigma \ D^2}{N \ (N^2 - 1)}$ Rank-difference correlation.

21. $\eta = \sqrt{\dfrac{\Sigma y_b{}^2}{\Sigma y_t{}^2}}$ The eta coefficient.

22. $r_{12.3} = \dfrac{r_{12} - r_{13} \ r_{23}}{\sqrt{(1 - r_{13}{}^2)(1 - r_{23}{}^2)}}$ Coefficient of partial correlation.

23. $R_{1.13} = \sqrt{\dfrac{r_{12} - 2r_{12} \ r_{13} \ r_{23} + r_{13}{}^2}{1 - r_{23}{}^2}}$

Coefficient of multiple correlation.

24. $\beta_{12.3} = \dfrac{r_{12} - r_{13} \ r_{23}}{1 - r_{23}{}^2}$ Beta coefficient.

25. $\beta_{13.2} = \dfrac{r_{13} \ r_{12} \ r_{23}}{1 - r_{23}{}^2}$ Beta coefficient.

26. $C.R. = Z \ score = \dfrac{\overline{X}_1 - \overline{X}_2}{S_{\bar{x}_1 - \bar{x}_2}}$ The critical ratio. Like t test but for large N.

27. $t = \dfrac{\overline{X}_1 - \overline{X}_2}{S_{\overline{x}_1 - \overline{x}_2}}$ The t ratio.

28. $S^2 = \dfrac{\Sigma x^2}{N} = \dfrac{\Sigma(X - \overline{X})^2}{N}$ Variance.

29. $S_{\overline{x}_1 - \overline{x}_2} = \sqrt{S_{\overline{x}_1}{}^2 + S_{\overline{x}_2}{}^2}$ Standard error of a difference for uncorrelated means.

30. $S_{\overline{x}_1 - \overline{x}_2} = \sqrt{S_{\overline{x}_1}{}^2 + S_{\overline{x}_2}{}^2 - 2r_{12}\,S_{\overline{x}_1}\,S_{\overline{x}_2}}$ Standard error of a difference for correlated means.

31. $\chi^2 = \sum \dfrac{(fo - fe)^2}{fe}$ Chi square.

32. $\phi = \sqrt{\dfrac{\chi^2}{N}}$ Phi coefficient.

33. $W = \dfrac{12\,\Sigma D^2}{K^2\,(N^3 - N)}$ Coefficient of concordance for measuring the agreement among judges.

34. $C = \sqrt{\dfrac{\chi^2}{x^2 + N}}$ Contingency coefficient for category data.

35. $A = \dfrac{\Sigma D^2}{(\Sigma D)^2}$ Sandler's A statistic often used in place of the matched group t test. D is the difference between two groups.

DICTIONARY
OF
PSYCHOLOGY

A

abasement: (*Murray*) the need to comply, to surrender, to confess, to atone, to accept punishment.

abclution: (*R. B. Cattell*) the rejection of acculturation. *Contr.* COMENTION.

abdominal reflex: a contraction of muscles in the abdominal wall in response to a sudden stroking of the skin in that region.

abducens or **abducent nerve:** the sixth cranial nerve. The abducens carries a motor component to the lateral rectus muscle of the eye and a sensory component mediating proprioception from the same muscle.

abducens nucleus: a mass of nerve cells in the fourth ventricle that gives rise to the abducent nerve.

aberration: a departure from normal; a temporary lapse from normalcy; idiosyncratic or peculiar behavior.

abience: avoidance. *Abient behavior* moves the organism away from a stimulus, in contrast to *adient behavior*, which moves the organism toward the source of stimulation.

ability: the power to perform an act. An ability may be innate or it may be the result of practice. *Ability*, as distinguished from *aptitude*, implies that an act can be performed now, whereas *aptitude* implies that training or education will be necessary before an act can be performed at some future time. *Capacity*, often used as a synonym for *ability*, usually implies an ability that can be fully developed in the future only under optimal conditions of training. In practice, an individual's capacity is rarely reached. See also GENERAL ABILITY; SPECIFIC ABILITY.

ability grouping: the practice of sectioning pupils into relatively homogeneous groups according to their scholastic ability.

ability test: a standardized examination for the purpose of measuring either general ability or some specialized ability.

ablation: removal of all or part of an organ (for example, the brain), for the purpose of studying its function. *Syn.* EXTIRPATION.

abnormal: 1. diverging widely from the normal; descriptive of behavior deviating markedly from what is considered normative, healthy or psychologically desirable from an adjustmental point of view. The term often carries a strong connotation of undesirability or pathology, but it is also occasionally employed to characterize extreme superiority or supernormality. 2. in statistical distributions, descriptive of scores that are atypical or outside the normal or expected range of scores.

The terms *abnormal* and *normal*, though used extensively in both technical and popular writing, are difficult to define precisely. Some authorities have suggested that abnormality be defined in statistical terms—that individuals who fall outside certain limits along the normal probability curve be considered abnormal. The difficulty with this definition lies in deciding where to establish limits or cutoff points. Others have suggested that normalcy and abnormality be defined in terms of cultural standards, thus allowing considerable latitude for cultural relativity. Some writers have suggested that normalcy be defined partly in subjective terms, or in terms of the individual's feelings of adequacy, happiness, and relatedness to others. In applying such a definition, considerable latitude must be allowed for clinical judgment. See also NORMAL; NEUROTIC; PSYCHOTIC; ADJUSTMENT; MALADJUSTMENT.

abnormal psychology: the branch of psychology that investigates abnormal behavior. *Syn.* PSYCHOPATHOLOGY.

aboulia: See ABULIA.

abreaction: (*Psychoan.*) the discharge of tension by reliving in words, feelings and actions a traumatic experience (the original cause of the tension) in the presence of an analyst. *Syn.* CATHARSIS. (*Abreaction* is the preferred technical term; *catharsis* is used more in nontechnical writing.)

abscissa: 1. the horizontal or *x* axis on a two-dimensional graph. In learning curves, for example, the independent variable of time or trials is usually plotted along the abscissa, and the dependent variable of errors or successes along the ordinate, or vertical axis. 2. the distance (*x* distance)

from a particular point to its origin, measured along a line parallel to the horizontal axis.

absolute accommodation: the accommodation of either eye separately.

absolute error: the observed value or score plus or minus the true value or score. The true value is usually taken to be the mean of the measurements. Thus, the absolute error is a positive or negative deviation on either side of the mean.

absolute impression: a judgment of intensity, brightness, weight, etc., when the stimuli are presented without any standard for comparison. The statement "This baby is heavy" illustrates an absolute impression. (To be distinguished from ABSOLUTE JUDGMENT.)

absolute judgment: in a series of judgments, an evaluation of the first of a pair of stimuli before the second is presented. Such judgments are made after the subject has become familiar with the series, and they are therefore not truly "absolute," but the result of his having built up a subjective scale against which he judges a given member of the series.

absolute-judgment method: a psychophysical method in which each stimulus in a series is judged by an absolute impression, or in the absence of any standard or comparison.

absolute luminosity: luminosity expressed in absolute terms, such as lumens per watt.

absolute measurement: 1. measurement taken without regard to algebraic sign. 2. a quantity or measurement derived from the thing being measured and not dependent upon comparison with other variables.

absolute pitch: 1. the pitch of a tone as a function of its rate of vibration. 2. the ability to recognize and name an isolated tone.

absolute refractory period: see RE-FRACTORY PERIOD.

absolute scale: a scale with an absolute-zero point and with intervals that are equal.

absolute sensitivity: the absolute threshold or minimal stimulus magnitude required to arouse a sensation. See also ABSOLUTE THRESHOLD.

absolute threshold: the minimally effective stimulus that will elicit a sensation on 50 percent of the trials. *Abbr.* RL (*Reiz Limen*—German for "stimulus threshold").

absolute value: the mathematical value of a number without regard to its algebraic sign.

absolute zero: 1. the point on a psychological scale at which the variable being measured ceases to exist. 2. the temperature at which all molecular motion ceases—equivalent to -273 degrees C. or -459 degrees F.

absorption: 1. a state of preoccupation or high degree of attention to one object or activity. 2. the condition of absorbing light by certain filters or surfaces. 3. the condition of absorbing sound, heat, or other kinds of physical stimuli.

abstract: 1. that which has been taken out of the whole or is being considered apart from its constituent elements. 2. that which is opposed to the concrete or particular. The concept of one's pet cat is a concrete concept; the concept *cat* as it is employed in referring to the cat family in general is an abstract concept. 3. (*verb*) to take out or separate a part or idea from the whole.

abstract ability: the ability to utilize abstract as opposed to concrete ideas in problem solving and in dealing with novel situations. See also: INTELLIGENCE; VERBAL SCALE; TEST; PERFORMANCE TEST.

abstract average: an average substituted for individual items in subsequent mathematical operations.

abstract idea: a generalized idea representing some aspect of a class or group of objects apart from particular or concrete objects themselves. *Mammal* is an abstract idea embracing a wide range of different vertebrates whose young are born alive and who are suckled after birth by the mother.

abstract intelligence: the ability to deal with abstract concepts and relationships effectively. *Contr.* CONCRETE INTELLIGENCE.

abstract set: the tendency to perceive things in terms of abstractions.

abstraction: 1. the process involved in developing or in isolating a concept from a class of objects or events. 2. a concept resulting from abstracting 3. preoccupation with one's own thoughts with consequent inattention to one's surroundings.

absurdity test: a task in which the testee must point out the incongruity or absurdity in a story or picture. Used at several levels on the Binet test.

abulia; aboulia: inability to come to a decision.

abundancy motive: a tendency to seek satisfactions beyond those involved in fulfilling deficits or eliminating needs. *Contr.* DEFICIENCY MOTIVE.

A–B variable: a variable describing the effectiveness of therapy. A therapists work best with schizophrenics, B therapists with neurotics.

acalculia: a type of aphasia in which the subject cannot carry out simple numerical calculations.

acanthesthesia: a variety of paresthesia in which the individual experiences pin pricks.

acarophobia: 1. fear of mites. 2. more generally, fear of small objects or animals.

acatamathesia: 1. inability to comprehend perceived situations. 2. impaired ability to understand speech.

acataphasia: the inability properly to connect words in a sentence. *Syn.* SYNTACTICAL APHASIA.

acceptance: 1. characterized by a positive or adient attitude. 2. in clinical practice, recognition of the individual's worth without implying either approval of his conduct or emotional attachment on the part of the therapist.

accessory nerve: the eleventh cranial nerve. This nerve is a helper, or accessory, to the vagus, or tenth nerve, and is distributed with it to the muscles of the pharynx and larynx.

accessory parts: all parts of sense organs except the receptor cells themselves. Accessory parts contribute to the more effective functioning of sense organs.

accidental error: error in measurment that results from variable and unknown causes and can neither be predicted nor controlled. If it is assumed that all measurements are, to some degree, inexact, then the means of a series of measurements is the best estimate of the true value. An accidental error is a deviation from this value. See also: CONSTANT ERROR; VARIABLE ERROR.

accident proneness: tendency toward accidents, presumably because of personality factors.

accommodation: 1. changes in the curvature of the lens of the eye in response to a change in distance. Ac-commodation results from the action of the ciliary muscle, which allows the lens to become spherical for near objects and flat for far objects. Accommodation of either eye separately is referred to as *absolute accommodation;* accommodation of both eyes simultaneously is referred to as *binocular accommodation.* 2. (*infrequent*) sensory adaptation or the raising of the absolute threshold in response to constant stimulation. 3. adjustment. 4. (*Piaget*) the child's adjustment of his schemes for understanding the world to the object or event at hand.

accommodation time: the lapse of time between a change in viewing distance and the achievement of accommodation.

accomplishment quotient: see ACHIEVEMENT QUOTIENT.

acculturation: 1. the process by which the individual child learns the behavior patterns characteristic of the group. 2. learning the social patterns of an alien group. 3. the acquisition by borrowing or diffusion of cultural patterns of a group. For example, the American Indian's borrowing of the use of firearms from white men.

accuracy compulsion: (*Rorschach*) a tendency on the part of the subject to be dissatisfied with his own responses and to be overly concerned with the form of the ink blots.

ACE test: the American Council on Education test of intelligence, designed primarily for college freshmen. The test yields an *L*, or language score, a *Q*, or quantitative score, and a total score.

acetylcholine (ACH): a complex organic compound liberated at the endings of parasympathetic fibers and at muscle end plates. Acetylcholine is a neurotransmitter.

acetylcholinesterase (ACHE): the enzyme that breaks down acetylcholine at the transmitter site, thus stopping its effects.

achievement: 1. accomplishment or attainment. 2. that which has been attained. 3. a specified level of success on a learning task or a certain level of proficiency in scholastic or academic work. Educational, or academic, achievement is a specified level of attainment or proficiency in academic work as evaluated by teachers, by standardized tests, or by a combination of both.

achievement age: the calendar or chronological age equivalent to a given level of proficiency on an achievement test.

achievement battery: see ACHIEVEMENT TEST.

achievement motive: 1. the tendency to strive for success or the attainment of a desired end. 2. the individual's ego-involvement in a task. 3. the expectation of success in a given task as revealed by the subject's responses on tests of fantasy. 4. (*Murray*) The motive to overcome obstacles or to strive to do difficult things difficult things quickly and well.

achievement quotient: the ratio of achievement age as measured by actual performance in school or on a standardized test and the level of performance expected. *Abbr.* A.Q. The expected level of performance may be indicated by the child's chronological age or it may be estimated by finding his mental age.

achievement test: a measure of the individual's present ability to perform a task. Achievement tests measure how well the subject has profited by learning and experience as compared to others. Achievement tests are not designed to measure the individual's future potential, which is measured by aptitude tests. However, it is recognized that it is impossible to measure aptitude without measuring achievement. Moreover, because it is impossible to measure all aspects of a complex skill or group of skills by means of a single test, batteries or groups of achievement tests are commonly employed in educational and industrial practice.

achluophobia: fear of darkness. *Syn.* NYCTOPHOBIA.

achromatic: 1. lacking in chroma; colorless. Achromatic stimuli lack hue and saturation and consequently vary only along the dimension of brilliance. 2. a term applied to a lens corrected for chromatic aberration.

achromatic color: a visual quality lacking in hue and saturation and varying only in brilliance. The white-gray-black series are the achromatic colors.

achromatic color response: (*Rorschach*) a category for responses determined by black, white, or gray.

achromatic response: (*Rorschach*) includes several subcategories for responses determined by texture, shading, or any factor not involving color.

achromatism: total color blindness due to the congenital absence of cones. All colors are experience as grays. *Syn.* ACHROMATOPSIA.

achromatopsia: see ACHROMATISM.

acmesthesia: seeing sharp points as touch, but lacking the perception of pain usually associated with such stimulation.

acoasm; acouasm; acousma: an auditory hallucination consisting of an indefinite sound or sounds such as buzzing or roaring.

acoustic filter: a device for screening out certain sound frequencies.

acoustic pressure: the force per square centimeter exerted upon the eardrum.

acoustic spectrum: the range of sounds audible to the human ear—from 20 to 20,000 Hz in young adults.

acoustics: 1. the science of sound. 2. the properties of a room that influence the distinctness with which sounds can be heard.

acquiescent response set: the tendency to agree with an item on an attitude scale or questionnaire regardless of its content.

acquired: characteristic of behavior learned through practice or experience, in contrast to behavior that is innate or inherited. Since psychologists believe that all behavior is a joint function of both heredity and environment, the terms *acquired* and *innate* are ordinarily not used as absolute qualifiers. When responses, such as reflexes, are primarily the result of the individual's biological endowment, they are characterized as innate; when responses, such as riding a bicycle or talking, are primarily dependent upon learning, they are characterized as acquired.

acquired characteristic: 1. a structural modification that arises as a result of the organism's own activities or because of environmental influences. 2. a learned modification of behavior.

acquired drive: 1. a drive that has been learned. Drug addiction is a well-known example of an acquired drive. 2. a species of drive satisfied by learned techniques or satisfiers. For example, the homosexual's drive is acquired in this meaning of the term. *Contr.* PRIMARY DRIVE.

acquisition: 1. a new response added to the organim's repertory of responses through learning. 2. (*Murray*) gaining of possessions; stealing or grasping things; working or bargaining for goods.

acquisitiveness: the tendency to acquire or to hoard possessions. In the older systems of psychology acquisitiveness was treated as an instinct.

acroanesthesia: loss of sensitivity in the extremities.

acroesthesia: abnormal sensitivity in the extremities.

acrocinesia; acrocinesis; excessive motility as observed in patients suffering from manic-depressive psychoses.

acromegaly: enlargement of the extremities, particularly the head, hands, and feet, as a result of hypersecretion of the anterior pituitary gland in adulthood.

acroparesthesia: numbness of the extremities.

acrophobia: fear of heights.

act: 1. a pattern of purposive behavior directed toward a goal. 2. (*Act Psychology*) conscious processes involved in cognition (sensing and perceiving), conation (striving, willing, desiring), and feeling (loving, hating). For the structuralists, mental processes are contents—in seeing a color, the conscious experience of the color is content and the proper subject matter for psychology. For the act psychologists, the processes of seeing, hearing, judging, desiring, etc., are acts, not contents, and are the proper subject matter of psychology. Acts lead to contents, but content itself is physical, not psychological. To study processes as acts, the act psychologists employed phenomenological observation, is contrast to Wundt and Titchener, who employed introspection.

acting out: (*Psychoan.*) carrying into action repressed impulses, which are brought to a conscious level in the course of analysis. Often the manifest behavior of symbolic or an earlier behavior pattern. For example, transference, or the patient's strong emotional attachment for the analyst, is a symbolic acting out of his earlier Oedipal attachment for the parent.

action: 1. the result of acting or activity. 2. purposive behavior, or behavior with intent, as in social action, for example. 3. a complex pattern of behavioral acts, such as walking. 4. the functioning of an organ, such as in sympathetic action. 5. the effect of a drug, such as the action of lysergic acid.

action current: the change in electrical potential in nerves and muscles that is correlated with activity. The term is often used as a synonym for ACTION POTENTIAL, and sometimes, incorrectly, for SPIKE POTENTIAL.

action potential: the change in electrical potential associated with the activity of nerves and muscles. *Syn.* ACTION CURRENT.

action research: a program of research whose ends are practical as opposed to theoretical.

action system: the complex of nerves, muscles, and glands that participate in a response.

activation: arousal or preparation for action. The term is generally used to characterize the influence of one organ on another. For example, the reticular formation alerts or activates the cerebral cortex, and for this reason is sometimes called the reticular activating system.

Activation-Deactivation Adjective Checklist: a personality inventory designed to assess the testee's customary level of activation.

activation pattern: on the electroencephalogram, a fast, irregular wave pattern accompanying arousal.

activation theory of the emotions: the assumption that the emotional processes are not special or unique processes but instead lie at one end of a continuum ranging between sleep (no activity) and violent emotion (maximum activity).

active analysis: (*Psychoan.*) a technique of psychoanalysis advocated by Steckel in which the analyst takes a more active role, giving advice, offering interpretations, and suggesting lines of inquiry for free association.

active avoidance: a learning situation in which the subject must perform a specific act in order to avoid punishment.

active introversion: (*Jung*) a voluntary, deliberate withdrawal from reality.

active therapy: 1. (*Psychoan.*) an analysis in which the therapist assumes a more directive or active role than is customary, for the purpose of breaking down resistance. 2. more generally, *active therapy* implies any psychotherapeutic situation in which the therapist takes an active, as opposed to a passive, or nondirective, role.

activity: 1. movement or behavior on the part of an organism. 2. any mental or physiological process. *Syn.* FUNCTION. The term *activity* is often qualified, as in the phrases *general activity, random activity, specific* *activity*. Sometimes the term does not imply a high degree of purpose or intent, as in *aimless* or *random activity*. More typically, some degree of direction and organization on the part of the organism is implied.

activity analysis: the study of a complex pattern of behavior by breaking it down into small units.

activity inventory: a list of acts performed in a particular job. Part of a complete job analysis.

activity cage: a cage with some means of recording an animal's general activity. The most common form is a living cage with an attached cylindrical wheel in which the animal can run. A mechanical counter records the revolutions of the wheel.

activity cycle: a rhythm or cycle of activity as measured over a period of time. Many of these are associated with drives such as hunger, thirst, sex.

activity drive: 1. the hypothetical drive to account for an animal activity even though all physiological drives are satiated. 2. the tendency to engage in activity or to utilize abilities or learned skills.

activity quotient: a proposed index of emotionality utilizing the ratio of activity words (primarily verbs) to qualifiers (primarily adjectives) in a sample of the individual's speech or writing.

activity sampling: the determination of what an individual does during a specified period of time.

activity system: a group of closely interrelated behaviors that serve the same general function. For example, crawling, running, walking, and hopping are all forms of locomotor behavior and constitute an activity system. *Syn.* BEHAVIOR SYSTEM.

actone: 1. (*Murray*) an action pattern considered from the point of view of the action itself and without regard to its effects. Actones may be *motones* (or muscular patterns) or *verbones* (verbal-action patterns). 2. a simple, reflexlike response.

act psychology: a viewpoint taken by Franz Brentano (1838–1917) to the effect that the subject matter of psychology should be acts, as opposed to contents. Brentano held that mental acts referred to contents, but were not identical to them. If, for example, we see a color, the act of seeing is a process that leads to a content of what is seen. However, the content itself was held to be not psychological, but physical. Act psychology arose in opposition to structuralism, founded by Wilhelm Wundt (1832–1920), which held that the subject matter of psychology was conscious contents to be studied by means of the method of introspection. The act psychologists rejected introspection in favor of phenomenological observation. Act psychology made no important positive contributions to psychology, but was important as a challenge to the dominant structuralism of the times and as a forerunner of functionalism.

acting out: reducing hostility, anxiety, or other emotions by expressing them in overt behavior.

act regression: the reappearance of a previously extinguished conditioned response when a barrier is interposed to a conditioned response related to the extinguished response.

actual neurosis (*Psychoan.*) a neurosis resulting from an organic difficulty.

acuesthesia; acuaesthesia: see ACME-STHESIA.

acuity: sharpness of perception. See also SENSORY ACUITY; VISUAL ACUITY.

acuity grating: a printed square of closely spaced, alternating black and white lines used to determine the minimum separability of objects necessary for their perception as two. Employed as a measure of visual acuity.

acupuncture: an ancient Chinese analgesic and anesthetic technique consisting of inserting needles of various lengths into certain sites on the body. The needles may be rotated or a weak electric current applied.

acute: 1. capable of fine discriminations, as in acute sense of smell. 2. severe, as in acute pain. 3. sudden in onset and likely to be of relatively short duration, as in acute mental disturbances.

acute brain disorders: a disease syndrome resulting from temporary impairment of the brain due to drugs, injury, or organic disease.

acute preparation: an animal that must be destroyed for humane reasons at the termination of an experiment involving radical surgical procedures.

adaptation: 1. structural or functional change that enhances the organism's survival value. 2. decreased sensitivity through the raising of the absolute threshold in the course of prolonged stimulation. 3. elimination of emotional or other irrelevant behavior during the early stages of learning.

adaptation level: 1. a subjective point of equality at which stimuli are indifferent or neutral. *Abbr.* AL. Stimuli above the AL are complementary in quality to those below the *AL.* 2. a state of homeostatis associated with emotional neutrality. See also AFFECTIVE-AROUSAL THEORY.

adaptation syndrome: profound physiological changes in the endocrine and other organ systems resulting from stress. There are three stages: ALARM REACTION; RESISTANCE; EXHAUSTION.

adaptation time: the elapsed duration between the onset of a stimulus and the cessation of the consequent changes in the sense organ being stimulated.

adaptive: 1. appropriate; suitable. 2. promoting adaptation.

adaptive act: In Carr's system of functionalism, the basic unit of behavior involving a motivating stimulus and a sensory situation leading the animal to make responses that reinforce behavior leading to a goal, thus satisfying the motivating condition.

adaptive behavior: 1. appropriate response. 2. behavior that helps the individual interact more effectively with his environment.

adaptometer: a device for measuring changes in sensory adaptation.

addiction: the state of being physically dependent upon a drug. In general, addiction implies increased tolerance to a drug, physical and psychological dependence, and withdrawal symptoms when administration of the drug is stopped. See also DRUGS AND BEHAVIOR.

additional score: (*Rorschach*) content reported or withdrawn after the primary or main response.

additive scale: a scale whose units can be summated since they are equal at all points along the scale. A yardstick is an additive scale. Mental-age scales cannot be added unless transformed into z scales, or ratio scales.

additive W: (*Rorschach*) detail response that culminates in a whole response.

adenohypophysis: the anterior pituitary gland.

adequate stimulus: stimulus that excites a receptor. *Contr.* INADEQUATE STIMULUS.

adience: behavior that moves the organism toward the source of stimulation, in contrast to *abient* behavior, which moves the organism away from a stimulus.

adipocytes: fat cells. Obese people possess more adipocytes, a possible causative factor in obesity.

adipsia: a pathological condition characterized by failure to drink when body water level is low.

adjustment: 1. variation in the activities of the organism in order to surmount a barrier and satisfy needs. 2. establishment of a harmonious relationship with the physical and social environment. The first definition implies a problem-solving situation in which the organism or individual has a need that cannot be met by habitual means. In such situations behavior is varied until a response brings satisfaction. Such a response may, in turn, become a habitual way of responding. The second definition puts less emphasis on skills or learning and instead approaches the idea of social accommodation or conformity. The terms *adjustment, accommodation*, and *conformity* are sometimes used interchangeably. However, *adjustment* implies a more active role on the part of the individual. *Accommodation* and *conformity* are more passive and imply a "giving in" in order to achieve harmony.

adjustment inventory: a questionnaire for assessing the quality of an individual's adjustment. Such inventories typically consist of a large number of questions indicative of good and bad adjustment. The subject is asked to agree, disagree, or indicate that he cannot answer the question. The pattern of answers is then scored and compared with norms based on large samples of individuals.

adjustment mechanism: see MECHANISM OF ADJUSTMENT.

adjustment method: a psychophysical technique in which the subject manipulates a variable stimulus in relation to a constant or standard stimulus. For example, he might be required to draw a line the same length as a standard line given by the experimenter. On some trials the subject is likely to draw the line too short, on others too long. The mean of the series of observation is taken at the most representative score. The standard deviation or some other measure of variability is also calculated in order to assess the subject's variability. *Syn.* METHOD OF AVERAGE ERROR.

adjustment of observations; measurements: 1. statistical correction involving weighting or reinterpreting observed data to allow for atypical conditions. 2. utilization of the method of least squares to determine the best or most probable value of a series of measurements.

adjuvant therapy: supplementary or corollary techniques used in therapy.

Adler, Alfred: Austrian psychiatrist, founder of Individual Psychology (1870–1937). Adler, an opthalmologist, became interested in the then controversial theories of Sigmund Freud, and in 1902 he joined the Vienna Pscyhoanalytic Society, which Freud had founded. Adler's formulations concerning inferiority feelings and compensatory striving for power as basic factors in personality development precipitated an open break with Freud in 1911. With a substantial group of followers, Adler established a new theoretical system which became known as Individual Psychology (q.v.). In his lectures and books he addressed himself not only to specialists in his field, but also to intelligent laymen, educators, and all those concerned with the welfare of children. He also founded a number of child-guidance clinics, several of which are still active. His influence, long overshadowed by that of Freud, has in recent years achieved increased recognition, and his teachings can be seen to underlie many contemporary developments in personality theory and psychotherapy.

Adlerian psychology: see INDIVIDUAL PSYCHOLOGY.

adolescence: the period between puberty and maturity. The approximate ages, are: 12–21 for girls, who mature earlier than boys, and 13–22 for boys.

adrenal cortex: the outer portion of the adrenal glands. See also ADRENAL GLANDS.

adrenal glands: a pair of endocrine glands located over the kidneys. The dark, central portion is called the medulla; the yellowish, outer portion, the cortex. The adrenal medulla produces epinephrine and norepinephrine (commonly called adrenaline and noradcnalinc), which are important in the body's reaction to stress. In general the effects are the mobilization of the body's resources to meet an emergency or stressful situation, by the release of sugar from the liver, increased heart rate, increased blood volume in the muscles, and inhibition of digestion. The adrenal cortex produces a number of hormones called steroids, which are of vital importance in the regulation of bodily metabolism and sexual functions. *Syn.* SUPRARENAL GLANDS.

adrenaline: a proprietary name for epinephrine, a hormone secreted by the adrenal medulla. See also ADRENAL GLANDS.

adrenergic: 1. having an adrenaline-like action. 2. characterizing the action of autonomic fibers of the sympathetic nervous system which secrete sympathin, an andrenalinclike product.

adrenergic-response state: (*R. B. Cattell*) a dimension of personality characterized by rapid pulse, high blood pressure, high blood sugar level, and general indication of the secretion of high levels of adrenaline.

adrenin: see ADRENALINE.

adult intelligence: the measured intellectual level at which the curve of mental growth has ceased to rise. It is estimated at between 16 and 19 by most authorities, but some would advance the point to the early twenties.

advantage, law of: the principle that of two or more inconsistent responses, one has an advantage and is more reliable.

advantage by illness: the gain enjoyed by the individual because of illness. In psychiatric literature a distinction is made between paranosic and epinosic gains. Paranosic gain is the direct advantage from illness, such as excuse from military duty. Epinosic gains are secondary gains exploited by the patient in an attempt to gain sympathy or some other advantage. For example, the sick child may utilize his illness to get undue attention from the mother.

adventitious deafness: deafness caused by injury, as opposed to CONGENITAL DEAFNESS.

adynamia: weakness. *Syn.* ASTHENIA.

aerial perspective: the loss of distinctness and fading-out of colors with increased distance. Aerial perspective is a monocular cue to depth perception.

aerophagia: gulping of air, a common symptom of neuroses.

aerophobia: fear of drafts.

aesthesiometer: see ESTHESIOMETER.

aesthetics: the branch of psychology concerned with the experimental study of beauty.

affect; affection: 1. a broad class of mental processes, including feeling, emotion, moods, and temperament. Historically, *affection* was distinguished from *cognition* and *violition*. 2. (*Titchener*) pleasantness and unpleasantness.

affect display: feelings and emotions conveyed by means of facial expressions.

affective-arousal theory: a theory proposed by D. C. McClelland that assumes motives arise from changes in the affective states. Specifically, it is held that motives arise when learned cues reinstate emotional or affective states originally associated with discrepancies in the individual's level of adaptation. Mild discrepancies result in pleasant states; extreme discrepancies in strongly unpleasant states.

affective congruency: consistency between an individual's feelings about a segment of his self concept and related behavior and the feelings of others toward these same components.

affective experience: an emotional experience.

affective logic: sequences of judgments or reasoning that superficially resemble logical chains of reasoning but upon closer examination are found to be linked by emotional factors.

affective psychosis: psychotic reaction especially characterized by severe emotional disturbances, such as occur in manic-depressive reaction.

affective ratio: (*Rorschach*) the ratio of the total number of responses to the colored cards to the total responses to the uncolored cards. The affective ratio is held to be an index of emotionality.

affective state: 1. an emotional state. 2. (*Titchener*) pleasantness or unpleasantness.

affective tone: 1. the feeling tone associated with any experience. 2. (*Titchener*) the pleasantness or unpleasantness associated with a stimulus. 3. the subjective correlate of adient and abient behavior. *Syn.* HEDONIC TONE.

affectivity: 1. emotionality; tendency toward emotional reactions. 2. generalized emotional reaction not readily identifiable with a particular stimulus situation.

afferent: conducting nervous impulses toward the brain or spinal cord. *Syn.* SENSORY.

afferent code: the pattern of neural input to the brain corresponding to the pattern of environmental stimulation.

afferent stimulus interaction: (*Hull*) the postulate that all afferent impulses interact in such a way as to modify one another. The principle attempts to provide a behavioristic explanation for patterning, configurational effects, and other Gestalt-like phenomena.

affiliation: (*Murray*) need for friendly association with others; formation of friendships; joining of groups; loving; cooperation.

afterdischarge: a continuing discharge of neural impulses after cessation of the stimulus. Believed to be the result of multiple pathways and synapses.

aftereffect: 1. the continuation of a sensory experience after cessation of a stimulating condition. 2. an aftersensation. 3. in learning, the strengthening of a stimulus-response connection by the satisfying consequences of a reward.

afterexplusion: see SECONDARY REPRESSION.

afterimage: continuation of a sensory experience after removal of the stimulus. In visual experience, afterimages may be positive or negative. If positive, they are of approximately the same hue and brightness as the original stimulus. If negative, they are less saturated, duller, and approximately the complementary color of the original stimulus.

aftersensation: continuation of a sensory experience after cessation of the stimulus. Most obvious in the visual modality, where they are commonly called afterimages.

AGCT: see ARMY GENERAL CLASSIFICATION TEST.

age equivalent: the level of development of any trait expressed in age units.

age-equivalent scale: a test on which the scores are expressed in age units. For each age, norms or averages expressed in units of years or months must be available for evaluating the performance of the individual being tested.

age-grade scaling: standardizing a test by establishing norms on a sample of children who are at the normal age for their grade in school.

age norm: 1. the average or normal score made by a large, representative sample of children on a standardized test. 2. the age on a test at which a given score is expected.

agent: the sender in a telepathy experiment.

age ratio: chronological age at one test administration divided by chronological age at a later testing. Used as a rough index of the predictive power of aptitude tests. Two factors influence test predictive power: (1) the age at which the test is given—the younger the age the poorer the predictive power; and (2) the interval between tests—the further apart the tests, the poorer the prediction from one to the other. Thus, prediction for ages 6 to 8 yields a ratio of 6:8, but prediction from ages 3 to 8 of only 3:8. In general, tests given before school age (6 years) have little or no predictive power.

age regression: in hypnosis the subject's reliving through fantasy events based on early memories.

age scale: see AGE-EQUIVALENT SCALE.

age score: the individual's score on a test expressed in terms of what is normal or average for that age. *Syn.* age-equivalent score.

ageusia: a deficiency in taste sensitivity.

aggregate: a totality or mass of distinct units.

aggregation: a crowd or collection of people not bound together by unity of purpose.

aggregation theory: a theory of intelligence that postulates abilities as a function of dispersed localized areas in the cerebral cortex.

aggression: 1. an attack; hostile action directed against a person or thing. 2. (*Freud*) the conscious manifestation or projection of the death instinct, or Thanatos. 3. (*Adler*) the manifestation of the will to power over other people. 4. any response to frustration (FRUSTRATION-AGGRESSION HYPOTHESIS). 5. an intrusive or bold pursuit of one's ends. 6. (*Murray*) the need to assault or injure another, to belittle, harm, ridicule, or accuse maliciously, to punish severely, or to engage in sadistic practices.

aggressiveness: 1. habitual tendency to display hostility. 2. self-assertiveness; the vigorous pursuit of one's goals. 3. social dominance, particularly where carried to an extreme.

agitated depression: a pathological condition characteristic of certain psychotics in which there is restlessness, apprehension, delusions of self-depreciation, feelings of worthlessness, and despair.

agitated melancholia: a psychotic state of profound depression accompanied by anxiety. Typically occurs in later life.

agitation: 1. extreme restlessness. 2. urgent or active verbal argument or propagandizing.

agitolalia: cluttered, excessively rapid speech due to emotional excitement or stress. *Syn.* agitophasia.

agnosia: partial or total inability to attach meaning to sensory impressions. Agnosia may occur in any sensory modality and is usually the result of brain injury.

agonist: 1. pharmacological compound that mimics the effect of a neurotransmitter at the synapse. 2. a muscle opposite in function to another. The biceps is an agonist to the triceps.

agoraphobia: morbid fear of open places.

agrammatism; agrammatologia; agrammata; agrammataphasia: loss of ability to speak coherently. May be due to brain injury or to a severe mental disturbance, particularly to schizophrenic reactions.

agraphia: the inability to write, because of brain damage.

agreement coefficient: 1. a measure of the agreement of a single item with the rest of a scale. The formula is:

$$CAg = \frac{{}^a1 + {}^a2 + {}^a3 \ldots + {}^an}{N}$$

where CAg = coefficient of agreement
$\quad {}^a1$ = total number of first subject's responses that are in agreement with that subject's responses to the item in question.
$\quad {}^a2$ = the same for the second subject's responses . . . and so on
$\quad N$ = the total number of responses

2. a measure of the degree of agreement among ratings given by the formula:

$$CA = 100 \cdot \frac{1 - \Sigma T - \Sigma B}{\frac{N}{2(H-L)}}$$

where CA = coefficient of agreement
$\quad T$ = the top 50% of the rankings
$\quad B$ = the bottom 50% of the rankings
$\quad H - L$ = the highest minus the lowest ranking
$\quad N$ = the number of cases

agrypnia: inability to sleep. *Syn.* INSOMNIA.

aha or **ah-ah experience:** the reaction accompanying the moment of insight in problem solving situations.

ahedonia: absence of pleasure.

ahistorical: a theoretical point of view emphasizing contemporary factors in the causation of behavior.

ahypnia; ahypnosia: severe insomnia; inability to sleep.

aichmophobia: fear of pointed objects.

ailurophobia: fear of cats. *Syns.* GATOPHOBIA; galephobia.

aim: 1. a goal to be attained by voluntary effort. 2. intent or purpose. 3. (*Freud*) the individual's desire to remove or reduce a source of tension. The external aim of the instinct-causing tension is an activity or object that will satisfy the internal aim, which, in turn, is some form of somatic modification. The external aim of the sex instinct is another individual who will satisfy the tensions associated with the drive and cause them to disappear temporarily.

akinesia, akinesis: loss or impairment of voluntary movement, usually of a functional nature.

akinesthesia: loss or impairment of the kinesthetic (muscle, tendon, and joint) sense.

alalia: functional absence of speech.

alarm reaction: the first stage of the general adaptation syndrome characterized by an emergency reaction involving the mobilization of energy through adrenal and sympathetic activity. See also ADAPTATION SYNDROME.

albedo: the reflection power of a surface measured in terms of the ratio of reflected light to the total illumination falling on the surface.

albedo perception: the discrimination of perception of surfaces according to their reflecting power while disregarding the general illumination. Albedo perception is a form of brightness constancy.

albinism: the congenital absence of pigmentation in the hair, eyes, and skin. The albino is color-blind.

alcoholic: one who suffers from alcoholism (*q.v.*).

alcoholic dementia: SEE KORSAKOV'S PSYCHOSIS; ALCOHOLIC PSYCHOSIS.

alcoholic psychosis: a severe mental disorder characterized by acute or chronic inflammation of the brain, delirium, hallucinations, impairment of memory, and general deterioration of judgment. The are two important types of alcholic psychosis: delirium tremens and Korsakov's psychosis. In delirium tremens, the individual exhibits marked anxiety, trembling of the extremities, excitement, and hallucinations. In Korsakov's psychosis the characteristic symptoms are confabulation, or the unsystematic falsification of memory, and loss of retention.

alcoholism: 1. personality disorder characterized by compulsive drinking. 2. the state or condition of an individual who drinks excessively and habitually.

aldosterone: a hormone produced by the adrenal cortex that aids the kidney in the maintaining the balance of electrolytes.

alertness: 1. attentiveness; a condition of preparedness or watchfulness. 2. speed of reactivity. 3. a neurological condition in which the electroencephalogram reveals a high degree of cortical activity as a result of natural or artificial stimulation of the reticular formation.

alexia: a form of aphasia or language deficiency in which the individual suffers from the inability to read or understand written or printed language. Alexia is usually caused by organic damage to the brain. *Syn.* word blindness.

algedonic: pertaining to the pleasantness-unpleasantness dimension of feeling or emotion.

algesia; algesis: 1. The sense of pain. 2. the ability to experience pain, particularly a heightened sense of pain.

algesimeter; alegesiometer: a calibrated needle for measuring sensitivity to pain. The needle is pressed against the skin.

algesthesia: the experience of pain.

algesthesis: the sense of pain.

algolagnia: sexual pleasure aroused by administering or receiving pain.

algophilia: receiving pleasure from pain. *Syn.* MASOCHISM.

algophobia: 1. a morbid fear of pain.

algorithm: a technique for problem solving that involves the specification and tryout of all possible solutions. *Contr.* HEURISTIC.

alienation: 1. the feeling of apartness; strangeness. 2. the absence of warm or friendly relationships with people. 3. (*Existentialism*) a separation of the individual from the real self because of preoccupation with abstractions and the necessity for conformity to the wishes of others and the dictates of social institutions. The alienation of contemporary man from others and from himself is one of the dominant themes of the existentialists. 4. an old term for mental disorders, now found chiefly in medicolegal writing.

alienation coefficient: an index of the degree of absence of a relationship between two variables. The coefficient is calculated according to the formula:

$$k = \sqrt{1-r^2}$$

where k is the coefficient of alienation; and

     r is the product moment correlation coefficient between the two variables

alienist: a medicolegal term for a physician, usually a psychiatrist, who is a qualified specialist in mental disorders.

allachaesthesia; allesthesia: the localization of a touch sensation in a place remote from the point stimulated.

allele: one of a pair of genes located at corresponding positions on a pair of chromosomes. Each pair of alleles controls or influences a specific trait, such as eye color. One allele is usually dominant and the other recessive:

allergy: a condition of heightened sensitivity to foreign substances that would be harmless to most people but, in the susceptible individual, causes reactions ranging from mild irritation to shock and, in rare cases, death. In many allergic reactions there is believed to be a psychological component. See PSYCHOSOMATIC DISORDER.

alliaceous: pertaining to a class of odors similar to garlic.

allied reflexes: two or more simultaneous reflexes that combine into a unitary response.

allocentric: characterizing the objectively oriented senses, such as vision and audition. *Contr.* AUTOCENTRIC.

allochiria; allocheiria: a condition in which touch is referred to a corresponding point on the opposite side of the body being stimulated.

alloeroticism; alloerotism: the direction of erotic or sexual tendencies toward others. *Contr.* AUTOEROTICISM.

alloplasty: (*Psychoan.*) the turning of the libido outward toward the environment. *Contr.* AUTOPLASTY.

allopsychosis: a psychological disorder directed toward the outer world. Allopsychic delusions are those in which the individual projects his own impulses into others. *Contr.* AUTO-PSYCHOSIS.

all-or-none law: the principle that individual neurons and muscle fibers react with maximum strength or not at all. There is no gradation of response, and the intensity of the stimulus, provided it is of threshold strength, does not affect the magnitude of the response.

Allport, Gordon W: American psychologist (1897–1967). Allport studied at Harvard and, after obtaining his doctorate, at Berlin, Hamburg, and Cambridge, returned to the United States in 1924 to teach at Harvard. He is widely known as the proponent of a system of personality which emphasizes the individual while at the same time utilizing the trait approach to make possible a quantitative science of personality. His works include two widely used tests—the A–S Reaction study (with F. H. Allport) and a Study of Values (with P.E. Vernon 1931; revised with P. E. Vernon and G. Lindzey, 1951)—a number of books—among them, *Personality: A Psychological Interpretation* (1937), *Becoming: Basic Considerations for a Psychology of Personality* (1955), and *Pattern and Growth in Personality* (1961)—and many contributions to psychological journals. See also ALLPORT'S PSYCHOLOGY OF INDIVIDUALITY.

Allport A–S Reaction Study: a personality inventory designed to measure ascendance-submission.

Allport's Psychology of Individuality: G. W. Allport's psychology of individuality defines personality as the "dynamic organization within the individual of those psychophysical systems that determine his characteristic behavior and thought." By dynamic organization Allport means that the human personality is a developing and changing organization of habits, attitudes, and traits. The choice of the term *psychophysical* to characterize personality systems recognizes the fact that both mental and physical processes must be taken into account. Allport believes that motivational systems are functionally autonomous, that is, are not dependent upon the antecedent conditions from which they arose. Thus, a good craftsman, may continue to make fine objects of furniture even though his income no longer depends upon it. Similarly, the businessman may amass wealth, not because he needs it, but because his motivation to do so has become habitual and independent of the needs that originally stimulated it.

The importance of functional autonomy in Allport's system is this: it divorces his system from historical and genetic factors in the explanation of present behavior. Unlike the psychoanalysts who seek the causes of behavior in the past, Allport seeks them in the present.

Allport favors the trait as the best and most valid concept for the study of personality. Traits are systems that have the capacity to make a variety of stimuli functionally equivalent and to initiate and guide behavior. Thus, the prejudiced individual will react to *all* members of a minority group (stimuli) as though they were identical (functionally equivalent) when, in fact, they are not. Moreover, we can expect such an individual to react consistently in approximately the same manner. Thus, traits are similar to habits.

Some traits are primarily individual traits or traits that are more or less specific to a given individual. Common traits, on the other hand, are those that are found in most individuals to some degree, such as sociability or dominance, and which therefore make measurement possible. However, the personality is not a mere collection of traits. Central to Allport's system is the concept of the *proprium*, which includes what traditional psychology has included under the terms *self*, *ego*, and *style of life*. Of first importance is the related concept of *propriate striving*, which refers to motivated behavior which is central to the self or proprium. Propriate striving includes all forms of behavior that attempt to realize the self's potentialities, the goals of life, the struggle to realize ideals.

Allport's system is characterized by emphasis on abundancy motivation, as opposed to deficiency motivation. It emphasizes man seeking new horizons going forward and always becoming something new as opposed to systems that emphasize man as seeking equilibrium or homeostasis. The system may also be characterized as relying on social as opposed to biological factors, although the latter are not excluded. Finally, it is a system that tends to emphasize the individual as a whole or self rather than as a congregation of parts or mechanisms.

Alpha, Beta, Gamma hypotheses: three hypotheses that state the relationship of frequency of repetition to rate of learning. Alpha: frequency promotes learning; Beta: frequency has no influence; Gamma: frequency hinders learning.

alphabet content: (*Rorschach*) a scoring code used when letters of the alphabet are given in response to the inkblots.

alpha block: the inhibition of the resting alpha wave of 8–10 Hz by asynchronous and rapid beta waves when a novel stimulus is presented.

Alpha Examination: a group verbal test consisting of eight subtests; the Army Alpha Test was administered extensively to military personnel during World War I.

alpha motor neuron: one of the large motor neurons that controls the voluntary or skeletal muscles.

alpha movement: see APPARENT MOVEMENT.

alpha response: in conditioning, a response believed to be due to sensitization rather than to true conditioning or learning.

alpha rhythm: the most conspicuous of the brain waves. The alpha rhythm has a normal frequency of 8–12 cycles per second and an amplitude of 5–15 microvolts. It is affected by age, drugs, mental activity, sleep, and sensory stimuli. *Syns.* BERGER RHYTHM; alpha wave.

altercasting: influencing the role of another by choosing a specific role oneself, thereby reducing alternative behavior for the other.

alter ego: a very intimate friend so close as to be "another self."

alternate form: a scale of items so similar to another scale that the two are regarded as different versions of the same test.

alternate-response test: any test that presents two responses for each question, the subject's task being to choose which alternative is correct.

alternating personality: a dual personality, one component of which tends to alternate in its appearances with the other component. See also MULTIPLE PERSONALITY.

alternating perspective: a drawing that creates a sense of the third dimension in that part of the figure alternately closer and farther away as the figure is fixated. See illustration of AMBIGUOUS FIGURE.

alternating psychosis: see MANIC-DEPRESSIVE PSYCHOSIS.

alternating response or **reflex:** two responses, sometimes antagonistic, that follow each other. For example, flexion-extension alternation in walking.

alternating vision: the use of first one and then the other eye in seeing. For most purposes one of the eyes is dominant over the other, whose sensory information is suppressed.

alternative reinforcement: reinforcement delivered according to a fixed-ratio or fixed-interval schedule, whichever is satisfied first. For example, the arrangement might call for either 100 responses or a 5-minute interval. If the 100 responses occurred before the 5 minutes elapsed, a reinforcement would be delivered; if not, reinforcement would occur after a 5-minute period elapsed.

altitude: a proposed dimension of intelligence measured by the level of difficulty of problems solved by the subject on a power test.

altitude test: a test designed to measure the maximum difficulty level the individual can achieve.

altruism: the disposition to act in behalf of others for unselfish reasons.

Alzheimer's disease: a form of premature senility resulting from brain deterioration.

amacrine cells: retinal cells that interconnect the bipolar or second-order neurons. Believed to be of importance in summation effects.

amathophobia: fear of dust.

amaurosis: loss of sight due to diseases of the optic nerve, but without changes in the structure of the eye.

amaurotic idiocy; amaurotic family idiocy: a rare type of severe mental deficiency accompanied by amaurosis. Believed to be inherited.

amaxophobia: fear of being in a vehicle.

ambidextral: pertaining to the use of both sides of the body, particularly the hands.

ambidextrous: equally skilled or proficient with both hands.

ambiequal: (*Rorschach*) well balanced in extratensive and introtensive tendencies; neither egocentric nor excessively dependent upon others.

ambiguity tolerance: the ability to withstand conflicting or complex situations without undue psychological distress. It has been suggested by Lewin, Fromm, and others that intolerance for ambiguity is symptomatic of the authoritarian personality—that is, one who demands unquestioning obedience—and of those who feel most comfortable under authoritarian atmosphere.

ambiguous: 1. equivocal; having two possible meanings or interpretations, as in *ambiguous figures*. 2. vague; lacking in clarity.

ambiguous figure: a figure drawn in such a way as to have two perspectives or as to be capable of two interpretations.

FIG. 1. *An ambiguous figure*.

ambiguous perspective: the alternation of perspective observed in a reversible figure. In general, the figure is designed in such a way as to give the illusion of changing depth, with one part alternately closer and more distant.

ambisexual: 1. characterized by absence of sexual dominance in traits. 2. possessing traits belonging to both sexes.

ambivalence: 1. the existence of contradictory attitudes or emotions, such as love and hate, in the same individual. 2. rapidly shifting or alternating emotional attitudes toward another. 3. (*Lewin*) the condition of being impelled or drawn toward two mutually antagonistic goals at the same time.

ambiversion: a personality type in the middle area between introversion and extroversion.

amblyopia: indistinct vision in the absence of defects in the refracting mechanism. Associated with drugs and other toxic conditions.

amblyscope: instrument for determining the fusion point of separately presented visual stimuli.

ambrosiac: odor classification of which musk is an example.

ambulatory psychotherapy: outpatient treatment of persons suffering from psychological disorders.

ament: one who has amentia, or mental deficiency.

amentia: an old term for mental deficiency or feeblemindedness.

American Sign Language (ASL): a system of gestures and hand signs used by the deaf for communication.

Ames demonstrations: a series of complex illusions of depth designed by Adelbert Ames, Jr., which are employed in studying visual depth perception. The most famous of these demonstrations is the distorted room, which looks normal from a certain vantage point but in which objects and people appear distorted in size.

ametropia: any defect in the refractive apparatus of the eye.

amimia: loss of ability to communicate by means of gestures.

amitosis: cell division without the splitting of the chromosomes characteristic of mytosis.

amnesia: 1. loss of memory, either partial or total, due to any cause. 2. functional inability to recall the personal past. The inability to recall, in functional amnesia, suggests that the forgetting is motivated; that is, because of severe conflicts of psychological trauma, the individual seeks escape through forgetting. However, amnesia also may be caused by cerebral shock, such as may occur in injuries to the head. Because this type of amnesia is typical for events just preceding the injury or immediately following, it suggests that the neurons of the cortex need a period of consolidation of functioning in order to form the necessary circuits for memory.

amnesic: pertaining to amnesia.

amniocentesis: the technique of removing a sample of amnionic fluid from a pregnant woman for determining whether the fetus suffers from genetic defects.

amphetamines: a group of synthetic central nervous system stimulants that increase general activity, suppress appetite, and may generate feelings of well-being. Employed medically as anti-obesity and antidepressant drugs.

amphigenous inversion: a form of sexual abnormality in which the individual has relations with members of both sexes.

amplitude: 1. the amount or magnitude of a cyclic variable at any specified period of time. 2. (*Sensory Psychology*) the height of a wave from the base line or zero point. The amplitude of sound and light waves is primarily related to the respective psychological dimensions of loudness and brilliance.

ampulla: the enlarged portion of each of the semicircular canals at the point of connection with the vestibule of the inner ear. Each ampulla contains sense organs in the form of hair cells whose excitation by movements of the lymphlike fluids in the canals gives rise to nervous impulses interpreted by the brain as acceleration and declaration of the head.

amygdaloid nucleus; amygdala: an almond-shaped mass of gray matter located within the cerebrum approximately at the anterior limits of the temporal lobe. The amygdaloid nucleus is believed to be associated with the control of aggressive behavior. Its removal renders the subject passive or submissive.

amyotrophic lateral sclerosis (ALS): a degenerative disease of motor neurons in the brain and spinal cord. There is progressive loss of motor function with accompanying loss of emotional control. Affects mostly males between 35 and 70.

Amytal; sodium amytal: 1. proprietary name for one of the barbiturates used extensively as a sedative and hypnotic. 2. "truth serum," so-called because under its influence inhibitions may be lowered with the result that the individual will discuss his problems more freely. Contrary to popular opinion, criminals do not confess against their will when given hypnotic drugs.

anabolism: conservation phase of bodily metabolism in which tissues are restored and built up, in contrast to catabolism or the expenditure and breaking down of tissue.

anaclisis: emotional dependence on others, usually employed in reference to infantile dependency

anaclitic choice: (*Psychoan.*) the choice of an adult love object modeled on the mother or mother substitute.

anaclitic depression: depression caused by the loss of a person upon whom the individual is dependent, such as a mother or father.

anaclitic identification: the tendency for children to identify with parents who are warm and nurturant.

anacusia; anacusic: deafness.

anaesthesia: see ANESTHESIA.

anaglyph: stereoscopic picture printed in two slightly offset complementary colors and viewed through correspondingly colored lenses, one over each eye. The resulting effect is stereoscopic, or depth, vision.

anaglyptoscope; anaglyphoscope:

device used to demonstrate the importance of shadows and lights in perspective by reversing the light and shadow on a test object as the subject observes the process.

anagogic: (*Jung*) pertaining to the moral, spiritual, or ideal tendencies of the unconscious.

anal: pertaining to the anus or exterior opening of the large intestine.

anal character: (*Psychoan.*) personality characterized by stinginess, orderliness, and compulsive behavior. Anal characteristics are presumed to be due to infantile fixation on the anal region and the process of defecation. See also ANAL-EXPULSIVE STAGE.

anal eroticism: (*Psychoan.*) erotic or sexual pleasure obtained from the activities associated with stimulation of the anal region, particularly in defecation.

anal-expulsive stage: (*Psychoan.*) in a formulation of developmental stages by Abraham, one of the two anal stages, the other being the *anal-retentive* stage. In the anal-expulsive stage, pleasure is obtained by expelling the feces; fixation of this level may lead to a personality syndrome of conceit, ambition, and aggressiveness. In the anal-retentive stage, pleasure is obtained by retaining the feces and by defying the mother's attempts at training; fixation at this level may result in a personality that is parsimonious and prudish.

analgesia: the absence of pain sensation.

anal impotence: (*Psychoan.*) inability to excrete in the presence of others.

anality: the libidinal component that seeks pleasure by localizing in the anal region.

analogies test: an examination in which the testee must supply a missing relationship of the form *A* is to *B* as *X* is to ——.

analogy: 1. a functional correspondence in organs that are anatomically different or occur in different species. 2. a logical or assumed relation between two things.

anal-retentive stages: see ANAL-EXPULSIVE STAGES.

anal sadism: (*Psychoan.*) a form of sadism originating in an individual's resentment because of punishment he received during toilet training.

anal-sadistic stages: (*Psychoan.*) an infantile period of development characterized by anal eroticism and sadistic impulses directed toward the parent.

anal stage: (*Psychoan.*) an infantile period of development during which the individual derives libidinal satisfaction from activities associated with defecation. See also ANAL-EXPULSIVE STAGE.

anal triad: (*Psychoan.*) the three traits of obstinacy, stinginess, and excessive orderliness, growing out of fixation at the anal development.

analysand: the individual being psychoanalyzed.

analysis: 1. the process of reducing a complex phenomenon to its simplest or most elementary parts. 2. the process of psychoanalysis involving the use of free association and dream interpretation. See also PSYCHOANALYSIS.

analysis of covariance: the use of the analysis-of-variance technique to include two or more variables. See also ANALYSIS OF VARIANCE.

analysis of variance: a statistical technique for determining whether differences in variance (σ^2) found in the dependent variable under two different experimental conditions exceed the differences to be expected by chance.

analyst: 1. a practitioner of psychoanalysis. 2. a follower of Freud's or of one of the deviant schools of psychoanalysis.

analytical psychologist: a practitioner of Jung's system of psychology.

analytical psychology: 1. any system of psychology that attempts to reduce phenomena to their constituent elements. 2. Jung's system of psychoanalysis. Analytical Psychology, founded by Carl Jung of Zurich, Switzerland, was originally modeled after Freud's psychoanalysis. However, almost from the beginning, Jung began to deviate from Freud, and the final break came in 1912 with the publication of *The Psychology of the Unconscious*, in which Jung presented his new interpretation of the libido. The libido, according to Jung, is the general life energy of "life urge," and this primal energy is not, as Freud had argued, necessarily manifested as the sexual drive; it may show itself at one time as sexual energy, at another as a creative or artistic form of behavior, or in still another setting as a striving for superiority. The psychological process by which libidinal energy is transformed into cultural activities is the symbol. Symbols emerge in the unconscious part of the psyche. Some of these belong to the primitive, collective unconscious modern man has inherited from his jungle ancestors. Others belong to the personal or individual unconscious, which develops out of repression from the individual's past. The primal symbols Jung called *archetypes* and these are universal. Some of the more common archetypal symbols are those for the Mother, the Hero, the Flood, the Cross, which are found again and again in the world's myths and literature. As these are made available to the conscious mind they become a powerful guiding force in a man's behavior, particularly in its religious and ethical aspects.

Archetypes of special significance in the individual personality are the persona, the shadow, the anima and animus, and the self. The persona is the mask that the individual presents to the world. The shadow is the dark, destructive side of personality. The anima is the female component of the male personality representing a kind of ideal woman which the man seeks. The animus is the corresponding male archetype in the woman. The self is the core of personality around which the other archetypes are integrated.

Jung also emphasized the bipolar nature of mind. The best-known of these dimensions is the introversion-extroversion polarity, or the inward- and outward-directed poles of personality. Extroverts are those whose personalities are directed outward, along social lines—men of action, rather than men of thought, finding value in objects and persons rather than in their own psyches. Introverts, on the other hand, are directed inward, finding value in their own ideas and feelings, and tending to avoid the world of action and social affairs.

Jung also believed that there were four main kinds of mental activity constituting two pairs of polar opposites: thinking, and feeling, and sense perception and intuition. Combining the four main types of mental activity with extroversion and introversion, Jung developed his theory around eight basic types of individuals. (See illustration).

The masculinity-femininity dimension of the psyche is another important bipolar opposite. In treating his patients, Jung attempted to bring to consciousness the repressed side of the psyche. Thus, in treating men, the feminine unconscious could be made available and its intuitive, artistic aspects utilized in enriching the individual's life. Jung's system of therapy, like Freud's, consisted of the use of free association and dream interpretation. However, Jung used dream analysis in order to understand the individual's current problems and future aspirations rather than solely as a basis for understanding the role of past experience as a cause of psychic difficulties. Jung also emphasized a more active form of therapy than Freud's, not hesitating to intervene with interpretations and suggestions. Finally, he emphasized man's essentially religious nature and encouraged his patients to seek to discover God.

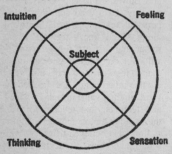

FIG. 2. *A figure to illustrate Jung's four types.*

analytical scale: a test that is used for diagnostic purposes.

analytic therapy: see ANALYTICAL PSYCHOLOGY.

analyzer: (*Pavlov*) a receptor and its central neuronal connections. Pavlov employed the concept to account for differential or selective sensitivity.

anamnesis: 1. recollection. 2. a medical history up to a specified time, such as the onset of an illness or admission to a hospital.

anamorphic: characterizing pictures constructed in such a manner as to appear normal when viewed from angles other than normal or perpendicular.

anancasm: repetitious, stereotyped behavior which if not carried out results in anxiety. *Syn.* COMPULSION.

anancastia; anankastia: an obsession in which the individual feels he is forced to act or think against his will.

anandria: absence of male characteristics.

anaphia: loss of the sense of touch.

anaphrodisiac: pertaining to lack of sexual feeling: *Contr.* APHRODISIAC.

anaphylaxis: 1. a type of allergy in which there is excessive hypersensitivity to foreign substances introduced into the body. 2. Hypersensitivity to a traumatic experience in such a manner that, when the experience is repeated, the individual suffers serious psychological distress called psychological anaphylaxis.

anarthria: defective articulation in speech as a result of a lesion in the motor speech area of the brain.

anatomy response: (*Rorschach*) a scoring code for internal anatomical detail.

anchor; anchorage: reference point of standard against which the subject makes judgments. In some experiments anchor points are provided by the experimenter, whereas in others they are developed by the subject as he becomes familiar with the series.

anchoring effect: an interrelation among attitudes such that an attack on any one threatens the entire structure, thus producing a high level of resistance.

anchoring of ego: identification of an individual with other persons for the purpose of finding security.

anchoring point: reference point on a subjective scale which provides an observer with a criterion against which to judge a series of stimuli. For example, the subject might be asked to think of the most pleasant odor that he could and to assign it a rating of 10. The stimuli in a test series would then be ranked according to his anchoring point.

androgen: the male sex hormone responsible for the structural and functional changes associated with "maleness" at maturity.

androgenic: causing or inducing maleness.

androgyneity: in anthropology, the concept based on the assumption that the individual has bipolar potentiality in sex until he is turned into a definite sex by tribal ritual.

androgynous: 1. characteristic of a male who shows structures characteristic of the female. 2. by extension, demonstrating qualities associated with both male and female roles.

andromania: nymphomania, or excessive sexual desire in a female.

anecdotal evidence: uncontrolled and unsystematic observations. The early reports appraising the abilities of children and animals were largely based on anecdotal evidence.

anechoic: echo-free

anemotropism: an orienting response of the body as a whole to air currents.

anencephalia: congenital absence of the brain.

anergasia: a loss of function.

anergia: weakness; loss of energy.

anesthesia; anaesthesia: complete or partial loss of sensitivity to external and/or internal stimuli due to drugs, lesions, or functional causes.

Angell, James Rowland: American psychologist and leader in the functionalistic movement (1876–1949). Angell studied at Michigan under John Dewey and at Harvard, where he came under James's influence. After graduate study at Halle, Germany, he taught for one year at the University of Minnesota, and then spent the next twenty-five years as a teacher and administrator at the University of Chicago. It was there that he assumed leadership of the functionalist school. Upon leaving Chicago, Angell became president of Yale—the first president of that institution who was not an alumnus. Following his retirement from academic life in 1937, he served as educational counselor with the National Broadcasting Company.

Angell is notable among the functionalists for developing the movement into a full-fledged school of psychology. He is also recognized for his administrative ability in making the department at Chicago the most influential of its day. Among his many students and associates were John B. Watson and Harvey Carr, both of whom became leaders of schools in their own right.

anger: an acute emotional reaction elicited by any of a number of stimulating situations, including threat, overt aggression, restraint, verbal attack, disappointment, or frustration, and characterized by strong responses in the autonomic nervous system, particularly by emergency reactions of the sympathetic division and by implicit or overt attack responses that may be either somatic or verbal. See also AGGRESSION; HATE; RAGE.

anginophobia: fear of choking or suffocation.

angiotensin: a protein produced in the blood that helps to regulate blood pressure and water balance.

angiotensinogen: a protein secreted in the liver that acts on renin (*q.v.*) to produce angiotensin.

angstrom unit: a unit employed in specifying the wavelength of light, equal to 1/10,000 micron.

angular gyrus: a convolution of the cerebral cortex located in the posterior portion of the lower parietal region near the posterior end of the upper temporal fissure. Broadmann's number 39. Believed to be associated with speech functions.

anhedonia: absence of hedonic tone or pleasantness-unpleasantness in situations that normally elicit such emotional reactions.

aniconia: absence of mental imagery.

anima: 1. in Jung's early formulations, the part of personality in close contact with the unconscious, in contrast with the persona, which represents the social self. 2. in later formulations, an archetype representing the feminine characteristics, in contrast to *animus*, which represents masculine characteristics.

animal: 1. a member of one of the two divisions of living organisms distinguished from plants (the second of the two) primarily by lack of photosynthesizing ability. In psychology, references to animals typically mean organisms lower than man. 2. the subject of psychological experiment. Animals are employed in experiments involving the use of genetic controls, where surgical procedures are employed, and where the psychologist wishes to study processes at simpler levels than they can be observed in man.

animal content: (*Rorschach*) a scoring category for animal references.

animal magnetism: an obsolete term for hypnotism originated by Friedrich (or Franz) Anton Mesmer, who held that the hypnotic state was induced by the flow of magnetism from the operator to the subject.

animal psychology: the branch of psychology concerned with the systematic study of animal behavior, particularly from a comparative point of view.

animatism: a primitive belief attributing life to inanimate objects. *Animatism* is considered more primitive than *animism* (*q.v.*), in which spirits or souls are attributed to inanimate objects.

animism: 1. attributing spirits or souls to inanimate objects. 2. the belief in the existence of a soul or spirit as distinct from matter and having separate characteristics. 3. (*McDougall*) the assumption of a separate mental factor that interacts and cooperates with the brain.

animus: 1. thought, spirit, purpose. 2. the spirit of hostility or the disposition to a hostile attack. 3. (*Jung*) an archetype representing masculine characteristics in a woman.

aniseikonia: inequality in the size and shape of the retinal images.

anisocoria: inequality in the size of the pupils.

anisometropia: inequality in the refractive power of the eyes.

anisotropy: 1. the quality of being unequally refractive when presented in different directions. 2. the apparent change in the length of a line when rotated in space.

ankle clonus: a sign of central neurological damage involving a rhythmic contraction of the muscles of the calf to sudden flexion of the toes.

anlage: 1. an inherited organization of cells from which an organ develops. 2. a basis, foundation, or predisposing factor in development.

annoyer: (*Thorndike*) a stimulus or condition that gives rise to unpleasantness the animal seeks to terminate. *Contr.* SATISFIER.

annulment: (*Psychoan.*) the process of converting painful ideas into daydreams, or otherwise rendering them ineffective.

annulospiral endings: the sensory endings of muscle spindle cells that mediate stretch reflexes.

anodal current: current flowing outward across the cell membrane ahead and behind the nervous impulse, or, in ephapses, the currents flowing inward.

anode: 1. the positive pole in a battery. 2. a conductor by means of which positive current flows into an electrolyte.

anodyne: an analgesic, or agent to reduce pain.

anoegenetic; anoetic: 1. a primitive state of consciousness, such as feeling, which does not lead to cognition. 2. not self-evident.

anomaloscope: instrument for measuring color deficiency by use of the Rayleigh equation, or the proportion of red and green necessary to equal yellow.

anomalous dichromatism: partial color blindness in which only two colors (usually blue and yellow) are seen.

anomalous stimulus: see INADEQUATE STIMULUS.

anomalous trichromatism: color weakness in the red-green region resulting in atypical ratios of red and green in color mixtures.

anomaly: marked deviation from what is typical or normal but without the implications of pathological condition.

anomia: 1. a type of aphasia in which there is an inability to recall names. 2. a defective moral sense.

anomie: the disorganization of social and personal values during times of catastrophic stress.

anopia: defective vision, blindness.

anorexia: a pathological loss of appetite. Anorexia is a common symptom in mental disorders. *Contr.* BULIMIA.

anorexia nervosa: an emotional disorder affecting mostly young women in their teens in which the individual diets or stops eating altogether to the point of severe malnutrition, and in some cases, death. Some anoretics "binge and purge," that is, eat excessively and then induce vomiting.

anorthopia: 1. a visual defect in which objects appear distorted. 2. STRABISMUS.

anosmia: absence or deficiency of the sense of smell.

anosognosia: unwillingness on the part of a patient to recognize a sensory or motor defect.

anoxia: an oxygen deficiency in such quantity as to seriously interfere with normal metabolism.

antabuse: a drug that induces nausea in persons who ingest alcohol while the drug is in the bloodstream.

antagonist: 1. a compound that blocks

the action of a neurotransmitter. 2. an opposing muscle. The biceps and triceps are antagonists.

antagonistic: opposite in quality or effect; counteracting one another. Used in reference to muscles, reflexes, or colors.

antagonistic colors: 1. the assumption that sensations of the color pairs black-white, red-green, and blue-yellow are aroused by antagonistic metabolic processes in the retina. 2. more generally, complementary colors.

antagonistic muscles: muscles, such as flexor and extensor pairs, which exert their effects in opposite directions.

antecedent: a condition that precedes a phenomenon and is usually considered to bear a causal relationship to it.

antedating goal response: see FRACTIONAL ANTEDATING GOAL RESPONSE.

antedating response: response that occurs earlier in a sequence than it normally should.

anterior: 1. preceding, temporally. 2. in front of, spatially. *Contr.* POSTERIOR. In primate anatomy, *anterior* is sometimes used as a synonym for *ventral*, and *posterior* is used synonymously with *dorsal*.

anterior horns: the ventral portion of the gray matter in the spinal cord. The anterior horns are the site of origin on the large motor neurons controlling muscular movement.

anterior-posterior gradient: the difference in metabolic rate and correspondingly more rapid rate of growth in the head region of the organism. The anterior-posterior gradient is responsible for the cephalocaudal sequence in development.

anterograde amnesia: failure to recall events occurring after the onset of amnesia.

anterograde degeneration: see WALLERIAN DEGENERATION.

anthropocentrism: the view that man is the central or most important fact in the universe.

anthropoid: manlike. Commonly used in reference to the higher apes.

anthropology: the science of man, including his physical characteristics, his cultures, and his races. Broadly, anthropology is divided into *physical anthropology*, which includes the study of anatomy and the anthropometric characteristics of various groups, and *cultural anthropology*, which is the study of nonliterate cultures.

anthropometry: the science of measurements of bodily form, particularly the proportions and relative frequency of occurrence of physical characteristics among the different races, cultures, sexes, etc.

anthropomorphism: 1. attributing human characteristics to gods, animals, or inanimate objects. 2. interpreting the behavior of lower forms in terms of human abilities or characteristics.

anthropopathy: attributing human feelings or emotions to gods or animals.

antianxiety drug: any of a broad class of drugs used for the relief of anxiety. See also DRUGS AND BEHAVIOR.

anticathexis: the attachment of an opposite feeling or idea to a repressed impulse. Thus, one may show overt hate toward another that he unconsciously loves.

anticipation: 1. mental set, or readiness, to receive a stimulus. 2. anticipatory reaction to a stimulus.

anticipation method: a technique in verbal learning where the subject is prompted upon hesitation and corrected upon making an error. The measure of learning is the number of anticipations or prompts necessary to master the material.

anticipatory error: a premature response in serial learning.

anticipatory maturation: the development of an organ or function before the organism has need for it. In the fetus, many sensory functions are well developed long before birth.

anticipatory response: a reaction or response occurring prematurely or in advance of the stimulus. Anticipatory responses are exemplified by runners who jump the gun.

anticonformity: behaving in ways contrary to social expectancies.

antidepressant: a drug that elevates mood, possibly by increasing the availability of norepinephrine and serotonin in the central nervous system.

antidiuretic hormone (ADH): a hormone released by the posterior pituitary that increases the capacity of the kidney tubules to reabsorb water, thereby reducing urinary output.

antidromic impulse: passage of a nervous impulse in a reverse direction, from axon to dendrite. Antidromic impulses do not occur naturally, but are induced for experimental reasons.

antisocial personality: a behavioral disorder characterized by truancy, delinquency, promiscuity, theft, vandalism, fighting, violation of common social rules, poor work record, impulsiveness, irrationality, aggressiveness, reckless behavior, and inability to plan ahead. The particular pattern of behavior varies from individual to individual.

antonym tests: a test in which the subject must give the opposites to a series of words.

anvil: one of the small bones in the middle ear. *Syn.* INCUS.

anxiety: 1. feeling of mingled dread and apprehension about the future without specific cause for the fear. 2 a chronic fear of mild degree. 3. strong, overwhelming fear. 4. a secondary drive involving an acquired avoidance response. In the presence of the conditioned stimulus (usually shock) the animal subject displays behavior interpreted as evidence of anxiety, including urination, defecation, attempting to flee the apparatus, etc. 5. (*Kelly*) The inability to predict the future or to resolve problems because the individual's construct system (*q.v.*) does not seem to apply to ongoing events.

anxiety equivalent: (*Psychoan.*) a strong sympathetic response, such as rapid heartbeat, that takes the place of conscious anxiety.

anxiety fixation: (*Psychoan.*) maintenance or carryover of an anxiety reaction from an earlier stage of development into a later stage.

anxiety hierarchy: in systematic desensitization (*q.v.*), a list of situations ranked from the least to the most anxiety producing.

anxiety hysteria: nerurosis characterized by fears and by conversion symptoms or by the manifestation of conflicts in the form of somatic disorders.

anxiety neurosis: a neurosis in which the most prominent symptom is anxiety that cannot be identified with any particular cause and which in many cases is pervasive and affects major areas of the individual's life.

anxiety object: the displacement of anxiety to an object that represents the person who originally caused the anxiety.

anxiety reaction: complex response pattern characterized by strong feelings of anxiety and accompanied by somatic symptoms, such as palpitations of the heart, choking, tightness of the chest, trembling, faintness, etc.

anxiety-relief responses: in behavior therapy, a technique in which the word "calm" is associated with the termination of an electric shock with the objective that the patient will eventually be able to reduce anxiety by thinking of the word in anxiety-arousing situations.

anxiety tolerance: the level of anxiety the individual can stand without serious psychological harm or maladjustment.

apareunia: inability to have sexual relations.

apathy: 1. lack of feeling or emotion in situations normally arousing such responses. 2. indifference to one's surroundings, as in severely depressed states.

aperiodic reinforcement: a form of irregular, intermittent reinforcement, as opposed to continuous reinforcement.

aperture: 1. an opening, such as the pupil of the eye. 2. the diameter of a lens.

aperture color: color as seen in holes in neutral screens. Aperture colors are classified as film colors.

aphagia: inability to eat. *Contr.* HYPERPHAGIA.

aphasia: partial or complete loss of ability to use language, as a result of cerebral damage. Many specific types of aphasia are distinguished, including: (a) motor, in which there is an inability to utter words; (b) sensory, or the inability to understand written or printed words (visual aphasia) or spoken speech (auditory aphasia); (c) syntactical, or the inability to put together words and phrases properly; (d) nominal, or the inability to find the proper word to use; (e) amnesic, or the inability to remember words; (f) global, or combined sensory and motor aphasia. See also ACATAPHASIA; ALEXIA; AGRAPHIA; EXPRESSIVE APHASIA; RECEPTIVE APHASIA; RECEPTIVE-EXPRESSIVE APHASIA.

aphemia: an inability to speak. May be a form of motor aphasia or a functional disturbance due to emotional disorders.

aphonia: loss of speech resulting from laryngeal defects or emotional disorders.

aphrasia: the functional inability or refusal to utter correct words or phrases even though separate words may be spoken.

aphrodisiac: anything that excites sexual desire.

apnea: a transitory cessation in breathing.

apomorphine: a drug that mimics the action of dopamine (*q.v.*) at the synapse. It may be used to induce vomiting.

apopathetic behavior: actions influenced by the presence of others but not directed toward them. For example, showing off.

apoplexy: loss of consciousness and motor control as a result of a cerebral hemorrhage or blocked blood vessel.

apostilb: one tenth of a millilambert.

apparent: 1. obvious, readily sensed or understood. 2. perceived but not objectively real. For example, *ap-*

parent motion, such as experienced in moving pictures.

apparent movement or **motion:** the illusion of motion, most commonly when stationary stimuli are presented in rapid succession, as in moving pictures. There are a number of types of apparent movement, including: *alpha movement*, which is the apparent change in size of an object when parts are presented successively; *beta movement*, in which there is an apparent movement of successive stimuli which differ in size or shape; *delta movement*, object movement which occurs when the illumination is suddenly changed.

appeal: an attempt to arouse emotion or motivation by verbal or pictorial communication.

apperception: 1. clear perception in which there is recognition. 2. recognition of relationships between a presented object and the apperceptive mass or existing body of knowledge.

appersonation; appersonification: a delusion in which the individual assumes the characteristics of another.

appetite: 1. a desire, motive, or impulse based on changing physiological states. 2. an instinct. Appetites may be modified through learning.

applied psychology: that branch of psychology that utilizes the principles and discoveries of psychology for practical ends. The applied psychologist may "borrow" principles or discoveries from the theoretical psychologist, or he may conduct his own research program. Discoveries in practical fields are then added to the general fund of psychological knowledge. Thus, applied psychology and theoretical psychology are complementary, each contributing to the other.

apprehension: 1. act of becoming aware of something. 2. anxiety about the future.

apprehension span: the number of objects that can be correctly perceived at a single brief exposure. *Syn.* ATTENTION SPAN.

apprehensiveness: mild, fear, anxiety, or uneasiness about the future.

approach-approach conflict: a situation in which the individual is drawn toward equally attractive but incompatible goals. For example, a college senior might receive equally attractive offers from two graduate schools to which he has applied.

approach-avoidance conflict: a situation in which there are both attracting and repelling aspects to the same goal. For example, a woman wishes to marry but fears sexual relations.

approach gradient: the increasing attractiveness of a goal as it is approached. The gradient of approach may be measured by the strength of pull on a harness as the animal approaches the goal.

approach response: movement toward a goal or stimulus: *Syn.* adient response.

approach type: (*Rorschach*) a response classification according to how the subject handles the blots. That is, does he deal with wholes or parts? Is he more concerned with color or with shading?

approximation conditioning: a procedure by means of which an animal can be conditioned to make an unusual and complex response by having him make a series of responses of increasing difficulty, each more and more like the final response. This is the essence of the technique by means of which a seal can be trained to play "My Country 'Tis of Thee" on pipes. *Syns*. SHAPING; SUCCESSIVE-APPROXIMATIONS METHOD.

appurtenance: 1. interaction between parts of a field, as in simultaneous contrast. 2. belongingness in perceptual fields.

apraxia: inability to perform a series of purposeful movements due to lesions in the motor area.

a priori validity: see FACE VALIDITY.

aprosexia: inability to give prolonged attention.

aptitude: the capacity to perform in the future; potential ability.

aptitude test: a series of standardized tasks designed to give a quantitative estimate of a subject's ability to profit by training. *Aptitude tests* measure future achievement, while *achievement tests* measure ability to perform in the present.

aqueduct of Sylvius: the midbrain canal that connects the third and fourth ventricles.

aqueous humor: the fluid that fills the anterior chamber of the eye.

aquaphobia: fear of water in bathing or swimming.

arachnoid layer: the delicate membrane intermediate between the pia mater and dura mater in the brain and spinal cord.

arbitrary response: (*Rorschach*) response that ignores the character of the inkblot on which it is based.

arbor vitae: treelike tissues of the cerebellum when seen in longitudinal section.

arc de circle: a bending of the body in the form of a bow. The arc de circle was described in the older clinical literature as a prominent feature of hysteria and was interpreted as symbolic of the flexion of the body in sexual intercourse.

archetype: (*Jung*) the primeval content of the racial unconscious consisting of inherited ideas and predispositions.

arcuate nucleus: a thalamic nucleus where sensory nerves from the tongue and face terminate.

area: 1. a region of the brain in which a function has been localized. 2. a region under the normal probability curve bounded by two vertical lines specifying a certain number of cases.

area sampling: in psychological surveys, the use of all respondents in a given geographical area. For example, all respondents in a square mile in a given city. *Contr*. QUOTA SAMPLING.

arbitrary weight: a weight assigned to a factor or measure upon a priori grounds.

Argyll-Robertson pupil: a pupil that contracts in accommodation and convergence but does not respond to light. A clinical sign of neurological damage.

Aristotle's illusion: the perception that an object, such as a marble, brought into contact with the tips of the crossed middle fingers is two.

arithmetic mean: a measure of central tendency, which is calculated by finding the sum of the scores or values and dividing by their number. The formula is:

$$\bar{X} = \frac{\Sigma X}{N}$$

where $\bar{X}$ is the mean
    X is a score
    ΣX is the sum of all of the scores
    N is the number of cases

arithmomania: 1. obsessive desire

to count. 2. unreasonable preoccupation with numerical or quantitative relationships to the exclusion of other modes of thought.

Armed Services Vocational Aptitude Battery: a general aptitude test used by the armed services to aid in classification of enlistees.

Army General Classification Test: the group intelligence test employed by the United States Army during World War II for the purpose of classifying inductees. The tests covered several aspects of intelligence, including numerical, verbal, reasoning, and perceptual relations. The raw point score was converted into an IQ.

Army tests: the Army Alpha, a group verbal test, and the Army Beta, a group performance test used in World War I.

aromatic: an odor classification. Typical examples are camphor and menthol.

arousal; arousal function: general state of cortical alertness following sensory stimulation. *Arousal*, or *alertness*, does not imply a specific reaction typical of stimulus-reponse conditions, but a more diffuse and more enduring cortical response. *Arousal* and *alertness* are believed to be mediated by corticofugal fibers from the recticular formation.

array: 1. a series of values in order of magnitude. 2. a row of values in a table.

arrest of development: 1. cessation of growth at a certain level of development as a result of unfavorable environmental conditions or disease. 2. a fixation at a relatively immature level of development.

arhythmia: lack or loss of rhythm.

arteriosclerosis: thickening and hardening of the arteries, particularly in the brain. Arteriosclerosis leads to destruction of tissue with consequent loss of memory, inattention, deterioration of judgment and personality.

Arthur Scale: a performance test of intelligence for children. It utilizes concrete, nonverbal materials, such as form boards, incomplete pictures, and block designs. Useful for testing deaf children or the foreign-born.

articulation: 1. audible speech. 2. specifically, the production of consonants in speaking.

artifact: 1. a man-made object, as opposed to a natural object. 2. misleading or incorrect information as a result of improper experimental conditions or the improper treatment of data.

artificial intelligence: the solution by computers or information processing systems of tasks that normally require human intelligence.

artificialism: child's tendency to explain natural phenomena in terms of intentions. For example, when asked why the clouds move, the child answers, "The clouds move because they want to."

artificial pupil: a screen with a small aperture to control the amount of light into the eye.

artificial selection: the process of choosing animals or plants for experimental breeding. *Contr.* NATURAL SELECTION.

A-scale: a questionnaire designed to measure intolerance for ambiguity.

ascendance; ascendant behavior: the tendency to dominate others or to assume the role of leadership in a group. *Contr.* SUBMISSION; SUBMISSIVENESS.

ascendance-submission: a bipolar continuum which assumes that the individual's behavior in relation to others may be located somewhere along a normal distribution, with extreme dominance at one end and extreme subordination at the other end.

ascending-descending series: in the method of limits for the determination of the absolute and/or differential threshold, stimuli presented first in increasing magnitude away from the standard or the approximate threshold, and then in decreasing magnitude away from the standard or the approximate threshold.

ascending reticular activating system: see RETICULAR ACTIVATING SYSTEM.

Asch situation: a test of conformity in which the subject is falsely led to believe that his perceptions are different from those of all other subjects in order to test the effect of the group's judgments on the individual.

asemia; asemasia: the inability to use or understand language.

asexual: 1. reproduction not involving the union of sex cells from two different individuals. 2. sexless, without sex organs.

"as if" hypotheses: 1. the tentative assumption that something is true, usually made for the purpose of discovering the consequence of such an assumption. 2. the philosophical position espoused by Hans Vaihinger which assumes that many of our most valuable ideas, categories, concepts, mathematical theorems and the like, are useful hypotheses that have not been proven or are contradictory. Adler was influenced by Vaihinger and developed the concept of the guiding fiction from Vaihinger's philosophy of "as if." 3. (*Adler*) the assumption that the goal of superiority has been reached.

asitia: revulsion at the sight or thought of food.

asocial: 1. lacking in social customs or social sense. 2. without social or communal value.

A/S ratio: see ASSOCIATION-SENSATION RATIO.

A-S scale: an opinion scale for measuring anti-Semitism.

assertiveness training: in behavior therapy, conditioning the individual to be less passive or fearful in certain situations.

assets-liabilities technique: a method of counseling wherein the subject lists his assets and liabilities for the purpose of gaining understanding and eventually eliminating liabilities.

assignment therapy: (*Moreno*) the utilization of small work or play groups for the purpose of psychotherapy. The individual may be assigned to the group after a sociometric study of the group as a whole.

assimilation: 1. (*Physiol.*) the absorption and storage of food. 2. (*Hering*) the anabolic buildup of retinal materials upon stimulation of the blue, red, or green substances. 3. (*Herbart*) the interpretation of new facts by associating them with existing knowledge. 4. the amalgamation and modification of newly perceived materials into the already existing cognitive structure; one of Wulf's three laws of memory, the other two being leveling and sharpening. 5. (*Jung*) the alteration of an object or situation to fit the individual's needs. 6. (*Thorndike*) the animal's utilization of a learned response in a new situation when the old and new have elements in common. 7. (*Piaget*) the child's application of a cognitive schema to a particular object, person, or event.

assimilation, law of: the principle that the organism will respond to a new situation in the same manner in which it responds to a familiar situation.

assimilative illusion: an illusion in which the entire percept is influenced by the context in which it is seen, or by attitudinal factors. Thus, an apprehensive person walking home in the darkness tends to mistake bushes for crouching men.

association: 1. a functional relationship or connection between two psychological phenomena, established through learning or experience. 2. bond or connection between ideas.

association, laws of: the principle formulated by the associationists to account for the functional relationshhips between ideas. Aristotle postulated the laws of contiguity, similarity, and contrast. Others added laws of coexistence, casuality, and succession. The law of contiguity, which states that of two experiences which occur close together in time, the subsequent occurrence of one will tend to elicit the other, proved to be the most fundamental of the laws and still plays a role in theories of verbal learning, animal learning, and conditioning.

association area: areas of the cerebral cortex that are not specific projection areas. The exact function of an association area may not be known, or it may mediate complex functions associated with memory, perception, judgment, language, etc.

association by contiguity: the principle that if two experiences occur close together in time, the subsequent occurrence of one tends to evoke the other. See also CONTIGUITY, LAW OF.

association center: a neural center where incoming, or sensory, impulses are correlated with outgoing, or motor, impulses. See also BRAIN.

association coefficient: an index of the relationship between discontinuous variables that are measurable only in categories, such as pass-fail, tall-short, etc.

association fiber: see ASSOCIATION NEURON.

associationism: the psychological doctrine that the mind is made up of simple elements in the form of ideas that come from sensory experience. These ideas are held together and are related by associations. The doctrine of associationism began with Aristotle's essay on memory and became a dominant theme in British philosophy during the seventeenth and eighteenth centuries. Throughout this period, British philosophy, and a significant segment of Continental philosophy, became strongly empirical in orientation. The empiricists sought to explain mind as a product of ideas, which in turn were considered the residuum of sensory experience. Empiricism was in opposition to the doctrine of innate ideas, which held that some ideas, at least, were innate. In order to account for the relatedness of ideas, the doctrine of associationism was invoked by the empiricsts. The crystallization of associationism as a formal school of philosophy took place under the leadership of David Hartley (1705–1757). However, the foundations had been laid by Thomas Hobbes (1588–1670), John Locke (1632–1704), George Berkeley (1685–1753), and David Hume (1711–1776). It reached its highest development in the works of James Mill (1773–1836). All of these philosophers emphasized contiguity and similarity as the basic laws of association, a position taken by Aristotle, although they presented varying interpretations of the laws and stated different corollary principles. In present-day psychology there is no school of associationism as such, but its influence remains in theories of verbal and animal learning. See also: THORNDIKE; CONTIGUITY; REINFORCEMENT.

association neuron: one of the neurons in the central nervous system that connect sensory and motor neurons or, more generally, connect any two centers in the brain.

association of ideas: see ASSOCIATIONISM.

association psychology: see ASSOCIATIONISM.

association-reaction time: the elapsed time between a stimulus word and the response in a word association test.

association-sensation ratio: (*Hebb*) the ratio of the mass of association cortex to the total sensory cortex. *Abbr.* A/S. The A/S ratio is an index of the learning ability of organisms, since the larger the ratio the greater the amount of cortex available for learning.

association test: a psychometric or experimental procedure designed to assess the subject's reaction to stimuli of various sorts. In word association tests the subject is instructed to respond with another word. In color naming, another variety of association test, the subject is asked to name a series of colors as rapidly as possible. In *free association* tests, the subject is allowed to respond with any word that comes into his mind. In *controlled association* tests he must respond according to a predetermined

category, such as synonyms, antonyms, etc.

association time: 1. association-reaction time. 2. association-reaction time minus simple reaction time. An obsolete technique for measuring the time required to associate a stimulus with a response. It was assumed that simple reaction time measured the duration of time required for the nervous impulse to travel over the sensory-motor routes. The rest was supposedly devoted to association.

associative chain theory: the assumption that one act is the cause of another in a sequence of acts.

associative facilitation: a process in which an established association makes the learning of another easier.

associative illusion: an illusion in which part of the stimulus pattern is misperceived because of the influence of other parts. Many of the line illusions come under this category, since they involve misperceptions of the length of the line because of the influence of other lines.

associative inhibition: 1. the weakening of an established association through the formation of a new association involving one of the members of the old. 2. difficulty in establishing a new association because of an already established association.

associative learning: learning as the formation of bonds between ideas, or stimulus-response units.

associative memory: the remembering of a past experience or an idea by recalling something associated with it. Thus, revisiting a town after many years' absence may recall a series of long-forgotten incidents each associated with one or more of the others.

associative shifting: (*Thorndike*) the

principle that responses learned to one set of stimuli may be learned to a new set provided that the overall situation is kept similar. Thorndike considered conditioning a form of associative shifting.

associative strength: the strength of a stimulus-response connection in verbal learning as measured by the frequency with which a given stimulus evokes the response, or as measured by its persistence in memory.

associative thinking: thinking that depends on past associations. A train of thought where one idea leads to another illustrates this form of thinking.

assonance: similarity of vowel sounds, as in *leach* and *reach*.

assumed mean: in the shortcut method of calculating the mean from a grouped distribution of scores, an aribitrary value in the distribution that is assumed to be close to the true mean. The algebraic sum of the deviations from the assumed mean divided by their number is then added or subtracted to the assumed mean in order to arrive at the exact mean. *Syn.* GUESSED MEAN.

assumption: a premise or supposition that something is true for the purpose of theoretical development. The term includes *hypothesis*, a principle to be tested experimentally, and *postulate*, a principle assumed to be true for the purpose of developing a theory.

astasia-abasia: a functional inability to stand or walk without loss of function for other uses of the limbs. Associated with hysterical reactions.

asterognosis: inability to recognize objects or geometric forms by touch. Associated with lesions in the posterior parietal lobe.

asthenia: weakness; lack of vitality.

asthenic: characteristic of feelings or emotions that are depressed or inhibited.

asthenic body type or **physique:** the long, slender body. A physique Kretschmer believed to be associated with the schizoid personality.

astigmatism: the failure of the light entering the eye to come to a focal point because of irregularities in the curvature of the refracting mechanism, chiefly the cornea.

astrocyte: a star-shaped glial cell found in the brain that serves a supportive function to the cerebral neurons. May also act as a transport cell in neuronal metabolism and in the formation of scar tissue.

asymbolia: a form of language disorder characterized by the inability to use and understand symbols.

asymmetrical distribution: a statistical distribution in which the two halves, as determined by the median or mean, are dissimilar because of bunching of the values toward one extreme. *Syn.* SKEWNESS.

asymptote: a theoretical limit that a curve approaches but never reaches.

asynergia: inability to carry out complex motor activities involving coordination between different muscle groups.

ataractic drug: a tranquilizer.

ataraxy: the absence of anxiety; calmness.

atavism: 1. a genetic throwback in which a characteristic reappears after an absence of several generations. 2. primitive or violent forms of behavior, such as tantrums, screaming, biting, etc., observed in autistic children.

ataxia: 1. incoordination of voluntary movement as a result of brain damage. 2. lack of coordination between ideas or thought processes.

ataxiameter: a device for measuring the involuntary movements made by an individual when he is attempting to stand motionless.

ataxic writing: uncoordinated writing with deficient characters due to brain damage or lack of skill.

atherosclerosis: narrowing or obstruction of blood vessels with consequent impairment of circulation.

athetosis: slow, recurrent movements of the arms, legs, and especially of the fingers and toes, due to brain damage.

athletic type or **physique:** the well-proportioned body. Kretschmer believed the athletic physique was associated with normalcy or personality.

atmosphere effect: 1. pertaining to the phenomenon wherein inappropriate responses are produced by habits of responding associated with a certain stimulus or stimulus pattern. For example, devout persons sometimes inadvertently cross themselves or genuflect in a theater. 2. in thinking, errors made because of an impression created by the premises or statement of the problem.

atomism: the theory that psychological phenomena are best studied and understood when reduced to their constituent parts or elements. The term is chiefly used with derogatory implications by the opponents of this point of view. *Syn.* ELEMENTARISM; MOLECULARISM.

atony; atonia; atonicity: lack of tone in the musculature.

atrophy: a wasting away, such as may occur in paralyzed muscles.

atropine: a drug that acts to block the action of acetylcholine at certain synaptic sites. Once widely used in eye examinations to relax the iris and in research on thirst to block salivation.

attachment: 1. an emotional attraction or dependence between two persons. 2. in anatomy, the connection between two parts, particularly muscles and their bones. 3. stimulus-response connections or bonds.

attachment bond: a strong and enduring affectional bond between two organisms, especially a parent and child.

attack: 1. the sudden and often temporary manifestation of a disorder, such as an epileptic seizure. 2. violent or aggressive behavior. 3. verbal censure or criticism. 4. the initiation of behavior, as in an attack on a problem.

attainment: see ACHIEVEMENT.

attend: to respond preferentially to a stimulus.

attensity: (*Titchener*) sensory clearness.

attention: 1. the process of preferentially responding to a stimulus or range of stimuli. 2. the adjustment of the sense organs and central nervous system for maximal stimulation. 3. (*Titchener*) a state of sensory clearness with a margin and a focus.

attention-getting: behavior, particularly in children, that seeks recognition from others as its goal.

attention level: the degree of clarity of an experience ranging from unconsciousness (total lack of awareness) to focal attention (vivid awareness).

attention reflex: a change in pupillary diameter upon a sudden fixation of attention.

attention span: see SPAN OF ATTENTION.

attenuation: 1. a reduction in the amount or degree of anything. 2. the reduction of the correlation coefficient because of the unreliability of measurements.

attitude: a relatively stable and enduring predisposition to behave or react in a certain way toward persons, objects, institutions, or issues. Looked at from a slightly different point of view, attitudes are tendencies to respond to people, institutions or events either positively or negatively. Attitudes typically imply a tendency to classify or categorize. Thus, one with a favorable attitude toward the Democratic party is likely to react favorably to all Democrats, disregarding their unique characteristics as individuals. Similarly, if the individual holds the attitude that "All Jews are aggressive" he will respond to Jewish people as if they were aggressive, whether or not they are in fact aggressive.

The source of attitudes are cultural, familial, and personal. That is, we tend to assume the attitudes that prevail in the culture in which we grow up. A large segment of these are passed on from generation to generation within the family structure. But some of our attitudes are also developed as adults on the basis of our own experience. Social psychologists believe that important sources of adult attitudes are propaganda and suggestion from authority, business, educational institutions, and other agencies that seek to influence conduct. Because attitudes differ in degree as well as in kind, psychologists have devised techniques for the measurement of attitudes. Several types of attitude scales have been developed for use with individuals and groups, and mass techniques of public-opinion polling have been developed

for the assessment of national attitudes.

attitude scale: a device for measuring the degree of strength of attitudes or opinions. Of the several techniques that have been employed, two are basic, the Thurstone and the Likert. In the Thurstone-type scale a number of statements of different degrees of strength are presented, and the subject indicates agreement or disagreement with them. The items are selected in such a way as to range along an equal-interval scale from extremely favorable to extremely unfavorable. In the Likert-type, a series of simple questions is presented, each question being rated on a five-point scale: strongly agree, agree, undecided, disagree, strongly disagree. See also LADDER SCALE.

attitude survey or **test:** a study utilizing a questionnaire-type instrument designed to discover the attitudes of a group.

attitude type: one of Jung's classifications of people according to their reactive dispositions. Basic types are the *introvert*, who is inwardly oriented and the *extrovert*, who is outwardly oriented. See also EXTROVERT and INTROVERT.

attitudinizing: 1. assuming certain attitudes for their effect on others. 2. in psychiatric literature, the catalepti-form postures assumed by catatonic schizophrenics.

attraction: anything having the qualities that elicit adient behavior.

attribute: 1. a fundamental or characteristic property of anything. 2. in structuralism, any of the most fundamental characteristics of sensations as identified by introspective analysis. According to Titchener, those attributes common to all sensations are quality, intensity, and duration. Some sensations possess additional attributes, such as extensity and clearness. 3. an independent dimension of a sensation as shown by discrimination tests.

attribution theory: the position that without necessarily being aware of doing so, individuals employ a number of tests to determine whether another person's words and deeds reflect his underlying characteristics or are merely forced responses to a given situation.

A-type personality: a personality pattern characterized by competitiveness, aggressiveness, high achievement, impatience, and restlessness. Presumed to be associated with proneness to coronary disease. *Contr.* B-TYPE PERSONALITY.

atypical: differing markedly in some characteristic. The term may refer to a score in a distribution that deviates markedly from the average, or it may be employed to characterize an individual who stands out from others of his age or class.

Aubert-Fleishel paradox: movement perceived as slower when a moving target is fixated than when the background is fixated.

Aubert-Förster phenomenon: the principle that smaller objects can be distinguished over a larger area of the retina when near than can distant objects, even though the latter subtend the same visual angle as the former.

Aubert phenomena: the apparent displacement of an isolated vertical line in the direction opposite to which the subject's head is tilted.

audibility limit: see ABSOLUTE THRESHOLD.

audile: 1. one whose comprehension is based primarily on hearing. 2. one whose mental imagery is largely in the auditory modality.

audio-frequency: mechanical or electrical oscillations that lie within the range of audibility, that is, 16–20,000 Hz.

audiogenic: produced by sound.

audiogenic seizure: a convulsion, similar to an epileptic seizure, induced by high-frequency sound waves.

audiogram: a record of the individual's auditory sensitivity as measured on an audiometer.

audiogravic illusion: an error in sound localization made by blindfolded individuals who have undergone rapid rotation. *Syn.* AUDIOGYRAL ILLUSION.

audiogyral illusion: see AUDIOGRAVIC ILLUSION.

audiometer: an instrument for determining auditory acuity. Measurements are typically taken in decibels of loss at various frequencies within the range of normal audibility.

audio-oscillator: an electronic instrument for producing a wide range of pure frequencies of desired intensity.

audition: the sense of hearing. The receptors are the ears. The sense cells are hair cells located along the basilar membrane. The hair cells are capable of converting mechanical energy into nervous impulses which are transmitted to the primary auditory area in the temporal lobes. The range of human hearing is approximately 16–20,000 Hz. See also EAR.

audito-oculogyric reflex: a turning of the eyes in the direction of a sudden sound.

auditory: pertaining to hearing. *Syns.* AURAL; OTIC. The term *aural* is typically used in connection with the ears or devices used in research on the ears; *otic* refers to the sense cells themselves or their nervous connections.

auditory acuity: the sensitivity of the ear as measured by the minimal stimulus intensity, at any given pitch, that can be detected 50 percent of the time.

auditory flicker: the perception of an intermittent auditory stimulus as discontinuous. Analogous to visual flicker.

auditory flutter fusion: the rate at which an intermittent tone is perceived as continuous. Analagous to visual flicker fusion.

auditory labyrinth: the portion of the labyrinth of the ear concerned with hearing. The expression is often used incorrectly for the labyrinth as a whole.

auditory nerve or **acoustic nerve:** the portion of the eighth cranial nerve that mediates auditory sensation.

auditory ossicles: the chain of small bones in the middle ear that conducts sound waves from the eardrum to the cochlea. In man there are three: the malleus, or hammer; the incus, or anvil; the stapes, or stirrup. Conduction deafness results when the ossicles become rigidified as a result of disease.

auditory projection area: the region of the temporal lobe where the auditory nerve terminates and where sound perception is mediated. Experiments on animals show that the auditory projection area is organized tonotopically, that is, one part of the region is sensitive to high frequencies, another to intermediate frequencies, and one to low frequencies.

auditory regression: see RECRUITMENT OF LOUDNESS.

auditory space: space as perceived by the sense of hearing.

auditory spectrum: see ACOUSTIC SPECTRUM.

auditory threshold: see AUDITORY ACUITY.

auditory type: see AUDILE.

aura: 1. the sensations that precede an epileptic seizure. 2. in psychic research, the hypothetical emanations given off by the body of an individual to which the operator is sensitive.

aura cursoria: aimless running around sometimes associated with epileptic attacks.

aural: see AUDITORY.

aural microphonic: see COCHLEAR MICROPHONIC.

Austrian school: a group of psychologists under the leadership of Franz Brentano, who emphasized the study of acts as opposed to contents. Also called the Würzburg school; a forerunner of functionalism. See also ACT PSYCHOLOGY.

authoritarian atmosphere: (*Lewin*) a term employed to characterize an extremely autocratic form of leadership relation in which the leader makes all decisions and keeps interpersonal interaction among members of the group to a minimum. *Contr.* DEMOCRATIC ATMOSPHERE; LAISSEZ-FAIRE.

authoritarian personality: a personality pattern characterized by strongly held beliefs, prejudices, and ethnocentrism. Such individuals tend to be highly conventional, submissive to authority, puritanical in sexual attitudes, disciplinarians, and inflexible in attitudes and behavior.

autia: (*R. B. Cattell*) a personality dimension characterized by nonconformity, impracticality, and dissociative behavior. *Contr.* PRAXERNIA.

autism: 1. thinking governed by personal needs or by the self. 2. perceiving the world in terms of wishes as opposed to reality. 3. extreme preoccupation with one's own thoughts and fantasies. See also INFANTILE AUTISM.

autistic child: an extremely withdrawn child. Autistic children may sit and play for hours with their own fingers or bits of paper; they appear to be lost in a world of inner fantasy.

austistic thinking: 1. thinking characterized by autism. 2. wishful thinking; thinking governed by the self or self-needs.

autocentric: 1. self-centered. 2. denoting senses that are subject-centered, with emphasis on the affective reactions. Smell and taste are autocentric senses. *Contr.* ALLOCENTRIC.

autochthonous: originating within the individual independently of outside influence and of the normal trains and modes of thoughts. Characteristic of schizophrenic thinking and obsessive states.

autochthonous Gestalt: a perceptual unity arising from innate factors as opposed to stimulus factors.

autochothonous variable: any change that results from factors within a system.

autoeroticism; autoerotism: sexual behavior utilizing one's own body, as in masturbation.

autogenic; autogenous: originating within the self; self-generated.

autogenic reinforcement: the strengthening of a response by factors within the organism so that the resulting response is stronger than could be accounted for by stimulating conditions. Autogenic reflexes strengthen muscular responses in walking each time the foot touches the ground.

autogenous: see AUTOGENIC.

autohypnosis: hypnosis that is self-induced.

autohypnotic amnesia: (*Jung*) repressive or artificial forgetting.

autokinesis: movement initiated by organism factors, as in proprioceptive responses.

autokinetic effect; autokinetic illusion: the apparent or illusory movement of a spot of light in a dark room. The movement is slow and irregular, extending as much as 45 degrees from the point of origin for some subjects.

automatic: 1. relatively independent of external stimulation, as in certain glandular responses and the hearbeat. 2. machinelike, requiring little attention or deliberation, as in automatic speaking and automatic writing.

automatic speaking: 1. involuntary speech associated with extreme emotional states, hypnosis, and senility. 2. speech that has been overlearned, such as the alphabet, days of the week, etc., and which can be uttered without a high degree of conscious control.

automatic writing: 1. writing while the attention is concentrated on content rather than on the act of writing itself. 2. writing carried out without conscious control. Under experimental conditions, automatic writing is elicited while the subject is made to engage in some other activity and the writing hand is hidden behind a screen.

automatism: an act or process performed unconsciously, as a reflex. In sensory automatism, illusions and hallucinations are produced by prolonged, concentrated stimulation. The clairvoyant's hallucinations produced by crystal gazing are sensory automatisms.

automatization: development of a process or skill to a degree in which acts become so routine as to require little or no conscous effort.

automatograph: an instrument used to record automatic movements.

automaton: 1. a manlike machine. 2. a person whose behavior is machinelike.

automorphic perception: perceiving others as like the self, while ignoring differences that may exist.

autonomic: functioning independently; self-regulating, as the autonomic nervous system.

autonomic balance: the normal complementary interaction between the sympathetic and parasympathetic branches of the autonomic nervous system in the regulation of bodily functions.

autonomic conditioning: conditioning designed to achieve conscious control of processes normally regulated by the autonomic nervous system.

autonomic function: a physiological process primarily under the control of the autonomic nervous system.

autonomic nervous system: one of the chief divisions of the nervous system, consisting of a large outflow of peripheral, efferent fibers, which regulate visceral and glandular responses. The system consists of two divisions, the sympathetic and parasympathetic. The sympathetic fibers arise from a chain of ganglia on either side of the spinal cord and innervate the various bodily organs. The parasympathetic fibers arise from the medulla and the sacral portion of the spinal cord and innervate all visceral organs except the adrenal glands. The sympathetic division is dominant in emergency conditions and initiates widespread and profound body changes, including acceleration in heartbeat, dilation of the bronchioles, discharge of adrenaline into the bloodstream, inhibition of digestion, and elevation in blood pressure. The parasympathetic is the system dominant in digestion, elimination, and sexual arousal. In general, the sympathetic is a catabolic system associated with emergencies; the parasympathetic, an anabolic system associated with vegetative processes. The sympathetic system is also known as the thoraciolumbar division and the parasympathetic as the cranial-sacral division, because of their anatomical origin.

autonomic reflex: a reflex involving the autonomic nervous system.

autonomous complex: one of Jung's partial systems or complexes that originate in the unconscious but subsequently become conscious.

autonomous morality: (*Piaget*) moral attitudes characteristic of children over eight years of age, who view moral rules as relativistic and partially dependent upon intentions. *Contr.* HETERONOMOUS MORALITY.

autonomy: the state of self-regulation.

autonomy; autonomy drive: the freedom of the human individual to choose, to be a self-governing entity.

autophilia: love of self. *Syn.* NARCISSISM.

autophobia: fear of the self, as in fear of being alone.

autopsychosis: any psychosis in which the disordered ideas are centered around the self as opposed to the environment.

autorivalry: see AUTOCOMPETITION.

autoscope: any instrument or device used to magnify small muscular movements, such as the automatograph and the divining rod.

autosome: a chromosome other than a sex chromosome.

autosuggestion: self-suggestion.

autotelic: characteristic of traits associated with the defense of self, self-preservation, and self-realization.

auxiliary ego: 1. one who identifies himself with all of another's expression and purposes. 2. in psychodrama, a person who substitutes for another in enacting a role.

auxiliary solution: (*Horney*) a defense mechanism or partial solution to a conflict, such as COMPARTMENTALIZATION; EXTERNALIZATION; and INTELLECTUALIZATION.

availability principle: see READINESS.

average: 1. a general term for several measures of central tendency. The commonly employed averages are the arithmetic mean, the median, and the mode. 2. the arithmetic average or mean; equal to the sum of the scores divided by their number.

average deviation: a deviation mean that yields the most representative estimate of the deviation of the individual values from their mean. *Abbr.* AD. It is found by dividing the sum of the deviations, ignoring sign, by their number.

average error: the average amount by which a series of observations differs from a standard. See also: ADJUSTMENT METHOD.

averages, law of: the generality that random errors of measurement will occur equally often in either direction away from the true value and consequently that the mean, which is the average error, is the best estimate of the true value.

average variation: average deviation.

aversion: 1. a turning away from something in disgust or dislike. 2. a negative reaction to a specific food.

aversive control: escape or avoidance conditioning achieved by employing negative reinforcement, e.g., animals escaping a shock by pressing a lever upon a signal.

aversive stimulus: a noxious stimulus, such as an electric shock, which the organism will avoid if possible.

aversive therapy: in behavior therapy, a technique that reduces the frequency of maladaptive behavior by associating it with real or imagined aversive stimuli during a conditioning procedure.

avoidance-avoidance conflict: a situation in which the individual finds himself equally repelled by two alternative courses of action. For example, the soldier who is suffering from combat fagitue may be repelled by the idea of further combat and contemplate deserting. But fear of the consequences of deserting is equally repelling. Such conflicts are highly disruptive and may result in "leaving the field," that is, escaping the situation. Many soldiers in World War I developed hysterical illness, a socially acceptable way of leaving the field.

avoidance gradient: the decreasing attractiveness of a negative goal accompanied by abient behavior or the tendency to draw away from it.

avoidance learning: a general term referring to any learning situation where the correct response allows the organism to escape punishment.

avoidance response or **reaction:** abient behavior in which the individual moves away from a stimulus.

awareness: 1. consciousness; alertness. 2. cognizance of something; a state of knowledge or understanding of environmental or internal events.

axial: pertaining to the longitudinal axis or dimension of the body.

axial gradient: a change in metabolism or in the rate of development along the axis of the body. For example, in the embryo the head region develops faster than the tail region.

axiom: 1. a self-evident truth; 2. a proposition not capable of either proof or disproof but which is universally accepted as true.

axis: 1. a reference line along which distances are measured or that defines spatial relations. 2. a line with which a coordinate line defines a point. The horizontal axis is typically identified at the X axis, the vertical as the Y axis. 3. an anatomical line of reference such as the cephalocaudal or head-to-tail axis. 4. a line around which a body moves; the axis of rotation.

axis cylinder: the central, conducting core of a neuron.

axoaxonic synapse: a synapse between two axons. This type of synapse mediates presynaptic inhibition.

axodendritic synapse: the synapse of an axon on a dendrite.

axon; axone: the relatively elongated part of a neuron that conducts impulses away from the cell body.

axon reflex: a peripheral reflex presumed to be mediated by collateral branches of afferent neurons that activate receptors. Axon reflexes have been used to account for certain vascular effects.

axosomatic synapse: a synapse between an axon of one neuron and the cell body of another.

B

babble: the meaningless speech sounds of the infant.

Babinski reflex or **sign:** extensions of the toes when the sole of the foot is lightly stroked. Normally the toes contract (pantar reflex). The Babinski reflex is manifested by normal infants and by those afflicted with diseases of the nervous system and as a sign of lack or loss of function of the upper motor neurons.

bacillophobia: fear of germs.

background: 1. the portions of a picture depicted as being in the rear or at some distance from the figure. The background is typically less distinct, may be less sharply contoured, and may lack pattern. Syn. GROUND. 2. the aggregate of events or experiences that influence a situation or form part of a case history. 3. that portion of a sensory experience that does not constitute the figure or focus of experience.

backward association: in verbal learning, the connection that exists between a given item in a series and a preceding item. *Contr.* FORWARD ASSOCIATION.

backward conditioning: a procedure whereby the conditioned stimulus follows the unconditioned stimulus. The procedure is unreliable, and some psychologists consider such conditioning an artifact.

backwardness: 1. a condition of mild intellectual retardation. 2. less than the normal rate of intellectual development. 3. scholastic retardation not the result of intellectual deficiency.

bad trip: a colloquial expression for an unpleasant experience resulting from the use of hallucinogenic drugs, especially LSD.

balance: 1. the maintenance of stable, upright posture. 2. in aesthetics, the harmonious relationship between parts of an artistic production. 3. emotional equilibrium or absence of eccentricities.

balanced scale: a scale with each half of the items scored in opposite directions. If half of the items are scored true, the other half will be false.

balance theory: the position that people prefer to hold consistent and compatible beliefs while avoiding those that are inconsistent and incompatible.

ballistic movement: a smooth, projectilelike movement in which the limb "follows through." Time-and-motion experts consider ballistic movements more efficient than other types of movements.

Bandura, Albert: American psychologist. Bandura was born December 4, 1925, in Mundara, Alberta, Canada. He grew up in the Province of Alberta, where he received his early schooling. He received his B.A. degree from the University of British Columbia in 1949, earning his M.A. (1951) and Ph.D. (1952) from the University of Iowa. He served a year's clinical internship at the Wichita Guidance Center after receiving his doctorate and then accepted an appointment to the department of psychology at Stanford University, where he has remained ever since. In 1974 he was awarded the endowed chair, The David Starr Jorgan Professor of Social Science.

Throughout his career at Stanford, Bandura has been a leader in developing social learning theory, an attempt to apply a modified form of behaviorism, stressing a cognitive approach, to the understanding of human behavior with clinical applications. See SOCIAL LEARNING THEORY.

Bandura has published numerous technical articles in professional journals and several influential books, *Social Learning and Personality* (1963), *Principles of Behavior Modification* (1969), *Aggression (1973)*, *and Social Learning Theory* (1977).

In 1972 he received the Distinguished Scientist Award from the American Psychological Association, and in 1974 was elected president of that organization.

bandwagon effect: a phenomenon in social groups where increasingly large numbers of individuals associate themselves with the prevailing majority opinion. Bandwagon effects often occur in political campaigns when voters switch their allegiance in order to identify with the majority.

bandwidth: the frequency range of a group of sound stimuli.

Barany test: stimulation of the semicircular canals by rotating the individual in a special chair.

barbiturate: any one of a class of drugs such as phenobarbital or seconal, which act as central nervous depressants, inducing drowsiness and muscular relaxation.

bar diagram or **chart:** a graphic method of representing scores or magnitudes by means of narrow rectangles of uniform width but different lengths. If the bars are made contiguous, the vertical lines are usually omitted and the result is called a *histogram*.

baresthesis; baraesthesia: the sense of pressure.

Barnum effect: the tendency for people to believe general descriptions about personality or behavior, such as astrologers' forecasts.

barotropism; barotaxis: an orienting response in which the organism heads into the current, such as may occur in fishes that inhabit currents of water.

barrier: a real or imagined impediment to movement toward a goal. Barriers may be physical, social, or the result of the individual's physical or mental limitations.

basal age: on tests standardized in mental age units, the age level at which all items are passed.

basal ganglia: a number of masses of gray matter in the subcortex of the cerebral hemispheres which are important in motor coordination.

basal metabolism: the minimum heat production during rest, measured after 14–18 hours of fasting. The basal metabolic rate represents the minimum energy expenditure, measured in calories, which is necessary to maintain vital functions.

base line: 1. the abscissa or horizontal axis. 2. a characteristic level of performance that can be used to assess changes in behavior resulting from experimental conditions.

basic anxiety: (*Horney*) the child's feeling of being alone and helpless in a potentially hostile world.

basic conflict: (*Horney*) the conflict between the fundamental neurotic

trends of moving toward, moving away from, or moving against people.

basic need: a fundamental or primary need that is vital to the organism and from which all others may be derived, according to some theorists.

basic personality: the constellation of personality traits common to individuals in a given culture which results from common childhood experience and training.

basic skills: a term used in educational literature to refer to the fundamentals of reading, writing, and arithmetic, whose mastery is needed to progress normally at higher levels.

basilar membrane: the membrane in the cochlea upon which the organ of Corti rests. The hair cells of the organ of Corti convert mechanical energy (movements of the basilar membrane) into nervous impulses which are then transmitted to the auditory centers in the temporal lobes.

basket cell: a type of interneuron found in the cerebellum.

basophobia: a morbid fear of standing erect or walking.

bathophobia: a pathological fear of the depths.

bathyesthesis; bathyesthesia: deep sensitivity.

battle fatigue: see COMBAT FATIGUE.

beat: periodic fluctuation in sound intensity produced when two tones of slightly different frequencies are sounded together.

beat tone: a rough tone intermediate in pitch between two tones, differing slightly in pitch, and are sounded simultaneously.

becoming: (*Allport*) the restlessness and desire for activity and the tendency toward growth, characteristic of one whose basic or primary drives are satisfied.

before-after design: an experimental condition in which both the experimental and control groups are given a pretest and an aftertest.

behavior: 1. any response(s) made by an organism. 2. specifically, parts of a total response pattern. 3. an act or activity. 4. a movement or complex of movements.

Although American psychologists are generally in agreement that the subject matter of psychology is behavior, there is considerable divergence of opinion as to precisely what ought to be included under the category of behavior. Taken in its broadest sense, behavior includes anything the individual does or experiences. Ideas, dreams, glandular responses, running, maneuvering a space ship—all are behavior. In a narrower sense, *behavior* can be defined to include only objectively or publicly observable responses. This definition would exclude such conscious phenomena as thinking, perceiving, judgment, and the like, except as these may be studied through their consequences in behavior. Few psychologists today define their subject matter so rigidly as to exclude any major segment of human activity. Most behaviorists, however objectively oriented they may be, believe that there is room in psychology for inferred or intervening variables. Thus, the term *behavior* no longer implies the strict behaviorism championed by Watson and the opponents of structuralism. In general, American psychology has become behavioristic in method, but in spirit it is sufficiently broad to include the study of all important segments of human activity.

behavioral: a term used to distinguish sciences whose aims and methods are objective as opposed to subjective or mentalistic.

behavioral contagion: the lessening of restraint as a result of observing others behave in a certain way.

behavioral dynamics: the pattern of motives that underlies behavior.

behavioral genetics: a branch of psychology concerned with the investigation of genetic or hereditary influences on behavior.

behavioral homology: the generalization that behavioral patterns form a continuity from species to species. Thus, fear responses in lower forms correspond in function and pattern to fear in man.

behavioral oscillation: (*Hull*) variations in reaction potential from moment to moment. Behavioral oscillation follows the normal frequency curve.

behavioral pattern: any complex act made up of recognizably individual components that are organized into a whole. Riding a bicycle is an example of a complex behavioral pattern made up of mounting, pedaling, steering, braking, etc.

behavioral rehearsal: in behavior therapy, the utilization of role playing by therapist and patient with the goal of helping the patient overcome deficits in interpersonal behavior.

behavioral sciences: the sciences that study the activities of man and the lower animals by means of naturalistic observation and experimentation. These include psychology, sociology, and social anthropology.

behavior determinant: (*Tolman*) any variable that is a necessary antecedent condition for behavior to occur. See also PURPOSIVE PSYCHOLOGY.

behavior disorder: a general concept referring to any type of abnormality that is functional in origin.

behavior exchange model: the position that in social interactions people are engaged in rational efforts to achieve mutually satisfying states of affairs for both parties to an exchange.

behavior field: any environmental condition or stimulus that influences the individual at a given moment in time.

behavior genetics: the science of the inheritance of behavioral characteristics.

behaviorism: a theoretical point of view that holds that the subject matter of psychology is behavior without reference to consciousness or mentalistic constructs. The point of view is old, but behaviorism as a formal school of psychology had its inception in the work of John B. Watson (*q.v.*). The formal launching of the movement occurred in 1913 with a paper that appeared in the *Psychological Review*. In it Watson gave his definition of psychology as follows: ". . . a purely objective experimental branch of natural science. Its goal is the prediction and control of behavior . . . The time seems to have come when psychology must discard all reference to consciousness; when it need no longer delude itself into thinking that it is making mental states the object of observation." The foundations of Watsonian behaviorism are to be found in the work of the early animal psychologists and the physiologists. The former were stimulated by Darwin to discover the origins and evolution of mind by the comparative study of the lower forms and man. The Russian physiologists, Pavlov, Bekhterev, and Sechenov worked to expand the newly discovered method of conditioning into a research tool that would enable them to investigate complex phenomena such as thinking, sleep, mental conflicts, and the neuroses. Watson was particularly influenced by Pavlov's work and made the method of conditioning one of the chief techniques of the behaviorist. Mention must also be made of the pioneer work of E. L. Thorndike (*q.v.*), who stimulated a generation of followers in the area of animal psychology. Although Watson was not directly influenced by his work, the broad movement of American behaviorism owes much to Thorndike.

Although Watson's behaviorism was the dominant behavioristic program in psychology between 1919 and the mid-1930's, when the schools as such disappeared, there were a number of prominent psychologists whose general orientation was behavioristic and who lent support to Watson. Edwin B. Holt (1873–1946) contributed strong philosophical support to the movement in his writings. Walter S. Hunter (1889–1953) contributed a number of methodological procedures, making possible the investigation of the higher mental processes in animals. Karl S. Lashley (1890–1958), a former student of Watson's, became one of the world's leading physiological psychologists. His work on brain functions in animals lent support to an objective psychology. Among the contemporary theories and systems whose overall orientation is behavioristic are E. C. Tolman's purposive behavior, C. L. Hull's behavior system, B. F. Skinner's descriptive behaviorism, and E. R. Guthrie's contiguity theory.

behaviorist: an adherent of behaviorism.

behavioristic: 1. pertaining to behaviorism. 2. objective, nomentalistic.

behavior method: a derivative of behaviorism, which like the parent school rejects introspection and mentalistic concepts but does not identify itself with the extremely negative point of view of Watsonian behaviorism toward anything not directly observable. Thus, most behavioral psychologists accept the study of intervening variables as explanatory constructs. However, they insist that these must be carefully anchored to stimulus and response and defined in operational terms. See also BEHAVIORISM; OPERATIONISM; INTERVENING VARIABLE.

behavior modification: changing human behavior by the application of conditioning or other learning techniques. The term is often used as a synonym for behavior therapy (*q.v.*).

behavior object: anything toward which reactions tend to be standardized, such as a toothbrush, a chair, or a shoe.

behavior rating: the report of the presence of a specific behavior or class of behavior. Often quantitative estimates are given. For example, the rater might be asked how often the child attempts to contact other children in the play group during a specified period of time.

behavior sampling: a record of what an individual does during a specific period. The period chosen is designed to be representative of the totality of the behavior under consideration.

behavior segment: the smallest descriptive unit of a response to a stimulus.

behavior space: see LIFE SPACE.

behavior therapy: the systematic application of learning principles and techniques to the treatment of behavior disorders. Behavior therapists assume that disorders are learned ways of behaving that are maladaptive and consequently can best be modified in more adaptive directions through relearning. In contrast to traditional forms of psychotherapy, behavior therapy minimizes the client's verbal explorations toward the eventual restructuring of personality by removing repressions and achieving insight. Instead, a direct attack is made on the client's symptoms. Thus, if the client complains of anxiety, the behavior therapist does not attempt to trace the history of the problem back to childhood but instead initiates a program of reconditioning designed to alleviate the symptoms of anxiety in those situations in which the client finds them most troublesome.

Behavior therapy is based on experimental studies of conditioning, both of the classical and operant varieties. Josph Wolpe's publication, *Psychotherapy by Reciprocal Inhibition* (1958), is considered one of the landmarks in the development of behavior therapy. Utilizing the concept of reciprocal inhibition, which refers to the discovery that a response incompatible with another will inhibit the former, Wolpe demonstrated that individuals suffering from anxiety reactions could be trained to overcome their problem by pairing imagined anxiety-producing situations with physical relaxation. Because anxiety and relaxation are incompatible responses, as relaxation increases, anxiety decreases. Care is taken to ensure that the imagined anxiety-producing situations are introduced in a hierarchy of low to high anxiety-induction in order to ensure gradual learning to cope with even the most severe situations.

Desensitization may also involve the gradual introduction of feared stimuli or situations. Fear of snakes has been overcome by introducing the subject to snakes in a cage at a distance, then having the subject gradually approach and touch the cage. The therapist may then remove the snake and handle it as the client watches. The client eventually is encouraged to touch and handle the snake himself.

Aversive techniques may also be employed by behavior therapists to overcome undesirable behaviors such as excessive smoking, drinking, or homosexuality. For example, the alcoholic may be given a drug (antabuse) that induces nausea if the ingestion of alcohol occurs while the drug is in the bloodstream. After a number of such pairings of the drug with alcohol ingestion, drinking becomes aversive. Similarly, electric shock paired with nude photographs of the same sex may be used in the treatment of homosexuality.

Among operant techniques derived from the experimental analysis of behavior by B. F. Skinner and his associates, the most widely used is the token economy, which involves a program of contingency reinforcement for behavioral responses that the therapist considers desirable. For example, a mentally retarded child may be trained to brush his teeth by reinforcing him with a token which can be "spent" for candy, television watching time, etc. Similarly, the adult mental patient may be reinforced with tokens for behaving in ways that the staff deems desirable or more adaptive. The utilization of the token economy is based on the theory of generalized reinforcers that acquire their reinforcing effect through association with primary reinforcers (*q.v.*).

For additional techniques available to the behavior therapist see entries under the following headings: ANXIETY-RELIEF RESPONSES; ASSERTIVENESS TRAINING; BEHAVIORAL REHEARSAL; CONDITIONED SUPPRESSION; COVERT EXTINCTION; COVERT REINFORCEMENT; EMOTIVE IMAGERY; IMPLOSIVE THERAPY; REPLICATION THERAPY; SELF-DESENSITIZATION; SHAME AVERSIVE THERAPY; THOUGHT STOPPING; and TIME OUT FROM REINFORCEMENT.

bel: See DECIBEL.

belief dilemma: an attitude or opinion whose positive and negative components are in a state of imbalance.

belief-value matrix: (*Tolman*) the system of expectancies and value judgments that the individual brings to his dealings with the environment.

Bell Adjustment Inventory: a personality questionnaire that yields scores on home, health, social, and emotional adjustments. Grades 9–16 and adult.

Bellevue Test or **Scale:** see WECHSLER-BELLEVUE SCALE.

Bell-Magendie law: the principle that the ventral roots or spinal nerves are motor in function and the dorsal roots, sensory.

bell-shaped curve: the normal-distribution curve.

belongingness: 1. the feeling of being accepted by another person or by a group; the feeling of being identified with a group. 2. (*Thorndike*) the property of one item being closely related to or an integral part of another. The names Washington and George exhibit the characteristic of belong-ingness.

belongingness, principle of: (*Thorn-dike*) the assumption that the connec-tions between items in learning are more readily formed if these are re-lated in some way. Belongingness was a supplementary principle to the laws of exercise and effect.

Bender-Gestalt Test: a test consist-ing of nine designs that the individ-ual is asked to copy. Analyses of the spatial errors are held to be signifi-cant for diagnosing psychological disorders.

beneceptor: a receptor, or sense organ, whose stimuli are in some way beneficial to the organism. *Contr.* NOCICEPTOR.

benign: pertaining to the milder forms of mental disorders.

Bennett Differential Aptitude Test: tests of numerical, verbal, mechan-ical, and abstract reasoning; spatial relations; clerical speed and accuracy; language usage. Grades 8–12.

Bennett Test of Mechanical Com-prehension: a test of mechanical aptitude, utilizing mechanical prob-lems in printed form; designed for high-school students and adults. Sev-eral levels of difficulty are available.

benzedrine: a synthetic compound used as a central nervous stimulant.

berdache: 1. an American Indian who dresses and assumes the occupa-tion of a woman. 2. a transvestite.

Berger rhythm: see ALPHA RHYTHM.

Bernreuter Personal Adjustment Inventory: a questionnaire-type in-ventory designed to yield measures of six traits: neurotic tendency, self-sufficiency, introversion-extrover-sion, dominance-submission, self-confidence, and sociability.

best fit: see GOODNESS OF FIT.

bestiality: sexual intercourse with animals.

beta coefficient: see BETA WEIGHT.

beta movement: see APPARENT MOVE-MENT.

beta response: a delayed eyelid re-sponse following the presentation of the conditioned stimulus. *Contr.* AL-PHA RESPONSE.

beta rhythm; beta waves: brain waves of 13–25 Hz observed on the electroencephalograph, which are faster than the alpha waves and of lesser amplitude.

Beta test: a group performance test designed for illiterates and used dur-ing the First World War.

beat weight: in multiple correlation, the weights are the multipliers of pre-dictors that will yield the highest correlation. *Syn.* BETA COEFFICIENT; beta regression coefficient.

Betz cell: any of the large pyramid-shaped cells of layer V of the motor cortex. *Syn.* pyramidal cell.

Bezold-Brücke phenomenon: a shift in hues containing red and green toward the yellow and blue side of the spectrum as the intensity of illumination is increased.

bias: 1. a prejudice. 2. a distorting factor or error in a set of data or in an experimental design.

Bidwell's ghost: see PURKINJE AFTER-IMAGE.

bifactoral theory of conditioning: the hypothesis that attitudes deter-mine the probability or incidence of conditioning, and stimulus properties determine the magnitude of the re-sponse.

bifactor method: a factor-analysis technique in which a general factor is extracted first, followed by the extraction of group factors, which are factors of more limited scope.

bilateral: pertaining to two sides; two-sided.

bilateral transfer: transfer of a skill from one side of the body to the other.

bimodal distribution: a distribution having two peaks or maxima.

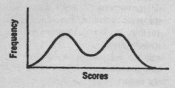

FIG. 3. *A bimodal distribution.*

binaural: pertaining to the two ears acting together, as in ordinary hearing.

binaural beat: a periodic fluctuation in sound intensity produced when two tones of slightly different frequencies are led into the two ears separately.

binaural fusion: the combined effect of stimuli simultaneously presented to the two ears.

binaural ratio: the ratio of sound intensity at the two ears.

binaural shift: see BINAURAL BEAT.

Binet, Alfred: French psychologist, developer of the first standardized test of intelligence (1857–1911). Binet studied law, medicine, and biology at the University of Paris and became attracted to psychology while collaborating at the Sorbonne with H. E. Beaunais, whom he later succeeded as director of the psychology laboratory. Discarding the then dominant "brass instrument" psychology of the structuralists, Binet studied the higher mental processes by means of simple paper-and-pencil tests, and 1866 he published his *Psychology of Reasoning*, based on his investigations. A number of technical articles followed, on hypnosis, suggestibility, and pathological alterations in personality. About 1900 Binet began his researches on individual differences, which culminated in the development of his famous scale of intelligence in 1905. Using his daughters as subjects, he attempted a systematic study of how they differed in their mental processes, employing pictures, verbal tests, and inkblots—the latter paving the way for the projective techniques so popular in contemporary clinical psychology. See also BINET TEST; STANFORD-BINET SCALE.

Binet Test or Scale: the individual verbal scale developed by Alfred Binet and Theodore Simon in 1905; the Simon-Binet Test. The original scale was designed to assess the relative intellectual ability of French school children. The test has been widely adapted for use in other countries. See also BINET TEST; STANFORD-BINET SCALE.

binocular: pertaining to the simultaneous functioning of the two eyes.

binocular accommodation: the simultaneous accommodation of the two eyes.

binocular color mixture: the simultaneous presentation of two different colors to the two eyes by means of a stereoscope.

binocular disparity: the slight difference between the two retinal images when viewing a solid object. The effect is caused by the separation of the two eyes with the consequent difference in visual angle. The importance of binocular disparity in depth perception is demonstrated in stereoscopic vision.

binocular fusion: the blending of two images falling on the separate retinas into a unitary experience.

binocular parallax: the disparity in the two retinal images caused by the separation of the eyes. In binocular parallax the right eye sees more of the right-hand side of an object on the right side and the left eye more of the left-hand side of an object on the left side.

binocular perception: perception with the two eyes interacting in such a way as to achieve fusion of the two visual fields.

binocular rivalry: the alternation of sensations between the two eyes when stimulated separately by two colors or figures that cannot fuse into a unitary experience.

binocular vision: seeing with both eyes focused on the same object.

bioelectrical potential: the electrical potential shown by living tissues, such as neurons, the brain, and the heart.

biofeedback: the control of internal processes, such as heart rate, brain waves, or the galvanic skin response, through conditioning.

biogenic law: see RECAPITULATION THEORY.

biographical method: the utilization of personal-background information in investigating the cause-and-effect relationships between events in the individual's life and development.

biometry: the utilization of statistical techniques for the study of living organisms.

bionegativity: a personality constellation in which a part is not harmoniously related to the whole, thus impairing the functioning of the organism.

bionomic factors: those factors, external to organisms, that influence development.

biopsychic: pertaining to psychological phenomena as they are related to the life of the individual.

biopsychology: see PSYCHOBIOLOGY.

biosocial: 1. pertaining to the interrelationships between biological and social phenomena. 2. both social and biological in nature. Psychology, for example, has been characterized as a biosocial study.

biotype: a group of organisms that share a common complex of hereditary factors.

bipolar: 1. having branches arising from both ends of a cell body, as bipolar neurons. 2. characterizing traits that can be expressed as opposites, such as dominance and submission.

bipolar neuron: a neuron with two processes, an axon and a dendrite, extending in opposite directions away from the cell body.

birth cry: a reflex vocalization associated with the initiation of respiration immediately after birth.

birth order: the relative age of children in a given family. Alfred Adler considered birth order an important factor in the development of personality. See INDIVIDUAL PSYCHOLOGY.

birth symbolism: (*Psychoan.*) a symbolic representation in a neurotic symptom or other form of behavior, which stands for the separation of the newborn child from the mother.

birth trauma: 1. (*Psychoan.*) the anxiety experienced by the infant upon being flooded with stimuli at birth. This primal anxiety is held to be the prototype of all neurotic anxiety. 2. a physical injury at birth.

biserial correlation: a relationship in which one variable is divided into two classes and the other into many classes. Thus, to correlate the answer to the question "Are you a Democrat?" (Yes or No) with economic status as estimated in ten distinct classes would require a biserial correlation.

bisexuality: 1. having the anatomical or psychological characteristics of both sexes. 2. the state of being equally attracted to both sexes.

bisexual libido: (*Psychoan.*) fixation of the libido on both masculine and feminine objects. *Syn.* psychosexual hermaphroditism.

bit: in information theory a unit of information that, when put into an assemblage of variables, reduces the alternative outcomes of an event by one half.

bivariate method: (*R. B. Cattell*) the classical experimental design involving the manipulation of an independent variable to observe its effect on the dependent variable, as applied to personality research.

black: an achromatic color of minimum brilliance. Black constitutes the extreme lower limit of the gray series. The arousal of black often depends upon contrast effects; that is, a stimulus of very low brilliance surrounded by a background of relative high brilliance is perceived as black.

black box: a term used to refer to models that seek to explain the behavior of organisms by drawing analogies between the organism and a piece of apparatus capable of receiving stimulation (input) and of making responses (output). The psychologist's problem is to develop constructs that, given a certain input, will account for output.

blackout threshold: the point at which an individual under conditions of oxygen deprivation loses consciousness.

Blacky Pictures: a series of cartoons depicting situations in the life of a family of dogs with obvious analogies to human family problems. The child is asked to tell stories about this situations, which are analyzed for context as possible indicators of family conflict, repression, etc. The test is psychoanalytically slanted.

blame avoidance: (*Murray*) the motive to avoid blame, censure, and social disapproval.

blank experiment: a type of experimental control in which an irregular condition is occasionally introduced in order to prevent the subject from becoming automatic in his responses. The results of blank experiments are not counted.

blast injection technique: see AUDIOGENIC SEIZURE.

blend: 1. a fusion of sensory experiences, such as the taste blend experienced in lemonade. 2. (*Rorschach*) a multidetermined response.

blind alley: a maze passage without an exit. *Syns.* blind; CUL-DE-SAC.

blind analysis: a diagnosis made from test results or descriptive protocols but without direct knowledge of or contact with the testee.

blindism: mannerisms, such as rubbing the eyes, that are characteristic of the blind.

blind-matching technique: validation procedure wherein an observer attempts to match the description of a person from one set of protocols to another. For example, selection of the appropriate Rorschach description through information derived from a number of other tests.

blindness: the inability to see: specifically, having less than 20/200 vision corrected. *Functional blindness* is an inability to see, caused by other than organic defect. This condition can be induced under hypnosis and may be a symptom of hysteria.

blind spot: a small area in the retina that is insensitive to light. It lies in the horizontal plane 12–15 degrees to the nasal side.

Bloch's law: see BUNSEN-RASCOE LAW.

block: 1. a barrier, either physical or psychological. 2. mechanical or chemical barrier to nervous transmission, as in *spinal blocks*. 3. a complete stopping of speech in stutterers. 4. a temporary failure of memory. 5. a group of trials.

block design: the division of experimental subjects into homogeneous categories according to some predetermined criterion. Each block of subjects is then treated as a unit for the purposes of the experiment.

block-design test: any test making use of colored blocks in which the testee is required to match designs.

block sampling: 1. the grouping of respondents or elements to be sampled into categories representative of the population and selecting from each category a certain number of cases for the final sample. 2. area sampling or taking a respondent from each geographic area.

blood-brain barrier: a protective mechanism that prevents certain substances carried by the blood from entering brain tissue.

blood pressure: the force exerted by the blood against the arteries. Systolic pressure is the maximum phase, which results from the surge of blood from the left ventricle; the diastolic phase is the minimal or resting phase. The two are often reported in the form of a ratio. For example, 120/80 means a systolic pressure of 120 and a diastolic of 80.

blue: a color experience associated with a wavelength of about 478 nanometers.

blue blindness: see TRITANOPIA.

blue-yellow blindness: a rare form of partial color blindness in which there is confusion between blue and yellow. The color experiences of the blue-yellow blind are limited to reds, greens, and grays.

body: 1. the central portion of an organism bearing the appendages and head. 2. an organ or organized mass of tissue, such as the mamillary body in the brain. 3. the material substance of the individual as distinct from the mental.

body build: the individual's structure from the point of view of the proportions of trunk and limb length to girth.

body-build index: the relation between stature and transverse chest diameter according to the formula

$$I = \frac{\text{stature} \times 100}{\text{transverse chest dia.} \times 6}.$$

The body-build index is used in studies of the relation of bodily build and psychoses. Distinction is made between leptomorphs, persons one SD (standard deviation) above mean of approximately 100; mesomorphs, within one SD, and eurymorphs, one or more SD's below the mean.

body concept or **body image:** the individual's idea of how his body appears to others. Sometimes the concept of how the body functions is included.

body language: the communication

of conscious and unconscious feelings through gestures and posture.

body size: the standard score for height times transverse chest measurement. Distinction is made between macrosomatics, persons whose size is one SD (standard deviation) above the mean; mesosomatics, within one SD of the mean; and microsomatics, those one or more SD's below the mean.

body type: any scheme for classifying individuals on the basis of certain defined physical characteristics. See CONSTITUTIONAL TYPE for an example.

Bogardus social distance scale: a scale designed to measure the social distance that people desire to maintain between themselves and members of other races or ethnic groups.

Bogen cage: a mazelike test of intelligence in which the testee is required to move a ball toward the exit by the shortest route using a stick inserted between slats of the apparatus.

bond: the hypothetical *O*-factor responsible for the association between stimulus and response. Some psychologists assume that bonds are neurological modifications brought about by practice; others are noncommittal as to the nature of the bond. *Syn.* CONNECTION.

bonding: the strong attachment of the mother to infant and infant to mother that develops shortly after birth.

bone conduction: transmission of sound into the inner ear by way of the bones of the skull. Hearing aids placed behind the ear utilize this mode of conduction.

bone-conduction test: a determination of how well a person can hear sounds through the skull bones. Greater ability to hear by bone conduction than by air conduction points to defects in the eardrum or auditory ossicles.

boomerang effect: a shift in an attitude away from the position advocated by others.

borderline: a descriptive term applied to any class of phenomena lying between two categories. The term is frequently applied to individuals who are at or near the dividing line between normalcy and mental deficiency.

borderline intelligence: an intellectual level between retardation and normalcy. An IQ in the 70's may be characterized as borderline, but the determination of normalcy or retardation must always be an individual matter, taking into account not only the measured intellectual level but social and legal factors as well.

boundary: (*Lewin*) 1. any limitation or hindrance to moving from region to region within the life space. 2. a region separating two psychological systems.

bound energy: (*Psychoan.*) energy that is available to the ego process for dealing with reality, as opposed to energy utilized in wasteful ways, such as the fantasy or in maintaining repressions.

bouton terminal: see SYNAPTIC KNOB.

bovarism: failure to differentiate between daydreams and reality. The concept is taken from the book *Madame Bovary* by Flaubert.

brachycephalic: broad-skulled; having a short front-to-back ratio. *Contr.* DOLICHOCEPHALIC.

bradyarthia: slow, hesitating speech due to a brain lesion.

bradyscope: a device for presenting visual stimuli at a slow rate of speed.

Braille: a system of lateral and numerical representation by means of embossed dots to enable the blind to read.

brain: the mass of nervous tissue within the skull. Its principal parts are diagrammed in the accompanying figure. Working up from the top of the spinal cord, we first come to the *medulla,* which is essentially an enlargement of the upper cord where it connects with the brain. Running through the medulla on the way to and from the brain are the various spinal pathways. The medulla also contains a number of *nuclei,* or centers, that are important in the regulation of vital functions, such as respiration and circulation. To the rear of the medulla lies the *cerebellum,* or "little brain." The cerebellum is the chief organ for the control of coordination and posture. It receives fibers from the kinesthetic and vestibular pathways and has abundant interconnections with the cerebrum. The *pons* (Latin for "bridge") lies above the medulla and is a bridge between the two halves of the cerebellum in that fibers connecting the right and left hemispheres of that organ pass through the pons. The pons also has a number of nuclei or centers for the origin and termination of cranial nerves serving the head. The *midbrain* connects the pons and medulla to the brain proper and also contains reflex centers important in vision and hearing. The rest of the brain is known as the *forebrain* and is the most highly developed part of the brain both in man and the higher animals. Referring again to the figure, we see that the thalamic region of the forebrain lies above the midbrain. The *thalamus* is a great relay station where incoming sensory impulses are shunted to appropriate higher centers. The *hypothalamus* lies downward and forward from the thalamus. It is not a lower extension of the thalamus with similar functions. It is important in a number of *motivational* and *emotional* aspects of behavior.

An important part of the forebrain is the *limbic system,* which consists of the *cingulate cortex,* an old part of the cortex that lies deep within the longitudinal fissure, the *septal region,* the *fornix,* the *hippocampus,* the *amygdala,* and according to some authorities, the hypothalamus. The limbic system is important in emotional reactions. For example, the destruction of the amygdala nuclei will turn ferocious animals into docile creatures. The septal region has been identified as one of the so-called pleasure centers of the brain. The hippocampus has been implicated in conditioned fear reactions and possibly in short-term memory storage. The functions of the cingulate gyrus and fornix are not yet completely understood.

The *reticular formation* is a loosely organized network of cells extending from the region of the medulla upward to the level of the thalamus and hypothalamus. This system is a nonspecific cluster of centers that receives afferent impulses as they branch off from afferent neurons arriving from the various sense organs. From the reticular formation impulses are relayed to subcortical centers and to the cerebral cortex, which contains the higher brain centers. Conversely, neurons originating in the higher centers and in the subcortical nuclei give

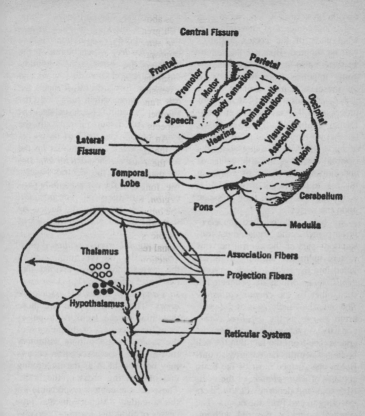

FIG. 4. *The human brain—a side view. The top figure shows the external structures: the bottom figure the internal structures.*

off branches as they travel through the reticular formation before entering the spinal cord. Thus, the reticular system acts as a two-way communication center intermediate between the great stream of incoming sensory impulses and the rest of the brain.

One function of the reticular formation is to serve as a cortical activation center. When bursts of sensory impulses are streaming in from the peripheral sense organs, the system goes into activity, thus "alerting" the rest of the brain. It is possible that the system may also serve as a switching center that determines to what parts of the cortex impulses will be shunted. Because the reticular system also mediates between outgoing impulses from the cortex to the muscles, it may well be that it also determines to what extent motor processes will be aroused by environmental stimulation. It is even possible that we may have to modify some of our traditional thinking about the cerebral cortex as the sole center of consciousness in favor of assigning this role to the effects of the reticular activating system as they impinge upon the cortex.

We have now reached the *cerebrum*, which is the largest, most conspicuous part of the central nervous system in higher animals. It is divided into the *right* and *left cerebral hemispheres*, which are connected to each other by the *corpus callosum*. The outer half-inch layer of the cerebrum known as the *cerebral cortex* consists of *gray matter* and takes its appearance from the fact that the cell bodies of neurons have a grayish tint. Below the surface most of the brain consists of *white matter*, or the whitish axons and dendrites of the fibers traveling to and from the cortex. The cerebral cortex is covered with invaginations, or fissures, which provide natural anatomical landmarks by means of which various lobes and functional areas can be distinguished. Neurologists believe that the cerebral cortex became invaginated in the course of evolution when it developed so rapidly that it could not fit inside the skull without folding. It has also been suggested that by wrinkling, more tissue surface is exposed to the cerebral blood supply—an advantage

for an organ that demands a large volume of blood. The most important of these invaginations is the *central fissure*, which begins in the center of the cortex at the longitudinal fissure and runs downward and somewhat forward until it meets the *lateral fissure*, which runs along the side of the brain. The tissue ahead of the central fissure makes up the *frontal lobe*. The mass of tissue below the lateral fissure makes up the *temporal lobe*. The *parietal lobe* lies to the rear of the central fissure, roughly under the corresponding parietal bone of the skull. The *occipital lobe* is not precisely delineated by fissures, but is located in the back of the brain.

Functional areas of the cortex. Traditionally, the functional areas of the cortex have been divided into two broad categories: (1) *primary sensory and motor areas;* (2) *associative areas*. The primary areas are those that either receive (sensory) impulses from lower centers or, in the case of the motor areas, initiate voluntary movements. The association centers may be thought of as the integrating and interpreting areas of the brain. These are the centers responsible for the so-called "higher" mental processes of thinking, learning, perceiving, etc. We shall examine each of these two kinds of cortical areas in some detail.

The motor system can be broadly divided into two main divisions, *pyramidal* and *extrapyramidal*. The pyramidal system originates in the precentral gyrus in the frontal lobes of the cerebral cortex. It takes its name from the fact that the cell bodies of the cortical neurons are shaped roughly like a double pyramid. From the cortex the fibers stream downward through the medulla, where approximately 80 percent cross over before continuing to the lower parts of the spinal cord. The remaining 20 percent cross just before terminating in the spinal cord. Consequently, the pyramidal system is completely *contralateral*, in that the right precentral gyrus controls the left side of the body and the left gyrus controls the right side. Moreover, the upper part of the motor area of the cortex controls the lower limbs, while the lower portion of the gyrus controls the muscles in the head. There is a disproportionate amount of tissue devoted to more mobile parts of the body such as the thumb, eyes, and mouth. The larger, less mobile portions of the body are represented by the relatively small amounts of cortex. If the precentral gyrus is stimulated by a weak electric current, movements are elicited in the corresponding part of the body. Indeed, our detailed knowledge of this area's functions was largely determined in this manner. If the area is destroyed, as frequently happens in older persons as a result of a stroke (cerebral hemorrhage), then the limbs and face on the opposite side become partly or totally paralyzed, depending on the extent of the damage.

The extrapyramidal system is made up of all the other areas of the brain that contribute to muscular movements. Of these, the most important is the *premotor association area*, which lies immediately in front of the primary motor area. Its function is to lend skill and coordination to voluntary movements. When the area is removed in animals, the animal shows weakness and poor coordina

tion on the affected side, and an inability to carry out skilled acts. Clinical studies of human patients with brain injuries in the motor association area and nearby regions often reveal the presence of *apraxias*, or the inability to carry out purposeful acts, such as lighting a cigarette, playing a piano, or solving a simple motor problem. These difficulties are much more likely to occur if the injury is on the *dominant* side of the brain. The most important of the primary sensory areas are the *somaesthetic*, *visual*, and *auditory*. The somaesthetic (*soma* = body; *esthetic* = feeling) region lies just beyond the central fissure in the postcentral gyrus. A *gyrus* (pl. *gyri*) is a strip of cortical tissue lying between two folds. It receives impulses from all over the body, mediating touch, pressure, temperature, sensitivity, and kinesthesis. Again, as is true of the motor region, the relationship is a crossed-over and upside-down one. In individuals whose somaesthetic region has been exposed during surgical operations, electrical stimulation of the area results in verbal reports to the effect that the patient feels sensations of warmth, numbness, and muscle movements in various parts of the body. Destruction of the somaesthetic region results in reduced tactile sensitivity and a greatly raised two-point threshold. Apparently the sense of pain is not represented cortically. The somaesthetic (and other areas of the brain) can be cut, stimulated, or destroyed without arousing pain. Indeed patients undergoing brain surgery are usually conscious, the only anesthesia employed being local, to the scalp. Pain, therefore, is apparently mediated by sub-cortical centers in the thalamus.

The primary visual area is located in the occipital lobe. The optic neurons from the retina terminate in the very tip of the occipital lobe, where the nervous impulses arising in the retina are interpreted as lights. Careful studies of the relationship between the retina and the primary visual areas indicate that there is a point-for-point correspondence between the retina and the occipital cortex. However, the optic neurons partly cross on their way to the brain. Consequently, injury to one of the primary visual centers results in one-half blindness in each eye (hemianopsia). If, for example, the right visual cortex were destroyed, the individual would be blind in the right half of each retina. Since the lens refracts light entering the eye in such a way that it crosses over, the left half of each visual field would be affected. Electrical stimulation of the primary visual area gives rise to reports of pinpoints of light, whirling colors, starlike patterns, and, sometimes, particular colors. The primary auditory area is located in the temporal lobe. Each auditory cortex receives fibers from both ears, and because of this, destruction of one cortex causes partial deafness in both ears. Electrical stimulation of the auditory cortex causes sensations of humming or buzzing. Interestingly, there is evidence that the organization of high-, medium-, and low-pitch appreciation found in the cochlea is preserved in the auditory cortex. If pitch is dependent on the place stimulated in the sense organ, as Helmholtz supposed, then some kind of localization in the cortex would be demanded in order to

preserve the organization of high, medium, and low pitches found in the cochlea. The centers for taste and smell are not so clearly localized, are highly complex, and are only poorly understood. We need not attempt to trace them here. It is interesting to note, in light of evolutionary theory, that the centers for smell are extensive in man and are located in the older portions of the brain, phylogenetically speaking, where they have been overshadowed by evolutionarily more recent parts of the cerebral cortex.

The associative areas of the cortex are less specifically localized than the primary sensory areas. However, it is possible to state a general principle to the effect that with each primary area there is a nearby region of the cortex whose functions are associative. Thus, there are *somaesthetic*, *auditory*, and *visual association* areas adjacent to their corresponding primary areas. The association areas are able to retain information from past stimulation and relate it to incoming impulses. If, for example, we are shown a common object, such as an orange, the impulses generated by the retina and transmitted to the primary visual area are relayed to the visual association area. This "information" about the color, texture, and shape of an orange has been retained from past experience and we therefore recognize the stimulus as an orange. Persons with injuries in the association areas are said to suffer from *agnosia*, a condition characterized by an inability to recognize objects on the basis of the affected sense modality. A person with *visual agnosia*, for example, might not recognize a key visually even though he could tell what it was if he were allowed to feel it. Similarly, if blindfolded, persons suffering from *somaesthetic agnosia* would be unable to distinguish among a number of blocks of different geometric shapes.

Closely related to the motor and premotor areas of the cortex is a complex center known as *Broca's area*, or the *speech center*. This center is usually located on the left side of the brain and in this respect is unlike other cortical centers, such as Wernicke's area in the upper temporal region, which are represented bilaterally. Injuries to the speech center and to other language centers have been studied exhaustively since World War I, when many soldiers suffered lesions of the brain in combat. Speech disorders that are a consequence of such injuries are called *aphasias* and may involve (1) *motor aphasia*, or the inability to pronounce words, or if words are pronounced fluently, to put them together in meaningful sentences; (2) *alexia*, or the inability to read; (3) *agraphia*, or the inability to write; (4) *amnesic aphasia*, or the inability to remember words. Because of the actual destruction of cortical tissue in aphasias, patients suffering from these disorders are very difficult to retain, although some relearning if possible if the damage is not too extensive. Finally, there is a relatively large mass of tissue on the frontal poles of the brain known as the *frontal association area*. This region, unlike the other association areas, is not closely linked with a specific primary area. Instead, its functions are general and involve the planning, management, and control of behavior. Persons suffering injuries to the frontal lobes are likely to be impulsive, inconsiderate, excessively emotional, and lacking in good judgment. In a sense, then, the prefrontal association areas are the general headquarters of the brain, exerting an overall controlling and guiding function on behavior.

Recent studies of persons whose brains have been "split," that is, whose corpus callosum has been cut, reveal that the two cerebral hemispheres have different functions. In general, the left side of the brain is the dominant or major side, the right, the minor side. The left side functions primarily in language, analytical thinking, and mathematical skills. The right side functions in spatial perception, in musical and other forms of artistic appreciation.

The fibers of the brain. A detailed description of the neurons of the brain would carry us far afield. However, brief mention will be made of several features. Microscopic sections of the cerebral cortex show that it is exceedingly complex. It has been estimated that the cortex alone contains some nine billion neurons. The cell bodies of the cortical neurons are connected with the lower centers by *projection fibers*, which stream up and down from the midbrain and fan out upon the cortex as if they were "projected" like a picture on a screen. The cortical neurons are also richly interconnected by *association fibers*, which travel from the anterior of the cortex to the occipital regions and to all points between. The right and left hemispheres are also interconnected across the corpus callosum. Thus, while emphasis has been put on localization in this article, the brain also acts as a whole.

brain center: any interconnected group of neurons in the brain that perform a specific function. For example, the speech center in the cerebral cortex functions in motor speech. See also CORTICAL CENTER.

brain lesion: damage to the brain caused by injury, disease, or surgical procedures.

brain localization: see LOCALIZATION.

brain potential: the electrical potential of the brain. See also ELECTRO-ENCEPHALOGRAM.

brain stem: the portion of the brain remaining after the cerebrum and cerebellum are removed.

brainstorm: 1. an emotional upheaval. 2. a new idea originating in an exciting movement of insight.

brainwashing: conversion of an individual from an established orientation (usually political) to another. The word derives from two Chinese words meaning "to wash the brain" and implies the use of physical and/or psychological duress.

brain waves: the rhythmic, spontaneous electrical discharges of the living brain. See also ELECTROEN-CEPHALOGRAM.

b reaction test: in reaction-time experiments, a test in which the subject is required to discriminate or choose between two stimuli.

break phenomenon: a sudden shift in response from one rival stimulus to another under conditions of fatigue.

breakthrough: 1. any major step foward in research or theoretical knowledge. 2. in psychotherapy, a sudden and significant modification in attitudes after a period of little or no progress.

Briggs-Meyers Type Indicator: a questionnaire designed to measure introversion-extroversion and the think-

ing, feeling, sensing, and intuiting modes of Jung.

brightness: 1. the intensity dimension of visual experience primarily dependent upon the amplitude of the light wave. 2. that characteristic of a color by which it can be located on the white-gray series. *Syn.* BRILLI-ANCE. 3. a high degree of intelligence. 4. a quality ascribed to certain nonvisual sensations because of their light, brilliant character. High tones, for example, are said to be bright or brilliant.

brightness adaptation: a decrease in the brilliance of stimuli as a result of increasing the general or incident illumination.

brightness contrast: the intensification of the apparent brightness of a stimulus object as a consequence of either simultaneous or prior stimulation.

brightness threshold: the minimal intensity of visual stimulation for any specified wavelength that is recognized as brighter than the surrounding unstimulated field. See also DIF-FERENTIAL THRESHOLD.

bril: a subjective unit of brightness.

brilliance: 1. the dimension of a color that enables the subject to locate it on the black-white-gray series. *Syn.* BRIGHTNESS. *Brightness* is now preferred to *brilliance* for this usage. 2. a high degree of intelligence.

brilliance contrast: see BRIGHTNESS CONTRAST.

Brodmann's areas: regions of the cerebral cortex to which Karl Brodmann, a German anatomist, assigned a system of numbers.

Brodmann's area 18: the area immediately forward and around the primary visual area (area 17). Area 18 mediates complex visual process. It is of central importance in Hebb's theory of perceptual learning.

Brodmann's area 17: the primary visual area where the optic neurons streaming back from the retina terminate. See also entries above.

Broca's area: the "speech center," located in the inferior frontal gyrus in the left cerebral hemisphere of right-handed individuals. The area is now known to be only one of many involved in language functions. It is primarily concerned in articulated or spoken speech.

broken home: a home in which one parent is absent because of death, divorce, desertion, etc.

brontophobia: fear of thunder. *Syn.* ASTRAPHOBIA.

Brown-Peterson paradigm: a design for measuring short-term retention in which a distraction stimulus is used to prevent rehearsal.

Brown-Séquard syndrome: paralysis on one side of the body accompanied by sensory anesthesia on the side opposite the lesion following sectioning of the lateral half of the spinal cord.

Brunswik ratio: a measure of perceptual constancy that relates the subject's responses to the stimulus variable under differing environmental conditions. For example, in studying the constancy of visual brightness, the subject is asked to match stimuli under varying degrees of illumination. Three variables are involved: (1) S, or the stimulus percent reflectance for a stimulus match; (2) A, or the albedo percent reflectance of the objects to be matched; (3) R, or the response percent reflectance of the subject's matching sample. The degree of constancy is found by the formula:

$$\text{Brunswik ratio} = (R{-}S)/(A{-}S)$$

brusixm: a tendency to grind the teeth during sleep.

B-type: 1. a personality pattern associated with low aggressiveness, competitiveness, and achievement motivation. B-type persons are believed to be less prone to coronary attacks than A-types (*q.v.*). 2. (*Jaensch*) a person whose eidetic imagery is flexible, imaginative, and under voluntary control. Such individuals are believed by Jaensch to be predisposed to exophthalmic goiter.

buffer: 1. a storage structure or process that provides for holding information for brief periods, as in short-term memory. 2. unscored items in a test which are included in order to minimize interaction between other items.

bulb: the medulla oblongata.

bulimia: a pathologically excessive appetite.

bulky color: See VOLUME COLOR.

bundle hypothesis: a concept employed by the Gestalt psychologists to characterize the structuralistic and behavioristic view that the whole is no more than the sum of its parts.

Bunsen-Roscoe law: the principle that the visual threshold is a function of the duration of the stimulus multiplied by its intensity. The principle holds only over a narrow range of stimulus durations.

burnout: a disorder of professional individuals engaged in helping others characterized by impaired performance, loss of concern, poor morale, emotional problems, and drug abuse. Burnout is presumed to be the result of prolonged high levels of demand and stress suffered by the victim.

burnt: an odor quality typified by the smell of burnt wood.

bystander effect: the discovery that people are less likely to help in an emergency when they are with others than when alone.

C

cable properties: characterizing the ability of axons to conduct impulses passively in a decremental fashion.

cachexia; cachexis: a condition of extreme malnutrition.

CAL: computer-assisted learning.

calcarine cortex: the cerebral cortex surrounding the calcarine fissure in the occipital lobe. The calcarine cortex contains the primary visual area (area 17).

calcarine fissure: an invagination on the medial surface of the occipital lobe which separates the cuneus from the lingual gyrus.

calendar age: see CHRONOLOGICAL AGE.

California Psychological Inventory: Ages 13 plus. Similar to the MMPI for use with normal populations. Contains 480 items to be answered "true" or "false." Yields scores on Dominance, Self-Acceptance, Responsibility, Socialization, Self-Control, Achievement, and Femininity.

California Test of Personality: a questionnaire type of personality inventory yielding scores on self-reliance, personal worth, sense of freedom, belongingness, various social skills, and total adjustment. Available for all grade levels and adults.

caloric nystagmus: nystagmus in-

duced by irrigation of the ears with warm or cold water.

campimeter: a chart used in mapping the visual field.

canalization: 1. the narrowing or restricting of alternative ways of behavior so as to select one in preference to others. 2. (*Murphy*) the tendency to satisfy drives in particular ways. 3. the hypothetical strengthening of a neural pathway by use.

cancellation test: a speed test in which the subject is required to cancel out a certain symbol whenever it appears scattered at random among a pattern of similar symbols.

candala: photometric unit replacing candle.

candle: the unit of measure of luminous intensity of a light source. It is equal to 1/16 of the luminance per square centimeter of a complete radiator at the temperature at which platinum solidifies.

cannabis sativa: Indian hemp. The female plant is the source of marijuana and hashish.

Cannon, Walter Bradford: American physiologist (1871–1945). Cannon attended Harvard University, where he received the degree of Doctor of Medicine in 1900. His entire career was spent at that institution. Cannon's influence in psychology came about as a result of his interest in the emotions and in the hunger and thirst drives. He viewed the emotions as emergency reactions, mobilizing the organism for critical situations. As a result of his own and his associates' experiments on the hypothalamus, he identified that portion of the brain as the center for the emotions. His views on hunger and thirst centered around his *local theory*, in which he attributed the hunger and thirst drives to local factors: stomach contractions in the case of hunger, and dryness of the mouth for thirst. Cannon is also responsible for introducing the concept of homeostasis into psychology. It means "steady state" and is used to characterize the remarkable stability of the internal environment. He believed that drives arise in response to imbalances in homeostasis. Although he was a physiologist, Cannon's wide range of interests led him into psychology and even social theory A great deal of contemporary research into the mechanism of the emotions and physiological motives of hunger and thirst has been stimulated by his pioneer work.

cannula: a small tube inserted into the body for the extraction or introduction of substances.

capacity: the full power of an individual in respect to any function. Capacity is dependent both upon native endowment and favorable environmental conditions for its optimal development. See also ABILITY.

Capgras syndrome: a delusion frequently observed in female psychotics in which the patient believes that people known to her have been replaced by doubles.

carbachol: a chemical that stimulates thirst when injected into the hypothalamus.

carbon dioxide therapy: The inhalation of a mixture of 30 percent CO_2 and 70 percent O_2 to the point of unconsciousness several times weekly. Claimed by its proponents to alleviate psychotic symptoms.

cardinal point: (*Fechner*) that point in a quantitative series of sensations at which the differential threshold begins to increase in accordance with Weber's law—that is, in proportion to the magnitude of the stimulus rather than in an absolute sense.

cardinal trait: (*Allport*) a pervasive and outstanding characteristic that influences all or nearly all of an individual's behavior.

cardiograph: an instrument for recording the rate and amplitude of the heartbeat.

cardiovascular: pertaining to the heart and blood vessels.

card sorting: a test of discrimination or learning in which the subject is required to sort cards into piles or bins according to sample.

carpal age: the degree of bony development as judged by ossification of the carpal, or wrist, bones.

Carr, Harvey: American psychologist (1873–1954). Carr studied at DePauw, at Colorado, and at Chicago, where he received his Ph.D. in 1905 under John Dewey and James Rowland Angell. After a brief period at Pratt Institute, he accepted an appointment at Chicago, where he succeeded John B. Watson. He remained at Chicago until 1938, the last twelve years as chairman of the department. There he became the leading exponent of the functionalist point of view, and his textbook in general psychology is considered the best exposition of the point of view of the Chicago School of Functionalism. He was an outstanding teacher, and under his leadership the department at Chicago became the best in the United States at that time.

case: 1. an example or circumstance. 2. a person who exemplifies a behavior disorder or disease.

case history: a compilation of information that includes all available data on background test results, interviews, ratings, diagnoses, etc., concerning an individual subject of a study. The case-history method is most frequently utilized in psychopathology and social casework for the practical purpose of diagnosis and prognosis. However, after the study of a number of individual cases, the clinician or sociologist may formulate theoretical principles or generalizations about some aspect of behavior. In this way the case-history method becomes part of the broader clinical method. See also CLINICAL PSYCHOLOGY; CLINICAL METHOD.

caste: a group separated socially from others by social, racial, or religious barriers.

castration: the surgical removal of the testes or ovaries. For the female, the term *spay* is more common.

castration complex: (*Psychoan.*) in the male, the infantile fear of losing the genital organs. In the female, the fantasy that the girl once possessed the penis but lost it by castration. The castration complex is presumed to be a result of the infant's fear of losing the genitals in retaliation for his forbidden sexual desires toward the parent of the opposite sex.

catabolism: the processes involved in tearing down tissues and expending energy, with the resulting accumulation of waste products. *Contr.* ANABOLISM.

catalepsy: 1. a trancelike state in which the muscles are held rigid for long periods. 2. a condition of waxy flexibility (*flexibilitas cerea*), in which the patient's limbs may be placed in any position. Characteristic of catatonic schizophrenics and of some forms of hysteria.

catalexia: a reading disorder in which words are reread.

catamnesis: a case history beginning with the onset of an illness up to admission to the hospital.

cataplexy: immobility caused by extreme fear or shock.

catastrophic reaction: a failure to come to terms with the environment in such a way as to result in a breakdown. The organism experiences anxiety and feelings of inadequacy and is unable to cope with the problem.

catathymic amnesia: amnesia limited to certain events or to a brief period of time.

catatonia: 1. any reaction in which there is a marked deviation of motor behavior in the direction of inhibition of movement, waxy flexibility, and negativism. 2. a form of schizophrenic reaction characterized by extreme negativism, mutism, the assumption of postures, waxy flexibility, withdrawal, and sometimes excitement.

catatonic schizophrenia: a form of schizophrenia in which there are severe disturbances of the motor processes. There may be extreme restlessness, and excessive motor activity or extreme motor inhibition accompanied by negativism and stupor.

catatonic stupor: a stuporous condition that is the most prominent symptom of catatonia and catatonic schizophrenia. Patients suffering from this disorder show extreme negativisim, stereotyped mannerisms, and inaccessibility to outside stimuli.

catecholamines: a group of amines including epinephrine, norephinephrine, and dopamine, which act as neurotransmitters and are important in coping with stress.

category: 1. a class or description of objects or events with common attributes. 2. in statistics, a qualitative grouping.

catelectrotonus: the state of heightened excitability of a nerve or muscle in the region of the cathode as a steady current is passing through the tissue.

catharsis: 1. (*Aristotle*) the purging of the spirit of morbid and base ideas or emotions by witnessing the playing-out of such emotions or ideas on the stage. 2. (*Psychoan.*) the release of tensions and anxieties by reliving and unburdening those traumatic incidents which, in the past, were originally associated with the repression of the emotions. *Syn.* ABREACTION. 3. the assumption that impulses that are inappropriate at a later stage of development are worked off in early play activity.

cathexis; cathection: 1. (*Psychoan.*) the investment of the libido on an object, on another person, or on the self. 2. concentration of mental energy on an emotion, idea, or line of action; giving such emotion, etc., importance or significance.

cathode: the negative electrode. *Contr.* ANODE.

Cattell, James McKeen: American psychologist (1860–1944). Born in Easton, Pennsylvania, the son of a professor of classics, Cattell attended Lafayette College, where he received his bachelor's degree in 1880. His first graduate work was done in Europe at Göttingen, and later at Leipzig under Wilhelm Wundt, the founder of experimental psychology.

Cattell, however, rejected Wundt's introspective psychology and turned to the study of individual differences, a subject that occupied him the rest of his life.

After taking his doctorate at Leipzig in 1886, Cattell taught at Bryn Mawr, the University of Pennsylvania, and at Cambridge in England. In 1888 he was appointed to a professorship of psychology at Pennsylvania, the first such appointment anywhere in the world, breaking the tradition of appointing psychologists as professors in the department of philosophy.

In 1891 he became professor of psychology and head of the department at Columbia University. There he became famous for introducing the concept of mental tests and for utilizing in his research a variety of motor, sensory, and simple association tests to study individual differences among college students. Later he turned his attention to the study of individual differences among scientists, utilizing the method of the order of merit in which distinguished scientists ranked each other, the average rank for each being calculated in order to determine final rank orders.

Cattell is also known for his influence as a teacher, with more psychologists-in-the-making having studied at Columbia during his tenure than at any other American institution.

His third major contribution was in editorial work. As editor of *Science*, he made it the leading general scientific publication in the United States.

He also founded the *Psychological Review*, a distinguished journal of review articles.

In the area of administrative work he helped found the American Association of University Professors, served as president of the American Psychological Association, and organized the Psychological Corporation in 1921, an organization devoted to the development of scientific tests useful for the professions and industry.

Cattell's major contributions in psychological research may be summarized under three headings: his investigations of reaction time, psychophysics, and the psychology of individual difference. More generally he is credited with turning the attention of American psychology away from preoccupation with the narrow experimental psychology of structuralism, toward mental testing and its practical applications.

Cattell, Raymond B.: American psychologist (1905–). Cattell's early education and university training were all taken in his native country, culminating in the Ph.D. degree from the University of London in 1929. After several professional appointments in England he came to the United States in 1937, to Teachers College, Columbia University. Following appointments at Clark University and Harvard, he accepted a position as a research professor at the University of Illinois, an appointment he has held since 1944.

Cattell has contributed numerous technical articles on the measurement of personality to psychological journals and has written a number of books, including: *A Guide to Mental Testing* (1936), *General Psychology* (1941), *Description and Measurement of Personality* (1946), *Personality: a Systematic, Theoretical, and Factual Study* (1952), *The Meaning and Measurement of Neuroticism and Anxiety* (1961), *Motivation and Dynamic Structure* (1975), *Personality and Learning Theory* (1980), and *The Inheritance of Personality and Ability* (1981).

Cattell Infant Scale: a scale of infant development and intelligence covering the range from 2 to 30 months. Developmental items are used on the lower level, and from 22 months on, developmental items are intermixed with items from the Stanford Binet.

Cattell's Factorial Theory of Personality: a system of personality based on the identification of personality traits and their measurement through factor analysis. Cattell defines personality in terms of "that which permits a prediction of what a person will do in a given situation." He believes that prediction is best achieved by the identification and measurement, through objective tests and rating scales, of those traits which lie at the source of the behavior patterns that make up personality.

Ordinary tests, questionnaires, rating scales, and other such devices measure what Cattell calls surface traits. Only when the results of large-scale samplings of surface-trait testings are subjected to factor analysis does the psychologist arrive at source traits. In such studies surface traits are revealed as correlation clusters, groups of tests that show high correlations with each other and relatively low correlations with other clusters. Source traits are relatively independent factor loadings that have been identified in a number of studies as fundamental modes of behavior. Among those source traits that have been repeatedly verified are: A, sizothymia vs. affectothymia; B, general mental ability vs. mental defect; C, emotional stability vs. emotional instability; and D, dominance vs. submissiveness.

Some traits such as sizothymia-affectothymia are constitutional traits—that is, are traceable to hereditary influences. Others are environmentally determined, such as conservativism-radicalism. Some traits are dynamic, and others are ability or capacity traits.

Personality is further characterized by the operation of ergs, or innate dispositions to react to certain objects and to continue to react until a goal is reached. Metaergs are similar to ergs, except that they are environmentally determined rather than innate. The most important of the metaergs are sentiments or dynamic attitudes.

Cattell has borrowed heavily from psychoanalysis in developing his theory of personality growth and development. The individual must learn to satisfy ergs and in doing so successfully, develops characteristic modes of behavior. Deprivation, blockage, and frustration are important crossroads that the individual must meet and cope with. Adolescence is the period during which the greatest demands are put upon the individual in learning how to cope with problems. Maturity is the learning of social interests in place of family and individual interests. The prediction of the individual's personality must take into account the institutions and social context in which he develops.

Cattell has recently extended his theory of personality into the area of neurotic patterns of personality in an attempt to bring together his factor-analysis findings and those from the clinic, to make possible more exact descriptions of the latter. These studies have resulted in the identification of new traits and measuring techniques, which should prove useful in the measurement of anxiety and neurotic reactions.

caudad: toward the tail.

caudal: pertaining to the tail.

caudate nucleus: a mass of gray matter which in the subcortical region of the cerebral hemispheres forms part of the corpus striatum. The caudate nucleus is believed to play a role in voluntary motor movement.

causal explanation: explanation in terms of antecedent conditions which account for a given phenomenon.

causalgia: a sensation of burning pain caused by irritation of the nerves.

causal texture: (*Tolman; Brunswik*) a sequence of events being related in a mutually dependent way. The events appear in causal relationship, not as certainties but as probabilities.

causation: 1. the act or process of causing. 2. the cause-and-effect relation where a given event, the cause, produces the effect. Contemporaneous causation stresses the search for antecedents in the present. Historical causation stresses factors in the past. Multiple causation emphasizes the principle that many factors determine a given event.

ceiling: the maximum score attainable in any test.

cell: 1. the structural units from which living organisms are built. 2. in statistics, a comparment or class formed by the intersection of two arrays of scores.

cell assembly: (*Hebb*) a hypothetical functional organization of neurons formed by repeated stimulation during practice. According to Hebb, cell assemblies are further organized into more complex assemblies, or phase sequences, which mediate learned experiences and skills. It is assumed that such assemblies need not be constantly active in order to mediate a memory but are activated by incoming impulses. Thus, to use Hebb's example, seeing part of a triangle will activate an entire phase sequence and give the perception of triangularity.

cell assembly, Mark II: a revision of Hebb's theory of the cell assembly based on an association-of-ideas paradigm that postulates inhibitory mechanisms and a theory of sensitization to account for association.

cell body: the central part of the cell that governs the life process of the entire cell.

cenotrope; coenotrope: an acquired behavior pattern shown by all members of a biological group in a common environment and assumed to be a joint product of hereditary endowment and common experiences.

censorship: (*Psychoan.*) the process responsible for selecting, accepting, or rejecting from consciousness ideas, memories, and impulses arising from the unconscious. The process of censorship is a joint function of the ego and superego.

cent: a unit of pitch equal to 1/1200 of an octave.

centile: a percentile, or point, in a distribution of scores on a scale of 1 to 100. Thus a score with a centile rank of 40 exceeds 40 percent of the scores in the distribution and represents the relative rank of that score. See also PERCENTILE.

central: 1. pertaining to the center, particularly in reference to the body or nervous system. *Contr.* PERIPHERAL. 2. of the greatest importance or significance, sometimes said of values, ideas, tradition. 3. the essential part, sometimes said of the inner core of personality.

central canal: the small opening in the center of the spinal cord which runs throughout its entire length. The canal is filled with cerebrospinal fluid and is believed to serve a nutritive function.

central conflict: (*Horney*) the conflict between the real self and the idealized self, the latter being the neurotic self with its unrealistic image of the self, its capabilities, and its limitations.

central fissure: a deep groove that begins in the middle of each cerebral hemisphere and runs downward and slightly forward. It divides the frontal from the parietal lobe and also serves as an important landmark separating the precentral and postcentral gyri. See illustration accompanying article on BRAIN. *Syn.* fissure of Rolando.

central inhibition: the process in the spinal cord or brain by means of which ongoing behavior is interrupted or action is prevented from occurring.

centralism: centralist psychology: the position that behavior as defined in its broadest sense is a function of the central nervous process—in short, of the brain. By contrast, the *peripheralist* stresses events that take place on the periphery—that is, in the receptors, the muscles, and the glands. The centralist denies that behavior is nothing but effector processes. He points to the brain as the control and integrating center mediating stimulus and response. Even those centralists who are willing to make effector behavior the fundamental unit of psychology seeks its explanation in the central nervous system. They emphasize cognition, attitudes, and problem solving, while the peripheralists stress drive, habit, and motor responses.

The middle-of-the-road psychologist sees room for both points of view and stresses the interaction between central and peripheral processes. He emphasizes behavior as dependent upon the interaction of environmental and organismic factors. The environment, he points out, can influence the organism only by way of the peripheral receptor mechanisms as these feed impulses to the brain. But the effectors, which in turn influence the environment, are under the direction of the central nervous system. Moreover, he points to the fact that behavior is not simply response to stimuli but response to stimuli as influenced by the organism. Thus, all three factors, environmental, peripheral, and central, are important. See also PERIPHERALISM.

central motive state: hypothetical processes in the central nervous system employed in accounting for the physiological motives and certain other forms of behavior. Central motive states are persistent and do not require additional outside stimulation once under way. They result in selectivity of reception and response and are sometimes responsible for the direct emission of behavior, such as that which occurs in response to releasers.

central nervous system: the brain and spinal cord. *Contr.* PERIPHERAL NERVOUS SYSTEM. See also NERVOUS SYSTEM.

central process: process that takes place in the central nervous system. *Contr.* peripheral or automatic process.

central tendency: 1. the general tendency for judgments, ratings, or estimates to gravitate toward the center of a scale. 2. the tendency for biological traits to revert toward the center of a distribution of those traits. Thus, the sons of very tall men are not as tall as their fathers.

central tendency measures: statistical indices that attempt to provide a representative value for a distribution of scores. Since errors of measurement are presumed to distribute themselves randomly about the center of a distribution with extreme deviations further and further away from the center, the true score is best approximated by a value that lies close to the center of the distribution. The most common measures of central tendency are the mean, median, and the mode.

central theory of thinking: the position that thinking is exclusively a cerebral process. *Contr.* PERIPHERAL THEORY OF THINKING.

central vision: vision that takes place in and around the fovea. *Contr.* PERIPHERAL VISION.

centrifugal: flying or moving out from the center. Sometimes used to describe fibers or nervous impulses originating in the central nervous system and going out toward the periphery. *Contr.* centripetal.

centrifugal nerve or **neuron:** an efferent or motor nerve or neuron.

centripetal nerve or **neuron:** an afferent or sensory nerve or neuron.

centroid factors: in factor analysis, the factors extracted by the centroid method described by Thurstone.

centroid method: a factor-analysis technique, essentially geometric in principle, developed by Thurstone. The correlation clusters may be represented by plots on the surface of a sphere, and the first axis is passed through the center of the cluster. Other axes are said to be *orthogonal*, or at right angles to the first, and therefore uncorrelated. However, by rotation, the axes can be made oblique and correlations among factors revealed.

cephalad: toward the head.

cephalic: pertaining to the head.

cephalic index: the ratio of head breadth to length multiplied by 100. Long heads are called *dolichocephalic;* medium heads *mesocephalic,* and broad heads *brachycephalic.*

cephalization: see ENCEPHALIZATION.

cephalocaudal: pertaining to the dimension of the body between the head and tail.

cephalocaudal development: the principle that growth and behavior develop sequentially in a head-to-tail manner. Thus, the head develops more rapidly in the fetus than the legs, and in the infant comes under control faster than the legs and arms.

cerea flexibilitas: the waxy flexibility of the limbs characteristic of the catatonic.

cerebellar cortex: the gray, outer covering of the cerebellum.

cerebellar peduncle: a band of fibers by means of which the cerebellum is attached to the brain stem. There are three such bands, the superior, the middle, and the inferior.

cerebellum: the smaller of the two main divisions of the brain. The cerebellum is an important organ of motor coordination.

cerebral aqueduct: the midbrain canal connecting the third and fourth ventricles.

cerebral cortex: the surface layer of the cerebrum. The cortex consists of cell bodies lending it its characteristically gray appearance. It has been estimated that the cortex contains about nine billion cells. Localized in the cortex are the primary sensory centers, the centers for motor control, and the complex areas that govern the higher mental processes. See also BRAIN.

cerebral dominance: 1. the principle that the cerebrum is the highest control center in the nervous system. *Syn.* CORTICALLIZATION. 2. the theory that the most complex behavioral functions are located in the dominant hemisphere, normally the one controlling the preferred hand.

cerebral integration: the theory that the cerebrum serves as an organ of integration between stimuli and responses, or more generally, serves to integrate and unify all parts of the body.

cerebral palsy: a form of paralysis caused by a lesion in the brain. It is frequently a cogenital defect in children.

cerebral peduncle: either of two bundles of nerve fibers that pass from the pons to the cerebral hemispheres connecting the spinal cord to the cerebrum.

cerebration: physiological activity in the cerebrum.

cerebrospinal fluid: a straw-colored, lymphlike fluid that fills the ventricles of the brain and the central canal of the spinal cord. It also surrounds the brain and spinal cord in their bony cases. It is believed to serve a nutritive function.

cerebrospinal system: the portion of the nervous system consisting of the brain and spinal cord along with all peripheral nerves, exclusive of those associated with the autonomic nervous system.

cerebrotania: see SHELDON'S CONSTITUTIONAL THEORY OF PERSONALITY.

cerebrum: the largest and most important division of the brain. It consist of two hemispheres, each containing a number of cortical (surface) and subcortical centers that mediate sensory, motor, and complex ideational activities. See BRAIN for further anatomical details and illustration.

certifiable: in medicolegal psychology, a term indicating that the individual is in need of treatment for a mental disorder.

cerveau isolé: characterizing an experimental animal whose brain has been transected at the upper level of the midbrain between the inferior and superior colliculi. The procedure isolates the cerebral hemispheres from the rest of the brain. *Contr.* ENCÉPHALE ISOLÉ.

C factor: the factor of cleverness, quickness in thinking, revealed in some factor analyses of intelligence tests.

C group: the control group in an experiment or study.

chain behavior or **reflex:** a sequential form of behavior in which one response provides the cue for the next. Thus, in walking, the process involved are linked by proprioceptive cues. In reciting a list of nonsense syllables or a poem, one item becomes the cue for the following.

chained reinforcement: a type of intermittent reinforcement in which the stimulus changes. For example, if a pigeon is trained to peck at a yellow key and a fixed interval of reinforcement is followed, the color may be changed and the reinforcement delayed until additional responses are given.

chance: 1. the probability of occurrence of an event as calculated on the basis of the theory of probability in light of the knowledge of certain basic conditions. Thus, the theoretical fall of coins may be predicted. 2. randomness of occurrence.

chance difference: any statistical difference between two measures that can be attributed to random factors.

chance error: measurement error that cannot be attributed to known factors and is therefore attributed to chance factors. Such errors are presumed to form a normal distribution around a mean with most of the errors near the mean and a few near the extreme. *Syns.* RANDOM ERROR, VARIABLE ERROR.

chance variations: genetic variations whose antecedent conditions are unknown.

change of life: the menopause in a woman.

channel: in information theory, a system for transmitting signals from an input to an output. The nervous system is a channel for transmitting coded signals (nervous impulses) from inputs (sense receptors) to outputs (effectors).

channel capacity: the maximal volume of information a channel can provide.

character: 1. a consistent and enduring property or quality by means of which a person, object, or event can be identified. *Syns*. TRAIT; characteristic. 2. the integration of synthesis of individual traits into a unity. This is the meaning intended in the Freudian literature by *anal* and *oral characters*. 3. the individual's personality considered from an ethical or moral point of view.

character analysis: 1. an analysis carried out by characterology. See also CHARACTEROLOGY. 2. a training analysis undergone by those studying to be psychoanalysts.

character armor: (*Reich*) the individual's system of defenses.

character neurosis: 1. (*Horney*) a long-standing neurosis or disorder originating in childhood. 2. a psychological disorder marked by vacillation in will. *Contr*. SITUATION NEUROSIS.

characterology: 1. the field of psychology concerned with the study of character and personality. 2. a pseudoscience that attempts to discover character traits by means of external signs, such as hair color, length of fingers, nasal configuration, etc.

character structure: the unity of integration of character traits.

character trait: 1. a relatively consistent and persistent form of behavior as viewed from the moral or ethical point of view 2. (*Psychoan*.) an inherited tendency.

charisma: a special quality of personal appeal or magnetism leading to effective leadership.

Charpentier's bands: the appearance of alternate black and white bands on slowly rotating black disks with a white sector. If the rotation is more rapid, a viewer will discern various patterns of pastel colors, which are called subjective colors, or Fechner's colors.

Charpentier's law: the product of the area of the image and the light intensity is a constant for threshold stimuli in the fovea.

chemical sense: a sense, such as taste, smell, or the common chemical sense, whose stimuli are chemical, and which react with receptors in such a manner as to produce nervous impulses.

chemoreceptors: sense organs, such as those for taste and smell, that are capable of reacting with chemical stimuli.

chemotherapy: the use of drugs in the treatment of mental disorders.

chemotropism: an orienting response of the organism as a whole toward a chemical stimulus.

Cheyne-Stokes breathing: labored breathing characterized by alternate increases and decreases in the rate of respiration. Characteristic of pathological conditions, and sometimes observed in premature infants.

chi: the Greek letter χ, used in various statistical formulas.

chiaroscuro: the distribution of light and shade in a picture or photograph in such a way as to produce the impression of depth or distance.

chiasm: see OPTIC CHIASM.

child: one who has not reached maturity. Depending on the nature of the reference, the term may signify an individual between birth and puberty or one between infancy and puberty.

child-centered: 1. characteristic of activities in school that are designed to meet the needs of the child, as opposed to those activities formulated with a view of teaching the child as a future adult. 2. characteristic of homes where the child's needs are allowed to dominate the family constellation.

child development: the study of the child from the development point of view in which the emphasis is placed on growth, rate of change, and social interaction in the family and among peers.

child-guidance clinic: an organization with a trained professional staff qualified to deal with adjustmental problems in children.

child-parent fixation: (*Psychoan.*) a strong emotional attachment of love or hate, or a mixture of love and hate, toward one of the parents. See also OEDIPUS COMPLEX, a specific type of fixation.

child psychology: the branch of psychology concerned with the development of the mental and behavioral processes from birth to maturity.

Children's Apperception Test: a test, similar to the THEMATIC APPER-CEPTION TEST, suitable for children.

chi square (χ_2): a statistical test for determining whether an obtained distribution differs significantly from the theoretical or expected distribution and thus may be attributable to the operation of factors other than chance.

chi-square test of goodness of fit: the comparison of an observed sample distribution with a theoretical frequency distribution to determine whether the observed sample conforms to the theoretical or expected sampled.

chlordiazepoxide: a tranquilizer sold under the trade name of Librium.

chlorolabe: a green-sensitive pigment in the cones of the retina.

choc: an uncoordinated response elic-

ited by a sudden stimulus for which the organism is not prepared.

choice reaction or **experiment:** a form of reaction or discrimination in which the organism must respond differently to various stimuli. A simple form of choice reaction would involve pushing one switch whenever a green light appeared and another whenever a red light appeared.

choice point: a place in a maze or a discrimination apparatus where the organism must make a choice between two alternative behavior patterns.

choleric: a type of temperament with a low threshold for outbursts of anger or rage.

cholinergic: 1. pertaining to organs stimulated by acetylcholine; 2. pertaining to postganglionic neurons of the parasympathetic system whose effects are mediated by acetylcholine.

cholinesterase: a complex organic compound that acts as an enzyme to hydrolize acetylcholine, the chemical transmitter of impulses.

Chomsky, Noam: American linguist (1928–). Born in Philadelphia, Chomsky was educated at the University of Pennsylvania, where he received the Ph.D. degree in 1955. He has been at the Massachusetts Institute of Technology since 1955, where he is professor of modern languages and linguistics. Chomsky's work in linguistics, although technical and specialized, has had a profound influence on psychologists. His criticism of the traditional learning theory basis for language acquisition has culminated in his espousal of a nativistic point of view stressing a language acquisition device (LAD) that all children the world over are born with. Utilizing the LAD, the child generates his own rules and early grammar, from which he can develop an infinite variety of phrases and sentences. Chomsky's major publications include: *Syntactic Structures* (1957), *Aspects of the Theory of Syntax* (1965), *Topics in the Theory of Generative Grammar* (1966), *Language and the Mind* (1968), *Logic Structure of Linguistic Theory* (1974), and *Reflections of Language* (1975).

chorda tympani: a branch of the seventh, or facial, nerve containing a sensory component for mediating taste and a motor component to the submaxillary and sublingual glands.

chorea: a neurological disorder of the motor system characterized by jerky, spasmodic movements. Sydenham's chorea is caused by rheumatic diseases and results in delirium and restlessness. Huntington's chorea is a sign of lesions in the corpus striatum. Chorea is popularly called St. Vitus's dance.

choreiform: pertaining to movements similar to those observed in chorea.

choreomania; choromania: an epidemic of frenzied dancing; specifically that which appeared in Europe in the fourteenth century, in the wake of the Black Death.

choroid coat: the intermediate layer of the eye between the inner retinal layer and the outer sclerotic layer. The choroid layer is dark and absorbs light.

chroma: 1. saturation or depth of color in the Munsell system. 2. color or hue. 3. in music, a semitone.

chromatic aberration: the failure of rays of light to come to a focal point, due to the fact that the various wavelengths are refracted, or bent, differently as they pass through a lens.

chromatic adaptation: 1. a decrease in hue and saturation upon prolonged exposure to a stimulus color. Under such conditions the fixated color may eventually lose saturation to the point where it becomes a neutral gray. 2. raising of the absolute threshold of sensitivity to hue.

chromatic brightness coefficient: the ratio of hue or color to brightness, ranging from a maximum in the violet region of the spectrum to a minimum in the yellow region.

chromatic color: a color possessing the attributes of hue and saturation. *Contr.* ACHROMATIC COLOR.

chromatic contrast; color contrast: the intensification or differences in hue between two colors when these are presented simultaneously or in close succession.

chromatic dimming: the decrease in saturation with a sudden diminution in the intensity of light after a period of fixation. The effect is due to successive contrast.

chromatic flicker: flicker, or intermittency in visual sensation, due to rapid periodic changes in hue, saturation, or both.

chromaticity; chromaticness: the dimension of a color stimulus specified in terms of its wavelength and purity.

chromatics: 1. the science of color. 2. the chromatic scale.

chromatic scale: a sequence of tones through an octave, each tone differing from the preceding tone by a semitone. The chromatic scale is the basis of Western music.

chromatic valence: the power of a stimulus to produce hue in mixtures.

chromatism: see PHOTISM.

chromatopseudopsia: see COLOR BLINDNESS.

chromatopsia: seeing objects as colored under abnormal conditions, such as drugging, or as an aftermath of intense visual stimulation. The blue tint seen after exposure to bright snow is an example of chromatopsia.

chromesthesia; chromaesthesia: a form of synesthesia in which the individual experiences colors upon hearing sounds. Certain sounds typically have special colors associated with them. One subject, for example, consistently, experienced blue whenever B-flat was sounded. See also SYNESTHESIA.

chromosome: a dark staining body in the nucleus of the cell. These bodies carry the genes or elementary units of heredity. In the human species there are 22 pairs of chromosomes plus the two sex determiners, or a total of 46. In the female, the sex determiners form an additional pair, the XX chromosomes; in the male they are unpaired, the XY chromosomes.

chronaxie: a measure of tissue excitability where the speed of reaction is calculated for stimulation with a current twice the threshold voltage.

chronic: pertaining to diseases and mental disorders of slow onset and long duration. *Contr.* ACUTE.

chronograph: an instrument for measuring elapsed durations of time and recording them graphically.

chronological age: the life age, or the age of the individual from birth to the time specified. *Abbr.* CA. *Syn.* CALENDAR AGE.

chronometer: a timepiece especially designed for uses (such as measuring reaction time) requiring great accuracy.

chronoscope: a clocklike instrument for measuring short durations of time.

chunk: an organized unit of informa-

tion such as a telephone number or nine dots in three rows of three each.

ciliary muscle: a circular mass of smooth muscle surrounding the lens of the eye. Its action governs the accommodation or focusing of the lens for near and far seeing.

cingulate gyrus: a fold of cortical tissue deep between the longitudinal fissure and lying above the corpus callosum. It is believed to be a part of the limbic system. See BRAIN.

cingulectomy: a form of psychosurgery in which the cortex is undercut in the middle portion of the frontal areas.

circadian: pertaining to rhythmic biological cycles occurring at approximately 24-hour intervals.

circular reaction or response: a type of behavior, either voluntary or reflex in nature, that provides the stimulation for a repetition of the same response.

circular reasoning: thinking in which one conclusion rests upon another which in turn refers back to the first— "Alcoholism results from too much drinking; too much drinking is the cause of alcoholism."

circumscribed amnesia: amnesia that is restricted to a certain set of events or to a specific period of time.

circumvallate papilla: see LINGUAL PAPILLA.

clairaudience: a form of cryptesthesia consisting of the alleged power of mediums to hear sounds without the use of the ears. Analogous to CLAIRVOYANCE.

clairvoyance: 1. the hypothetical power of seeing without the use of the eyes. 2. more generally, awareness of past, present, and future without the use of the senses. See also CRYPTESTHESIA.

clan: a social group having common descent.

clang: a tone that is the fundamental tone along with its overtones. The tonal quality of a clang depends upon which overtones the sounding body accentuates.

clang association: an association of words that sound alike. Thus *clang* might elicit the associated term *bang* because of their similarity in sound.

clarification: in nondirective counseling, a statement by the counselor that summarizes and makes clearer in meaning what a client has just said. It is considered important for the counselor not to reveal his own attitudes of approval and disapproval while clarifying.

class: 1. a grouping of objects, persons, or events according to some distinguishing characteristic that sets them apart from other classes or groups. 2. in biology, a group of plants or animals, between phylum and order. Class is more inclusive than phylum but less inclusive than order. 3. in statistics, a grouping of values according to equality or approximate equality of magnitude.

classical: 1. in aesthetics, that which is traditional, authoritative, and follows long-established forms. 2. first, older, authoritative. For example, Pavlovian conditioning is often referred to as classical conditioning.

classical conditioning: see CONDITIONING.

classical psychoanalysis: psychoanalysis based on Freudian doctrine and procedure.

classification test: 1. a test that requires the subject to sort objects into categories. 2. a test used to classify people, such as an aptitude test when employed for the purpose of classifying students into instructional sections.

classificatory scale: a simple nominal scale in which names or classifications are assigned to objects. *Syn.* NOMINAL SCALE.

class inclusion: (*Piaget*) the ability on the part of the child to reason simultaneously about part of a whole and the whole itself.

class interval: in statistics, the range of scores within a given division or class in a frequency distribution.

class limits: the upper and lower boundaries of a class interval.

class structure: the manner in which a given society is divided into classes.

class theory: the assumption that objects have properties or characteristics because they belong to a certain class.

claustral complexes: (*Murray*) a number of related complexes dealing with the unconscious effects of prenatal experiences or of the trauma of birth upon subsequent behavior. One manifestation of the claustral complexes is the desire for security.

claustrophilia: the desire to be enclosed.

claustrophobia: fear of closed spaces.

clearness: 1. one of the attributes of sensations and images. The clear sensation or image stands out or is in the focus of attention. *Syn.* ATTENSITY. 2. the degree to which a phenomenal or cognitive experience is separated off from another experience. 3. in thinking, the property of being understandable.

clerical test: a vocational test of the abilities required in clerical work. Included are arithmetic computation, spelling, alphabetizing, filing, and some machine operations.

Clever Hans: one of a group of

horses known as the Elberfeld Horses, which were trained in such a way that they appeared to be solving complex mathematical problems when, in fact, they were responding to subtle stimuli from their trainers.

cleverness: quickness and versatility of apprehension. See also C FACTOR.

client: in nondirective systems of psychotherapy the counselee, or person, who is undergoing treatment.

client-centered therapy: a system of psychotherapy based on the assumption that the client or subject is in the best position to resolve his own problems provided that the therapist can establish a warm, permissive atmosphere in which the client feels free to discuss his problems and to obtain insight into them. In client-centered therapy, the therapist assumes a nondirective role; he does not advise, interpret, or intervene except to offer encouragement and occasional restatements of the client's remarks for the purpose of emphasis and clarification. For further discussion of the theoretical basis of client-centered therapy see. ROGERS' SELF THEORY OF PERSONALITY.

climatric: see MENOPAUSE.

clinic: 1. a place organized for the diagnosis and treatment of physical and mental disorders. 2. a part of the hospital where outpatients can receive treatment. 3. a demonstration for instructional purposes utilizing patients.

Psychological clinics are similar in organization and function to medical clinics. Frequently there is some degree of specialization among the members of the staff, or the entire clinic may specialize, as in the case of a child-guidance clinic. or a marriage counseling clinic.

clinical: 1. pertaining to a clinic. 2.

characterizing a method of approach to the study of the individual that emphasizes the investigation of background factors, the analysis of family relations, test results, and staff consultation culminating in a diagnosis and prognosis of adjustmental disorders.

clinical grouping: the classification of persons into relatively homogeneous groups according to their symptomatic behavior.

clinical method: a variety of techniques including interviews, questionnaires, tests, projective techniques, and diagnostic observation. The purpose of the clinical method is the practical one of diagnosing the cause of a disorder and prescribing for its treatment. In addition, most clinics maintain training and research programs for the transmission and diffusion of knowledge.

clinical psychology: the branch of psychology that specializes in the application of clinical methods to persons suffering from behavior disorders.

clinical type: an individual whose physical or behavioral symptoms correspond to a recognized clinical pattern.

clitoris: a small, erectile organ that forms part of the external genitalia of the female and is the analog of the male penis.

cloaca theory: (*Psychoan.*) the belief, not uncommon among young children and ignorant adults, that birth takes place through the anus.

clonus: rapid, rhythmic contraction and relaxation of muscles.

closed system: a theoretical system that does not admit additions or changes. *Contr.* OPEN SYSTEM.

closure, law of: a Gestalt principle

of organization that holds that perception, memories, thinking—mental and behavioral processes in general—tend to completeness, good definition, and symmetry of form. See illustration.

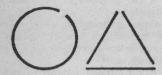

FIG. 5. *Illustrating closure. The figure on the left is perceived as a circle; the figure on the right, as a triangle, in spite of gaps.*

clouding effect: (*Jung*) a psychological barrier that prevents understanding between persons of different types.

clouding of consciousness: a partial loss of orientation, with faulty perception, lack of attention, and confusion. Characteristic of pre-epileptic attacks, delirium, and psychosis.

clue: see CUE.

cluster analysis: a technique for the determination of the presence of clusters in a correlation table of matrix.

coacting group: a group working side by side on a common project but without communication or interaction between the members.

coarctation: 1. the process of narrowing or inhibiting. 2. (*Rorschach*) the inhibition of responses or ego-limiting effects on the responses.

cocaine: a local anesthetic that, if injected or swallowed, may act as a stimulant inducing excitation, talkativeness, and muscular tremors.

cochlea: the part of the ear containing the organ of hearing. The coch-

lea is a bony, snail-like organ consisting of three tubes, the SCALA VESTIBULI, the SCALA MEDIA, and the SCALA TYMPANI. See EAR.

cochlear canal: the tube of the cochlea containing the organ of Corti; the SCALA MEDIA.

cochlear microphonic: an electrical response generated in the cochlea of the inner ear by stimulation. Up to relatively high frequencies, the cochlear microphonic follows the frequency of the stimulus. It is believed that cochlear microphonics arise from the hair cells and may serve as generator potentials for triggering auditory nerve impulses.

coconsciousness: coexisting mental states with no awareness or incomplete awareness between them. Morton Prince coined the term to describe cases of dissociation in which multiple personalities exist in the same individual with only incomplete awareness of each other.

code: 1. a set of symbols used to transform sets of data into another form. The use of special computer symbols in data processing machines illustrates this form of code. 2. standards of conduct.

code capacity: an information theory, the maximum rate at which a given volume of information can be transmitted through a channel.

coding: see ENCODING.

codeine: a morphine derivative that acts as a central nervous depressant.

code test: a test in which the subject must translate one set of symbols into another. For example, the testee might be instructed that given a code where $A = 2$, $B = 3$, $C = 4$, and so on, he must write "Washington" in code.

coding: 1. the process of transforming scores into another form. 2. in information theory, the transformation of messages into signals.

coding key: a list of the categories and their appropriate symbols for a code.

coefficient: 1. a factor by which a value is multiplied. 2. an expression of the degree to which a given characteristic occurs in a specified instance. Thus, the correlation coefficient expresses the closeness of a relationship between two variables.

coenesthesia: coenaesthesia; coenesthesis: the mass of undifferentiated sensations from within the body which forms the basis for bodily feelings.

cognition: a general concept embracing all forms of knowing. It includes perceiving imagining, reasoning, and judging. Traditionally, cognition was contrasted with conation or willing and with affection or feeling.

cognitive-awareness level: a construct in diagnosis and psychotherapy that is useful, noncontradictory, and acceptable to the client.

cognitive dissonance: an uncomfortable psychological state in which the individual experiences two incompatible beliefs or cognitions. Cognitive dissonance theory holds that the individual is motivated by the attendant discomfort to act in such a manner as to reduce dissonance.

cognitive map: (*Tolman*) An animal's conceptualization of a maze. The cognitive map is built up of sign-Gestalts which are learned relationships between environmental cues and the animal's expectations. That is, the animal comes to expect a series of spatial relationships on the basis of its experience with a maze or other apparatus. Tolman and his associates found evidence for cognitive maps and sign-Gestalt learning in experiments on place learning, latent learning, and reward expectancy.

cognitive need: a motive or desire to observe and know the environment. Cognitive needs are the basis of curiosity and exploratory behavior.

cognitive psychology: 1. the branch of psychology that includes the study of processes involved in sensing, perceiving, remembering, and thinking. 2. a point of view in psychology that stresses the importance of purpose, knowing, understanding, and reasoning in behavior. The cognitive point of view was first emphasized by the Gestalt psychologists in their investigations of perception, learning, and thinking, particularly as they opposed traditional associationistic theories and methods of research involving these processes. For decades beginning in the 1930s, Jean Piaget, the famous Swiss psychologist, emphasized the cognitive approach in his research on the development of understanding in the child. In the 1930s and 1940s, E. C. Tolman attempted to make the cognitive point of view compatible with behavioristic methods in the study of animal learning. Using the maze as a model, he argued that the animal learns by developing a cognitive map of the apparatus. More recently cognitive psychology has come to be identified with the point of view that the organism is an information-processing system analogous to electronic detection, storage, and retrieval systems. For specific examples of cognitive approaches, see GESTALT PSYCHOLOGY, INFORMATION PROCESSING THEORY, PIAGET'S THEORY OF COGNITIVE DEVELOPMENT, TOLMAN'S PURPOSIVE BEHAVIORISM.

cognitive schema: 1. a perceptual

organization of past experiences to which present and future experiences are related. On the simplest level the Gestalt principles of grouping exemplify cognitive schemas. A more complex example is in one's perception of the Republican party. 2. (*Tolman*) the organism's expectancies or sets; a cognitive map.

cognitive structure: the organization of the perceptual world into a unified and hierarchical pattern of beliefs, attitudes, and expectancies.

cognitive style: the pattern of perceptual and cognitive behavior characteristic of an individual employed in coping with information, problems, and the physical and social environments. Some individuals, for example, are more analytical than others; some are more inclined to take risks than others.

cognitive theory of emotion: see EMOTION.

cognitive theory of learning: any theory of learning that postulates intervening variables of a cognitive nature in order to explain learning. In contrast, stimulus-response theories emphasize reinforced responses and avoid the use of central cognitive constructs as explanatory concepts. For an example of a cognitive theory, see TOLMAN'S PURPOSIVE BEHAVIORISM. For an example of stimulus response theory, see GUTHRIE'S CONTIGUOUS CONDITIONING.

cognizance need: (*Murray*) the need to explore, ask questions, satisfy curiosity, listen, read, and seek knowledge.

cohesion; cohesiveness: the quality of hanging together or being mutually attractive. The term may be applied to social groups, perceptual phenomena, or to items in learning.

cohesion, law of: in learning, the generality that acts that occur close together in time and space tend to integrate into more complex acts.

coition; coitus: sexual intercourse; the union of the male and female genitals with orgasm. Coition is the process in general, coitus a specific act of intercourse.

coitus more ferorum: literally, intercourse in the manner of wild beasts—that is, from the rear.

coitus reservatus: 1. coitus in which the male delays until the female experiences orgasm. 2. complete withholding of orgasm on the part of the male as a method of birth control.

coitus interruptus: interrupted coition on the part of the male, usually to prevent pregnancy.

cold: the sensation normally aroused by a stimulus whose temperature is below skin temperature, which on the exposed surfaces of the body is about 89.6 degrees Fahrenheit, or 32 degrees Centigrade.

cold emotion: a concept used to characterize the stirred-up organic state resulting from the injection of a drug such as adrenaline. The emotion is said to be *cold* since there is an absence of conscious emotional feeling.

coldness: frigidity, or the inability to enjoy sexual feeling.

cold spot: a point, on the skin or mucous membrane, that is sensitive to cold stimuli.

collateral: a branch of the axon of a neuron.

collective: characteristic of a group judgment, attitude, or reaction.

collective consciousness: the group or crowd mind. Psychologists no longer accept the idea of a group mind.

collective image: (*Jung*) a racial image which is part of the collective unconscious.

collective memory: see RACIAL MEMORY.

collective mind: 1. a consensus. 2. the group mind.

collective psychology: see SOCIAL PSYCHOLOGY.

collective representation: collective ideas, or ideas held in common by members of a social group as a result of their common experience.

collective unconscious: (*Jung*) the part of the unconscious that is inherited and common to all men. It is the seat of the archetypes.

colliculus: a hump or prominence in the nervous system. The superior and inferior *colliculi* form the corpora quadrigemina in the brain stem. The superior colliculus is believed to mediate visual reflexes, the inferior, auditory reflexes.

colligation: a combination of distinct units that remain distinct, as contrasted with fusion, in which the units do not remain distinct. A chord of music as printed is a *colligation*, but as played typically *fuses*.

color: the quality dimension of light. Broadly, colors are divided into *chromatic*, which are analyzable into three dimensions of hue, saturation, and brightness, and *achromatic*, which possess only the attribute of brightness. The latter are grays, blacks, and white.

Colors are associated with the physical dimension of wavelength so that it is possible to specify the length of the wave that gives rise to a psychological experience of color. Waves at the long end of the spectrum in the region of 700nm give rise to red. At the short end, at about 400nm, the corresponding experience

is violet. Blue lies at about 470nm and yellow at 580nm.

color adaptation: see CHROMATIC ADAPTATION.

color antagonism: see COMPLEMENTARY COLOR.

color attribute: any of the basic or fundamental characteristics of color sensation: hue, saturation, and brightness.

color blindness: a congenital visual defect characterized either by the partial or total inability to see colors. Total color blindness is known as *achromatism*, or *achromatopsia*. The totally color-blind are incapable of distinguishing among any color combinations and see only shades of gray. Most common is a form of partial color blindness known as red-green blindness, which is the inability to discriminate between red and green under certain conditions. There are two major forms of red-green blindness, *protanopia* and *deuteranopia*. In protanopia, red is seen as a whitish gray with the luminosity of the spectrum abnormally low at the red end. In deuteranopia, red and green are confused, but the relative brightness value of the spectral colors is unchanged. Blue-yellow color blindness is extremely rare and of little practical importance.

color circle: a representation of the

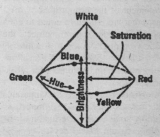

FIG. 6. *A color circle.*

spectral colors in the form of a circle with the dimension of hue on the periphery and the dimension of saturation and brightness represented by radii extending from a netural gray in the center to maximal on the periphery. See illustration.

color constancy: one of the perceptual constancies describing the fact that colors tend to remain the same despite relatively wide variations in the conditions of illumination.

color contrast: the fact that any color is affected by, and in turn affects, any other color in the surrounding field. Contrast takes two major forms: simultaneous and successive. *Simultaneous contrast* occurs between colors experienced at the same time. Fundamentally it consists of the enhancement of complements by each other. Thus, yellow seen against a blue background is yellower and the blue bluer where it immediately surrounds the yellow. *Successive contrast* occurs when a color is fixed for a period of time and the point of fixation is then shifted to a neutral background. The approximate complement of the original color is then seen.

color deficiency: COLOR BLINDNESS.

colored hearing: see CHROMESTHESIA.

color equation: in color mixing, a statement of the proportions of mixtures that are judged as equal to each other. Thus, for a given subject, the following might hold: 40% white + 60% black = 45% blue + 55% yellow.

colorimeter: an instrument for measuring colors.

color mixer: 1. an electric apparatus that rotates interleaved colored discs rapidly so as to achieve fusion of the colors. 2. an optical device capable of producing relatively homogenous lights, which are projected onto a screen in such a way as to overlap.

color mixture: the process of combining two or more colors in such a way as to achieve a fusion or combination. There are several basic methods of accomplishing color mixture: (1) interleaved sectors of standard-colored papers may be rotated rapidly on a color mixer; this is known as *retinal mixture*. (2) colored lights may be projected onto a screen in such a way that they overlap; this is called *additive mixture*. (3) pigments may be mixed as the artist mixes paints; this technique is called *subtractive mixture*, since the pigments subtract all wavelengths except the one reflected. Because the mixing of pigments gives results that are different from those produced by the other methods, it is not for scientific purposes.

color naming: (*Rorschach*) a scoring category for naming the colored cards with appropriate color names as a form of response.

color primary: 1. one of those colors that, when mixed in proper proportions, yield all other colors including white; within this definition, red, green, and blue are the primaries. 2. one of those colors that cannot be broken down by introspective analysis; red, green, yellow, and blue are primary, according to this criterion, and some authorities would add white, black, and gray, because other colors cannot be seen in them. The artist's primaries are red, blue, and yellow, since, by mixtures of these pigments, he obtains all other colors.

color purity: see SATURATION.

color pyramid: a three-dimensional schematic representation, in the form

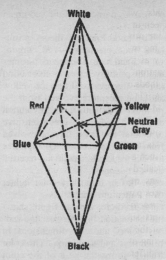

FIG. 7. *A color pyramid.*

of a double pyramid, of the dimensions of both chromatic and achromatic color experience. The vertical axis from black at the bottom to white at the top represents the dimension of brightness. The base of the pyramid represents hue, with the fundamental colors—red, green, yellow, and blue—at the corners. The radii extending outward from neutral gray at the center represent saturation, that is, depth of color. By moving up and down along the surface of the vertical axis, we obtain various tints or shades of color. As we move in toward the center, the tones becomes less saturated but of equal brightness. The pyramids are also arranged so that colors or tones that are opposite each other are complementary.

color response: (*Rorschach*) a scoring category for responses determined by the color of a blot.

color shade: a series of colors of the same hue and staturation which vary only in the dimension of brightness.

color shock: (*Rorschach*) a scoring category for an emotional response to a colored card.

color solid: 1. any geometric solid representing schematically the several dimensions of color experience. 2. the color pyramid.

color-sorting test: a test for the detection of color blindness. See HOLMGREN TEST.

color spindle: see COLOR PYRAMID.

color square: see COLOR PYRAMID.

color surface: a plane surface obtained by cutting through a color pyramid or triangle at right angles to the vertical axis. All possible hues and saturations will be found on the surface at that level of brightness.

color temperature: the temperature of a black body, or nonselective complete radiator, at which it yields a color matching that of a given sample of radiant energy. The temperature is measured on the Kelvin or absolute scale.

color theories: systematic attempts to organize the facts and hypotheses concerning color vision into a framework that will account for visual phenomena. Broadly, any theory must account for the following: (1) the phenomena of color mixture; (2) primary colors and complementary colors; (3) simultaneous and successive contrast effects; (4) color weakness and color blindness; (5) transduction or the converting of light energy into nervous impulses, their encoding and transmission to cortical centers.

There are several well-known theories of color vision, including the Young-Helmholtz, the Ladd-Franklin, and the Hering. The Young-Helmholtz theory assumes that there are three fundamental color receptors or cones in the retina corresponding to the physical primaries red, green, and blue. Each receptor is stimulated by any wavelength but responds maximally to the wavelength to which it is most sensitive. White is accounted for as the simultaneous arousal of all receptors. Individual color experiences are accounted for as the separate arousal of one conal process, or in the event of nonprimaries, of two processes. Thus, yellow is accounted for as a mixture of red and green processes. Color blindness is assumed to be due to the absence of cones, either a total absence in the case of total color blindness or of the red-green processes in the case of red-green blindness. The Young-Helmholtz theory received empirical support from the discovery in the 1960s of three types of cones sensitive to red, green, and blue wavelengths, respectively.

The Hering theory postulates six primaries: black, white, red, green blue, and yellow. These qualities are presumed by Hering to be mediated by three processes in the retina, a black-white, a red-green, and a blue-yellow. Catabolic, or destructive, excitation gives rise to the white, red, and yellow sensations; and anabolic, or constructive metabolic, stimulation gives rise to black, green, and blue sensations. Mixtures are explained by the simultaneous arousal of pairs of the nonantagonistic processes. Complementary colors are the antagonistic pairs that, when aroused simultaneously, give rise to gray. Color blindness is assumed to be the lack of one or more of the chromatic

processes, particularly the red-green process.

The Ladd-Franklin theory postulates four primaries—red, green, yellow, and blue. The theory assumes that the primitive eye was color-blind (a cone-free eye) and that the yellow and blue receptors evolved from the primitive rods with further evolution producing red- and green-sensitive receptors, the latter having evolved from yellow processes. Of the three theories the Ladd-Franklin has received the least support.

color tint or **tone:** any color lighter than a medium gray.

color triangle: a plane figure showing the relationships between the various colors and the dimensions of brightness and saturation. The color triangle forms the base of the color pyramid (*q.v.*)

color value: the dimension of brightness.

color weakness: less than the normal ability to discriminate hues. The term is a broad one and may be used to refer to color blindness as well as to diminished sensitivity to colors.

color wheel: see COLOR MIXER.

color zones: regions of the retina that respond differentially to different hues. For normal individuals all colors are seen in the foveal or central region of the retina. In the middle zone, blue and yellow and the grays can be seen, and in the outer zone only achromatic responses are given. However, the zones are not sharply defined and show considerable overlap, particularly in the blue-yellow region.

Columbia Mental Maturity Scale: general intelligence test utilizing pictorial classifications designed for children ages 3½ to 10. Items are printed on cards, requiring the examinee to select the one that does not belong.

column: 1. a bundle of neurons of the same general structure and function that travel for some distance longitudinally in the central nervous system. 2. a row of values in a statistical table of matrix.

columns of Goll: the large nerve tracts in the posterior spinal cord that carry touch and proprioceptive impulses. The columns are made up of the two tracts known as FASCICULUS GRACILIS and FASCICULUS CUNEATUS.

coma: a state of profound unconsciousness with abolition on most reflexes and voluntary behavior.

combat fatigue: a traumatic neurosis characterized by anxiety reactions and somatic disturbances brought on by long exposure to combat. In World War I, the equivalent disorder was called *shell shock* and was typically characterized by the presence of functional paralyses and anesthesias.

combat neurosia: See COMBAT FATIGUE.

combination, law of: 1. the generality that two or more stimuli presented together or in close succession may combine to elicit response. 2. the generality that two or more responses that are made either simultaneously or in close succession will tend to occur together when the stimulus for either is presented alone.

combination tone: a tone generated when two tones are sounded together. There are two types: *difference tone*, which in frequency is the difference between the two original tones, and *summation tone*, which in frequency is the sum of the two generating tones.

comention: (*R. B. Cattell*) a personality dimension characterized by con-

formity to cultural standards, acceptance of authority, and frequently, repression. *Contr.* ABCLUTION.

commissural fibers: the neurons that make up a commissure.

commissure: a tract of nerve fibers connecting two regions on the opposite side of the brain.

common chemical sense: a sense mediated by receptors in the nose that arise from endings of the trigeminal nerves which are sensitive to irritating vapors.

common factor: in factor analysis, a group factor.

common fate, law of: (*Wertheimer*) principle that elements in perception that function in the same way or move or change in the same way tend to be apprehended together. *Syn.* factor of uniform density.

common personality: (*Murray*) the most commonly repeated and consistent patterns of behavior during a given period of life. See also LIFETIME PERSONALITY; MOMENTARY PERSONALITY.

common sense: 1. the practical understanding and good judgment that folklore attributes to the common man. 2. (*Adler*) social sense; social interest, as opposed to private interest and striving for personal superiority. 3. the common characteristics or attributes of the various senses; that is, spatiality, temporality, and number.

common-sense validity: see A PRIORI VALIDITY; FACE VALIDITY.

common sensibility: the undifferentiated and poorly localized mass of visceral sensations. *Syn.* COENESTHESIA.

common trait: (*Allport*) a trait that is possessed to some degree by all members of a culture.

communication: 1. the transmission of energy changes from one place to another, as in nervous transmission. 2. the process of transmitting or receiving signals or messages. 3. a message or signal. 4. information given by a patient to a psychotherapist.

communications theory: the branch of psychology that deals with communication in all its phases—human, mechanical, institutional. The related disciplines of physiology, neurology, and electronics are included as they apply to communications. Particular emphasis is lent to developing models and parallels between human communication and machines.

communications unit: in communications theory, an ensemble consisting of a *sender*, which encodes messages that are then transmitted in signal form through a *channel* to a *receiver*, where they are then decoded. Analogies are drawn between electronic communications units and the human organism. The sense organs are receivers that transform stimuli (encoding) into signals (nervous impulses) that are sent through the channels of the nerves to the brain, where they are interpreted (decoded).

community-of-content theory: the assumption that in each complex stimulus situation there are a number of elements in common with other situations. Community of content is utilized in explaining consistency of response from situation to situation.

comparable form: see ALTERNATE FORM.

comparable group: two or more groups that are representative samples of a population. Such groups need not be equal in every respect but must be valid samples of the population they have been chosen to represent.

comparative judgment: a report by a subject of how two or more stimuli are alike or different on a given dimension. For example, the subject might be asked to compare a series of variable weights to a standard weight.

comparative judgment, law of: (*Thurstone*) the assumption that in judging two items with respect to any dimension, the psychological difference between the two can be measured by the relative dispersion of the items in their frequency distributions. The unit of the scale of measurements is the standard deviation of the discriminal dispersions.

comparative psychology: the branch of psychology that investigates behavioral differences among the various species from a comparative point of view.

comparison stimulus: a stimulus, or part of a series of stimuli, that is compared with or judged against a standard stimulus.

compartmentalization: the isolation and blocking-off of ideas, feelings, values, and attitudes. The businessman who is a pillar of the church on Sunday but on Monday forces a shopowner out of business in order to obtain a franchise on a block of property that will be sold to the city at a fantastic profit, is demonstrating compartmentalization.

compatible: 1. capable of harmonious coexistence. 2. in logic, not contradictory. 3. descriptive of two persons who are temperamentally and sexually suited to each other in marriage.

compensating error: an error that cancels out another error.

compensation: the process of engaging in substitutive behavior in order to make up for social or physical frustration or a lack of ability in a certain area of personality. Freud considered compensation a mechanism for covering up awarness of an undesirable impulse. Adler considered the process one of reacting to feelings of inferiority; the concept was central to his system of INDIVIDUAL PSYCHOLOGY (*q.v.*).

compensation idea: (*Adler*) the substitution in fantasy or in dreaming of a superior image for an inferior one.

compensatory movement or reflex: a movement, often reflexive, that seeks to restore a normal position or equilibrium. For example, when a cat is dropped upside down, the animal will show rapid compensatory righting movements.

compensatory trait: a trait, usually found in a high degree that is serving as a substitute for a trait that is possessed to a low degree. In general, psychologists do not believe in a strict law of compensation among ability or personality traits; more commonly accepted is the rule that good things tend to go together rather than bad with good.

competence: 1. appropriateness or ability of training for a task. 2. in forensic psychology, a state of mind qualifying a person be responsible for his actions.

competition: mutual striving between two individuals or groups for the same objective. *Competition* implies strong personal involvement in a struggle. *Rivalry* ordinarily does not imply a personal antagonism but only a friendly and parallel desire to excel, as in *sports*. However, in *sibling rivalry* there may be a strong element of personal opposition.

complement: one of a pair of complementary colors.

complementary color: any combination of colors that when mixed in proper proportion, yields gray.

complementary instinct: (*Psychoan.*) instincts of opposite polarity, such as eros and thanatos. Both Freud and Jung tended to think in terms of polarities, and in their formulations each instinct had its opposite.

complementary probabilities: the sum of probabilities of an event's occurring and not occurring.

$$p + q = 1.00$$

complete-learning method: a technique in which the material to be learned is presented until it can be reproduced without an error. After each presentation, the subject attempts to repeat the material correctly.

completion test: test designed in such a way that the subject must supply the answer by filling in blank spaces.

complex: 1. group of interrelated or associated ideas. 2. (*Psychoan.*) a group of associated ideas strongly toned with emotion and that may be wholly or partly repressed.

The term *complex* has come to have pathological connotations because of its wide usage among psychoanalysts and psychiatrists to characterize clusters of ideas and impulses (such as the OEDIPUS COMPLEX) that are in strong conflict with other aspects of personality. However, the concept does not necessarily carry the implication of abnormality and may be used to characterize associations of desires, impulses, and sentiments in normal persons.

complex cell: a cell in the visual area of the cerebral cortex that responds to a bar of light on edge and will also respond to a moving bar or edge in a particular orientation.

complex indicator: (*Jung*) in a word-association test, a response that arises from a repressed complex. Indicators may take the form of blushing, stammering, or stereotyping of responses.

complex reaction: a form of the reaction-time experiment in which the subject is required to make a choice or discrimination between two or more stimuli.

compliance: yielding; making one's desires conform to the wishes of others but without changing one's private attitudes.

compliant character: (*Horney*) one who is overly self-effacing and yielding and who shows an extreme tendency to move toward people.

complication: 1. a combination of sensations derived from different receptors, such as the sight and smell of a rose. 2. the occurrence of a second disease condition during the course of a primary disease.

complication experiment: an experiment in which two events are attended simultaneously, such as observing a dial and listening for the ring of a bell, with one being in the focus of attention. The event that receives only marginal attention will be displaced in time. Thus, in the example given above, the bell will seem to have sounded later than it actually did. Conversely, if the bell is attended, the dial will be judged to have moved more than it actually did.

component instinct: (*Psychoan.*) a fusion of two instincts into one. Thus, the sex instinct is said to be a combination of a number of instincts, among which are sadism, self-destruction, and exhibitionism.

composite: a whole composed of parts, traits, or features that belong to different persons or things. Thus, in a dream, a person may be a composite of several individuals.

composite figure: a dream figure or image made up of traits that belong to two or more real persons.

composite image: an image derived from a number of memory images.

composite norm: a norm obtained by combining two or more scores.

composite score: an average score made up of several subscores. Sometimes the individual scores are weighted.

compos mentis: competent, not legally insane or mentally deficient. *Contr.* NON COMPOS MENTIS.

compound: a mixture or blend of elements or independent parts.

compound eye: a type of eye found extensively in insects; it consists of a number of rudimentary optical systems that focus images at slightly different points so as to form a mosaic instead of a single image.

compound reaction: forms of the reaction-time experiment in which the subject either must recognize the stimulus before reacting or must discriminate between two or more stimuli. For example, he might be instructed to react only to a white light and not to a yellow. See also REACTION TIME.

compound tone: a tone made up of two or more simple or partial tones.

comprehension: understanding, grasping; the process of reacting intelligently in a problem situation.

comprehension test: 1. a type of aptitude test, first employed by Binet, in which the subject is asked what he would do in a given situation. For example, the question might involve what to do if one awoke smelling smoke. 2. an achievement test that measures the subject's understanding of a printed passage by means of a series of questions about the selection.

comprehensive examination or **test:** an examination that measures a student's achievement in an entire field or over a long period of time in a number of subjects.

comprehensive solution: (*Horney*) the identification of the real self with the idealized image in order to resolve conflicts. In extreme form, the psychotic resolves conflicts by identifying with his fictionalized concept of self.

compromise formation: (*Psychoan.*) a form of behavior that represents a fusion between the repressive forces of the psyche and the repressed impulse. The mechanism is essentially one of modification of the repressed impulse in such a way as to enable it to escape the censorship of the ego.

compulsion: 1. a psychological state in which an individual acts against his own will or conscious inclinations. 2. the forcing of an individual to act against his own wishes.

compulsiveness: 1. the trait of repetitiveness of behavior often inappropriate or contrary to the individual's inclinations. 2. the trait or characteristic of rigidity and lack of flexibility in behaving.

compulsive-obsessive neurosis: see OBSESSIVE-COMPULSIVE NEUROSIS.

compulsive personality: an individual who is excessively orderly, rigid, and pedantic.

conation: striving; acting; willing. The conative aspect of the personality is that which is characterized by

purposive behavior and the impulse to act.

concaveation: placing nonpregnant animals with young. Maternal behavior may be induced in female animals by this procedure.

concept: 1. a general idea or meaning usually mediated by a word, symbol, or sign. 2. an idea that combines several elements from different sources into a single notion. The concept *mammal* refers to a variety of divergent species, all of which have several attributes in common. Concepts are formed by a process of abstraction, which is then followed by a process of generalization. A child, for example, abstracts the concept of roundness from his limited experiences with balls, oranges, and the moon. He then learns to generalize the concept to all objects having the same characteristic shape. Abstract concepts are concepts, such as number, goodness, or quality, that cannot be attributed to a specific object or finite number of objects or events. Concrete concepts involve a particular instance or object, as opposed to a general instance or quality of many objects.

concept formation: the process of learning concepts. It involves abstracting a quality of property of an object or event and then generalizing that quality or property to all appropriate objects or events. Thus, we learn that the term *mammal* applies to viviparous organisms that suckle their young and possess hair. The concept can then be applied to all creatures—shrews, elephants, men, whales—however disparate they may otherwise be, provided they meet these criteria.

conception: 1. the process of imagining or thinking. 2. the process of forming a concept. 3. a general idea of related group or ideas such as one's conception of communism. 4. the fertilization of an ovum.

conceptional or **true age:** age as reckoned from the estimated day of conception.

conceptualization: 1. the process of thinking or imagining. 2. the formation of a concept or ideal.

conceptual learning: the learning of new concepts or the modification of existing concepts.

conceptual model: a schematic or diagrammatic representation of a concept.

conceptual nervous system: a model or system of hypothetical constructs by means of which the neural correlates for behavior can be visualized. As is true of any model, the conceptual nervous system is an analogy that is useful for stimulating research and does not necessarily represent reality.

concha: the concavity of the outer ear that leads into the external canal.

concomitant variation: 1. a correlation. 2. a method of inductive reasoning that assumes that where two phenomena vary together they are casually related in some way, either directly or indirectly, by being related to a thrid variable.

concordance: the appearance of the same trait in both members of a pair of twins. *Contr.* DISCORDANCE.

concordance coefficient: a statistical measure of the degree of which a group of judges is in agreement in ranking.

concordance ratio: in genetics, the percentage of relatives who show the same trait as a given individual.

concrete: 1. pertaining to the specific or particular instance, as opposed to the general or abstract. 2. practical, utilitarian, and is sometimes said of intelligence.

concrete image: a memory image that is recalled in terms of the sensory qualities of an object, such as the feel of a hammer or the odor of a skunk.

concrete intelligence: the ability to deal effectively with practical or concrete situations and relationships.

concrete operational stage: (*Piaget*) the stage of development during which the child is able to use rules based on concrete instances but cannot deal with abstract qualities.

concurrent reinforcement: two or more independent schedules of reinforcement operating at the same time.

concurrent validity: a measure of how well a test measures what it was designed to measure by finding out how well people do on the test who are in occupations for which the test is presumed to be valid.

concussion: a general term meaning a loss of consciousness due to a blow on the head. Concussion may be accompanied by shock, temporary paralysis, amnesia, and variable aftereffects.

condensation: (*Psychoan.*) the fusion of several latent elements in a dream into a single manifest element. The process is held to be an unconscious one that represents the dream work's attempt to get by the censor.

condition: 1. a circumstance antecedent to a given effect. Thus, lightning is a condition for thunder. 2. the state of a person or thing with respect to a particular function or general health. 3. (*verb*) to establish conditioned response. 4. (*verb*) to cause or promote learning.

conditional probability: the frequency with which an event is likely to occur as dependent upon the presence of another event.

conditional reflex: see CONDITIONAL RESPONSE.

conditioned: 1. describing responses that, through learning, have been made dependent or conditional upon the presentation of a previously neutral stimulus. 2. dependent or contingent upon something.

conditioned avoidance response: a conditioned response that prevents the appearance of a noxious or painful stimulus.

conditioned emotional response: an emotional reaction that has been associated with a certain stimulus pattern by means of conditioning procedures.

conditioned escape response: a conditioned response that allows an animal to escape from a noxious or painful stimulus.

conditioned inhibition: the suppression of a conditioned response by pairing it with an indifferent stimulus in the absence of reinforcement. Thus, the indifferent stimulus becomes a signal for nonreinforcement and the conditioned response is suppressed.

conditioned reflex: see CONDITIONED RESPONSE.

conditioned response: 1. the learned responses to an indifferent stimulus that has been attached to it by repeatedly pairing the stimulus with a reinforcer. Thus, Pavlov, the discoverer of conditioning, attached the dog's salivatory response to the sound of a tuning fork by repeatedly pairing it with food. Salivation to the sound of the tuning fork is called a *conditioned response*.

conditioned reinforcement: see SECONDARY REINFORCEMENT.

conditioned reward: a secondary reward. See DELAYED REWARD.

conditioned stimulus: the neutral or indifferent stimulus that through conditioning becomes effective in eliciting the conditioned response. *Abbr*. CS.

conditioned suppression: the utilization of an aversive or painful stimulus in conjunction with a neutral stimulus in a series of conditioning trials, with the result that the subject will show a decrease in the magnitude of the previously neutral stimulus alone.

conditioning: 1. classical conditioning; Pavlovian conditioning; Type-S conditioning. The process discovered by Pavlov in which an originally neutral or indifferent stimulus repeatedly paired with a reinforcer comes to elicit a response. The neutral stimulus is called the conditioned stimulus, or CS; the reinforcer is the unconditioned stimulus, or US; the natural or unlearned response is called the unconditioned response, or UR; and the learned response the conditioned response, or CR. As Pavlov used the term, a reinforcer is any agent, such as food, that reduces, or partly reduces, a need. Thus, the dog naturally salivates (UR) to food in the mouth (US). When a neutral stimulus, such as a bell (CS), is presented with the food, it elicits salivation (CR). 2. instrumental conditioning; operant conditioning; Type-R conditioning—a type of conditioning where the reinforcement is made contingent upon the animal's reponses. Thus, when a rat learns to press a lever to get a pellet of food, an instrumental conditioned response has been established.

Because instrumental reinforcement can be negative, the animal's learning to escape a noxious stimulus is also instrumental conditioning. In the food-pellet experiment, the lever is the conditioned stimulus; the depression of the bar is the conditioned response; the food is the unconditioned stimulus; and the eating of the food is the unconditioned response. In classical conditioning, several measures are possible: latency, or the time between the conditioned stimulus and the appearance of the conditioned response; magnitude of response; probability of response; and resistance to extinction. In operant conditioning, rate of conditioning is the most widely employed measure of conditioning, with resistance to extinction also being used by some experimenters. See also SKINNER'S OPERANT CONDITIONING.

conduction: 1. the transmission of the nervous impulse from one place in the nervous system to another. 2. the transmission of sound waves through the ear.

conduction aphasia: a speech disorder involving the inability to repeat words as a result of damage to the conduction pathways between Wernicke's area and Broca's area (*q.q.v.*).

conduction deafness: deafness caused by a defect in the conducting mechanisms, that is, the eardrum or auditory ossicles. *Contr.* NERVE DEAFNESS.

conduction unit: (*Thorndike*) a system of neural connections or bonds that function in a certain adaptive act.

conductivity: the ability of a neuron or nerve to transmit nervous impulses. Conductivity varies with size and metabolic conditions of the neuron.

cones: specialized receptor cells in the innermost portion of the retina that are capable of transforming the energy of light into nervous impulses. The cones function in photopic or daylight vision and mediate both chromatic and achromatic responses.

confabulation: 1. compensation for loss of memory by the fabrication of details. 2. (*Rorschach*) unorganized, rambling responses.

confederate: a person who is supposedly a subject in an experiment, but unknown to the real subjects, is an accomplice of the experimenter's.

confidence interval: the distance in sigma units between the fiducial limits, or limits outside of which an event is not expected to occur by chance.

confidence limits: see FIDUCIAL LIMITS.

configuration: see GESTALT.

confirmation: (*Tolman*) the fulfillment of an expectancy. *Confirmation* is Tolman's substitute for *reinforcement*.

confirming reaction: the hypothetical reaction within the organism that takes place when a goal is reached.

conflict: the simultaneous occurrence of two or more mutually antagonistic impulses or motives. An *actual conflict* precipitates a mental crisis and is to be distinguished from a *root conflict* which has existed from childhood in a dormant condition.

confluence: 1. (*Adler*) the fusion of several instincts into one. 2. the flowing-together, or fusion, of perceptual elements, motives or responses.

conformity: 1. a tendency to allow one's behavior to be governed by prevailing attitudes and opinions. 2. a personality trait that tends toward allowing the opinions and attitudes of others to govern one's behavior.

confound: to vary irrelevant variables in an experiment in such a way that they will be counterbalanced.

confusion: disturbed, emotional, and unclear thinking. In serious cases there may be perceptual disorientation and hallucinations.

congenital: pertaining to something (usually a condition or characteristic) originating at the time of birth or during fetal development. Congenital is to be distinguished from *hereditary*, which denotes an origin in progenitors.

congenital deafness: deafness already existing at birth due to the defects in the development of the middle or inner ear.

congruence: (*Rogers*) the conscious integration of an experience to become a part of the self.

congruent: being mutually agreeable or conforming: harmoniously coexistent.

congruent points: points on the two retinas that are referrable to the same stimulus point.

conjugate movements: coordinated movements of the two eyes acting together.

conjunctiva: the mucous covering of the eyeball and inner eyelid.

conjunctival reflex: the closing of the eyelid when the cornea is stimulated.

conjunctive concept: a concept defined by the joint presence of several attributes.

conjunctive motivation: striving for real and permanent satisfactions, as opposed to *disjunctive motivation*, which seeks substitute or temporary satisfactions.

conjunctive reinforcement: a type of intermittent reinforcement in which both the requirements of a fixed-ratio and a fixed-interval schedule must be satisfied. For example, reinforcement might be made contingent upon 5 minutes elapsing and 100 responses being given between reinforcements.

conjunctivity: (*Murray*) the coordination and organization of motives and purposes with action.

connection: 1. any linking between two phenomena, whether physical or mental. 2. specifically, the hypothetical bond between neural units that mediates a learned association.

connectionism: (*Thorndike*) the doctrine that the functional mediators between stimulus and response, or between associations are neural bonds, or links, that can be either inherited or acquired through learning.

connector: 1. a neuron that lies between a receptor and an effector. 2. any neuron lying between two other neurons.

connotation: 1. the aspect of meaning is suggestive of the emotional content of a word. 2. the implied meaning of a word in addition to its explicit meaning. See also SEMANTIC DIFFERENTIAL.

conscience: 1. the individual's system of moral values; the sense of right and wrong in conduct formerly believed by the theologians to be an innate character but now generally held by psychologists to be learned. 2. the superego or introjected set of moral and ethical values acquired from the parents.

conscious: 1. characterizing awareness or knowing. 2. able to respond to stimulation. 3. pertaining to the process of being aware, or characterizing a reaction of which the individual is aware. 4. (*noun*) that which is observable by introspection. 4. (*Psychoan.*) that which is part of the perceptual conscious, that is, the portion of mind aware of the immediate environment.

conscious experience: in popular usage, awareness of a mental process of perception, emotion, motivation, etc. More generally the term *experience* is used as an equivalent for learning.

conscious need: a need of which the individual is aware.

consciousness: 1. the state of awareness. 2. the totality of experience at any given moment, as opposed to mind, which is the sum of past consciousness. 3. awareness of acts, activities, and reactions. 4. the subjective aspect of neurological activities. 5. self-knowledge; self-awareness.

conscious state: 1. the totality of mental processes at any given time. 2. a condition of mental awareness.

consensual actions: reflex and involuntary acts of which the individual is aware.

consensual eye reflex: the contraction of a shaded pupil when the other pupil is stimulated by light.

consensual validation: the use of mutual agreement as a criterion for the truth or reality of a phenomena. Consensual validation is sometimes employed in psychotherapy to ascertain whether the patient is showing improvemenet.

conservation: 1. memory or retention. 2. (*Piaget*) a child's ability to ignore irrelevant transformations. Thus, the child at a certain level of development realizes that the amount of water is not changed by pouring it into glasses of different shapes.

consistency: see RELIABILITY.

consistency index: see RELIABILITY INDEX.

consolidation: 1. the hypothetical continuation of the neurophysiological activities involved in learning after the cessation of practice. The necessity for assuming consolidation of some sort is based on the facts of retroactive inhibition and retrograde amnesia. 2. the hypothesis that learning occurs in two phases, an initial short-term phase which, through practice or repetition, is converted into long-term memory.

consonance: 1. a harmonious combination of tones. *Contr.* DISSONANCE. 2. the degree to which elements within an attribute are harmonious with each other.

constancy: the tendency for objects in perception to resist change in spite of wide variations in the conditions of observation. See also OBJECT CONSTANCY and COLOR CONSTANCY.

constancy hypothesis: the assumption that there is a one-to-one relationship between stimulus variables and responses regardless of surrounding conditions, provided that the sense-organ-stimulus relationships remain the same. The constancy hypothesis is attributed to the structuralistic and behavioristic schools of psychology by the Gestalt psychologists, who take a relativistic point of view and hold that responses are always relative to the total complex of stimulating conditions as they interact with organismic factors.

constancy of internal environment: (*Cannon*) the tendency for various metabolic processes to remain constant—that is, for levels of heat, blood sugar, salt, pressure of the blood, etc., to remain constant (within narrow limits). *Syn.* HOMEOSTASIS.

constancy of the IQ: the tendency for the ratio of mental age to chronological age to remain constant from test to retest, provided that the same, or approximately the same, test is used. Constancy of the IQ is also a function of the length of test-retest interval, age, and environmental conditions.

constant: 1. a mathematical value that does not change. 2. an experimental condition that is not allowed to vary.

constant error: an experimental error that is continuous and in one direction. For example, most subjects, when judging the length of a vertical line tangential to a horizontal line, overestimate the length of the vertical line. See illustration.

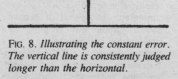

FIG. 8. *Illustrating the constant error. The vertical line is consistently judged longer than the horizontal.*

constant method; constant stimulus method: a psychophysical technique for measuring accuracy of judgment or discrimination. The method is characterized by the presentation of a constant stimulus to which a large number of similar stimuli differing in varying degrees of magnitude must be compared. Thus, a

constant tone might be paired in chance order with tones of progressively different pitches for comparison. The problem is then one of calculating the minimal stimulus difference, or threshold, that can just be detected 50 percent of the time.

constellation: 1. a complex of ideas held together by association. 2. (*Psychoan.*) a nonrepressed complex or group of emotionally charged ideas.

constellatory construct: (*Kelly*) a construct that is rigid and invariable and that determines the manner in which experiences fit into its elements. *Contr.* PROPOSITIONAL CONSTRUCT.

constitutional: pertaining to relatively enduring dispositions and traits whose foundations lie in organic or hereditary factors. *Contr.* situational or environmental.

constitutional inferior: characterizing an individual suffering from any of an ill-defined category of disorders—including chronic thievery, pyromania, homicidal tendencies, and sex perversions—that are assumed to be based on poor hereditary characteristics.

constitutional trait: a trait that is inherited or is part of one's basic biological equipment. *Contr.* ENVIRONMENTAL-MOLD TRAIT.

constitutional type: 1. complex of anatomical, physiological, and psychological traits that fall into a natural cluster or grouping and are believed to constitute a basis for classifying people. 2. the behavioral characteristics believed to be correlated with certain types of physique. See SHELDON'S CONSTITUTIONAL THEORY.

constriction: 1. diminished or narrowed spontaneity. 2. being overly determined by external factors. 3.

(*Rorschach*) poor form (F) responses. 4. (*Kelly*) the narrowing of the individual's construct system (*q.v.*) in order to reduce incoming experiences to a minimum.

construct: 1. a concept that represents relationships between empirically verifiable events or processes. Empirical constructs are based on observed facts or data and represent real and presently measurable variables. Hypothetical constructs are processes that are inferred to have real existence and to give rise to measurable phenomena. 2. a scientific model. 3. a piece of apparatus. 4. (*Kelly*) the individual's perception of interpretation of an event.

construction need: (*Murray*) the need to organize and to build things.

constructive: 1. creative. 2. pertaining to thinking or criticism that attempts to improve rather than to destroy.

constructive play: play that reveals the imaginative creation of new materials out of old, or that utilizes incomplete materials as though they were complete.

construct system: (*Kelly*) the hierarchy or total organization of the individual's constructs (*q.v.*).

construct validity: validity as determined by the extent or degree to which the items making up a test both individually and collectively are true measures of the construct or process being tested. For example, in designing a test of achievement in algebra, a board of experts would analyze each test item in terms of its validity for measuring some aspect of the field of algebra.

construe: (*Kelly*) to perceive or interpret events.

consultant psychologist: a psychologist who gives professinal advice to organizations for the solution of psychological problems.

consulting psychologist: a psychologist who gives professional help in the areas of mental health and vocational and educational needs and opportunities.

consummatory communication: in communications theory, messages that serve their purpose by expressing the feelings or ideas of the sender and do not require feedback from the receiver.

consummatory response: the final response in a series of responses that brings the organism into a state of adjustment. The animal's eating response at the end of a maze run constitutes an example of a consummatory response.

consummatory stimulus: a stimulus that serves to initiate a consummatory response, or a response bringing the organism into adjustment with those conditions that initiated behavior.

contact desensitization: in behavior therapy, a technique in which the therapist maintains physical contact with the patient during systematic desensitization (*q.v.*).

contagion: the spread of behavior patterns through a social group as a consequence of suggestion.

contamination: 1. allowing the investigator's knowledge of the dependent and independent variables to create a spurious relationship between them. Thus, an investigator who knows the body build of a number of subjects and subsequently rates them on personality or temperamental traits is allowing his knowledge of both variables in question to contaminate the correlation, making it spuriously high. 2. (*Rorschach*) a combination of responses that do not belong together.

contemporaneous-explanation principle: the assumption that causation is ahistorical, that is, that only present events can influence behavior.

content: 1. that which is in consciousness. 2. the material in a test or document. 3. the material expressed by a patient in an analytic session. 4. (*Guilford*) one of three dimensions of intelligence, the other two being operations and products. Content ability utilizes figures, symbols, meaning, and the behavior of others.

content analysis: the study of a document or a communication in terms of the frequency with which certain terms, ideas, or emotional reactions are expressed. An attempt may also be made to get at the degree of expression of feelings in the content.

content psychology: the structuralistic and phenomenological systems of psychology, which investigate conscious experience.

content response: (*Rorschach*) the subject's report of what he sees in an inkblot—animal, landscapes, anatomical details, etc.

content validity: a method for determining the validity of a test by assessing how well the various items correspond to the behavior the test is designed to measure or predict.

context: 1. conditions that surround a mental process and thus influence its meaning or significance. 2. the related verbal material that qualifies or clarifies the meaning of a word, phrase, or statement.

context theory of meaning: (*Titchener*) the assumption that the meaning of an experience is brought to it by a group of mental images habitually associated with the sensation.

Thus, the meaning of fire is the fusion of the habitual mental images of heat, pain, withdrawal, and light. Originally these meanings arose through actual kinesthetic and sensory contact with fire. With more and more experiences, the reactions are transformed into images, and even the verbal stimulus "fire" elicits the original meaning. Because well-established meanings may be very rapid, almost instantaneous, the images are perceived only in a kind of shorthand manner. In short, meaning is a sensation plus the context of mental images that form around the core of sensation giving it meaning.

contiguity: the proximity of two objects or events in space or time.

contiguity, law of: (*Aristotle*) a principle of associationism and learning that holds that those events occurring close together temporally or spatially tend to be associated or learned. There is general agreement among psychologists that contiguity of stimulus and reponse is a necessary condition for learning. Some theorists hold that it is both a necessary and sufficient condition. Others argue that contiguity must be supplemented by a principle of reward or reinforcement. A considerable amount of research in the area of learning has been devoted to attempts to identify the relative contribution of these two factors.

continence: 1. self-restraint in sex. 2. complete abstinence from sexual activity. 3. the ability to retain the urine and feces.

contingency: a statistical expression meaning the degree of relationship between the two variables.

contingency coefficient: a measure of the association between two sets of data. The measure employed is the degree to which one set is found to be nonindependent of the other more often than can be expected by chance. The mean square contingency coefficient is given by the formula:

$$C = \sqrt{\frac{X^2}{n + X^2}}$$

contingency contracting: in behavior therapy, a contract or reward based on cooperative responses in which the patient understands that he must perform a certain act in order to be reinforced or rewarded.

contingency table: a table showing the frequencies of occurrence of categories of events in vertical and horizontal rows.

continuity: condition or quality of being without interruption or break in duration or progress, usually with the implication of changes in related elements.

continuity theory of learning: the postulate that in discrimination learning there is an increment of learning for every rewarded or reinforced response to the stimulus.

continuous: 1. without gaps or breaks. 2. pertaining to a curve or line that changes by infinitely small steps. *Contr.* DISCRETE; DISCONTINUOUS.

continuous scale: a scale in which the increments of gain are on a continuum. For practical purposes the divisions may be stepwise, as on a temperature scale or graphic rating scale, but the function being measured is assumed to be or is known to be continuous.

continuous variable: a variable whose

course of change shows no jumps, gaps, or breaks.

continuum: a variable, graph, or curve without discrete gaps between points.

contour: the boundary of a perceptual figure. One of the criteria of a good figure is a distinct contour.

contractility: one of the fundamental properties of living tissue whereby it shortens upon stimulation. Contractility is a specialized property of muscle tissue.

contracture: a state of temporary or permanent failure of a muscle to return to its resting length after contraction.

contralateral: pertaining to the opposite side of a body.

contrast: 1. the intensifying of a difference between two sensations by the simultaneous or successive juxtaposition of two stimuli. For example, the sour taste of lemon in lemonade is heightened when the liquid is taken after eating candy. 2. the heightened awareness of differences between any two experiences by bringing them into juxtaposition.

contrasuggestibility: the tendency to act in a manner opposite to that which has been suggested.

control: 1. (*noun*) a factor in an experimental situation that is treated in such a way as to prevent its influencing the experimental or independent variable. 2. (*verb*) to arrange experimental conditions in such a manner as to insure that the experimental or independent variable under investigation is solely responsible for the results obtained.

control experiment: a special experiment carried out in order to test the effect of a variable that was either not controlled or inadequately controlled in another experiment.

control group: a group of subjects carefully selected so that they are equal in every respect to the members of the experimental group, except that the experimental or independent variable is not applied to the control group.

controlled analysis: (*Psychoan.*) analysis performed by a trainee under supervision of a qualified analyst.

controlled association: a test in which the experimenter limits the responses to be given to a series of words. For example, opposites might be required.

controlled sampling: sampling procedures in which factors that may influence the results are not left to chance.

controlled variable: a variable subject to regulation by the experimenter; the independent variable.

control series: a series of measurements or experiments designed to test the validity of a previous experiment or set of observations.

convention: a social custom that is not rigidly binding but is widely observed.

conventional stage of moral development: the stage during which the child attempts to maintain the expectations of family, social groups, and nation in his moral behavior. See also POSTCONVENTIONAL STAGE.

convergence: 1. the rotation of the two eyes inward toward a source of light so that the image falls on a corresponding part of each retina. 2. the coming together of a number of neural influences on a common path. 3. the interaction of hereditary and environmental factors in the causation of behavior. 4. a coming together of judgments or attitudes.

convergent thinking: (*Guilford*) the kind of thinking or ability involved in solving test problems with a single correct answer as established by test standardization. *Contr.* DIVERGENT THINKING.

conversion: 1. a rapid, often dramatic, change in religious beliefs. 2. the transformation of psychological conflict into physical symptoms. 3. the transformation of scores from one scale to another.

conversion of affect: (*Psychoan.*) the transformation of a repressed impulse or conflict into a physical manifestation. The physical symptom is said to be symbolic of the repressed desire or conflict.

conversion reaction: a form of hysteria in which the underlying psychic conflict is transformed into a sensory or motor symptom, such as functional anesthesia, deafness, blindness, or paralysis.

convolution: a fold of the cerebral cortex.

convulsion: a general seizure involving rapid spasmodic contraction and relaxation of the musculature.

convulsive therapy: any form of somatic therapy in the treatment of mental disorders that utilizes induced convulsions.

coordination: 1. smooth, harmonious functioning of bodily parts, particularly muscles. 2. arrangement of data or classes in such a manner that they bear the same relationship to another class.

coping behavior: the characteristic manner in which the individual deals with his social and physical environment, particularly as he mobilizes his resources to handle stress.

coprolagnia: sexual excitement generated by the sight or smell of feces.

coprolalia: the obsessive use of obscene words.

coprophagy: the ingestion of excrement or filth.

coprophilia: an attraction to, or excessive interest in, feces.

coprophobia: fear of excrement or filth.

copulation: sexual intercourse: *syn.* COITION.

cord: the spinal cord.

core construct: (*Kelly*) a basic or vital construct (*q.v.*) that determines one's identity and is highly resistant to change.

corium: the outer portion of the derma, or layer, that lies under the epidermis.

cornea: the anterior, transparent part of the sclerotic coat of the eye.

corneal lens: a small plastic corrective lens that floats on the tears over the cornea: corneal lenses are popularly called contact lenses.

corneal-reflection technique: method of studying eye movements by photographing light reflected from the cornea.

corneal reflex: the closing of the eye upon stimulation of the cornea.

coronal: pertaining to a plane of the head passing through the two ears.

corporal: bodily; pertaining to the body.

corpora quadrigemina: the two paired masses of tissue that form hillocks near the rear portion of the midbrain. The anterior mases, called *superior colluculi*, contain reflex centers for vision. The posterior masses, called *inferior colliculi*, contain centers for audition.

corpus callosum: a band of white fibers connecting the two cerebral hemispheres.

corpuscle: 1. a free-floating cell in the blood. 2. a small, specialized organ in the skin such as a touch corpuscle.

corpus striatum: literally, striate body; a part of the forebrain consisting of the caudate nucleus, lenticular nucleus, and internal capsule.

correction: 1. the manipulation of data in such a way as to minimize errors of observation and chance. 2. the application of lenses to the eye to improve vision.

correction for guessing: in objective tests, penalties imposed for incorrect answers in order to discourage guessing. For example, on a four-alternative multiple-choice test, the formula for scoring might be R-1/4W.

correlate: 1. (*noun*) a variable related in some way to another variable. 2. (*verb*) to calculate the coefficient of correlation. 3. (*verb*) to relate two things in any manner.

correlated: characterizing a relationship that is greater than zero.

correlation: 1. any relationship between two variables. 2. (*statistics*) concomitant variation between two variables in such a way that change in one is associated with change in the other. See also CORRELATION COEFFICIENT.

correlation cluster: a group of variables more closely related to each other than to other groups. When plotted geometrically on the surface of a sphere, such correlational groupings form clusters.

correlation coefficient: a numerical index of the degree of relationship between two variables. Correlation coefficients range between .00 and 1.00 and may be either positive or negative. The numerical size of the correlation coefficient is an expression of the strength of the relationship and may be interpreted according to the following stable:

Correlation coefficient	Degree of Relationship
±.00 to ±.20	none to negigible
±.20 to ±.40	negligible to moderate
±.40 to ±.70	moderate to moderately high
±.70 to ±.90	moderately high to very high
±.90 to ±1.00	very high to perfect.

The sign of the correlation coefficient is an indication of the direction of the relationship. Positive correlations indicate that high standing on one variable is associated with high standing on the other variable; negative correlations indicate that high standing on one variable is associated with low standing on the other variable.

correlation hierarchy: a correlation table in which the magnitude of the coefficients falls off progressively from one corner to the other three. In such cases, the correlations could be accounted for as originating from a general factor and specific factors.

correlation matrix: a table that includes all the correlations of a set of variables with each other. Usually each test's correlation with itself (the reliability coefficient) is also included. Correlation matrices are basic to factor analysis.

correlation ratio: an index of the degree to which a correlation is nonlinear.

correlation table: a statistical technique for showing the relationship between two variables to be correlated. One variable is represented according to values along horizontal rows, the other according to values along vertical columns. A given variable is then entered where the two scales intersect for that value. *Syns.* TWO-WAY TABLE; SCATTER DIAGRAM.

correspondent inference: the relationship that is assumed to exist between another's behavior and the motives for that behavior. Correspondence is perfect if the same items can be used to characterize both the individual's behavior and his disposition or motives to behave.

corresponding points: retinal points in the two eyes that give rise to a single visual impression when stimulated simultaneously.

cortex: 1. the outer layer or covering of any organ. 2. the cerebral cortex.

cortical: pertaining to the cerebral cortex.

cortical center: 1. an area in the cerebral cortex from which motor fibers originate that control certain sets of muscles. 2. an area in the cortex in which the afferent or sensory fibers from a sense organ terminate.

cortical control: the regulation exerted by the cortical centers on subcortical centers.

cortical deafness: deafness resulting from injury to the areas for hearing in the cerebral cortex.

corticalertia: (*R. B. Cattell*) speed and alertness in handling reactions.

cortical field: see ISOMORPHISM.

cortical induction: the arousal of activity in one part of the cortex as a result of activity in an adjacent part.

cortical inhibition: the blockage of nervous impulses by centers in the cortex.

corticalization: the tendency for more and more processes to come under control of the cerebral cortex as we ascend the phylogenetic scale. Corticalization is related to the corresponding tendency of functions to come under the control of the brain, which is called encephalization of function.

corticotrophic hormone: a hormone secreted by the anterior pituitary, which regulates the functions of the adrenal cortex.

cortin: a complex secretion of the adrenal cortex containing several hormones. *Cortin* is important in the control of salt intake and in the regulation of the gonads.

cortisol: hydrocortisone; generic name for 17-hydrocorticosterone.

cortisone: a hormone produced by the adrenal cortex.

cosaturation: the satisfaction of one drive by the fulfillment of another.

cost-benefit analysis: the theory that in deciding whether to engage in altruistic behavior, the individual weighs the cost (negative consequences) versus the benefits (positive factors).

cotwin control method: the use of one twin from a pair as a standard to which the outer twin can be compared after having been subjected to some kind of special training. In this way the control twin serves as a control on heredity, while the effects of learning on the experimental twin can be evaluated.

counseling: a broad name for a wide variety of procedures for helping individuals achieve adjustment, such as the giving of advice, therapeutic discussions, the administration and interpretation of tests, and vocational assistance.

counseling interview: an interview whose purpose is counseling or the giving of guidance in the area of personality, vocational choice, etc.

counseling ladder: the progressive stages or steps taken by a counselor in guiding the progress of counseling.

counseling psychologist: a psychologist who is professionally trained in the area of personality, marital, and vocational problems.

counselor: a psychologist or other professional individual who practices counseling.

counteration need: (*Murray*) the need to refuse to accept defeat; the need to select difficult tasks and overcome them.

counterbalancing: an experimental procedure for eliminating the effect of irrelevant variables by presenting them in a different order along with the independent variable. For example, the effect of fatigue on variable x might be eliminated in a series of trials by presenting x at the beginning, in the middle of the series, and at the end. Thus, the effect of fatigue on x could be evaluated by comparing performances without fatigue, with moderate fatigue, and with severe fatigue.

countercathexis: see COUNTERINVESTMENT.

countercompulsion: the development of one form of compulsive behavior in order to resist another. For example, the anxious person may maintain a high degree of muscular tension or engage in mannered behavior in order not to reveal a nervous tic.

counterconditioning: the elimination of a response through conditioning an incompatible response to the same stimulus.

counterego: the unconscious part of the self that acts antagonistically toward the ego or self.

counteridentification: (*Psychoan.*) the analyst's identification with the patient as a reaction to the patient's identifying with the analyst.

counterinvestment: (*Psychoan.*) attaching an opposite feeling to a repressed idea or impulse. For example, showing hatred for a person whom one unconsciously loves. *Syns.* ANTI-CATHEXIS; COUNTERCATHEXIS.

countersuggestion: a suggestion given to counteract a previous suggestion.

countertransference: (*Psychoan.*) the analyst's experience of emotional attachment for the patient.

counterwill: the ability to say no to others and to one's own impulses. In Otto Rank's system of Will Therapy, the concept of the counterwill is central.

couvade: the custom among nonliterate peoples of the father taking to bed at the birth of a child as if he were suffering the pains of childbirth.

covariance: a condition where change in one variable is associated with change in another. Where *x* and *y* are the deviations from the means of the paired values in the series, then covariance is given by the formula where N is the number of cases.

$$\frac{\Sigma xy}{N}$$

covariation: see CORRELATION.

cover memory: see SCREEN MEMORY.

covert: 1. hidden, concealed. 2. that which cannot be directly observed without the use of instrumentation. The term *covert* is employed as the opposite of *overt* in referring to behavior. Overt behavior consists of publicly observable responses; covert behavior refers to responses that cannot be directly observed, such as thoughts, feelings, glandular reactions, etc. The objective behavioristic psychologists favor the study of overt responses; the subjective phenomonological psychologists favor the study of covert behavior. *Syn.* IMPLICIT. *Contr.* overt.

covert conditioning: the introduction of imagination, thinking, or feeling in behavior therapy to facilitate changes in targeted behaviors. Thus a client might imagine a change in behavior (not smoking) and its consequences (freedom from the habit, better health) in order to bring about that change.

covert extinction: in behavior therapy, the imagined elimination of reinforcement for maladaptive behavior.

covert reinforcement: in behavior therapy, a technique in which the patient imagines a reinforcement following the successful handling of an anxiety-producing situation.

C–P–C cycle: (*Kelly*) a sequence of construing (*q.v.*) involving circumspection, preemption, and control. Circumspection involves construing an event or situation in various ways, followed by focusing on one construct (preempting), and finally, choosing the pole of the construct that will allow for prediction and control of events.

cranial: pertaining to the cranium.

cranial capacity: the cubic content of the cranium. Cranial capacity is taken by anthropologists as one index of race.

cranial division: the upper part of the craniosacral or parasympathetic division of the autonomic nervous system. See AUTONOMIC NERVOUS SYSTEM.

cranial index: the cephalic index as taken on a bare skull.

cranial nerves: The twelve pairs of nerves that have points of origin or termination within the cranium.

cranial reflex: a reflex mediated by one of the cranial nerves.

craniometry: the measurement of the skull.

craniosacral division: the division of the autonomic nervous system that arises out of the medulla and lower spinal cord. The craniosacral division governs vegetative, anabolic organic processes. *Syn.* parasympathetic division. See also AUTONOMIC NERVOUS SYSTEM.

craniscopy: the study of areas of the skull; PHRENOLOGY.

cranium: the skull, particularly the brain pan.

crawling: infantile locomotion in a prone position by means of the arms pulling the body forward as the legs or knees push.

C reaction: the response of an embryo to stimulation by bending the body into a C shape.

creative: pertaining to productive mental application or functioning— usually with the implication of employment of information derived not from direct experience or learning but from conceptual extension of such sources—in the solution of problems or the development of artistic or mechanical forms.

creative fantasy: (*Jung*) the solution of personal problems by the fusion of opposites.

creative imagination: the pattern of ideas accompanying the solution of a problem or the development of a new form. See CREATIVE.

creative resultants: (*Wundt*) the position that the whole of a mental process may be greater than the mere summation of its elemental processes.

creative synthesis: (*Wundt*) the process in apperception in which elements are brought together into more or less meaningful relationships ranging from a new ensemble to a concept.

creativity: the ability to produce new forms in art or mechanics or to solve problems by novel methods.

credibility: the perceived characteristic of a communicant—such as trustworthiness or expertise—that makes his message believable.

creeping: prone infantile locomotion on the hands and knees.

Crespi effect: a disproportionate increase in habit strength as compared to increase in reinforcement.

cretinism: a condition resulting from thyroid insufficiency in childhood and characterized by severe mental retardation, stunting, patchy hair, protruding abdomen, and a severely underdeveloped personality.

criminal psychology: that branch of psychology dealing with the study of criminal behavior.

criminal type: category comprising individuals who repeatedly engage in criminal or antisocial behavior, supposedly because of a strong, possibly constitutional tendency in that direction.

criminology: the science of crime, criminals, and penology. The social, psychological, and psychiatric aspects of the problem are usually included.

crisis: 1. a turning point marked by sharp improvement or sharp deterioration. 2. a decision or event of great psychological significance for the individual.

crisis intervention: therapeutic techniques for helping individuals experiencing a crisis.

criterion: 1. an independent, outside measure against which a test can be validated. 2. a standard of judgment or belief. 3. a level or goal by which behavior can be judged. 4. the dependent variable.

criterion behavior: a behavior standard against which another behavior is judged.

criterion group: a group whose characteristics are known and whose members are given a test for the purpose of validation. It is assumed that if the criterion group performs on the test according to expectation, the test is valid. For example, in validating neurotic inventories, diagnosed groups of neurotics are used as criterion groups.

criterion score: a score to be predicted, the dependent variable.

criterion variable: a standard against which another value, score, or test can be evaluated.

critical: 1. pertaining to an important or crucial judgment or evaluation. 2. a decisive point or the point of transition in a phenomenon or event.

critical flicker-fusion frequency: the rate of frequency at which a flickering stimulus fuses into a smooth, continuous stimulus.

critical incident technique: the observation of special samples of behavior believed to be indicative of the behavior of the individual as a whole.

critical ratio: the ratio of the difference between two statistics to the standard error of that difference. *Abbr.* CR. The most commonly employed critical ratio involves the difference between two means. The formula for uncorrelated means is:

$$CR = \frac{M_1 - M_2}{\sqrt{\sigma_{M1}^2 + \sigma_{M2}^2}}$$

where M = mean
σ = the standard error of the mean or
$\sigma_{dist}/\sqrt{N-1}$

CR must be three or more before the difference is accepted as being statistically significant.

critical score; critical level: a score that divides an array of scores into two groups with reference to some criterion. For example, a score of 80 on a medical-school entrance test might be taken as a minimal passing mark.

cross-adaptation: the generalized effect of raising the absolute threshold for one stimulus to sensitivity to other stimuli.

cross-conditioning: 1. incidental conditioning to any irrelevant stimulus that occurs along with the unconditioned stimulus. 2. the attachment of postural or tonic reflexes or responses to a commonly present stimulus.

cross-correspondence: in psychic research, messages in automatic writing by one medium that must be interpreted by a different medium.

cross-cultural approach: the observation of several cultures in order to study the effect of common environmental conditions or social practices. One of the most frequently studied behavioral patterns by this technique is child rearing.

crossed reflex: a reflex in which the response is elicited by a stimulus to the opposite side of the body. *Contr.* DIRECT REFLEX.

cross education: a type of transfer in which practice given to one side of the body is carried over to the other side.

cross modality: 1. pertaining to matching experiments in which the stimulus intensity in one sense is subjectively equated to a different stimulus in another modality. 2. pertaining to transfer of training utilizing two different sensory avenues.

crossparental identification: a strong attachment for the parent of the opposite sex.

cross-sectional method: a technique for studying a large number of representative persons or variables at a given period of time, as opposed to the longitudinal method, which follows the individual's development over a long period of time. Cross-sectional methods are frequently employed in the establishment of normative data. See also AGE NORM.

cross-validation: a technique for determining the validity of a procedure by testing it for a second time on another sample after its validity has been demonstrated on an initial sample.

crowd: a temporary collection of people who share a common interest and whose emotions may be readily and uncritically aroused. A mob is distinguished from a crowd on the basis of its domination by strong emotions and often aggressive behavior.

crowding: the sensation of stress and unpleasant feelings associated with settings involving a high density of people.

crucial experiment: a test or experiment critical for the acceptance of rejection of a hypothesis or theory.

crude mode: the midpoint of the class interval that contains the greatest number of cases in a frequency distribution.

crude score: 1. a raw score; a score

that has not been transformed into another form. 2. an approximation.

crus cerebri; crura cerebri: see CEREBRAL PEDUNCLE.

cryptesthesia: the general term for any form of perception without the use of known receptors. It includes clairvoyance, or seeing objective phenomena without the use of the eyes; clairaudience, or hearing without the ears; telepathy, or communication without sensory mechanisms; and premonitions.

crytpomnesia: 1. apparently new memories whose basis in experience has been forgotten or repressed. 2. apparently novel or creative thinking originating from forgetting ideas.

crystallized intelligence: (*R. B. Cattell*) intellectual ability as dependent on cultural factors and learning as these interact with fluid intelligence (*q.v.*).

cue: 1. a learned signal for guiding or controlling behavior 2. a stimulus used by the organism in making a discrimination. The term often implies a faint or obscure secondary stimulus that serves as a means of recognition or discrimination, although it may not be fully discriminated.

cue reduction: the ability of a portion of a stimulus pattern to elicit a response after learning has sufficiently progressed.

cue reversal: an experiment in which the stimulus that originally serves as a cue for the reward is interchanged with the stimulus that serves as a cue for nonreward.

cul-de-sac: 1. a blind alley in a maze. 2. a blind ending or barrier in thinking.

Culler's phi process: a method for finding the difference threshold in which the momentary difference thresholds are equated with the probable errors of the ogive distribution. The method is presumed to be more reliable than the Urban method and also takes into account the subject's willingness to make doubtful judgments.

cult: 1. a body of beliefs, rites, and customs associated with an object or person. The objective of the cult is usually religious, and magical powers are attributed to its agents. 2. collectively, those who hold strong beliefs associated with the teachings of a leader.

cultural anthropology: that branch of anthropology concerned with the structure and functioning of nonliterate societies.

cultural assimilation: the process of learning the customs and other group characteristics that make it possible for the individual to be fully incorporated into a group.

cultural conflict: the opposing forces that impinge upon individuals or groups who hold allegiance to two different cultures.

cultural determinism: the assumption that culture is responsible for the development and limitations in behavior patterns characteristic of a society.

cultural items: test items that are heavily loaded with information that can be acquired only in a specific culture or subculture and are therefore unfair to anyone not of that culture.

cultural lag: the carryover of customs, attitudes, and cultural products after these become dated or obsolete relative to the standards set by another culture or subculture.

cultural norm: a standard or set of standards in a given culture derived from the behavior of the generality of the individual members of that culture; an ordinarily expectable behavioral manifestation or pattern, against which an individual's behavior is judged.

cultural relativism: the view that cultural products—art, literature, music, mechanical inventions—can be judged only in relation to the culture from which they originated and not in any absolute sense. 2. the view that standards of behavior can be judged only in relation to the culture. 3. the view that the laws of psychology have only cultural, not universal, validity.

cultural transmission: the passing on by one generation of cultural standards and products to the next. *Syn.* ACCULTURATION.

culture: 1. the totality of the customs, arts, science, and religious and political behavior taken as an integrated whole that distinguishes one society from another. 2. a society or group of persons whose customs, arts, etc., set them apart from another group. 3. the intellectual and artistic aspects of life as opposed to the purely material or technical.

culture area: a geographical division showing common cultural patterns.

culture complex: an organized set of social attitudes and behavior patterns that form an integrated whole; for example, all activities associated with the hunting, preparation, and eating of meat.

culture conflict: 1. clash between two social groups from differing cultures who live in close proximity. 2. the individual's experience of conflicting motives and behavior patterns arising because of loyalties divided between two cultures. This kind of conflict is experienced frequently by immigrants.

culture-epoch theory: 1. the hypothesis that all societies tend to evolve in the same way. That is, all societies pass through the hunting, pastoral, agricultural, and industrial stages of evolution. 2. the theory that the individual child tends to pass through stages typical of his race and that his education should be planned accordingly.

Culture Fair Intelligence Test: general ability tests designed to be culture-fair, utilizing perceptual tests, completing progressive series, classifying and completing designs. Scales available for ages 4 to adult. See CULTURE-FAIR TEST.

culture-fair test: a test relatively free from invalidating biases caused by questions favorable or unfavorable to certain social classes, cultures, or ethnic groups.

culture-free test: a test designed in such a manner that all items depending upon cultural factors have been eliminated. No such test has thus far been developed.

culture trait: 1. a consistent and fundamental aspect of a given culture, such as marriage rites. 2. a personal trait attributable to cultural factors.

cumulative: 1. constituting the totality of that which has been summed successively as each new quantity is added. 2. any totality up to a given point.

cumulative distribution: a type of frequency distribution in which each plot shows the total number of cases falling below each successive magnitude. If the distribution is normal, the resulting curve will be S-shaped, or ogival.

cumulative frequency: a numerical or graphic count of cases wherein each new case is added to the preceding total.

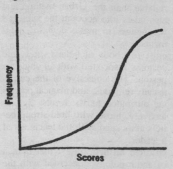

FIG. 9. *A cumulative frequency curve.*

cumulative frequency curve: a graphic representation of the sums of the frequencies of a series of scores arranged in order of magnitude. See illustration.

cumulative record: a continuous record to which data are added in summative form. Operant-conditioning records are cumulative records.

cumulative scale: an attitude scale in which the items have been arranged in such a manner that a response to any given item may be taken as indicative of agreement with all items of lower rank. *Syn.* GUTTMAN SCALE.

cuneus: a triangular lobe at the extreme back of the cerebrum behind the parieto-occipital lobe and above the calcarine fissure.

cunnilingus; cunnilinctus: the stimulation of the female genital organs with the mouth or tongue.

cunnus: the external genitals in the female.

curare: a vegetable extract used as

an arrow poison by Indians in Central and South America. Because it blocks nervous transmission, it has been employed in research on transmission at neuromuscular junctions.

curiosity: the tendency to explore, to investigate, to seek knowledge. Curiosity is regarded by some psychologists as one of the primary drives, along with sex, hunger, thirst, etc.

current of injury: the electrical current produced in injured tissues measured by placing one electrode on the outside of the membrane and the other on the injured surface.

curricular validity: the degree to which the items making up a test are a representative sample of the area for which the test is designed. For example, if the test measures achievement in algebra, then the items must measure a representative sample of the field of algebra.

curve: 1. a line between two contiguous surfaces. 2. the path of a point as defined by an equation. 3. a representation of a series of values, such as the number of errors made by an animal during the course of a learning experiment.

curve fitting: the process of identifying the curve that best fits obtained data. The fitting may be done by means of visual inspection and drawing a line that seems to pass through the data so as to be most representative of the maximum number of cases, or it may be done by mathematical techniques such as the method of least squares.

curve of rest: in the psychogalvanic skin response, the gradual dropping-off of the response curve from a high to a low during a state of no stimulation.

curvilinear: pertaining to a line that is bent, as distinguished from a straight-line function.

curvilinear correlation: a relationship that is represented by a curve rather than a straight line. The degree of such a relationship is estimated by a correlation ratio.

curvilinear regression: regression in which the equation for the line of regression is a curve rather than a straight line.

curvilinear relationship: any relationship that, when plotted, is represented by a curved line.

custodial care: minimal institutional care of mental patients without therapy.

custodial case: an individual who requires institutional care because of mental illness or criminality.

custom: a mode of relatively permanent behavior characteristic of a society. Customs are held to be complex habit patterns learned during the course of acculturation.

cutaneous: pertaining to the skin or sense organs in the skin.

cutaneous sense: any sense whose receptors lie beneath the surface of the skin or mucous membranes.

cutis anserina: goose pimples.

cutting score: a critical score that serves as a dividing point in a distribution of scores. Most tests have a cutting score for pass-fail.

cyan: bluish-green color.

cybernetics: the science of control mechanisms and their associated communications systems. Cybernetics cut across engineering, psychology, physiology, economics, and medicine. Illustrative problems that have been studied by cyberneticists, such as control systems in guided missiles, the production of artificial limbs, and the development of machines enabling the blind to read.

cycle: 1. a recurrent series of events. 2. a complete vibration in sound or light waves.

cyclic disorder: a mental disorder, such as manic-depressive psychosis, that tends to recur periodically.

cycloid: characterizing a personality pattern that shows relatively marked alternations of depression and excitement. The cycloid is the normal equivalent of the manic-depressive.

cyclopean eye: an imaginary single eye in the middle forehead that combines the functions of the two eyes. The concept of the cyclopean eye is useful in discussions of coordinated eye movements and space perception.

cyclophoria: a muscular imbalance of the eyes resulting in a tendency for one eye to move out of position when not fixated on a stimulus.

cycloplegia: paralysis of the ciliary muscle.

cyclothymia: 1. a tendency toward alternating periods of elation and depression which, in serious cases, is manifested as manic-depressive psychoses. 2. (*R. B. Cattell*) a constitutional source trait identified by factor analysis of correlation clusters and manifested as abnormal swings in mood.

cynolabe: a blue-sensitive pigment in the cones of the eye.

cytoarchitecture: the organization and patterning of cells within the cerebral cortex.

cytology: the branch of biology concerned with the study of cells.

cytoplasm: the protoplasmic substance of cells exclusive of the material in the nucleus.

D

DA: see DOPAMINE.

dactology: the art of communication by means of signs made with the fingers.

Daltonism: an old name for red-green color blindness, after John Dalton (1766–1844), a chemist, who suffered this defect and was the first to describe it.

damping: the checking or attentuation of vibrations in a sounding body by internal and external friction.

dancing mania: an epidemic of obsessive dancing which has appeared from time to time in Europe, notably following the Black Death. *Syn.* CHOREOMANIA.

dark: characterizing a state of color of low illumination or brilliance.

dark adaptation: a process of rod adjustment whereby the retina becomes over a million times more sensitive to dim light. The process depends upon the resynthesis of visual purple, a rod-stimulating substance, which is broken down under bright light. Complete dark adaptation requires about four hours; however, most of the process takes place in approximately one-half hour.

Das ein: "the one"; the field of being.

Daseinanalyse: see EXISTENTIAL ANALYSIS.

data: a collection of facts or numerical values.

datum: 1. the singular of *data*; a fact or value. 2. that which is sensed or perceived.

day blindness: an abnormality of the foveal region of the retina in which the individual sees better in dim light. In such cases the individual finds bright light uncomfortable.

daydream: a waking fantasy or reverie. Daydreaming is frequently wish-fulfilling in function and differs from night dreaming in that the expression of wishes is not hidden.

daylight vision: see photopic vision.

daymare: an acute anxiety attack.

day residues: (*Psychoan.*) remnants of experiences that play a part in determining the content of dreams.

dB: see DECIBEL.

deaf mute: a person who cannot speak because of deafness.

deafness: the partial or complete inability to hear. Total deafness is the inability to hear all sounds regardless of their loudness. Partial deafness may involve a decreased sensitivity to the entire range of sounds, or it may involve only inability to hear certain pitches. Adventitious deafness is caused by injury to the ears, as opposed to congenital deafness, which is caused by developmental defects, and central or cortical deafness, which results from injury to the areas for hearing in the cerebral cortex.

death feigning: see TONIC IMMOBILITY.

death instinct: (*Psychoan.*) the instinct for destruction and death, and when fused with pleasure, inward and outward directed drives for pain. The death instinct was not precisely described by Freud, who considered it difficult to access in the unconscious. However, like the life instinct, or Eros, it originates from the libido, which is the source of all energy in the individual.

deceleration: a slowing down; a decrease in velocity. The term is often used to characterize a decrease in the rate of learning as shown by a learning curve.

deception experiment: an experiment whose purpose is not revealed to the subjects in order to prevent such knowledge from influencing the results.

decerebrate: an animal whose cortex has been removed.

decerebrate rigidity: exaggerated contraction of the extensor muscles and postural reflexes following decerebration. It is caused by the loss of control of upper motor neurons.

decerebration: the removal of the cerebrum.

decibel: a unit of measurement of the perceived differences in sound. The standard sound exerts a pressure of .0002 dynes per cm^2 on the eardrum. This is of approximately average threshold value for a tone of 1,000 Hz. The decibel is a $10 \times \log_{10}$ of the ratio between this sound and a comparison sound. A bel is ten times the threshold intensity. Because the scale is logarithmic, two bels are 100 times threshold intensity. A whisper is about 10 decibels, conversation about 60, and thunder about 120. Thunder, then, represents a 10-million-fold increase in relative sound energy. *Abbr.* dB.

deciduous teeth: the first, or baby teeth, which give way to the permanent teeth.

decile: in a distribution of ranked scores, a division that contains one tenth of the cases.

decile rank: the rank order of the decile divisions of a distribution of scores. The first decile rank is the rank of all cases below the first decile point; the sixth decile, of those below the sixth decile point; and so on.

decoding: an information theory, the process by means of which a receiver translates signals into messages. By analogy, stimuli may be treated as signals, which the receptors encode into nervous impulses, which are decoded by the brain.

decompensation: 1. a progressive loss of normal functioning in favor of psychotic behavior. 2. disorganization of the personality under stress.

decorticate: an animal whose cerebral cortex has been surgically removed.

decorticate conditioning: a conditioned response established in the absence of the cerebral cortex.

decortication: the experimental removal of the cerebral cortex of an animal.

decrement: 1. a decrease or falling-off of anything. 2. a loss in retention as revealed by a change in the slope of a curve of retention. Contr. INCREMENT.

decremental conduction: see CABLE PROPERTIES.

decussation: 1. a crossing-over of nerve tracts from one side of the nevous system to another. 2. specifically, the crossing of the fibers of the pyramidal tracts in the medulla.

deduction: 1. an inference made from formal premises or propositions. 2. the formulation of a hypothesis or set of hypotheses.

deep: 1. characteristic of sensations that arise from proprioceptors in the muscles and organs. 2. pertaining to tones of relatively low rates of vibration. 3. pertaining to highly saturated colors.

deep-pressure sensitivity: the sense of pressure arising from subcutaneous receptors upon intense stimulation of the skin.

deep reflex: a muscular reflex elicited by tapping a tendon or the bone of attachment of a muscle. Syns. TENDON REFLEX; MYOTATIC REFLEX.

deep sensibility: sensitivity that arises from subcutaneous receptors and receptors associated with the muscles, tendons, and joints.

deep structure: in psycholinguistics, the idea underlying a sentence. Contr. SURFACE STRUCTURE.

defect: 1. the lack or absence of anything; an imperfection. 2. failure to come up to a standard, as in mental defectives.

defective: 1. incomplete; lacking in some manner. 2. having less than normal intellectual ability.

defective delinquent: a juvenile delinquent or adult criminal who is also subnormal intellectually.

defective speech: see SPEECH DISORDER.

defendance: (Murray) the need to defend oneself against blame or criticism, or to justify one's actions.

defense: 1. (Psychoan.) behavior that protects the ego against guilt, anxiety, and shame. 2. the act of protecting oneself. 3. excusing or rationalizing one's actions.

defense mechanism: any behavior pattern that protects the psyche from anxiety, shame, or guilt. Some common defense mechanisms are: REPRESSION; REGRESSION; PROJECTION; IDENTIFICATION; FANTASY; COMPENSATION; SUBLIMATION; REACTION-FORMATION; and AGGRESSION.

defense reaction: see DEFENSE MECHANISM.

defense reflex: a reflexive response, such as the sudden withdrawal of a limb to a painful stimulus.

defensiveness: 1. the personality characteristic of being overly sensitive to criticism. 2. engaging in behavior that turns an observer's attention away from one's deficiencies or from behavior which, if noticed, would cause embarrassment or guilt.

deference: (*Murray*) the need to admire and follow a leader, or to serve a superior gladly.

deficiency motive: a tendency to satisfy a need rather than to seek satisfaction beyond needs or deficits. *Contr.* ABUNDANCY MOTIVE.

definition: a boundary between two classes or phemonema. For example, a figure may be said to have good definition if it stands out clearly from the background as a result of having a well-defined border.

definitional validity: the assumed validity of a test whose items are taken as the definition of the variable to be measured.

definition of the situation: see SOCIAL REALITY.

deflection: (*Psychoan.*) a defensive form of behavior in which a thought or idea is diverted from consciousness.

defusion: (*Psychoan.*) a separation of the life and death instincts usually fused in the unconscious.

degenerate: one who deviates markedly from normal standards of conduct acceptable in a given society. The term is frequently applied to individuals who have committed sexual offenses and in such cases implies a constitutional deficiency.

degeneration: 1. retrogression or deterioration in an organ. 2. a moral decay or deterioration.

degrees of freedom: the number of observations—scores, test items, trials, etc.—in a sample set of observations minus the number of restrictions put on the observations. The number of restrictions is equal to the number of independent calculations used in arriving at a given statistic. For example, let us assume the problem involves fitting a straight line to 10 data points. A straight line by definition will fit two points, a and b, with no residuals. Therefore, there are eight degrees of freedom in determining the values since two of the observations are used up in making the determination.

dehoaxing: revealing any deceptions practiced on a subject during an experiment.

deindividuation: a feeling of anonymity as a result of being in a crowd. May account for aggressive or other atypical behavior on the part of otherwise stable individuals.

Deiters' cells: elongated supporting cells in the outer portion of the organ of Corti in the cochlea.

déjà vu: the illusion of familiarity in a strange place. It is believed to be due to the presence of familiar but subthreshold cues. For example, in walking in a strange town, some features may be similar to those experienced elsewhere—a church steeple, a chain store, a shop front. etc. As one glances at these, the presence of a subtle but familiar odor may be sufficient to trigger the *déjà vu* illusion.

delayed conditioned response: a conditioned response that is established by presenting the conditioning stimulus over a relatively long period of time, such as a minute, and delaying the reinforcement until near the end of the stimulus presentation. The animal's reponse, which at first occurs with the onset of the conditioned stimulus, comes to be delayed until near the end of the presentation.

delayed instinct: an instinct that does not appear until some time after birth or until development has reached a certain level.

delayed reaction: a response in a reaction-time experiment that does not occur immediately. In discrimination reaction time, for example, more complex conditions than are found in simple reaction time may lead to a short delay. The delay was formerly attributed to ideational pocesses.

delayed reinforcement: 1. in classical conditioning, reinforcement that is not administered until a period of time has elapsed between the presentation of stimulus and the emission of a response. 2. In operant conditioning, a delay between the emission of a response and the administration of the reinforcement.

delayed response: an experimental situation wherein an animal reacts to a stimulus a considerable time after the stimulus has been removed. For example, the stimulus might be food placed under one or two cups while the animal watches but is restrained from approaching until a specified delay period has passed. The ability to delay is a function of phylogenetic level.

delayed reward: the presentation of the reward following an interval of time after the subject has made his response.

delinquent: 1. a juvenile offender, usually under age 18 according to most state laws. 2. one who commits an offense that is not a serious crime.

delinquency: 1. relatively minor offense against the legal code, especially by a minor. 2. the characteristic of being a repeated offender.

délire du toucher: a compulsion to touch objects.

delirium: a state of mental confusion accompanied by delusions, illusions, and hallucinations. Delirium may be induced by fevers, drugs, or shock.

delirium tremens: an acute alcoholic condition characterized by tremors, anxiety, hallucinations, and delusions.

delta movement: see APPARENT MOVEMENT.

delta rhythm: an electroencephalographic wave of 1–3 Hz of high voltage (150 microvolts) which is characteristic of deep sleep.

delusion: a false belief that cannot be modified by reasoning or a demonstration of the facts. Persistent and systematic delusions are characteristic of psychotic states. Delusion should be distinguished from *illusion*, which is a distorted perception, and from *hallucination*, which is a false perception.

delusional: characterizing the condition of one who suffers from delusions.

delusional speech: speech marked by the presence of delusions.

delusions of grandeur: the belief, usually psychotic, that one is a great or powerful person.

delusion of persecution: a delusion, characteristic of the paranoid individual, that he is the victim of efforts to injure him or to cause him to fail in some way. The belief often takes the form of an imagined conspiracy in which the patient's physician and family are thought to have joined in the effort to damage the patient.

delusion of reference: a false belief that the behavior of others has malign significance for the self.

demand: any aspect of the environment or any internal condition that arouses drives in the organism.

demand character: a Gestalt concept characterizing the need-arousing attributes of objects. A shiny red apple "demands" to be eaten; a striking painting "demands" to be looked at.

demand characteristics: those features of an experiment or of an experimenter's behavior that suggest to participants the desired outcome of an experiment.

demand feeding: see SELF-DEMAND SCHEDULE.

dementia: a deterioration of intellectual, judgmental, and emotional processes characteristic of certain forms of senility and psychoses. *Dementia* should be distinguished from AMENTIA, which denotes failure to develop intellectually.

dementia infantilis: a degenerative disease of the neurons of the cerebrum. There is loss of speech and some impairment of motor function. *Syn.* HELLER'S DISEASE.

dementia paralytica: general paresis. See also PARESIS.

demenetia praecox: see SCHIZOPHRENIA.

democratic atmosphere: (*Lewin*) a leadership situation in which the members of a group are allowed to participate in planning, are told in advance what the group's goals are, and are encouraged to discuss and criticize group activities. *Contr.* AUTHORITARIAN ATMOSPHERE.

demography: the study of population variables including geographic distribution, vital statistics, physical situations, and the like.

demonomania: the delusion on the part of an individual that he is under the influence of a demon or evil spirit.

demophobia: fear of crowds.

dendrite: the fiber(s) of a neuron conveying impulses toward the cell body; dendron. Sensory neurons have a single dendrite, motor neurons many.

dendrodendritic synpase: a synapse between two dendrites.

dendron: see DENDRITE.

denervation: the removal of the nerve sypply to an organ or part of the body.

denotation: the object or objective events designated by a word; the dictionary meaning of a word. *Contr.* CONNOTATION. See also SEMANTIC DIFFERENTIAL.

density: the attribute of solidity or compactness which, according to some psychologists, tones possess.

dental age: a measure of the child's dental development comparing the number of permanent teeth that have erupted to the average number for the child's age.

dentate nucleus: a semicircular mass of cell bodies, shaped like a set of teeth, in the cerebellum.

dentition: the development and eruption of the teeth in a child.

deoxyribonucleic acid (DNA): an extremely complex molecule composed of substructures of phosphates, bases, and sugars. The particular sequence of these subunits determines the genetic information carried by the chromosomes and regulates all metabolism.

dependence: 1. a relationship of

causality between two phenomena, such that a change in one is accompanied by a change in the other. 2. reliance on a social group for the formation of ideas and opinions; subordination to the opinions of others.

dependency: 1. a condition in which one individual must rely upon another, or upon society, for his maintenance. 2. the tendency to rely upon others in making decisions; lack of self-reliance.

dependency construct: (*Kelly*) perceptions about others that are interpreted as necessary to one's survival.

dependent: that which is influenced by another or is contingent upon the appearance of another event. The dependent variable, or subject's reaction, in a psychological experiment is dependent upon the independent variable.

dependent personality: a personality pattern characterized by lack of independence, passivity, low self-confidence, and a tendency to submit to others.

dependent variable: 1. the subject's reaction. 2. a variable in which changes are consequent upon changes or antecedent conditions in another (experimental or independent) variable.

depersonalization: 1. a pathological condition in which the individual experiences a feeling that he or his body is unreal. 2. a cultural state in which natural phenomena are no longer regarded as manifestations of a supernatural agency. 3. in existential and sociological writings, the feeling attributed to contemporary man of being a cog in a vast, impersonal machine.

depolarization: 1. the breakdown of the ionic equilibrium across the cell membrane in a neuron so that negative ions flow outward across the membrane. The propagated depolarization of the neuron is the electrical sign of the passage of a nervous impulse. 2. used figuratively to indicate a discharge of emotional tension or coloring.

depression: 1. in the normal individual, a state of despondency characterized by feelings of inadequacy, lowered activity, and pessimism about the future. 2. in pathological cases, an extreme state of unresponsiveness to stimuli, together with self-depreciation, delusions of inadaquacy, and hopelessness.

depressive reaction: a transient neurotic condition precipitated by a severe loss and characterized by anxiety, depression, and self-depreciation.

depressor nerve: 1. generally, an afferent nerve whose function is to retard motor or glandular activity. 2. specifically, a branch of the vagus that depresses blood pressure.

deprivation: 1. the loss or removal of something desired or loved. 2. the removal of food from animals for experimental purposes.

deprogramming: a procedure for reversing the effects of extreme indoctrination characteristic of brainwashing in cults. The victim is encouraged to think critically, flexibly, and independently after removal from the cult.

depth: in vision and audition, the perceived dimension of distance away from the observer.

depth analysis: the analysis of the contents of the unconscious. *Contr.* EGO ANALYSIS.

depth interview: an interview that attempts to get at underlying or dynamic factors that motivate the individual and are responsible for observed behavior patterns. Adjuncts to the depth interview are the projective techniques, dream analysis, and free association.

depth perception: 1. awareness of the distance between an observer and an object. 2. the awareness of three dimensionality or the solidity of perceived objects.

depth psychology: a system of psychology that assumes behavior is to be explained in terms of unconscious processes. The Freudian and Jungian systems of psychoanalysis exemplify depth psychology.

dereistic: characterizing thinking that is autistic or governed by personal factors.

derivative: (*Psychoan.*) characterizing behavior that is disguised or distorted by the ego to permit its expression without anxiety.

derived emotion: an emotional reaction associated with the outcome of any intense motive or instinct, such as joy or despair.

derived need: a need that has developed out of one of the primary needs. The behaviorists hold that the need for socialization (derived need) is derived from the infant's close contact with the mother during feeding (primary need).

derived primary attention: habitual, nonvoluntary, or passive attention.

derived property: in Gestalt psychology, the postulate that parts derive their characteristics from the whole.

derived scale: a scale whose values have been transformed into some kind of derived score, such as a standard score based on the standard deviation.

derived score: a score arrived at on the basis of statistical treatment or

manipulation from a raw score. The standard score is an example of a derived score.

derma; dermis: the skin under the epidermis.

dermal: cutaneous.

dermal sense; dermal sensitivity: the sensations associated with receptors in the skin.

dermatitis: inflammation of the skin. Some authorities hold that it is a psychosomatic ailment.

dermatographia: skin writing; the appearance of raised welts on the skin upon being lightly stroked. Dermatographia is believed to be due to hyperirritability of the dermal capillaries.

dermatome: a section of the skin innervated by a particular spinal nerve root.

dermographia: an incorrect, but sometimes used, spelling for dermatographia.

Descartes, René: French philosopher, mathematician, and scientist (1596–1650). Descartes is important in the history of psychology chiefly for his views on the interactionism of mind and body and for his mechanistic concept of the nervous system. He taught that mind and body are different substances but that they interact at the site of the pineal gland, a small gland deep within the brain. He believed that mind triggers animal spirits to course along the nerves and stimulate the muscles to action. Descartes's theory of interactionism was a precursor of Wundt's and Titchener's parallelistic account of consciousness, and his theory of the animal spirits was a forerunner of our contemporary understanding of the nervous impulse. Descartes is also important in the history of thought for being the father of modern existential philosophy. He separated phenomena into existence and essence, giving existence priority over essence in his famous doctrine of *Cogito ergo sum*.

description: 1. a report of observed phenomena without any attempt at identifying causal relationships or antecedent conditions. *Contr.* EXPLANATION. 2. in introspective psychology, a report on the contents of consciousness without attribution of meaning to them.

descriptive average: a rough estimate of the average on the basis of incomplete data.

descriptive principle: a generalization that does not attempt to explain in terms of cause and effect but does characterize the phenomenon under consideration and may make possible its prediction and control.

desensitization: 1. lessened reactivity. 2. a decreased emotional sensitivity with respect to a personal defect or social problem after counseling.

desexualization: removing sexual significance from an object or activity.

design: 1. a plan involving forethought. 2. a graphic or schematic representation. 3. the plan of an experiment in light of its purpose, including the choice of subjects, the procedure, and the treatment of the results.

designatory scale: see NOMINAL SCALE.

desire: 1. a conscious longing or want. 2. a conscious wish to be rid of an unpleasant or aversive stimulus or situation.

destination: in information theory, the place where messages arrive.

destruction method: see EXPIRATION.

destructiveness: a tendency, usually on the part of a child, to express underlying frustration by aggressive attacks on objects.

destrudo: (*Psychoan.*) the energy associated with the death instinct.

desurgency: (*R. B. Cattell*) a source trait in personality revealed by factor analysis and characterized by anxious, agitated brooding and a tendency toward seclusiveness. *Contr.* SURGENCY.

detached affect: (*Psychoan.*) an idea separated from its emotional component and maintained apart from other associations. The detachment serves to free the affect from its unbearable idea. Such detached affects were used by Freud to explain obsessions and compulsions. The unbearable or painful affect attaches itself to a new idea (the obsession).

detachment: 1. an attitude of freedom from involvement with another person or another's problems. 2. (*Horney*) a neurotic characteristic involving a lack of feeling for others, lack of social involvement, and a tendency to view one's problems objectively, as if emotional feelings were irrelevant.

deterioration: a progressive impairment or loss of function. The deteriorative psychoses are those in which the predominant system pattern is one of loss of judgment, emotional and intellectual deterioration, and progressive loss of memory.

deterioration index: an estimation of the approximate amount of loss with age of certain mental abilities as measured by the Wechsler-Bellevue tests. The tested functions that decline most rapidly are digit span, digit symbol, block design, and similarities. These are called "Don't hold" functions. The functions that show little decline are vocabulary, information, object assembly, and picture completion. These are the "Hold" functions. The deterioration quotient

$$= \frac{\text{Hold–Don't hold} \times 100}{\text{Hold}}$$

determinant: 1. a cause or anteced-ent condition. 2. a factor that is deci-sive or final in a cause-and-effect relation. Determinants may be *orga-nismic*, in which case they are caus-ative factors arising from within the organism or individual; they may be *environmental*, in which case they arise from the environment; or they may be *situational*, in which case they arise from an immediate event or circumstance that acts as an ante-cedent condition to behavior.

determiner: 1. a causal agent or an-tecedent condition. 2. in genetics, a factor whose presence in the germ plasm results in a hereditary charac-teristic in the offspring; a gene.

determining tendency: 1. a set. 2. goal direction; the arousal and main-tenance of a behavior sequence by a goal.

determinism: the doctrine that for every effect there is a cause. It is assumed that all behavior is a func-tion of causal factors either in the individual's environment or within himself. According to determinism, given a complete knowledge of the individual's past and of present envi-ronmental conditions, his behavior could be predicted precisely. Some degree of determinism is postulated by all schools of psychology. *Contr.* Free will. *Hard determinism* is a strict deterministic point of view allowing no room for freedom of choice or

indeterminism. Classical psychoanal-ysis exemplifies such a point of view. *Soft determinism* allows for a limited freedom of choice. The soft deter-minist believes that, within the limi-tations of one's constitution and past, it is possible to choose one's future programs of action. Contemporary ex-istential psychologists take a posi-tion of soft determinism.

detour behavior: any form of indi-rect action that leads to a goal.

detour problem: a problem-solving situation in which the goal must be reached by an indirect route.

detoxification: medical treatment for eliminating alcohol or other drugs from the body.

detraction: the lessening of atten-tion without loss of the focal point of what one is attending to.

detumescence: the subsidence of swelling or erection in the genitals following sexual excitement.

deuteranomaly: color vision that is weak in the region of green, demon-strated by the large amounts of green required in matching mixtures.

deuteranopia: a form of red-green blindness in which weakness for green is the predominant symptom. Shades of gray are seen in place of red and green, but the relative brightness value of the spectral colors remains un-changed.

development: 1. the progressive and continuous change in the organism from birth to death. 2. growth. 3. changes in the shape and integration of bodily parts into functional parts. 4. maturation, or the appearance of fundamental patterns of unlearned behavior.

developmental age: 1. any measure of development stated in age units.

2. a combined index of all developmental estimates or scores.

developmental level: a division of the span of life according to arbitarily fixed chronological ranges. The period of infancy lasts from birth to approximately one year; childhood from 1 to 12 years; adolescence from 12 to 21 years; maturity from 21 to 65 years; and old age from 65 years to death. Some authorities also distinguish subdivisions of these periods for special purposes, such as the neonatal period from birth to about one month, or the preadolescent from 10 to 12 years.

developmental norm: a norm based on the representative performance to be expected of children at a given age or developmental level.

developmental psychology: that branch of psychology that studies the processes of pre- and post-natal growth and the maturation of behavior. The developmental psychologist is interested in the various stages of development, the principles or laws of maturation, and the effects of early experience and later practice on development. In its broadest sense, developmental psychology includes the periods of infancy, childhood, and adulthood.

developmental quotient: the developmental age, or any measure of development divided by the chronological age.

developmental scale: an inventory of behavior for the purpose of assessing the level of development reached by a child. Many of the infant scales that attempt to measure intelligence utilize developmental inventories.

developmental sequence: the order of appearance of maturational patterns characteristic of the species. The cephalocaudal sequence of development, in which the head region develops faster than the tail, is characteristic of a number of species.

developmental stage: a period in the life of the individual in which specific traits or behavior patterns appear. The well-known Freudian designations, *anal, oral* and, *genital* stages, exemplify the concept of developmental stage.

developmental tasks: skills, levels of achievement, and social adjustment considered important at certain ages for the successful adjustment of the individual.

developmental unit: in a scale of measurement, an interval that is equal or approximately equal at different ages. IQ intervals derived from mental-age scales can be applied as developmental units. Thus, a gain of 10 IQ points at five years of age should equal a gain of 10 points at eleven years of age. In practice, most scales of intelligence do not meet the criterion of equality in intervals of measurement.

developmental zero: the hypothetical point at which development starts; the point of fertilization of the ovum.

deviate: 1. one who differs markedly from normal, or whose standards of conduct and attitudes are sharply in conflict with accepted standards. 2. a sexual pervert.

deviation: 1. in statistics, the degree to which a measure (or average of a number of such measures) departs from a reference point such as the mean or median. 2. a departure from normal. 3. (*Optics*) the bending of light rays from a straight line.

deviation IQ: a standard score on an intelligence test such as the Stanford-Binet. The interpretation of the deviation IQ is similar to that of the conventional IQ.

deviation score: the difference between any raw score and the mean of the raw scores.

Dewey, John: American philosopher, educator, and psychologist (1859–1952). John Dewey attended the University of Vermont and Johns Hopkins University, where he received a Ph.D. in philosophy in 1884. Dewey was one of the founders of the functionalistic movement in psychology, which subsequently became one of the leading schools of the 1920s and 1930s. His functionalistic point of view grew out of his instrumentalistic philosophy, which held that ideas are plans for action that arise in response to a problem and accomplish their purpose by solving the problem. He attacked molecularism and reductionism in psychology and physiology and pleaded for a psychology of acts or functions. His continued interest in psychology led him to write one of the first textbooks in the field. His influence stimulated James Rowland Angell and Harvey Carr to develop functionalism as a formal school.

dexterity test: a test that requires both speed and accuracy in manual operations. Dexterity tests typically utilize peg boards and simple assembling operations.

dextrad: toward the right side of the body.

dextral: pertaining to the right side of the body. *Contr.* SINISTRAL.

dextrality: 1. preference in handedness for the right hand or more generally, for the right side of the body. 2. sidedness in motor activity. *Contr.* ambidextrality.

dextrosinistral: characterizing an individual originally left-handed who has been retrained to use the right hand.

diad: see DYAD.

diagnosis: 1. the determination of the nature of an abnormality or disease. 2. the classification of an individual on the basis of a disease or abnormality.

Diagnostic and Statistical Manual of Mental Disorders 3rd ed. (DSM III): A classification of mental disorders with incidence, symptomatology, sex differences, etc., published by the American Psychiatric Association.

diagnostic interview: an interview whose purpose is to determine the probable cause of a behavioral disorder, its treatment, and its prognosis.

diagnostic test: any test utilized in an effort to determine the nature and source of an individual's difficulties. For example, a reading test may be diagnostic of such possible sources of difficulty as poor comprehension, slowness of reading, or vocabulary deficiency.

diagnostic value: the utility or validity of a test used for diagnostic purposes.

diagnostic word test: an intensity-threshold test for spoken words to determine the loudness level at which speech can be understood.

diagrammatic: pertaining to drawings in which only the essential parts are shown, often in a distorted or simplified fashion for the sake of clarity.

dialectic: reasoning, particularly an extensive train of deductive reasoning.

Diana complex: (*Psychoan.*) the repressed wish of the woman to become a man.

diarchisis: generalized temporary impairment following brain injury.

diary method: the daily recording

of observations about the development of a child.

diachisis: a temporary increase in the threshold for excitability in a nerve center.

diastole: the period of ventricular dilation in the cardiac cycle during which the ventricle fills with blood. *Contr.* SYSTOLE.

diathesis: an inherited predisposition toward a certain disease.

diathesis-stress: the hypothesis that persons who are genetically predisposed will, under stress, manifest abnormal behavior.

diazepam: a tranquilizer.

dichotic: pertaining to differential stimulation of the two ears. *Contr.* DIOTIC.

dichotomy: a division in two classes according to some predetermined criterion.

dichromatism; dichromatic vision; dichromatopsia: partial color blindness in which the hues seen are reduced to combinations of two, typically blue and yellow, more rarely red and green.

didactic analysis: analysis undergone by those in training for professional careers in psychoanalysis, in fulfillment of Freud's dictum that all analysts should be analyzed.

diencephalon: the interbrain; the region of the brain located between the prosencephalon and mesencephalon. It is composed primarily of the thalamus and hypothalamus.

difference threshold: see DIFFERENTIAL THRESHOLD.

difference tone: a tone heard when two tones are sounded simultaneously. The frequency of the difference tone is the difference in frequency between the two original tones.

differential: 1. (*adjective*) pertaining to factors or features that make one thing different from another. 2. (*noun*) an increment or change in one variable that occurs concomitantly with a change in a related variable.

Differential Aptitude Test: a battery of eight tests primarily for use in educational and vocational guidance in grades 8 through 12. There are tests of verbal reasoning, number ability, abstract reasoning, space relations, mechanical reasoning, clerical speed and accuracy, and language usage.

differential conditioning: the establishment of a conditioned response to one of two or more stimuli by selectively reinforcing the desired conditioning stimulus and not reinforcing the rest.

differential diagnosis: the process of distinguishing between two similar diseases or abnormalities by discovering a critical symptom present in one but not in the other.

differential extinction: the selective extinction of one response while another is being maintained. *Contr.* DIFFERENTIAL CONDITIONING.

differential growth: growth or development of an organ at a rate different from that of other organs in the same organism. Such differentials are particularly marked in the early stages of development and are typified by the rapid selection growth of genital tissue at puberty.

differential inhibition: (*Pavlov*) the gradual development of inhibitory tendencies to stimuli resembling the original conditioning stimulus. *Contr.* STIMULUS GENERALIZATION.

differential prediction: a prediction made on the basis of empirical evidence about the probable outcome of one variable as opposed to another.

differential psychology: the branch of psychology that investigates individual differences, their consequences, causation and magnitude among groups.

differential reinforcement: the application of reinforcement to one of two alternative responses. For example, if an animal is responding to both a tone of 256 Hz and one of 280 Hz, rewarding only the 256 Hz tone would be differential reinforcement leading to a discriminated response.

differential response: any response that is elicited by a particular stimulus among many possible different stimuli. For example, an animal may be trained to salivate to a tuning fork of 256 Hz by selective reinforcement and not to forks of closely related frequencies.

differential scoring: the scoring of a test battery in several ways in order to obtain measures of several different variables. The Strong Interest Blank, for example, is scored along more than thirty dimensions in order to obtain the individual's relative interests in that number of different occupations.

differential threshold: the minimally effective stimulus difference that is reported correctly as a difference 75 percent of the time. *Abbr.* DL. The statistical convention requiring a 75 percent judgment has been generally adopted since the individual would guess a difference correctly 50 percent of the time.

differentiation: 1. the process by means of which a mass of homogeneous cells develops into specialized tissues. 2. the change in a psychological field from homogeneity to heterogeneity. 3. in conditioning, the process by means of which an animal is

trained to discriminate between two stimuli or two different responses. 4. sensory discrimination. 5. in mathematics, the process of obtaining a differential.

differentiation of life space: (*Lewin*) the organization of the life space into different regions, such as the past, the present, and the future, and on the levels of reality and unreality.

difficulty scale: a test whose items are arranged and graded in the order of difficulty. *Syn.* POWER TEST.

difficulty value: a measure of the discriminating power of a test item in terms of the percentage of individuals who passed the item.

diffraction: the bending of a light or sound wave by a lens or obstacle.

diffraction grating: a polished surface ruled by fine lines, used for producing a spectrum.

diffuse: lacking in specificity or coordination, such as the diffuse reponses in infants that show a lack of goal direction and coordination.

diffusion: 1. the spread of cultural traits from one group to another. 2. the spread of a stimulus through cutaneous tissues. 3. the scattering of light in the eye because of spherical aberration.

diffusion circle: a circular area of sensitivity on the skin generated by the spread of a cutaneous stimulus.

diffusion of responsibility: see BYSTANDER EFFECT.

diffusion response: (*Rorschach*) a scoring code for responses stimulated by the shading of the inkblots.

digital: 1. pertaining to the fingers or toes. 2. pertaining to the digits, that is, the numbers from 0 to 9.

digit-span test: a test of immediate recall in which the subject repeats a random series of digits following a single presentation. The score is the maximum number that can be recalled correctly.

diglottic: the simultaneous stimulation of two areas of the tongue with the same substance.

dilantin: anticonvulsant drug used in the treatment of epilepsy.

dilation: (*Kelly*) broadening of a construct system (*q.v.*) to make it more comprehensive.

diminishing returns, law of: the principle that holds that improvement becomes progressively less with each increment of application. For example, in many learning situations, each practice session brings increasingly smaller increments of gain.

dimming effect: the intensification of an afterimage by reducing the intensity of the field upon which it is projected.

dingdong theory of language: the hypothesis that language originates in the mimicry of natural sounds.

Dionysian: 1. orgiastic. 2. pertaining to the emotional as opposed to the intellectual side of life. The term comes from the cult of Dionysus, the Greek god of wine, whose followers held orgiastic rites.

diopter: a unit of measurement applied to the power of a lens to bring light rays to a focal point. The measure for any lens is the quotient obtained by dividing unity by the focal distance of the lens.

diotic: pertaining to the stimulation of the two ears.

diplacusis: an auditory disorder in which a tone is heard as two tones differing slightly in pitch in the two ears.

diplegia: paralysis on both sides of the body. *Contr*. HEMIPLEGIA.

diploid: characterizing the two sets of chromosomes present in all cells except the gametes. *Contr*. HAPLOID.

diplopia: double-image vision, usually because of imperfections in the coordination of the extrinsic muscles of the eye.

dipsomania: uncontrollable craving for alcohol, usually manifested in periodic attacks.

direct aggression: an attack upon the source of frustration. *Contr*. DISPLACED AGGRESSION.

direct apprehension: a form of recognition in which objects are identified but without full recognition.

direct association: memory bonds between items without intermediary connections. For example, the linkage between $2 \times 2 = 4$ is direct. Remembering one's anniversary by a roundabout mnemonic device of associating it with one's street number is indirect association.

directed movement: movement related to a specific stimulus. *Contr*. RANDOM ACTIVITY.

directions test: a series of ordered tasks given to examinees as items on an intelligence test on the assumption that the ability to carry out verbal instructions is one indication of intelligence.

directive counseling: counseling in which positive advice and interpretation are given and where the counselor suggests the area of personality to be explored.

directive therapy: see ACTIVE THERAPY.

direct measurement: measurement made by immediate comparisons or by use of a scale that does not have to be transformed into another scale. *Contr*. INDIRECT MEASUREMENT.

direct reflex: any reflex where the receptor and effector involved are

homolateral, or on the same side of the body. *Contr.* CROSSED REFLEX.

dirhinic stimulation: the simultaneous stimulation of both nostrils.

disability: a severe, handicapping, loss, or impairment of a bodily organ, with corresponding functional loss.

disarranged-sentence test: a test item involving the rearrangement of a jumbled sentence so as to make sense. For example, the subject might be presented with the following scrambled words to put in order: *late of car we failure because were*.

discharge: 1. the firing of a neuron upon stimulation. 2. the expression of pent-up emotion or tension. 3. reduction of the tension associated with drives upon making a consummatory response. 4. the emission of a response.

discharge of effect: (*Psychoan.*) the reduction of emotion through giving it expression.

discharge of anxiety: (*Psychoan.*) the relief of tensions associated with anxiety through daily action without correcting the underlying cause.

discipline: 1. a branch of knowledge. 2. control of subordinates. 3. punishment. 4. self-control, for the purpose of holding undesirable impulses or habits in check.

discomfort-relief quotient: the ratio of verbal expressions of self-satisfaction, or of satisfaction with one's environment, to expressions of dissatisfaction. The discomfort-relief quotient is utilized in the analysis of documents, news accounts, etc.

discontinuity theory of learning: the assumption that in learning that involves discrimination, the required discrimination cannot be learned until the organism relates it to the problem as a whole. *Contr.* CONTINUITY THEORY OF LEARNING.

discontinuous: 1. lacking continuity; characterized by gaps or breaks. 2. pertaining to measures that do not form a continuum of infinitely small steps but represent instead whole numbers.

discontinuous variable: a variable that changes in discrete steps. *Contr.* CONTINUOUS VARIABLE.

discord: a combination of musical tones that sounds harsh or inharmonious. *Contr.* HARMONY.

discordance: failure of a trait to appear in both members of a twin pair. *Contr.* CONCORDANCE.

discrete measure: a measure taken from separate or discontinuous values. The number of people at a rally is a discrete series made up of individuals, whereas the Fahrenheit temperature scale is continuous.

discrete variable: see DISCONTINUOUS VARIABLE.

discrimen: a sensory difference, whether perceived or not.

discriminability: the characteristic of being capable of being distinguished or discriminated.

discriminada: (*Tolman*) things to be discriminated; the property or characteristic of being discriminable.

discriminal dispersion: the scatter or spread of discriminated responses around a given mean.

discriminal process: the activity of making a discrimination.

discriminate: 1. to be aware of differences. 2. to respond in such a way as to indicate an appreciation of differences.

discriminated operant: (*Skinner*) a conditioned operant to a generalized stimulus, or stimulus associated with the original reinforced stimulus. A discriminated operant in the analog of a generalized response in classical conditioning.

discriminating power: 1. the ability of a test item to distinguish between two criterion groups. For example, if the test is a neurotic inventory, each item in the test should be responded to differentially by known neurotic and normal groups. 2. the power of a test as a whole to distinguish between two groups along the dimension being measured.

discriminating range: the spread of scores at which a test separates or measures subjects on the dimension measured. Very low scores lie outside the discriminating range because of the possibility that they may be caused by chance factors.

discrimination: 1. the process of distinguishing between two objects. 2. the process of distinguishing differences between stimuli. 3. prejudice, particularly prejudice based on racial, religious, or ethnic considerations.

discrimination, index of: a graphic or numerical expression of the extent to which a test or test item separates subjects according to the degree to which they possess the trait being tested.

discrimination-reaction time: a form of the reaction-time experiment in which the subject must make a distinction between stimuli before responding. For example, the instructions might require him to respond with the left hand to a green light and the right hand to a red light.

discriminative learning: learning in which the task is to make choices or judgments between alternatives. For example, discriminative learning is involved when an animal must learn

to go right when hungry and left when thirsty.

discriminative stimulus: a stimulus in operant conditioning that releases a response.

discussion leader: in small groups, one whose function is to promote discussion. Discussion leaders often have special training for their work.

disease: 1. an abnormal condition within the body, involving a serious impairment of function. 2. by extension, a serious abnormality or deviation in behavior. Many psychologists oppose the use of the term to characterize behavioral disorders, because of the organic implications of the term.

disgust: the emotional feeling accompanying attitudes for repulsion, rejection, and withdrawal. Disgust may be accompanied by nausea in extreme cases.

disinhibition: 1. the temporary removal of inhibition as a result of introducing an outside or irrelevant stimulus. In conditioning experiments, the phenomenon is shown when an animal no longer salivating to the sound of a bell (original conditioned stimulus) because of lack of reinforcement will salivate to the sound of a buzzer introduced unexpectedly. 2. a loss of self-control upon overindulgence in alcohol or while under the influence of drugs.

disintegration: the disruption of an organized system; the fragmentation of a unified whole.

disjunctive concept: a concept that contains at least one element from a larger class of elements. For example, a strike in baseball has the common element of being a pitch that (1) is in a certain zone, (2) is struck at and missed, (3) results in a foul ball provided there are not two strikes against the batter, or (4) is an unsuccessful bunt after two strikes.

disorder: 1. disease. 2. lack of organization or meaningful relations among phenomena. 3. aberrant social behavior.

disorganization: lack of meaningful or orderly relations among objects, people, or events.

disorganized behavior: characteristic of extreme emotional conditions where the individual's behavior lacks harmony and may show unintelligible relationships with environmental conditions, such as occurs in hysterical laughter induced by a tragic loss or disaster.

disorientation: lack of loss or ability to locate oneself spatially or temporally.

disparate retinal points: points on the retinas whose stimulation leads to different spatial impressions. *Contr.* CONGRUENT POINTS.

disparation: the doubling of images nearer or farther than the point of fixation. If the finger is held before the face and fixated, objects in the background are double. If a background object is fixated, the finger is seen as double.

dispersion: the scatter of a group of scores plotted in a frequency distribution or on a scatter diagram. Dispersion is measured by the range, average deviation, standard deviation, variance, or the interquartile range.

dispersion circle: a circle of light or color produced by a lens when the rays emanate from a point source of light.

dispersion coefficient: see VARIATION COEFFICIENT.

displaced aggression: an attack against a person or object other than the source of frustration. Displaced aggression occurs when the actual source of frustration is unavailable or is likely to retaliate. *Contr.* DIRECT AGGRESSION.

displacement: 1. the distortion of an eidetic image in which there is inversion and reversal of the image. 2. (*Psychoan.*) the transference of an affect or emotional attachment from its proper object to a substitute. 3. the substitution of one response for another when the first is blocked, such as occurs in displaced aggression. 4. (*Rorschach*) attention to insignificant detail as a means of avoiding response that might be revealing.

displacement activity: in ethology; seemingly irrelevant behavior manifested by an animal in a situation in which two other conflicting fixed action patterns are evoked.

displacement of affect: (*Psychoan.*) the attachment of emotion to an object other than the one to which it belongs. In dreams an unimportant object may assume disproportionate emotional significance because the dream censor does not permit direct emotional expression in relation to the real object.

disposition: 1. the organized totality of the individual's psychophysical tendencies to react in a certain way. See also TEMPERAMENT. 2. an arrangement or organization of elements or parts so that a functional connection exists between them, such as occurs in neural dispositions. 3. an enduring emotional attitude, such as is implied in the phrase "a happy disposition."

Attitudes, sets, dispositions, traits, instincts, drives, predispositions, prepotent responses, tendencies, habits, and temperament are among the many concepts employed by psychologists in trying to account for the relatively enduring and consistent quality of behavior. These constructs are valid and useful only in the sense that they have arisen from valid operations and procedures of measurements, or that they are treated as hypothetical intervening variables to be tested.

disposition rigidity: the tendency to maintain a response or pattern of behavior beyond the point of its adaptive utility.

disregulation: the assumption that disorders of the psychophysiological type are the result of failure of the body's regulatory system.

dissected-sentence test: see DISARRANGED-SENTENCE TEST.

dissimulation: 1. catabolism, or the breaking down of tissues during metabolism. 2. (*Jung*) the adjustment of the individual to an object other than the self.

dissociation: separation from the personality as a whole of a complex pattern of psychological processes which may then function independently of the rest of the personality. The multiple personality illustrates dissociation in its extreme form. However, it also is present in some degree in hysteria, amnesia, and schizophrenia.

dissonance: the harsh, unpleasant effect produced by two notes sounded simultaneously that do not blend or fuse. See also COGNITIVE DISSONANCE.

distal: away from the reference point or away from the center of the body.

distal effects: responses that alter the environment in some manner. *Contr.* proximal effects.

distal response: any response that alters the environment beyond the manipulative boundaries of the organism. For example, throwing a brick through a window. *Contr.* PROXIMAL RESPONSE.

distal stimulus: a stimulus as it emanates from environmental objects. *Contr.* PROXIMAL STIMULUS.

distal variable: a variable whose origin is a stimulus in the environment that does not act directly on a receptor but is mediated through a proximal stimulus. Thus the energy of sound at its source is a distal variable; sound as it impinges on the ear is a proximal variable.

distance: 1. the distance between a source of stimulation and the organism. 2. on graphic rating scales, the linear distance between two data points. 3. the degree to which the individual feels apart from others or experiences difficulty in forming close, meaningful relationships. 4. (*Adler*) any of several techniques for coping with situations in which one may reveal his shortcomings. These techniques include functional illness, indecision, erecting false barriers, and ceasing to try.

distance receptor: the visual, auditory, and olfactory receptors that, among the body's receptors, are those capable of responding to stimuli at a distance. *Syn.* TELERECEPTOR.

distance vision: the visual discrimination of objects more than twenty feet distant from the observer.

distorted room: a room constructed in such a way that the subject perceives it as rectilinear when, in fact, it is not. Objects or persons in the room will be distorted. See also TRANSACTIONAL THEORY OF PERCEPTION.

distortion: 1. the bending of an image, such as the retinal image, by a lens. 2. (*Psychoan.*) the disguising or modification of unacceptable impulses so that they can escape the dream censor.

distractibility: tendency to be drawn away from that to which one is attending; capacity or ability to draw someone's attention away from an object on which it has been fixed.

distraction: 1. an extraneous stimulus that draws attention. 2. the condition of having one's attention drawn away by an extraneous stimulus.

distractor technique: in short-term memory, the interpolation of material in order to prevent rehearsal between presentation and recall. *Contr.* PROBING TECHNIQUE.

distress-relief quotient: the number of verbal expressions of distress or discomfort divided by the number of statements expressive of relief. The distress-relief quotient is utilized in therapy and counseling situations as an index of improvement.

distributed practice: the spacing of periods of practice over a period of time rather than massing the practice in one long learning session. Distributed practice is usually found to be more efficient than massed practice, in relation to learning time for most tasks. *Syn.* distributed learning.

distribution: a table or graph of the frequency of scores plotted against their appropriate numerical values. The scores are typically plotted on the horizontal axis, the frequencies on the vertical axis.

distribution curve: a frequency curve where the values are plotted on the base line and the frequency of their occurrence is plotted on the vertical axis.

disulfiram: see ANTABUSE.

disuse, law of: in learning, the assumption that responses or associations that are not practiced will weaken and disappear.

diurnal: occurring during daylight hours.

divagation: a tendency to disgress and ramble while speaking confused thought.

divergence: 1. the turning outward of the two eyes when shifting fixation from a very close object to a more distant object. *Contr.* CONVERGENCE. 2. a permanent turning outward of one eye with respect to the other. *Syn.* EXOTROPIA; WALLEYE.

divergent thinking: on tests of intelligence or creativity, giving novel and diverse responses rather than a single correct response as determined by test standardization. *Contr.* CONVERGENT THINKING.

divination: foretelling the future by magical or supernatural means.

divining rod: see DOWSING.

dizygotic twins: fraternal twins, or twins that arise from two separate eggs. *Contr.* MONOZYGOTIC TWINS.

dizziness: the sensation of falling or whirling often accompanied by nausea. *Syn.* VERTIGO.

DNA: see DEOXYRIBONUCLEIC ACID.

docile: 1. teachable; easily controlled. 2. (*Tolman*) characterizing molar behavior; readily teachable to organisms.

doctrine: a teaching; a set of beliefs, usually without adequate supporting evidence but with the implication that given further research adequate supportive evidence will be forthcoming. Cf. DOGMA.

dogma: a statement or belief that must be accepted on faith from authority. The term *dogma* is rarely used in science except in a derogatory manner. *Doctrine* is used to characterize a theory or principle advocated by a school of psychology or a prominent theorist. Thus, *Freudian doctrine* refers to authoritative statements made by Freud or his followers on the assumption that present or future work will support the doctrine. *Dogma*, on the other hand, implies acceptance on the basis of pure authority without supporting evidence.

dogmatic: stated on authority as a matter of faith.

dogmatism scale: a questionnaire designed to measure rigidity and inflexibility in thinking.

dolicocephalic: long-headed: having a cephalic index below 77. *Contr.* BRACHYCEPHALIC.

dolichomorphic: tallness and thinness in body build.

dolorimeter: a device for measuring the threshold for pain.

domal sampling: literally, home sampling; a form of area sampling in which certain predetermined homes in a given area are selected for sampling and in which a designated member of the household is questioned, such as the head of the house.

dominance: 1. the trait of desiring to be on top. *Contr.* SUBMISSION. 2. prepotency; the relative strength that causes one response to win out in a conflict of responses. For example, flexion of the limb in withdrawal to a painful stimulus is dominant over an extension reflex. 3. in genetics, the capacity of one trait to suppress a recessive trait. 4. the preferential use of one hand or one side of the body over the other. 5. the tendency for one side of the brain to be more important than the other in the control of the body.

dominance hierarchy: a series of behaviors or responses that occur in the form of a rank order of importance or dominance.

dominance need: (*Murray*) the need to control others or to lead or dictate to others.

dominance-submission: a bipolar continuum that measures the degree to which some individuals seek to be on top, to control others, while some, by contrast, avoid positions of control and authority. Presumably, most people are midway between these two extremes. *Syn.* ASCENDANCE-SUBMISSION.

dominant: 1. in music, the fifth tone (*sol*) of the diatonic scale. 2. in genetics, the appearance of DOMINANCE (3) in a trait.

dominant wavelength: the spectral wavelength that, when mixed with white, will match a sample hue.

dominator-modulator theory: in vision, the theory that a special dominant receptor exists for brightness vision and that chromatic vision is mediated by receptors that modulate the response of the dominant receptor.

Donders' law: a principle of visual fixation stating that regardless of how an ocular position is reached, every position of the line of fixation corresponds to a definite, invariable angle of torsion of the eyes.

dopamine: one of the catecholomines important in neural transmission. Also used in the treatment of depression and in Parkinson's disease.

doppler effect: the shit in hue or pitch when a source of light or sound is moving rapidly in reference to an observer. The effect may be noticed in listening to the whistle of an approaching or receding locomotive.

dorsad: toward the back.

dorsal: pertaining to the back.

dorsoventral: the axis extending from

the back to the ventral side of the body.

dotting test: a paper-and-pencil test of mechanical ability in which the subject is required either to make as many dots as possible (tapping test), or to put dots in small circles as quickly as possible (aiming test).

double-alternation problem: a situation in which the subject is required to respond twice in one way, then twice in another way, in the absence of sensory cues to signal the changes. The temporal maze can be used to study double-alternation responses.

double bind: the hypothesis that schizophrenia may develop from a situation in which a basically hostile parent reacts one way (positively) toward a child on one level of communication and another way (negatively) on another level of communication. Thus, the child is "damned if he does and damned if he does not."

double-blind technique: in drug experiments, a technique in which neither the subject nor the experimenter knows whether or not a drug has been administered or what the drug is. The purpose of the technique is to control possible psychological assumptions about the effects of the drug.

double-entry table: a statistical table in which the values are entered both by rows and columns. The scatter diagram is a form of double-entry table.

double images: 1. the duplication of images on the retina as a result of optical defects. 2. the doubling of images in the distance when fixating on near objects or of near images when fixating on far objects.

double representation: the failure of an object color and illumination

color to fuse or blend when they are different.

double sampling: the use of two or more techniques for selecting a sample at different stages in an investigation. *Syn.* mixed sampling.

double vibration: see VIBRATION.

double vision: see DIPLOPIA.

doubtful judgment: in psychophysical experiments, a judgment of difference between stimuli of which the subject is uncertain.

Down's syndrome: a congenital physical defect associated with mental retardation. The tongue is thick and fissured, the face flat, the eyes slanted. *Syn.* mongolian idiocy.

dowsing: locating underground sources of water or minerals by prospecting with a divining rod or forked twig held by the two branches in the two hands. When the rod or twig dips toward the earth, the dowser takes this as a sign of success. Psychologists generally account for the phenomenon as unconscious muscle movements.

drainage hypothesis: the theory that neural facilitation and inhibition can be explained as the drawing-off of neural impulses to areas of greater or lesser activity, just as water will flow in to or out of areas of lessened or increased pressure.

drama therapy: see PSYCHODRAMA.

dramatization: (*Psychoan.*) the transformation of repressed wishes or impulses into symbolic forms, as in dreams.

Draw-a-Man Test: see GOOD-ENOUGH DRAW-A-MAN TEST.

Draw-a-Person Test: see MACHOVER DRAW-A-PERSON TEST.

d reaction test: in reaction-time experiments, a test in which the subject is required to withhold his response until he has identified which of two stimuli has been presented.

dream: a more or less coherent train of imagery and ideas occurring during sleep, or in drugged or hypnotic conditions.

dream analysis: see DREAM INTERPRETATION.

dream content: (*Psychoan.*) the images and ideas expressed in the dream. These are held to be of two fundamental types: (a) the manifest content, or content as it occurs to the dreamer; (b) the latent, or hidden, content, which must be interpreted by the technique of dream interpretation.

dream determinant: (*Psychoan.*) any factor in the environment that plays a part in the causation of a particular dream and lends it its particular flavor.

dream ego: (*Jung*) the portion of the ego responsible for dreaming.

dream instigators: see DAY RESIDUES.

dream interpretation: the process of deciphering the meaning of a dream. The procedure employed by psychoanalysts is to have the patient free-associate around the dream content until its wish-fulfillment nature has become apparent. Considerable use is also made of dream-symbol interpretation. Some symbols are held to be universal and immediately interpretable, such as pointed objects, which are phallic symbols, and running water, which symbolizes birth. Many other symbols are peculiar to the individual dreamer and must be interpreted by the process of free association.

dream wish: (*Psychoan.*) the symbolic representation of a repressed or unconscious wish in a dream.

dream work: (*Psychoan.*) the process of adapting the unconscious or repressed wishes into acceptable form so that they may be expressed in consciousness. The most important ways in which the transformation is accomplished are (a) by condensation, which abbreviates the manifest dream and makes it less rich in content; (b) by displacement, which makes the latent elements more distant or turns them into symbols; and (c) by secondary elaboration, which adds details to the dream, making it more coherent and changing its form.

drill: practice by systematic repetition to the point of mastery. Drill implies a lack of insight and a consequent necessity for rote repetition.

drive: an aroused, goal-directed tendency of an organism based on a change in organic processes. Drives may be generated by deprivation or by noxious conditions that give rise to pain. The behavior associated with drives is directed toward eliminating deprivation or moving away from noxious stimuli.

drive arousal: the activation of a drive by an internal or external condition, or, more typically, by a combination of both.

drive displacement: the arousal of behavior appropriate to one drive upon the frustration of another. Thus, the sex-starved person may eat sweets to excess.

drive reduction: diminution of drive behavior and associated intraorganic conditions. Typically, drive reduction is accomplished by satiation or consummatory behavior at the goal.

drive-reduction theory: the assumption that (a) all motivated behavior arises out of drives, and (b) responses that satisfy drives are strengthened or reinforced. Drive-reduction theory in various forms has played a major role in theories of learning, notably Thorndike's and Hull's. Drive reduction is also assumed to be the factor serving as a reinforcer in classical conditioning procedures. Contiguity theorists, on the other hand, de-emphasize drive reduction and stress contiguity as the most important factor in learning. In most situations both factors are operating to some degree, and it may be very difficult to separate them experimentally.

drive specificity: the assumed relationship between DRIVE STIMULI (*q.v.*) and the responses that satisfy the drive.

drive state: the hypothetical intraorganic condition that gives rise to drive behavior. Such states are assumed to reach a certain critical level before initiating goal-seeking behavior. They may consist of cellular conditions, neural states, or localized peripheral factors, such as dryness of the mouth or stomach contractions.

drive stimuli: (*Hull*) the afferent nervous impulses that are assumed to arise in organs in a drive state. *Symbol S_d.* It is the reduction of these stimuli that, in Hull's modified behavior system, are associated with reinforcement.

dromomania: an abnormal impulse to travel.

drug abuse: the use of a drug to the degree that it produces impairment in social adjustment or physical and psychological health.

drug addiction: the habitual use of drugs, with psychological and physiological dependence.

drug effect: any change in behavior or in a psychological state that is systematically related to drug dosage.

drugs and behavior: the alteration of states of consciousness and behavior by drugs has been observed for centuries. Some of the commonly abused drugs in our society, such as alcohol, caffeine, nicotine, mescaline, and hashish, were utilized by man both for medicinal and nonmedicinal purposes generations before pharmacology became a scientific adjunct to modern medicine. With the development of the various synthetic drugs, such as the barbiturates, amphetamines, and tranquilizers, the use and abuse of drugs has become a serious medical, social, and psychological problem. In many cases the actions of drugs on the central nervous system or their long-range effects on the individual are only poorly understood. However, several general effects of excessive drug usage have been reliably reported and these will be described before considering specific classes of drugs and what is known about their short- and long-term effects.

Some degree of *tolerance* occurs with repeated usage of most drugs. Tolerance refers to the fact that the individual's response to a drug tends to decrease with repeated doses. Consequently, in order to obtain the same effect the user tends to gradually increase the dosage.

Many drugs, particularly the sedatives and narcotics, create *physical dependence*, a condition characterized by withdrawal symptoms if usage of the drug is terminated. The pattern of tremor, convulsions, and hallucinations characteristic of delirium tremens as observed in withdrawal from alcohol is a familiar example.

Associated with most drugs is some degree of *psychological dependence,* or a strong drive to use a drug for the effect that it induces. It is difficult in some cases to determine to what degree preexisting personality factors make the individual vulnerable to psychological dependence and to what degree such dependence is induced by the chronic use of the drug itself. Moreover, social factors, such as peer pressure and environmental conditions, may contribute significantly to preoccupation with drugs leading to physical and psychological dependence.

Some drugs show *cross-tolerance* and/or *cross-dependence*. Cross-tolerance refers to the fact that tolerance for one drug leads to a diminished response to another drug of the same class. Cross-dependence means that withdrawal symptoms may be prevented by administering another drug in place of the withdrawn drug. For example, methadone prevents the withdrawal symptoms associated with the cessation of heroin administration.

Technically, *drug addiction* refers to physical dependence on a drug with tolerance, and, if usage stops, withdrawal symptoms. However, the term is also popularly, if incorrectly, employed to mean preoccupation with drugs and psychological dependence.

Drugs are commonly classified as sedatives, opiate narcotics, stimulants, tranquilizers, and hallucinogens or psychedelics. The specific effects of each of these classes of drugs will be considered next.

The more common sedatives include alcohol, the barbiturates (phenobarbital, nembutal, seconal), chloral hydrate, and the bromides. Medicinally, the sedatives are used to induce relaxation or sleep, relieve anxiety, and alleviate muscular spasm or tension. Many individuals utilize sedatives, especially alcohol, to induce a state of relaxed disinhibition in social or recreational settings. In general, users of sedatives develop increased physical and psychological dependence with chronic usage. There is also cross-tolerance and cross-dependence for the sedatives. The sedatives, among other drugs, may show *potentiation effects*, with one drug accentuating the effects of another. Thus, many individuals have accidentally lost their lives by ingesting alcohol before taking barbiturates.

Opiate narcotics include such drugs as opium, morphine, codeine, and the synthetics, Demerol and methadone. These drugs induce states of euphoria (feelings of well-being), nausea, drowsiness, apathy, and lethargy. Medically some of the narcotics are useful in the relief of pain (morphine, codeine, and Demerol). Chronic users of drugs of this class are subject to increasing tolerance and severe physical and psychological dependence. The psychological dependence on this class of drugs is strong and difficult to treat. Physical dependence on heroin, the most addictive of the opiates and the drug responsible for serious social problems, may be treated with methadone, a legal drug, which, although itself addictive, prevents withdrawal symptoms associated with heroin dependence.

The more commonly used stimulants are caffeine, nicotine, the amphetamines (Benzedrine, Dexedrine, and Methadrine), and cocaine. Caffeine is legally and widely used in coffee and tea, and nicotine in various tobacco products. Some authorities believe that some degree of physical dependence on caffeine and nicotine is present in chronic and heavy users of these drugs. Many individuals are strongly dependent psychologically on these drugs and find them difficult to give up.

The amphetamines have been employed medically in the treatment of narcolepsy, depression, and obesity. They have also been used with hyperkinetic (extremely overactive) children. Although stimulants, the amphetamines may have a paradoxical calming effect on such children. In treating obesity the drugs are administered because of their appetite-suppressant effect.

The amphetamines cause increased alertness, loss of appetite, insomnia, and sometimes euphoria. Chronic usage may cause irritability, loss of weight, agitation, paranoid reactions, and depression upon withdrawal.

Cocaine, whose medical use is that of an anesthetic in dentistry and ophthalmology, is stimulating in the same general way as the amphetamines when it is sniffed or taken orally. Neither the amphetamines nor cocaine produce physical dependence with chronic usage, but many result in psychological dependence.

The tranquilizers include chlorpromazine, reserpine, and lithium salts, all of which are anti-psychotic agents. Also included are the anti-anxiety agents, Valium, and Miltown or Equanil (both trade names for meprobamate).

The antipsychotic drugs relieve tension, suppress hallucinations and delusions, and markedly improve the functioning of psychotics. These drugs are employed in mental institutions and on an outpatient basis for the treatment of psychotics and for-

mer psychotics for whom they are prescribed to prevent symptom recurrence.

The milder tranquilizers or anti-anxiety agents are widely prescribed for the relief of anxiety and tensions among people in the population at large who suffer from these symptoms. The illicit use of tranquilizers is negligible. However, since they may produce some physical and psychological dependence as well as undesirable side effects, they are legally restricted to medical prescription.

The hallucinogens or psychedelic drugs include LSD (lysergic acid diethylmide), mescaline (derived from the peyote cactus), psilocybin (from Mexican mushrooms), hashish (from Indian hemp), and marijuana (from Cannabis sativa, a widely distributed weed).

The hallucinogens arouse or enhance visual imagery, cause increased sensory awareness, anxiety, impaired coordination, and feelings of expanded consciousness in some instances. Medically their use is restricted to experimental work. Popularly, their use has been widespread in part due to publicity among young people seeking escape or expanded consciousness and to ready availability through the extensive illicit traffic that exists for such drugs.

There is some potential for increased tolerance with the hallucinogens, especially LSD. There is no serious physical dependence, but strong psychological dependence may occur for this class of drugs in some individuals who become preoccupied with drugs. Occasionally psychotic-like reactions ("bad trips") have been reported in individuals who are unprepared for the hallucinogenic states induced by such drugs. There appears to be little evidence that the use of marijuana, the most commonly used of the hallucinogens, leads to addiction to hard drugs, such as heroin.

Treatment for drug abuse may include singly, or in combination, supportive drug therapy, institutionalization, group and individual psychotherapy. Many authorities believe that educational programs in public schools about the undesirable effects of drug abuse are a positive step toward preventing the abuse of drugs.

D sleep: see REM SLEEP.

DSM III: See DIAGNOSTIC AND STATISTICAL MANUAL OF MENTAL DISORDERS.

dualism: 1. a philosophical position whose chief exponent was Plato. Dualism holds that there are two fundamentally different substances in the universe, mind and matter. 2. the psychological position that mind and body are separate processes. In psychological dualism, differences in the nature of mind and body may or may not be implied. *Contr.* MONISH. See also PSYCHOPHYSICAL PARALLELISM.

dual memory theory: the assumption that there are two fundamental types of memory: short-term memory (*q.v.*) and long-term memory (*q.v.*).

dual personality: a multiple personality consisting of two components. See also MULTIPLE PERSONALITY.

ductless gland: one of the endocrine glands whose products are poured directly into the bloodstream.

dull: 1. pertaining to sensations, such as color, tones, and touch, that are lacking in brilliance or in sharpness.

2. pertaining to deficiency of intelligence.

dullness: a state of low intelligence, usually implying an IQ somewhere between 70 and 90. *Contr.* BRIGHTNESS.

dull normal: a category for persons whose IQ's are between 70 and 90.

dumbness: an inability or unwillingness to speak.

duplicity theory: the theory—now regarded as established fact—that there are separate visual receptors for brightness vision (rods) and for color vision (cones).

dural sinus: the space between layers of the dura mater, or hard outer covering of the brain, which carries blood from the cerebral veins into the neck.

dura mater: the tough, outermost membrane covering the brain and spinal cord. Lying underneath it are the arachnoid layer and the pia mater.

durance: (*Murray*) an interval of time during which a life activity occurs.

duration: 1. the time of occurrence of an event. 2. the temporal attribute or characteristic of sensations.

Dvorine test: a test for defective color vision similar to the Ishihara test (*q.v.*).

dyad; diad: 1. a social group consisting of two persons. 2. a chord composed of two tones.

dynaception: the self-perception of one's own need state.

dynamic: 1. pertaining to systems of psychology that emphasize motives. 2. pertaining to change or that which initiates change. 3. pertaining to depth psychology or systems that stress the unconscious causation of behavior.

dynamic-effect law: (*R. B. Cattell*) a generalization stating that when goal-directed behavior becomes disperse, attention to new stimuli and the accompanying responses will become habitual in proportion to the extent that they shorten distance to the goal.

dynamic equilibrium: a generally stable organization of forces or energy. Changes in one part of a system in dynamic equilibrium are reflected by a rearrangement of the energy distribution in the whole, and are further characterized by constant change and activity. The concept of dynamic equilibrium has been applied by Gestalt psychologists to the cerebral cortex.

dynamic lattice: (*R. B. Cattell*) a graphic representation of the interrelations among goal-seeking behaviors and motives.

dynamic psychology: any system of psychology, such as field theory or psychoanalysis, emphasizing the search for cause-and-effect relationships in motives and drives.

dynamics: in field theory, the forces that act upon a psychological field.

dynamic-situations principle: a principle of contiguous conditioning expressing the constant change in stimulus patterns due to responses, visceral changes, fatigue, and uncontrolled variation in the stimulus.

dynamic subsidiation: a sequence of subgoals leading to a final goal.

dynamic system: a system in which the parts are interrelated in such a way that a change in one part will influence the entire system. A dynamic system is analogous to a field of force that, if disturbed at any point, reflects that disturbance throughout. A static system, by way of contrast, does not necessarily reflect changes in all parts. A telephone switchboard is a type of static system.

dynamic theory: (*Köhler*) the theory that the brain's action is characterized by constant changes of energy and that there is no fixed point-for-point correspondence between events in the cerebral cortex and environmental stimuli. See also DYNAMIC EQUILIBRIUM.

dynamic trait: a trait that has motivating characteristics or is manifested in goal-directed behavior.

dynamism: 1. a relatively persistent and consistent mode of behavior employed in drive satisfaction or in protecting the self from psychological distress. 2. a mechanism of adjustment.

dynamogenesis; dynamogen: 1. the initiation of motor responses as a result of sensory stimulation. 2. the correlation of effector responses with receptor activities.

dynamograph: a recording dynamometer.

dynamometer: a device for measuring the strength of a muscular response; typically a hand-grip device on which a scale is employed.

dyne: a unit of force defined as the force necessary to accelerate a gram of material one centimeter per second.

dysacousia: a psychological condition wherein ordinary noise causes discomfort.

dysarthia: speech impairment resulting from brain lesions. *Syn.* DYSPHASIA.

dysbasia: ataxia, or incoordination.

dysbulia: difficulty in concentration, impaired ability to maintain a train of thought.

dyseneia: defective articulation of words, resulting from deafness.

dysesthesia: a diminished sensitivity to pain.

dysfunction: a malfunction, impaired function.

dysfunctional: maladaptive. See MAL-ADAPTATION.

dysgenic: 1. pertaining to influences detrimental to heredity. 2. biologically deficient.

dysgeusia: a perversion of taste.

dysgraphia: inability to write, due to cerebral lesions.

dyslalia: defective speech without demonstrable brain damage.

dyslexia: inability to read; impairment of the reading function.

dyslogia: 1. impairment of speech due to mental deficiency. 2. difficulty in speaking or expressing ideas because of mental disorders.

dysmnesia: impaired memory.

dyspareunia: 1. lack of capacity to enjoy sexual intercourse. 2. painful sexual intercourse.

dysphagia: inability to swallow as a result of functional spasms of the throat muscles.

dysphasia: aphasia; impairment or inability in any of the language functions.

dysphoria: depression accompanied by anxiety. *Contr.* EUPHORIA.

dysphrasia: impairment in writing or speaking because of mental disorders.

dysphrenia: an old term for mental disorders.

dysplasia: abnormal growth resulting in an abnormal physique.

dysplastic type: an irregular body build difficult or impossible to classify according to one of the type theories.

dyspnea: difficult breathing.

dyspraxia: impairment in coordination; inability to carry out skilled movements.

dysrhythmia: 1. irregularity of brain waves. 2. irregular speech.

dysthymia: despondency in mood.

dystonia: a lack of muscular tonus. *Syn.* ATONY.

dystrophy: faulty nutrition leading to wasting and muscular weakness.

E

ear: the organ that contains the receptors for hearing. It is divided into three main parts: the outer, middle, and inner ears. The outer ear consists of the pinna and the external auditory canal, which terminates in the eardrum, or tympanic membrane. The middle ear consists of three auditory ossicles—the hammer, anvil, and stapes—the third of which articulates with the cochlea at the oval window. The eustachian tube, a pressure equalizer, enters into the middle ear from the mouth. The inner ear consists of the cochlea, which contains the receptors for hearing and the organs connected with the static sense and the sense of movement. The cochlea consists of three canals: the scala tympani, the cochlear canal, and the scala vestibuli. The organ of Corti, containing the receptor cells for hearing, rests on the basilar membrane. See illustration.

eardrum: the tympanic membrane that is stretched across the inner part

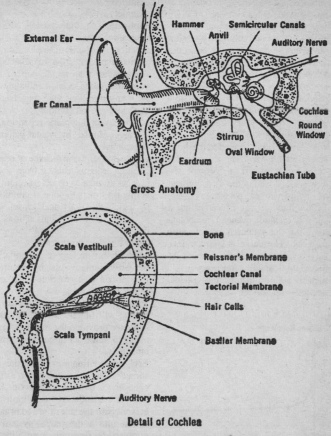

Gross Anatomy

Detail of Cochlea

FIG. 10. *The ear*

of the external auditory canal and articulates with the auditory ossicles. Its function is to vibrate in resonance with external sounds, setting up vibrations in the ossicles.

early infantile autism: see INFANTILE AUTISM.

Ebbinghaus, Hermann: German pioneer in the field of learning (1850–1909). Ebbinghaus attended the Universities of Bonn, Halle, and Berlin. After graduating from Bonn he studied independently for the next seven years. It was during this period, after reading Fechner's *Elements of Psychophysics*, that he launched an investigation of the higher mental processes, following Fechner's quantitative lead. He invented the nonsense syllable and, using himself as a subject, explored the memory process for the next several years. In 1885 he published his results in a slim volume entitled *Concerning Memory*. In the years that followed, he published several other books and, with Arthur König, founded the *Journal of Psychology*. He also devised the completion test, a form of test now widely used in the measurement of intelligence and personality.

Ebbinghaus' curve of retention: a curve of retention obtained by Ebbinghaus for the retention of nonsense material. The curve is characterized by a sudden drop in the amount retained immediately after practice and then by a slow, increasingly gradual decline with further time. See illustration.

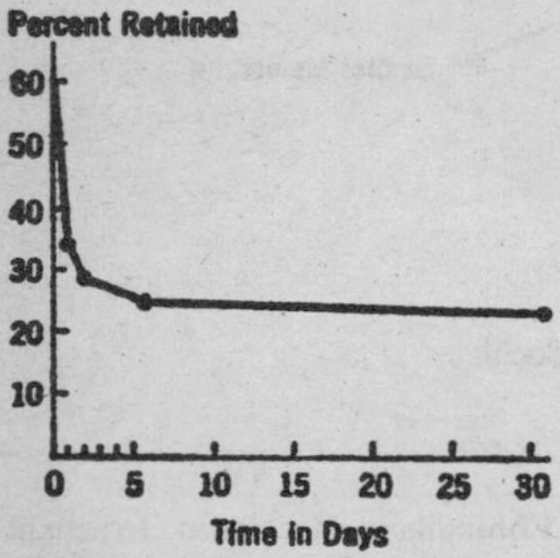

FIG. 11. *Ebbinghaus' curve of retention.*

ecbatic: a result or outcome without purpose. *Contr.* TELIC.

eccentric: characterizing a deviation from normalcy, usually not to the degree that the individual is considered psychotic.

eccentric projection: the location or referring of sensation to objects in space rather than to the part of the body stimulated. Vision and audition are the senses that give the clearest experience of projection.

echolalia: an automatic repetition of words or phrases by mental patients; echophrasia.

echolocation: the avoidance of obstacles by utilizing echoes from those objects as cues to object location.

echopathy: a pathological condition in which the individual senselessly imitates the words and actions of others.

echophrasia: see ECHOLALIA.

echopraxia: the automatic imitation of movements made by another. Echopraxia is a reaction sometimes found in catatonics.

echo principle: the hypothesis that an animal will imitate another animal's behavior provided the two have been engaged in the act in question simultaneously.

E/C intervening variable: the assumed factor to account for differences in the outcome of experimental (E) and controlled (C) conditions.

eclecticism: the selection and organization into a theoretical system of compatible findings from diverse sources. Sometimes there is an attempt to reconcile incompatible findings or points of view. *Contr.* SYNCRETISM.

ecmnesia: 1. the inability to recall recent events, without memory impairment for remote events. 2. anterograde amnesia.

ecology: 1. the study of biological

forms in relation to their physical environments. 2. (*Lewin*) the study of those aspects of the individual's environment that are important parts of his life space.

ecomania: a pathological attitude toward members of one's own family. It is characterized by irritable, domineering behavior.

economics: (*Psychoan.*) pertaining to the development, distribution, and utilization of psychic energy.

economy, principle of: see PARSIMONY, PRINCIPLE OF.

ecphory; ecphoria: the reactivation of a memory trace through stimulation.

ectoderm: the outermost embryonic layer that develops into the skin, nervous system, fingernails, and hair.

ectomorphic: see SHELDON'S CONSTITUTIONAL THEORY OF PERSONALITY.

ectoplasm: in psychic research, a substance said to emanate from the body of a medium.

edge detail: (*Rorschach*) a scoring category for responses determined by the contour or the edge of the blot.

edging: (*Rorschach*) a tendency on the part of the subject to turn the cards edgewise.

Edipus complex: see OEDIPUS COMPLEX.

educability: the potentiality for learning, particularly for formal, scholastic learning.

educational acceleration: faster-than-normal educational progress, either through grade skipping or by means of enriched curricula.

educational age: the grade level of a child as measured by standardized achievement tests scored in age units.

educational guidance: the process of discovering the child's educational capacities and liabilities and matching these to a suitable program.

educational measurement: the use of tests, both standardized and unstandardized, in assessing the abilities of pupils; the evaluation of educational procedures; the construction and validation of standardized tests for use in schools.

educational psychology: the investigation of psychological problems in the area of education and the application of formalized methods for solving these problems.

educational quotient: the ratio of the educational age to chronological age times 100.

$$EQ = \frac{EA}{CA} \times 100$$

The educational quotient is interpreted as an index of educational achievement. *Abbr. EQ*.

eduction: the process of developing new relations in thinking on the basis of perceived fundamental relations between items. For example, in the problem *Black is to white as night is to ——*, the fundamental relation *Black is to white* immediately educes *day* in response to *night*.

Edwards Personal Preference Schedule: a preference test employing a forced-choice technique to obtain scores on selected Murray's needs.

effect: 1. an event or phenomenon that follows another in a causal relationship. 2. (*Thorndike*) the result of a satisfying or unsatisfying state on a learned bond or connection. See also EFFECT, LAW OF.

effectance motive: an over-all motive embracing all specific intrinsic motives. The biological significance of the effectance motive is to attain competence in dealing with the environment.

effective-habit strength: (*Hull*) the strength of a given learned reaction as a function of the number of reinforcements.

effective-reaction potential: (*Hull*) the strength of a reaction potential (habit strength times drive) minus any inhibitory tendencies that may be operative.

effective stimulus: a stimulus that produces a response.

effect, law of: (*Thorndike*) the principle that other things being equal, the animal will learn those habits that lead to a satisfying state and will not learn or will only slowly learn those that result in an annoying state.

effector: a muscle or gland that acts in response to impulses arriving over efferent neurons.

efferent: pertaining to neurons or nerves leading outward from the central nervous system. Efferent nerves transmit motor impulses to muscles and glands. *Syn.* MOTOR.

efficiency: the ratio of output to input; the ratio of the amount of energy expended to the effect or result obtained.

efficient cause: the totality of antecedent conditions leading to a given effect.

effort: 1. the subjective feeling of strain associated with problem solving or strenuous physical activity. 2. increased tension or activity in the face of obstruction or frustration. 3. voluntary, as opposed to involuntary, work.

effort syndrome: a type of anxiety neurosis characterized by palpitations and circulatory, respiratory disorders. *Syn.* SOLDIER'S HEART; neurocirculatory asthenia.

E-F scale: a subscale of thirty items from the Minnesota Multiphasic Inventory of Personality, used to measure ethnocentric and authoritarian attitudes.

egg: the female germ cell; the ovum.

ego: 1. the self, particularly the individual's conception of himself. 2. (*Psychoan.*) the superficial portion of the id, or primitive infantile mind, that develops out of the id in response to stimulation from the infant's physical and social environments. The chief functions of the ego are (a) reality testing, or learning to distinguish between self and environment; (b) mediating between the demands of the id and the superego, which embodies the critical and moral aspects of the self.

ego-alter theory: 1. a theory that the origin and functioning of social institutions is the result of deliberate self-interest, which, in turn, is generated by the instinct for self-preservation. 2. a theory that social conduct is determined by the manner in which the individual (ego) perceives others (alters).

ego analysis: (*Psychoan.*) the analysis of the ego as opposed to the id. Ego analysis concentrates on the relative strengths and weaknesses of the ego, is less concerned with deeply repressed processes in the id, and is shorter than a conventional analysis.

ego anxiety: anxiety generated by the conflicting demands of the ego, the id, and the supergo.

ego block: anything that prevents the enhancement of the ego.

ego cathexis: the directing of the libido toward an object in the reality domain of the ego.

egocentric: 1. concerned or preoccupied with the self. 2. (*Piaget*) pertaining to speech and thinking directed by individual needs or concerns.

ego complex: (*Jung*) a group or cluster of emotionally toned psychic elements centered about the self.

ego defense: (*Psychoan.*) the utilization of psychic energy arising from the id in order to protect the ego. See also DEFENSE MECHANISM

ego-dystonic: unacceptable to the ego.

ego failure: (*Psychoan.*) 1. failure of the ego to check impulses arising from the id. 2. failure on the part of the ego to harmonize the demands of the id and the superego.

ego function: (*Psychoan.*) any activity or process that belongs to the ego. For example, dealing with the demands of society or mediating between the id and the superego are both ego functions.

ego ideal: that part of the ego that consists in the individual's identification with loving and reassuring parents or parental substitutes. The ego ideal represents positive and desirable standards of conduct. In contrast, the superego represents negative or forbidden aspects of identification with the parents; it is the equivalent of conscience.

ego instincts: (*Psychoan.*) the instincts associated with the need for self-preservation as opposed to the sexual instincts whose aim is reproduction.

ego-integrative: tending to harmonize the personality and organize it into a healthy whole.

ego-involvement. 1. committing the self to a task. 2. condition in which the individual identifies the self with the situation.

egoism: 1. the tendency for one to behave for self-advantage. 2. the so-

cial philosophy that all behavior is motivated by self-interest.

egoistic: conceited; motivated primarily by self-interest.

ego libido: (*Psychoan.*) psychic energy restricted to the service of the ego or attached to the ego.

egomorphism: the tendency to attribute one's own needs, desires, motives, etc., to others. *Cf.* PROJECTION; AUTISM.

ego neurosis (*Psychoan.*) a neurosis whose symptoms are primarily ego disturbances.

ego-object polarity: the tendency to distinguish between self and not self.

egopathy: hostile behavior arising from an exaggerated sense of self-importance.

ego resistance: (*Psychoan.*) the tendency on the part of the ego to resist recognizing repressed impulses during analysis and to resist giving up defense mechanisms.

ego strengths: (*Psychoan.*) the hypothetical strength of the ego as determined by the amount of psychic energy available to it. Ego strength is an important factor in determining whether or not the individual will break down under unfavorable conditions.

ego structure: the pattern of enduring personality traits.

ego-syntonic: consistent with ego ideals or with the individual's evaluation of himself.

ego threat: the danger, as perceived by the ego, in the demands of the id or in the emergence of a repressed impulse.

egotistic; egotistical: conceited; the tendency to overevaluate the self or one's own accomplishments.

eidetic imagery: uncommonly vivid imagery, as though actually perceived.

Eidetic imagery is common in childhood but in nearly all cases disappears during adolescence.

Eigenwelt: in existentialist terminology, man's relationship with himself. *Cf.* UMWELT; MITWELT.

Einstellung: a set; an attitude. Einstellung connotes a strong predisposition to behave in a certain way.

eisotrophobia: a fear of mirrors.

ejaculation: the discharge of the male semen at orgasm.

ejaculatio praecox: premature ejaculation.

Elberfeld horses: a group of horses trained in Elberfeld, Germany, seemingly able to carry out difficult mathematical operations when, in fact, they were responding to subtle cues on the part of the trainer.

Electra complex: (*Psychoan.*) the incestuous desire of the daughter for sexual relations with the father. The Electra complex is the female counterpart of the OEDIPUS COMPLEX.

electric-shock therapy: see ELECTROSHOCK THERAPY.

electrocardiogram: the graphic record of the electrical activity associated with the heartbeat. *Abbr.* EKG. It is used as a diagnostic tool.

electroconvulsive therapy: see ELECTROSHOCK THERAPY.

electrode: a metallic device used to apply current to tissue. The positive pole is the anode; the negative, the cathode.

electrodermal response: see GALVANIC SKIN RESPONSE.

electroencephalogram; electroencephalograph: a graphic record of the electrical currents developed by the cerebral cortex. *Abbr.* EEG. The most conspicuous of these is the alpha wave, recorded in the occipital cortex. It has a frequency range of 8–12 per second and an amplitude of 5–15 microvolts.

electromyogram; electromyograph: the recorded action currents in a muscle.

electronarcosis: a form of shock therapy that produces a comatose condition following the convulsive phase.

electroretinogram: the recorded electrical potential changes that occur on the retina of the eye. *Abbr.* ERG.

electroshock therapy: a form of somatic therapy consisting of the application of weak electric currents to the head in order to produce convulsion and unconsciousness.

electrotherapy: the use of electricity for therapeutic purposes.

electrotonus: the altered electrical and physical condition of a nerve or muscle in response to the application of an electric current.

element: 1. (*Wundt; Titchener*) the simplest constituents of consciousness; sensations, images, and affective states. 2. a construct or concept abstracted out of the use of another construct. 3. in information theory, an item in an ensemble or collection of items.

elementalism; elementarism: 1. the doctrine that mental processes or behavior are analyzable into their constituent parts and that such analysis is properly within the province of psychology. 2. used derogatorily by those who favor a holistic point of view, to imply losing sight of the whole in overconcern with the parts. *Syns.* ATOMISM; MOLECULARISM. *Contr.* HOLISM; GESTALT.

Elgin checklist: a list of behavior patterns found in psychotics.

ellipsis: the omission of one or more words; the omission of ideas, as in free association during psychoanalysis.

embedded figure: a form of ambiguous figure in which the outline of a person or object is carefully blended into the background so as to be difficult to perceive. Camouflage is a practical application of the principle of embedded figures. *Syn.* HIDDEN FIGURE.

Embedded Figures Test (EFT): a test of cognitive field dependence-independence consisting of embedded figures.

embryo: the earliest stage of development. In man the embryonic period is held to extend from the time of conception to (variously) 6–12 weeks of intra-uterine life. The fetal stage follows the embryonic.

embryology: the branch of biology concerned with the study of organisms from conception to birth.

embryonic: pertaining to the embryo.

emergency theory of the emotions: (*Cannon*) the theory that the emotions and the associated sympathetic activity in the autonomic nervous system prepare the organism for emergencies. Essentially, the theory proposes that the visceral responses of increased heart rate, increased blood flow to the muscles, inhibition of digestion, expansion of the air sacs in the lungs, and other related processes characteristic of emotional states, prepare the organism for flight or fight according to the evaluation of the situation made by the cortex.

emergent: characteristic of anything that cannot be predicted from its constituent parts or from the properties of antecedent conditions.

emergent evolution: the doctrine that new forms of functions evolve from the interactions of simpler forms.

emission: 1. the making of a response that is not associated with a specific identifiable stimulus. 2. the discharge of the semen, particularly in nocturnal discharges.

emit: to make a response in the absence of a specific or identifiable stimulus.

Emmert's law: the generality that the size of an afterimage or an eidetic image increases in proportion to the distance it is projected onto a ground.

emmetropic; emmetropism: normal vision.

emotion: variously defined by psychologists of different theoretical orientations, but with general agreement that the emotional state is a complex reaction involving a high level of activation and visceral changes, and accompanied by strong feelings, or affective states.

Feelings are conscious experiences activated either by external stimuli or by various bodily states. We smell a rose and experience a pleasant feeling. The taste of sugar is pleasant. Similarly, many sensory stimuli are intrinsically pleasant. Many, on the other hand, are unpleasant. Organic and kinesthetic stimuli arising from the organs and muscles can also give rise to feelings of pleasantness and unpleasantness. There are the common pleasant feelings associated with a good dinner, mild exercise, sexual satisfaction. Commonly experienced unpleasant feelings are associated with such conditions as illness, fatigue, and ingestion of certain chemicals.

Emotions may be defined as an aroused state of the organism involving conscious, visceral, and behavioral changes. Emotions are therefore more intense than simple feelings, and involve the organism as a whole. Where a mild feeling of anger or annoyance may go unobserved by another, rage is accompanied by such profound visceral, expressive, and other behavioral changes as to be clearly distinguishable even to a casual observer.

Although the early psychologists put a great deal of effort into their attempts to relate feelings to nervous and organic processes and, at the same time, into discussions of the differences between feeling and emotion, contemporary psychologists treat the two as aspects of the same fundamental process. Feelings are always a part of emotions. Both involve visceral and conscious changes, and, in the last analysis, the two are primarily distinguishable on the basis of the greater intensity of emotional states. It might also be added that in recent research more attention has been given to emotions than has been given to feelings, largely because the bodily changes accompanying the emotions are more readily observable and therefore lend themselves to laboratory investigation.

A problem of definition that has loomed large in recent psychological discussion of the emotions is that of the relationship between feeling and emotion on the one hand and motivation on the other. Common experience tells us that when we are motivated we are also emotionally aroused. A strong desire to escape is accompanied by fear. A motion to destroy or attack, by anger or rage. The sexual goal, too, has its characteristic emotional state. Indeed, so close is the relationship between motives and emotions that some psychologists believe we do not need both terms. Although we need not become involved in what is still a

controversial theoretical issue, there can be no disagreement that emotions, once aroused, impel us to activity. One psychologist has, in fact, suggested an *activation theory* of emotion that stresses the high level of neural activity in the reticular system and cerebral cortex during strong emotional states. Using the electroencephalograph to record brain waves, he compared the low level of nervous excitation in sleep, coma, and drowsiness with the relatively high level of arousal in rage, pain, and excitement. Activation, as it is used to describe such states, is almost synonymous with motivation.

However, if we change our frame of reference, several differences between motives and emotions may be pointed out, demonstrating that although emotional and motivational processes are closely related, there are, nevertheless, differences. To begin with, the primary motives or drives are cyclic in their appearance, dependent as they are upon changing physiological rhythms. Emotions, on the other hand, are likely to be more dependent on stimulus situations and their personal significance for the individual. The normal person does not show periodic outbursts of anger, rage, love, grief without provocation. Rather, the arousal of these emotions depends upon outside circumstances—what others say or do, how our work goes, what happens to our finances, and so on.

Secondly, drives and motives are geared to habitual patterns of satisfaction. Emotional reactions, on the other hand, are more typically aroused by situations for which we have no ready-made pattern of response. Thirst, hunger, and sex, for example, are usually satisfied by learned patterns of behavior that become more or less habitual in the normal adult. But should we lose a loved one, inherit a fortune, or meet a bear while strolling in the woods, we have no habitual modes of reacting to enable us to cope with such situations in a stereotyped, semiautomatic fashion.

Finally, emotional behavior is frequently disorganized and disturbed, whereas motivated behavior is typically goal-directed. In the more acute, emergencylike states of rage, terror, wild grief, and the like, the individual's behavior becomes completely disorganized, lacks a goal, and is characterized by extreme behavioral reactions. Nonemotional motivated behavior, on the other hand, is well organized, is goal-directed, and shows a level of arousal commensurate with the task in hand.

The chief problems in arriving at an agreed-upon definition of the emotions are those of associating emotional with other types of behavior and of distinguishing between emotional and other types of behavior. High activation levels, strong visceral responses, and conscious states of feeling may separately and in combination enter into other processes and behavior patterns. In general, few psychologists would disagree that such traditional emotions as fear, rage, love, joy, disgust, grief, and the like are phenomena to be explained. The problem is how to relate them to the organic and conscious changes in a meaningful way and one that is operationally valid. See also EMERGENCY THEORY; JAMES-LANGE THEORY; THALAMIC THEORY.

emotional: 1. pertaining to the expres-

sion of the emotions or the visceral changes that accompany the emotions. 2. characterizing individuals who are readily stimulated to emotional behavior.

emotional bias: a prejudice stemming from emotional causes.

emotional blockage: inability to remember or to think logically because of emotional disturbances.

emotional control: an attempt on the part of the individual to govern his or another's emotions.

emotional disorder: a mental disorder in which chronic, inappropriate emotional reactions predominate.

emotional expression: the muscular, glandular, visceral, and behavioral changes associated with the emotions.

emotional immaturity: 1. a tendency to display emotional reactions inappropriate to one's age. 2. a loose term for any maladjustment.

emotional instability: a tendency to display rapid and unpredictable changes in emotionality.

emotionality: the tendency or degree to which a person reacts emotionally.

emotional maturity: a state or condition of having reached an adult level of emotional development and therefore no longer displaying emotional patterns appropriate to children. The term emotional maturity often carries with it the implication of emotional control. Most adults experience the same emotions as children but suppress or control them better, particularly in social situations.

emotional pattern: the hypothetical characteristic set of behavioral, peripheral, and visceral responses associated with a given emotion.

emotional release: an outpouring, sometimes explosive, of pent-up emotions. *Syns.* ABREACTION; CATHARSIS.

emotional stability: freedom from wide variations or alternations in mood; the characteristic of having good emotional control.

emotional state: the visceral, behavioral, and conscious states characteristic of the emotions.

emotive: pertaining to emotion-provoking stimuli.

emotive imagery: in behavior therapy, a technique in which the patient imagines anxiety-producing stimuli in the context of strong, positive ideation in order to inhibit anxiety reactions.

empathy: 1. projecting one's own feelings into an event, a natural object, or an aesthetic product. For example, to its occupants, a car may seem to strain as it climbs a hill, and they may "help" it by leaning forward. 2. the realization and understanding of another person's feelings, needs, and suffering.

empirical: 1. derived from naturalistic observation or from experimental procedures. 2. experimental. 3. pertaining to EMPIRICISM (*q.v.*). 4. pertaining to curves or equations developed out of experimental findings.

empirical construct: a construct based on observed facts.

empirical equation: an equation derived from a set of observations, as contrasted with a *rational equation*, which is derived by deductive means.

empirical law: a principle, based on experimental findings, attempts to state a general relationship. Weber's law, which holds that the just-noticeable difference between two stimuli is a certain constant fraction of the total magnitude, is an empirical law. *Contr.* a priori law; deductive law.

empirical psychology: 1 act psychology (*q.v.*). 2. any system of psychology that emphasizes dependence on facts.

empirical test: an appeal to facts or experimentation in order to test a hypothesis.

empirical validity: validity from the point of view of how well a test actually measures what it is designed to measure, as determined by correlating that test with a criterion or outside, independent measure.

empiricism: 1 the philosophical position that experience is the source of all knowledge. The School of British Empiricism began with John Locke (1632–1704). Among its advocates were George Berkeley (1685–1753), famous for his *New Theory of Vision*; David Hume (1711–1776), who advocated associationism to account for complex ideas; David Hartley (1705–1757) and James Mill (1773–1836), under whom associationism became a separate school of thought and heavily influenced psychology. 2. the position that psychology (or science in general) can deal only with objective facts and that these, in turn, must be discovered through naturalistic observation and experimentation. Strong emphasis is placed on the desirability of operational definitions of mental constructs, and equal emphasis on keeping theory to a mimimum and relating it to experimental findings.

employment psychology: see VOCATIONAL SELECTION.

empty organism: a term employed by the opponents of stimulus-response systems of psychology to indicate their dissatisfaction with the lack of emphasis on organism factors in such systems.

emulation: a striving to equal the performance of another.

enactive mode: (*Bruner*) the most basic or primitive way that people convert immediate experience into a mental model. It is nonverbal and based on action or movement.

enantiodromia: (*Jung*) the play of opposites; the theory that everything eventually goes over into its opposite.

encéphale isolé: a brain transected at the junction of the brain and spinal cord. The entire brain is isolated from the rest of the nervous system. *Contr.* CERVEAU ISOLÉ.

encephalitis: an acute inflammation of the brain or the covering of the brain. *Epidemic encephalitis* and *encephalitis lethargica*, popularly called sleeping sickness, leave serious aftereffects in the form of personality changes, which frequently require institutional care for the victim.

encephalization: the principle that the brain becomes more and more important in mediating nervous functions as we go up the phylogenetic scale. Closely related to encephalization is the process of corticalization, whereby more and more functions are localized in the cortex as we move up from birds and reptiles, where the cortex first appears, to the mammals and eventually the primates, where it reaches its highest development.

encephalon: the brain.

encephalopathy: any disease of the brain.

encephalopsychosis: psychosis associated with cerebral lesions.

encoding: 1. the transformation of messages into signals, as in the punching of scores into IBM cards. 2. the process of transforming information into a form suitable for storing in memory.

encopresis: functional, involuntary defecation. Encopresis is sometimes observed in children as a result of improper toilet training or emotional conflicts.

encounter group: a form of psychotherapy seeking to encourage personal growth and improvement in interpersonal communication through intensive interpersonal experience in a small group. Encounter group leaders encourage openness, honesty, emotional expression, sensitivity to the feelings of others.

enculturation: the process of adapting to a new culture.

end: 1. the goal or objective result aimed at in purposive behavior. 2. an implied purpose or goal.

endbrain: see TELECEPHALON.

end brush: the highly branched termination of an axon. *Syn.* TELODENDRION.

end button; end foot: an enlargement of a fibril of the end brush where it makes contact with the body of a succeeding cell at the synapse; terminal button.

endocathection: (*Murray*) preoccupation with one's own thoughts, feelings; withdrawal from the practical life. *Contr.* EXOCATHECTION.

endocrine gland: one of the ductless glands, such as the pituitary or thyroid, that pour their products directly into the bloodstream. *Contr.* EXOCRINE GLAND.

endoderm: the innermost of the three embryonic layers. The endoderm develops into the visceral organs. *Syn.* ENTODERM. *Contr.* ECTODERM; MESODERM.

endogamy: the custom of confining marriage to members of a community, a caste, a clan, or a consanguineous group.

endogenous: 1. originating within a body or biological group. *Contr.* EXOGENOUS. 2. characterizing forms of mental deficiency determined by heredity.

endolymph: the straw-colored fluid within the semicircular canals and structures of the inner ear.

endomorphy: SEE SHELDON'S CONSTITUTIONAL THEORY OF PERSONALITY.

endophasia: silent or internal speech.

endopsychic: pertaining to that which is in the mind. *Contr.* EXOPSYCHIC.

end organ: a receptor or sense organ, particularly one that arises as a specialized or encapsulated afferent neuron in the cutaneous tissues.

endorphins: a class of neurotransmitters whose properties are similar to morphine. Believed to function as natural narcotics or opiates in the body.

end plate: the ending of the motor neuron at its junction with the muscle. Here the nervous impulse is transmitted from axon to muscle fiber.

end plate potential: the electrical potential developed on motor neurons at the myoneural junction.

end pleasure: (*Psychoan.*) 1. the intensely pleasurable sensation that occurs with orgasm. 2. the final organization of the libido at the genital stage.

end spurt: a rise in performance shortly before the termination of work or practice.

enelicomorphism: act or practice of attributing adult characteristics to children.

enervate: 1. to weaken; to diminish energy. 2. to remove nerves surgically.

engineering psychology: the branch of psychology concerned with relating men to machines and to work. Of particular concern to the engineering psychologist is the design of machines for maximum efficiency and safety of operation.

engram: a hypothetical trace left in the nervous system as a result of learning. The concept of the engram is employed to account for retention.

enkephalin: a type of endorphin (*q.v.*).

entelechy: 1. something that realizes or contains an end or final cause. 2. an immaterial agency that regulates material processes.

enteroceptor: SEE INTEROCEPTOR.

entity: a being or object that has autonomy or is independent of other beings or objects.

entoderm: SEE ENDODERM.

entoptic: 1. inside the eye. 2. characterizing visual responses that do not arise from light waves but are generated by mechanisms or chemical processes with the eye.

entropy: 1. (*Psychoan.*) the degree to which psychic energy cannot be transferred once it has been invested in an object. 2 in information theory, the number of possible outcomes a given event may have. 3. the tendency for social progress to become static because each succeeding change uses up energy that is then unavailable for further progress.

entry: the placement of a number or value in a table or frequency distribution.

enucleation: surgical removal of an organ—as an eye—without cutting into it.

enumeration: a form of classification obtained by identifying each member of a group in turn.

enuresis: involuntary discharge of urine; bed-wetting.

environment: totality of, or any aspect of, physical and social phenomena that surround or affect an individual organism or part of an organism. Psychologists recognize several types of environment: (1) the *postnatal* environment, which is the environment after birth and is understood when the term is not qualified; (2) the *prenatal* environment, or the environment of the individual before birth; (3) the *cellular* environment, consisting of the blood and electrolytic fluids and other cells that surround any given cell; (4) the internal environment, or the environment of the cells inside the body.

environmentalism: the viewpoint that emphasizes the role of environmental factors in the causation of behavior.

environmental psychology: the branch of psychology concerned with the relationship between behavior and the environment in which it occurs, with special emphasis on the variables of space, architecture, crowding, and noise.

envy: unpleasant feeling or emotion aroused by the desire to have what another possesses.

enzygotic twins: identical twins. *Syn.* MONOZYGOTIC TWINS.

environmental-mold trait: (*R. B. Cattell*) a personality trait developed through environmental influences. *Contr.* CONSTITUTIONAL TRAIT.

eonism: the pathological desire to wear the clothes of the opposite sex, usually in association with sexual excitement. *Syn.* TRANSVESTISM.

ependyma: the lining of the brain ventricles and the central canal in the spinal cord.

epicritic: pertaining to pressure, touch, and mild temperature sensitivity, as opposed to *protopathic*, which includes pain and extreme temperature sensitivity. Henry Head, the famous British neurologist, proposed that protopathic sensitivity is phylogenetically older and cruder than epicritic sensitivity.

epidemic: a rapid spread of a social phenomenon, such as a dancing mania or a fad.

epidermis: the outermost layer of the skin.

epigastric: pertaining to the region over the stomach.

epigenesis: the hypothesis that in embryonic development new properties emerge that were not contained in the original fertilized cell but develop out of prenatal environmental influences and intracellular interaction.

epilepsy: any of a group of nervous disorders characterized by either focal or generalized convulsions. The chief forms are *petit mal*, in which there may be only an extremely transitory loss of consciousness accompanied by blinking of the eyes or an automatic act; *grand mal*, or seizures in which the individual falls to the ground and suffers generalized convulsions; and *psychomotor attack*, in which there are outbursts of violent activity, sometimes destructive in nature, for which the individual is amnesic. See also FOCAL EPILEPSY; PATHIC EPILEPSY; MASKED EPILEPSY; SYMPTOMATIC EPILEPSY.

epileptic equivalent: see MASKED EPILEPSY.

epileptic furor: in epilepsy, a state of conscious confusion followed by a blind, maniacal attack for which the patient has no memory.

epileptic stupor: a state of near-unconsciousness or difficulty of arousal often following a grand mal attack.

epileptiform seizure: 1. a convulsive disorder resembling epilepsy, but caused by a disease or injury. 2. a hysterical condition in which the subject has epileptoid convulsions.

epileptoid personality; epileptoidism: epileptic character; a cluster of personality traits and behavior patterns believed to be associated with epilepsy. Among those suggested are stubbornness, irritability, and unco-operativeness.

epinephrine: see ADRENALINE.

epinosic: (*Psychoan.*) pertaining to indirect advantage gained by illness. See also ADVANTAGE BY ILLNESS.

epiphenomenalism: the doctrine that consciousness is the by-product of neural activities, that the cause of conscious activities is to be found in antecedent or parallel activities of the nervous system.

epiphenomenon: an event that accompanies another event but bears no causal relation to it.

epiphysis; epiphysis cerebri: the pineal gland.

episcotister: a disc that has variable open and closed sectors and is rotated between an observer and a stimulus for studying short exposure intervals.

epithalamus: that portion of the brain dorsad to the thalamus. It contains the pineal body and the habenula.

epithelium: the thin cellular layer covering the exposed inner surfaces of the body, the organs, and the hollow linings of the body.

epsilon movement: motion that is perceived when a white line on a black ground is changed into a black line on a white ground.

equal-and-unequal-cases method: in psychophysics, a variety of the constant methods in which pairs of stimuli are judged to be either equal or unequal.

equal-appearing-intervals method: a psychophysical technique in which the subject must adjust the magnitudes between pairs of stimuli in such a way that the sensed intervals are equal. The method has been applied to weight lifting, to aesthetic judgments, and by extension to attitude scaling.

equal-interval scale: a scale whose zero point is arbitrarily chosen but on which the intervals are equal. The Fahrenheit temperature scale is an equal-interval scale.

equality, law of: (*Gestalt*) the principle of perceptual grouping that parts of a figure that are equal tend to go together and form a whole.

equalization of excitation: a tendency for nervous excitation to spread out equally over all parts of a system.

equally noticeable differences: just-noticeable differences, or differences adjudged just perceptible half of the time.

equal-sense-differences method: see EQUAL-APPEARING-INTERVALS METHOD.

equated scores: scores from two different tests that have been reduced to a common basis by weighting.

equation method: the psychophysical method of average error.

equilibration: 1. the achievement of a balance between two opposed forces. 2. in Piaget's theory of development, the process by which cognitive structures change from one state to another, seeking equilibrium.

equilibrium: 1. a condition of stability or balance in a system. *Syn.* HOMEOSTASIS. 2. the maintenance of an upright posture.

equipotentiality: 1. the capacity of any part of early embryological tissue to develop into any part of the mature organism. 2. the generalization that any portion of the cerebral cortex can, with proper training, function for any other part in general learning. 3. the hypothesis that one sensory cue may substitute for another cue.

equity theory: the assumption that individuals seek a fair share of rewards or outcomes in a relationship.

equivalence: a relationship between two variables or stimuli or responses, of such a nature that one can substitute for another.

equivalence belief: (*Tolman*) a behavioral response on the part of the animal that shows it is perceiving a subgoal as the equivalent of the main goal. See also SECONDARY REINFORCEMENT.

equivalence coefficient: the correlation coefficient between two equivalent forms of the same test given to the same group. High coefficients of equivalence are taken as evidence of reliability.

equivalence test: a test to determine which aspects of a stimulus pattern may be altered without destroying the equality of the pattern. Patterns that elicit the same response are considered equivalent.

equivalent form: an alternate form of a test constructed with similar items so as to render the two forms as nearly the same in function as possible. Equivalent forms are useful in test-retest situations where it is desired to avoid practice effects.

equivalent groups: two or more groups that are matched with respect to all known variables. Within narrow limits, the means, standard deviations, and range of scores should be the same. Equivalent groups are used in experiments where an experimental group or groups will be compared with a control group. The groups must, therefore, be equivalent on all variables except the experimental variable.

equivalents method: a form of the method of average error in which the subject must adjust a variable stimulus until it appears equal to a standard.

erection: swelling of erectile tissue, that is, the penis, clitoris, or nipples.

erethism: exaggerated sensibility or irritability in a part of the body.

erg: 1. a unit of work. 2. (*R. B. Cattell*) innate predisposition to engage in certain activities in response to certain stimuli.

ergasia: a general concept referring to the totality of psychophysical functioning.

ergic: purposive; pertaining to drives or innate predispositions. *Ergic behavior* may also involve attitudes and feelings.

ergic trait: a dynamic trait; a trait that causes the individual to seek a goal.

ergograph: a device for recording muscular movement, usually in fatigue experiments involving a restricted member, such as the finger.

ergonomics: the science of fitting the man to the job and the job to the man. Ergonomics deals with the customs, habits, and laws of work and their relationship to employees.

ergotropic: characterized by drive or arousal.

Erikson, Erik H.: American psychoanalyst (1902–). Born in Frankfurt, Germany, Erikson studied psychoanalysis with the Freudians and graduated from the Vienna Psychoanalytic Institute in 1933. He became a United States citizen in 1939 and has taught at Yale, the University of California at Berkeley, and Harvard, where he was professor of human development and lecturer on psychiatry from 1960 to 1970. Erikson is noted for his extensive writings on child development, the development of the concept of the "identity crisis," and his modification and extension of Freud's theory of psychosexual development. His best-known works are *Childhood and Society* (1950), *Young Man Luther* (1958), *Insight and Responsibility* (1964), *Identity: Youth and Crisis* (1968), and *Gandhi's Truth* (1969).

Erikson's Ego Psychology: Erikson's theory of personality development is similar to Freud's (*q.v.*); however, he has cast his theory into a psychosocial form, added a number of stages, and emphasizes the ego rather than the id.

Stage one is the oral-sensory stage during which the child learns basic trust or mistrust depending on the success of the first encounter with the parents. In stage two, the muscular-anal stage, the child learns autonomy if successful, or shame and doubt if unsuccessful. The locomotor-genital stage is the third, and the child's learning is initiative or guilt. The fourth stage is the latency stage, during which industry and inferiority are the alternative modes of development. In puberty and adolescence, the fifth stage, they are identity versus role confusion. In young adulthood, which is the sixth stage, intimacy or isolation will be the result of the crisis in development. The seventh stage is adulthood and presents the alternatives of generativity versus stagnation.

In the final, eighth stage, maturity, ego-integrity, and despair are the alternatives.

In each of these stages are crises that must be coped with either successfully or unsuccessfully. Each represents an encounter between the child and the demands of society. Of particular importance for a successful, healthy adult personality is the successful resolution of the identity crisis during puberty and adolescence.

erogenous zone: an area of the body that gives rise to sexual feeling when stimulated.

Eros: (*Psychoan.*) a term adopted by Freud from the name of the Greek god of love to mean all of the life, or self-preservation, instincts.

erotic: 1. pertaining to sexual feeling or sensation. 2. pertaining to the stimuli that give rise to sexual excitement. 3. more generally, pertaining to love in all its manifestations.

eroticism; erotism: 1. sexual excitement. 2. a predisposition to be interested in sexual matters or to experience sexual excitement more readily than the average individual. 3. pertaining to sexual excitement arising from nongenital members, such as the mouth, anus, and lips.

erotization: (*Psychoan.*) the process whereby a part of the body, such as the oral or anal region, takes on sexual importance.

erotized anxiety: a paradoxical response to anxiety in which the patient moves toward the source of anxiety and appears to enjoy it.

erotomania: pathologically exaggerated sexual interest. In the male the condition is called satyriasis; in the female, nymphomania.

error: 1. mistaken or distorted belief. 2. in statistics, a deviation from a true score. 3. in experimental procedures, a deviation from the true value, because of inadequacies in the design, apparatus, or methodology. 4. an inappropriate or incorrect response delaying arrival at the goal.

error-choice technique: see FORCED-CHOICE TECHNIQUE.

error of estimate: 1. in using regression equations, the error involved in making estimates from one variable to another. 2. in a psychophysical experiment, the point of subjective equality in comparative judgments minus the standard stimulus. 3. the error of prediction from an individual test score on a criterion variable due to imperfect test validity.

error of expectation: 1. in psychophysical experiments involving ascending and descending series, a tendency on the part of the subject to anticipate a stimulus that he knows is coming or to believe he senses it after it is no longer above threshold value. 2. an error of anticipation; "jumping the gun."

error of measurement: 1. the deviation of any given measurement from its true value. The true value is usually estimated by taking the mean of the measurements. 2. an error due to the unreliability of an instrument. *Syn.* error of observation.

error of refraction: the degree to which the lenses of the eye fail to bring the image to a focus on the retina.

error variance: variance due to such uncontrolled factors as test unreliability or sampling errors.

erythrogenic: pertaining to radiant energy that gives rise to the sensation of red.

erythrolabe: the red-sensitive cone pigment in the retina.

erythropia; erythropsia: a tendency toward red vision due to overexposure to intense white light. A common aftermath of skiing in bright sunlight.

Es: (*Psychoan.*) German for *id*. The term is occasionally used in its untranslated form in psychoanalytic writing.

E scale: an attitude scale designed to measure ethnocentrism.

escape from reality: 1. behavior that enables the individual to substitute fantasy or daydreams for real satisfactions. 2. any behavior involving the avoidance or retreat from the problems and conflicts inherent in living.

escape learning: learning situations in which the regulating drive is punishment; the desired response brings relief from punishment.

escape training: learning in which the animal is subjected to a noxious or painful stimulus that may be avoided by escaping into another compartment or by withdrawing a limb from a grid.

esophoria: see HETEROPHORIA.

estotropia: an inward deviation of one eye.

ESP: abbreviation for extrasensory perception.

essential hypertension: high blood pressure not related to an organic condition. The qualifier *essential* is sometimes used to distinguish the condition from high blood pressure due to renal insufficiency.

establishment: (*Murray*) a division of personality. Murray borrows and modifies the concepts of the ego, the id, and the superego as the establishments of personality. The id is not wholly animalistic and unacceptable; the ego is not wholly inhibitory; the superego, as is true in psychoanalysis, is a culture introjection that functions as the moral establishment of the psyche.

Estes' Statistical Model of Learning: a theory of learning that assumes all stimuli are composed of a large number of elements and only a fraction of these can be effective at any given time. Only those portions that are effective can enter into associative learning. The fraction of stimuli effective in the learning situation is represented by θ, which has some value less than 1.00. If, in a given learning situation, θ has a value of .25, then on any one trial there will be added to the components of the stimulus already associated with the response in question, one-fourth of the remaining portions of the stimulus complex, in this instance a relatively high proportion. Lower values of θ mean slower rates of learning. It is assumed that extinction means that fractions of the stimulus complex originally attached to the response have become attached to another response. The theory allows for the use of rate of response, resistance to extinction, latency, etc., as measures of the probability of learning. The fundamental equation that measures the change in the probability of response from trial n to trial $n + 1$ is as follows:

$$Pn + 1 = Pn + \theta(1 - Pn)$$

That is, the probability of response on the following trial will equal the probability on the trial in question plus a fraction of the remaining probability (θ) needed to reach probability 1.00. The generalized equation for Pn is given as follows:

$$Pn = 1 - (1 - P_1)(1 - \theta)^{n-1}$$

esthesiometer; aesthesiometer: a compasslike device for measuring the two-point threshold on the surface of the skin.

esthetics: see AESTHETICS.

estimate: 1. a value arrived at by subjective judgment, usually after careful inspection of the data on which the estimate is based. 2. a statistical inference about a population based on a sample measurement.

estrogen: any of the female hormones that regulate the estrus cycle and are instrumental in stimulating the development of the secondary sexual characteristics at puberty.

estrus or **estrous cycle:** the periodic appearance of sexual desire and accompanying physiological changes in the female animal.

eta coefficient (η): the correlation ratio or measurement of the degree to which a correlation line is curvilinear.

ethereal: pertaining to the class of odors represented by the volatile substances, such as chloroform and ether.

ethnic: 1. pertaining to racial divisions. 2. pertaining to any division of man, social or biological.

ethnocentrism: 1. the characteristic of holding one's own racial or national group to be superior. 2. a personality syndrome characterized by strongly conventional attitudes, power-oriented personal relations, and a tendency to project hostile impulses to others.

ethnology; ethnography: the study of ethnic groups, their geography, customs, and culture.

ethnopsychology: the comparative psychology of nonliterate peoples.

ethogram: a record of an animal's behavior as it occurs in the natural habitat.

ethology: 1. the science of ethics, particularly the comparative study of ethics among different racial and national groups. 2. the experimental or empirical study of character. 3. the study of behavior from a comparative point of view. The study of imprinting and releasers exemplifies psychobiological ethology. 4. the study of customs, folkways, and mores.

ethos: the character of a national or radical group.

etiology: the investigation of casual relations in diseases.

eugenics: the biosocial movement to improve the hereditary characteristics of man by eliminating propagation among the unfit and encouraging propagation among superior individuals.

eunuch: a castrate; a male whose testes have been removed.

eunuchoidism: a condition in which the individual has the characteristics of a eunuch because of testicular atrophy due to disease.

eupareunia: coitus during which orgasm is achieved. *Contr.* DYSPAREUNIA.

euphoria: a psychological state, often pathological, of extreme well-being, optimism in outlook, and heightened motor activity. Euphoria is characteristic of manic states.

eupsychia: (*Maslow*) 1. (*noun*) a psychological utopia in which self-actualized people could live in harmony.

eupsychic: (adj.) characterizing a psychologically healthy environment.

eurymorph: a person of short, heavy build. See also BODY BUILD INDEX.

eustachian tube: a valved tube connecting the middle ear and the mouth. Its purpose is to permit equilibrium of atmospheric pressure between the outside and the middle ear.

euthenics: the science concerned with the improvement of man by improving the environment. *Contr.* EUGENICS.

euthymia: a feeling of well-being or tranquility. *Contr.* DYSTHYMIA.

evaluation: a comparison and determination of the relative importance of a phenomenon, score, or test result.

event: 1. an occurrence or phenomenon that may become a psychological datum. 2. (*Murray*) any incident in life that is related to a PRESS or NEED.

eviration: in a male, the delusion that he has turned into a woman or lost his masculinity.

evocative therapy: any form of therapy in which the primary technique involves the interpretation of the patient's verbal productions.

evoke: to elicit or call forth, as a response. *Syn.* stimulate.

evoked potential: an electrical discharge in one part of the nervous system that has been generated by stimulation in another part.

evolution: 1. the theory that the systematic, orderly changes in the phylogenetic species have arisen by the operation of genetic mutations with survival of the best-adapted mutants. 2. more generally, the orderly development of anything, such as a theory or system of thought.

exceptional: pertaining to individual differences in ability, usually in reference to children of very high or very low intelligence.

exchange theory: see SOCIAL EXCHANGE THEORY.

excitable: 1. pertaining to highly reactive nervous tissue. Large, peripheral neurons are highly excitable. 2. more generally, in reference to living tissue, having the capacity to respond to stimulation. 3. overly emotional or easily aroused to emotional reactions.

excitant: a stimulus; an agent capable of eliciting a response.

excitation: 1. physiological change induced in a receptor or in neurons by stimulation. 2. a hypothetical central nervous state induced by a stimulus.

excitation gradient: see GENERALIZATION GRADIENT.

excitatory agent: a stimulus.

excitatory field: an active region of the brain or a field near the termination of a neuron.

excitatory irradiation: (*Pavlov*) the spreading out of excitation from an active neural center.

excitatory postsynaptic potential (EPSP): the potential developed by partial depolarization of cell bodies and dendrites resulting from the release of an excitatory transmitter substance at synaptic knobs.

excitatory potential: (*Hull*) the strength of a tendency to respond. Excitatory potential is a multiplicative function of drive and habit strength.

excitatory synapse: a synapse in which transmission results in the firing of the postsynaptic neuron. *Contr.* INHIBITORY SYNAPSE.

excitatory tendency: the capacity of a stimulus to elicit a response.

excitement: a highly emotional state characterized by motility, impulsive verbal and motor behavior, and feelings or tense anticipation.

excitement-quiescence: one of the dimensions posited by Wundt's tri-dimensional theory of feeling. The other dimensions are pleasantness-unpleasantness and tension-relaxation.

executive area: a cortical area that exerts a high level of integrative control over other areas in the cortex.

exercise: 1. in learning, practice or the repetition of an act or verbal skill to mastery. 2. physical activity for muscular training.

exercise, law of: (*Thorndike*) the principal that other things being equal, such as motivation or knowledge of results, the more an act is practiced, the faster and surer the learning.

exhaustion: 1. a depleted metabolic condition characterized by extreme fatigue, underactivity, and minimal responsiveness to stimulation. 2. the final state of the adaptation syndrome characterized by severe metabolic depletion.

exhaustion delirium or **psychosis:** a delirious condition with quasi-psychotic behavior occurring under conditions of physical exhaustion.

exhibitionism: 1. a compulsive tendency to expose parts of the body, usually the sex organs, for the purpose of sexual excitement. 2. a tendency toward calling attention to one's self. See also EXHIBITIONISTIC ATTITUDE.

exhibitionistic attitude: (*Murray*) the need to attract attention to oneself, usually by attempting to amuse, to stir, or to shock others.

existential analysis: a form of therapeutic analysis practiced by the adherents of existential psychology. Its aim is to restore to the patient a sense of freedom and responsibility for his own choices. See also EXISTENTIALISM.

existential anxiety: the anxiety that arises from facing a choice involving the unknown.

existentialism: a dominant twentieth-century European philosophical and literary movement, whose chief tenets are that philosophy ought to be concerned with man's existence, his situation in the world, his freedom to choose his goals and projects, and the meaning of his life. The modern origins of existentialism are to be found in the works of Sören Kierkegaard, Friedrich Nietzsche, and Martin Heidegger. Literary existentialism is associated in the popular mind with the works of Jean-Paul Sartre, Simone de Beauvoir, Albert Camus, and Gabriel Marcel. Existentialism has strongly influenced European psychoanalysis. See also EXISTENTIAL PSYCHOLOGY.

existential psychology: 1. the school of psychology, primarily championed by Wundt in Europe and Titchener in America, that held that the subject matter of psychology was conscious content to be investigated by the method of introspection. For a further discussion of the school see STRUCTURALISM. 2. the system of psychology associated with the philosophical position of existentialism. Its adherents oppose what they term the abstractions of both academic psychology and classical psychoanalysis and emphasize instead that existence takes precedence over essence; that freedom of choice is paramount over determinism.

existential psychotherapy: existential psychotherapy is not a unified set of procedures or techniques for helping the individual find a better way of living. Some existential therapists favor a modification of the analytic technique of free association; some utilize the client-centered or face-to-face approach. Others have developed their own specialized techniques. Moreover, those who practice existential therapy are not agreed upon a systematic body of theory out of which clinical practice evolves. Rather, there are certain more or less commonly accepted existential themes that form the basis of therapy.

Because the most basic of all existential themes is that of *being*, therapy must deal with the problems of being or being-in-the-world. The patient's relationship to the world of things, to other people, and to his own internal world of consciousness must be explored. Being, it is emphasized, is conscious *existence* that is never fixed but always becoming. Existence is therefore free to determine the future. Non-being is *essence* that is fixed and without freedom to determine its future.

Because existence is free to choose, anxiety arises. The individual without choice has no reason to fear. Those who must face alternatives and take risks experience fear. To escape anxiety the individual may adopt inauthentic modes of existence such as becoming detached or alienated, pursuing pleasure, or losing the self in conformity to the demands of society. It follows that an essential goal of therapy is to examine being in all its manifestations and particularly to explore the patient's inauthentic modes of living. Anxiety and inauthentic modes of being can be overcome by commitment, not to egotistical goals, but to those that favor humankind.

Existential psychotherapy rejects the unconscious determinism of classical psychoanalysis. The individual who is living a maladaptive mode is not forever determined to do so because of his past. The goal of therapy is not merely to make him more comfortable with his disability, but to show him that he can choose a new mode of being and free himself from the past. Therefore emphasis in therapy is on the present and the future and not on the past. Fulfillment, not the resolution of conflicts, is the model for personality. Ultimately the patient must experience a transformation in the meaning and values that he attaches to living. He does this through the analysis of his own being and his relationship and commitment to his fellowman.

exocathection: (*Murray*) occupation with external events; willingness to participate in the world of practical affairs. *Contr.* ENDOCATHECTION.

exocrine gland: one of the duct glands whose products do not enter directly into the bloodstream. *Contr.* ENDO-CRINE GLAND.

exogamy: marriage outside one's own group, *Contr.* ENDOGAMY.

exogenous: originating outside the body. *Contr.* ENDOGENOUS.

exolinguistics: in information theory, the study of the relationships between messages and senders and receivers.

exophoria: a muscular imbalance that causes the eyes to deviate outward. See also HETEROPHORIA.

exophthalmic goiter: a disease of the thyroid gland so named because of proturberant eyeballs associated with the disorder. The disease is also marked by rapid heart rate, excessive energy output, restlessness, and fatigue. *Syns.* Basedow's, GRAVES'S, and Parry's disease.

exopsychic: pertaining to mental activity that has effects outside the individual. *Contr.* ENDOPSYCHIC.

exosomatic method or **technique:** the utilization of skin resistance to an electric current in measuring the psychogalvanic response. *Syn.* Féré's method. *Contr.* Tarchanoff's method.

exotropia: walleyedness; the turning of one of the eyeballs outward due to muscular imbalance.

expansive delusion: delusions of gran-

deur accompanied by extreme feelings of well-being and excitement.

expansiveness: a personality trait characterized by an outerdirected orientation to others, loquaciousness, and overreactivity.

expectancy: 1. the probability of an occurrence. 2. an attitude, or set, characterized by attentiveness and heightened muscular tension. *Syn.* SET.

expectancy theory: see TOLMAN'S PURPOSIVE BEHAVIORISM.

expectation: 1. a state of anticipation; an emotional attitude of watchful waiting. *Syn.* ANTICIPATION. 2. the statistical probability of the occurrence of an event.

experience: 1. an event that has been lived through. 2. (*Titchener*) the totality of present consciousness. 3. knowledge or skill derived from practice or learning.

experience balance: (*Rorschach*) the ratio of movement (M) to color (C) indicative of the experience type. See also EXPERIENCE TYPE.

experience type: (*Rorschach*) the dimension of introversion-extroversion or extratensive-introversive. Several indices are available for estimating the experience type. A preponderance of M (movement) responses over C (color) responses is indicative of introversion. Similarly, FM (animals in action) indicates introversive tendencies.

experiment: a series of observations carried out under controlled conditions for the purpose of testing a hypothesis. In an experiment, there are several variables: the experimental or independent variable, which is manipulated by the experimenter and is applied to the subject in order to assess its effect; the dependent variable, or the subject's reaction to the

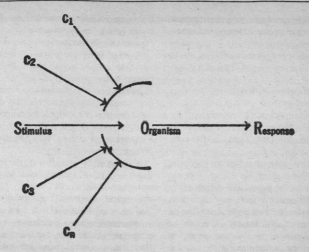

FIG. 12. *The scheme of an experiment. A stimulus is directed toward an organism, who makes a response. Other factors, C_1, C_2, C_3. . . .C_n, that might influence the response are held constant.*

independent variable; and the controlled variables or conditions, to be held constant in order to prevent them from influencing the dependent variable and confusing the result.

experimental control: the application of the principle that all conditions and variables in an experiment must be known and regulated in such a manner that the influence of the independent variable will be unambiguous. This involves excluding or holding constant any variable or environmental conditions that might influence the dependent variable. Some experimental conditions call for the use of control groups.

experimental design: see DESIGN.

experimental error: a deviation in a measurement, or a false value in a series of measurements, due to an inadequate design, method, or apparatus employed in the experiment.

experimental extinction: see EXTINCTION.

experimental group: a group of subjects who are subjected to the independent or experimental variable in an experiment. The experimental group is matched in all respects with the control group, which is treated in the same manner as the experimental group except for the application of the experimental variable.

experimental method: the technique of discovering information by means of experimentation.

experimental neurosis: a state of stereotyped behavior involving compulsions or fixations, refusal to respond, extreme emotionality or lack of emotionality, and inability to solve problems similar to those that induced the abnormal behavior. Experimental neuroses are created in animals by giving the animal impossible problems to solve, particularly problems involving severe punishment for failure.

experimental series: 1. true trials, as opposed to trials used in a pretest or as a pilot series. 2. procedures applied to the experimental group, as opposed to those applied to the control group.

experimental variable: an independent variable whose effect is being tested on the dependent variable.

experimenter effect: any distortion in the results of an experiment caused by the experimenter's behavior or attitudes.

expiatory punishment: (*Piaget*) the belief held by children that a wrongdoer should suffer punishment in proportion to the seriousness of the offense even though not necessarily related to it.

explanation: 1. the discovery of those antecedent conditions that account for a given phenomenon. 2. rendering a complex statement or description into simpler terms.

explicit: 1. that which is made clear or stated directly. 2. overt, as in overt behavior.

explicit behavior: action or conduct that is outwardly manifest, as in physical motion.

explicit response: an overt response that can be observed directly without the aid of instrumentation.

exploitation: the tendency for one person to make use of another person to satisfy the needs of the former without regard to the needs of the latter.

exploitive character: one who practices exploitation or who forces others to accede to his wishes.

exploratory behavior: movements or locomotor behavior engaged in by organisms seeking to orient themselves in new situations.

exponent: 1. in mathematics, a number written as a superscript that denotes the power to which the number or expression is to be raised. 2. an advocate of a theory or systematic point of view.

exposition attitude: (*Murray*) the tendency to explain, lecture, relate facts, or to demonstrate.

expression method: the investigation and measurement of feeling and emotion through bodily changes that accompany these states. In the earlier literature, the aim was to correlate a characteristic set of changes with each emotion; more recently, it is recognized that this was an oversimplification of the problem.

expressive: 1. pertaining to any response made by an organism. 2. pertaining to the facial, vocal, and gestural responses characteristic of the emotions.

expressive aphasia: aphasia in which the individual cannot speak, write, or make intelligible gestures. *Contr.* RECEPTIVE APHASIA.

expressive functions: see EXPRESSIVE.

expressive movements: distinctive movements, particularly facial and postural movements.

expressive therapy: a form of therapy in which the patient or client is encouraged to talk out his problem and freely express his feelings.

extension: 1. the spatial character of physical phenomena. 2. the straightening or supporting movements of a limb.

extensity: the attribute of spatiality;

the psychological correlate of physical extension. Extensity is a quantitative, not a qualitative attribute.

extension: a muscle whose function is to straighten a limb. *Contr.* FLEXOR.

extensor thrust: a reflex extension of the leg elicited by stimulating the sole of the foot.

external auditory meatus: the canal that leads from the external ear into the middle ear. (See EAR for illustration.)

external inhibition: (*Pavlov*) the reduction in the magnitude of a conditioned response that is observed when an external or extraneous stimulus is presented along with the conditioning stimulus.

externalization: 1. the arousal, through learning, by external stimuli of a drive previously aroused by internal stimuli, 2. in children, the process of differentiating between self and not self. 3. the projection of one's own psychological processes to the environment, such as occurs in paranoid or hallucinatory states.

external rectus: one of the extrinsic eye muscles. The external rectus rotates the eyeball outward.

external sense: a receptor system, such as the eye or ear, stimulated by external sources of stimulation. *Syn.* EXTEROCEPTOR. *Contr.* INTEROCEPTOR.

external validation: the process of establishing validity by discovering an outside criterion against which a measure can be correlated. Thus, if the problem is to validate a medical school aptitude test, then the external criterion against which the test can be correlated, and hence validated, is grades in medical school.

external world: the totality of physical phenomena outside the body; the totality of objects and events not a part of the self.

exteroceptor: a sense organ whose stimuli arise outside of the body. *Contr.* INTEROCEPTOR; PROPRIOCEPTOR.

extinction: the gradual diminution in magnitude or rate of a conditioned response upon withdrawal of the reinforcement or of the instrumental reward.

extinction ratio: the ratio of unreinforced responses emitted by an animal in reconditioning under conditions of periodic reinforcement.

extinguish: to bring about the experimental extinction of a response.

extirpation: the removal or destruction of a part of the nervous system for the purpose of studying its function: *Syn.* ABLATION.

extraception: (*Murray*) a down-to-earth, skeptical attitude; a disposition to adhere to facts. *Contr.* INTRACEPTION.

extrajection: (*Psychoan.*) attributing one's own characteristics to another. *Syn.* PROJECTION.

extramural: pertaining to an event outside the institution, such as a psychiatric investigation of a patient conducted in his own neighborhood.

extrapolate: to estimate a variable beyond the given data. Extrapolation frequently takes the form of extending a curve beyond its plotted range.

extrapunitive: characterizing a reaction to frustration in which the frustrated individual shows aggression toward the source of frustration. *Contr.* INTROPUNITIVE; IMPUNITIVE.

extrasensory perception (ESP or psi): perception without the mediation of sensation. There are two main classes of phenomena included under the general heading of extrasensory perception: (1) *extrasensory percep-*

tion that in turn includes (a) *telepathy*, or direct thought transference from one individual to another without the intervention of any known exchange of physical energy, (b) *clairvoyance*, or the ability to know objects and objective events by some means other than the senses, and (c) *precognition*, or knowledge of future events; (2) *psychokinesis* (PK) or the ability to influence objects by direct mental manipulation.

Telephathy is typically investigated by means of an experimental arrangement involving two people, one of whom (the sender) attempts to send a message to the other (the percipient) without the aid of sensory cues. The message is a symbol from a pack of ESP (Zener) cards consisting of 25 cards, the face of each marked with one of the following symbols: star, cross, circle, square, wavy lines. Since each pack has 5 cards bearing each of the 5 symbols, the percipient could only get 5 correct by chance. If on many runs the subject scores consistently above chance, the result is attributed to ESP. Great care must be taken to avoid inadvertent sensory cues (preferably by isolating the sender and percipient in different buildings) and errors of recording by having independent checkers.

In clairvoyance experiments no sender is involved. Instead the subject attempts to guess the sequence of a pack of cards that lies facedown on the table. A record of the subject's guesses is made before the cards are examined. In precognition experiments the percipient attempts to guess what is *going* to be sent on the *next* trial. In psychokinesis experiments the subject attempts to influence the throw of dice. In all of these procedures standard statistical methods are employed to evaluate the significance of the results.

On the average only small differences are found between observed guesses and chance expectations. However, such differences are statistically significant if a large number of runs is involved. Nevertheless, most psychologists remain skeptical of ESP because of the lack of consistency in subjects (even the best subjects appear to lose their ability after a number of runs), the finding that the tighter the experimental controls the less evidence of ESP, and the fact that the evidence for such phenomena is based only on statistical inference involving very large numbers of runs.

extraspectral hue: a color or hue not found in the spectrum. Purple, intermediate in hue between red and blue, is an extraspectral hue.

extratensiveness: (*Rorschach*) the personality characteristic of the individual who is highly responsive to his environment, is creative in relation with others, and is reactive toward the world rather than striving. *Contr.* INTROVERSIVENESS.

extraversion; extroversion: a tendency to direct the personality outward rather than inward toward the self. The extravert is social, a man of action rather than a man of contemplation, and one whose motives are conditioned by external events. *Contr.* INTROVERSION.

extraversion-introversion: (*Jung*) a bipolar personality dimension along which people can be divided into types. Extraversion is characterized by outward-directedness (see EXTRAVERSION) on the one extreme and inward-directedness on the other extreme (see INTROVERSION). Careful testing of large groups of people has not substantiated the dimension as a unitary trait or type; rather, the distribution of scores approximates a normal probability curve.

extravert: an individual who shows the personality characteristics of extraversion.

extrinsic: 1. characterizing that which is outside or external. 2. pertaining to that which is not an inherent part of something but is related to it. *Contr.* INTRINSIC.

extrinsic behavior: see INTRINSIC BEHAVIOR.

extrinsic eye muscles: a set of six eye muscles that rotate the eyeball in various directions.

extrinsic interest: attributing value to an object or activity because of its relationship to some other object or activity. *Contr.* INTRINSIC INTEREST.

extrinsic motivation: motivation not inherent in the behavior itself. Engaging in activities for the material rewards they bring is *extrinsic* motivation; engaging in activities because one enjoys them is *intrinsic motivation.*

extrinsic reward: a reward external to the behavior itself. See also EXTRINSIC MOTIVATION.

extrinsic thalamus: thalamic nuclei that serve as relay stations for incoming impulses. *Contr.* INTRINSIC THALAMUS.

extroversion: see EXTRAVERSION.

extrovert: see EXTRAVERT.

exvia: (*R. B. Cattell*) extraversion.

eye: the receptor for vision. In cross section (see illustration) the eye is seen to consist of three coats; the sclerotic, a tough layer, which constitutes the white of the eye along the sides and rear and is modified in front into the cornea, a clear lens that fo-

cuses light; the choroid coat, a dark, middle layer, whose function is to absorb light; and the retina, the innermost layer, which contains the rods and cones. The center of clearest vision is the fovea at the rear of the retina on the line of regard. Toward the front of the eye is the lens, whose function is to regulate incoming light. The lens is regulated in turn by the ciliary muscle; the iris is a muscular diaphragm capable of self-regulation. The rods mediate brightness vision; the cones mediate color or daylight vision.

eyedness: eye dominance.

eye contact: looking directly into the eyes of another. Frequency of eye contact may be used as a measure of attraction.

eye dominance: the tendency for one eye to be used in preference to the other in sighting or fixating objects.

eye ground: the back of the eye as seen through the pupil with the aid of an opthalmoscope.

eye-hand coordination: the working together of the eyes and hands in grasping or manipulating objects.

eye movements: the changes in the position of the eyes as a result of the action of the extrinsic eye muscles. See also CONVERGENCE; DIVERGENCE; FIXATION; OCULAR PURSUIT.

eye muscles: see EXTRINSIC EYE MUSCLES; INTRINSIC EYE MUSCLES.

eye span: see READING SPAN.

eye-voice span: the distance in letters by which the eye leads the voice in oral reading.

Eysenck Personality Inventory: for grades 9–16 and adults. An instrument designed to measure extraversion and neuroticism.

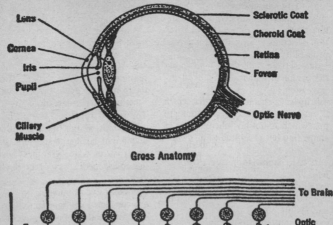

FIG. 13. *The human eye*.

F

fables test: a test in which the subject must interpret fables. Fable tests have been used as items on the Stanford-Binet intelligence scale and also as projective techniques.

fabulation: a falsehood; concocting and telling falsehoods as if they were true; fabrication.

face-to-face group: a group whose members are in such close proximity that direct interaction between them is possible.

face validity: the validity of a test as determined by an evaluation of the relevancy of the test to the variable being measured. Thus, a coordination test involving the manipulation of a stick and rudder bar has face validity as one of a battery of tests measuring aptitude for pilot training.

facial nerve: the seventh cranial nerve. It consists of an efferent component to muscles in the face and an afferent component mediating taste from the anterior two thirds of the tongue.

facial nucleus: a mass of cells in the pons that gives rise to the facial nerve.

facial vision: discernment of obstacles, most often by the blind, by means of tactile appreciation of air currents on the face.

facilitation: 1. increased ease of performance, as measured by efficiency. 2. increased ease of transmission across a synapse because of practice. 3. increased ease of transmission across a synapse due to summation effects. 4. a condition where the maintenance of one reflex, or of a voluntary response, increases the strength of another reflex. Grasping a hand dynamometer increases the strength of the knee jerk.

facilitator: a professional therapist or layman who serves as a leader for a group experience.

factor: 1. a cause of antecedent condition in bringing about a phenomenon. 2. one of the products of factor analysis, such as a verbal factor. 3. in genetics, a gene.

factor analysis: the process by means of which the smallest number of factors (products that can be multiplied together) that can account for a correlation matrix is found. Such factors

are presumed to represent intellectual traits if the correlations came from ability tests, as personality traits, if the correlations came from measures of personality. Thus, a number factor might be postulated that could account for the intercorrelations among tests of multiplication, division, subtraction, etc. A dominance factor might be postulated account for intercorrelations among tests of ascendance, dominance, etc.

factor axes: a set of coordinates that shows the relationship of factors to each other and to the correlations in the table or matrix. These axes are discovered by a process of rotation and represent the best solution for a given factorial study for discovering the minimal number of factors that can explain the matrix.

factor coefficient: see FACTOR LOADING.

factor configurations: in centroid factor analysis, the positions of the system of vectors or lines that represent the various tests in the correlation matrix. The angle of the vectors with respect to each other represents the correlation. A right angle is a zero correlation; the more acute the angle, the higher the correlation.

factorial design: an experimental series in which the effects of several experimental variables are assessed in turn. Thus, in an experiment on retroactive inhibition, the effect of length, temporal placement, and makeup of the interpolated material might be studied.

factorial invariance: the degree to which the patterning and loading of a set of factors remains unchanged when new tests are introduced into the correlation matrix and the analysis repeated.

factorial validity: the validity of a test as determined by correlating the test with a factor isolated by factor analysis.

factoring: carrying out a factor analysis.

factor loading: the degree to which a given factor is correlated with the various tests that make up the set of correlations on which a factor analysis has been carried out.

factor matrix: a table of factor loadings that is the end product of a factor analysis.

factor reflection: changing the algebraic signs among the factor loadings in order to maintain consistency among the factors in the matrix.

factor resolution: (*R. B. Cattell*) the outcome of a factor analysis when the positions and relationships for the test vectors have been coordinated with the factor axes. *Syn.* SIMPLE STRUCTURE.

factor rotation: the process of manipulating the axes in a centroid analysis so that they will pass through the maximum number of correlations.

factor structure: (*Thurstone*) the end product of a factor analysis when the position and interrelationships among the test vectors have been established. *Syn.* FACTOR RESOLUTION.

factor theory: an analysis of intellectual abilities or personality structure in terms of factors derived from the factor analysis of a group of tests. For further discussion of types of theory, see R. B. CATTELL; SPEARMAN; THURSTONE.

factor theories of learning: in general, theories that learning can be resolved into two or more fundamental processes or factors. For example, a number of authorities believe that conditioning represents one kind of learn-ing, and instrumental problem solving another fundamental type. The basic division appears to be an emphasis on a "mechanical" factor in conditioning as opposed to an "understanding" factor in other types of learning.

factor weight: see FACTOR LOADING.

faculty psychology: the discredited doctrine that mind is constituted of a number of powers or agencies, such as intellect, will, judgment, and attentiveness, which produce mental activities.

failure: 1. in an experiment, not obtaining the anticipated result. 2. an individual who has either not achieved a minimum economic status or who has failed to achieve his own goals. 3. one who has failed a test or a course of study.

faintness: 1. weakness in intensity. 2. a temporary condition bordering on loss of consciousness with dizziness, weakness, and sometimes nausea.

faith healing: alleviation of physical or mental disorders through the patient's belief in the power of divine intervention whether through direct prayer or the mediation of a healer.

fallacy: an error in reasoning or thinking that gives a conclusion that is seemingly true but actually false.

fallectomy: cutting of the Fallopian tubes as a means of preventing conception.

false negative: a case excluded by tests (or other criteria) but that is, in fact, qualified. Thus, a trade test, because of its imperfect validity, might exclude otherwise qualified people who make a low score on the trade test.

false positive: the inclusion of unqualified cases because of imperfection in the selecting criterion. Thus, an unqualified student may be admitted to college because of imperfect selective standards.

familial: pertaining to the family, occurring in all members of a family.

family: 1. a group of individuals related by marriage or blood, typically including a father, mother, and the children. 2. a group of persons living in a single household. 3. a group of closely related genera that constitutes a subdivision of an order. 4. a closely related group, such as a family of curves or languages.

family constellation: (*Adler*) the age, pattern, and functional relationships among members of the family. Adler considered the family constellation an important factor in the development of the style of life.

fantasm: a vivid representation of a form or person believed by the perceiver to be a disembodied spirit.

fantastic: pertaining to, or a product of, fantasy. 2. distorted, wild, unbelievable.

fantasy; phantasy: the process of imagining objects or events in terms of imagery. Fantasy takes the form of both day and night dreaming. In its normal range it serves both a creative and adjustive function.

fantasy formation: the process of daydreaming or creating fantasies.

far point: the point of greatest distance distinctly visible to the eye under conditions of relaxed accommodation.

farsightedness: inability to see near objects clearly. The most common cause is hyperopia, in which the light rays come to a focus behind the retina.

fasciculus: a bundle of nerve fibers that make up a tract in the spinal cord.

fasciculus cuneatus: with fasciculus gracilis, an important tract in the dorsal part of the spinal cord for the mediation of proprioception and possibly touch.

fasciculus gracilis: with fasciculus cuneatus, an important tract in the dorsal part of the spinal cord for the mediation of proprioception and possibly touch.

fast component: see NYSTAGMUS.

father complex: see ELECTRA COMPLEX.

father figure: a person who takes the place of a real father. Often used in reference to a person who is unrelated but with whom another person identifies. *Syn.* FATHER SURROGATE.

father fixation: an excessively strong, sometimes pathological, emotional attachment to the father.

father imago: the father figure.

father surrogate: one who takes the place of a father; one who is reacted to as if he were a father. *Syn.* FATHER FIGURE.

fatigue: 1. behaviorally, the decreased ability to do work. 2. a subjective feeling of tiredness after prolonged work or nervous tension. 3. impaired sensory or nervous activity following prolonged stimulation, such as occurs in retinal or auditory fatigue.

fear: 1. a strong emotional reaction involving subjective feelings of unpleasantness, agitation, and desire to flee or hide, and accompanied by widespread sympathetic activity. Fear is a reaction to a specific present danger; anxiety to an anticipated danger. Phobia is a persistent, irrational fear. The terms *fear, anxiety,* and *phobia* are loosely used as synonyms. 2. (*Kelly*) the reaction experienced when a new construct (*q.v.*) is about to enter the construct system.

feature profile test: a concrete performance test in which the testee must put blocks together to form a profile or head.

Fechner, Gustav: German physiologist, philosopher, psychologist (1801–1887). Fechner took his degree in medicine at Leipzig in 1822, but he conceived an interest in the physical sciences, and within a decade he had achieved prominence as a physicist. In his work with light, Fechner developed a side interest in sensation, which eventually resulted in the development of the science of psychophysics. In his *Elemente der Psychophysik*, published in 1860, he defined the new discipline as the exact science of the functional relations between mind and body. Fechner's definition reveals his deep philosophical concern with the problem of relating the mental to to the material, a subject on which he wrote a number of volumes. His most enduring work, however, appears to be the discovery of the psychophysical methods that remain as the most fundamental of the experimental methods in the study of the sensory processes and in attitude scaling.

Fechner's colors: subjective colors seen when a black and a white sector are rotated together on a color wheel. Rotation must not be too rapid or the stimuli will fuse into a neutral gray.

Fechner's law: a law formulating the relation between stimuli and sensations as $S = K \log R$, where S is a sensation, K a constant, and R is the stimulus (*Reiz* is the German for "stimulus"). *Syn.* WEBER-FECHNER LAW. See also WEBER'S LAW.

Fechner's paradox: the increase in brightness of a figure viewed binocularly when one eye is suddenly occluded.

feeblemindedness: an obsolete term for mental retardation (*q.v.*)

feedback: 1. in a machine or electronic system, a means of regulating input by linking it to output. Thus, a governor on a steam engine or a thermostat in a home regulates output by reacting negatively to increasing output. 2. in neurology, the afferent impulses from proprioceptive receptors that give rise to motor movements. Feedback from such receptors is believed to be important in aiming, grasping, and placing reactions. 3. more generally, any kind of return information from a source useful in regulating behavior.

feeding problem: a persistent difficulty in getting a child to eat adequate amounts of food. Such problems are common and are usually indicative of emotional stress.

feeling: 1. most generally any conscious state or experience. 2. specifically an affective, or emotional, state. 3. (*Titchener*) one of the elements of consciousness. The primary dimensions of feeling is pleasantness-unpleasantness. *Syn.* AFFECTIVE STATE. 4. the sense of touch. 5. an intuitive belief.

feeling tone: the affective component of experience; pleasantness-unpleasantness.

feeling type: (*Jung*) one who is dominated by affective states. See JUNG'S ANALYTICAL PSYCHOLOGY.

fellatio: sexual stimulation by introduction of the penis into the mouth.

felt need: a conscious need.

femininity: the generality of the characteristics peculiar to the female sex; the quality of, or the state of being, a female.

feminization: the process of becoming like a female.

fenestra ovalis: the membraneous oval window in the cochlea where the stapes articulates with the inner cochlea.

fenestra rotunda: the round window, a membraneous opening in the cochlea that serves as a pressure equalizer in response to pressures applied through the oval window.

fenestration: the process of making an artificial opening into the cochlea for the purpose of correcting conduction deafness.

feral child: child allegedly reared by animals.

Féré method: see GALVANIC SKIN RESPONSE.

Ferry-Porter law: the generalization that the critical flicker-fusion frequency increases as a function of the log brightness of the stimulus.

fertility: 1. capacity for bearing children. 2. creativity.

fertilization: the union of the egg and sperm.

fetishism: 1. the veneration of inanimate objects believed to have magical power. 2. a pathological condition in which sexual arousal and gratification is induced by handling objects or nonsexual parts of the body belonging to a member of the opposite sex. Fetishes are typically articles of clothing (stockings, lingerie, etc.), handkerchiefs, the hair, or the feet.

fetus: the late embryo; after the sixth week.

F factor: (*R. B. Cattell*) the personality dimension of surgency-desurgency; cheerful, social, energetic versus depressed, seclusive, subdued, dull.

FSH: see FOLLICLE STIMULATING HORMONE.

fiber: 1. a single neuron. 2. the axon or dendrite of a neuron.

fibril: a thread or filament that runs through the cell body of the neuron and outward through the peripheral processes.

fiction: 1. an imaginary construct taken as true for the sake of argument. 2. a paradoxical self-contradictory construct or concept in thinking that is useful, such as the $\sqrt{-1}$. 3. (*Adler*) a complex determining the individual's style of life. The overall guiding fiction functions to lead the person from a state of persistent feelings of inferiority to a state of feelings of superiority and mastery.

fiducial limits: the limits on either side of the mean (or other measure of central tendency) beyond which a statistic is not expected to occur except by chance a stated percentage of the time. The fiducial limits express in standard deviation units how far on either side of the mean the statistic may fall and still be within a given level of reliability.

field: 1. the psychological representation in consciousness or perception of a physical situation. 2. the complex of social, personal, and physical forces within which an individual functions.

field cognition mode: (*Tolman*) a combination of perceiving, thinking, and remembering that gives rise to a specific manner in which an organism knows the environment.

field dependent: characterizing an individual who has difficulty in ignoring factors in a perceptual field that are irrelevant to a task. *Contr.* FIELD INDEPENDENT.

field force: (*Lewin*) energy manifestations on the part of the individual that are considered in relation to the entire field. See also FIELD THEORY.

field independent: characterizing an individual who can ignore factors in a perceptual field that are irrelevant to a task. *Contr.* FIELD DEPENDENT.

field of attention: that to which the individual is attending at any given time.

field of consciousness: the totality of which the individual is aware. *Syns.* PHENOMENAL FIELD; field of awareness.

field of regard: all of the external world that can be seen by the moving eye.

fields of psychology: divisions or branches of psychology in which psychologists specialize. There are eight main fields of psychology: *Abnormal psychology* is concerned with mental disorders, their causes, treatment, and prevention. *Child* (or *developmental*) *psychology* specializes in the development of children and of immature animals; the child psychologist is particularly interested in discovering the principles that govern changes in the behavior of immature forms as they develop. *Comparative psychology* and *physiological psychology* are two closely related specialties; the comparative psychologist studies animals, striving to discover principles of behavior that apply to all animals, including man, and the physiological psychologist is interested in the relationship between behavior and the nervous system and endocrine glands. *Clinical psychology* is concerned with the diagnosis, treatment, and prevention of adjustmental problems. *Educational psychology* applies the principles of psychology to educational problems. *General experimental psychology* is concerned with the establishment of general laws of behavior. *Industrial psychology* applies the principles of psychology to industrial and military problems.

field structure: 1. the patterning of relations among the various parts of the psychological field. 2. the hierarchy of parts that lends rigidity and stability to the psychological field.

field theory: a systematic point of view in psychology developed by Kurt Lewin (*q.v.*), an associate of Wertheimer and Köhler at the University of Berlin. Lewin was completely dissatisfied with traditional associational and structuralistic psychology and became attracted to the Gestalt point of view. However, he found the strong interests of Wertheimer and Koffka in perceptual theory, and Köhler's interests in brain theory, insufficient to develop a system that would take into account motivational factors in behavior. Field theory can, therefore, be considered a close relative of Gestalt psychology, but a system in which motivational and social factors are considered of paramount importance.

The psychological field is the individual's life space, or the space containing the individual and his environment. Psychologically, the environment is the environment only as perceived by the individual in relation to his needs, goals, and purposes. His perception is therefore highly selective. Some objects and persons will be ignored, some considered of little importance, and others of great importance. If an object is of importance to the individual it will have positive valence, that is, it will be attractive; if it has negative valence, the object is one that the individual will avoid if possible.

The individual is shown in the life space as directed toward or away from objects by means of vectors, or directed lines. A vector tends to produce movement toward or away from objects or persons, but it is sometimes impeded by a barrier, particularly in conflict situations.

Lewin used the rudiments of topology for mapping the life space—showing the individual, his goals, and the routes to the goal. Vector analysis was brought into the system in order to represent needs, motives, tensions, or, in general, motivational states. Lewin's use of the mathematics of topology and vector analysis has been controversial. However, his work and that of his associates on such problems as level of aspiration, regressive behavior at barriers, democratic versus authoritarian atmospheres, conflict, and the tensions associated with interrupted tasks, have proved challenging to psychologists of every theoretical point of view.

figural aftereffect: a perceptual phenomenon illustrating the principle that there is a tendency to maintain stability in the figure-ground relationship. An inspection figure is fixated and then the gaze is shifted to a test figure. The test figure will be distorted, due to the aftereffect of the inspection figure.

figural cohesion: the tendency for all parts of a figure to maintain mutual attractiveness and to "hang together" perceptually. Thus, a disjointed picture or cartoon is perceived as a recognizable whole despite the fact that it is no more than a collection of broken lines.

figural openness: in Gestalt psychology, a condition in which the area of a configuration is not enclosed with a figure. Thus in a swastika, the area between the arms is "open," while the area within the boundaries of the arms is "closed."

figure: a unitary perceptual experience that occupies the center of atten-

tion and is characterized by having good contour, depth, and solidity.

figure-ground: the principle that perceptions are fundamentally patterned into two aspects: (a) the figure, which stands out, has good contour, and gives the appearance of solidity or three-dimensionality; and (b) the ground, which is indistinct and whose parts are not clearly shaped or patterned.

filial regression, law of: the principle that the characteristics of the members or filial generations tend to revert toward the mean. Sons of very tall fathers are not so tall as their fathers; very short fathers, on the other hand, tend to have sons who are taller.

film color: a texture-free soft color difficult to localize, such as might be seen when looking through colored glass.

filter: 1. a lens or slide that transmits only specified and relatively homogenous wavelengths. 2. a capacitor or choke circuit, or combination of both, that smooths out the flow of current. 3. any device or procedure that screens out or selects information.

final: 1. last in a series of terms or trials. 2. telic; purposive.

final common path: the bundle of motor neurons upon which all the influences from higher centers impinge. The lower motor neurons serving the arms and legs are final common paths for cortical, subcortical, and cerebellar influences.

finalism: 1. the doctrine that behavior has purpose. 2. teleology, or the assumption that behavior should be interpreted in terms of its goals.

finger painting: a form of projective test in which the subject is allowed to spread pigments or cold cream with the fingers. The results are believed to be expressive of personality.

firing: the triggering of a nervous impulse by a receptor or mechanical stimulus.

first-order correlation coefficient: a partial correlation in which the influence of only a single variable has been held constant. See PARTIAL CORRELATION.

first-order factor: a factor derived from a table of intercorrelations. *Contr.* SECOND-ORDER FACTOR.

Fisher's test: a test for determining the significance of an obtained correlation coefficient for a given size of sample. Coefficients that do not meet the test may have arisen by chance and are not considered significant.

fission: reproduction in which the adult splits into two parts, each of which becomes a mature cell; characteristic of unicellular animals.

fissure: any of the deep grooves on the surface of the brain. The more shallow grooves are called *sulci*.

fistula: an opening, either natural or artificial, into an internal organ. Esophageal and gastric fistulas have been used in the study of hunger and thirst.

fit: 1. a seizure, such as an epileptic seizure. 2. in statistics, the conformity of obtained data to a predetermined standard. 3. adjustment of data to conform to a standard.

fixation: 1. a persistent mode of behavior that has outlived its usefulness or has become inappropriate. 2. the strengthening of a learned habit. 3. a strong and relatively enduring emotional attachment for another person.

fixation pause: the brief periods during which the eyeball is not moving. It is during these periods that seeing takes place in reading. See also READING SPAN.

fixation point: the point on the fovea, at the end of the line of regard, where an object comes to a focus.

fixation of affect: (*Psychoan.*) a developmental abnormality in which the individual retains an attachment for feelings more appropriate to an earlier phase of development.

fixed alternative: in a test or questionnaire, one of several limited alternatives among which the subject must choose. *Contr.* OPEN-ENDED QUESTION.

fixed idea: a strongly held and usually irrational idea. Fixed ideas are typical of obsessive neuroses and paranoiac states.

fixed-interval reinforcement: a type of intermittent reinforcement in which the animal is given reinforcement, such as a pellet of food, at specific intervals.

fixedness; functional fixedness: a lack of flexibility in problem solving. Fixedness is illustrated when the individual finds it difficult to change sets or to utilize objects in new ways in pursuit of solutions.

fixed-radio reinforcements: a type of intermittent reinforcement in which the animal is given the reinforcement after making a certain number of responses. Thus, an animal might be given a pellet of food after ten bar presses.

fixed role therapy: (*Kelly*) a system of therapy in which the therapist develops a script or role for the individual to act out for purpose of discovering and utilizing more effective ways of perceiving and interpreting events and situations.

flaccid: soft, without tone, as in flaccid paralysis in lower motor neuron disorders in which the muscles atrophy.

flagellation: the practice of submitting to whipping, whether for penitential purposes or to arouse sexual feelings.

flagellomania: sexual excitement aroused by whipping.

Flanagan Aptitude Classification Tests: Nineteen tests oriented toward vocational guidance for grades 12–16 and above.

flattening of affect *or* **emotion:** in pathological states, the absence of appropriate emotional responses, as when the schizophrenic smiles upon being informed that his house has burned.

flavor: a combined experience from the olfactory, gustatory, and cutaneous senses.

Flesch index: an index of the reading difficulty of a passage.

flexibilitas cerea: waxy flexibility observed in pathological states, particularly in catatonia. The limbs can be molded, and the imposed posture will be retained for long periods.

flexible: 1. characterizing a person who is readily adaptable. 2. charateristic of one who is able to change a set or line of thinking readily.

flexion: the bending of a limb.

flexor: a muscle that bends a limb.

flicker: a relatively rapid alteration in visual perception induced by a corresponding change in the stimulus. Flicker is typically measured in terms of a threshold called the critical flicker-fusion frequency, a point at which a flickering stimulus fuses into a continuous one.

flight from reality: 1. a type of adjustment in which imaginary satisfactions are substituted for real satisfactions. 2. a retreat into psychotic behavior in order to escape the problems of living.

flight of colors: The afterimage of white or the succession of colors that occurs as a response to the prolonged fixation of white.

flight of ideas: a rapid succession of unrelated thoughts; disconnectedness in ideas as expressed in verbal speech.

floating affect or **feeling:** (*Psychoan.*) a feeling or emotion set free from its original object, such as occurs in free-floating anxiety.

flooding: a therapeutic technique in which the individual is made to confront the situation he fears until his anxiety is extinguished.

flower spray ending: stretch receptors located in skeletal muscles.

flowery: a class of odors represented by the odor of flowers.

fluctuation: 1. oscillation; a cyclic change in a function due to chance factors. 2. changes or variations in a species. 3. changes in the value of statistical constants taken from successive samples.

fluctuation of attention: periodic changes in sensory clearness under conditions of constant stimulation.

fluency: the ability to think of words and word associations rapidly. Word fluency is measured by such tests as the number of words a subject can make out of *Washington* in a given span of time.

fluid intelligence: (*R. B. Cattell*) the ability to grasp relationships in novel situations quickly and to make correct deductions from them. Relatively culture-free. *Contr.* CRYSTALLIZED INTELLIGENCE.

F-minus-K index: an index of the degree to which a subject's score on the Minnesota Multiphasic Inventory of Personality is an attempt to fake or obtain a socially desirable score.

focal: pertaining to the point at which rays of light come to a focus.

focal epilepsy: Jacksonian epilepsy, in which there is no loss of consciousness and the convulsions affect only a limited area of the body or an individual limb. Focal epilepsy is caused by local irritation in the motor region of the cerebral cortex.

focal length: the specified distance from a given lens to the point at which it brings parallel rays of light to a focus.

focus: 1. (*noun*) a point at which rays of light are made to converge by a lens. 2. (*verb*) to adjust an optical system so as to bring rays of light to a point of convergence. 3. (*verb*) to center one's attention on a stimulus.

focus of attention: the clearest or most vivid portion of an experience.

focus of convenience: (*Kelly*) events or situations best interpreted by a construct or construct system (*q.q.v.*). See also RANGE OF CONVENIENCE.

foliate papilla: a leaflike type of papilla found along the sides and back of the tongue. See also PAPILLA.

folie à deux: the occurrence of psychosis in two persons who are closely associated, such as husband and wife.

folie à trois: psychosis or a delusion suffered by three; an extension of FOLIE À DEUX.

folium: a fold or convolution of the cerebellum.

folklore: the traditions, customs, legends, songs, etc., that have survived in a culture from the past.

folk psychology: the social psychology of nonliterate peoples.

folkways: traditional patterns of behavior in a given culture or social group.

follicle stimulating hormone (FSH): one of the tropic hormones released by the anterior pituitary gland. It controls the maturation of eggs in the ovary and sperm in the testes.

following reaction: a species-specific (instinctive) form of behavior that is the tendency of the young to follow the mother after imprinting has occurred.

fontanel: the soft, unossified area in the center of the skull of an infant.

foot anesthesia: see GLOVE ANESTHESIA; STOCKING ANESTHESIA.

foot candle: a unit of illumination defined as the illumination produced on a surface by a standard candle that is one foot away.

foot-in-the-door technique: inducing compliance for a larger commitment by first obtaining compliance for a small commitment.

foot-lambert: a unit of luminance or brightness defined as the luminance reflected by a perfectly diffusing and reflecting surface whose brightness is one foot candle everywhere.

footrule correlation: a coefficient of correlation based on gains in rank from the first to the second variable. The formula is:

$$R = 1 - \frac{6 \times \Sigma g}{N^2 - 1}$$

where *g* is a gain by an individual from rank 1 to rank 2.

foramen magnum: the opening in the occipital bone through which the spinal cord passes.

forced-choice technique: on rating scales or personality questionnaires, the use of alternatives neither of which seems acceptable but one of which must be chosen. For example, the subject might be asked to choose whether he is more noisy or more lazy. Even though he may feel that neither alternative applies, he must nevertheless choose the least objectionable or the one that fits best. The forced-choice technique is frequently utilized in order to equate the social desirability of items.

forced fantasy: (*Psychoan.*) an emotionally charged fantasy that has been deliberately stimulated by the analyst.

forced movement: a tropism, or orienting response, to an external stimulus.

forced vibration: see RESONANCE.

forebrain: the anterior portion of the embryonic brain that divides into the telencephalon and diencephalon. The telencephalon becomes the olfactory bulbs, the cerebral hemispheres, and the corpus striatum. The diencephalon becomes the thalamus and hypothalamus.

forecasting efficiency, index of: a measure of the degree to which predictions may be made from one correlated variable to another. *Abbr.* E. The formula is:

$$E = 1 - \sqrt{1 - r^2}.$$

foreconscious: see PRECONSCIOUS.

forencis: pertaining to the courts. Thus, *forensic psychology* treats of the psychology of the law, of courts, and legal procedures, particularly of the nature of evidence and its reliability.

foreperiod: the initial period in any experiment, particularly the interval between a ready signal and the presentation of a stimulus.

foreplay: mutual sexual stimulation by two individuals as a prelude to sexual intercourse.

forepleasure: (*Psychoan.*) the sexual pleasure aroused by stimulation of an

erogenous zone preparatory to intercourse. *Contr.* END PLEASURE.

foreshortening: 1. the apparent shortening in the length of a line regarded lengthwise. 2. the perceptual effect of shortening in a painting or photograph.

foresight: the ability to think ahead, to imagine events as they probably will occur.

forgetting: loss of ability to recall, recollect, or reproduce what has been previously learned. Various theories of forgetting emphasize different possible causes of the process. The retroaction and proaction hypotheses assume that learning that comes either before or after the test sample causes interference with the retention of that sample. The Gestalt psychologists have emphasized the modification of the memory trace with the passage of time according to the principles of reorganization into good Gestalts, just as original perceptions tend toward good Gestalts. The psychoanalytic school emphasizes motivated forgetting. Any complete theory of forgetting must take into account all of these factors. For further discussion of these factors see RETENTION.

form: 1. the shape or outline of an object. 2. the spatial arrangement of parts into a unitary whole. *Syn.* SHAPE, CONFIGURATION, GESTALT. See also GESTALT PSYCHOLOGY.

formal discipline: the now discredited doctrine that certain subjects should be studied not for their own sake but for the purpose of strengthening the mind. Mathematics and the classics were recommended for this purpose.

formal exercise: 1. drill based on the assumption that exercise is valuable for strengthening the mental processes involved. 2. drill without interest on the part of the learner.

formal operational stage: (*Piaget*) the stage of thought beginning about age 12. It is a period characterized by logical thinking, abstract thinking, and conceptualization. See also CONCRETE OPERATIONAL STAGE; PREOPERATIONAL STAGE; SENSORIMOTOR STAGE.

formant: 1. the timbre, or quality, that makes one vowel sound different from another. 2. concentrations of speech sounds that appear as dark bands or smudges on a sound spectrogram.

form board: any of a class of tests that utilize removable geometric forms to be fitted into place as quickly as possible. Many of the shapes are similar and may require putting together several in order to complete a single missing shape.

form determinant: (*Rorschach*) the form or shape the subject perceives in an inkblot and that determines his response.

formication: a vague, diffuse sensation as of ants crawling on the surface of the body.

formula: 1. in statistics or mathematics, a symbolic statement of a set of operations or relations. 2. a set of rules, laws, or principles.

fornix: a bundle of nerve fibers in the brain that form a tract between the thalamus and hippocampus.

forward association: in verbal learning, the connection of a given item in a series with a subsequent item. *Contr.* BACKWARD ASSOCIATION.

foster: pertaining to persons who either provide or receive care although not related to each other by blood or marriage, such as foster parents or foster children.

foster-child fantasy: the mistaken belief among children that one's parents are foster parents instead of true parents.

fourfold table: a statistical table having two sets of columns and rows.

Fourier's law: the mathematical principle that any complex wave, such as a sound wave or a light wave, may be analyzed into simple sine waves.

fovea; fovea centralis: the small depression in the center of the retina that is the area of fixation and the center of clearest vision.

foveal vision: seeing with the fovea. *Contr.* PERIPHERAL VISION.

fractional antedating goal response: a reaction that occurs progressively earlier in conditioning a series of responses and thus may come to serve as a conditioned stimulus for subsequent responses. *Abbr.* r_G.

frame of reference: 1. a standard or attitude against which actions or results are judged. Thus, a *classical frame of reference* would ensure the acceptability of classical art or music but the rejection of modern forms. 2. a perceptual schema that influences perceived meaning. Thus, in autokinetic movement, placing additional lights around the stimulus light will retard or stop the movement.

fraternal twins: twins that develop from two eggs fertilized at the same time. From the point of view of heredity they are no more alike than ordinary sibling combinations. *Contr.* IDENTICAL TWINS.

F ratio: in statistics, an index used to determine whether the differences between two variances (σ^2) is statistically significant. The F ratio is found by dividing the larger variance by the smaller

$$\frac{\sigma_1^2}{\sigma_2^2}$$

and looking up the result in a table of significance.

free association: 1. (*Psychoan.*) the reporting of whatever comes to the mind of the person being analyzed, regardless of how painful, embarrassing, or irrelevant it might seem. 2. a condition in a word-association test where no restrictions are put on the nature of the subject's response.

free-association test: a test in which the subject is asked to speak a word as rapidly as possible in response to a stimulus and response and the nature of the words given are taken into consideration in evaluating the results.

free-floating anxiety: pervasive and chronic anxiety not attached to specific objects or situations.

free nerve ending: an unencapsulated afferent nerve ending found in the skin and believed to be associated with pain and possibly with temperature sensitivity.

free play: play that is not directed by a supervisor.

free-will doctrine: the philosophical and religious position that behavior is ultimately directed by volition regardless of external influences. *Contr.* DETERMINISM.

frequency: 1. the number of cycles per second of a sound wave. 2. The number of times a score or phenomenon occurs. In statistical work there are a number of techniques for representing frequency numerically or graphically; among the most common are: (a) the frequency distribution, which shows the number of cases falling within a given class interval or range of scores; (b) the frequency polygon, which is a graphic outline of the frequency distribution made by connecting the plots of the midpoints of the class intervals; (c) the histogram,

which represents the frequency of scores within each class interval and is constructed by erecting rectangles whose height is proportional to the frequencies.

frequency curve: a curve that connects the midpoints of a frequency distribution and whose height is proportional to the frequency of cases.

frequency diagram: see FREQUENCY 2.

frequency distribution: see FREQUENCY 2.

frequency graph: see FREQUENCY 2.

frequency, law of: the principle that, other things being equal, the more an act or association is practiced, the more rapid the learning. See also EXERCISE, LAW OF.

frequency polygon: a figure constructed by erecting ordinates from the midpoints of the class intervals of a frequency distribution and connecting these with either continuous or rectilinear lines. See illustration.

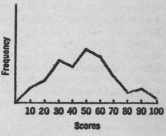

FIG. 14. *A frequency polygon.*

frequency table: a statistical tally of the number of times a score or event occurs.

frequency theory of hearing: see HEARING, THEORIES OF.

Freud, Sigmund: Viennese neurologist, founder of psychoanalysis (1856–

1939). Freud took his medical degree at the University of Vienna in 1881 and planned a specialist's career in neurology. Lack of means forced him to abandon his research interests for a clinical career. His interest in what was to become psychoanalysis developed during his collaboration with Josef Breuer in 1884, which resulted in *Studies in Hysteria*. *The Interpretation of Dreams* appeared in 1900, *Three Contributions to the Theory of Sex* in 1905, and the *General Introduction to Psychoanalysis* in 1916—a book that contained the evolving theory of the libido and the unconscious. In subsequent years Freud's outlook became increasingly broad as revealed by the titles of his later works: *Beyond the Pleasure Principle* (1920), *The Future of an Illusion* (1928), and *Civilization and Its Discontents* (1930). As early as 1906 Freud had also interested himself in founding an organization to promote the diffusion of psychoanalytic knowledge. Men who were to become famous in their own right joined with him—Adler, Brill, Ferenczi, Jones, Jung, and Stekel. By 1908 the first International Congress of Psychoanalysis had convened, and by 1910 there were branches in all important countries in the world. In 1938, when the Nazis entered Austria, Freud was forced to flee to England, where he died of cancer of the mouth on September 23, 1939. He left his influence on every department of thought. See also PSYCHOANALYSIS.

Freudianism; Freudism: the psychoanalytic doctrine as originally propounded by Sigmund Freud.

Freudian slip: an error in speaking or writing that unintentionally reveals the speaker's or writer's true meaning.

Freud gives the example of a Vienna newspaper that once referred to an unpopular member of the royal family as the "Clown Prince."

frigidity: in women, the inability to experience sexual desire or to experience orgasm during intercourse.

fringe of consciousness: see MARGINAL CONSCIOUSNESS.

Froelich's syndrome: a pathological condition characterized by metabolic disturbances, poor skeletal development, obesity, and infantilism in appearance and behavior. The condition is due to a lack of the anterior pituitary factor. *Syn.* adiposogenital dystrophy.

frontal: pertaining to the anterior part of the body or brain.

frontal lobe: the portion of the cerebral hemisphere anterior to the central fissure.

frottage: a sexual perversion in which orgasm is achieved by rubbing against the clothing of a member of the opposite sex in a crowd.

fruity: a category of odors typified by the fruits.

frustration: 1. blockage or thwarting of goal-directed behavior. 2. an unpleasant state of tension, anxiety, and heightened sympathetic activity resulting from blockage or thwarting.

frustration-aggression hypothesis: the assumption that frustration always leads to some kind of aggressive reaction whether explicit or implicit.

frustration response: (*R. B. Cattell*) a factorial personality trait showing at its positive pole anger, depression, and attempts at control.

frustration tolerance: the ability to suffer being thwarted without undue psychological harm.

F scale (Fascism scale): a scale designed to measure readiness to accept antidemocratic ideologies.

F score: a score on the Minnesota Multiphasic Inventory of Personality that indicates whether or not the subject has followed the directions.

F test: a test of variance between two samples to determine whether the difference could be due to chance.

fugue: an amnesiac flight. The individual leaves home, changes his mode of living, and in some cases his occupation. There is complete amnesia for the flight.

Fullerton-Cattell law: the generalization that the error of observation and j.n.d.'s are proportional to the square root of the magnitude of the stimulus. It is proposed as a substitute for Weber's law.

full organism: the point of view that the organism is, in part, self-determining and not a passive respondent to external stimulation. *Contr.* EMPTY ORGANISM.

function: 1. in statistics, a quantity that varies in some way with another quantity. 2. the activity of an organ or organism, such as the transmission function of a neuron. *Contr.* STRUCTURE. 3. a behavioral act or activity. *Contr.* conscious content. 4. the purpose or end product of an organ. The function of the thyroid gland is the production of thyroxin. 5. a heading or category for activities. For example, the functions of the cortex are learning, sensory processes, intelligence, etc.

functional: pertaining to functions, particularly to functions as psychological or physiological activities.

functional autonomy principle: (*Allport*) the generalization that motives tend to become independent of their origins. For example, a child may reluctantly practice the piano because of fear of parental reprisal. Later, when he becomes an accomplished musician, he plays for the satisfaction it provides and not to escape from fear.

functional deafness: deafness caused by malfunctioning of the auditory mechanism, without any structural defect in the ear.

functional defect: a deficiency or pathological condition for which no organic basis has been discovered or for which it has been definitely established that there is no organic basis. The functional disorders are illustrated by the neuroses. There is no known organic disease in the neurotic. His symptoms are believed to be the result of his failure to adjust. However, the absence of known organic pathology is not final proof that subtle organic factors may not be involved. For decades schizophrenia was classified as a functional psychosis, in contrast to general paresis and alcoholic psychosis, which are both organic disorders. However, there is increasing evidence that schizophrenia may be hereditary or may involve hormonal factors. If this proves to be the case, the disorder will have to be reclassified. See also PSYCHOSOMATIC DISORDER.

functional fixedness: a tendency on the part of the individual toward inflexibility in problem solving, with the result that objects used one way are not perceived as usable another way.

functionalism: a school of psychology that emphasized mental acts or processes as the proper subject matter for psychology, as opposed to structural psychologies, which emphasized conscious contents. The functional point of view held that mind should be studied in terms of its usefulness to the organism in adapting to its environment. It emphasized the study of mind from the "is for" point of view rather than from the "is" point of view.

Functionalism as a school in Europe was less well developed than in the United States. However, in Germany and Austria, the act psychologists led by Franz Brentano were precursors of functionalism in their opposition to Wundt's structuralism. In the United States, William James (*q.v.*) took a strongly functionalistic stand in criticizing the aims, methods, and findings of the structuralists. John Dewey (*q.v.*) adopted James's point of view and in developing his system of psychology became the official founder of functionalism as a definite movement in American psychology. In an article on the reflex are published in 1896, Dewey announced that the study of the organism was the proper subject matter for psychology.

Functionalism became a formal school of psychology at the University of Chicago under James Rowland Angell (*q.v.*) and Harvey Carr (*q.v.*). Angell and Carr both prepared textbooks setting forth their basic premises for the new functionalism and attempted to relate their experimental findings in learning, perception, thinking, emotion, and so forth, to their theoretical point of view. Functionalism proved to be a popular system of psychology in America and eventually came to overshadow the once dominant structuralism. American psychologists and students of psychology were attracted to the strongly pragmatic and practical flavor of functionalism. In fact, the school was so successful, it was absorbed into the mainstream of American psychology and disappeared as a separate school. Today American psychology is strongly functionalistic in spirit, although its methodology is behavioristic. See also PROBABLISTIC FUNCTIONALISM.

functionalistic: characterized by emphasis on functionalism as a point of view.

functional pain: pain for which there is no organic cause.

functional pleasure: the exercise of a trait or ability for the pleasure involved. See also FUNCTIONAL AUTONOMY; SELF-ACTUALIZATION.

functional psychology: see FUNCTIONALISM.

functional psychosis: psychosis for which no known organic basis has been discovered. Schizophrenia, paranoia, and the manic-depressive reactions have traditionally been defined as functional. According to this point of view, they are extreme forms of maladjustment.

functional relation: a dependency between two variables so that a change in one is accompanied by a change in the other.

functional unity: the operation of different traits or process in such a manner as to produce an integrated whole. The factor analysts assume that various surface traits are related to factorially identifiable source traits of which they are functional parts.

function engram: (*Jung*) an inherited imprint upon the nervous system that gives archetypal symbols their meaning.

function types: (*Jung*) the generic terms for Jung's various types: thinking, feeling, sensing, and intuitive. The attitude types (extraversion-introversion) may be combined with function types.

fundamental color: hues that are assumed to be more important or basic for any given theory of color vision. For example, in the Helmholtz theory, the fundamental colors are red, green, and blue—the physical primaries.

fundamental-response processes: the hypothetical retinal processes presumed to underlie color fundamentals.

fundamental skill: a skill needed before further progress can be attained in a given area.

fundamental tone: the basic or lowest tone in a compound tone.

furor epileptica: see EPILEPTIC FUROR.

fusion: a union into a whole; a complete blending, such as color fusion, in which the components are no longer distinguishable.

future shock: the disorientation and anxiety consequent upon rapid social and technological changes.

G

GABA: see GAMMA-AMINOBYTURIC ACID.

gain: an increment, such as an increment of learning.

Galton bar: an instrument for determining the just-noticeable difference for visual distance.

galvanic nystagmus: nystagmus induced by passing an electric current through the labyrinthine region.

galvanic skin response: changes in the electrical resistance of the skin as detected by a sensitive galvanometer. *Abbr.* GSR. In measuring the response, a weak electric current may be impressed on the skin and the resistance of the skin to that current may be measured (Féré phenomenon), or the weak current generated by the body may be measured on the surface of the skin (Tarchanoff phenomenon). In either case, what is probably being measured is the electrical activity associated with vascular changes in the arterioles and veinules. The GSR has been correlated with emotional states, strain, and tension, but in no clear-cut manner; it is best thought of as an index of the level of activation. *Syns.* ELECTRODERMAL RESPONSE; PSYCHOGALVANIC RESPONSE (PGR); and PSYCHOGALVANIC REFLEX.

galvanometer: an instrument for measuring the strength of an electric current. Measurements are made in amperes and milliamperes.

galvanotropism: an orienting movement of the body toward an electric current.

gamete: a sex cell that, combined with another sex cell, forms the zygote or the beginning of a new individual.

game theory: the utilization of the structure of games, such as chess, to better understand action in conflict situations wherein the opponents seek maximal gain and minimal personal loss.

gamma (γ): in psychophysical measurements, the distance of a stimulus from the threshold.

gamma-aminobyturic acid: an inhibitory neurotransmitter of the central nervous system.

gamma efferent: small motor neurons, particularly those innervating the muscle spindles.

gamma movement: see APPARENT MOVEMENT.

gang: social unit consisting of individuals whose common interests bind them together. Gangs may be composed of people of any age, but are very common among children. Frequently, but not necessarily, gangs are antisocial in outlook and activities.

ganglion: 1. a group of nerve cells whose cell bodies are located outside the brain or spinal cord. 2. a cluster of cell bodies in the subcortical regions of the brain.

Ganser syndrome: a hysterical reaction in which the patient fails to answer questions correctly, however simple they may be and regardless of the fact that they are understood. It is accompanied by bizarre beliefs, paralyses, and hallucinations. Often observed among prisoners who hope to be treated leniently. *Syn.* nonsense syndrome.

Ganzfeld: a homogeneous visual field.

gargalesthesis: the sensation of tickle.

gating: the inhibition of one sensory channel by another. Gating occurs during attention, when there is a selective focusing of the sensory apparatus.

gatophobia: fear of cats. *Syn.* AILUROPHOBIA; galephobia.

Gaussian or **Gauss's curve:** see NORMAL PROBABILITY CURVE.

gay: a colloquialism referring to homosexuals.

gender: sex—male or female.

gender identity: one's sense of being male or female.

gender role: the set of behaviors that a given culture expects of each sex.

gene: any of the hypothetical particles living along the chromosomes which are believed to be the elementary units of heredity. See also DEOXYRIBONUCLEIC ACID; RIBONUCLEIC ACID.

gene pair: the combination of genes from the parents that determines a specific hereditary trait. Members of pairs that determine traits in the same way are homozygous; if the members exert opposite effects, they are said to be heterozygous.

general ability: 1. an ability that is common to all intellectual tasks and is measured to some degree by all cognitive tests. *Abbr.* G or g. Fundamentally, G is the ability to perceive relations and educe correlates. *Contr.* SPECIFIC ABILITY. 2. general intelligence.

general-ability test: a general-intelligence test.

general adaptation syndrome: see ADAPTATION SYNDROME.

general aptitude: 1. capacity or potentiality to achieve proficiency in a variety of subjects or skills. 2. intelligence.

General Aptitude Test Battery: a test developed by the United States Employment Service for use by their counselors. The battery consists of verbal-aptitude, numerical-aptitude, spatial-aptitude, form-perception, clerical-perception, motor-coordination, and manual-dexterity tests.

general factor: a factor common to all tests and, by extension, to all intellectual tasks. (*Abbr.* G). Charles Spearman believed that the G factor represents the general ability to perceive relationships and to educe correlates from them. *Contr.* SPECIFIC FACTOR.

general image: an image that the subject considers to represent any one of a class of objects.

general intelligence: see INTELLIGENCE.

generalization: 1. the process of forming an idea or judgment applicable to an entire class of objects, people, or events. 2. the process of applying a general idea to new data. 3. A broad principle or law in science.

generalization gradient: the principle that a stimulus similar to the original stimulus evoking a response will also evoke a response but that the latter will be weaker than the former. The more alike the stimuli, the more effective the generalized stimulus in evoking the response and the less steep the gradient. The same gradients are found in response generalization. That is, responses similar to original responses will be evoked in proportion to how similar they are to the original response.

generalized: pertaining to objects, symbols, principles, etc., formulated in such a manner that they have wide applicability.

generalized inhibitory potential: (*Hull*) conditioned inhibition resulting from stimulus generalization.

general paresis: see PARESIS.

General Problem Solver: a computer program capable of solving a variety of problems by setting up subgoals and testing the validity of solutions to these subgoals eventually to discover the final solution.

general psychology: 1. the broad branch of psychology that seeks to discover the laws and principles that apply to persons in general, as opposed to differential psychology, which seeks to discover the ways in which people differ. 2. the broad synthesis of all findings and theories

in the field as typified by an introductory textbook or course.

general semantics: the study of human responses to signs and symbols.

generation: 1. the act of creating. 2. the average interval between stages in descent, conventionally given as 33 years for the human being.

generator potential: voltage change that occurs in a receptor cell upon stimulation. Generator potentials trigger nervous impulses in sensory neurons connecting receptors to the central nervous system.

generic: 1. pertaining to a biological genus. 2. having wide application in the sense of applying to all members of a class.

genetic: pertaining to the origin and development of an organism or an entire species.

genetic code: the sequence of molecules in deoxyribonucleic acid that carries the genetic information determining the appearance of genetically determined traits.

geneticism: the point of view that behavior is inborn. The doctrine of instincts and the Freudian stages of psychosexual development illustrate geneticism.

genetic method: explanation or understanding of behavior in terms of its hereditary origins and developmental history.

genetic psychology: developmental psychology; that branch of psychology that studies behavior by the genetic method.

genetics: the branch of biology concerned with heredity and its relation to evolutionary theory.

genetic sequence: the order in which structures or functions appear during development.

genetic theory or viewpoint: the point

of view that present behavior is to be understood in terms of its hereditary origins and developmental histories.

geniculate bodies: paired, oval-shaped masses, to the rear of the thalamus. The lateral geniculate bodies are important synaptic stations for the optic neurons on their way to the occipital cortex.

genital: pertaining to the reproductive organs or to the sensations arising from those organs.

genital character: (*Psychoan.*) the adult stage of psychosexual development representing a fusion or synthesis of the earlier stages of oral, anal, and urethral eroticism.

genital eroticism: 1. obtaining sexual excitement and pleasure from the stimulation of the genital organs. 2. (*Psychoan.*) one of the three stages of eroticism: oral, anal, and genital.

genital stage: see PHALLIC STAGE.

genital primary stage: (*Psychoan.*) the final stage of psychosexual organization wherein emphasis is on the act of intercourse and the pleasure-giving possibilities of the genital organs.

genitals: the sexual organs or external organs of reproduction.

genital sensations: sexual sensations arising from the genital organs.

genital zones: the external genitals and the immediately adjacent structures capable of giving genital sensations.

genius: 1. very high intellectual or creative ability manifested in the execution of new forms. 2. a person possessing such ability.

genomotive: a need that results in an introspectively apparent motive. *Contr.* PHENOMOTIVE.

genotype: 1. the traits or characteristics common to a biological group. 2. a trait or the totality of traits that can be transmitted by an individual. 3. any of those hereditary factors exerting a causative influence on development. 4. (*Lewin*) behavior as explained in causal terms. The totality of causes for a phenomenon. *Contr.* PHENOTYPE.

gens: an anthropological term used to characterize the division of an ethnic group whose line of descent runs through the male.

genus: a biological classification embracing closely related species. The various genera make up the next higher category of family.

geometric: pertaining to the members of a series that increase by a certain constant ratio or proportion.

geometric illusions: a class of illusions depending upon distorted and misrepresented lines. The illusions are chiefly of size and distance. For an example, see MÜLLER-LYER ILLUSION.

geometric mean: the nth root of the product of n number of means. Thus,

$$M_G = \sqrt[N]{M_1 \times M_2 \times M_3 ... \times M_n}$$

The geometric mean is used in averaging a number of means that are distinctly different but whose standard deviations are comparable. More generally, the geometric mean of any series of numbers involving ratios, rates of change, etc., is calculated in preference to the arithmetic mean.

geotropism: an orienting response to gravity.

geriatrics: the branch of medicine specializing in the treatment of diseases of old age.

geriopsychosis: see SENILE PSYCHOSIS.

germ cell: a reproductive cell during any stage of its development.

germinal period: the very early stage

of embryonic life, approximately the first 14 days.

gerontology: the science of old age. It embraces the sciences of geriatrics, psychology, sociology, and anthropology.

Gesell Development Scales: inventories of development based on the systematic study of infants and preschool children in the Yale Clinic of Child Development. Two scales, the Infant Schedule and the Preschool Schedule, are available. The inventory at each level consists of entering plus or minus scores for the presence or absence of motor, adaptive, linguistic, and social-behavior samples.

Gestalt (pl. *Gestalten*): 1. form, figure, or configuration. 2. an integrated whole greater than the sum of its parts.

Gestalt factor: any condition that favors the perception of a Gestalt or a unitary figure. Proximity, similarity, contrast, contiguity, etc., are all Gestalt factors that promote perceptual organization.

Gestalt psychology: the school or systematic position within the field, to the effect that the proper subject matter for psychology is behavior and experience studied as wholes. Some degree of analysis is permissible but should be of the phenomenological variety, since molecular or elemental analysis would destroy the unitary quality of that which is undergoing analysis. Similarly, conscious experience cannot be meaningfully resolved into structuralistic elements, nor can behavior be reduced to combinations of reflexes or conditioned responses and still retain its uniqueness and meaningfulness. The Gestalt psychologists also object to treating the nervous system as a static, machinelike structure capable only of responding piecemeal to incoming stimuli. Rather, the cerebral cortex is viewed as analogous to a field of force in active equilibrium and in which each incoming stimulus affects the entire field. Cortical events, moreover, are isomorphic to external events. That is, there is a point-for-point correspondence between cortical events and objects in the environment, but the correspondence does not represent an identity. Instead, the two are related in the same manner in which a road map is related to a highway. The map distorts the landscape and the twists and turns in the road are smoothed out for simplicity, but the essential relations remain valid.

The best-known of the Gestalt contributions are in the field of perception and learning. The perceptual concept of figure and ground, the laws of primitive organization of perception—proximity, contrast, similarity, and contiguity—the principles of transposition, closure, good figure, and *Prägnanz*, are all contributions of the school. In learning, the Gestalt psychologists are noted for their studies of insight in apes and the extension of their theories into productive thinking in human subjects. The chief exponents of the Gestalt school were MAX WERTHEIMER, WOLFGANG KÖHLER, and KURT KOFFKA (*q.q.v.*)

Gestaltqualität: form quality; the unitary characteristic of a whole as dependent upon the configurational patterning of the parts.

Gestalt therapy: psychotherapy in which there is emphasis on the principles of Gestalt psychology (*q.v.*) as applied to the treatment of behavioral disorders. Healthy personality functioning is seen as the patient's perception of experiences as meaningful wholes, with fluid relationships existing between focal or figural experiences and background experiences. Emphasis is placed on attention, self-awareness, spontaneity of perception, involvement in experiences, overcoming gaps or distortions in experience believed to produce anxiety, compulsive behavior, and loss of zest. The approach is phenomenological and emphasizes contemporaneous factors in the causation of neuroses more than traditional psychoanalysis does.

gesture: a movement of a bodily part for the purpose of communication.

geusis: the process of tasting.

G factor: see GENERAL FACTOR.

G force: one gravity; the force needed to overcome the pull of the earth's gravity. At about 3–4 G's the individual experiences "redout" because of the rush of blood to the eyes, and at 5–6 G's unconsciousness, or "blackout."

giantism: an abnormal increase in size or stature due to malfunctioning of the anterior pituitary gland.

gifted: 1. possessing a high degree of intellectual ability; having an IQ of 140 or more. 2. possessing a nonintellective talent, such as musical talent, to a high degree.

gland: an organ that specializes in the secretion of a substance either utilized within the body or discharged from it. Distinction is made between endocrine and exocrine glands, or glands of internal and of external secretion. The endocrine glands discharge their products directly into the bloodstream, while the exocrine glands discharge their products to the outside or into the gastrointestinal tract. Endocrine glands are known also as ductless glands, and exocrine glands as duct glands. A third fundamental type of gland is the cytogenic, or cell-producing gland, such as the sex glands or the lymph glands. Some cytogenic glands, such as the sex glands, also produce hormones.

glans: the bulbous end of the penis or clitoris.

glare: characteristic of a smooth, bright surface or of strong incident light making visual discriminations difficult.

glassiness; glass sensation: the apparently filled quality of a transparent solid.

glaucoma: an pathological condition of the eye caused by increased internal pressure from the liquids or humors. Glaucoma is an important cause of blindness.

glia cells: specialized supporting cells within the cerebrospinal axis.

glioma: a brain tumor.

global: taken as an entirety. A *global system* attempts to embrace the entire field, in contrast to a *miniature system*, which attempts only to encompass a limited part of a field.

globus hystericus: a hysterical symptom involving the sensation of having a lump in the throat or of having a mass arise from the stomach to choke the victim.

glomeruli: synapses in the olfactory bulbs where sensory neurons from the olfactory receptors terminate.

glossiness: a quality of a surface that determines the degree to which it reflects light.

glossolalia: speech in a fabricated language such as occurs in religious ecstasies (speaking in tongues), or in hypnotic and mediumistic trances.

glossopharyngeal nerve: the ninth cranial nerve, which contains afferent components mediating taste from the posterior third of the tongue and efferent components to muscles in the throat.

glossosynthesis: the fabrication of nonsense words.

glottis: the opening between the vocal cords.

glove anesthesia: a functional loss of sensitivity in the hand or forearm (parts usually covered by gloves). This was a common symptom of conversion hysteria and can be induced or removed under hypnosis.

glucocorticoids: hormones produced by the adrenal cortex important in carbohydrate metabolism.

glucomate: a possible neurotransmitter of the central nervous system.

glucostatic theory: the position that a low level of blood sugar stimulates hypothalamic cells to initiate eating behavior.

goal: 1. the end result toward which the organism is striving or moving. 2. a place containing an incentive, such as the goal compartment at the end of a maze. 3. a consummatory response. 4. (*Adler*) an objective, such as superiority, toward which the individual strives and that determines his style of life. *End* and *purpose* are often used synonymously with goal, but *purpose* implies a subjective state that makes the goal attractive.

goal-directed behavior: behavior interpretable only in terms of the organism's seeking a goal. The term is often used by behavioristic psychologists to avoid the implication of purpose.

goal gradient: (*Hull*) the tendency for an animal to speed up as it approaches the goal, and the concomitant tendency for the errors nearest the goal to be eliminated first.

goal object: the final objective as contrasted with means or subgoals.

goal orientation: 1. the condition of being directed toward the goal. 2. in maze learning, entering runways that are in the direction of the goal, whether or not these are blinds or part of the true path.

goal response: 1. goal-directed behavior. 2. in conditioning, the response made toward an instrumental reward.

goal set: a readiness or anticipation of a goal.

goal stimulus: a proprioceptive stimulus that arises from goal-directed behavior.

golden section: the dividing of a line or area into two parts so that the ratio of the smaller to the larger is equal to the ratio of the larger to the entire line or area. The golden section is supposed to have aesthetic value.

Goldstein-Scheerer tests: several tests of concept formation or abstracting ability, such as the ability to copy color designs using cubes or to sort common objects into appropriate categories. The tests are often used in the diagnosis of brain injuries.

Golgi apparatus: irregular structures within nerve cells which undergo changes during Wallerian degeneration. See also WALLERIAN DEGENERATION.

Golgi-Mazzoni corpuscle: a bulbous, encapsulated nerve ending that may mediate pressure sensations.

Golgi tendon organ: a nerve ending in the tendon near the point of attachment to muscles. Golgi organs are believed to respond to changes in tendon tension and thus function as proprioceptors.

Golgi type I neuron: a multipolar neuron with an elongated axon that carries impulses from one part of the central nervous system to another.

Golgi type II neuron: a multipolar neuron with a short, branched axon that carries nervous impulses to nearby neurons.

gonad: a sex gland. The gonads in the male are the testes, which produce sperm, and in the female the ovaries, which produce eggs.

gonadotropic hormone: a fraction from the pituitary gland which stimulates activity in the gonads.

goniometer: an instrument for measuring sway.

good continuation: (*Gestalt psychology*) the principle that a line tends to maintain its direction. For example, the lines in the accompanying illustration do not appear as broken by each other but as smooth, continuous lines.

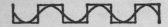

FIG. 15. *Good continuation. The wavy and rectilinear lines are seen as unbroken.*

Goodenough Draw-a-Man Test: a test of intelligence in which the subject is asked to draw the best possible picture of a man. The result is scored according to the amount of detail present and the total points are converted into mental-age norms. The test is used for subjects up to age eleven.

good Gestalt: a simple, symmetrical, and stable configuration.

goodness of fit: a measure of the degree to which any statistical constant conforms to a standard or theoretical value. For example, a distribution of intelligence test scores can be fitted to the normal probability curve

and an index of the goodness of fit calculated.

good shape: (*Gestalt psychology*) the principle that figures or patterns are perceived in such a way as to be as uniform as possible.

Gordon Personal Inventory: for grades 8–16 and adults. A self-report inventory that yields scores on cautiousness, original thinking, personal relations, and vigor.

Gordon Personal Profile: a self-report inventory for grades 9–16 and adults yielding four scores: responsibility, emotional stability, ascendancy, and sociability.

Gottschaldt figures: simple geometric figures hidden in more complex figures for the purpose of testing the perception of form.

Grace-Arthur Performance Scale: a general intelligence test consisting of a number of performance tests, such as block designs, form boards, figure-completion tests, etc. The scale yields an IQ.

gradation methods: those psychophysical methods that make use of equal steps or units of change, such as the method of just-noticeable differences and the method of minimal changes.

grade: 1. a class or division in a series of measurements or on a scale. 2. in elementary and secondary schools, a division representing one academic year. 3. a rating or score on a test or on a semester's work.

graded potential: less than threshold potentials or electrical disturbances induced in a neuron. When graded potentials reach threshold, an action potential is generated.

grade equivalent: a type of norm that assigns achievement on a test or battery of tests according to grade norms. Thus, performance on a test might be assigned the equivalent of sixth-grade work even though the testee is actually in the seventh grade. Grade-equivalent scores are useful supplements to ratings given by teachers.

grade norm: a standard of performance that represents the average performance of a group of pupils in a given grade. Frequently the norm is taken to be equivalent to the range of scores between the 40th and 50th percentiles.

grade scale: a standardized scale scored in terms of grade norms.

grade score: a score expressed in terms of grade level for which the individual's achievement is average. Thus, a grade score of 7 means the individual's performance was comparable to that of the average seventh-grader.

gradient: 1. any magnitude that shows a gradual slope in steps or degrees from high to low. 2. a gradual and continuous change in a variable. 3. in states of conflict, a graded difference in the strength of motivation that increases as one goal is approached and correspondingly lessens in intensity in respect to the other goal until a state of equilibrium is reached. 4. a rate of change in any magnitude.

gradient of effect: the principle that S–R sequences that either closely precede or follow reinforced sequences have a greater probability of occurrence than those that are remote. The probability of occurrence falls off in a gradient as the sequences are increasingly removed from the reinforced sequence. See also SPREAD OF EFFECT.

gradient of reinforcement: the principle that the closer a response is to the reinforcement, the stronger it becomes.

gradient-of-response generalization: the generalization that if a response is learned to a given stimulus, that stimulus will elicit similar responses; the greater the similarity in a response, the more often will the stimulus elicit it.

gradient-of-stimulus generalization: the generalization that when an animal has learned to make a response to a stimulus, it will respond to similar stimuli; however, the response may not be as strong or as frequent. This is the gradient of generalization.

Graduate Record Examination: a combined aptitude and achievement test is believed to be of selective value in choosing candidates for admission to graduate school.

grand mal: a form of epilepsy involving generalized convulsions and loss of consciousness.

granular layer: 1. the fourth layer of the cerebral cortex, containing a large number of small cells with short peripheral processes. 2. the fifth or seventh layer of the retina.

graph: a representation by means of lines or geometric figures of the relationship between two variables.

graphic alignment: the angle of letters in relation to the base line in writing. Claimed by graphologists to be a significant diagnostic variable.

graphic analysis: the utilization of graphs for the purpose of discovering significant relationships among variables.

graphic individuality: the pattern or characteristics of a person's handwriting that make it unique and establish the identification of the writer.

graphic language: communication by means of symbols, such as the pictorial writing characteristic of the ancient Egyptians.

graphic method: 1. a technique for recording responses for subsequent analysis. 2. the use of graphs to present or to analyze data.

graphic rating scale: a form of rating scale in which the rater can check the individual's characteristics on a series of graphs representing gradations of the trait in question. The graphs typically take the form of a series of straight lines calibrated with different degrees of the trait or characteristic in question. The rater then checks the line above the degree he believes the individual possessed. See illustration.

graphic score: a score represented by a line, bar, histogram, pie chart, or other visual device.

graphodyne: a device for recording pressure in handwriting.

graphology: 1. the scientific investigation of handwriting for purposes of personal identification or for personality analysis. 2. a pseudo science that makes exaggerated claims for the diagnostic value of handwriting.

graphomania: a pathological and obsessive desire to write.

graphometry: a projective technique in which the subject, blindfolded, is asked to draw something and then is asked to describe it, once with blindfold in place and again with blindfold removed.

graphomotor technique: a projective method in which the subject moves a pencil freely over a piece of paper. The result is interpreted by a clinician.

graphorrhea: a meaningless flow of written words sometimes observed in pathological states.

grasping reflex: a reflexive grasping or clutching of any small object with the fingers or toes, which stimulates the palm of the hand or the sole of the foot.

gratification: 1. the pleasant state immediately following drive reduction or the achievement of a desire. 2. sexual satisfaction.

Grave's disease: see EXOPHTHALMIC GOITER.

gray: an achromatic visual sensation that lies between the limits of black and white. The grays possess neither the attribute of hue nor that of saturation, hence they are said to vary only along the dimension of brightness.

gray matter: the masses of neural tissue made up primarily of cell bodies. Gray matter is found both in the spinal cord and in the brain. In the cord, the central, H-shaped region is gray, and consists of cell bodies; in the brain, gray matter makes up the cerebral cortex as well as a number of important subcortical nuclei. Masses of cell bodies outside the brain and spinal cord are called ganglia; inside the brain, or medulla, they are called nuclei, with the exception of the gray matter of the cerebral cortex, which covers the brain.

gray-out: a partial or incomplete loss of consciousness.

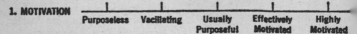

FIG. 16. *An item from a graphic rating scale. The rater checks along the line according to where he feels the subject falls.*

GRE: an abbreviation for the GRADU-ATE RECORD EXAMINATION.

Greek love: homosexuality among males; so called because of the prevalence of homosexuality among the ancient Greeks.

green: a visual sensation elicited by wavelength at or near 500 nanometers.

gregariousness: 1. the tendency in certain species to congregate in herds or to live in flocks. 2. the human tendency to want to belong to groups, to enjoy group activity, or to find satisfaction in group work.

grief: a strongly unpleasant emotional state associated with loss or deprivation and often accompanied by sobbing or weeping.

grooming: in certain species, particularly the monkeys, the removal of parasites from the fur by picking.

gross: 1. large. 2. crude; dependent more on strength than on fineness of coordination. The term is employed to characterize muscular responses, coordination, and large anatomical parts.

gross score: a score reported in the original units of measurement. *Syn.* RAW SCORE.

ground: The background in figure-ground relations.

group: 1. a collection of scores, objects, data, events, etc., that can be treated as a whole. *Syn.* CLASS, CATEGORY, CLASSIFICATION. 2. a social group (see SOCIAL GROUP). 3. (*verb*) to place in a category or bring together for some purpose.

group acceptance: the willingness of members of a group to accept a new member within the group. Group acceptance to some extent determines the status or role of a new member, but the individual may also impress his role on the group.

group analysis: a study of the social pathology of a group.

group atmosphere: the feelings and attitudes expressed by or within a group.

group behavior: 1. the actions of a group treated as a whole. 2. the actions of an individual member of a group as influenced by his being a member of the group. 3. behavior characteristic of individuals within a group but not of the same individuals when isolated or removed from the group.

group boundary: rules or regulations that determine group membership or group activities.

group consciousness: 1. the awareness that one individual in a group has for the other members or for the group as a whole. 2. a consciousness or mind attributed to groups that is more than the sum of the individual consciousnesses or minds. This concept, now discarded, was once employed to explain group behavior.

group contagion: the rapid spread of emotional reactions or behavior patterns through a group as a result of heightened suggestibility.

group decision: a conclusion arrived at by a group. The conclusion rendered may be an informally determined consensus or a majority vote of membership.

group differences: deviations or differences with respect to any measured variable between two or more groups taken as wholes. For example, the average difference between large samples of rural and urban children on an intelligence test would constitute a group difference.

group dimension: an attribute or characteristic by means of which a group may be described or measured.

group dynamics: the investigation of cause-and-effect relationships within groups; the study of the interrelationships between members of the group, how it was formed, and how it reacts to other groups. Group dynamics includes studies of cohesiveness, leadership, decision making, and subgroup formation.

grouped distribution: a frequency distribution in which the values are entered in ranges. For example, in tallying the weight of young adult males, the ranges in pounds might be 90–99; 100–109; 110–119; 120–129; 130–139, etc.

group experiment: an experiment carried out on a large number of individuals in mass. This is frequently done by employing college classes.

group factor: in factor analysis, any factor present in two or more tests that constitute the correlation matrix. Thus, the group factor of numerical ability might be found in tests of multiplication, division, subtraction, and addition.

group identification: the sense that one is a member of a group, that he shares the group's ideals, standards.

grouping: 1. the process of combining scores into categories or intervals. 2. the process of assigning pupils to relatively homogeneous classes.

grouping error: the error introduced into a set of statistical data when they are grouped into class intervals. Grouping requires the assumption—not always true—that the data are uniformly distributed around the midpoint of each class interval.

group interval: a class interval.

group interview: the application of the interview technique to several individuals at once.

group measures: measures that fall within certain statistical intervals or classes, as opposed to an array of individual scores.

group mind: an assumed mind or consciousness attributed to a group for the purpose of explaining behavior that supposedly cannot be explained on the basis of the behavior of individuals making up the group.

group morale: the degree to which a group shows a favorable spirit and willingness to presevere in achieving its stated goals.

group norm: 1. the norm that represents the performance in a specified group. 2. a social norm.

group processes: the methods by which groups resolve problems and meet objectives.

group rigidity: the tendency of a group to resist change. Closely knit, cohesive groups tend to be more rigid than loosely organized groups.

group structure: the relationship between members of a group, between subgroups within the main group, between the leader(s) and the members of the group, and the degree of cohesiveness or rigidity characteristic of the group.

group superego: that portion of the superego derived from peer groups, as opposed to that portion derived by introjection from the parents.

group test: a test designed to be administered to more than one individual at the same time. *Contr.* INDIVIDUAL TEST.

group therapy: any form of collective therapeutic treatment. Frequently the process involves group meetings of patients with the therapist, who acts as a discussion leader. It is assumed that hearing other people's problems and how they are being resolved may have both cathartic and therapeutic effects on the individual. In the psychodrama—a specialized form of group therapy—patients, with the help of others, actually act out their difficulties on a stage in the presence of the therapist.

groupthink: thinking so dominated by the desire to maintain unanimity of thought in a group that critical thinking is suspended or rendered ineffective.

growing pains: 1. pains in the legs typically experienced at bedtime or during the night by adolescents and presumed to be due to overly rapid development of bones and muscles. 2. metaphorically, any period of development that involves stress.

growth: 1. an increase in the size of bodily parts or of the organism as a whole. 2. development; the change and functional differentiation in bodily parts. 3. the incremental or continuous increase in a function or curve.

growth curve: a graphic representation in the rate of growth of any function.

growth differential: differences in the rate of growth or development between two individuals.

growth hormone: a hormone secreted by the anterior pituitary that stimulates growth.

growth principle: see ROGERS' SELF-THEORY OF PERSONALITY.

guessed mean: see ASSUMED MEAN.

guidance: the procedures used to assist individuals to find maximum satisfaction in their educational and vocational careers. Guidance involves the utilization of interviews and tests, and the study of background information, in order to arrive at a systematic plan of educational or vocational pursuits. Counseling procedures bordering on therapy may be utilized by some guidance counselors.

guiding fiction: (*Adler*) an idealized conception of the self by means of which the individual guides his conduct and selects his goals. In the normal person, the guiding fictions are not far removed from reality and are flexible. In the neurotic they are unrealistic and inflexible, and the psychotic, in a manner of speaking, has literally become his guiding fiction. *Syn.* IDEALIZED IMAGE.

Guilford-Zimmerman Temperament Survey: a personality inventory that measures ten traits identified through the use of factor analysis.

guilt: 1. the emotional feeling associated with the realization that one has violated an important social, moral, or ethical regulation. According to the psychoanalysts, guilt need not be conscious, and some guilt may be imaginary; in the latter instance it is assumed that the imagined guilt is symbolic of real, repressed guilt. 2. (*Kelly*) the awareness that the individual's core role (*q.v.*) no longer applies.

gust: a unit of taste equal to the subjective strength of a one percent solution of sucrose.

gustation: the sense of taste whose stimuli are substances in solution and whose receptors are on the tongue and soft palate.

Guthrie, Edwin R.: American psychologist (1886–1959). Guthrie attended the University of Nebraska, where he earned B.A. and M.A. degrees in 1907 and 1910 respectively. His Ph.D. degree was granted by the University of Pennsylvania in 1912. Guthrie remained at the University of Washington during his entire professional career except for periods in the military service and temporary appointments at a number of institutions. During World War II, Guthrie served with the Office of War Information and was chief consultant to Military Intelligence Service from July 1941 until September 1942. After the war he returned to Washington as dean of the graduate school. Guthrie wrote numerous articles for professional journals, as well as several books, among the most important of which are *The Psychology of Learning* (1935, revised 1953), *The Psychology of Human Conflict* (1938), and, with G. P. Horton, *Cats in a Puzzle Box* (1946).

Guthrie's Contiguous Conditioning: a systematic treatment of learning based on an instrumental conditioning model. The basic law of acquisition states that "a combination of stimuli which has been accompanied by a movement will on its recurrence tend to be followed by that movement." Thus, the theory subscribes only to the principle of contiguity to account for learning and does not invoke a law of effect or reinforcement. A corollary principle to the law of acquisition states that learning is complete on one trial. By this Guthrie means that in simple learning situations, movements involved in learning a skill are learned the first time the animal succeeds in performing the skill. Reward prevents the animal from doing things that would interfere with the newly acquired response and thus cause extinction by interference. In the case of more complex skills many trials may be needed, because of the large number of variable elements in the situation. Gradually all the correct responses, each of which has reached its full associative strength on a single trial, will fall into a sequential pattern and the habit will become stereotyped.

Guthrie's position on transfer is similar to that formulated by Edward L. Thorndike, namely, that only in those learning situations in which there is an identity of elements from one to the other can there be any significant amount of transfer. Despite his conditioning orientation, Guthrie does not subscribe to the principle of extinction by lack of reinforcement. Rather, he holds that old learning is obliterated only upon the acquisition of new learning and that habits not subjected to interference will last for years. Guthrie's theory has provided a challenging model to account for skill learning and has been extended by its originator and his associates into the area of human learning and conflict.

Guttman scale: see CUMULATIVE SCALE.

gynandromorphism: the coincidence of male and female characteristics in the one individual or organism.

gynandry: the tendency of the female to possess masculine characteristics.

gyrus: a fold on the surface of the cerebral cortex. The gyri are bounded by the sulci. *Syn.* CONVOLUTION.

H

Haab's pupillary reflex: the contraction of both irises when the gaze is directed toward a source of light in a darkened room.

habenula: a collection of fibers in the epithalamus.

habit: 1. an acquired response. 2. an activity that has become relatively automatic through prolonged practice. 3. relatively consistent pattern of thought or attitudes. 4. a characteristic form of behavior; a trait. 5. an acquired drive, such as drug addiction.

habit deterioration: a symptom observed in a number of psychotic conditions, particularly the schizophrenic reactions, in which the individual's characteristic manner of living disappears or is replaced by lower-order forms of behavior more appropriate to an earlier age.

habit family hierarchy: (*Hull*) the arrangement in a preferential order of alternate routes to a goal. When the most preferred route or response is blocked, a less favored one will appear.

habit hierarchy: the organization into a hierarchial form of a number of simpler habits into progressively higher-order systems. Used by learning theorists to explain plateaus in learning curves for complex sensorimotor tasks, such as typewriting. See also PLATEAU.

habit interference: a conflict of two or more incompatible responses that results in mutual weakening of the

eventual domination of one response over the other.

habit pattern: a number of habits combined into a unified activity.

habit strength: Hull's term for learning. Habit strength is dependent upon the number of reinforcements, the amount of reinforcement, and the spatial interval between stimulus and response and between the response and the reinforcement.

habituation: 1. the elimination with practice of useless, emotional responses in animal learning. 2. becoming adapted to a stimulus or to an interfering response, such as the ballet dancer's becoming adapted to the tendency toward dizziness upon whirling around.

hair cells: a type of cell that acts as a receptor, such as the hair cells in the organ of Corti in the inner ear.

halfway house: a self-governing facility for discharged mental patients who no longer require hospitalization but who do need the support of a restricted social community to assist them in the transition back to society.

hallucination: a false perception; the acceptance of ideational phenomena as real. Hallucinations are indicative of abnormality but are occasionally experienced by normal persons.

hallucinatory image: a mental image taken for reality.

hallucinogen: any of a group of chemical compounds that induce hallucinations or other altered states of consciousness.

hallucinosis: any disorder in which the patient is subject to hallucinations. Hallucinosis is particularly typical of acute alcoholism or other toxic conditions.

halo: a band or ring of light around a stimulus.

halo effect: the tendency to rate individuals either too high or too low on the basis of one outstanding trait. The halo effect is a characteristic defect in rating scales.

halving method: see EQUAL-APPEARING-INTERVALS METHOD.

hammer: one of the small bones in the middle ear. *Syn.* MALLEUS.

Hampton Court maze: a famous maze of yew hedges in Hampton Court, England, whose pattern was copied in early animal mazes in the United States.

handicapped: having less than normal ability or having an anatomical or functional defect that makes it difficult for one to compete with his peers.

Hanfmann-Kasanin Concept Formation Test: a test of the subject's ability to arrange blocks of various colors, shapes, heights, and widths into four categories. The performance is analyzed in terms of the types of solutions attempted and the subject's ability to conceptualize and verbalize. The test is believed to be useful in the diagnosis of mental impairment.

haphalgesia: a sensation of pain when the skin is touched by a normally nonirritating stimulus.

haploid: pertaining to cells with half the number of chromosomes typical of somatic cells. The haploid cells are normally the sex cells, the ovum, and sperm. *Contr.* DIPLOID.

haptic: pertaining to the proprioceptive and cutaneous systems of senses.

haptics: the investigation of the cutaneous system of sensation.

haptometer: an instrument for measuring sensitivity to touch.

hard colors: the reds and yellows that subjectively are most easily separated from grays of equal brilliance and saturation. *Contr.* SOFT COLORS.

hard of hearing: having deficient auditory acuity. Many persons who are hard of hearing may benefit from a hearing aid. *Syn.* HYPACUSIA.

Harlow, Harry F.: American psychologist (1905–1981). Harlow was educated at Reed College and Stanford University, where he was granted the Ph.D. in 1930. During his entire professional life he was at the University of Wisconsin, with which he became associated in 1930.

Harlow is noted for his extensive research on rhesus monkeys. Critical of the deprivation-reinforcement models of drive, he showed that monkeys are motivated by curiosity and manipulative drives to solve problems in the absence of food reward. He is also noted for his experiments on problem solving in monkeys from which his concept of "learning to learn" as an alternative to insight explanations was developed. He is most famous for his research on wire- and terry-cloth surrogate mothers. In many articles and lectures he has explored the nature of the affectional systems in monkeys as revealed by his work with these substitute mothers.

harmavoidance: (*Murray*) the need to avoid harm, injury, illness, danger, and death; taking protective measures for one's safety.

harmonic: 1. (*noun*) an overtone, or partial, whose frequency is a multiple of the fundamental one. 2. (*adj.*) pertaining to combinations of tones into chords.

harmonic analysis: the resolution of a complex wave into simple sine and cosine components by means of a harmonic analyzer or the application of Fourier's law.

harmonic mean: the reciprocal of the arithmetic mean of the reciprocals of a series of values.

harmony: 1. any arrangement of forms, figures, parts, etc., wherein the units are combined into a pleasing and balanced whole. 2. in music, the combination of tones into chords that have musical effects when put into an ordered sequence. 3. the absence of discord; good working relations.

harp theory: see HEARING THEORIES.

harria: (*R. B. Cattell*) a factor trait characterized by toughness, decisiveness, assertiveness, and realism in outlook.

harshness: 1. an unpleasant quality of sounds arising from aperiodic or irregular wave forms. 2. a personality trait manifested in abruptness of manner and speech and lack of sympathetic understanding.

hashish: cannabis indica, or Indian hemp, a narcotic.

hate: a strongly aversive attitude involving anger, ill will, and the desire to inflict injury on the object of hatred. *Contr.* LOVE.

Hawthorne effect: the tendency of people to work harder when experiencing a sense of participation in something new and special.

Healy Picture Completion Test: a performance test requiring the assembling of incomplete pictures by selecting the correct parts from a large number of possibilities.

hearing: the perception of sounds through the ear. *Syn.* AUDITION.

hearing loss: the loss of ability to hear tones at various frequencies. The loss may be reported in terms of the percentage of normal acuity present, or in absolute terms in decibels of loudness.

hearing theories: comprehensive theories that attempt to explain how the auditory mechanism functions. The most prominent of the various theories may be classified into the *resonance theories*, the *frequency theories*, and the *volley theory*. The best-known of the resonance theories is that of Helmholtz, who accounts for pitch by assuming that the short fibers of the basilar membrane are selectively tuned to high-pitched sounds; the long, loose fibers are tuned to the low-pitched sounds; and the fibers in the middle of the membrane are tuned to sounds of medium pitch. Intensity is accounted for by assuming that more neurons are excited at a given place by loud sounds, or that the excited neurons fire more rapidly. Because of its emphasis on place excitation, the theory is also known as the *piano theory* or the *harp theory*. It is classified as a resonance theory because it emphasizes that the fibers of the basilar membrane operate by a principle of sympathetic resonance.

A frequency theory was first proposed by Rutherford, who assumed that the basilar membrane responded in its entirety to incoming pitches in the same manner in which a telephone diaphragm vibrates as a whole. Analysis, therefore, occurs not in the cochlea but in the brain. No adequate account of loudness appreciation was offered by Rutherford.

The volley theory propounded by

Wever and Bray proposes that the neurons of the basilar membrane fire in squads or volleys rather than acting in unison. In this way much faster rates of firing can be accounted for. Loudness is explained as the number of neurons taking part in a given volley. The chief advantage of the volley theory is in accounting for the observed finding that the basilar membrane responds to incoming pitches up to several thousand per second by generating an equal number of outgoing impulses over the auditory nerve. Only by assuming a squadlike action on the part of the nerve can such high rates of speed be accounted for.

Among the other types of theories of hearing, Max Meyer's hydraulic theory has achieved some prominence. It assumes that different tonal components involve different lengths of the basilar membrane. Pitch is accounted for in terms of the frequency of impulses arriving at the brain. Presumably loudness is accounted for by the number of neurons involved in a segmental response.

heat: 1. a sensory experience that occurs when the skin is stimulated in such a way that both warm and cold receptors are excited simultaneously. The device used for this purpose consists of alternate pipes of warm and cold water which take the form of a heat grill. Heat is often confused with warm but most authorities believe they are distinct sensations mediated by different nervous processes. 2. a state of sexual receptivity in female animals.

Hebb, Donald O.: Canadian psychologist (1904–). After his graduate training at Dalhousie University, Hebb earned his M.A. degree at McGill in 1925 and his Ph.D. at Harvard in 1936. He has held appointments at Harvard, the Montreal Neurological Institute, Queen's University, and the Yerkes Primate Laboratory. Since 1947 he has been at McGill University as professor of psychology and chairman of the department. His theory of perceptual learning was first systematically presented in his *Organization of Behavior* (1949). He has contributed extensively to technical journals and is the author of a *Textbook of Psychology* (1958). See also HEBB'S THEORY OF PERCEPTUAL LEARNING.

Hebb's Theory of Perceptual Learning: an attempt to account for perceptual learning and other psychological processes on the basis of the formation of cell assemblies and phase sequences in the cerebral cortex. The cell assembly is a functionally related group of cells that work together in a coordinated and highly organized manner. Cell assemblies are built up through practice. That is, it is suggested that some kind of metabolic change, or possibly the growth of additional terminal buttons at the synapse, may account for the development of cell assemblies with practice. Hebb uses as his model of learning the acquisition of the concept of a triangle, which is not, as common sense would have us believe, a simple process. Rather, the learning of each angle and each side requires the formation of a separate cell assembly. These separate assemblies are finally related to each other in a superordinate structure called a *phase sequence*, which is the functioning of the various assemblies. Phase sequences mediate the totality of a learned perception such as triangularity. Because the process becomes highly mechanical with practice, there is no sense of the separate functioning of the various assemblies, only the total experience. Hebb allows for the operation of Gestalt-like laws such as *Prägnanz*, since if parts of the stimulus pattern are missing, or if part of a cell assembly is destroyed, it is postulated that alternate paths may take over. Moreover, new learning may be effective in modifying old phase sequences by being recruited into the system of new cell assemblies. Motivation and emotionality are related to the phase-sequence theory by assuming that motivation is a persistent state of sequential activity in a phase sequence. Pleasure is associated with the formation of new sequences, and fear with the disruption of cell assemblies. Hebb has related a large amount of empirical research in learning, intelligence, perception, motivation, and emotion to his theory.

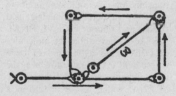

FIG. 17. *A cell assembly. Once the impulse has entered the assembly of cells, it can continue indefinitely. Note alternate path (x).*

hebephrenia; hebephrenic schizophrenia: obsolete terms for disorganized schizophrenia, a category characterized by incoherence in speech and flat, incongruous, or silly emotional reactions. There is a tendency for social withdrawal and oddities of behavior for there is an absence of systematized delusions and hallucinations typical of other forms of the disorder.

hedonic: pertaining to feeling or to the dimension of pleasantness-unpleasantness.

hedonic tone: the quality of an experience as described along the dimension of pleasantness-unpleasantness. *Syn.* FEELING TONE.

hedonism: 1. the psychological theory that the individual acts in such a way as to seek pleasure and avoid pain. 2. the ethical theory that pleasure or the pursuit of pleasure ought to be the goal of conduct.

Heinis constant: a measure of the rate of mental growth found by converting mental age units by absolute scaling into theoretically equal units and dividing the result by chronological age. *Syn.* personal constant.

Heinis law of mental growth: the generalization that intelligence increases with age according to the exponential law as given by the formula where *y* is attained intelligence; *e* is the base of the natural logs; and *CA* is chronological age.

$$y = 429 \left(1 - e^{\frac{CA}{6.675}}\right)$$

helicotrema: a small opening at the apex of the cochlea where the scala vestibuli communicates with the scala tympani.

hellotropism: an orienting movement of the body as a whole toward a source of light.

helix: the curved portion of the outer ear.

Heller's disease: see DEMENTIA INFANTILIS.

Helmholtz, Hermann von: German physicist (1821–1894). After receiving his medical degree in Berlin,

Helmholtz became an army surgeon, but left the service after a short time in order to begin his fruitful career as a pure scientist at Königsberg. During the next thirty years he held appointments, first as a physiologist, then as a physicist, at Bonn, Heidelberg, and Berlin. During this period he developed his famous theories of hearing and vision, provided the mathematical background for the law of the conservation of energy, invented the ophthalmoscope, and developed his outstanding *Sensations of Tone* (1862), and *Physiological Optics* (1866). Helmholtz lent strong support to the development of an empirical psychology and is part of the great empiricist tradition in perception and sensation.

Helmholtz theory of hearing: see HEARING THEORIES.

Helmholtz theory of vision: see COLOR THEORIES.

hemeralopia: see HEMERALOPSIA.

hemeralopsia: variously used by different authorities to refer to both day blindness and night blindness.

hemiopia: blindness in one half of the visual field. *Syn.* hemianopia.

hemiplegia: paralysis of one side of the body.

hemispheres: the two symmetrical halves of the cerebrum or cerebellum.

hemispherical dominance: see DOMINANCE.

hemophobia; hematophobia: a fear of blood.

Henmon-Nelson Tests of Mental Ability, 1973 Revision: group tests of general ability designed for elementary and secondary-school children.

Herbartian psychology; Herbartism: a system of educational psychology formulated by J. F. Herbart in 1825 and based on the assumption that ideas are competitive in their struggle to arrive in the center of consciousness. Its central doctrine is the doctrine of apperception, which holds that new sense impression striving for recognition has to be related to the body of previously acquired ideas (the apperceptive mass) before it can become meaningful. The doctrine of apperception was taken over by Wundt and the structuralists.

herd instinct: see GREGARIOUSNESS.

hereditarianism: the point of view that emphasizes the biological determination of behavioral characteristics. See also NATIVISM.

heredity: the totality of characteristics transmitted from the parents to the offspring. The transmission of genetic characteristics is a function of the CHROMOSOMES and GENES (*q.q.v.*). The exact mechanism of hereditary transmission was not known until the discovery of deoxyribonucleic acid (DNA) and ribonucleic acid (RNA). It is now believed that the molecules of DNA serve as a kind of code whose built-in program influences the developing tissues through the agency of RNA, which serves in turn as a messenger for DNA. However, the concept of the gene as a determiner remains useful in describing dominant, recessive, and sex-linked characteristics. Dominant characteristics are those that will appear in the offspring as actual or manifest traits. Recessive characteristics may be present but do not appear in the offspring unless both parents are the carriers of recessive genes. Sex-linked characteristics are those transmitted by the sex-determining chromosomes and may only appear in the presence of the male sex hormone. Color blindness and baldness in men are examples of such sex-linked characteristics. These traits are carried by women but do not become manifest except in the presence of relatively high levels of the male sex hormone. In general, heredity interacts with environment to produce the individual; all traits are a product of the combined interaction of the two factors. *Syns*. HERITAGE; INHERITANCE.

hereditary predisposition: an inherited tendency toward a certain disorder. Whether or not the disorder appears will be determined by environmental conditions.

Hering afterimages: the positive afterimage that follows a bright stimulus and is of the same hue and saturation as the original.

Hering grays: a set of fifty gray papers arranged in subjectively equal steps to represent the achromatic series from extreme white to extreme black.

Hering theory of color vision: see COLOR THEORIES.

heritability: characterizing that portion of the total variability in a trait that can be attributed to genetic differences.

heritage: 1. the sum total of biological traits transmitted by the parents. 2. the social transmission of customs, folkways, and mores from one generation to the next.

hermaphrodite: an individual who possesses both the male and female reproductive organs. One set is usually developed more completely than the other.

hermaphroditism: the condition of having both male and female sex organs.

heroin: a morphine derivative that is one of the most widely used of the addictive drugs. Its effect is that of a narcotic.

hertz (Hz): one cycle per second. Used in measuring sound waves, EEG waves, etc.

heterochronia; heterochrony: difference in rate between two processes, such as in differences in the speed of nervous impulses in different types of fibers.

heteroerotic: pertaining to attraction for the opposite sex. *Contr*. autoerotic.

heterogeneous: characteristic of groups, sets of data, or individuals who show differences or dissimilarities.

heteromorphic: deviating from the normal.

heteronomous morality: (*Piaget*) characterizing the moral attitudes of young children (4–7) who view moral rules as absolutes given by authority. *Contr*. AUTONOMOUS MORALITY.

heteronomy: 1. the guidance of one individual by another such as occurs in hypnosis. 2. pertaining to activities originating outside the self.

heterophilic: attracted to the opposite sex.

heterophoria: a condition of muscular imbalance between the two eyes with the result that one of the eyes deviates from its normal position.

heteroscedasticity: quality or condition of a matrix in which the arrays show significantly different standard deviations. *Contr*. HOMOSCEDASTICITY.

heterosexuality: 1. attraction toward members of the opposite sex. 2. a developmental stage in which attraction toward members of the opposite sex is achieved. *Contr*. HOMOSEXUALITY.

heterotropia: strabismus; cross-eyedness.

heterozygous: pertaining to an organism possessing a trait whose genetic makeup consists of both dominant and recessive genes. *Contr.* HOMO-ZYGOUS.

heuristic: leading to the discovery of, or the search for, new thought formulations, solutions, or conclusions.

Heymans' law: the principle that the threshold value of a stimulus is increased in proportion to the intensity of a simultaneously acting inhibitory stimulus.

hidden-cue test or **situation:** a task in which the learner must discover the feature of a stimulus situation that will lead to the reward.

hidden figure: see EMBEDDED FIGURE.

hidden observer: (Hilgard) a part of consciousness that monitors external events even during deep hypnosis.

hierarchy: an organization of persons, habits, elements, ranks, etc., arranged in such a manner that all components below a given rank are subordinate. Thus, a hierarchy of habits implies that the habit at the top of the hierarchy is dominant over all others and will appear first. If it does not meet the demands of the situation, then the second-highest habit will appear, and so forth.

higher centers; higher brain centers: the brain centers of the cerebral cortex concerned with the more complex processes, such as memory, imagination, intelligence, and learning.

higher-level skills: work or behavioral-pattern techniques or abilities applicable to a wide variety of tasks rather than to one particular task.

higher mental processes: thinking, judgment, imagination, intelligence—in contrast to primary sensory processes or simple motor responses.

higher-order conditioning: a kind

of type-S, or classical, conditioning, in which the conditioned stimulus in one series of trials is used as the unconditioned stimulus in a second series of trials. For example, a dog might be conditioned to salivate to the sound of a bell; then a light would be flashed as the bell was sounded without any further reinforcement. The dog's eventual response to the light is a higher-order conditioned response.

higher response unit: integrations of simpler acts into more complex acts. For example, a phrase is a higher unit than a word but must be built up of words.

high-grade defective: an individual of subnormal intelligence who requires a minimum of supervision and who can perform useful tasks. Most high-grade defectives are morons. *Contr.* LOW-GRADE DEFECTIVE.

hindbrain: the division of the brain made up of the cerebellum, pons, and medulla.

hippocampus: a curved nerve tract consisting mostly of gray matter in the floor of the inferior horn of the lateral ventricle. In shape it resembles a sea horse, hence the name hippocampus. The hippocampus is believed to function in olfactory, visceral processes and short-term memory.

hircine: having a goatlike or cheese-like smell.

histogram: a graphic form of the frequency distribution in which the number of cases within each class is represented by a vertical bar whose height is proportional to the number of cases within the class.

histology: the branch of biology that deals with the structure of body tissue.

historical approach: in counseling, the recounting of events up to the onset of the problem. Occasionally the client is asked to write out a biographical account of his life up to the initiation of therapy.

historical explanation: explanation in terms of the totality of previous events leading up to the phenomenon under study. *Contr*. CONTEMPORANE-OUS EXPLANATION.

historical method: the study of the individual by tracing his life history. *Contr*. AHISTORICAL METHOD.

hodological space: psychological space, or space as defined by the dynamic factors involved. Hodological space is not the same as Euclidian space.

hodology: the geometry of vectors, paths, and the space in which they occur. In his field theory, Kurt Lewin utilizes hodology as a model of behavior. Vectors, or directed lines, are employed to represent motivation and tensions; paths are the routes over which behavior occurs in moving from one space to another; and the concept of hodological space is employed in the sense of dynamic space with its psychological properties.

holergasia: a psychosis that involves the entire personality.

holism: the doctrine that a living being or its behavior cannot be explained solely in terms of the behavior of the parts.

Holmgren test: a test of color blindness in which the testee must sort a number of skeins of colored wool into three basic piles according to a sample set. The test has also been used by Goldstein and his associates as a test of abstracting ability.

holophrastic stage: the period in development when the child's speech is characterized by one-word utterances that often function as sentences.

homeostasis: 1. the tendency for the organs of the body and the blood to maintain constancy. For example, the blood must maintain a relatively stable level of salt, sugar, electrolytes, etc., or illness and death will eventually supervene. 2. the tendency of the organism as a whole to maintain constancy or to attempt to restore equilibrium if constancy is disturbed. For example, the adrenalectomized rat will ingest more salt than normal in an attempt to overcome a sodium insufficiency brought on by the operation.

homoerotism: sexual desire for a member of one's own sex.

homogamy: inbreeding among members of a genetically isolated group resulting in the development of similar traits among the various members.

homogeneity: 1. similarity or likeness among members of any group, data, or variables. 2. the degree to which a test measures a single variable.

homogeneous grouping: 1. grouping students according to ability on the basis of standardized tests and measures of school performance. 2. arranging any set of variables into like categories.

homogeneous reinforcement: the simultaneous presentation of a stimulus with another stimulus evoking the same or a similar response. For example, the presentation of a bell simultaneously with food will lead in both cases to salivation.

homolateral: pertaining to the same side, such as a homolateral reflex.

homologous organs: organs that have the same essential structure but differ in function — for example, the fin of a fish and the hand of a man.

homonomy drive: the human motive

to fit into social groups, such as the family, society, and nation.

homoscedasticity: the property of having equality in variability (applied to matrices and scatter diagrams).

homosexuality: 1. sexual intercourse between members of the same sex. 2. sexual attraction for members of the same sex. Homosexuality may involve the entire range of behavior from overt sexuality—that is, mutual masturbation, cunniliction, fellatio, or anal intercourse—to repressed desires toward members of the opposite sex. Overt homosexual practices are still regarded as perversions, from a legal point of view in some communities. However, the presence of homosexual tendencies is considered within the normal range by clinicians.

homozygous: containing two genes of the same type, that is, either two dominant or two recessive genes.

Honi phenomenon: in the Ames distorted room, the failure of a well-known individual, such as a husband or wife, to appear distorted in size.

hope: an attitude characterized by an expectation of the favorable outcome of an event. The accompanying emotional tone is often one of fear mixed with anticipated joy. *Contr.* DESPAIR.

horizontal group: a group that draws upon only a single social class. *Contr.* VERTICAL GROUP.

horizontal growth: the increase in the number of activities or skills on the same level of difficulty attained by the subject.

horizontal mobility: the change from one role or position to another within the same social class.

hormic psychology: a system of psychology advocated by William McDougall (1871–1938), whose fundamental assumption was that behav-

ior is characterized by purpose, or a tendency to seek goals. Basically, goal-seeking behavior is motivated by propensities that are instincts or sentiments. Instincts are innate propensities, such as flight, curiosity, pugnacity, reproduction, acquisition, and self-assertion. All instincts are describable in terms of their three fundamental characteristics or attributes—*cognitive, affective,* and *conative.* That is, all instincts have a sensory, a motivational, and an emotional component. Instincts may be modified into sentiments, such as love, jealousy, or patriotism, which are combinations of instincts and, through experience, become associated with complex stimulus situations.

McDougall's hormic psychology was popular among those psychologists, anthropologists, and sociologists in the early 1920s who found the structuralistic and behavioristic systems sterile. His introductory textbook went through fourteen editions. However, as the concept of instinct came into disrepute under the attack of the behaviorists, McDougall's system rapidly lost ground.

hormone: a chemical substance produced by one of the endocrine glands and conveyed to the other organs by the bloodstream.

Horner's law: the principle that the most common form of red-green color blindness is transmitted from male to male through the female.

Horney, Karen: American psychoanalyst (1885–1952). Karen Horney received her M.D. degree from the University of Freiburg, Germany, in 1913. She came to the United States in 1932. In the course of her professional career she held appointments at the Institute for Psychoanalysis in

Berlin and at the Chicago Institute for Psychoanalysis; and she lectured at the New School for Social Research in New York City. She was appointed Dean of the American Institute for Psychoanalysis in 1941, a post she held until her death. She was a leader in the school of neo-Freudian psychoanalysis. Impressed with the role of cultural conflicts in the formation of the neuroses, she rejected Freud's extreme emphasis on sexuality and stressed the child's feeling of insecurity and his search for security through modal behavior patterns that lead to inner conflicts and a neurotic life style. In her emphasis on insecurity and the drive for superiority, she closely resembles Adler, who held that feelings of inferiority were the driving force behind neuroses. Horney's influence in the world of psychoanalysis was felt through a number of brilliantly written books and technical articles. Her books include *The Neurotic Personality of Our Time* (1936), *New Ways in Psychoanalysis* (1939), *Self-Analysis* (1942), *Our Inner Conflicts* (1945), and *Neurosis and Human Growth* (1950).

horopter: the locus of all points in the field of vision that fall on identical or corresponding points in the two retinas.

hostility: 1. the tendency to wish to inflict harm on others; the tendency to feel anger toward others. 2. (*Kelly*) trying to force others to behave in such a way as to prove the correctness of one's constructs in the face of evidence to the contrary.

House-Tree-Person Test: a projective technique for ages five and older, requiring the subject to draw a house, a tree, and a person in that order. The examiner notes sequences of detail,

speed, comments made by the subject, and general behavior.

H scaling: in constructing attitude scales, the utilization of several items of equal acceptability as if they were one item, in order to increase reliability.

H test: a test of the significance of differences between two sets of data when the observations are ranked.

hue: the dimension of visual sensation primarily related in the wavelength of the stimulus. Hue is secondarily related to wave amplitude, since colors change to some degree as the intensity of the stimulus changes. Hues are specified by names such as red, green, blue, etc., or by wavelength in nanometers. See also SPECTRUM.

Hull, Clark L.: American psychologist (1884–1952). Hull studied at the University of Michigan and at the University of Wisconsin, where he was granted the Ph.D. degree in 1918. He was the principal of a public school in Sickels, Michigan, from 1909 to 1911, taught at the University of Wisconsin from 1916 to 1929, then joined the Institute of Human Relations, at Yale, where he remained for the rest of his life. Hull's early interests were diverse. He wrote on concept formation and on the influence of tobacco smoking on psychological processes. His *Hypnosis and Suggestibility*, published in 1933, is considered a classic in its field. His interests in learning theory resulted in the publication of the *Mathematico-Deductive Theory of Rote Learning*, with Hovland, Perkins, and Fitch, in 1940; *Principles of Behavior* (1943), *Essentials of Behavior* (1951), and *A Behavior System* (1952). He also wrote numerous articles for professional journals.

Hull's Mathematico-Deductive Theory of Learning: a systematic treatment of learning based on classical conditioning theory and stated in the form of deductive postulates and corollaries. The fundamental law of acquisition assumes that habit strength is gradually built up in increments of habit by contiguous reinforcement of S-R units. Habit strength is sensitized into performance by drives. In the absence of drive, performance will drop off to zero. In the absence of habit strength, performance will also be zero, since drive and habit strength are related to each other in a multiplicative function. As is true of all theories based on the principles of conditioning, Hull's makes use of extinction and inhibition in order to account for diminution of response. Extinction is brought about by nonreinforced repetition of responses. Stimuli closely associated with a response undergoing extinction, themselves become capable of inhibiting that response. Forgetting verbal material is presumed to be a decay function with the passage of time.

For measuring the course of learning, Hull offers several possibilities: (1) latency of response, or the speed with which a response appears following presentation of the stimulus; (2) probability of response; (3) number of repetitions needed to bring about extinction. In the early statements of his theory Hull emphasized drive and primary reinforcement. In later revisions he placed more emphasis on drive stimulus reduction and secondary reinforcement. The theory was also extended to account for discrimination learning and problem-solving behavior. Of the conditioning theories, Hull's has proved to be one of the most provocative of research, particularly in the investigation of the role of reinforcement in the establishment of conditioned responses. Hull is also recognized as being one of the earliest theorists to attempt a highly quantified theory of learning.

human engineering: an applied branch of psychology and engineering concerned with problems of machine design, working conditions, skills, learning ability, and efficiency.

humanistic psychology: a theoretical and therapeutic system of psychology that emphasizes particularly human processes—the uniqueness of the individual, the validity of subjective experience, freedom of choice, and the tendency for each individual to strive to realize his potential. Humanistic psychology grew out of the work of ABRAHAM MASLOW, a personality, theorist, and the clinical practice of CARL ROGERS.

human nature: the characteristics of all mankind. The term implies innate rather than acquired characteristics and is often used to rationalize or excuse failings.

human potential movement: an offshoot of humanistic psychology (q.v.) that emphasizes the development of the individual's potential and the ultimate improvement of society.

Humm-Wadsworth Temperament Scale: a personality questionnaire designed to measure relative standing on paranoid, hysteric, manic-depressive, and schizoid tendencies.

humor: 1. a pleasant, affable attitude. 2. any glandular or organic secretion.

Humphrey's paradox: the generalization that a learned response is more resistant to extinction if the response has not been reinforced on every trial.

hunger: 1. appetite; a desire for food.

2. hunger pangs; a mass of sensations from the stomach, described as an aching, gnawing sensation. 3. a craving for any thing, as *hunger* for affection.

hunger drive: a hypothetical state due to food deprivation and causing general restless and goal-seeking behavior.

hunger pangs: the subjective sensation of associated sensation associated with strong hunger contractions in the stomach.

Huntington's chorea: a neurological disorder characterized by progressively more serious loss of coordination, spasmodic, jerky movements, and mental deterioration. The disease is hereditary.

Hunt-Minnesota Test for Organic Brain Damage: a test for use with individuals sixteen years of age or older involving the vocabulary test of the Stanford-Binet, which is relatively insensitive to brain damage, and six memory and recall tests relatively sensitive to brain damage, with nine interpolated tests for the detection of uncooperativeness or such severe deterioration as to preclude testing

hybrid: 1. the offspring of two parents belonging to two different species. 2. the offspring of parents only one of whom has a certain unit character.

hydraulic theory of hearing: see HEARING THEORIES.

hydrocephalus; hydrocephaly: an abnormal condition of the cerebrospinal fluid in which there is a marked excess of fluid, resulting in both inward and outward pressure. The skull enlarges in response to the pressure and the brain may be damaged.

hydrophobiaphobia: fear of hydrophobia.

hydrotherapy: treatment by means of water packs, baths, and hot water bottles.

hypacusia; hypacusis; hypacousia: impaired sense of hearing; partial deafness.

hypalgesia: impaired sensitivity to pain.

hyperalgia: greatly increased sensitivity to pain.

hyperergasia: a state of restlessness, overactivity, and excessive motility associated with manic-depressive psychosis. *Contr.* HYPOERGASIA.

hyperesthesia: increased sensitivity to touch.

hypergnosis; hypergnosia: the projection of conflicts to the environment.

hyperkinesis: excessive motility or restlessness.

hyperkinesthesia: pathological sensitivity to sensations arising from the muscles, tendons, and joints.

hypermnesia: unusual ability to remember. Hypermnesia may occur under hypnotic states or during free association.

hyperopia: farsightedness; a condition in which the rays of light entering the eye come to a focal point behind the retina because of shortness of the eyeball.

hyperorexia: an excessive appetite for food. *Contr.* ANOREXIA.

hyperosmia: unusually acute sensitivity to odors. *Contr.* ANOSMIA.

hyperphagia: extreme overeating. *Contr.* APHAGIA.

hyperphrasia: excessive volubility; a pathological condition in which the patient speaks excessively.

hyperprosexia: a compulsive desire to attend to a stimulus, such as the dripping of a faucet.

hypersomnia: an uncontrollable urge to sleep; excessive sleepiness.

hypertension: 1. excessive muscular

tension. 2. high blood pressure not due to any known organic cause.

hypertelorism: a disease of the eye characterized by increased interpupillary distance. *Syn.* Grieg's disease.

hyperthymia: excessive emotionality. *Contr.* HYPOTHYMIA.

hyperthyroidism: a condition of excessive secretion by the thyroid gland. Hyperthyroidism is associated with a greatly elevated metabolic rate, restlessness, excessive motility, and apprehension. If neglected, the condition is fatal.

hypertonicity: a high degree of tension in a muscle.

hypertropy: excessive development in an organ.

hypertropia: a form of strabismus in which one eye fixates normally and the other deviates in the upward direction.

hypesthesia; hypaesthesia: decreased sensitivity or raising of the threshold.

hypnagogic: pertaining to sleep or to a drowsy state.

hypnagogic image: a vivid image of almost hallucinatory character experienced while falling asleep or during a drowsy state.

hypnoanalysis: psychoanalysis carried on while the patient is in a hypnotic trance.

hypnogenic: 1. sleep-producing. 2. inducing hypnosis.

hypnoidal: a mild state of hypnosis; a quasi-hypnotic state.

hypnopompic: pertaining to the drowsy state following awakening from a deep sleep.

hypnosis: a sleeplike state induced artificially by a hypnotist and characterized by greatly heightened suggestibility. For this reason the hypnotized individual shows extreme responsiveness to suggestions made by the hypnotist. As many of the early investigators observed, paralyses, anesthesias, and hyperesthesias may be induced under hypnosis. The possibility of anesthesia under hypnosis has been put to practical use in childbirth, surgery, and dentistry. Because the patient is relaxed and more subject to suggestibility under hypnosis, the state has been utilized for therapeutic purposes since the time of Charcot, Freud, and Breuer. The patient is encouraged to remember and verbalize his difficulties, and supportive suggestions are given.

hypnotherapy: the utilization of hypnosis as a means of physical or mental therapy.

hypnotic: 1. pertaining to hypnosis. 2. pertaining to drugs that induce sleep.

hypnotic rigidity: an induced state of muscular rigidity brought about by suggestion during hypnosis.

hypnotic set: see POSTHYPNOTIC SUGGESTION.

hypnotism: the systematic investigation and practice of hypnosis.

hypnotize: to induce a hypnotic state.

hypochondria; hypochondriasis: an exaggerated concern about one's health.

hypochondriac: an individual who suffers from hypochondria.

hypoergasia: the depressive phase of manic-depressive psychosis. *Contr.* HYPERERGASIA.

hypofunction: less than the normal degree of function.

hypoglossal nerve: the twelfth cranial nerve. Its chief component is motor to the muscles of the tongue.

hypoglossal nucleus: a mass of cell bodies in the lower medulla. The origin of the hypoglossal nerve.

hypoglycemia: a condition of abnormally low blood sugar.

hypoglycemic therapy: a form of shock therapy induced by artificially lowering blood-sugar level.

hypokinesis: a condition of subnormal motor motility.

hypologia: a lack of capacity for speech due to neurological or functional disorders.

hypomania: a mild degree of mania characterized by excitement, energetic behavior, restlessness, and high productivity.

hypophrasia: lack of speech characteristic of the depressed phases of the psychoses.

hypophrenia: mental deficiency.

hypophysectomy: the surgical removal of the pituitary gland.

hypopituitarianism: a deficiency in the amount of secretion of the pituitary gland.

hypoprosexia: inadequate attention.

hypostatization: the attributing of existence or reality to anything

hypothalamic-hypophyseal portal system: the network of blood vessels connecting the hypothalamus and anterior pituitary gland. Hypothalamic hormones reach the pituitary via the system.

hypothalamus: the lower part of the thalamus, consisting of a group of nuclei believed to be important in the regulation of hunger, temperature, emotional control, and other visceral functions.

hypothesis: 1. an assumption that serves as a tentative explanation. Looked at from another point of view, a hypothesis may be considered as a question put to nature to be answered by an experiment or series of observations. 2. an inferred variable in animals to account for the fact that the

animal can learn complex discriminations. Tolman and Kreschevsky have both used the concept to account for the animal's behavior at choice points in mazes.

hypothetical: characteristic of ideas or explanations that are tentative or take the form of "as-if" propositions.

hypothetical process: an inferred process invoked to explain behavior; an intervening variable.

hypothetico-deductive method: a scientific method in which the investigator begins with a few empirical facts and on the basis of these deduces a number of postulates or hypotheses to be proved. If the postulates are substantiated, they become scientific principles or laws. Newton made use of the deductive method in establishing his system of celestial mechanics. Hull utilized the technique in his mathematico-deductive theory of learning.

hypothymia: a lowering of emotional responsiveness.

hypothyroid: deficient in the production of thyroxin.

hypothyroidism: a disorder of the thyroid gland in which there is an insufficiency of thyroxin. Hypothyroidism in children may lead to cretinism, a condition in which the child is extremely subnormal mentally, is stunted in growth, and lacks personality. In adults, the disorder leads to low motivation, loss of the sex drive, and a subnormal metabolic rate. *Contr.* HYPERTHYROIDISM.

hypotonic: lacking in muscle tone.

hypovolemia: a decrease in the volume of extracellular fluids. Believed to be a causative factor in thirst.

hypoxemia: a deficiency of oxygen in the bloodstream.

hysteria: a complex neurosis that

takes a number of forms. In general, the disorder is characterized by emotional instability, repression, dissociation, and suggestibility. The more important varieties of the disorder are: (1) conversion hysteria, in which mental conflicts are converted into physical symptoms, such as paralyses, blindness, and anesthesias; (2) somnambulism, or sleep walking; (3) the fugue or flight, in which the individual becomes amnesiac for his personal past; (4) multiple personality, in which the individual's personality splits into two or more distinct personalities with dissociation of consciousness.

hysterical: 1. pertaining to the symptoms associated with hysteria. 2. characterizing a functional disorder, such as blindness, deafness, the paralyses and anesthesias typical of conversion hysteria.

hysterical deafness: deafness resulting from strong psychological conflicts. There are often advantages to the patient from hysterical deafness in the sense that he may become dependent on others and receive considerable sympathy from physicians and friends.

hysterics: an attack of uncontrollable laughing and weeping.

hysteriform: pertaining to disorders of functional origin that resemble hysteria.

hysteroid: resembling hysteria.

I

iatrogenic illness or **neurosis:** a functional disorder brought on by the physician's diagnosis or suggestions.

icon: 1. an image or pictorial representation. 2. a brief image representing persistent activity in sensory channels following stimulation. 3. in interpersonal relations a strategy for impressing others that takes the form of mentioning important names and places.

iconic mode: (*Bruner*) a method of converting immediate experience into mental models using sensory images.

ICSH: see LUTENIZING HORMONE.

ictal emotions: emotions that occur suddenly and disappear quickly.

ictus: 1. a stroke. 2. an epileptic seizure of sudden onset that is unaccompanied by an aura. 3. the accentuation of a tone or syllable.

id: (*Psychoan.*) that division of the mind, or psyche, that is the seat of the libido. From it arise the animalistic, chaotic impulses that demand gratification. The id is not in contact with the outside world, only with the body, and thus centers its demands on the body. It is governed entirely by the pleasure principle and attempts to force the ego, which is governed by the reality principle, to accede to its wishes regardless of the consequences. See also PSYCHOANALYSIS.

idea: 1. a thought or cognitive process not directly sensory in nature. 2. mental content that is not simply a perceptual process. 3. a mental image. 4. a plan of action; a hypothesis.

idealized image: (*Horney*) an ideational construct of the self that supplies unity and striving in the world of people and things. The idealized image is a false and exaggerated estimate of one's true potentialities and abilities and is derived more from fantasy and wishes than from reality.

ideation: the process of forming ideas.

ideational: pertaining to ideas or cognitive processes in general.

ideational learning: learning in which there is a high degree of understanding or the comprehension of concepts, as opposed to learning that is rote or involves relatively meaningless material such as nonsense syllables.

idée fixe: fixed idea.

idée force: the principle that ideas have dynamic properties and can serve as the mainsprings of action.

id-ego: (*Psychoan.*) the organization of the psyche into the original primitive mind of the infant (*id*) and the reality-oriented aspect of mind that develops out of it (*ego*).

identical direction, law of: in binocular vision, the principle that objects are localized as if seen by a single eye in the median plane of the head.

identical-elements theory: (*Thorndike*) a theory that transfer in learning will occur only to the extent that there are similar or identical components in the two learning situations.

identical points: points on the retinas of the two eyes that receive the same stimuli from the same objective distance or infinity. *Syn.* CORRESPONDING POINTS.

identical twins: twins that develop as the result of the splitting of an already fertilized egg. The heredity of identical twins is identical. *Syns.*

monozygotic twins; monochorionic twins. *Contr.* FRATERNAL TWINS.

identification: 1. the process of recognition. 2. placing objects or individuals in a class according to certain characteristics. 3. the process of reacting in one situation in the same manner in which one reacted in a previous situation. 4. associating oneself closely with a group or cause. 5. (*Psychoan.*) the process whereby the child models his or her behavior on that of the parent of the same sex.

identification test: a test on a verbal-intelligence scale in which the examiner points to a picture of a part of an object and asks the subject to name it.

identity: 1. the individual self. 2. the personality. 3. the conditions of being the same in all essential characteristics.

identity formation: (*Psychoan.*) achieving adult patterns of personality through the process of identification.

identity crisis: see ERIKSON'S EGO PSYCHOLOGY.

ideogram: a symbolic representation of an object by a single symbol. For example, a key might signify the gateway to knowledge. *Syn.* PICTOGRAPH.

ideokinetic apraxia: the inability to carry out seriatim or sequential functions. Individual motor responses may be intact, but the patient is unable to put them into a correct sequence.

ideomotor act: a response initiated by an idea.

idiocy: obsolete term formerly employed to characterize the most severe level of mental retardation. The IQ range was defined as 0–20. In law idiots were considered so deficient as to be unable to profit from ordinary education or to avoid the ordinary dangers of life. As a result they were institutionalized. See also MENTAL RETARDATION; AMAUROTIC IDIOCY.

idiodynamics: the point of view that the individual selects those aspects of the environment relevant to his personality. Idiodynamics opposes the point of view that responses are elicited by whatever stimuli may be present and above threshold.

idiographic: 1. pertaining to the individual. 2. characterizing any system of psychology that searches for individual laws of behavior in order to explain individual cases. *Contr.* NOMOTHETIC.

idiopathic: pertaining to diseases that arise entirely within organs, as opposed to those that are the result of outside influences.

idiopathic epilepsy: epilepsy without a known organic basis.

idiophrenic: 1. pertaining to mental disorders due to diseases of the brain. 2. psychogenic in origin.

idioretinal light: the gray perceived in darkness due to the metabolic processes within the retina or brain.

idiosyncrasy: 1. a peculiarity of behavior characteristic of an individual. 2. something unusual or odd.

idiot: an individual suffering from idiocy.

idiotropic: turning inward toward the self; introverted or introspective.

idiot savant: a mentally deficient individual with a highly specialized talent in some area such as rapid calculation, memory, or the execution of music.

I/E ratio: the rate of inspiration divided by the rate of expiration. The I/E ratio is held to be an index of emotionality and may be used as part of the lie-detecting process. Low I/E ratios are believed to be indicative of lying.

I. E. Scale: a special scoring key for the Minnesota Multiphasic Inventory of Personality, which yields scores on the dimension of introversion and extroversion.

I–E Scale: a scale developed by Julian Rotter to measure the individual's principal locus of control—internal or external.

I fraction: the ratio of the duration of inspiration to the total cycle of inspiration-expiration.

illiteracy: 1. the inability to read and write, due to lack of proper education rather than mental deficiency. The U.S. Census Bureau defines illiteracy as the inability, after ten years of age, to read or write in any language. 2. metaphorically, gross ignorance in any field.

illuminance: the intensity of light energy or flux that falls on a surface. Illuminance is measured in foot candles.

illumination: 1. illuminance, or the amount of light falling on a surface. 2. a sudden solution of a problem following a period of no conscious or obvious attempts at a solution.

illusion: a mistaken or distorted perception. Illusions are of various sorts. Some are illusions of movement, such as stroboscopic movement, autokinetic movement, and induced movement. Illusions of perspective refer to the apparent coming-together of parallel lines in the distance. Other illusions involve the misrepresentation of spatial figures, such as the Müller-Lyer, Poggendorff, and Zöllner illusions. Still other illusions involve reversible perspectives, such as the Peter-Paul Goblet and the staircase illusion. *Illusions* are to be distinguished from *hallucinations*, which are false perceptions. Illusions always involve the distortion of stimulus patterns; hallucinations are generated within the individual and are generally considered evidence of abnormality. *Illusions* are also to be distinguished from *delusions*, which are mistaken beliefs.

illusory movement: see APPARENT MOVEMENT.

image: 1. a central or conscious experience similar to sensory experiences, but less vivid, and recognized as arising from memory. 2. a likeness, copy, or reproduction. 3. a picture of an object formed by a condensing lens. 4. (*Titchener*) one of the three elements of consciousness, the other two being affective states and sensations. 5. an attitudinal or judgmental reaction toward a business, institution, or nation. 6. an afterimage (*q.v.*). 7. a component of dreams (see DREAM).

imageless thought: an idea or thought that lacks sensory content. The Würzburg school of psychology held that introspective analysis revealed the existence of imageless thoughts. This contention was denied by Titchener and the structuralists, who held that at least traces of sensory content could be found in all thinking.

imagery: 1. images taken collectively. 2. the type of imagery characteristic of an individual. See also EIDETIC IMAGERY.

imaginal: pertaining to images or to the process of imagination.

imaginary companion: a playmate created in the fantasies of a child and treated as if it were real. The child will talk to the imaginary companion, set a place at the table for it, and "play" with it.

imagination: the process of creating objects or events without the benefit of sensory data. Imagination involves the creation of new objects as a plan for the future, or it may take a fanciful form strongly dominated by autistic or wishful thinking. This kind of imagination is observed in dreams or daydreams.

imagine: 1. to think in terms of objects not present to the senses. 2. to think or to plan.

imago: (*Psychoan.*) an idealized memory of a beloved person, formed in childhood and not subjected to correction by subsequent events.

imbecile: obsolete term formerly employed to characterize a severe level of mental retardation. The IQ range was 20–50. See MENTAL RETARDATION.

imipramine: a drug that retards the uptake of norepinephrine and serotonin by the terminal buttons. Used as an antidepressant.

imitation: copying the actions of another intentionally.

immanent justice: (*Piaget*) the child's belief that misdeeds will naturally lead to punishment.

immature: 1. characteristic of an organism or parts of an organism that have not achieved full development. 2. characteristic of behaviors more appropriate at an earlier age.

immediate experience: 1. (*Wundt*) the conscious process dealt with by psychology, in contrast to the mediate experiences with which the physical sciences deal. 2. a thought or sensation without psychic antecedents.

immediate memory: the memory for material presented within the past few moments. See also MEMORY SPAN; SHORT-TERM MEMORY.

immobility: 1. a condition of the organism in which there is no visible motion. 2. tonic immobility, or "freezing," a reaction manifested by certain species upon being frightened.

impairment: 1. a deterioration in function. 2. a weakening of function or partial loss of function, due to disease or injury.

imperceptible: too weak to be observed or too weak to result in a just-noticeable difference.

imperception: agnosia; lack of perception.

impermeable construct: (*Kelly*) a construct (*q.v.*) that does not permit the addition of new elements. *Contr.* PERMEABLE CONSTRUCT.

impersonal: not concerned with feelings; objective in attitude toward others.

impersonation: the deliberate assumption of the identity of another.

implantation: the attachment of the fertilized ovum to the walls of the uterus. Implantation is believed to occur about 72 hours after fertilization.

implicit behavior: behavior that cannot be directly observed without the aid of instrumentation, such as glandular secretions or the movements of the larynx during speech. Watson used the term to characterize subvocal speech movements, glandular secretions, and deep-seated changes within the body not easily observable. He also believed that thinking could be reduced to implicit subvocal behavior.

implicit response: a covert response that cannot be observed directly.

implosive therapy: in behavior therapy, a technique in which anxiety-arousing stimuli are presented in imagination while the patient is encouraged to experience anxiety as intense as possible. Since the situation is lacking in objective danger, anxiety responses are not reinforced and are gradually extinguished.

impotence: 1. the inability of the male to perform the sex act. 2. a lack of fertility. 3. a feeling of inability to control events.

impression: 1. the theoretical neurological results of stimulation. 2. a phenomenological observation or an unanalyzed sensation. 3. a vague judgment or conclusion.

impression formation: the association and integration of various perceptions into a single impression. Employed especially in reference to how an observer forms impressions of others.

impression method: a procedure in which the subject reports the feelings aroused by a stimulus pattern.

imprinting: a behavioral response acquired early in life, not reversible, and normally released by a certain triggering stimulus or situation.

improvement over chance: a level of improvement in the dependent variable as compared with the average amount of improvement that might have been expected by chance.

impuberty: condition of not having reached puberty.

impulse: 1. an act directed by the id or by another instinct. 2. a sudden incitement to act. 3. a motive or propensity. 4. an awareness of a tendency toward action.

impulsion: a state that predisposes the individual to action.

impulsive: characterizing activity engaged in without due reflection or that cannot be suppressed.

impulsiveness: a more or less chronic tendency to act on impulse or without reflecting upon the consequences of action.

impulsive obsession: *see* OBSESSIVE-COMPULSIVE REACTION.

impunitive: characterizing a reaction

to frustration in which the individual denies the frustration, minimizes it, or condones the reason. *Contr.* INTROPUNITIVE; EXTRAPUNITIVE.

inaccessibility: a condition characteristic of the severe depressive states in which the individual is not responsive to stimuli or verbal commands.

inaccessible memory: a memory, such as a repressed one, that cannot be recalled by ordinary means, but has not been lost.

inadequacy: 1. a feeling or conviction of inferiority or inability. 2. (*Psychoan.*) sexual inadequacy or psychic impotence.

inadequate character: the dependent, socially inadequate individual whose adjustment is built upon dependency relationships.

inadequate personality: an individual lacking good judgment, initiative, and motivation; a social failure.

inadequate stimulus: a stimulus for which the receptor is not highly selective. For example, mechanical pressure on the eyeball will give rise to the sensation of weak light in the retina.

inattention: a state in which there is no focus of attention or in which attention wanders unselectively. See also SELECTIVE INATTENTION.

inborn: innate, as opposed to *acquired* or *learned*.

inbreeding: procreation among close relatives. Inbreeding is deliberately arranged in certain strains of animals in order to maintain hereditary characteristics.

incentive: 1. an external object that tends to arouse motivation and to maintain goal-directed behavior. 2. an extrinsic reward on the way to a main goal. Supplementary rewards are frequently used with school chil-

dren in order to maintain good study habits.

incest: sexual relations between persons of the opposite sex who are closely connected by blood relationship. The degree of relationship is governed by law and social custom.

incest barrier: (*Psychoan.*) the prohibitions placed upon sexual relations with members of the family, particularly with the parent of the opposite sex, and that eventually lead to freeing the libido from familial attachments and to making an external object choice.

incest dream: (*Psychoan.*) a dream having an incest theme, whether symbolic or literal.

incest taboo: the prohibition against sexual intercourse between close relatives.

incidence: the frequency of occurrence of any condition or event.

incidental learning: learning that takes place without intent to learn or in the absence of formal instructions. Whether or not incidental learning can occur is of considerable importance for theories of motivation and learning. If it can, then contiguity would seem to be a sufficient condition for learning; if it cannot, then some motivation and reward are necessary for learning to occur. In practice there is great difficulty in designing experiments in which all motivation is absent.

incidental memory: a memory that occurs without intent to remember.

incidental stimulus: a stimulus not intentionally a part of an experimental arrangement. Sometimes subjects may learn to respond to incidental stimuli. See INCIDENTAL LEARNING.

incident region: in topological psychology, a class of activities that can be reached directly from another class without the necessity of going through an intermediate class.

incoherence: a state of lack of organization or integration, particularly in reference to disconnected speech.

incommensurable: characterizing magnitudes or units of measurement that are incompatible because they are based on different scales.

incompatible response: a response that cannot take place at the same time as another response. Flexing and extending the arm are incompatible responses.

incompetent: lacking the necessary ability or qualification properly to carry out a task. In psychiatric literature, *incompetence* refers to a state characteristic of insane or mentally deficient persons who, because of their deficiency, are not legally responsible.

incomplete-pictures test: any test that makes use of a series of drawings that show more and more of the object in question. The subject's task is to identify it as quickly as possible.

incomplete-sentence test: 1. an item on a test of general intelligence in which sentences are presented with words missing, particularly with relational words such as *but*, *for*, and *and*. 2. a type of projective technique in which the subject completes a sentence stem, such as, "When I am at home I————." The responses are analyzed for significant themes.

incontinence: 1. inability to govern defecation or urination or both. 2. inability to restrain sexual impulses.

incoordination: 1. the failure of balance or harmony in the functioning of bodily parts. 2. lack of balance or impairment in the static sense.

incorporation: taking into the body or making a part of the self.

incorrigible: characterizing an individual whose behavior is not capable of being corrected or improved.

increment: the amount of increase or decrease in a magnitude or variable.

incubation: a period of no activity, or apparent inactivity, in thinking, during which a solution to a problem may occur.

incus: one of the auditory ossicles. The incus is midway between the malleus and the stapes. *Syn.* ANVIL.

indecency: 1. conduct generally considered contrary to social customs. 2. conduct considered contrary to legal codes, particularly conduct involving sexual behavior or exposure of the body.

independence: 1. a state of absence of known causal or correlational relations between two variables. 2. an attitude characterized by self-reliance. *Contr.* DEPENDENCE.

independence, test of or **index of:** in statistics a measure of the degree of agreement between actual and expected frequencies in a plot of two variables. *Syn.* test for homogeneity.

independent variable: 1. the variable controlled by the experimenter and applied to the subject in order to determine its effect on the subject's reaction. 2. in simple correlations, the criterion variable with which the measured variable is to be correlated.

indeterminate: 1. in mathematics, pertaining to values that are not fixed or that cannot be specifically evaluated in magnitude. 2. undetermined or undeterminable.

indeterminism: the position that man is able to act independently of antecedent conditions and present stimuli when confronted with choice situations. *Contr*. DETERMINISM.

index: 1. a significant value that can be used to identify a category. 2. an exponent that shows the power (or root) of a number. 3. in statistics, a number indicating a change in a series of magnitudes.

index case: in genetic research, the individual in a family who shows the trait under investigation. *Syn*. PROBAND.

indifference: a state of neutrality with respect to two opposing psychological states, such as pleasantness and unpleasantness.

indifference point: a transition zone between two opposing variables, such as warmth and cold, or pleasure and pain.

indifferent stimulus: a stimulus, such as a bell in conditioning, that has not yet elicited the response under investigation.

indirect: 1. not taking the shortest path in a maze or discrimination apparatus. 2. more generally, proceeding through intermediate steps or in a roundabout manner.

indirect measurement: measurement in which the obtained values must be converted to another scale or where the quantification must be carried out through intermediary processes. The estimate of infant intelligence by means of absolute scaling techniques illustrates the use of indirect measurement.

indirect vision: seeing with any part of the retina other than the fovea.

indissociation: a stage in the development of the child's perception of the physical world in which phenomena are not clearly distinguished from one another or from the self.

individual difference: any trait or quantitative difference in a trait by which any individual may be distinguished from other individuals.

individualism: 1. strong attitude of personal independence. 2. the doctrine that the individual is of paramount importance. 3. the theory that individual effort and initiative should take precedence over governmental or social action.

individuality: 1. that which distinguishes the individual from all other individuals. 2. the unique qualities of the individual; the integration of an individual's traits.

individualization: the process of becoming an individual.

individual psychology: the branch of psychology that investigates differences among individuals. *Syn*. DIFFERENTIAL PSYCHOLOGY. The latter term has comes to be preferred. The first is chiefly historical.

Individual Psychology of Alfred Adler: a system of psychology founded by Alfred Adler, whose aim is the understanding, prevention, and treatment of mental disorders. As an early associate of Freud's, Adler became dissatisfied with the former's emphasis on sexuality in the development of personality and the neuroses, and he emphasized the childhood weakness and helplessness that lead to feelings of inferiority and, in severe cases, to an inferiority complex. Feelings of inferiority are greatly accentuated if the child has either a real or imagined organic inferiority, is a member of the female sex, or is a member of a minority group. Such accentuated feelings of inferiority lead to compensatory activity and a style of life characterized by active striving to overcome the minus situation of inferiority by achieving a plus situation of superiority. Compensatory behavior is likely to lead to overcompensation with attempts to dominate others, to generate hostility toward competitors, and to develop asocial or antisocial attitudes such as are characteristic of the delinquent, criminal, or withdrawn individual. Individuals suffering from excessive feelings of inferiority are also driven by an exaggerated notion of their own worth, which takes the form of an unreasonable guiding fiction toward which they strive and that dominates their style of life. The great gap between the reality of the individual's life and the idealized guiding fiction creates anxiety, further striving, and more overcompensation, and so a vicious circle is generated.

Adler laid great emphasis on the family constellation as the chief factor in the development of the lifestyle. The oldest child is particularly vulnerable to developing feelings of inferiority if another child comes along and dethrones him from his position of preeminence. The mother, who holds the critical position as the first social contact the child experiences, must be on guard against either inadvertently or consciously rejecting the older child in favor of a younger. Equally important, she must avoid pampering the child and thus preventing him from developing an independent, self-reliant spirit. In treating a patient, Adler first sought to determine the patient's style of life, to determine the cause of his going astray and discover where the patient began to seek to dominate people instead of mastering his inferiority feelings in a socially constructive manner. Of considerable importance in arriving at a diagnosis is the individual's earliest memory, which reveals the first attempts to solve problems. Adler also accepted dream analysis but, unlike Freud, did not emphasize the sexual nature of dreams; instead he interpreted them as another instance of the individual's attempts at problem solving. Adler strove to help the patient realize his mistaken style of life and to seek sound, socially satisfying adjustments in the marital, vocational, and social aspects of living.

Adler's system of Individual Psychology became popular in the years immediately after its founding, and Adler attracted a number of followers who helped him in the establishment of centers for the practice of Individual Psychology. With his death the system went into an eclipse in the spreading shadow of Freudian psychoanalysis. But Adlerian concepts of personality formation, the causation of the neuroses, and therapeutic theory and practice have been enjoying a rebirth in recent years and are found with increasing frequency in the literature on these subjects.

individual response: in association tests, a response not commonly given.

individual test: a test that must be given to a single individual, typically by a specially trained person. The Binet and Wechsler intelligence tests are examples of individual tests.

individuation: 1. the process by which parts differentiate out of the whole. 2. the process of individualization. 3. the emergence of partial patterns of behavior out of the totality of behavior. 4. in social groups, a condition in which the names and personal characteristics of participants are known to each other.

induced color: a color change in a part of the visual field that is not due to direct stimulation but to the stimulation of an adjacent area.

induced tonus: muscular tone caused by contraction in another part of the body.

inducing color: a stimulus that induces a contrast effect. See also COLOR CONTRAST.

induction: 1 in logic, reasoning from the particular to the general. 2. a form of parental discipline in which explanations are given to the child as to why he should modify his behavior. 3. in physiology, the arousal of an activity in one part as a result of the spread of activity from an adjoining area. See also NEURAL INDUCTION.

induction coil: an electrical device consisting of two coils, the primary and the secondary, from which high voltages at very low amperages can be induced in the secondary coil for physiological stimulation and for the application of shock in psychological experiments.

induction test: a test employed on general intelligence scales in which the testee must deduce a general principle from a number of specific instances.

industrial psychology: that branch of psychology concerned with applying the methods and findings of psychology to the solution of industrial problems. Areas of concern are: employment and personnel practices, working conditions, fatigue, morale, rewards for work, and efficiency. In its broadest sense, industrial psychology is extended to include the areas of business, advertising, and the military.

ineffective stimulus: a stimulus incapable of arousing a receptor.

inertia: a property of receptors and neurons manifested by the fact of a time lag between the stimulus and the onset of activity in the organ in question.

infancy: the early period of postnatal life in which the individual is relatively helpless and dependent upon the parents. The term is usually applied only to the first year.

infantile: 1. pertaining to infancy. 2. characterized by immature, childlike behavior on the part of an older child or adult.

infantile amnesia: (*Psychoan.*) the inability to recall events of the first two or three years of life because of repression.

infantile autism: a serious developmental disorder of infancy, childhood, and adolescence. It is characterized by an almost total lack of responsiveness to others, with gross impairment of linguistic development, bizarre behavior involving repetitive movements, and self-abusive behavior such as head banging. The disorder is relatively rare, involving 2–4 children per 10,000 and about three times more prevalent in males than females.

The identification of the disorder occurs when the parents discover that the child appears cold and unresponsive, does not smile, and fails to begin to speak at the normal age. Such children may play with the same toy for hours, make irrelevant and repetitive movements such as hand clapping, head banging, or turning light switches on and off endlessly. They appear disturbed if their routines are changed, and seem to prefer being left alone. As they grow into adolescence and adulthood, only 15 to 20 percent make an adequate adjustment. Most remain totally dependent on others and many are institutionalized.

The causes of infantile autism are unknown. Originally believed to be associated with cold, unresponsive mothers, it is now thought to be due to other factors, since many autistic children have warm, caring mothers. The psychoanalytic school has emphasized a failure to develop through the oral, anal, and early genital stages with consequent inability to establish contact with reality and the lack of ego development. Others have suggested that the disorder is an early form of schizophrenia. Some investigators have argued that it has an organic basis but have been unable to demonstrate precisely where the physiological deficit lies.

Treatment has taken the form of attempting to provide an intensely warm, high contact environment in order to encourage the child to emerge from his inner world. Recent behavioral techniques involving reinforcement of positive social responses have been tried with some success. However, the overall success of treatment programs remains poor.

infantile birth theories: the belief on the part of children that babies emerge from the navel, the anal opening, or are dissected out of the mother.

infantile perversion: (*Psychoan.*) the doctrine that the infant shows forms of sexual behavior that in an adult would be considered perversions.

infantile sexuality: (*Psychoan.*) the capacity of infants for sexual desire and experience. The best-known of the various manifestations of infantile sexuality are the behaviors associated with the oral, anal, and early genital phases of development.

infantile speech: baby talk; speech in which many words are omitted and many sound substitutions occur.

infantilism: 1. a condition of arrested development. 2. regression to a level of behavior more appropriate to an early stage of development.

infant psychology: the branch of psychology concerned with children under one year of age.

infant test: any test of behavioral development used as an index of normalcy in behavioral or intellectual development. See also GESELL DEVELOPMENTAL SCALES.

infavoidance motive: (*Murray*) the motive to avoid failure, shame, ridicule, or tasks likely to lead to failure.

inference: 1. a conclusion arrived at on the basis of previous conclusions rather than through direct observation. 2. the process of drawing a conclusion based on other conclusions.

inferior: 1. designating a lower part of the body or a posterior part of an organ such as the brain. 2. of lower degree or quality.

inferiority complex: a term used by Adler in two ways: (1) to refer to unconscious intensified feelings of being insignificant, insecure, or unable to cope with life; (2) a conscious excuse or rationalization for failure or unwillingness to strive or cope.

inferiority feelings: feelings of insecurity, of being insignificant, helpless, incomplete, and unable to cope with the demands of living. The minus situation of the inferiority feelings leads the child to strive for a positive situation of superiority through compensation.

inferior oblique: one of the extrinsic eye muscles. The inferior oblique rotates the eyeball upward.

infertile: 1. sterile; having no offspring. 2. having few offspring.

inflection: 1. a bending or change in the shape of a curve. 2. a change in the pitch of the voice. 3. change in word forms to express grammatical modifications.

informal test: a test that has not been standardized but which gives a crude index of the individual's ability.

information: 1. a set of facts or ideas gained through investigation, experience, or practice. 2. a characteristic of a cue or stimulus utilized by an organism in learning situations. 3. in information theory, a quantitative property of a collection or ensemble of items that enables the items to be classified in some way. The *bit* is the unit of information in information theory.

information processing theory: deals with the input, processing, storage, and retrieval of information in men and machines. Stimulated by the invention of computers and other devices for processing data efficiently, information processing theory attracted the attention of psychologists who believe that an analysis of the problems involved in developing machines that simulate sensing, memory, learning, and problem solving in human beings can be of help in understanding how the brain can carry out these functions.

On the input side, the brain is dependent upon the sense organs for detecting information from environmental stimuli and transducing it into nervous impulses. The sensory nerves and their pathways through the spinal cord and subcortical centers are analogous to channels in machines and, like the machine, have a limited channel capacity. This capacity is described in information processing theory as bits of information. Ordinarily the individual can detect only 5–9 bits of information of a random nature, such as the correct number of dots scattered on a sheet of paper or random digits pronounced orally to be repeated immediately. If, however, bits are combined into chunks, channel capacity is greatly increased. For example, if sixteen dots are arranged in random order the correct number

••• ••••• • ••• •• • ••

cannot be apprehended in a single act of perceiving. The same dots arranged in chunks of four are readily apprehended:

•••• •••• •••• ••••

The brain, like the digital computer, can recognize, select, or reject information on the basis of certain distinctive features. One type of detection system is template matching, a technique widely used in processing bank checks. Special numbers are printed on the checks which the computer can be programmed to recognize by means of determining whether they fit the correct template or pattern. Human memory is organized in such a manner that the individual can instantly recognize information presented to the "memory banks" in the brain. Psychologists are not yet ready to suggest that the brain makes use of template matching in retrieving information. The process is undoubtedly far more complex.

The greater complexity of the human organism is revealed in the fact that we can recognize information presented in unusual ways. Numbers and letters can be set in all kinds of type and still be recognizable. The machine, however, can recognize only special stylized type. Moreover, we can keep track of several streams of incoming information at the same time. This is known as parallel processing—an ability not possessed by machines that can deal only with one channel of information at a given time. This is called sequential processing.

Machines have been constructed that are capable of learning in the sense of modifying the sequence of processing on the basis of experience. Moreover, machines can solve problems by techniques known as algorithmic and heuristic processing. In algorithmic processing every possible solution to the problem is tried out and rejected until the correct solution is found. In making a possible chess move to counteract an opponent's, the machine might be programmed to run through every possible move before "deciding" on the most appropriate. By contrast, in heuristic problem solving the machine is programmed to try out certain predetermined combinations that are likely to be successful. The latter technique is clearly more effective than the former which for relatively simple problems can involve an astronomical number of possible combinations of choices.

Machines have been built that can play checkers and chess, solve mathematical equations, make crude or literalistic translations of foreign languages, and simulate various aspects of human learning and thinking. In developing such programs for machines, psychologists have arrived at a better knowledge of our input (sensory) system, our processing (learning and problem solving) systems, and our retrieval (memory) system.

information test: a test that samples the individual's knowledge in a given area or number of areas. The information sampled is usually of the incidental type, which theoretically should be common to everyone.

information theory: a branch of science and engineering dealing with the transmission of information and its measurable characteristics. Quantities of information are measured in units called *bits*. A bit tells which of two equally probable events has taken place. Information is analyzed in terms of signals and their characteristics and in terms of the effect of the structure of informational form on the reliability of communication.

infrahuman: 1. pertaining to species other than man, particularly animals other than man. 2. pertaining to behavioral characteristics typical of animals lower than man.

infundibulum: the stalk by means of which the pituitary gland is attached to the brain.

in group: a closely knit group with strong feelings of solidarity. *Syn.* WE GROUP. *Contr.* OUT GROUP; they group.

inherent: 1. belonging to or existing in an object or person as a permanent characteristic. 2. an unlearned characteristic.

inherit: 1. to receive from the parents through the agency of genetic transmission. 2. to receive property from the parents. 3. to receive the cultural heritage from parents and society.

inheritance: 1. heredity. 2. inherited property.

inherited: derived from the parents or one's ancestors; not learned.

inhibition: 1. in neurology, the stopping of an ongoing process or the prevention of a process from starting, as in the inhibition of antagonistic muscles. 2. a mental blockage; a hesitancy to behave, particularly in a somewhat unconventional manner. 3. (*Psychoan.*) the prevention, by the intervention of the superego, of libidinal impulses from reaching consciousness.

inhibition of delay: the lessening of the time interval between stimulus and response or between the conditioned stimulus and the conditioned response.

inhibitory postsynaptic potential (IPSP): an increase in internal negativity of a neuron resulting from impulses arriving over inhibitory neurons.

inhibitory potential: (*Hull*) conditioned inhibition. Conditioned inhibition is generated when stimuli closely associated with the cessation of a response become conditioned to the inhibition associated with the elicitation of that response.

inhibitory reflex: the reflexive relaxation of an antagonistic muscle pair upon stimulation of one member of the pair.

inhibitory synapse: a synapse where transmission results in the inhibition of firing in the postsynaptic neuron. *Contr.* EXCITATORY SYNAPSE.

initial spurt: the relatively high level of performance at the beginning of a series. *Contr.* END SPURT.

initiative: 1. the ability to act independently. 2. the action involved in beginning a series of events.

injury: damage due to disease, accident, or deliberate surgical intervention.

inkblot test: see RORSCHACH TEST.

innate: inborn; present in the individual at birth. The term *innate* does not necessarily imply that the behavior in question appears full-blown without practice or independent of environmental effects. All behavior is a joint product of the interaction of heredity and environment.

innate intelligence: the discredited theory that intelligence is hereditary or innate without regard to environmental influences.

inner ear: the portion of the auditory apparatus contained in the cochlea along with the utricle and saccule and the semicircular canals. The utricle, saccule, and semicircular canals are concerned with the sense of equilibrium, proprioception, and movement.

innervation: 1. the nerve supply to a muscle or gland. 2. the excitation of a motor unit by a nerve. Innervation is sometimes improperly used as synonymous with excitation.

innervation ratio: the number of muscle fibers in a motor unit per neuron. In high-speed phasic muscles the ratio is low; in low-speed postural muscles the ratio is high.

inoculation theory: the assumption that providing an individual with a weakened counterargument allows him to build up effective refutations to counterpropaganda.

input: 1. the amount of energy or effort put into a system. 2. in electronic circuits, the signal fed into a circuit from another circuit. 3. in information and communication theory, a signal fed into a receiver.

insanity: a serious mental disorder that renders the individual incapable of conducting his affairs in a competent manner. Insanity is a legal, not a psychological term. See also PSYCHOSIS.

insecurity: the feeling of being unable to cope; feeling unsafe, threatened, or anxious.

insensible: 1. characteristic of stimuli that are not sensed, either because they are inadequate or below the absolute threshold. 2. not responsive to stimulation, or incapable of responding to a certain class of stimuli. 3. a state of unconsciousness. 4. lacking in emotionality; unsympathetic.

inside details: a Rorschach scoring category for unusual detail involving responses based on areas inside larger areas which most subjects respond to as a whole.

insight: 1. in problem-solving and learning situations, a sudden solution characterized by high understanding, good retention, and high transfer. 2. a novel solution not based on previous experience. 3. in psychotherapy, the illumination, or bringing to awareness, of motives, relationships, feelings, impulses, etc., that had previously been poorly understood or about which the subject was totally unaware. 4. in the normal individual, self-understanding; awareness of one's major motivations, desires, feelings, etc.

insistence: a second-order attribute brought about by the concurrence of two simple attributes and resulting in forced attention.

insistent idea: a fixed idea.

insomnia: a chronic inability to sleep; agrypnia.

inspection: introspection. See also IMPRESSION.

inspiration: 1. the act of drawing air into the lungs. 2. the sudden solution to a problem or the occurrence of a creative idea without previous trial and error or reasoning.

inspiration-expiration: see I/E RATIO.

instability: 1. tendency toward excessive or rapidly changing emotional behavior. 2. a more or less chronic lack of personality organization or self-control.

instigation therapy: in behavior therapy, a technique in which the therapist provides a positive model for the patient as well as reinforces his progress in the development of self-regulatory and self-evaluative behaviors.

instinct: 1. a complex, unlearned response characteristic of a given species, such as nest building in the wasp. 2. a propensity or impulse toward a certain type of behavior. 3. a complex response or set of responses characteristic of a species and released by certain specified stimulus conditions. Ducks imprinted to a mother exemplifies this usage of the term. 4. innate or inherited tendencies that are the motive power behind all thought and action. *Syns.* ERG; PRIMARY DRIVE; SPECIES-SPECIFIC BEHAVIOR; PROPENSITY.

instinctive: 1. pertaining to instincts. 2. characterizing a behavior pattern that is not learned.

instinctual: 1. pertaining to behavior that is instinctive or species-specific. 2. impulsive, irrational. 3. (*Psychoan.*) impulses that develop out of the primitive id; strongly emotional or irrational impulses.

instinctual fusion: (*Psychoan.*) the integration of the life and death instincts in all behavior.

institution: 1. an organization, corporation, or establishment whose purpose may be political, economic, religious, educational, recreational, etc. 2. an organized mode of social behavior, such as the institution of marriage.

institutionalization: 1. the process of placing a person in an institution for corrective or therapeutic purposes. 2. the individual's adaptation to the patterns of behavior characteristic of an institution.

instruction: 1. teaching; the imparting of knowledge to others in a systematic manner. 2. directions to a subject in an experiment.

instrument: 1. broadly, any device utilized in measuring or recording data, such as apparatus, chronometers, tests, etc. 2. a means or a tool by which something is accomplished.

Instrumental: 1. pertaining to a form of behavior in which the subject's response is a means to an end, such as reactions in instrumental conditioning. 2. pertaining to that which is emphasized or valued as a means to an end.

instrumental conditioning: see CONDITIONING (2).

instrumental learning: learning in which the subject is directly involved in bringing about the reward or reinforcement. For example, if a dog must lift his foot in order to escape a shock, the response is instrumental in achieving the goal of escape from pain.

Insula: see ISLAND OF REIL.

insulin: a hormone secreted by the islands of Langerhans in the pancreas. The hormone acts in the utilization of carbohydrates.

insulin coma: a comatose state induced by an overdose of insulin taken accidentally by a diabetic or given to a mental patient for shock therapy.

insulin shock therapy: the utilization of insulin-induced coma and convulsions for the purpose of treating mental disorders.

integrate: 1. to bring together into a whole. 2. to give members of a minority group equal rights in a community, particularly in schools and places of public accommodation.

Integrating tendency: collectively, all patterns of behavior involved in satisfaction seeking.

integration: 1. process by which parts are unified into a whole. 2. in neurology, the process of coordinating impulses from several centers into a unified whole. 3. a personality condition, or condition of the entire organism in which all traits or parts work together in a smooth, coordinated whole. 4. the process of guaranteeing equal civil rights to members of a minority group hitherto segregated or discriminated against.

intellect: 1. the cognitive processes of thinking, relating, and judging. 2. mental ability or intelligence.

intellection: the process of thinking or judging.

intellectual: 1. pertaining to the intellect; pertaining to intelligence. 2. characterizing an individual whose interests are primarily in ideas and learning.

intellectual imbalance: an inequality in abilities or intellectual interests.

intellectualism: the doctrine that reduces all mental procedures to cognitive processes.

intellectual maturity: 1. the attainment of an adult state of intellectual development. 2. wisdom; a high degree of good judgment in the control and management of behavior.

intellectualization: the analysis of a problem in purely intellectual terms, primarily as a defense mechanism. In intellectualization, feelings and emotions are ignored. Horney gives the example of a patient who, in the course of analysis, looked at himself and exclaimed, "How interesting!"

intelligence: 1. the ability to meet and adapt to novel situations quickly and effectively. 2. the ability to utilize abstract concepts effectively. 3.

the ability to grasp relationships and to learn quickly. The three definitions are by no means independent; they merely emphasize different aspects of the process. In spite of the prevalence of intelligence testing, psychologists have found it difficult to define intelligence precisely. Binet, who originated the individual test, emphasized reasoning, imagination, insight, judgment, and adaptability as the mental processes involved in intelligent behavior. Some subsequent investigators have emphasized the ability to adapt quickly and effectively in novel situations, while others have stressed the ability to solve abstract problems. Many abstract problems require adaptability or flexibility in thinking. Conversely, man's great adaptability and his tremendous cultural, scientific, and technological achievements depend upon his capacity for abstract reasoning. However, most of the psychologists who developed the early tests sidestepped the problem of the precise nature of what they were measuring and attempted to make their scales good predictors of scholastic achievement. This approach made good sense, since the primary purpose of administering intelligence tests to children was (and still is) to determine their scholastic aptitude. Moreover, most psychologists think of intelligence in much the same way that physicists think of time. Time is what chronometers measure. By the same logic intelligence is what tests measure.

intelligence coefficient: the index of relative intelligence that is obtained when the testee's score on an intelligence test is divided by the norm for the chronological age. *Syn.* INTELLIGENCE QUOTIENT.

intelligence quotient (IQ): an index of the child's relative level of brightness as compared with other children his age. The intelligence quotient is obtained by dividing the mental age by the chronological age and multiplying by 100, or

$$IQ = \frac{MA}{CA} \times 100$$

A child or adult who receives an IQ of 100 is normal or average for his age. IQ's over 100 are above the statistical average, and IQ's below 100 are below the statistical average. However, an IQ must be more than one standard or probable error above or below the mean IQ of 100 to be considered significantly different from average. The following table may prove useful in making interpretive judgments about the significance of obtained IQ's.

IQ	Interpretation
0–20	Profound Retardation
21–35	Severe Retardation
36–50	Moderate Retardation
51–70	Mild Retardation
70–90	Dull, Slow Learner
90–110	Average
110–120	Superior
120–140	Very Superior
140–	Gifted

intelligence scale: a standardized intelligence test.

intelligence test: an intelligence test consists of a series of tasks of graded difficulty that have been standardized on a representative sample of the population. Tests are of two types: individual tests, which must be administered to a single subject by a trained psychologist; and group tests, which may be administered to large numbers of individuals simultaneously. However, the results of group tests should be interpreted and utilized only by trained individuals. Tests may also be divided into verbal and performance types. Verbal tests utilize language both in the administration and in the subject's responses. On the advanced levels of the test, the subject may be required to read. Performance tests utilize concrete, nonverbal materials, such as form boards, incomplete pictures, and colored block designs. In general, verbal tests, where applicable, are considered superior to performance tests, and individual tests are considered superior to group tests.

intelligibility: the quality of conveying meaning; that which can be readily understood.

intensity: 1. the quantitative attribute of a sensation that is correlated with the intensity of the stimulus, such as the brightness of a color or the loudness of a sound. 2. the strength of any behavior or experience, such as the intensity of an emotional response. 3. the strength with which an opinion or attitude is held.

intent analysis: see CONTENT ANALYSIS.

intention: 1. a striving, or planning to strive, for a goal. 2. the distinguishing feature of psychological processes which involves their reference to an object. See also ACT PSYCHOLOGY.

intentional: pertaining to intention; purposeful; conscious or voluntary.

intentional forgetting: forgetting due to repression or to an unconscious desire to forget.

intentionality; intentionalism: a characteristic of acts that refer to or in-

tend to something outside themselves. See also ACT PSYCHOLOGY.

intentional movement; intentional response: a preliminary, usually tentative, movement that precedes a hierarchy or chain of responses.

intentional tremor: a type of tremor that occurs during voluntary movement.

interaction: 1. a relationship between systems such that events taking place in one system influence events taking place in the other. 2. a social relationship between people of such a nature that individuals mutually influence each other.

interaction-process analysis: a technique for studying social groups by analyzing the members' reactions in terms of categories involving emotional and problem-solving responses.

interaction variance: variance that is the result of the interaction of two or more variables acting together.

interactive measurement: (*R. B. Cattell*) any measurement that reflects an interaction between the individual and his environment.

interbehavioral psychology: a system of psychology emphasizing the interaction between the organism and the environment. The subject matter of psychology is the *event* (perceiving, learning, discriminating, etc.) that is studied in terms of the history of its relations to stimuli and to other events.

interbrain: the diencephalon, consisting of the thalamus, epithalamus, and hypothalamus.

intercept: the distance from a point of origin to where a line crosses a reference axis.

intercorrelation: a correlation of one variable with another in a group of variables. Intercorrelations are often presented in tabular form in factor-analysis studies.

intercourse: 1. interaction between two individuals or groups. 2. coitus; sexual intercourse.

interest: 1. an enduring attitude that engages the individual's attention to make it selective toward the object of interest. 2. the feeling that a certain activity, avocation, or object is of worth or significance to the individual. 3. a state of motivation, or set, that guides behavior in a certain direction or toward certain goals.

interest inventory or **test:** an instrument designed to measure an individual's interests in a variety of activities. Many of the interests and preferences measured are peripheral or avocational. Because such interests are related to certain vocational areas, the results of interest inventories can be used in vocational guidance. The most widely used inventories are the Strong Vocational Interest Blank, which measures interests in a wide variety of specific occupations, and the Kuder Preference Record, which has been validated for a limited number of broad vocational areas.

interference: 1. a conflict of competing associations in learning or memory. 2. a decrease in the amplitude of a sound or light wave when two waves occurring simultaneously are out of phase. In audition, this phenomenon causes beats. 3. a conflict of incompatible interests, motives, activities, perceptual processes, ideas, etc. 4. the placing of barriers or difficulties in another's way.

interjection theory of speech: the theory that language arose out of the utterance of exclamations or interjections.

interlocking reinforcement: a type of intermittent reinforcement in which there is a decreasing ratio of required responses per reinforcement. For example, the schedule might demand 100 responses for the first reinforcement, then 90 for the second, 80 for the third, and so on.

intermission: a period of relative normalcy between periods of mental disturbance, such as often occurs in manic-depressive reactions.

intermittence tone: see INTERRUPTION TONE.

intermittent: not continuous; occurring periodically.

intermittent reinforcement: any pattern of reinforcement that is not continuous. See FIXED-RATIO REINFORCEMENT; FIXED-INTERVAL REINFORCEMENT; PERIODIC REINFORCEMENT; VARIABLE-RATIO REINFORCEMENT; CONJUNCTIVE REINFORCEMENT; INTERLOCKING REINFORCEMENT; TANDEM REINFORCEMENT; MULTIPLE REINFORCEMENT; CONCURRENT REINFORCEMENT.

internal: 1. within the body. 2. toward the central axis of the body. 3. subjective or mental as opposed to objective or behavioral.

internal capsule: a relatively large tract of nerve fibers that passes through the corpus striatum.

internal consistency: an index of the extent to which various parts of a test or other measuring device measure the same function. The degree of internal consistency can be estimated by correlating the two halves of the test or by applying the Hoyt or Kuder-Richardson formula.

internal ear: see EAR.

internal environment: the processes going on within the organism that tend toward maintaining constancy, or homeostasis. The functions of many organs are such that they automatically attempt to correct imbalances. *Syn. milieu interne*.

internal-external scale: (*Rotter*) a personality scale that measures the extent to which the individual believes he controls events as opposed to the extent he believes external forces control him.

internal inhibition: (*Pavlov*) any of the inhibitory processes in the nervous system that act contrary to excitatory processes and thus cause a gradual diminution in the magnitude of a conditioned response even though reinforcement is being given. When reinforcement is stopped, internal inhibition quickly gains in relative strength and the response is extinguished.

internalizaton: the incorporation of attitudes, standards of conduct, opinions, etc., within the personality. Freud believed that the superego, or moral aspect of personality, was derived from the internalization of parental attitudes

internal motivation: motivation arising from cyclic or rhythmic changes within the organism.

internal need: a need that arises directly out of the tissues or cyclic physiological changes.

internal rectus: one of the extrinsic eye muscles. The internal rectus rotates the eyeball inward.

internal reinforcement: an organismic process that serves to increase the probability of a response.

internal-secretion gland: see ENDOCRINE GLAND.

internal senses: the proprioceptive and interoceptive senses.

internal validation: the process of improving the validity of a measuring instrument by making sure that the various items correlate highly with the total score, on the assumption that the overall score is a valid measure.

internuncial neurons: neurons that connect sensory and motor neurons within the spinal cord. *Syn.* interneuron; connector neuron.

interoceptor: a sense organ within the body proper that gives information about visceral processes. *Contr.* EXTEROCEPTOR; PROPRIOCEPTOR.

interocular distance: the distance between the pupils of the two eyes as measured with the eyes in normal fixation.

interosystem: any system, such as the cardiac, respiratory, and parts of the digestive, that functions wholly within the organism and is controlled by the autonomic nervous system.

interpersonal: 1. that which takes place between persons. 2. characterizing processes that arise as a result of the interaction of individuals. 3. social.

interpersonal conflict: 1. a conflict between persons who seek the same goal. 2. a conflict within the individual that originates out of his relations with others.

interpersonal theory: the theory developed by Harry S. Sullivan that mental disorders and personality development are primarily determined by interpersonal interaction rather than by constitutional factors.

interpolated reinforcement: the introduction of a block of one schedule of reinforcements into another schedule for a brief period of time.

interposition: the partial obscuring of one object by another. Interposition is a monocular cue to depth perception.

interpretation: 1. explaining something in a meaningful way. 2. (*Psychoan.*). explaining the significance of freely associated material and of dreams.

interpretive hypothesis: (*R. B. Cattell*) an assumption as to the nature of a personality dimension or influence that could produce an observed pattern of variables consistently found to be related to a factor in factor-analysis studies of personality.

interpretive therapy: therapy in which the significance or meaning of the patient's productions is formulated by the therapist and given to the patient. The therapist will particularly seek to interpret resistances, repressions, and dream material. *Contr.* NONDIRECTIVE THERAPY.

interquartile range: the distance between the end of the first to the beginning of the third quartile. The interquartile range includes the middle 50 percent of the distribution of values.

interruption tone: tonal effect produced by the interruption of a tone of constant pitch. If the interruption is slow, beat is experienced; if the interruption is fast, a tone is heard whose pitch corresponds to the frequency of the interruption. *Syn.* INTERMITTENCE TONE.

intersexuality: having the characteristics of both sexes in a normally bisexual species.

interstitial cell-stimulating hormone: see LUTENIZING HORMONE.

intertone: a tone that may appear when two primary tones are producing beats. The intertone is intermediate in pitch between the primaries.

intertrial interval: the interval between successive presentations of stimuli, lists of nonsense syllables, etc.

interval: 1. the range of time between two events, tests, etc. 2. the distance between two objects. 3. the difference in pitch between two tones. 4. a class interval in a frequency distribution.

interval of uncertainty: the range between the momentary upper and lower thresholds in determining thresholds by the method of just-noticeable differences. *Abbr.* IU.

interval reinforcement: reinforcement presented at a fixed or variable temporal schedule.

interval scale: a scale that does not have an absolute zero point but whose intervals are equal. The Fahrenheit temperature scale is an interval scale. Most psychological scales are of the interval variety.

intervening variable: a hypothetical variable postulated to account for responses to stimulating conditions. Intervening variables have no independent existence except as they are observed in experimental situations. Some intervening variables may be assumed to have "real" existence in the sense that cortical modifications have been postulated to account for memory. Nevertheless, intervening variables are not physical constructs but processes defined and measured by appropriate instruments or techniques.

interview: a face-to-face conversation for the purpose of obtaining factual information, assessing the individual's personality, or counseling or therapeutic purposes. According to its purpose, the nature of the interview will be more or less directive. If the purpose is to obtain factual information, then the interviewer is likely to be highly directive, asking questions and recording the subject's answers. If the purpose is therapeutic, the nondirective interview is typically more favored, on the assumption that the subject is more willing to reveal himself in an atmosphere in which he is not questioned but is made to feel the warmth and understanding of the interviewer.

interviewer bias: the effect of the interviewer's own opinions and prejudices upon the course and interpretation of an interview.

intimacy principle: the principle that Gestalts are interdependent wholes, none of whose parts may be changed without changing the whole.

intolerance of ambiguity: see AMBIGUITY TOLERANCE.

intoxication: a state of either abnormal elation or abnormal depression, or alternate periods of depression and elation, caused by the ingestion of drugs, poisons, or alcohol.

intraception: (*Murray*) the dominance of feeling, fantasy, aspirations. A warm, humanistic outlook. *Contr.* EXTRACEPTION.

intrafusal fiber: specialized muscle cells within muscle spindles sensitive to stretch.

intraocular modification: any change that takes place in the visual stimulus due to structures within the eyeball. Distortions caused by the cornea, lens, humors, effects of diffusion, and the like, are included.

intraserial learning: the learning of associations between items within a list.

intrapsychic: taking place within the personality or mind, such as intrapsychic conflicts that are expressions of the existence of two opposing motivations or impulses within the individual.

intrapunitive: see INTROPUNITIVE.

intrauterine: taking place within the uterus.

intraversion: see INTROVERSION.

intrinsic: pertaining to a quality or property of something in itself, without regard to value arising from its relations to other objects, properties, etc. *Syn.* INHERENT. *Contr.* EXTRINSIC.

intrinsic behavior: behavior that expresses itself through a specific organ. For example, the knee-jerk reflex. Extrinsic behavior has no specialized response mechanism. For example, teaching may be carried out in a variety of ways using various response mechanisms.

intrinsic eye muscles: the iris and ciliary muscles. See also EYE.

intrinsic interest: attributing value to an object or activity for its own sake. Thus, learning to play a musical instrument for the enjoyment that it brings is demonstrating intrinsic interest in the activity. Learning to play because of the prestige it brings is learning because of extrinsic interest.

intrinsic motivation: motivation in which the satisfaction arises out of the behavior itself. For example, working a puzzle for the satisfaction of finding the solution. *Contr.* EXTRINSIC MOTIVATION.

intrinsic reward: a form of reward in which the activity itself is found interesting and rewarding. For example, assembling a model airplane.

intrinsic thalamus: thalamic nuclei whose incoming impulses originate in other thalamic nuclei. *Contr.* EXTRINSIC THALAMUS.

introjection: 1. (*Psychoan.*) the process of absorbing the superego from the parents; that is, the child incorporates the attitudes of the parents as his own. 2. the process of projecting one's own characteristics or mental processes into inanimate objects.

intropunitive: characterizing a reaction to frustration in which the individual blames himself and experiences feelings of shame and guilt. *Contr.* IMPUNITIVE; EXTRAPUNITIVE.

introspection: 1. (*Structuralism*) the objective description of conscious content in terms of its elements and attributes. 2. a description of one's experiences or patterns of behavior.

introspectionism: 1. a synonym for structuralism. 2. more generally, the doctrine that the aim of psychology is the introspective description of experience.

introversion: (*Jung*) orientation inward toward the self. The introvert is preoccupied with his own thoughts, avoids social contacts, and tends to turn away from reality.

introversiveness: (*Rorschach*) The personality of the individual who shows a well-developed imaginative function and reduced responsiveness to the outside world. The introversive individual reacts more with the cerebral and autonomic nervous systems than with the striped muscular system. *Contr.* EXTRATENSIVENESS.

introvert: (*Jung*) one who tends to withdraw from social contacts and whose interests are directed inward to his own thoughts and experiences. According to Jung the introvert directs his libido inward and is withdrawn into himself, particularly in times of stress. The introvert tends to be self-sufficient, while the extrovert needs people. *Contr.* EXTROVERT.

introverted: 1. directed inward toward the self. 2. (*Rorschach*) strongly introversive.

intrusion: in retention tests, 1. a recall error in which the individual makes an inappropriate response. 2. substitution of one part of a list for another in recall. 3. substitution of a response from an entirely different set of materials than those practiced.

intution: 1. direct or immediate knowledge without consciousness of having engaged in preliminary thinking. 2. a judgment made without preliminary cogitation. The term is more often used by laymen than by scientists.

intuitive type: (*Jung*) a classification of individuals who form opinions and judgments on the basis of intuition, as opposed to the *sensation type*, whose ideation activities are dominated by sensations.

invalid: 1. in reference to a test, failing to measure what it was designed to measure. 2. not logically correct; in reference to a conclusion, not properly following from the premises.

invalidate: 1. to render an experiment or a test worthless for scientific purposes because of improper procedure. 2. to discard data or test results as invalid or inappropriate. 3. to render an argument or conclusion invalid.

invariable color: a hue that does not change when seen toward the periphery or is not affected by change in luminosity. Invariable colors are a nonspectral purplish red; a blue green, an ultramarine blue; and a yellow. *Syn. Ur* color.

invariance: 1. the characteristic of remaining constant or invariable. 2. the tendency for an afterimage to retain its size despite changes in the distance to which it is projected.

inventory: an instrument for assessing the presence or absence of certain behaviors, interests, attitudes, etc. Inventories usually take the forms of lists of questions to be answered.

inventory test: a test that attempts to cover all major areas of pupil achievement in order to yield a profile of each testee's achievement.

inverse correlation: see CORRELATION.

inverse relationship: 1. a negative correlation. 2. more generally, any relationship wherein high standing on one variable is associated with low standing on another variable.

inverse factor analysis: see Q TECHNIQUE.

inversion: 1. a transposition, upside down or right to left, or both, of a variable, such as in the inversion of the retinal image. 2. a transposition of numerical values in a series. 3. a change in the direction of a curve. 4. sexual inversion, or the assumption of the role of the opposite sex. 5. (*Psychoan.*) homosexuality.

inversion of affect: a sudden switch in emotions from love to hate or vice versa.

invert: an individual whose sexual partners are members of the same sex.

inverted factor analysis: see Q TECHNIQUE.

inverted Oedipus complex: (*Psychoan.*) a reversal of parental roles in the Oedipus stage of psychosexual development so that the parent of the same sex is the object of libidinal attachment.

inverted sadism: (*Psychoan.*) the strong, active repression of tendencies toward sadism.

investment: (*Psychoan.*) the affective or emotional charge given to an object or person. If, for example, the patient fears his father, the father is the person in whom the fear is invested.

invia: (*R. B. Cattell*) the central or core meaning of the verbal concept of introversion.

inviolacy motive: (*Murray*) the de-

sire to prevent self-depreciation, to preserve one's good name, to redeem failures and to defend the self.

involuntary: characteristic of actions made without intent or carried out despite an attempt to prevent them.

involuntary movement: any movement made in spite of an effort not to make it.

involution: a retrograde change in development with deterioration in physiological and psychological functions.

involutional melancholia; involutional psychotic reaction: a mental disorder developing in relation to the climacteric, or menopause, and characterized by agitation, depression, worry, hypochondriasis, and delusions.

iodopsin: the photochemical pigment found in the cones.

IPAT Anxiety Scale: A self-report inventory for ages 14 and over designed to measure covert and overt anxiety.

ipsative scale: a scale that utilizes the individual's own characteristic behavior as a standard. For example, rating a mental patient as improved utilizes the concept of ipsative scaling.

ipsilateral: on the same side.

iris: the pigmented muscular disc surrounding the pupil of the eye. Contractions of the iris regulate the amount of light entering the eye.

iritic reflex: the action of the iris in regulating the amount of light entering the pupil of the eye.

irradiation: 1. the spreading of light rays or other wavelike forms of energy. 2. the apparent increase in the size of a small, bright stimulus against a dark background. 3. the diffusion or spread of an afferent impulse to adjacent neurons as the impulse travels toward the central nervous system. 4. the spread of excitation in muscle fibers. For example, excitation of the cardiac muscle spreads out from the auricular-ventricular node. 5. (*Pavlov*) the diffusion of impulses in the cerebral cortex away from a center of high activity. 6. (*Pavlov*) the spread of a conditioned response to stimuli of a similar class; stimulus generalization. 7. the exposure of tissues to radiation.

irradiation theory of learning: the theory that learning consists of the selective reinforcement of one of many responses occurring in a hierarchy of responses.

irrational: contrary to reason or logic; lacking the ability to reason.

irrational type: (*Jung*) a class of individuals who regulate their conduct by means of sensation and feeling. *Contr.* RATIONAL TYPE.

irreality level: (*Lewin*) the region in the individual's life space in which behavior is determined by needs, fantasies, prejudices, etc. *Contr.* REALITY LEVEL.

irreality-reality dimension: (*Lewin*) the measure of behavior in relation to the degree of its regulation by needs, desires, fantasy, etc., as compared to the reality demands of the environment or the objective situation.

irresistible impulse: a compulsion.

irresponsibility: in forensic psychology or in law, a basis for the avoidance of guilt on the grounds that the accused is not responsible for his conduct by reason of mental deficiency or mental disorder.

irreversibility of conduction, principle of: the property of the synapse that prevents the nervous impulse from traveling backward, that is, from dendrite to axon.

irritability: 1. a fundamental property of living matter that governs responses to stimulation. Irritability is a specialized property of nervous tissue. 2. susceptibility to irritation or stimulation. 3. a tendency toward oversensitivity to stimuli.

irritation: 1. inflammation of tissues. 2. the process of exciting tissue. 3. a mild degree of anger.

Ishahara test: a test for the detection of color blindness, consisting of a series of plates in which the figures are presented against a background of random dots of varying saturation and brightness. The central figure varies only in respect to hue and is therefore invisible to the color-blind eye.

island deafness: see TONAL-GAP DEAFNESS.

island of Reil: an invagination of the cerebral cortex lying near the bottom of the fissure of Sylvius. The island of Reil is characteristic only of primate brains.

isochronal: 1. equal in rate or frequency of occurrence. 2. having the same chronaxie.

isokurtic: not skewed. See SKEWNESS.

isolate: 1. to separate, as to house animals separately. 2. to abstract from a class. 3. (*Psychoan.*) to separate memories from their emotional component. 4. to set apart or to seek out, as to *isolate* a variable in an experiment.

isolation: 1. the condition of being isolated. 2. the habitual avoidance of social contacts. 3. (*Psychoan.*) blocking off a wish or memory from the rest of the psyche as a means of denying it. The process is similar to *repression*, except that in the latter there is lack of awareness of the process. 4. (*Psychoan.*) the separation of memories from their emotional components.

isolation amentia: mental defectiveness due to extreme paucity of social stimulation in early childhood.

isolation effect: in serial learning, the beneficial effect of isolating an item in the middle of the list. Ordinarily such items are the most difficult to learn because of associative interference. When the item is isolated, such as by printing it in a distinctive type or in color, it is much more easily learned. The Gestalt psychologists attribute the effect to perceptual differentiation.

isolation mechanism: (*Psychoan.*) in the compulsion-obsession neurotic, a period of inactivity following any word or act that is linked with an unpleasant memory or problem.

isometric contraction: a type of muscular contraction in which the muscle develops tension but does not shorten. Such a condition would occur if one were to push against a wall. *Contr.* ISOTONIC CONTRACTION.

isometric twitch: a slight muscular contraction made while the muscle is pulling against a rigid support; hence, a contraction in which the muscle cannot shorten.

isomorphism: (*Gestalt psychology*) the hypothesis that there is a point-for-point correspondence between the stimulus and excitatory fields in the cerebral cortex. This does not mean that objects in the environment are "pictured" on the cortex as they exist in physical reality. Rather, the map of the stimulus on the cortex may be likened to an automobile road map in which there is correspondence between the map and the road but not an identity. Isomorphism is the Ge-

stalt concept paralleling the concept of psychophysical parallelism is structuralistic psychology.

isophilic: characterizing affection directed toward a member of one's own sex. Isophilic behavior does not imply sexual manifestation or desire.

isophonic contour: a graphic representation of the relationship between physical sound waves and their corresponding auditory experiences.

isotonic contraction: a muscle contraction in which the muscle shortens, as, for example, in flexing the arm. *Contr.* ISOMETRIC CONTRACTION.

isotropic: 1. characteristic of attributes placed in a nonquantitative ordered series. 2. having the same properties in all directions.

item analysis: 1. the process of determining whether a test item shows discriminability—that is, does it distinguish between high and low groups or does it correlate highly with the total score? The assumption involved is that the test as a whole measures the function under consideration. Therefore, any item that correlates highly with the discriminative power of the test as a whole is valid. 2. more generally, the determination of any item characteristic, such as difficulty, level of ambiguity, time limits, etc.

item difficulty: the difficulty level of any test item as measured by the frequency with which the item is passed (or failed).

item scaling: the assignment of a test item or item on an attitude scale to its proper place relative to its level of difficulty.

item selection: the process of choosing items for a test or other measuring instrument. Such considerations as the difficulty level, freedom from ambiguity, scorability, validity, and reliability of the item must be taken into account.

item validity: the extent to which any given item of a test measures what it is intended to measure.

item weighting: the process of assigning to any given test item the proportion of the total score that item will determine.

J

Jacksonian epilepsy: a form of epilepsy characterized by localized convulsions that are usually limited to one limb. The cause of the disorder is localized irritation of the cerebral cortex.

Jackson's law: the principle that when intellectual functions are lost through disease, those that appear latest in evolution are lost first.

jactitation; jactation: extreme restlessness or tossing about.

James, William: American philosopher and psychologist (1842–1910). William James entered Harvard in 1861 to study medicine but interrupted his program to accompany Louis Agassiz on a biological expedition to South America and then, because of poor health, to spend a year in Europe. He returned to Harvard and received his medical degree in 1868. In 1872 he joined the faculty at Harvard as an instructor in physiology. In his courses he gave considerable attention to psychology, and in 1875 he established the first psychology laboratory in America. A few years later he began his great work, *Principles of Psychology*, which was published in 1890. Thereafter he turned his attention more and more exclusively to philosophy. His outstanding later works include *The Will to Believe and Other Essays* (1897), *Varieties of Religious Experience* (1902), *Pragmatism* (1907), and *The Meaning of Truth* (1909).

In psychology James is best known for the stream-of-consciousness approach to mental phenomena, which he held in opposition to the then dominant structuralism. As the phrase "stream of consciousness" implies, James believed that mental processes ought to be studied as processes and not as static bits of consciousness, as the structuralists had suggested. Because of the dynamic nature of his views, James's psychology was given the name *functionalism*. James is also famous for associating himself with the Danish physiologist Carl Georg Lange in formulating the James-Lange theory of the emotions (*q.v.*)

James-Lange theory of the emotions: a formulation that attempts to integrate the conscious and behavioral aspects of the emotions. Lange, a Danish physiologist, had argued that emotional processes are identical with changes in the circulatory system. James took this aspect of Lange's theory and incorporated it into his own theory, which holds that the emotional experience is the result of the visceral changes arising from the individual's reacting to an emotion-provoking experience. The essence of the theory is contained in the famous argument offered by James that upon meeting a bear in the woods we do not run because we are afraid, but are afraid because we run; that is, running stirs up a visceral reaction and this is the emotion.

Janet, Pierre: French clinical psychologist (1859–1947). Pierre Janet was educated in Paris, where he qualified at the school of medicine after completing his undergraduate training. Like Freud, he studied with J. M. Charcot and became a specialist in nervous and mental disorders. He taught in various schools in France and became director of the psychology laboratory at the Salpêtrière. In 1898 he was appointed lecturer in psychology at the Sorbonne and in 1900 professor at the Collège de France. He is known for his work in hysteria and multiple personality. He interpreted both of these states in terms of association theory, arguing that in hysterical persons a lack of cohesive force allows associations to split apart into conscious and unconscious parts. Janet's chief works are *The Mental State of Hysterics* (1892), *Neuroses and Fixed Ideas* (1898), and *The Major Symptoms of Hysteria* (1907).

J curve: a curve describing the frequency of compliance with a rule or standard. A commonly cited example is the manner in which automobile drivers comply with a stop sign. Some stop completely, some not at all, and some slow down to varying degrees. The curve representing the various degrees of compliance approximates the capital letter *J* in shape.

jealousy: an attitude of envy toward another because of affection that individual shows to a third person.

jnd; j.n.d.: see JUST-NOTICEABLE DIFFERENCE.

job analysis: an investigation of the ability requirements, working conditions, pay, opportunities for promotion, etc., that go with a particular job. Job analyses are helpful in employee-selection programs.

job placement: the assignment of an individual to a job on the basis of his abilities, experience, interests, and the requirements of the position.

job specification: a description of a job and the requisite abilities needed for success in the work involved.

Jocasta complex: the morbid attachment of a mother for her own son.

joint probability: the frequency of occurrence of an event that is a compound of two classes of events, *i* and *j*.

joint sense: see KINESTHESIS.

Jordan curve: a closed, nonoverlapping curve used to represent various aspects of the life space.

Jost's law: the principle that given two associations of equal strength but unequal age, practice will be of more benefit to the older. The law is based on the empirical finding that older associations lose strength less rapidly with the passage of time.

joy: a highly pleasant emotion associated with accomplishment, satisfaction, and gratification. *Contr.* GRIEF.

judgment: 1. the process of relating two or more objects, facts, or experiences. 2. a critical evaluation of a person, situation, or thing. 3. in psychophysical and related experiments, the process of deciding whether or not a stimulus is present or whether it is of greater or lesser magnitude than another stimulus. See also ABSOLUTE JUDGMENT; COMPARATIVE JUDGMENT.

Jukes: fictitious name for a family in New York State whose progeny included nearly a thousand feebleminded members. See also KALLIKAK.

Jung, Carl: Swiss psychoanalyst and founder of Analytical Psychology (1875–1962). Jung was educated in the schools of Basel and at the University of Basel, where he obtained his M.D. degree in 1900. Jung then studied with Janet in Paris and in 1906 became a member of Freud's circle. However, Jung eventually disagreed with Freud over the nature of the libido and the unconscious and, in 1913, broke away from Freud to found his own school of Analytical Psychology. Because Jung believed that the study of the racial unconscious could add to a man's understanding of the individual unconscious, he became interested in the study of the primitive peoples of the world—in their myths, religions, folkways, and mores.

Among his more important works are *Contributions to Analytical Psychology* (1928), *Psychological Types* (1933), *The Integration of Personality* (1939), and the *Undiscovered Self* (1959). See also ANALYTICAL PSYCHOLOGY (2).

just-noticeable difference (jnd; j.n.d.): the difference between two stimuli that is just barely perceptible 50 percent of the time in a series of trials.

just-noticeable-differences method: a psychophysical technique for determining the just-noticeable difference. A standard stimulus is presented along with a variable stimulus whose magnitude is gradually increased on some trials and decreased on other trials until the just-perceptible differences is reported by the subject. The average of the ascending and descending series is taken, and the threshold is calculated at that point where the difference can be recognized 50 percent of the time.

just-world hypothesis: the belief that people get what they deserve, and so can be held accountable for their behavior.

K

Kallikak: fictitious name for a family with two lines of descendants: one of normal and superior people, the other of delinquents, psychotics, and mental defectives. The family was studied by H. H. Goddard, a pioneer in the study of mental deficiency.

kappa effect: alteration in the apparent interstimulus interval when the distance between two successively presented stimuli is altered. *Contr.* TAU EFFECT.

katasexual: characteristic of sexuality in which dead partners are the sexual goals. *Syn.* NECROPHILIA.

K complex: a generalized cortical

response evoked by an auditory stimulus during sleep as revealed by the electroencephalogram.

Keeler polygraph: see LIE DETECTOR.

Kelly, George A., American psychologist (1905–1966). Born in a small Kansas town, Kelly attended public school in Wichita, then enrolled in Friends University, and later, Parks College. He was graduated from Parks in 1926, and in 1931 was awarded a doctorate in psychology by the University of Iowa.

Kelly's career as a professional psychologist began at Fort Hays State College, and included a traveling clinic for the State of Kansas. During World War II he served as an aviation psychologist in the United States Navy. Following the war he was appointed professor of psychology and director of the clinical program at Ohio State, where he remained until 1965, when he accepted an appointment to the Riklis Chair of Behavioral Science at Brandeis University. He died in 1966.

During his tenure at Ohio State he completed his major work, *The Psychology of Personal Constructs* (1955). He also authored a number of technical papers and contributed chapters to books dealing with personality and clinical psychology.

Kelly's constant process: a psychophysical method for fitting data to the normal ogive by using the standard deviation instead of *h*. The latter measures the steepness of a distribution, while the former measures its scatter or spread.

Kelly's Psychology of Personal Constructs: Kelly's theory of personality takes as its point of departure the assumption that ordinary people, like scientists, attempt to predict and control events. Toward this goal the individual construes events or interprets them on the basis of personal experience. This results in the individual constructing hierarchial organizations to explain the way he conceptualizes the world. Some constructs are superordinate, containing other or subordinate constructs. Some, such as strong biases or radical positions, are preemptive constructs that prohibit any other constructs from becoming part of their elements. Others are constellatory constructs or powerful determinants of the way in which other concepts may be applied. Prejudices and stereotypes exemplify constellatory constructs. Propositional concepts, by contrast, are open to change and can, therefore, be modified by experience.

Constructs, like scientific theories, have a focus and a range of convenience or applicability. For example, Sigmund Freud's psychoanalytic theory had a wide range of applicability but its focus was on sexuality. Similarly, an individual's construct system about good and bad will tend to have wide applicability but may focus on sexual or moral behavior.

Constructs may be verbal or preverbal. Most of our constructs can be verbalized, but those of young children often cannot be expressed in words. This same limitation also applies to the constructs of persons with serious behavioral problems. In formulating the distinction between preverbal and verbal constructs, Kelly allows for processes comparable to those regarded as conscious or subconscious by the psychoanalytic and related schools.

For the purpose of diagnosis and therapy, Kelly assesses the individual by means of the REP test (Role Construction Repertory Test), a special technique devised by him to evaluate the individual's important constructs in relation to significant others—parents, siblings, teachers, close friends, those in authoritative positions, and sought-after and rejected individuals.

Persons with behavior problems are likely to have poorly verbalized and submerged constructs that are narrow in range. Such individuals are also beset by anxiety and defensiveness about their constructs as a way of maintaining a restricted, and therefore "safe," way of interpreting events. Therapy consists in assigning the individual roles to play, much as an actor plays a role that may be quite different from his behavior in real life. The therapeutic role is carefully constructed to provide new modes of reacting to others and to encourage more effective ways of construing experiences.

Kelly's emphasis on constructs places him in the camp of cognitive theorists. His system is closely related to that of Carl Rogers, among contemporary personality theorists, and Alfred Adler, among the classical theorists.

Kent-Rosanoff Test: a standardized free-association test devised by Grace Kent and A. J. Rosanoff. It consists of 100 stimulus words and tables of relative frequency for responses to those words by 1,000 subjects. The results of an individual case may be compared with the tabular material for common, unusual, and doubtful responses.

keraunophobia: fear of lightning.

key: 1. a list of the correct answers used in scoring a test. 2. a devise for coding or decoding information. 3. in music, a system of tones based on their relationship to a keynote or tonic from which the key takes its name.

kinephantom: an illusion of movement, particularly in a shadow movement, such as that which occurs when the shadows of the spokes of a wheel are seen moving in the opposite direction from that of the wheel.

kinesics: the study of bodily language or communications by gestures and bodily positions and movements.

kinesimeter: a device for measuring the threshold of the sensation for movement.

kinesthesis: the muscle, tendon, and joint sense. Along with the static sense in the inner ear, this combination of senses yields information about the position of the limbs and body in space. The receptors for the muscle sense are called muscle spindles, which take the form of microscopic fibrils that wrap around muscle fibers. The tendon sense is mediated by Golgi tendon organs, which are specialized sensory neurons found in the tendons near their insertion, and the joint sense, by Pacinian corpuscles, which are encapsulated neurons embedded in the joints. The static sense depends on the semicircular canals and the action of hair cells in the utricle and saccule.

kinesthetic method: a technique for treating speech and writing disabilities by having the patient attend to the muscular sensations involved.

kinesthetic response: (*Rorschach*) a response category for projecting action into the blots.

kinetic information: gestures, expressive movements, posture, and tension patterns used in making judgments about persons.

Kjersted-Robinson law: the principle that the amount of material learned during equal portions of the learning time is relatively constant for different lengths of material.

kleptolagnia: sexual excitement associated with stealing.

kleptomania: an obsessive impulse or compulsion to steal.

Klinefelder's syndrome: a genetic abnormality where the sex chromosome pattern is XXY. Characterized by retarded gonadal development, mental retardation, and a tendency toward femininity.

Klüver-Bucy syndrome: a behavior pattern observed in monkeys whose temporal regions have been removed with involvement of the tissues deep in the frontolateral region. Such animals display "psychic blindness," or the inability to recognize objects, are aggressive, and suffer from hypersexuality.

knee-jerk reflex: the reflexive extension of the lower leg upon a sharp tap to the tendon just below the patella, or kneecap. *Syn.* PATELLAR REFLEX.

knowledge of results: information given to a subject about the correctness of his response. An important principle of learning holds that the learning of associations is facilitated by giving the learner information about his progress either immediately upon making a choice or at the end of a series of choices.

Knox Cube Test: a performance test in which the subject must tap a series of four cubes in various sequences according to a pattern presented by the experimenter.

Koffka, Kurt: pioneer Gestalt psychologist (1886–1941). Koffka was educated at the universities of Berlin and Edinburgh. After receiving a doctorate from the University of Berlin, he accepted a series of positions as an assistant to prominent psychologists. It was while working with Schumann at Frankfurt that Koffka met Wolfgang Köhler and, with him and Max Wertheimer, founded the Gestalt school of psychology. During the First World War Koffka worked with neurological patients at Giessen. After the war he came to the United States as a visiting professor at Cornell and Wisconsin. In 1927 he accepted an appointment at Smith College, where he remained until his death. Koffka's most important work is the *Principles of Gestalt Psychology* (1935), a difficult and scholarly book, in which he attempted to summarize and organize Gestalt psychology as a system.

Köhler, Wolfgang: pioneer Gestalt psychologist (1887–1967). Köhler was educated at the universities of Tübingen, Bonn, and Berlin. In 1910 he became associated with Max Wertheimer and Kurt Koffka, in investigations that led to the founding of the Gestalt school of psychology. Köhler spent the years 1913–1919 on the island of Tenerife, studying the intelligence of chimpanzees, developing his famous concept of insight learning. In 1920 he returned to Germany to accept an appointment at the University of Berlin. In 1934 he came to the United States to deliver the William James Lectures at Harvard. He decided to stay in America and accepted an appointment at Swarthmore, where he remained until his retirement. His best-known works are *The Mentality of Apes* (1925) and *Gestalt Psychology* (1929).

Kohs Block Design Test: a performance test of intelligence utilizing a set of one-inch colored cubes whose sides are painted red, blue, yellow, white, yellow and blue, and red and white respectively. Colored designs presented to the subject on seventeen test cards must be reproduced using the blocks. The test is part of the Arthur Performance Scale.

kolytic: inhibitory in action.

Korsakov's psychosis; Korsakov's syndrome: a mental disorder brought on by alcoholism and marked by neural irritation, disturbances of memory and orientation. See also ALCOHOLIC PSYCHOSIS.

Korte's laws: laws of apparent movement stating the following generalizations for the optimal movement of phi: (1) if intensity is held constant, the time interval for optimal movement varies directly with the distance between stimuli; (2) if time is held constant, the distance for optimal movement varies directly with intensity; and (3) if distance between stimuli is held constant, then intensity for optimal movement varies inversely with time interval.

Krause end bulb: an encapsulated neuronal ending believed by some authorities to be a receptor for cold.

K scale: a special scoring key for the Minnesota Multiphasic Inventory of Personality which detects malingering.

Kuder Form E General Interest Survey: grades 6–12. A vocational interest survey similar to the Kuder Preference Record—Vocational (*q.v.*).

Kuder Occupational Interest Survey: grades 11–12 and adults. An interest inventory that yields 114 occupational scores reported in terms of the relationship between the examinee's responses and those of successful groups in the occupations given.

Kuder Preference Record—Vocational: an early interest inventory that gives the subject's relative standing on ten broad areas of vocational interest, such as social service, science, art, etc.

Kuder-Richardson coefficients of equivalence: formulas for estimating the correlation between comparable forms of a test on the basis of one administration.

Kuhlmann-Anderson Test: a series of tests of general intelligence ranging from kindergarten to adulthood.

Kundt's rule: 1. the principle that divided or graduated lines or distances appear greater than nongraduated or undivided distances. 2. the principle that in attempting to bisect a horizontal line using the single eye, there is a tendency to place the intercept too near the nasal side of that eye.

kurtosis: the degree of flatness or peakedness of a frequency curve in the region of the mode.

kwashiorkor: a protein deficiency disease of infants and children, characterized by edema, pot belly, and skin lesions. Found chiefly in Africa.

kymograph: an instrument for tracing records of temporal variations in any variable on a smoked or lightly waxed drum.

L

labia: the folds surrounding the opening of the vagina.

labile: flexible; free in expression.

labyrinth: the portion of the inner ear containing the receptors for hearing (cochlear) and those for the static sense (uricle, saccule, and semicircular canals).

labyrinthine sense; labyrinthine sensitivity: see STATIC SENSE.

lactation: the process of milk production in mammals.

lacuna: a gap; a temporary lapse in memory.

ladder scale: a self-anchoring scale for measuring the individual's attitude toward the real world as contrasted with his attitude toward his ideal world.

Ladd-Franklin theory of color vision: see COLOR THEORIES.

lag: 1. a time delay between stimulus and response. 2. a brief period after the removal of a stimulus, when it is still perceived.

laissez faire: (*Lewin*) a kind of leadership in which a minimum of control is exerted.

lalopathy: any speech disorder.

lalophobia: fear of speaking.

laloplegia: paralysis of the speech muscles, with consequent inability to speak.

lalorrhea: see LOGORRHEA.

Lamarckism; Lamarckianism: the theory that structural changes acquired by an organism through use or disuse can be transmitted to the offspring.

lambert: a unit of luminance or brightness equal to the brightness of a perfectly diffusing surface emitting one lumen per square centimeter. The millilambert, which equals 1/1000 lambert, is more commonly used.

Lambert's law: a law stating the interrelation of incidence, emission, and reflection of light, to the effect that these factors vary directly as the cosine of the angle of the rays perpendicular to the surface.

Landolt circles: circles with gaps of varying degree used in the determination of visual acuity.

language: 1. any form of communication among people, whether verbal or gestural. 2. verbal behavior, either oral or written. 3. the symbols used in communication.

language acquisition device (LAD): the innate mechanism common to all human children which operates on linguistic data supplied by parents to produce a given language structure.

language behavior: behavior involving the use of language whether oral, written, or in the form of gestures.

language centers: a number of areas of the cerebral cortex that function in various aspects of spoken and written language and in music. Broca's area, or the speech center, is the best known of the language centers.

lanugo hair: delicate, downy hair that appears briefly during the later months of fetal development.

lapse: 1. a slip or error. 2. a brief period of forgetfulness.

lapsus linguae: a slip of the tongue.

laryngeal reflex: coughing caused by irritation of the larynx.

larynx: the upper part of the windpipe, which contains the vocal cords.

Lashley, Karl S.: American psychologist (1890–1958). Born in Davis, West Virginia, Lashley received his professional education at the University of Pittsburgh and at Johns Hopkins, where he received the Ph.D. degree in 1914. His first appointment was at the University of Minnesota, where he served as an instructor, assistant professor, and professor of psychology between 1917 and 1925. In 1926 he became associated with the University of Chicago, where he carried out his famous experiments on cerebral functioning in learning. In his latter years he was associated with Harvard University, and in 1942 was appointed director of the Yerkes Laboratories of Primate Biology. During his distinguished career Lashley authored numerous monographs and journal articles on the functions of the brain in maze learning, discrimination learning, and problem solving. From this research he developed his famous principles of mass action and equipotentiality (*q.v.*). His best known work is *Brain Mechanisms and Intelligence* (1927).

latah, lattah: a mental disorder characterized by excitement and great suggestibility, with hallucinations of sexual content. The disorder is frequently observed among women in Malaya.

latency: a condition of inactivity between the application of a stimulus and the onset of a response.

latency period or **stage:** (*Psychoan.*) a period extending from three and one half or four years of age until the onset of puberty. During the latency period, there is little or no manifest interest in sex. According to Freud, sexuality during latency is sublimated into the process of becoming socialized.

latent: 1. hidden; not manifest, as the latent material in a dream. 2. not manifest in development or behavior but potentially present. Sexual behavior in young children may be said to be latent in this sense. 3. genetic traits not manifest as characteristics in the individual but contained in the germ plasm.

latent content: (*Psychoan.*) the hidden content of a dream that must be brought out during analysis by means of free association. Presumably, some impulses and ideas are so incompatible with the individual's evaluation of himself that they must be hidden or disguised even in dreams. See also MANIFEST CONTENT; DREAM WORK.

latent learning: learning that is not manifested in performance. For example, nonhungry rats were allowed to explore a maze for ten days. On the eleventh day they were made hungry and found a food reward at the end of the maze. Within a day or two their performance was as good as that of the control group, which had been regularly rewarded. Evidently, then, learning had gone on during the ten-day interval but was latent until activated by a drive-reward situation.

latent period: a time interval between the reception of a stimulus and the onset of a response.

latent process: 1. a term formerly used for unconscious cerebration. 2. (*Psychoan.*) any psychic process, such as perception in the infant, not yet developed.

lateral: pertaining to the side of an organ or of the body.

lateral dominance: 1. the tendency for one side of the brain to be dominant over the other for most functions. 2. dominance or preferential use of one hand.

lateral fissure: a deep fissure in the temporal cortex, which divides the temporal lobe from the parietal and frontal lobes. *Syn.* fissure of Sylvius.

lateral inhibition: the inhibition of one neuron by an adjacent neuron. In the retina, lateral inhibition is believed to enhace edges and contrast effects.

lateral lemniscus: a bundle of nerve fibers in the medulla and pons which carry auditory impulses.

laterality: the preferential use of one side; sidedness.

lateral thalamic nucleus: a large mass of cell bodies on the lateral aspect of the thalamus. The nuclei are important relay stations for incoming sensory impulses.

Latin square: a type of experimental design that provides for as many trials as there are experimental conditions. Each subject is exposed to all conditions, but for the purposes of controlling order of presentation, the exposure order varies systematically for each subject.

latitude of acceptance: characterizing the range of attitudes or opinions about an issue that an individual is willing to accept. *Contr.* LATITUDE OF REJECTION.

latitude of rejection: characterizing the range of attitudes or opinions about an issue that an individual finds objectionable. *Contr.* LATITUDE OF ACCEPTANCE.

law: 1. a statement of a uniformity found in nature. Scientific laws are broad generalizations that describe cause-and-effect relations among variables and their antecedent conditions. 2. a legal or moral rule for the guidance of conduct.

lay analysis: psychoanalysis as practiced by one who does not possess a medical degree but who has undergone special training in the theory and technique of psychoanalysis.

layman: an individual who is not professionally trained in a given area.

L data: (*R. B. Cattell*) life record data obtained by rating the individual as he reacts to life situations. See also Q DATA and T DATA.

leader: 1. one who guides, directs, or controls the actions of others. 2. one who possesses the personality traits and other qualifications for leadership.

leadership: 1. the exercise of authority; the control, guidance, and direction of the conduct of others. 2. the qualities of personality and training that make for success in guiding and controlling the conduct of others.

leading eye: the eye that first turns toward an object of attention.

learned helplessness: a condition following a number of bad experiences, where the individual believes he is helpless to control events.

learning: 1. acquisition of any relatively permanent change in behavior as a result of practice or experience. 2. process of acquiring responses as a result of special practice.

Psychologists interested in the investigation of learning use a number of different procedures. In studying learning through conditioning, two models are available, *classical conditioning* and *operant conditioning*. In *classical conditioning* the essential process involved is the paired repetition of a conditioned (to be learned) stimulus and an unconditioned stimulus (also referred to as the reinforcement). Thus Pavlov utilized a bell or a tuning fork as a conditioned stimulus, which he paired with a puff of meat powder in the mouth eventually to train the animal to salivate to the sound of the bell. The process of salivation to food in the mouth is the unconditioned response; salivation to the sounding of a bell or any arbitrary stimulus is the conditioned response. In *operant conditioning* the animal is allowed to emit a response, which is then reinforced. Thus a rat might be put in a cage with a kind of slot-machine arrangement so that when he presses a bar, a pellet of food is delivered. The animal's rate of bar pressing is the measure of learning. Classical conditioning has been utilized to study the acquisition of simple habits and autonomic responses. Operant conditioning is utilized in a wide variety of investigations involving both simple habits such as bar pressing and complex habits such as learning lessons in teaching machines, a form of operant-conditioning situation.

Psychologists also utilize various types of puzzle boxes and mazes to study animal skills and place learning, and a large part of this research has been devoted to the investigation of the laws of learning. (For specific learning laws see entries cited at end of this article.) In studying human learning, psychologists utilize various types of mechanical puzzles, mazes, and verbal materials ranging from nonsense syllables to meaningful connected discourse. Performance in verbal learning has been found to be a function of the type of material learned, the conditions of practice, and the personal characteristics of the learner. See also CONDITIONING; MEMORIZING; INSIGHT; HABIT; and the following entries for special treatments of learning: GUTHRIE'S CONTIGUOUS CONDITIONING; HULL'S MATHEMATICO-DEDUCTIVE THEORY; SKINNER'S OPERANT CONDITIONING; THORNDIKE'S TRIAL-AND-ERROR LEARNING; TOLMAN'S PURPOSIVE BEHAVIORISM.

learning curve: a graphic representation of the course of learning with practice. Learning curves can be plotted with gains or errors on the vertical axis and trials on the horizontal

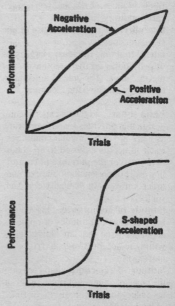

FIG. 18. *Several common types of acceleration in learning curves.*

axis. Curves may be individual or group; they may represent each trial plotted separately or they may be based on successive fractions of the total learning (VINCENT CURVE). See also NEGATIVE ACCELERATION; POSITIVE ACCELERATION.

learning, laws of: generalizations or principles that attempt to formulate the conditions under which learning occurs. For specific examples, see cross references under LEARNING.

learning set: 1. an intention to learn; active, as opposed to passive, learning. 2. the acquisition of a certain method or approach in learning, particularly in problem solving.

learning theory: formulation of laws and conditions of learning. For specific learning theories see entries under LEARNING.

learning to learn: acquiring skill at learning tasks through practice at learning. Some psychologists believe that learning to learn can account for behavior formerly classified under insight learning.

least action, law of: see LEAST-EFFORT PRINCIPLE.

least-noticeable difference: see JUST-NOTICEABLE DIFFERENCE.

least-effort principle: the generalization that an animal tends to follow that route to a goal that involves a minimum of effort.

Least Preferred Co-Worker Test: a test designed to measure whether a leader is people-centered or task-centered.

least square, law of: the assumption that the best estimate of a value is that for which the sum of the squares of the deviations is at a minimum.

least-square method: a procedure for fitting curves by discovering the line that ensures that the sum of the squares of the differences between the points to be fitted and the points of the line of fit are at a minimum.

leaving the field: (*Lewin*) a reaction to frustration or to conflict in which the individual resolves the dilemma by removing himself from the situation. Thus, a soldier caught between the terrors of combat and the fear of disgrace if he deserts may become functionally ill and thus escape his conflict.

legend: 1. a traditional belief about a person, place, or important event that is not supported by adequate historical evidence. 2. an explanation accompanying a graphic illustration or table.

Leiter International Performance Test: a nonverbal test of intelligence utilizing matching pictures and forms, color designs, number series, and concealed figures. It has been standardized for ages 2–18.

lens: to the transparent structure attached to the body of the eye by the ciliary muscle. The lens is capable of accommodation or adjustment for near and far vision and makes focusing possible.

lentiform or **lenticular nucleus:** the outermost of two large nuclei of the corpus striatum.

leptokurtic: in a frequency curve, possessing peaks.

leptomorphic: see BODY BUILD INDEX.

leptosome: a person of slender build.

lerema: the tendency of some types of psychotics to be talkative.

Lesbianism: homosexuality among women.

lesion: an injury to tissue from disease or surgical procedures.

lethargy: drowsiness; an apathetic condition of extremely low motivation and activity level.

leucotomy: see LOBOTOMY.

level: 1. a position or rank attained on a test. 2. a mental age or point score that all persons of a given chronological age should reach. 3. coordinating centers or divisions of the brain. Thus, it is proper to speak of a medullar level, brain-stem level, cortical level, etc. 4. the state or condition of reactivity of a receptor or neuron.

leveling: in memory, the tendency to reduce irregularities, to make drawings or stories less sharp, to leave out details. Concomitantly, sharpening and assimilation may occur with leveling to cause considerable distortion in the memory trace.

leveling effect: the tendency for repeated series of measurements to group or cluster about the mean, due to the reduction of extreme differences because of practice effects.

level of aspiration: a self-imposed standard against which a person judges his own performance. Level of aspiration is an index of confidence and varies with the pattern of success or failure.

level of confidence: in the t test (*q.v.*), an expression of the assurance with which the null hypothesis (*q.v.*) can be rejected, often expressed as a percentage. If the desired result could occur by chance one in 20 times, the level of confidence is 5 percent; if one in 10 times, 10 percent.

level of intelligence: the degree of tested intelligence on a standardized intelligence test. Generally speaking, when the term *level* is employed, it is implied that the test in question is of the mental-age type. 2. the functional level of intelligence as revealed in performance in everyday life.

level of significance: in the t test (*q.v.*), an expression of the confidence with which the null hypothesis (*q.v.*) can be rejected, usually expressed as a faction. If the desired result could occur by chance once in 20 times, the level of significance is .05.

levels of factuality method: a technique for classifying protocols according to how far they depart from objective fact along the dimension from bare fact to a strongly subjective reaction.

Lewin, Kurt: founder of Field Theory (1890–1947). Lewin was educated at Freiberg, Munich, and at Berlin, where he obtained the Ph.D. degree. At Berlin he began the long series of researches upon which his field theory was based, attempting to add a psychology of motivation to the existing Gestalt school. Lewin came to the U.S. in 1932, and in 1935 he accepted a permanent appointment at Iowa, where he launched the famous series of studies of children. During the Second World War, he worked for the Office of Strategic Services, and at the war's end, went to the Massachusetts Institute of Technology to head the Research Center for Group Dynamics, a position terminated by his untimely death. Among his more important works are *A Dynamic Theory of Personality* (1935) and *Principles of Topological Psychology* (1936).

Lewinian: pertaining to Lewin's system of psychology (field theory) or characteristic of Lewin's point of view.

LH: see LUTENIZING HORMONE.

libidinal development: the growth and differentiation of the libido through the various infantile stages of oral, anal, and early genital eroticism, the latency period, and eventually maturity.

libidinal object; libido object: (*Psychoan.*) the object choice of the libido; the object or person with which the libido is concerned.

libidinization: the process of becoming the object of libidinal attachment.

libido: 1. the sex instinct. 2. erotic desire or erotic pleasure. 3. more generally, the combination of the life instincts (eros) and death instincts (thanatos). As originally conceived by Freud, the libido was narrowly sexual in nature, but the concept was broadened to include all kinds of love and pleasure and finally to encompass both the life and death instincts. However, as it is most commonly used in the literature, it means sexuality. Other usages are usually clear from the context.

libido analog: any object that has become a substitute for a libidinal object.

librium: a tranquilizing or anti-anxiety drug.

lie detector: a collection of instruments designed to measure minute changes in emotionality that accompany the telling of lies. The changes measured are in respiration, blood pressure, heart rate, and the galvanic skin response. *Syns.* POLYGRAPH; KEELER POLYGRAPH; GSR.

life age: the age of the individual since birth; chronological age; calendar age.

life cycle: the typical pattern of birth, development, maturity, reproduction, and death that characterizes a given species.

life goal: (*Adler*) the goal of striving to overcome felt inferiority and to achieve superiority.

life history: a detailed description of an organism from birth to the present or to the death of the organism.

life instinct: (*Psychoan.*) eros; the tendency to preserve and reproduce the self. *Contr.* THANATOS; DEATH INSTINCT.

life lie: (*Adler*) the individual's rationalization that he cannot succeed because of obstacles or personal defects.

life plan: (*Adler*) the individual's style of life, including his guiding fiction, his attempts to achieve superiority, and to rationalize or explain failures.

life space: (*Lewin*) the totality of all possible events that influence the individual from the past, present, and future as it is being contemplated by the individual. See also DIFFERENTIATION OF LIFE SPACE.

life span: 1. the length of life characteristic of a species. 2. the life of an individual organism from birth to death.

lifetime personality: (*Murray*) the successive patterns of behavior that are repeatedly manifested from birth to death. See also COMMON PERSONALITY; MOMENTARY PERSONALITY.

light: the radiant energy that constitutes the stimulus to vision. Light is measured in nanometers (NM) or billionths of a meter. With various salient wavelengths are correlated certain primary or salient colors, such as red, approximately 700 nanometers; yellow, approximately 600 nanometers; green, approximately 500 nanometers; and blue, approximately 480 nanometers. Other colors are related to intermediate wavelengths, and white is a mixture of all wavelengths. The blacks, whites, and grays form the achromatic series.

light adaptation: the rapid adjustment of the eye to bright light. It involves narrowing of the pupil and the initiation of cone activity.

light induction: the effect on one

part of the visual field of stimulation applied to another part. One example of light induction occurs in color contrast.

lightness: 1. brightness or luminance of a color or of an achromatic stimulus. 2. a characteristic of weights of small size or minimal density.

light reflex: the pupillary response; the tendency of the pupil to decrease in diameter on exposure to a bright stimulus.

light wave: light regarded as a wave-like form of energy. See also LIGHT.

Likert scale: a type of attitude scale on which the subject is asked to indicate his degree of agreement or disagreement with stated attitudes on a three- or five-point scale. *Contr.* THURSTONE SCALE.

limbic system: a group of functionally related structures in the brain, including the allocortex, transitional cortex, and various subcortical nuclei, upon which there is not yet general agreement. The system is believed to be important in the regulation of emotional patterns and primary drives.

limen: the threshold. There are two types of limens, the absolute and the differential. See also ABSOLUTE THRESHOLD; DIFFERENTIAL THRESHOLD.

liminal: at or above threshold.

liminal stimulus: a stimulus just at the threshold or that barely evokes a response. Technically, a liminal stimulus is one that evokes a response on 50 percent of the trials.

limit: 1. the first or last value or score in a distribution of scores or in a step interval. 2. the end of any continuum, such as the limit of the range of hearing.

limits method: see JUST-NOTICEABLE-DIFFERENCES METHOD.

linear: 1. pertaining to a straight line.

2. pertaining to continuous, as opposed to discrete, functions.

linear correlation: a relationship in which the plot of the variables to be correlated on a scatter diagram results in a straight line.

linear-operator model of learning: (*Bush-Mosteller*) a probability, or stochastic, theory of learning that assumes organisms react only to a fraction of the total stimulus pattern available and that responses become associated with that fraction. Parameters, which increase or decrease the probability of correct responses over the course of a learning series, are assumed for both positive and negative operators.

linear perspective: the relative differences in size of an object at different distances from the eye. In looking down a railroad track, it will be noted that the ties in the distance become smaller and closer and the rails come together at a point in the far distance.

linear regression: a regression whose equation develops a straight line.

linear system: a system in which units of input summate in a simple straight-line manner or in which the response is the simple summation of individual responses to the separate elements of a stimulus complex.

line of direction: a line from an object through the nodal points of the eyes; the line of sight.

line of fixation: the straight line between an object of regard and the center of vision.

line of regard: the straight line from the center of the eye to the object being viewed.

lingual papilla: any of the papillae of the tongue, of which there are four varieties: (1) *circumvallate*, which are relatively prominent and are situated in the back of the tongue; (2) *filiform*, which are small, widespread, very numerous, and largely tactile; (3) *foliate*, which contain taste buds, are leaf-shaped, and located along the edges and back of the tongue; (4) *fungiform*, which are mushroom-shaped, largely in the front, and also contain taste buds.

linguistic relativity: the theory that cultural differences are created by linguistic differences; therefore, individuals in different cultures perceive and think about the world differently.

linguistics: the study of languages, their origins, structure, and evolution.

linkage: the tendency for characters to be inherited together. That is, the offspring will show both or neither.

link analysis: the design of efficient systems of controls attempting to identify links, or connections, among operations; "link values," or the movements made by an effector; and the minimal number of links for maximum link value. The design of an improved typewriter keyboard illustrates such a problem.

lip eroticism: a tendency to seek sexual satisfaction through stimulation of the lips.

lip key: a device for measuring the reaction time of speaking as detected by lip movements.

lip reading: a technique used by the deaf to understand spoken speech by watching the speaker's lips.

Listing's law: a principle of eye movement stating that if the eye moves from one primary position to another, the rotation of the eyeball in the new position is the same as if the eye had turned in a fixed axis which is at right angles to the initial and the final lines of regard.

literacy: 1. the ability to read or write. 2. by extension, knowledge-ableness in a given field.

literacy test: a test of the ability to read and write.

lithium carbonate: a compound of the element lithium; has been found useful in treating manic-depressive disorders.

little brain: the cerebellum. *Contr.* CEREBRUM.

Lloyd Morgan's canon: the principle that it is improper to interpret an act in terms of a higher mental process if that act can be interpreted as the outcome of a process lower in the psychological scale. Thus, it would be improper to interpret behavior in terms of thinking that could, instead, be attributed to conditioned responses or reflex processes.

load: 1. a weight or factor loading. 2. a caseload, or the number of patients or clients being cared for by a social worker or therapist.

loading: 1. the weight or relative importance given to a statistic. 2. in factor analysis, the degree to which a test is correlated with a factor.

lobe: a rounded projection or portion of an organ, particularly in reference to portions of the brain. See also BRAIN.

lobectomy: the surgical removal of the prefrontal region of the frontal lobes.

lobotomy: the cutting of the nerve fibers connecting the frontal lobes with the thalamus and hypothalamus. It is a technique sometimes used in the treatment of psychotic conditions; however, with the discovery of tranquilizers, it has come into disfavor, since the use of appropriate drugs can achieve the same results—namely, the improved manageability of behavior.

local excitatory potential or **state (LES):** the initial reaction of nervous tissue to stimulation, consisting of a localized increase in negativity on the surface of the membrane. If the stimulus is above threshold, the LES gives way to the spike potential.

localization: 1. the assigning of functions to particular places in the cerebral cortex or other parts of the nervous system. 2. the referring of a sensory or perceptual process to the place where they are originating. 3. the identification of a stimulated place on the surface of the body.

local norm: a norm based on a test sample drawn from a given locality. *Contr.* NATIONAL NORM.

local sign: an inherent attribute of a sense experience such that the experience can be distinguished from other sensations in space. It is believed that the inherent quality of local signs is attributable to the receptor processes, whose structure makes it possible to assign spatiality to experience. For example, the retina of the eye is capable of giving rise to a series of excitations upon the movement of a stimulus across the field of view, with the result that the stimulus is perceived as moving in space. The local-sign theory was developed by Rudolph Lotze (1817–1881) and became a fundamental assumption of all nativistic theories of perception.

location chart: (*Rorschach*) reproductions of the Rorschach inkblots included in the record blank so that the examiner may record the location of the subject's response.

locomotion: 1. the movement of an organism from one place to another. 2. (*Lewin*) psychological locomotion, or movement within the life space.

locomotor ataxia: *tabes dorsalis,* a disease involving the dorsal columns of the spinal cord (*fasciculus gracilis* and *fasciculus cuneatus*) resulting in loss of coordination, particularly in walking.

locomotor behavior: behavior involved in traveling from place to place.

locus: a place on an organ or on the surface of the body.

locus coeruleus: a portion of the pontis caudalis nucleus whose destruction abolishes paradoxical sleep.

locus of control: the degree to which the individual attributes the cause of his behavior to environmental factors or to his own decisions.

logagnosia; logamnesia: see APHASIA.

logarithmic curve: a curve in which one of the coordinates is the logarithmic value of a variable while the other coordinate is the natural value of a variable. For example, the equation $y = \log x$, yields a logarithmic curve.

logarithmic mean: see GEOMETRIC MEAN.

logarithmic scale: a scale in which the intervals are based on logarithms rather than on the original numbers.

logic: the branch of philosophy concerned with establishing rules for correct thinking. Logic includes the principles of reasoning, the use of syllogisms, errors of thinking, and deductive and inductive thinking.

logical: pertaining to logic; characterized by sound or correct reasoning.

logical approach: any attempt to solve a problem according to the principles of logic.

logical deduction: reaching a conclusion by deductive means; reasoning from the general to the specific. *Contr.* empirical reasoning, which is inductive reasoning, or reasoning from the specific to the general case.

logical positivism: the philosophical

position that meaningful statements in science must be defined operationally and that metaphysical statements are either meaningless or emotive in nature. In psychology, such a position would eliminate mentalistic concepts.

logical validity: see CONSTRUCT VALIDITY; A PRIORI VALIDITY.

logic-tight compartments: see COMPARTMENTALIZATION.

logomania: a pathological state of volubility or incoherent wordiness. Characteristic of mental disorders. *Syn.* LOGORRHEA.

logorrhea: incoherent bursts of talking; pathological volubility. *Syn.* LOGOMANIA.

logotherapy: a system of psychotherapy, founded by Viktor Frankl, based on existential principles. The goal of therapy is to help the patient overcome the "existential neurosis," to assume responsibility for his life and to reexamine his experiential, creative, and attitudinal values in order to achieve a more meaningful and productive style of living. Each patient must find his own solution to the problems of living, but each must do so in the context of his membership in society and responsibilities to one's fellowman.

long-circuiting: (*R. B. Cattell*) the renunciation of immediate satisfactions in favor of attaining remote goals.

longitudinal method: a technique in which changes in the same individual are studied over a long period of time or over the entire span of development. *Contr.* CROSS-SECTIONAL METHOD.

long-term memory (LTM): permanent memory or memory that endures for long periods, possibly for life.

looking-glass self: the self-impression the individual has based upon the way others react toward him and the opinions he hears from others about himself. See also SOCIAL SELF.

loose construct: (*Kelly*) a construct (*q.v.*) that permits variable, even contradictory, predictions. *Contr.* TIGHT CONSTRUCT.

lordosis: 1. a curvature of the spine in the forward direction. 2. in female animals, the arching of the spine and elevation of the posterior part of the body upon the approach of the male.

loudness: the intensity attribute of sounds that is primarily correlated with the amplitude of the sound wave. There is, however, a secondary correlation of loudness with wavelength, since the absolute threshold for sounds is lowest in the middle of the range.

love: 1. a strong feeling of attachment for a specific person, usually with a sexual component. 2. a sentiment whose dominant characteristic is a strong feeling of affection; exemplified by love of one's country. 3. (*Psychoan.*) the libidinal or erotic instincts that seek object gratification. 4. (*Watson*) with fear and rage, one of the three inherent, or primary, emotions. 5. in religious writings, a spiritual, mystical quality that unites the individual to a divine being.

love object: the person or thing toward which the libido is directed in seeking satisfaction.

low-grade defective: an individual of subnormal ability requiring institutionalization and close supervision; an individual of extremely limited learning ability. Most low-grade defectives are in the 0–50 IQ range and are profoundly moderately retarded. *Contr.* HIGH-GRADE DEFECTIVE.

LSD: see LYSERGIC ACID.

lucidity: 1. the quality of clarity in perception. 2. in a psychotic state, an interval or period of remission in which the patient appears normal and can be communicated with.

lues: syphilis.

lumbar: pertaining to the middle of the back or to one of the lumbar nerves rising from the spinal cord in that region.

lumen: the unit of luminous flux defined as the amount of light within a solid angle of a unit size originating from a source of one candlepower. For example, a standard candle placed in the center of a hollow sphere whose radius is one meter sheds one lumen of light on one square meter of the surface of the sphere.

luminance: light energy transmitted, reflected, or emitted from a source.

luminosity: the relative brightness or intensity of a light as dependent upon its reflectance, conditions of illumination, etc. Thus, a white paper in a dimly lighted room is more luminous than a gray paper. See also ABSOLUTE LUMINOSITY.

luminosity curve: the luminosity, or brightness value, of the various wavelengths plotted as curves with wavelength on the horizontal axis and luminosity on the vertical axis.

luminous: glowing; having the property of emitting light.

luminous flux: the rate of passage of light as determined by the experienced brilliance it produces in an observer.

luminous intensity: the luminous flux per unit solid angle emitted in a given direction from a source of light, usually one standard candle.

lunacy: a technically obsolete term still occasionally employed to refer to the condition of a person who is legally insane or psychotic. The term arose as a result of a mistaken association between psychoses and the influences of the moon.

Luria technique: in the measuring of emotional tensions, a method wherein the subject presses the fingers of one hand on a sensitive tremor recorder as he responds in a free-association test.

luster: the brightness or sheen characteristic of highly polished surfaces.

lutenizing hormone: a tropic hormone produced by the anterior pituitary, which stimulates ovulation, the growth of the corpus luteum, and the testes to produce androgen.

lux: the illuminance of a surface, one square meter in area, receiving a uniformly distributed flux of one lumen from a source of light such as a standard candle.

lycanthrophy: in psychiatry, the delusion that the patient can change himself into a wolf.

lying: making an assertion known to be untrue. The pathological liar may make statements he believes to be true or comes to believe to be true if he repeats them often enough.

lymph: a fluid derived chiefly from the blood but that may contain food products. The lymph travels slowly through a system of lymphatic ducts and vessels toward the large veins near the heart, where it empties into the bloodstream.

lymphocyte: a white blood cell found in the lymph.

lysergic acid diethylamide (LSD): one of a group of psychomimetic drugs that produce psychological changes resembling a psychosis.

lyssophobia: fear of becoming insane. *Syn.* MANIAPHOBIA.

M

Machiavellianism. 1. a belief that people can be manipulated through flattery, threats, and deceit. 2. the attempt to manipulate through such techniques.

machine theory: the point of view that behavior or nervous processes may be treated as if they were the expressions of an elaborate machine. The general point of view is called *mechanism* and is often contrasted with a *dynamic*, or *field-theory*, viewpoint.

Machover Draw-a-Person Test: a projective technique in which the subject is required to draw a person. Completion of the drawing is followed by requesting the subject to tell a story about the drawing. Analysis is based on the assumption that the child or adult projects his own body or self into the situation. Used with ages two and over.

Mach Scale: a test designed to measure the extent to which the individual endorses Machiavellianism.

MacQuarrie Test for Mechanical Ability: a paper-and-pencil test including the tracing of a line through a series of broken lines, tests of tapping, block analysis and counting, and pursuit. The test is heavily weighted for eye-hand coordination and spatial relations.

macrocephalic: having an abnormally large head, a condition usually correlated with mental deficiency. *Contr.* MICROCEPHALIC.

macromania: a pathological tendency to overevaluate the self. *Syn.* MEGALOMANIA.

macropsia: an increase in the apparent size of visual objects due to pathology of the visual apparatus. *Syn.* MEGALOPSIA.

macroscopic: 1. large enough to be seen without the aid of magnification. 2. considered as a whole or without regard to detail.

macrosomatic: a person whose general body size is one or more standard deviations above the mean of general body size as established by multiplying the standard score for height by the standard score for transverse chest measurement.

macrosplanchnic build: body build in which the trunk is disproportionately large.

macula acustica: structures found in the utricle and saccule consisting of masses of hair cells of unknown function.

macula; macula lutea: a yellowish area about 2 mm. in diameter in the center of the human retina. The macula contains the fovea.

Maddox rod test: a test of muscular imbalance in the eyes.

magenta: a purplish red with a wavelength of about 515 nanometers, the complement of green.

magic: 1. the art of producing illusory phenomena by means of sleight of hand. 2. the practice among primitive people of invoking supernatural powers to control natural phenomena.

magical thinking: a stage in a child's thinking in which he believes he is the cause of physical phenomena. Said to be characteristic of children between one and six years of age. *Contr*. rational thinking.

magnetropism: an orienting movement of the organism toward a magnetic field.

magnitude: the characteristic of objects, spatial extents, temporal durations, etc., in respect to which one may be larger, longer, or otherwise greater than another.

main score: (*Rorschach*) a score based on responses given during the test proper. Additional scores or withdrawals are given for responses that occur after the completion of the test proper.

mainstreaming: the practice of helping persons suffering from chronic mental disorders to adjust successfully to the community with the aid of support systems.

maintaining stimulus: a stimulus that continues to elicit a response as long as it is present. In the case of the spider, the absence of a complete web is sufficient stimulus to maintain spinning until the web is completed.

maintenance functions: the physiological functions that preserve the animal in a relatively constant, or homeostatic, state.

maintenance level: a stage of maturity when growth has ceased and the animal's size and developmental processes have reached a ceiling.

maintenance schedule: the provision of food and water in sufficient quantity to keep an animal in good physical condition and to prevent undue weight loss.

major hemisphere: in most individuals the left hemisphere of the cerebrum, controlling speech and logical functions. *Contr*. MINOR HEMISPHERE.

major scale: see DIATONIC SCALE.

major solution: (*Horney*) a tendency to repress one of the fundamental neurotic trends—moving toward, against, or away from people—in order to resolve a conflict.

Make-a-Picture Story: a projective technique, suitable for use with adolescents and adults, in which the subject is given materials consisting of backgrounds and figures. The experimenter gives the subject a background to which he must match a figure of his own choosing and about which he must tell a story. The stories are then analyzed for significant themes.

make-believe: a form of children's play in which situations are imagined and responded to as if they were real.

maladaptation: 1. failure of a species to develop the biological characteristics that make for successful survival. 2. an improper synonym for *maladjustment*.

maladjustment: 1. the inability of the individual to develop patterns of behavior, making for success in his environment. 2. loosely, a mental disorder.

malergy: (*R. B. Cattell*) a condition of the organism characterized by maladaptive, inefficient, or subnormal functioning.

malevolent transformation: the acquisition of the attitude that one is living among malevolent persons—a mother, a nurse, teacher, associates, etc.—who are perceived as causing potential harm.

malfunction: failure of an organ or mechanical system to function properly.

malingering: feigning illness or disability, usually for the purpose of escaping responsibility or unpleasant duty.

malleus: one of the auditory ossicles. The malleus is attached to the eardrum and articulates with the incus. *Syn.* HAMMER.

malpractice: 1. behavior on the part of a professional individual, such as a clinician or physician, that is contrary to ethical codes. For a clinician to reveal information given in therapy would constitute malpractice under this definition. 2. negligence on the part of a professional individual.

mammary gland: the gland that secretes milk in the female; the breast.

mammillary bodies: two small rounded bodies on the floor of the posterior hypothalamus.

mammilothalamic tract: a bundle of nerve fibers that projects from the mamillary bodies to the anterior thalamus.

mandala: (*Jung*) a magic, protective circle representing the unity of the self. The concept is taken from Hindu writings that show the *mandala* as a square in a circle; it is a symbol for meditation.

mand function: (*Skinner*) a type of verbal operant involved in imperative behavior or commands such as "Wait!" "Shh!" "Fire!" reinforced by a characteristic consequence and thus coming under the control of certain forms of deprivation or aversive stimulation.

mania: 1. violent, uncontrollable behavior characterized by excessive motor activity, excitement, and impulsiveness. 2. the hyperactive phase of manic-depressive psychosis.

maniacal: pertaining to mania or characterized by mania.

maniaphobia: fear of becoming insane. *Syn.* LYSSOPHOBIA.

manic: 1. (*noun*) an individual suffering from mania or manic-depressive psychosis. 2. (*adj.*) pertaining to mania.

manic-depressive psychosis: a severe mental disorder characterized by cyclic swings in emotion or mood. In the manic phase there is hyperexcitability, extreme elation, excessive motor activity, and a flight of ideas. In the depressive phase, depression, underactivity, unresponsiveness, retardation of ideas, anxiety, sadness, and sometimes suicidal impulses. In its classic form the disorder is an alternation between the two phases. However, the patient may show only periods of depression with intermittent periods of remission, or periods of mania with periods of relative remission. The disorder has been classified as a bipolar disorder in DSM-III.

manifest anxiety: (*Psychoan.*) anxiety that is apparent and presumed to be symptomatic of underlying repressions or conflicts.

Manifest Anxiety Scale: a questionnaire designed to measure anxiety as a general drive.

manifest content: content of the dream as it is experienced by the dreamer. This aspect of the dream is of far less significance than the *latent content*. See also LATENT CONTENT and DREAM WORK.

manifest need: any need that is observable or has consequences in behavior. *Contr.* latent need. See also MURRAY'S PERSONOLOGY.

manifold: 1. a collection of things having something in common. 2. a classification that includes two or more subdivisions.

manikin test: test frequently found

in performance scales in which the subject must put together a small manikin made of wood.

manipulanda: (*Tolman*) the characteristics of objects that support motor activity; such properties as lengths, widths, fluidity, solidity, etc., are *manipulanda*.

manometer: a device for measuring pressure in a liquid or gas. Manometers may be used in physiological experiments to measure blood pressure directly from an artery or vein.

manoptoscope: a device for testing eye dominance. The apparatus consists of a simple hollow cone through which the subject sights.

mantle layer: the embryonic layer of the neural plate that eventually develops into the gray matter of the cerebral cortex.

man-to-man rating: the comparison of an individual with a group of individuals who show different degrees of the traits being rated.

manual dominance: the preferential use of one hand or side of the body particularly in skilled acts.

manual method: the use of sign language for communication among the deaf and between deaf and normal persons. *Contr.* ORAL METHOD.

marasmus: 1. a progressive withering of tissues because of nutritional disease. 2. a progressive emaciation in infants, believed to be caused by lack of mothering.

marathon group: a group encounter of extended length, usually of 24 hours' duration or more.

margin: the periphery of two-dimensional figures.

marginal consciousness: experience that is not at the focus of attention, hence vague and unclear. *Syn.* FRINGE OF CONSCIOUSNESS.

marginal frequency: 1. the sum of the frequencies of a column or row recorded along the margin of the table. 2. the frequency of responses falling outside the modal response.

marginal group: a group that has not yet been assimilated into a culture.

marginal intelligence: intelligence intermediate between mental deficiency and normalcy. *Syn.* BORDERLINE INTELLIGENCE.

margin of attention or **consciousness:** those portions of the field of attention that are less clear or vivid.

marijuana: a habit-forming drug derived from the flower of the hemp plant, *Cannabis sativa*. Marijuana acts as a narcotic and gives a feeling of well-being with loss of inhibitions and a distorted time sense, slowing down the perceived passage of time. It is also known as bhang. The drug is frequently prepared in the form of cigarettes, "reefers," or "joints."

marker test variable: in factor analysis, a test whose factorial structure is known and can therefore be used to identify factors with which it is highly correlated.

market research: a systematic investigation of the buying habits and economic demand for a product.

Markov (or **Markoff**) **process** (or **chain**): a statistical model for representing conditional and sequential probabilities; transitions between states being measured are dependent only on the immediately preceding trial and not on earlier states.

Marlowe-Crowne Social Desirability Scale: a questionnaire designed to measure the tendency to respond in a socially desirable manner.

masculine protest: (*Adler*) 1. the desire of the female to be a male. 2. the desire to be strong, to dominate, to be superior. In the latter sense both men and women can develop the masculine protest; according to Adler, the misdirected desire for superiority is the driving force behind the neurosis.

masculinity; masculinism: 1. a state or condition of any organism that has male characteristics. 2. specifically said of females who exhibit masculine characteristics.

Mashburn Complex Coordinator: a devise for measuring eye-hand and eye-foot coordination. The subject must line up rows of lights with a stick and rudder bar, whereupon a new pattern appears. The score is the total number of matchings in a given unit of time.

masked epilepsy: epileptic equivalent, or a form of epilepsy in which the patient does not suffer true convulsive attacks but in which there is a substitute—a dreamy state of an outburst of anger.

masked obsession: (*Psychoan.*) an obsessive idea or impulse that has been disguised: in particular, pain of psychogenic origin is said to mask impulses toward forbidden pleasure.

masking: 1. the interference or blockage of one sensory stimulus by another. 2. the partial or complete obscuring of one tone by another. Low notes mask high notes better than high notes mask low notes.

Maslow, Abraham H.: American psychologist (1908–1970). Born in Brooklyn, New York, Maslow received his professional training at the University of Wisconsin, where he earned the Ph.D. degree in 1934. He taught at Wisconsin, Brooklyn College, and Brandeis University. Maslow is known for his advocacy of humanistic psychology, his studies of self-actualizers,

and his hierarchical theory of human motivation. His major publications include: *Principles of Abnormal Psychology* (1941), *Motivation and Personality* (1954), *Toward a Psychology of Being* (1962), and *Religion, Values and Peak-Experiences* (1964).

Maslow's theory of human motivation: Maslow rejected the dominant American schools of behaviorism and psychoanalysis as offering too narrow a conception of man, and championed a "third force" in psychology—humanism. As he conceived it, humanism concerns itself with higher human motives, and the need for self-realization, knowing, understanding; and with aesthetic needs. These Maslow characterized as abundancy needs in contrast to deficiency needs, which arise out of the physiological motives and feelings of insecurity and alienation.

The highest development of the abundancy needs is found in self-actualizers: individuals who include both outstanding historical figures, such as Thoreau, Beethoven, and Einstein, and people who exhibit such characteristics as spontaneity in living, a problem-centered rather than a self-centered approach to life, and a tendency toward mysticism, nonconformity, and creativity. Such individuals enjoy "peak experiences"—moments of great awe, understanding, and rapture. Peak experiences may be creative periods or they may be of a contemplative nature—a compassionate, nonactive, and noninterfering awareness. In his writing and lectures, Maslow urged people to recognize and encourage peak experiences for their value in healthy, happy living.

Maslow's views are closely related to those of Alfred Adler, Erich Fromm,

Rollo May, and Carl Rogers, who also espoused a humanistic psychology in contrast to psychoanalytic and behavioristic views.

masochism: 1. a sexual disorder in which the individual derives satisfaction from the infliction of pain upon himself. Pain may be a prelude to, or an accompaniment of, sexual relations or its application may be sufficient in and of itself to induce orgasm. 2. more generally, the enjoyment of suffering or a tendency to seek opportunities for being offended or hurt. 3. (*Psychoan.*) the turning inward of thanatos, the destructive tendencies. *Contr.* SADISM.

masochistic sabotage: (*Psychoan.*) openly destructive behavior designed to satisfy the unconscious motive to bring punishment on the self.

mass: 1. physically, the quantity of matter. 2. a collection or aggregate of persons or things, typically without formal organization. 3. characteristic of movements involving large muscles or segments.

mass action principle: the generalization that in learning the areas of the cortex function as a whole. The principle was established on the basis of studies of animal learning followed or preceded by cerebral destructions of various sizes and locations. It was found that the important factor was the size or mass of destruction and not its locus or site. However, the generalization must be accepted with reservations. For some types of learning some parts of the brain are more important than others. There are, moreover, species differences in the relative importance of localized areas of the cortex.

mass communication: the widespread dissemination of information, as by newspapers, radio, or television.

mass contagion: the rapid spread of behavior patterns among groups of people not necessarily in direct contact.

massed practice: the learning of material with little or no periods of rest between blocks of practice. *Contr.* DISTURBED PRACTICE.

Massformel: a German term meaning "measuring formula," used by Fechner to indicate the final formula he derived from Weber's law, $S = k \log R$, where S is sensation, k is a constant, and R is the stimulus.

mass media of communication: the apparatus or organs of communication, such as television, newspapers, radio, and books, which reach large numbers of people quickly.

mass method: any technique involving the measurement of large numbers of people at the same time, such as group intelligence testing.

mass movement: a unified attempt on the part of a large number of people to effect social action, such as demanding governmental reform or civil rights.

mass observation: sampling the opinions of large numbers of persons, as in public-opinion polling.

Masson disk: a white disk upon which black squares or rectangles are placed in such a way that when the disk is rotated, a series of concentric rings of diminishing grayness is seen. The first ring from within, which becomes indistinguishable from the background, measures the difference threshold of brightness vision.

mass polarization: techniques for focusing the attention of large numbers of individuals upon propaganda or other types of communications.

mass psychology: the study of crowd behavior or of the behavior of loosely organized groups.

mass reflex: indiscriminate and widespread reactions of muscles and glands to a stimulus. For example, the "freezing" reaction in fear is mass reflex.

mastery: 1. a high or nearly complete degree of proficiency in the execution of a skill. 2. the condition of being able to control one's own actions or the behavior of others.

masturbation: the induction of a state of erection of the genital organs and the achievement of orgasm by manual or mechanical stimulation.

matched dependent behavior: imitation.

matched group: one of two groups that have been made equivalent in all respects, usually for purposes of experimental control. One group will be given the experimental variable while the other rests or goes about its usual activities. The mean difference between the two groups is then taken as the measure of the influence of the experimental variable.

matched sample: any sample found to be identical with another sample on all known variables under consideration.

matching test: a test in which the subject is required to select the appropriate item from one list and match it with an item in a second list.

matching to sample: a test procedure in which the subject must choose one of two stimuli that is the same as a third sample stimulus.

mate: 1. to copulate. 2. to enter into a durable relationship with a member of the opposite sex, typically by marriage.

materialism: 1. a point of view that the only reality is matter. 2. an attitude that leads to the acqusition of goods and the cultivation of comfort at the expense of cultural or intellectual pursuits.

materialization: the production of a body or parts of a body by spiritualistic or supernormal means.

maternal behavior: the behavior involved in caring for the young.

maternal drive: the tendency of the female animal to engage in caring for the young. The maternal drive and its consequent behavior patterns were formerly regarded as instinctive. More recent studies indicate that many of the components of maternal behavior may be learned.

maternal impression: the now discredited theory that pregnant women can influence the fetus indirectly by engaging in certain experiences. Birthmarks were formerly attributed to frightening experiences.

mathematical axis: 1. a straight line around which a plane figure can be rotated to produce a solid. 2. a pair of lines or coordinates intersecting at right angles. The intersection or point of origin can be used to locate any point along the X or Y axis. See illustration.

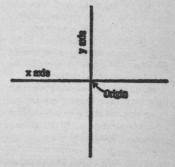

FIG. 19. *A simple mathematical axis.*

mathematical model: a system, or more commonly a theory, in some area of psychology that establishes a mathematical equation or set of equations whose parameters are related in an empirical or rational way to experimental data in the area in question. Ebbinghaus' equation of retention—$R = k \log t$—is a simple mathematical model of the course of retention.

mathematic-deductive method: the use of definitions, postulates, corollaries, cast in mathematical form in establishing a theory or system. For an example, see HULL'S MATHEMATICO-DEDUCTIVE THEORY.

mating behavior: the pattern of behavior involved in mating, including both preliminary courtship behavior, coitus, and postcoital behavior.

matriarchy: a society in which lincage is established through the female line.

matrilineal: pertaining to inheritance or descent through the female line.

matrix: 1. a table of numbers in rows and columns, such as a correlation matrix (*q.v.*), which is subjected to mathematical operations. 2. a context of framework.

maturation: 1. development; the process of attaining maturity. 2. developmental process that may be ascribed to heredity or constitutes species-specific behavior. Locomotor behavior, such as walking or swimming, illustrates this usage. 3. the ripening of the immature sex cells.

Sharp distinctions were formerly made between behavior attributable to learning and that which is attributable to maturation, or hereditary processes. *Maturation* is a term borrowed from biology, where it referred to the ripening of the immature sex cells. Psychologists believed it would

be preferable to *instinct* in describing unlearned behavior, since maturation implied the action of certain identifiable processes such as metabolism, exercise, food, and hormones in development. Many experiments have been carried out to assess the relative importance of maturation and learning in the production of mature behavior, with the recognition that all behavior is to some extent a product of both maturational and learned factors.

maturation-degeneration hypothesis: the theory that developmental is best described as a trajectory with functions reaching an optimal state sometime after birth and thereafter gradually declining.

maturation hypotheses or **theory:** the assumption that some modes of behavior are determined solely by heredity but are not capable of being elicited by appropriate stimuli until the organs and neural pathways involved have reached a certain level of maturity.

maturity: 1. the state of having reached a mature or adult form. 2. psychological maturity, or the full development of intelligence, emotional processes, etc.

maturity rating: an assessment of the degree to which the individual shows adult modes of behavior on the trait under investigation.

Maudsley Personality Inventory: a questionnaire designed to measure neuroticism and introversion-extroversion.

MAVA technique: (*R. B. Cattell*) the multiple abstract variance analysis method for determining the relative contribution of heredity and environment to personality traits.

maximal; maximum: the limit or highest degree of any variable. A maximal sensation is one for which increased stimulus values have no corresponding increase in sensation.

Maxwell disks: slotted disks that are interleaved on a color mixer for the purpose of mixing the hues represented.

Maxwell triangle: see COLOR TRIANGLE.

maze: a system of pathways with one correct path and a number of blind alleys or cul-de-sacs leading off the true path. The objective for the human or animal subject is to get from a designated starting point to a goal with a minimal number of errors. Mazes of any degree of complexity usually take many trials to master, and the criterion for learning is customarily two successive errorless runs.

Some of the more common types of mazes are: 1. The multiple-T or -Y maze, which consists of a number of T- or Y-shaped units that can be fastened together in a variety of forms; one arm of the T or Y leads on to the correct path, while the other is a blind. 2. The finger maze, consisting of either a slightly raised pathway of heavy wire or a depressed pathway the subject (usually blindfolded) follows with his finger. 3. The paper-and-pencil maze, which consists of pathways that must be traced with a pencil; recreational forms of this type are commonly seen in magazines and newspaper supplements. Mazes for animal subjects include: (1) alley mazes, which are runways enclosed at the sides with wood and covered over the top by wire mesh; and (2) elevated mazes, which are constructed of T-shaped strips of wood mounted on trestles rising several feet off the floor.

McCarthy Scales of Children's Abilities: a scale of general, intellectual ability consisting of six subscales—verbal, perceptual-performance, quantitative, general cognitive, memory and motor. Ages 2½–8½.

McNaghten rule: a definition of legal responsibility invoked in cases of insanity or mental deficiency. The rule holds that the individual is judged to be responsible for his actions unless it is proved that at the time of committing the act he was suffering from a serious defect of reason that rendered him incapable of appreciating the nature and quality of his actions and the distinction between right and wrong.

mean: 1. in general, any measure of central tendency, such as the average, or arithmetic mean. 2. specifically, when not qualified, the arithmetic mean or the sum of the scores divided by their number.

mean deviation: see AVERAGE DEVIATION.

mean-error procedure: see ADJUSTMENT METHOD.

mean-graduation method: see EQUAL-APPEARING-INTERVALS METHOD.

meaning: 1. that which is intended. 2. that which a given term or symbol stands for or designates. Thus the meaning of ♀ is female; of ♂ is male. 3. the significance, often the emotional or motivational significance, of something for an individual.

means: the activities engaged in by the organism between confrontation with a problem and the solution.

means-end capacity: (*Tolman*) the hypothetical ability to react to the relationships that exist between means objects and goal objects. Means-end capacity refers specifically to the animal's ability to deal with distances, directions, and any objects that serve as cues on the way to the goal.

means-end expectation: (*Tolman*) a state of readiness for a goal, resulting from the presentation of particular, immediate, means-object stimuli.

means-end relations: (*Tolman*) the intervening objects, distances, directions, etc., that exist between a means and an end or goal.

means object; means situation: (*Tolman*) an object or situation that results in bringing the animal closer to the goal. The means object or situation may be thought of as a sign, or cue, that arouses an expectancy.

mean square: the square root of the mean or average of the squares of all the values in a distribution of values.

mean-square contingency coefficient: a statistic calculated for the purpose of determining whether the entries in a two-way table could have been produced by the operation of chance factors. *Symbol* ϕ^2.

mean-square error: see VARIANCE.

mean variation: see AVERAGE DEVIATION.

measure: 1. a quantitative result obtained by measurement. 2. a standard in measurement.

measurement: 1. the quantification of variables. Quantification usually implies the assignment of numbers or numerical values to that which is being measured. 2. the comparison of any items or variable with a standard. 3. the placing of an item along a scale, such as an attitude scale. See also SCALE.

mechanical ability or **aptitude:** the capacity for dealing with mechanisms or machines, as opposed to ideas or abstract symbols. *Syn.* CONCRETE INTELLIGENCE.

mechanical-aptitude test: a test designed to evaluate the individual's ability to deal with mechanical devices and to understand mechanical relationships.

mechanical causality explanation: an explanation of movement offered by children in which objects are said to move because of contact with other objects that are moving, with consequent transfer of movement from one to the other.

mechanical intelligence: the ability to deal with concrete objects and problem situations involving machines.

mechanical stimulation: the activation of a receptor by means of pressure. Mechanical stimulation is the adequate stimulus for touch, pressure, and audition.

mechanism: 1. the theoretical point of view that all things in the universe, including living organisms, may best be understood as machines. Mechanism implies natural monism, or the assumption that all processes, including psychological processes, are ultimately reducible to physics and chemistry. Mechanism also typically implies determinism, or the exclusion of freedom of will or choice. 2. a machine or system that operates like a machine; that is, in a highly predictable cause-and-effect manner. 3. the means or manner in which something is accomplished. Thus, the mechanism of vision includes the physical stimulus and the physiological and neural processes involved. 4. a habitual or model form of behavior, particularly one that is adjustive. Thus, rationalization may be called a mechanism of adjustment to the threat of ego failure. 5. (*Psychoan.*) an unconscious drive or motive that directs behavior. The defense mechanisms, such as regression, aggression, and projection, exemplify this usage of the term.

mechanistic theory: see MECHANISM (1).

Medea complex: a compulsion to kill one's own children.

medial: toward the middle or midline of the body.

medial lemniscus: a bundle of somesthetic nerve fibers that ascends through the medulla and pons.

median: 1. the middle score in an array of scores arranged in order from highest to lowest. 2. toward the middle of the body or of an organ. *Abbr.* Mdn.

median deviation: the median or midpoint of the deviations from a measure of central tendency.

median gray: a gray halfway along the scale of brightness values from pure white to pure black.

median interval: the class interval that contains the median.

median plane: a line that runs through the body or an organ, dividing it into two symmetrical halves.

mediate: 1. (*adj.*) interposed between two items or processes. 2. (*adj.*) dependent upon an intervening process. 3. (*verb*) to act as a referee between disputants in an effort to reach an agreement. 4. (*verb*) to be a link or an intervening variable between two processes or events.

mediate association: an ideational connection linked indirectly by means of an intervening idea. The individual who remembers an anniversary by linking it with his house number is employing mediate association.

mediated generalization: a form of conditioning wherein a generalized response occurs to a stimulus not used in the original conditioning and not similar to the original. For example, the same response may be made to "man" that was originally conditioned to "boy." *Syn.* SEMANTIC CONDITIONING.

mediation theory: the assumption that stimuli do not initiate behavior directly but that intervening processes are aroused by stimuli which in turn are responsible for the initiation of behavior.

mediator: in information theory, the system that intervenes between a receiver and a transmitter. The organism may be thought of as a mediator between stimuli and responses. The nervous system is also often spoken of as a mediator in the same sense.

medical model: the conceptualization of behavior disorders and psychological abnormalities as diseases analogous to organic diseases.

mediation: 1. a sustained effort at thinking, usually of a contemplative variety. 2. reflection on the relationship between the mediator and God.

medium: 1. an agency through which something is accomplished. 2. that which fills the space through which something is being transmitted. 3. a person who professes to be controlled by a disembodied spirit during a trance.

medulla: the central portion of an organ, such as the medulla of the adrenal gland or the medulla oblongata (*q.v.*).

medulla oblongata: an enlargement of the upper portion of the spinal cord just before it enters the brain. The medulla oblongata contains a number of nuclei governing important vital functions. *Syn.* bulb.

medullary sheath: the myelin sheath, a thin fatty layer that covers peripheral sensory and motor neurons. It is believed to have an insulating function.

medullated: covered with a medullary or myelin sheath.

megalocephalic: see MACROCEPHALIC.

megalomania: an extreme overevaluation of the self.

megalopsia: an increase in the apparent size of visual objects because of retinal pathology or distortion of the lens. *Syn.* MACROPSIA.

megrim: see MIGRAINE.

Meier Art Judgment Test: a test designed to measure aesthetic judgment by means of 100 paired pictures. One member of each pair is a recognized masterpiece, the other an inferior alteration. The subject must choose between them.

meiosis: the cell division found in the gametes or sperm and ova, where the number of chromosomes is reduced by one half. *Contr.* MITOSIS.

Meissner corpuscle: an afferent neuron whose peripheral portion consists of an elliptical capsule. The Meissner corpuscles are found primarily on the hairless surfaces of the skin and are believed to mediate touch or light pressure.

mel: a unit in a subjective ratio scale for pitch constructed by setting a tone of 1,000 Hz at 1,000 mels. The steps in the scale are then arrived at by a process of fractionation, with the subject adjusting a variable tonal stimulus until it appears to be one half as high in pitch as the standard of 1,000 mels, and so on for the other fractions.

melancholia: a pathological state of depression accompanied by depressed motor functions and low reactivity to stimuli. See also INVOLUTIONAL MELANCHOLIA.

melancholic: 1. pertaining to melancholy. 2. pertaining to a type of temperament associated with frequent spells of depression and pessimism about the future.

melancholy: a mood characterized by sadness, loss of interest in one's pursuits, and underreactivity to stimulation.

melioristic: pertaining to that which improves or makes better.

membership character: a concept used by the Gestalt psychologists to characterize the dynamic interaction whereby a change in a member influences the whole, and a change in the whole influences the members.

membership group: a group in which the individual is an accepted member. *Contr.* REFERENCE GROUP.

membrane: 1. the outer covering of a cell. 2. the lining in a cavity of the body.

membrane theory of conduction: a theoretical explanation of the propagation of the nervous impulse in terms of electrochemical events occurring on the surface of the neuronal membrane.

memorizing: the process of committing verbal material to memory by repetition.

memory: 1. the function involved in reliving past experiences. 2. the totality of past experiences that can be remembered. 3. a specific past experience.

The memory process is measured by recall, reproduction, recognition, and relearning. In *recall* the subject must demonstrate that he can remember what has been learned without the aid of stimulus cues. An essay examination measures recall. In *reproduction*, he must show, by a drawing or by rearranging objects in their original order, that he can remember what was originally learned or perceived. In *recognition*, the subject must demonstrate that he can remember which of several alternatives were originally learned when all are presented together. The multiple-choice examination draws upon this type of memory. In *relearning*, the amount of time or number of trials saved is measured for the relearning of a passage learned in the past. See also RETENTION; FORGETTING.

memory afterimage: a perceptual experience that consists of a vivid revival or prolongation of an experience after it has passed. For example, one may seem to hear the shout of ''Fire!'' hanging in the memory after the shouting has ceased.

memory color: the color of an object as it is remembered and as it influences the perception of a present color. The effect of the memory color is often surprisingly strong. The remembered grass is much greener than the actual grass, the remembered hair less gray than the present hair.

memory curve: see RETENTION CURVE.

memory drum: a mechanical device for presenting items to be remembered at a constant rate of speed. It consists of a drum of metal advanced by a ratchet at a preselected speed. A paper is hung over the drum with the items to be learned typed or printed on it, and these appear singly or in pairs in a window.

memory illusion: 1. a deluded belief that another's experience is one's own. 2. a false memory.

memory image: a reconstructed object or event in the memory with recognition that the orginal percept was in the past.

memory span: the number of items that can be repeated correctly after a single presentation. The materials used are unrelated sequences of numbers,

letters, or symbols. Memory-span tests are commonly included as items on standardized intelligence tests.

memory trace: a hypothetical modification of the nervous system postulated to account for the relative persistence of memories. *Syns.* ENGRAM; MNEME; mnemonic trace.

menarche: the first menstruation in the girl.

mendacity: pathological lying or attempts to deceive others.

Mendelian ratio: the frequency in the offspring (from a specified mating) of those manifesting a trait as compared with those who do not manifest the trait. The best-known of the Mendelian ratios is the 3:1 ratio that comes from the crossing of purebred lines of parents possessing a dominant and a recessive trait respectively. There will be three cases that manifest the trait to one that does not.

Mendelism: a theory of inheritance based on the Mendelian principles of (1) the existence of unit characters that may be dominant or recessive; and (2) the assumption that the genetic material is segregated from somatic material and is therefore independent of change through learning or experience.

meninges: the three membranes that cover the brain and spinal cord. They are, from the outside in, the dura mater, the arachnoid layer, and the pia mater.

meningitis: inflammation of the meninges. *Contr.* ENCEPHALITIS.

meniscus: a lens that is concave on one side and convex on the other.

menopause: the period of life in a woman at which menstruation ceases. *Syns.* climacteric; change of life.

menses: the period of menstruation;

the material discharged during menstruation.

menstruation: the cycle discharge of blood and sloughed-off uterine material that occurs in mature females. *Syns.* menstrual cycle; catamenial discharge; period.

mental: 1. pertaining to mind or the processes associated with mind. 2. (*Structuralism*) pertaining to conscious content. 3. (*Functionalism*) pertaining to acts or processes. 4. (*Psychoan.*) pertaining to the conscious, the unconscious, and the preconscious. 5. pertaining to specific processes, such as sets, attitudes, impulses, and intellectual processes. 6. pertaining to hidden or covert, as opposed to public or overt, processes. 7. pertaining to that which originates as a result of psychological causation, such as mental disorders. *Syns.* PSYCHIC; CONSCIOUS; PSYCHOGENIC.

mental ability: intelligence.

mental age: level of mental development expressed in units of chronological age for which the mental development is judged normal. Mental age (*Abbr.* MA) is most effectively calculated for children up to the chronological age 15 and is ordinarily ascertained by the child's performance on an intelligence test. A child whose MA is significantly higher than his CA (chronological age) is brighter than normal; one whose MA is significantly lower than his CA is duller than normal. For the relationship of MA to CA in terms of IQ (intelligence quotient), see INTELLIGENCE QUOTIENT.

mental analysis: 1. a list of the components of mind or its attributes. 2. psychoanalysis. 3. the discovery of the components, attributes, or relationships in an object or objective situation without overtly dealing with

the object or situation. One who sits and analyzes a chess situation without actually moving the pieces is engaging in this type of mental analysis.

mental chemistry viewpoint: the view that mind behaves like chemical compounds, that mind is possessed of elements compounded by association into more complex processes that may no longer resemble the elements from which they arose. The term was invented to promulgate the view that mind is not a mere passive collection of elements but a synthesis or fusion of elements whose attributes may differ from the elements from which they are constituted.

mental conflict: see CONFLICT.

mental content: the conscious content of experiential data in mind at any given time.

mental defective: see MENTAL DEFICIENCY.

mental deficiency: see MENTAL RETARDATION.

mental deterioration: see DETERIORATION.

mental development: the progressive changes in the mental process that go on from birth to death. The term includes both changes due to maturation and changes due to learning, and it often implies intellectual development.

mental discipline doctrine: the theory that special training results in the improvement of a function or in a general improvement in mental ability. The study of mathematics and the classics was frequently recommended for such purposes. The doctrine has now been discredited.

mental disease: a general term for any serious psychotic reaction, whether psychogenic or organic in origin. The term *mental disorder* (or *behavioral* *disorder*) has come into favor as a replacement for *mental disease* because of the somatic or organic implication in the use of the term *disease*.

mental disorder: any serious maladjustment that is disabling in its effect. The disorder may be either psychogenic or organic in origin and includes both psychotic and the more serious neurotic reactions.

mental element: a psychological process that cannot be resolved into anything simpler. The structuralists found by means of introspective analysis that the mental elements were sensations, images, and affective states. The concept is now chiefly of historic importance.

mental evolution: the progressive changes in mental organization with increasingly higher levels of a complexity as we progress up the phylogenetic scale.

mental examination: 1. a comprehensive examination of an individual's abilities, usually for establishing normalcy or abnormality. 2. a mental test, such as an intelligence test.

mental faculty: see FACULTY PSYCHOLOGY.

mental function: 1. any activity or process that is mental in origin, such as sensing, thinking, or judging. 2. a specific process, such as the intellectual function.

mental growth: the increase with age in the depth and breadth of any psychological function, but particularly intellectual functions. See also HEINIS CONSTANT, HEINIS LAW OF MENTAL GROWTH.

mental-growth curve: a graphic plot of mental age and chronological age that shows the rate of mental development. Mental age is plotted on the vertical axis and chronological age on the horizontal axis.

mental healing: the healing of mental disorders and physical diseases by suggestion or faith. *Syns.* FAITH HEALING; mind cure; divine healing.

mental health: a state of good adjustment with a subjective state of well-being, zest for living, and the feeling that one is exercising his talents and abilities.

mental hygiene: the investigation and application of those measures that prevent mental disorders and promote mental health.

mental illness: any behavioral disorder, whether functional or organic, of such a degree of severity as to require professional help and (usually) hospitalization.

mental image: a conscious representation of something that is not present to the senses. See also IMAGE; CONCRETE IMAGE VERBAL IMAGE.

mentalism: the doctrine that a class of phenomena exists that cannot be reduced to physiological or physical phenomena. *Contr.* NATURAL MONISM.

mentality: 1. mind considered as characteristic of an individual or a species, as the mentality of the child. 2. an ability or power of mind.

mental level: 1. the individual's standing on a standardized test of intellectual ability. 2. (*Psychoan.*) one of the divisions of consciousness: conscious, preconscious, and unconscious. 3. (*Jung*) one of the three divisions of the psyche: the conscious, the personal unconscious, and the collective unconscious.

mentally handicapped: educationally and vocationally retarded because of subnormal mentality.

mental maturity: 1. the attainment of an adult level of general development and psychological functions. 2. an adult status on an intelligence test.

mental measurement: 1. the application of quantitative methods to the measurement or psychological processes, such as intelligence. *Syn.* MENTAL TESTING. 2. the process of developing scales on which responses can be assigned a position. 3. psychophysical measurements, such as the determination of thresholds.

mental mechanism: see MECHANISM 4, 5.

mental organization: 1. the individual's pattern of mental processes considered as a whole. 2. the hierarchy of interrelations among the individual's habits, attitudes, and general patterns of social behavior.

mental phenomena: 1. conscious processes. 2. the totality of the functions associated with mind, whether conscious or unconscious.

mental process: 1. activity on the part of an organism that is of a psychological nature or involves the mind. 2. the phenomena of consciousness.

mental ratio: an occasional synonym for the IQ, or intelligence quotient.

mental retardation: intellectual deficiency or subnormality of such degree as to seriously impair the individual's functioning in society. The most profound degree of mental retardation occurs in individuals whose IQ's are below 20. These people show poor motor development, often are unable to talk, and cannot learn to read or write. They are unable to care for their own personal hygiene and are totally dependent upon others. For these reasons the profoundly retarded are institutionalized.

Severe retardation occurs where the IQ range is 20–35 and is characterized by the inability to profit from ordinary education or vocational training. Severe retardates show serious motor, speech, and intellectual impairment. Some can be trained in simple health care and self-maintenance habits but must be kept under close supervision and are therefore usually institutionalized.

Moderate retardation (IQ range 36–50) offers the possibility of training in social and vocational skills, with some individuals completing the first two grades of schooling. Because many lack the skills for complete self-sufficiency, they are maintained in controlled or sheltered environments or are dependent upon their families for support.

Mild retardation characterizes persons whose IQ range is approximately 51–70. They are capable of profiting from elementary schooling and achieve sufficient levels of social and vocational skills to function in society with some guidance or assistance from family and friends.

The causes of retardation lie in genetic abnormalities, brain damage during the gestation period or at birth, nutritional deficiencies, or severe environmental impoverishment during early childhood. Retardation may also result from certain infectious diseases such as rubella, or German measles; encephalitis; and syphilis.

mental scale: see MENTAL TEST.

mental set: a preparation or readiness for a certain kind of activity. For example, if the instruction accompanying a set of problems is to multiply, the subject maintains that attitude and carries out the appropriate operation. If the problems call for addition, his set is to add. The influence of set is shown in mixed series, where the subject is considerably slower than in a simple series.

mental structure: 1. a hypothetical construct used to account for behavior. The id, for example, was used by Freud to account for the striving, animalistic, and instinctive nature of man. 2. the individual's personality viewed as a persistent and complex organization of traits.

mental synthesis viewpoint: a viewpoint associated primarily with structuralistic psychology, which reflected the attempt on the part of the structuralists to understand mind as a compounding of the mental elements.

mental test: 1. an intelligence test. 2. more generally, any test designed for measuring the degree to which a subject possesses a psychological trait.

mental work: energy expended in accomplishing tasks that are primarily mental in nature, such as solving problems.

menticide: literally, mind-murder; brainwashing; the systematic attempt to break down one's beliefs, attitudes, and allegiances, in favor of the ultimate adoption of those of another.

meprobamate: a mild tranquilizing drug sold under the trade name Miltown.

merit ranking: see ORDER OF MERIT.

merit rating: the appraisal of an individual's performance on a particular job. *Syns.* progress report; efficiency rating.

merit scale: a scale in which the individuals or items are ranked according to the average of the merits assigned by the judges or raters.

Merkel corpuscle: an encapsulated sense receptor located in the mouth and tongue and believed to be associated with touch and pressure.

Merkel's law: the generalization that

equal supraliminal (above-threshold) sense differences correspond to equal stimulus differences.

Merrill-Palmer Scale: a series of 93 items consisting of both performance and verbal materials designed to measure intellectual ability. The test is standardized for children 24–63 months of age.

mescal; mescaline: a narcotic drug derived from a cactus plant. It produces vivid hallucinations of color. Peyote is obtained from mescaline.

mesencephalon: the midbrain, consisting of the corpora quadrigemina, the cerebral peduncles, the tegmentum, and the nerve tracts called the crura cerebri. The mesencephalon is the middle portion of the embryonic brain.

mesial: medial.

mesmerism: an old name for *hypnotism*, from the name of Franz (or Friedrich) Anton Mesmer (1734–1815), an early hypnotist.

mesocephalic: a head with a median ratio of length to breadth, specifically with a cephalic index between 76 and 81.

mesoderm: the middle of the three embryonic layers. The mesoderm develops into muscle and bone. *Contr.* ECTODERM, ENDODERM.

mesokurtosis: the peakedness of a distribution curve characteristic of that found in the normal distribution curve.

mesomorphic: *see* SHELDON'S CONSTITUTIONAL THEORY OF PERSONALITY.

mesopic vision: vision intermediate between photopic (daylight) and scotopic (twilight) and therefore a joint function of both rods and cones.

mesosomatic: (*Eysenck*) an individual who is within one standard deviation of the mean of scores calculated by multiplying the standard score for height by the standard score for transverse chest measurement.

message: 1. in communications theory, the output of a transmitter fed into a receiver. 2. loosely, a nervous impulse.

messenger RNA: the ribonucleic acid molecule that is assembled on the DNA molecules in the cell nucleus that migrates to the ribosomes of the cell cytoplasm and forms a pattern for transfer RNA.

metabolism: broadly, the physicochemical changes in living organisms. More specifically, the physiological process involved in the anabolism, or building, of tissues.

metacontrast: a kind of backward masking in which the original stimulus and masking stimulus are presented in adjacent retinal areas.

metaerg: (*R. B. Cattell*) a motivational source trait that results from environmental influences rather than from constitutional factors. See also ERG.

metallic color: color sensation evoked by the reflecting surfaces of certain metals and of paints containing particles of metal, such as aluminium.

metamers: colors whose spectral characteristics differ but are nevertheless seen as identical under certain conditions.

metamorphosis: a rapid and radical change of form, such as observed in the development of the frog from a tadpole.

metaneeds: in the hierarchy of needs, those at the top, such as self-actualization, self-esteem, aesthetic needs, and the like, which can only be satisfied when lower order needs are satisfied.

metaphrenia: the mental condition of the individual in the modern state— one who is concerned with material products, is overly hygienic, is anxious, and whose libido is withdrawn from his family group.

metaphysics: the branch of philosophy dealing with the ultimate nature of existence. Metaphysics includes *ontology*, or the science of being, and *cosmology*, or the science of the nature of the universe.

metapsychics: 1. the study of supernormal phenomena, spiritual manifestations, clairvoyance, telepahty, etc. 2. parapsychology. For definitions of the branches of metapsychology or parapsychology, see PARAPSYCHOLOGY.

metapsychoanalysis: a system of psychoanalysis developed by Otto Rank that goes beyond the bounds of classical psychoanalysis.

metapsychology: 1. any branch of psychology dealing with phenomena that lie outside the province of empirical psychology, such as telepathy, clairvoyance, and psychokinesis. *Syn.* PARAPSYCHOLOGY. 2. (*Psychoan.*) a point of view that treats mental processes in terms of their dynamic, topographical, and economic significance for the individual. 3. a systematic attempt to formulate broad, comprehensive laws that will embrace the total field of psychology. *Syns.* nomothetic psychology; metasystem.

metempirical: pertaining to phenomena that lie beyond the limits of the empirical or beyond the possibility of empirical validation.

metempsychosis: transmigration of the human soul after corporal death into another body.

metencephalon: the portion of the embryonic brain that becomes the medulla oblongata.

methadone: a synthetic, addictive narcotic used to treat heroin addicts. Methadone reduces the symptoms of heroin withdrawal and blocks the euphoric effects of other narcotics.

methamphetamine: a powerful amphetamine that is addictive if taken intravenously.

method: 1. the systematic procedures involved in the investigation of facts and concepts. 2. one of the special techniques in psychology, such as the experimental method or the clinical method. The term implies the special procedures utilized in the investigation of facts and the formulation of concepts from the point of view as stated.

methodology: 1. the formulation of methods to be used in the search for knowledge. 2. the method employed in a particular investigation.

metonymy: a language disturbance in schizophrenia in which approximate or related terms are used instead of direct terms.

metrazol: a drug that produces convulsions. Metrazol is one of the agents employed in inducing convulsions in shock therapy.

metric methods: 1. the psychophysical methods. 2. any quantitative method.

metronoscope: a device that exposes printed material for short periods of time and is used to measure reading speed or to pace reading.

microcephalic: having an abnormally small head, with associated mental deficiency, due to interrupted or incomplete brain development.

micron: a unit of length equal to a thousandth of a millimeter or a millionth of a meter.

microphonic: see AURAL MICROPHONIC.

micropsia: a decrease in the apparent size of objects as a result of disease of the retina or a functional disorder.

microsecond: one one-millionth of a second.

microsomatic: an individual who is one or more standard deviations below the mean of scores calculated by multiplying the standard scores for height and transverse chest measurement.

microspectrophotometer: a device for measuring the hue and intensity of lights arising from microscopic areas.

microsplanchnic: describing a type of body with small trunk and relatively long limbs.

microstructure: the fine mixture of surface grain of objects that makes them qualitatively distinctive.

microtome: an instrument for cutting thin sections of tissue for the preparation of microscopic slides.

midbrain: the mesencephalon, consisting of the corpora quadrigemina, cerebral peduncles, and the tegmentum.

middle ear: the portion of the ear lying between the eardrum and the cochlea. It contains the auditory ossicles and is connected to the oral cavity by the eustachian tube.

midparent: any measure expressing the average for the two parents in respect to any characteristic, such as height, weight, intelligence, etc. Allowance is made for sex differences in height.

midpoint: the halfway point in a distribution or a step interval.

midrange value: the average of the highest and lowest scores in a distribution. The midrange is a crude measure of central tendency.

midscore: the median.

Mignon delusion: the delusion on the part of a child that his parents are mere substitutes and that his true parents are distinguished individuals.

migraine; migraine headache: a disorder, believed to be inheritable, characterized by severe and usually unilateral headaches accompanied by nausea and visual disturbances.

milieu: the environment, usually external, unless qualified.

milieu therapy: therapy that seeks improvement in a behavior disorder by providing a controlled and stimulating environment.

military psychology: the branch of applied psychology that investigates the selection and assignment of military personnel, training procedures, morale, the design of equipment, and other problems bearing on life in the armed forces that may have psychological aspects.

Miller Analogies Test: a test of verbal analogies used in the selection of candidates for graduate school.

millilambert: a measure of luminance equal to one thousandth of a lambert.

millimicron: one thousandth of a micron; millionth of a millimeter. *Symbol* μμ. The millimicron is a unit of measurement for light waves.

millisecond: one thousandth of a second.

Miltown: a trade name for meprobamate, a mild tranquilizer.

mimetic: 1. imitative. 2. responding to instinctive behavior or species-specific behavior without opportunity for previous learning.

mimetic response: responding by imitation; copying the response of another organism.

mind: 1. the organized totality of psychological processes that enables the individual to interact with his environment. 2. (*Structuralism*) the totality of conscious experiences. 3. the totality of enduring structures employed to account for conscious experience and psychological activities. 4. the self or psyche. 5. the intellect or intelligence. 6. a characteristic mode of behavior or manner of thinking, such as the *American mind* or the *mind of a savage*.

Although psychology has been traditionally defined as the science that deals with mental activities, there has been no commonly agreed-upon definition of mind. A canvass of a number of psychologists would turn up an equal number of definitions. Nevertheless, a large number—the majority—would associate mind with the *processes* of perceiving, thinking, remembering, and intelligent behavior. Today most psychologists do not concern themselves with the ultimate nature of mind, nor do they concern themselves with the exact relationship between mind and body, a problem that was once a central issue in psychology. See also MIND-BODY PROBLEM.

mind-blindness. see AGNOSIA.

mind-body problem: an issue in philosophy and psychology that extends back to classical Greece and one that has been wrestled with by all modern systematic psychologists. The central problem is the exact relationship between body and mind. Are they separate substance? Do they interact? Are they ultimately reducible to one? Traditionally, the view that mind and body are two separate substances with no interaction between them is called *dualistic*. Plato was the first dualist. The view that mind and body are of a different nature but interact is called *interactionistic* and is represented by Descartes's view that mind and body, though separate, interact at the site of the pineal gland. The structuralists posited that mind and body run along in parallel streams without interaction but with parallel influences. That is, anything that influences mind is reflected by a parallel influence in the body and vice versa. This view is known as *psychophysical parallelism*. The Gestalt psychologists assume an *isomorphism* between mind and body. Isomorphism holds that there is a point-for-point correspondence between conscious experience and the physical situation but not an identity. Thus, mind, like a road map, reflects what is out there but is not identical with it. More recently, largely as a result of the behaviorist influence, the issue has ceased to be a central one in psychology. The psychologist studies the psychological individual, his responses and mental processes, without concerning himself with the ultimate nature of the relation between mind and body. See also PSYCHOSOMATIC.

mind-dust theory: the assumption that mind is made of particles or atoms that exist everywhere in the universe and coalesce to form the individual mind.

mind reading: the alleged ability of one individual to know what is passing in the mind of another without direct communication. Mind reading depends upon the interpretation of subtle muscular movements and other deliberate or inadvertent cues.

mind-twist hypothesis: the theory that mental disorders are functional in nature, or the result of severe maladjustments, as opposed to the brain-spot hypothesis, which assumes that all mental disorders are organic.

miniature system: a set of facts and theoretical assumptions organized for the purpose of explaining a restricted area in psychology, typically some one psychological process, such as conditioning, perception, intelligence, etc. For an example, see HULL'S MATHEMATICO-DEDUCTIVE THEORY OF LEARNING or SKINNER'S OPERANT CONDITIONING.

minimal audible field: the minimum pressure that can just be heard, measured at the midpoint of the observer's head.

minimal audible pressure: the smallest amount of pressure on the eardrum resulting in an audible sound.

minimal brain dysfunction: a diagnostic category employed for individuals who show learning or behavioral disorders whose precise cause is unknown but is believed to be associated with central nervous system dysfunctions. Often used as a synonym for learning disorder and hyperkinesis.

minimal-changes method: a psychophysical technique in which the experimenter presents the variable stimulus in ascending and descending series, each presentation varying from the preceding by very small amounts. On each trial the variable stimulus is compared to the standard, and the differential threshold can be calculated from a number of such comparisons.

minimal cue: see REDUCED CUE.

Minnesota Clerical Aptitude Test: a test of aptitude for clerical work, involving number-and-name comparisons, spelling, computation, and speed of checking.

Minnesota Multiphasic Inventory of Personality: a personality inventory containing over 500 statements with which the subject indicates agreement or disagreement. Patterns of responses are scored for the individual's tendencies toward hypomania, schizophrenia, psychesthenia, paranoia, masculinity, psychopathic deviation, hysteria, depression, and hypchondriasis.

Minnesota Paper Form Board: a test of mechanical aptitude that presents in printed form the types of problems ordinarily presented on wooden form boards. The subject is shown two or more parts of a geometric figure. When the parts are correctly assembled, they will make a figure that must be selected from among five choices.

Minnesota Rate of Manipulation Test: a test of motor or manual aptitude consiting of pegboards into which multicolored cylindrical disks must be filled in a prescribed order.

Minnesota Spatial Relations Test: a test of mechanical aptitude consisting of a series of four boards with cutouts of various shapes and sizes to be fitted into the correct portions of the board as quickly as possible.

minor hemisphere: in most individuals the right cerebral hemisphere, controlling spatial activities and musical functions.

minority group: a population subgroup possessing social or religious interests that differ from those of the larger group. Minority groups are subjected to various kinds of segregation and unfavorable treatment that may be legal, quasilegal, or purely social.

minor scale: see DIATONIC SCALE.

miosis: see MYOSIS.

mirror drawing: a drawing made by viewing a design in a mirror. In the typical laboratory experiment involving mirror drawing, the task is to trace a pathway through a double-lined star as quickly as possible without touching the sides and looking only at the mirror.

mirror focus: an abnormal region of the cerebral cortex that develops seizurelike firing in response to abnormal firing in the same region on the opposite side.

mirror reading: reading backward; reading from right to left.

mirror reversal: the right-left reversal of objects as when they are viewed in a mirror.

mirror tracing: see MIRROR DRAWING.

mirror writing: writing in which the right-left relationships are reversed so that when viewed in a mirror, it is seen as ordinary writing. The notebooks of Leonardo da Vinci were written in mirror script. It is sometimes observed in children.

misogyny: a hatred of women.

misoplegia: revulsion or hatred for a paralyzed limb by a hemiplegic.

mising-parts tests: any test in which the testee must point out the missing parts in a picture. Missing-parts tests are used on the Stanford-Binet scale.

mitosis: cell division in which the chromosomes split, with one half of each chromosome going to the daughter cells. Mitosis is characteristic of cell division in the fertilized ovum. *Contr.* REDUCTION DIVISION.

Mitwelt: 1. in existentialist terminology, man's relationship with his fellowmen. *Cf.* EIGENWELT; UMWELT. 2. the age we live in; our times.

mixed cerebral dominance: the failure of one side of the brain to be clearly dominant over the other in motor control. The resulting conflict is held to be the cause of speech disorders by disrupting the delicate motor control normally exercised by the side that controls handedness.

mixed neurosis: a neurosis that involves the symptoms of both hysteria and obsessive-compulsive reactions.

mixed reinforcement: a type of multiple reinforcement in which the change is not signaled by a change in stimulus but must be detected by the subject by a change in the pattern of reinforcement.

mixoscopia: sexual excitement induced by witnessing a sexual act.

mneme: 1. the memory trace; the enduring and basic principle in mind that accounts for memory. 2. (*Semon*) the pervasive or characteristic modification of living organisms by learning and experience.

mnemonic system: a scheme for remembering, particularly verbal or numerical materials. Many people remember number facts by associating them with familiar numbers, such as house numbers, anniversaries, etc.

mnemonics: the art of improving the memory with the aid of artificial systems.

mnemonic trace: see MEMORY TRACE.

mob: a crowd of individuals acting under strong emotional conditions often leading to violence or illegal acts.

modal: pertaining to a MODE.

modality: see SENSE MODALITY.

mode: 1. the most frequent score in a distribution. 2. the peak (or peaks) in a frequency curve. 3. a sensory category (see SENSE MODALITY). 4. a characteristic way of behaving or satisfying motives.

mode interval: the class interval that contains the mode.

model: 1. a copy of anything. 2. an ideal form, or standard. 3. a physical representation of a system to show how that system works. Models of the ear and of neurons have been constructed to help visualize their working principles. 4. a set of assumptions or postulates, often in mathematical form, which attempts to provide a generalized working construct that can account for empirical data or relationships. See MATHEMATICAL MODEL; LINEAR-OPERATOR MODEL; HULL'S MATHEMATICO-DEDUCTIVE THEORY OF LEARNING.

modeling: learning to make a response by watching another make that response. Imitation.

mode of appearance: characteristic properties of certain colors, in addition to hue, saturation, and brightness, determining how they are perceived. The nature of the surface, film color, bulkiness, and metallic sheen exemplify mode of appearance.

mode pleasure: the satisfaction attained from the manner in which an activity is carried out, as opposed to the goal satisfaction to which the activity leads.

moderator variable: any variable that affects another variable.

modification: any change in structure or function due to internal, external, or hereditary influences.

modulator: a hypothesized retinal receptor that yields a certain sensation of hue. Depending on the species, Granit has found from one to four modulators by means of direct electrical stimulation of the retinal elements while recording optical responses.

molar: pertaining to the entire mass of material, to large units, or to relatively unanalyzable units.

molar behavior: 1. a large unit of behavior, such as solving a puzzle or running a maze. 2. holistic units of behavior that cannot be analyzed without destroying their unity. 3. behavior described in nonphysiological terms, as opposed to reflex behavior. 4. (*Tolman*) animal behavior that shows purpose and teachability; the unit of Tolman's Purposive Behaviorism (*q.v.*). *Contr.* MOLECULAR BEHAVIOR.

molarism: a preference for a molar approach to the study of behavior. *Contr.* MOLECULARISM.

molecular: 1. pertaining to molecules, such as the molecules of a gas. 2. pertaining to small units or units that are the result of analysis.

molecular behavior: 1. behavior described or analyzed into small units. 2. behavior described in terms of reflexes or segmented neuromuscular units. *Contr.* MOLAR BEHAVIOR.

molecularism: a preference for a molecular approach to the study of behavior.

molilalia: see MOGILALIA.

moment: 1. a minute interval of time. 2. in statistics, the average of deviations from the mean raised to a power.

momentary personality: (*Murray*) the patterning of behavior during one event in the individual's life.

momism: a term popularized by Philip Wylie and occasionally found in the technical literature to characterize excessive concern with motherhood and mothering.

monadism: the doctrine that reality is composed of independent units of being of both mind and matter.

monaural: pertaining to one ear.

monogolism: a congenital defect characterized by deficiency in intelligence, usually at the severely or moderately retarded level, and physical abnormalities that result in the individual's having a mongoloid appearance—slant eyes, a relatively flat skull, and stubby fingers. The tongue is furry and the individual has a tendency to dribble saliva. *Syns.* Down's syndrome; mongolian idiocy; mongolian imbecility.

monism: the point of view that there is basically only one kind of reality.

monitor: to watch or guard an individual or a machine for the purpose of making sure that functioning is normal.

monochorionic twins: see IDENTICAL TWINS.

monocular: pertaining to one eye; one-eyed; involving the use of only one eye.

monocular suppression: the tendency for one eye to dominate the other so that there is failure of binocular fusion, and useful information is obtained only from the dominant eye.

monocular vision: vision in only one eye. *Contr.* BINOCULAR VISION.

monoideism: a pathological obsession along a single line or thought.

monomania: an old term for paranoia, a disorder characterized by fixed ideas and delusions of persecution. See PARANOIA.

monorhinic: pertaining to smelling with one nostril.

monotic: pertaining to a single ear; characterizing a stimulus presented to a single ear.

monotonic: 1. having a single tone. 2. characterizing two variables related in such a way that for each value of one there is a single value of the other.

monovular twins: see IDENTICAL TWINS.

monozygotic twins: twins developed from a single, fertilized ovum; identical twins.

Monroe Diagnostic Reading Test: a reading-readiness test for kindergarten and primary-school children. The scale includes both visual and auditory tests.

mood: a mild, usually transitory emotion.

Mooney Problem Check List: an adjustment inventory for use in secondary schools and colleges that consists of a series of problems with which the student expresses agreement if they fit his condition. Useful as a screening device for selecting cases that may need attention.

moral: 1. pertaining to morals. 2. characterizing a person or group whose conduct is proper or ethical. 3. pertaining to laws or customs governing conduct.

moral code: the accepted set of rules for the guidance of conduct in a given society.

morale: the attitude or spirit characterized by the presence of confidence, strong motivation to continue, cheerfulness, and good organization.

moral realism: an attitude, characteristic of children, that the morality of an act is inherent in that act and can be perceived immediately by an observer as an objective fact.

morbid: 1. pertaining to a diseased or pathological condition. 2. relating to attitudes that result in excessive interest in pathological conditions.

mores: social customs regarded as essential to the welfare of the group.

Morgan's canon: see LLOYD MORGAN'S CANON.

moron: a now obsolete term used to characterize a mild degree of mental retardation (IQ 50–70). See also MENTAL RETARDATION.

Moro reflex: the infantile equivalent of the startle response. The infant shows clutching movements of the arms and legs if startled by a loud sound.

morpheme: the minimal linguistic unit with meaning.

morphine: a narcotic drug, the principal alkaloid of opium. The drug is a depressant useful in the relief of pain. It produces a state of euphoria and drowsiness.

morphogenesis: the development of the organism's form and structure.

morphological index: an index or relationship among bodily proportions, used to describe the individual's physique or body build.

morphologic inferiority: (*Adler*) a deficiency in general physique or in an organ.

mortido: the death instinct.

mosaic: a design made up of small parts. Mosaic tests may be employed on individual intelligence scales or in projective techniques.

mossy fiber: one of the excitatory types of fibers found in the cerebellum.

mother complex: a strong attachment to the mother, with overtones of sexual desire. *Syn.* OEDIPUS COMPLEX.

mother figure: a psychological substitute or surrogate for the mother.

mother surrogate: 1. a person who functions for the individual as if she were the mother. 2. one perceived as having the functions of a mother.

motile: 1. (*adj.*) characterizing organisms capable of moving from place to place. 2. (*noun*) an individual whose imagery is primarily kinesthetic.

motility: 1. the capacity to make movements. 2. the characteristic manner and speed of movement.

motion study: see TIME-AND-MOTION STUDY.

motivate: 1. to incite to action. 2. to serve as an incentive or goal.

motivated error: 1. a mistake or accident that reflects underlying motivation. 2. a slip of the tongue, or "Freudian slip."

motivation: an intervening variable used to account for factors within the organism that arouse, maintain, and channel behavior toward a goal. See also MOTIVATE.

motivational hierarchy: the theory proposed by Abraham Maslow that human motives form a hierarchy with the primary or physiological drives on the bottom; safety and security next; then gregariousness, love, and affection as the next highest category; prestige, power, and possession are immediately higher than gregariousness, love, and affection; self-actualization, the need for knowing, and aesthetic needs are the top of the hierarchy.

motivation research: the study of consumer motivation by advertisers and specialists in the field of psychology who attempt to discover the motives that make people buy the way they do and who strive to modify buying habits by discovering more effective appeals and making changes in packaging, or in the product itself, that will meet with more favorable attitudes.

motive: 1. a state of tension within the individual that arouses, maintains, and directs behavior toward a goal. 2. the conscious reason the individual gives for his behavior. 3. an unconscious reason for behavior. See UNCONSCIOUS MOTIVATION. 4. a drive. The term *drive* is used primarily to refer to the primary motives for which the bodily basis is known. 5. a set or attitude that guides behavior.

Of the many intervening variables that psychologists use, the concept of motive (or motivation) is among the most controversial and least satisfactory. There seem to be as many different major definitions as there are major theories of motivation. Some of the more common usages are included above. The concept is also freighted with a number of subtle connotations from general English usage and with specialized denotations from the literature of psychology. Some of these are reflected in the following list of related terms: APPETITE, ATTITUDE, COMPLEX, DESIRE, DETERMINING TENDENCY, DISPOSITION, DRIVE, EMOTION, END, ERG, GOAL, HABIT, IMPULSE, INCENTIVE, INSTINCT, INTEREST, LIBIDO, NEED, PREFERENCE, SENTIMENT, SET, TEMPERAMENT, URGE, VALENCE, WISH.

motone: (*Murray*) a muscular-motor action pattern.

motoneuron: a nerve cell or neuron that supplies a muscle or gland.

motor: pertaining to or characterizing muscular or glandular action.

motor aphasia: the inability to speak, caused by a lesion in the speech area.

motor apraxia: the inability, because of a lesion in the premotor area, correctly to carry out a series of acts.

motor area: the portion of the cerebral cortex, approximately enclosed by the precentral gyrus and known as Broadmann's area 4, which is responsible for the mediation of simple, circumscribed muscle movements.

motor cell: a motor neuron.

motor cortex: see MOTOR AREA.

motor diffusion: the tendency in infants to show widespread responses involving large segments of the body.

motor end plate: the point of junction of a motor neuron with a muscle.

motor equivalence: the principle that there are a number of identical or equal ways to carry out a specific act. One may reach B from A by crawling, walking, running, or, if conditions permit, by means of vehicular transportation.

motor function: any of the activities associated with muscles and glands.

motor habit: a habit described and studied in terms of the responses it involves.

motor incoordination: see INCOORDINATION.

motoric region: (*Lewin*) the aspect of personality manifesting itself in outward appearance and responses.

motor learning: learning skills or habits in which the processes involved are primarily muscular or are described in muscular or in glandular terms.

motor nerve: a nerve whose functions are associated with muscle or glands.

motor neuron: a neuron that conveys impulses toward a muscle or gland.

motor-perceptual region: in topological psychology, a boundary that must be traversed in going from the external environment into the inner, personal region.

motor point: see MOTOR END PLATE.

motor primacy theory: the theory that motor functions develop before sensory functions.

motor-reaction type: a class of reactions in which the subject's attention has been specifically directed toward the motor aspect of a stimulus-response situation.

motor root: any of the ventral or anterior roots of the spinal cord that are motor in function. *Contr.* SENSORY ROOT. *Syn.* ventral root.

motor sense: see KINESTHESIS.

motor set: 1. a readiness for a certain kind of response. 2. a preparatory adjustment of the muscles that orient and alert the individual for a certain kind of activity. Someone looking for a lost object, or runners at the starting line, illustrate this type of set.

motor theory of consciousness: the assumption that consciousness is the subjective correlate of muscular and glandular activity. This assumption was first widely promulgated by John B. Watson, the founder of Behaviorism. See also PERIPHERALISM.

motor unit: the neuron and its connected muscular or glandular terminal.

mouches volantes: literally, flying flies; specks in the vitreous or aqueous humor of the eye which seem to dance in the visual field.

movement: 1. motion apparent or real. 2. a change in position of the organism or any of its parts.

movement determinant: (*Rorschach*) the quality of the inkblot that causes the subject to see either human or animal movement.

movement illusion: the belief that the body or a part of it is in motion when, in fact, it is not.

movement response: (*Rorschach*) a response attributing human or humanlike movement on the part of an animal to one of the inkblots. Movement responses are interpreted as an indication of introversion and fantasy.

moving total method: a technique for smoothing or evening-out a series of items by substituting for each item the sum of the item and a certain number of adjacent items. Thus, a moving total computation for output on the last three working days of the week would enter for Friday the sum of the data for Thursday, Friday, and Saturday.

Mullerian system: in the embryo, the primitive sexual structures that will develop into female reproductive organs provided testes are not present. *Contr.* WOLFFIAN DUCT SYSTEM.

Müller, Johannes: physiologist, founder of modern experimental physiology (1801–1858). After receiving his medical degree, Müller taught at the University of Bonn, from 1824 until 1833, and then at the University of Berlin, where he wrote his famous *Handbook of Physiology*, recognized as the first systematic textbook in the field. It was in the *Handbook* that he stated his famous doctrine of the specific energies of nerves, to the effect that each nerve has its specific form of energy with which it responds, regardless of stimulus. By taking this position, Müller allied himself with the nativistic school of perception. Among his more important pupils were Helmholtz and Wundt.

Müller-Lyer illusion: the distortion in the length of a line enclosed in arrowheads or acute angles in comparison with a line of the same length enclosed by obtuse lines.

Müller-Schumann law: the principle that when two items have been associated, it is more difficult to form an association between one of the items and a third item.

Müller-Urban method: a psychophysical procedure for treating data gathered by the method of constant stimuli, which assumes that the best measure of the difference threshold is the median of the best-fitting ogive for the distribution of values.

Müller-Urban weights: a procedure in psychophysics for determining the best value of h, or the precision with which the data have been fitted. The value of h at a probability level of .50 is maximum and at either end of the distribution, $p + .01$ or $p + .99$, the weightings for h are at a minimum

multicellular: pertaining to an organism composed of many cells.

multigroup method: (*R. B. Cattell*) a factor-analysis technique in which all the factors are extracted from the correlation matrix simultaneously, rather than successively, as in the Thurstone centroid method.

multimodal: pertaining to a distribution that has more than one mode or peak.

multimodal theory of intelligence: the theory that intelligence is made up of a large number of specific abilities rather than a single general ability.

multiple-choice experiment: an experiment in which the individual or animal is confronted with several choices, only one of which leads to the reward. The choices are identified by a perceptual cue, and care is taken to ensure that the subject is not responding on the basis of spatial cues. For example, several doors might be employed with the symbols triangle, circle, and square painted on them. Only the square would lead to the reward. The position of the correct door would be shifted from trial to trial.

multiple-choice test: a test in which there are several alternative answers, only one of which is correct.

multiple correlation: a coefficient expressing the relationship between a dependent variable and a pool of independent variables. *Abbr.* R. Essentially, the multiple correlation is employed where relationships among variables are not simple, but rather where a given effect is due to multiple causation. The formula for a multiple correlation is:

$$R_{1.23} = \sqrt{\frac{r^2_{12} - 2r_{12}r_{13}r_{23} + r^2_{13}}{1 - r^2_{23}}}$$

multiple-determination coefficient (R^2): a coefficient expressing the percentage of a correlation between two variables in a multiple correlation to be accounted for by the effects of other variables.

multiple-factor: pertaining to either a theory or a method that assumes that in the function or process under consideration there is more than one variable responsible for the observed results.

multiple-factor inheritance: the determination of a genetic trait by the combined action of several pairs of genes.

multiple-group method: see MULTI-GROUP METHOD.

multiple personality: a pathological condition in which the integrated personality fragments into two or more personalities, each of which manifests a relatively complete integration of its own and is relatively independent of the other personalities. One of the earliest cases of multiple personality was that reported under the pseudonym of Sally Beauchamp by Dr. Morton Prince. In recent years the case reported in *The Three Faces of Eve* by Drs. Thigpen and Cleckley achieved international prominence.

multiple regression equation: an equation for computing the individual's score on a certain selected criterion on the basis of his scores on several correlated variables. The problem often involves predicting job success on the basis of several test scores.

multiple reinforcement: reinforcement programmed according to two or more schedules that alternate at random. A change in stimulus signals the change in reinforcement.

multiple response, principle of: the generalization that an animal reacts to a situation with a series of varied responses.

multiple sclerosis: a pathological condition of the brain and spinal cord in which hardening of the tissues results in impairment of function.

multipolar nerve cell or neuron: a neuron with several processes extending away from the cell body. *Contr.* unipolar; BIPOLAR.

multitrait measurement: measurement with no attempt made to single out the effect of any one trait but in which the combined effect of all traits is measured.

multivariate: pertaining to a measuring scale or technique that attempts to measure the effect of several variables or to demonstrate their effect in behavior.

multivariate analysis: any statistical technique, such as FACTOR ANALYSIS or ANALYSIS OF COVARIANCE, designed to test the effect of many variables acting simultaneously.

multivariate test: a statistical technique for determining the differences between groups in respect to all variables.

Munsell color system: an atlas of color samples arranged in such a way that colors of every hue, saturation, and brightness are systematically categorized. Any hue can be compared with its nearest value in the Munsell system and specified by a combination of numbers and letters.

Murray, Henry A.: American psychologist (1893–   ). Murray received degrees at Harvard, Columbia, and Cambridge. His interest in psychology developed during his stay at Cambridge, where he came upon Jung's *Psychological Types*. A personal visit to Jung revolutionized his attitude toward science and psychoanalysis, and he became a psychologist. His career began in 1927 as an instructor at Harvard, where he joined Morton Prince at the newly founded

Psychological Clinic. At Harvard Clinic he directed the extensive research project on normal personalities that culminated in the development of the widely used Thematic Apperception Test. During World War II, Murray served with the Army Medical Corps and directed an assessment service for the Office of Strategic Services. After the war he returned to Harvard as a professor of clinical psychology. He is currently professor emeritus at that institution. His chief works include: *Explorations in Personality* (1938), *Manual of Thematic Apperception Test*, with Christiana Morgan (1943), and *Assessment of Men* (1948).

Murray's Personology: Murray's definition of personality treats it as a "continuity of functional forms and forces manifested through sequences of organized regnant processes and overt behaviors from birth to death." By *regnant processes*, Murray means *brain processes*, reflecting his view that behavior is functionally dependent upon the central nervous system. The definition also emphasizes the longitudinal continuity of personality and its enduring patterns of behavior. Personality is also a dynamic process, as revealed by the many needs that play an important role in its organization and functioning. Some of the more important needs given by Murray are: needs for affiliation, deference, nurturance, succorance, harm avoidance; needs for avoiding inferiority feelings, blame, abasement; needs for passivity, seclusion, and inviolacy. There are, in addition, needs for aggression, autonomy, dominance, rejection, achievement, recognition, exhibition, sex, acquisition, cognizance, construction, and order. (Many of these needs are defined further under appropriate entries in this dictionary.)

Murray's list of human needs leans heavily on Freudian concepts, reflecting his lifelong interest in psychoanalysis. The needs are closely related to what Murray calls *perceptual press* (singular and plural), which reflects what significance an object or person has for the individual. Some of the more important press are: absence or death of parent, danger or misfortune, birth of a sibling, dominance by another; exposure to sex, illness, and awareness of inferiority feelings. Needs and press are interrelated in Murray's theory in that press depend upon needs. Specifically, if there is no existing need, an environmental object or person has no significance for the individual and therefore cannot be a press. Personality is revealed in the *proceedings*, or concrete activities, of the individual over a period of time. Proceedings may be internal—thoughts, memories, fantasies—or external, comprising the individual's attempts to cope with environmental events. The development of personality as it interacts with the environment and persons in that environment who have significance for the individual follows development envisaged by Freud. Murray accepts the ego, id, and superego, with some modifications. The concept of complexes is also taken from Freudian literature, with modifications and additions. Characteristic methods of study include the use of interviews, projective techniques. (Thematic Apperception Test), and psychoanalysis.

muscae volitantes: SEE MOUCHES VOLANTES.

muscarinic: characterizing a receptor responsive to acetylcholine that mediates inhibitory activities.

muscle: a structure composed of individual muscle fibers bound together into a contractile unit. The chief types of muscles are *striated*, or voluntary; *smooth*, or involuntary; and *cardiac*.

muscle balance: the tendency for either eye to maintain a position of fixation when fusion is artificially prevented.

muscle potential: the action potential generated in a muscle by the nervous impulse after it has crossed the myoneural junction, or synapse, between the neuron and the muscle.

muscle reading: the interpretation of slight involuntary movements by an experimenter in physical contact with the subject. A skilled "reader" can open a safe or find lost objects by correctly interpreting involuntary muscle movements on the part of the subject.

muscle sensation: awareness of muscular movements and tensions. Muscle sensation is part of the kinesthetic sense, or muscle, tendon, and joint sense.

muscle spindle: a type of receptor consisting of a specialized filament of an afferent neuron wrapped around a muscle fiber and which gives information about the contractions of the fiber. Muscle spindles are part of the kinesthetic system.

muscle tonus: the slight degree of contraction muscles maintain when inactive. Tonus keeps muscles in good condition and makes it possible for them to respond more readily than would otherwise be possible.

muscle twitch: 1. the sharp contraction of a nerve-muscle preparation upon being stimulated with a make-or-break shock. 2. a derogatory characterization of behaviorists by holistic psychologists because of the former's alleged concern with molecular units of behavior.

muscular imbalance: inequality in the tension exerted by a muscle group, with the result that the organ of movement may be adversely affected. Muscular imbalance often affects the eyes, a condition called *heterophoria*.

musculature: the totality of the striped muscles; more rarely, the entire muscular system, striated and smooth.

mutation: a sudden, inheritable genetic variation. Mutations are believed to be among the chief reasons for the evolution of the species.

mute: 1. (*noun*) an individual suffering from mutism. 2. (*adj.*) pertaining to an inability to speak because of mutism.

mutism: 1. lack of speech due to a failure of development of the necessary organs or because of deafness. 2. an emotional blockage resulting in a voluntary or involuntary inability to speak.

mutitas: see MUTISM.

myasthenia: a muscular weakness due to disease.

mydriasis: extreme dilation of the pupil of the eye, due to a pathological condition or drugs.

myelencephalon: the portion of the embryonic hindbrain that develops into the medulla oblongata.

myelin; myelin sheath: the white, lipoid material surrounding the medullated neurons.

myelination: the formation of the myelin sheath during embryonic development.

myelitis: inflammation of the spinal cord.

myelon: the spinal cord.

Myers-Briggs Type Indicator: a self-report inventory for grades 9–16 and adults, designed to measure Jung's personality types.

myoclonus: muscular spasms characterized by alternating periods of rigidity and relaxation.

myoesthesis: the muscle sense.

myogenic: having its origin in muscle tissue.

myograph: an instrument for measuring the force of a muscular reaction. An *isometric myograph* measures reactions against a strong opposing force that prevents contraction; an *isotonic myograph* measures muscular reaction that allows the muscle to shorten.

myokinetic: pertaining to muscle movement.

myoneural junction: the point at which a motor nerve comes into contact with a muscle.

myopia: nearsightedness; a condition in which the light rays come to a focus in front of the retina because the eyeball is too short. Vision is indistinct for far objects.

myosis: extreme pupillary contraction.

myotatic reflex: the contraction of a muscle produced by a sudden stretch.

myotonia: abnormal rigidity of the muscles; muscle spasms.

mysophilia: a pathological interest in filth or dirt.

mysophobia: an obsessive fear of dirt or contamination. Mysophobia is typically associated with a hand-washing compulsion.

mysticism: 1. the belief that knowledge can be obtained by avenues other than the senses. Mystical knowledge is held to be attained by means of contemplation. 2. used derogatorily to characterize beliefs arrived at by nonscientific techniques or techniques that allegedly cannot be described.

myth: 1. a traditional belief without historical verification. 2. a false belief widely accepted among the populace.

mythology: the body of myths in a given culture.

mythomania: a tendency to give exaggerated reports of imaginary adventures.

myxedema: a condition of hypothyroidism in adults, characterized by a low basal-metabolism rate, weakness, low motivation, and a puffy condition of the skin.

N

nail biting: a nervous habit, usually observed in children, in which the fingernails are chewed down to the quick.

naive: 1. lacking sophistication; childlike; inexperienced. 2. characteristic of subjects in experiments who are unaware of the nature of the experiment.

naloxone: a drug that inhibits the action of opiates and blocks the pain-relieving effect of endorphins.

Nancy school: a school of hypnotism founded by Bernheim in 1882. The Nancy school held that hypnosis was a normal phenomenon induced by suggestion, in contrast to older schools, which considered the hypnotic trance a manifestation of hysteria.

nanism: dwarfism.

nanometer (NM): a billionth of a meter. Used in measuring light waves.

narcissism; narcism: 1. self-love; exaggerated concern with the self. 2. (*Psychoan.*) an early stage in human development characterized by extreme concern for the self and lack of concern for others. Narcissism may persist into adulthood as a fixation.

narcissistic neurosis: (*Psychoan.*) a neurosis in which the libido regresses to a very early (pregenital) phase of development. Thus, the individual fails to develop an attachment for another person or object.

narcissistic object choice: (*Psychoan.*) the investment of the libido in the ego or in an individual similar to one's self.

narcoanalysis: a form of therapy in which a sleeplike state is induced with the aid of barbiturate drugs. The individual is encouraged to discuss his difficulties, and interpretations are given later. During the sleeplike state some suggestions may be offered by the therapist to aid in the alleviation of symptoms.

narcolepsy: a pathological desire for sleep.

narcomania: a pathological desire for relief from pain or discomfort.

narcosis: a state of pathological reduction in responsiveness of the individual as a whole and a marked deceleration of the physiological system as a result of narcotic drugs.

narcosynthesis: the interpretation of the patient's verbal productions obtained under the influence of narcotic drugs.

narcotherapy: the utilization of the narcotic state induced by drugs for the purpose of treating personality disorders.

narcotism: 1. state of being under the influence of narcotic drugs. 2. drug addiction.

nares: the nasal passages.

nascent: coming into existence; beginning to develop.

natal: pertaining to birth.

national character: characteristic behavior patterns, attitudes, values, etc., that are found in a nation.

national norm: a norm based on a representative sample drawn from an entire nation. *Contr.* LOCAL NORM.

native: inborn; inherited. *Contr.* ACQUIRED; learned.

nativism: a point of view that emphasizes the role of heredity, as opposed to environment, in the development of mental and behavioral processes. Nativism is a doctrine particularly associated with perception. Nativists held that space and time perceptions were dependent upon native factors, in opposition to the empiricists, who held that these qualities were learned. The nativistic point of view is also associated with intelligence by those who hold that the capacity for intellectual function is inherited. However, even those who emphasize the native inheritance of potential intelligence recognize that environment plays a crucial role in developing that capacity. See also EMPIRICISM.

naturalism: the point of view that mental processes, attitudes, and other psychological processes are part of the system of natural phenomena and therefore interpretable according to natural laws.

naturalistic observation: the oldest of the scientific methods, consisting of the observation and recording of events as they occur in nature. Naturalistic observation is frequently used in studying the development of children.

natural law: 1. a statement, often in mathematical form, of a consistently observed and predictable phenomenon of nature. 2. a well-established custom presumed to be discerned by reason without the necessity of artificial sanction by legal codes.

natural monism: the point of view that all sciences are ultimately reducible to physics and chemistry. Thus, psychology would be reducible to physiology, physiology to physics and chemistry.

natural sciences: the sciences dealing with physical and biological objects and processes. Psychology may be classified as a natural science or as a social science, depending upon the definer's point of view. To avoid the dilemma, some psychologists prefer the term *behavioral science* for psychology and allied disciplines.

natural selection: evolutionary process of "survival of the fittest"; natural process by which species capable of adjusting to their environment survive and those incapable of adjusting become extinct.

nature: 1. the innate or inherited characteristics of an individual. 2. the phenomena of the universe taken as a totality. 3. the qualities of an individual that make up his personality and temperament. Thus, it is sometimes said of an individual, "That is his nature."

nature-nurture problem or **controversy:** the problem of deciding the relative contribution of heredity and environment to the development of individual differences.

nausea: 1. a complex disturbance of the gastric, vasomotor, and sebaceous systems involving dizziness, sweating, a tendency toward vomiting, and feelings of weakness. 2. metaphorically, disgust.

NE: see NOREPINEPHRINE.

near effect: the degree of excitation of a neuron depending upon how close the neuronal system is to the point of application of the stimulus and how appropriate that stimulus is for the system in question.

near point: 1. in visual accommodation, the nearest point at which an object can be seen clearly. 2. in convergence, the nearest point at which an object can be seen in clear fusion with two eyes focused on it.

nearsightedness: see MYOPIA.

near vision: the visual discrimination of objects at about two feet or less from the eye.

Necker cube: an ambiguous figure consisting of a cube whose edges fluctuate in perspective. See illustration.

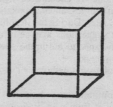

FIG. 20. *The Necker cube. A type of ambiguous figure.*

necromania: morbid desire, usually sexual, for a dead body.

necrophilia; necrophilism: sexual attraction to corpses.

necrophobia: a fear of corpses.

need: 1. a cellular substance that organisms must have in order to remain healthy. 2. more generally, any lack or deficiency felt by the individual to be inimical to his welfare. 3. a motive. 4. a hypothetical tissue deficiency measured in terms of hours of deprivation for a needed substance. 5. an animal drive or physiological motive.

need cathexis: the investment of a need in a specific object or person

need-drive-incentive pattern: a theoretical model of behavior stating that needs dependent upon deprivation give rise to drives directed toward incentives for their satisfaction.

need gratification: the reduction of a need by consummatory behavior at a goal.

need-integrate: (*Murray*) a representation of movements, pathways, behavior patterns, or goal objects that may be analyzed to discover an individual's needs. See also MURRAY'S PERSONOLOGY.

need-press: see MURRAY'S PERSONOLOGY.

need reduction: the state of having a need reduced by consummatory behavior.

need state: the hypothetical condition of the organism as a result of a need or period of deprivation.

need tension: the tension or emotional feeling that accompanies a need.

neencephalon: the new brain or cerebral cortex, in contrast to the *paleencephalon*, or phylogenetically older portions of the brain.

negation: 1. the disproof or denial of a statement or suggestion. 2. negativism.

negative: 1. in mathematics, characteristic of a quantity less than zero. 2. pertaining to denial, negation, disputatiousness, and attitudes of hostility. 3. pertaining to correlations in which one variable is inversely related to another, or where high standing in one variable is related to low standing in another. 4. pertaining to the cathode, or cathodal current, or to electricity in which the elementary units are electrons.

negative acceleration: a decrease in the rate of growth or change in a function with time or practice.

negative adaptation: 1. gradual loss in sensitivity due to prolonged stimulation. 2. gradual weakening of a response as a result of repeated or prolonged stimulation.

negative feedback: in a complex system, a signal that diminishes or stops output. For example, in a furnace the thermostat sends a signal to the burner, shutting it off when the house reaches the desired temperature. *Contr.* POSITIVE FEEDBACK. See also FEEDBACK.

negative fixation: the learned avoidance of a class of responses because of punishment or social disapproval. Many food aversions in children are accounted for in this manner.

negative induction: (*Pavlov*) the intensification of inhibition in a system because of the influence of preceding excitation.

negative narcissism: underevaluation of the self.

negative phase: characterizing any period marked by withdrawal of the individual or negativism during development or during the course of a disease.

negative practice: deliberately practicing an error in order to overcome it. As the individual practices he repeats to himself that what he is doing is incorrect. The method has also been used to overcome bad habits under clinical supervision.

negative reinforcement: in operant

conditioning, reinforcement contingent upon the termination of an aversive stimulus. For example, the cessation of punishment can be made contingent upon the bar-pressing.

negative reinforcer: any stimulus whose removal increases the probability of a response.

negative response: an abient response, or response that removes the organism from the source of stimulation.

negative reward: a stimulus, situation, or verbal statement leading to dissatisfaction, withdrawal, or a decreased probability of response.

negative sensation: (*Fechner*) a subthreshold sensation.

negative suggestion: a suggestion designed to prevent or inhibit another's behavior.

negative transfer: see TRANSFER.

negative transference: (*Psychoan.*) a state of hostility toward the psychoanalyst that commonly follows the stage of positive transference.

negativism: an attitude of resistance to the suggestions or commands of another. Negativism is most commonly observed in children and in individuals suffering from certain forms of mental disorders.

neoanalyst: see NEO-FREUDIAN.

neobehaviorism: a derivative of the older school of behaviorism, which retains the point of view that behavioral responses are the fundamental data of psychology but lacks the militant objections to certain molar concepts characteristic of the parent school and is more tolerant of verbal reports and the use of intervening variables.

neo-Freudian: 1. characterizing a psychoanalyst who follows Freud's major doctrines but has added theoretical formulations that depart significantly from Freud's original premises. 2. more loosely, characterizing any dynamic psychology or therapeutic system that emphasizes social factors, insecurity, and interpersonal relations in the causation of the neuroses. The term has been applied to the systems of Harry Stack Sullivan, Karen Horney, Clara Thompson, Alfred Adler, Erich Fromm, and others.

neographics: see NEOPHASIA.

neolalia: speech made up of many neologisms or words coined by the speaker.

neologism: 1. any newly coined word. 2. loosely, using an established word or phrase in an entirely new way. The use of neologisms is characteristic of certain psychotic reactions.

neonate: a newborn infant.

neopallium: the cerebral cortex exclusive of the olfactory cortex.

neophasia: the elaborate language sometimes developed by schizophrenics. The language may have fixed rules of grammar and its own special vocabulary. The written form is *neographics*.

nerve: a bundle of neurons. Nerves may be made up of sensory or motor components or be a mixture of both. Some nerves are classified as belonging to the central nervous system and others to the autonomic system.

nerve block: the stoppage of a nervous impulse by mechanical or chemical means.

nerve cell: 1. the cell known as a neuron, the elementary unit of the nervous system. 2. the cell body of a neuron.

nerve center: 1. any portion of the nervous system that serves as a point of transition from afferent (sensory) to efferent (motor) pathways. 2. a region in the nervous system that serves as an integrating area; a region of the nervous system in which a definite function is localized.

nerve current: see NERVOUS IMPULSE.

nerve deafness: deafness caused by malfunctioning or damage to the auditory nerve.

nerve ending: the end process of a neuron in an effector (muscle or gland).

nerve fiber: 1. the long, hairlike projection emanating from the cell body of a neuron. 2. loosely, a neuron.

nerve impulse: see NERVOUS IMPULSE.

nerve-muscle preparation: a muscle, such as the gastrocnemius muscle of a frog, with its attached nerve. Nerve-muscle preparations are used in the study of nervous and muscular functions.

nerve pathway: the route taken by a nervous impulse in a particular response.

nerve or **neural pattern:** a functional integration of neurons that operates in a unitary fashion.

nerve plexus: a complex mass of neurons closely associated with each other in a functional network.

nerve process: see NEURONAL PROCESS.

nerve root: a nerve connected directly with the brain or spinal cord; any of the pairs of nerves entering the spinal cord. The dorsal roots are sensory and the ventral are motor in function.

nerve tissue: the totality of nerve cells and their processes under consideration.

nerve trunk: a relatively large nerve. The term usually refers only to the bundle of axons or dendrites and not to the central or peripheral terminations.

nervism: (*Pavlov*) the hypothesis that

all bodily functions are controlled by the nervous system.

nervous: 1. pertaining to nerves or their functions. 2. characterizing individuals in a state of heightened emotionality, usually with visible signs of muscular tremor, hyperexcitability, and tenseness. 3. pertaining to diseases or disorders of the nerves or personality.

nervous arc: see NEURAL ARC.

nervous breakdown: in popular terminology, any type of psychotic or neurotic condition that is incapacitating and requires hospitalization.

nervous conduction: see NEURAL CONDUCTION.

nervous disease or **disorder:** 1. an organic disease of the nervous system. 2. a functional disorder. Because the term *disease* implies an organic condition, the phrase *nervous disease* should be restricted to such conditions.

nervous energy: in popular terminology, a high state of drive and activity.

nervous habit: a stereotyped form of activity that serves the purpose of reducing tension. Nail biting, bed rocking in infants, tics, and mannerisms are examples of nervous habits.

nervous impulse: the propagated electrical pulse that results from threshold stimulation of a neuron. The electrical pulse is due to the rapid change in permeability of the neuronal membrane to certain ions, particularly to sodium and potassium ions. The flow of ions across the cell membrane results in the electrical pulse, which is the most characteristic aspect of the nervous impulse. The impulse, once started, travels at a high rate of speed—up to 120 meters per second in large neurons—the entire length of the neuron. The impulse is an all-or-nothing process. That is, the impulse is as large as the condition and size of the neuron will permit. As a result of this all-or-nothing action of the neuron, the tissue is absolutely refractory for a brief period of time following transmission of the impulse and for this reason no stimulus, however strong, can excite the tissue for a few milliseconds. Following the absolute refractory stage, there is a brief period of relative refractoriness before recovery.

nervousness: 1. a state of restlessness with heightened emotionality and visible signs of muscular tremor, tenseness, and overactivity. 2. a popular but misleading term for any chronic and benign personality disorder.

nervous system: the totality of neural tissues. From an anatomical point of view the nervous system may be divided into (a) the *central nervous system* and (b) the *peripheral nervous system*. The central nervous system consists of the brain and spinal cord; the peripheral nervous system consists of all nerve fibers that connect the receptors and effectors to the central nervous system. From a functional point of view the nervous system may be divided into (a) the *somatic* and (b) the *autonomic* divisions. The somatic division is that which comprises all voluntary, conscious functions. The autonomic division is concerned with the innervation of visceral, automatic, nonvoluntary processes. Both of these schemes for dividing the nervous system have their utility. The anatomic scheme is most useful when the purpose of the investigation is fiber tracing, identifying specific structures, or in describing embryological development. The functional scheme is particularly useful when one is interested in the nervous system from the point of view of its actual functions, regardless of whether these are peripheral or central. See also AUTONOMIC NERVOUS SYSTEM; BRAIN.

nervous tissue: 1. the totality of nerves and neurons, including cell bodies and peripheral processes. 2. any mass of neurons and their cell bodies, as distinguished from other bodily tissues.

neural: pertaining to the structure or functioning of nerves or neurons.

neural arc: 1. at the simplest level, a sensory neuron connected to a motor neuron. *Syn.* REFLEX ARC. 2. more generally, any interrelated network of cells with their functional connections. Some type of neural arc is hypothesized to account for learned behaviors, perceptual and attitudinal processes, and any function that implies some kind of relatively permanent change in the nervous system as a result of practice or maturation.

neural bond: a hypothetical functional association between two neurons.

neural center: see NERVE CENTER.

neural circuit: 1. a neural arc. 2. the functional passage of a nervous impulse from one center within the nervous system to another.

neural conduction: the passage of a propagated disturbance, the nervous impulse, along a nerve fiber and from fiber to fiber across synapses.

neural crest: a ridge on the dorsal portion of the neural plate (or the mass of embryonic ectodermal cells that gives rise to the nervous system) that forms the spinal ganglia and sympathetic division of the autonomic nervous system.

neural current: the electrical disturbance that passes along the nerve fiber and from neuron to neuron across the synapse.

neural discharge: the excitation and propagation of a localized disturbance in a neuron or nervous center. The term usually implies a discharge into an effector, that is, a muscle or gland.

neural excitation: the process whereby a state of irritability is initiated in a neuron by an outside stimulus.

neural facilitation: see FACILITATION.

neural fold: the tissues on either side of the dorsal neural plate (embryonic nervous tissue) that grow up and over the neural groove.

neuralgia: a nervous disorder characterized by bursts of sharp pain usually localized to the field of innervation of one nerve.

neural groove: the embryonic groove along the neural plate that eventually forms the neural tube, whose walls develop into the central nervous system.

neural induction: the influence of one action system on another, either facilitating or inhibiting activity. In *negative induction*, inhibition in one system is enhanced by activity in another; in *positive induction*, inhibition in one system facilitates action in another.

neural impulse: see NERVOUS IMPULSE.

neural irritability: the fundamental property that makes nervous tissue responsive to stimulation. Irritability is dependent upon polarization of ions on either side of the cell membrane, with positive ions on the outside and negative on the inside. Threshold stimuli disturb this relationship with a consequent flow of ions across the membrane and propagation of the disturbance along the neuron. See also NERVOUS IMPULSE.

neural parallelism: the theory that for every mental event there is a corresponding neural activity.

neural plate: the layer of ectodermal tissue that forms the beginning of the embryonic nervous system.

neural reinforcement: strenghtening of one response by the simultaneous operation of another response. Thus, the grasp response strengthens the knee jerk.

neural reverberation: see REVERBERATORY CIRCUIT.

neural set: 1. in a reflex circuit, a temporary state of heightened sensitivity that favors the passage of impulses. 2. in the nervous system, a hypothetical adjustment corresponding to behavioral adjustment during set.

neural tube: the embryonic tube whose wall forms the brain and spinal cord.

neuraminic acid: an acid of unknown structure that can be isolated from the brain. It is said to be deficient in schizophrenics.

neurasthenia: a form of psychoneurosis characterized by excessive weakness, fatigue, complaints of visceral malfunction, and anxiety. Neurasthenia is considered a functional disorder.

neuraxis: the brain and spinal cord, which lie along the vertical axis of the body.

neurilemma: a thin covering of the myelin sheath in peripheral nerves. The neurilemma is necessary for regeneration of injured fibers, since it persists after injury and forms a hollow tube along which the regenerating fibrils grow.

neurin: 1. a protein extract of nerve tissue. 2. a hypothetical specific form of energy involved in nervous excitation.

neurite: 1. the axon. 2. a primitive, unspecialized neuron.

neuritis: inflammation of a nerve.

neuroanatomy: the anatomy of the nervous system.

neurobiotaxis: (*Kappers*) the phenomenon wherein the dendrites of neurons are stimulated to grow toward the axon endings of active neurons.

neuroblast: an embryonic neuron.

neurocirculatory asthenia: see EFFORT SYDNROME.

neurocyte: 1. a neuron. 2. the cell body of a neuron.

neurofibrillae: the fine filaments that make up the axis cylinder of the neuron.

neurogenic: 1. forming neural tissue. 2. having its origin in neural tissue or neural processes.

neuroglia: supporting tissues of the cerebrospinal axis. Recent evidence indicates that the neuroglial cells may have a functional as well as a supportive role in cerebral processes. *Syn.* GLIA CELLS.

neurogram: 1. an engram; a permanent change in nervous tissue resulting from stimulation. 2. a schematic model of the nervous system.

neurohumors: chemical agents, such as acetylcholine or norepinephrine, that serve as mediators of nervous activity.

neurology: the science of the structure and functioning of the nervous system.

neuromuscular: pertaining to any process that is a joint function of the muscles and nerves.

neuromuscular junction: see MYONEURAL JUNCTION.

neuron or **neurone:** the single cell that is the elementary building block of the nervous system. For a description of the parts of a neuron see legend accompanying illustration.

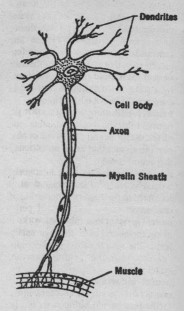

FIG. 21. *A typical motor neuron.*

Neurons may be classified as: (a) *afferent*, or *sensory*, that is, leading from receptors to the spinal cord or brain; and (b) *efferent*, or *motor*, that is, leading away from the spinal cord or brain to muscles and glands. A third large class of neurons is variously called *interneurons*, *association neurons*, *internuncial neurons*, *connector neurons*, and *adjustor neurons*. These neurons are of various sizes and shapes and connect neurons with other neurons or centers with each other.

neuronal periodicity: the tendency for neurons to fluctuate in their susceptibility to stimulation.

neuronal process: the fine terminal branching of a neuron.

neuropathic: 1. pertaining to an organic disease of the nervous system. 2. pertaining to a functional disorder of the nervous system. The terms *neurotic* and *psychogenic* are preferred to *neuropathic* for functional disorders.

neuropathology: the branch of medicine dealing with diseases of the nervous system.

neurophypophis: the posterior pituitary gland.

neurophysiology: the branch of physiology dealing with the functions of nervous tissues.

neuropile or **neuropil:** a network of nonmyelinated fibrils found at the synapse of a neuron.

neuroplexus: a network of peripheral nerve fibers. Such networks are common in the autonomic nervous system. *Syn.* PLEXUS.

neuropsychiatry: a medical specialty that deals with neurological and psychiatric disorders.

neurosis: a benign mental disorder characterized by (a) incomplete insight into the nature of the difficulty; (b) conflicts; (c) anxiety reactions; (d) partial impairment of personality; (e) often, but not necessarily, the presence of phobias, digestive disturbances, and obsessive-compulsive behavior. *Syn.* PSYCHONEUROSIS. Several general types of neurosis are recognized: generalized anxiety disorders, obsessive-compulsive disorders, phobias; conversion disorders including conversion hysteria, fugue, amnesia, and multiple personality. (*q.q.v.*). See also CHARACTER NEUROSIS; SITUATION NEUROSIS.

neurosyphilis: syphilis of the nervous system. Syphilis of the spinal cord attacks the tracts of fasciculus gracilis and fasciculus cuneatus, resulting in locomotor ataxia; syphilis of the brain results in general paresis.

neurotic: 1. pertaining to an individual suffering from a neurosis. 2. characterizing behavior or traits symptomatic of a neurosis.

neurotic anxiety: a chronic, nonspecific type of anxiety characteristic of the anxiety neuroses.

neurotic character: 1. (*Adler*) the combination of traits organized as a defense against feelings of inferiority. 2. a constitutional tendency toward neurosis. 3. an individual suffering from a neurosis.

neurotic contributory factor: (*R. B. Cattell*) in factor analysis studies of personality, a factor that discriminates between clinically diagnosed neurotics and normals.

neurotic fiction: (*Adler*) a guiding fiction so far removed from the possibility of real accomplishment as to be unachievable and to keep the individual pursuing unrealistic selfish goals.

neurotic inventory: a questionnaire designed to reveal tendencies toward neuroticism. Statements are taken from case histories, and the subject indicates his agreement or disagreement with the statement. Theoretically, the more statements with which the subject agrees, the more likely he is tending toward neuroticism.

neuroticism: 1. the state of being neurotic. 2. (*R. B. Cattell*) equivalent to neurosis but from Cattell's point of view emphasizing that neurotic traits vary continuously in degree throughout the population and are not merely characteristic of the abnormal.

neurotic-phase factor: (*R. B. Cattell*) dimensional states that change with time, and when high or in phase at the same time, can place the individual temporarily in the neurotic pattern.

neurotic process: (*Horney*) the central inner conflict in the neurotic between the idealized self and the real self.

neurotic-process factor: (*R. B. Cattell*) a characterological trait factor whose scores are of critical importance in influencing the severity of a neurosis.

neurotic-regressive debility: (*R. B. Cattell*) the low score or negative pole of a personality-factor dimension characterized by rigidity, exhaustion, incompetence, loss of interests, and inability to mobilize habits in following through a program.

neurotic solution: the resolution of a neurotic conflict by excluding the conflict from awareness.

neurotic trend: (*Horney*) an organization of tendencies oriented toward the achievement of maximum security. There are three primary neurotic trends: moving toward, moving away, and moving against people. The conflicts that develop between two or more of these are at the core of the neurosis.

neurovegetative system: the autonomic nervous system, particularly the parasympathetic division.

neutral: 1. characterizing an intermediate region between extremes of a variable, such as neutral gray, which is intermediate between black and white. 2. pertaining to an indifferent electrode.

neutral color: an achromatic color, one of the gray-white-black series.

neutral stimulus: a stimulus that produces an indifferent response; a stimulus that does not ordinarily elicit the response it is made to elicit after conditioning, when it has become a conditioned stimulus. The bell in Pavlov's famous experiment was a neutral stimulus until after conditioning, whereupon it became effective in eliciting the salivary response.

newborn: an infant less than one month of age.

nicotinic: characterizing receptors that mediate the excitatory effects of acetylcholine.

night blindness: subnormal vision under conditions of dim illumination; nyctalopia. Night blindness may be due to a deficiency in vitamin A or to a retinal defect.

nightmare: an anxiety dream; a dream depicting fearsome events.

night terror: see PAVOR.

night vision: vision under greatly reduced conditions of illumination, such as occurs at night.

nihilistic delusion: the delusion characteristic of some psychotics that the existing order of things has disappeared.

Nissl bodies: granular bodies found in the cell body of the neuron and in the dendrites. Nissl bodies are believed to have some function in regeneration of damaged cells.

nociceptor: a pain receptor. *Contr.* BENECEPTOR.

noctambulation: sleepwalking; somnambulism.

nocturnal: pertaining to night.

nocturnal emission: loss of semen in the male during sleep.

nodal point: a point in the eye through which all rays must pass that join points in the visual field with their corresponding points in the retinal image.

node: 1. a point in a wave, such as a sound wave, that has zero amplitude. 2. a protuberance or swelling.

noesis: 1. the intellective function. 2. cognition; particularly cognition or knowledge that is self-evident.

noise: 1. the auditory experience that arises upon stimulation with aperiodic sound waves. 2. any undesirable or undesired sound. 3. in electronic and communications systems, extraneous signals, static, or anything that interferes with output.

nomadism: a tendency to wander or change occupation or residence frequently.

nominal aphasia: the inability to utter or recognize the name of an object or person.

nominalism: 1. tendency to believe that by naming things they are made real. 2. philosphical position that all universal concepts or abstractions are but words and that only concrete particulars are logically real.

nominal scale: the simplest type of scale, which consists of a simple system of classifications, such as those employed in classifying fighter planes or members of an athletic team.

nominating technique: for the study of group structure or individual personality, a sociometric technique in which individuals are rated by the group according to a criterion. For example, the members of the group rate (*nominate*) the most popular, most able to work on a committee, etc.

nomogram; nomograph: a chart consisting of three parallel lines representing values of related variables in such a way that a straight line drawn through the first two will intercept the related third value. For example, given lines representing MA and CA, one could find IQ.

nomological: see NOMOTHETIC.

nomothetic: pertaining to the formulation of general laws and principles. *Contr.* IDIOGRAPHIC.

nomothetic: pertaining to the formulation of general laws and principles. *Contr.* IDIOGRAPHIC.

nonadditive: 1. pertaining to objects or variables that cannot be combined because of heterogeneity. Thus, IQ's and income cannot be added. 2. pertainining to wholes, or Gestalts, that cannot be obtained by adding the individual parts.

nonadjustive: pertaining to behavior that fails to bring the individual into harmony with his social or physical environment.

non compos mentis: a phrase used to characterize an individual legally not responsible for his conduct.

nonconscious: without consciousness, particularly in reference to inanimate objects.

nondetermination coefficient: that proportion of variance in the dependent variable that does not result from the independent variable.

nondirective: pertaining to counseling or therapeutic procedures in which a minimum of direction is given by the counselor or therapeutician. The latter attempts to create a warm, permissive atmosphere in which the client feels free to discuss his problems frankly. The counselor attempts to show that he understands, is not critical, and will, when necessary, reflect and clarify the client's expressions. See also CLIENT-CENTERED THERAPY.

noneducable: of persons who cannot be educated in the conventional sense.

nonlanguage test: a test making use of concrete, nonverbal materials, such as a series of mazes of increasing difficulty. *Syn.* PERFORMANCE TEST.

nonlinear: 1. not falling along a straight line. 2. curvilinear.

nonlinear regression: see CUVILINEAR REGRESSION.

nonliterate: pertaining to cultures or societies without a written language. In scientific writings, the term *nonliterate* is replacing *primitive*, *savage*, and *preliterate*.

nonparametric statistics: the branch of statistics dealing with distributions that are not normal.

nonrational: pertaining to considerations where rational arguments do not apply. *Syn*. IRRATIONAL.

nonsense figure: a figure without meaning or that does not resemble familiar objects.

nonsense syllable: a pronounceable combination of letters that do not make meaningful words, such as *lor*, *zuk*, *rul*. The nonsense syllable was devised by Hermann Ebbinghaus for his memory experiments (1885) and has been widely used in rote-learning experiments ever since.

non sequitur: a fallacy in logic; an invalid conclusion drawn from established premises.

nonsocial: 1. of one who is indifferent to or actively avoids social groups. *Syn*. ASOCIAL. 2. outside the sphere of society or social considerations.

nonspecific system: the projection of fibers from the reticular activating system to the cerebral cortex.

nonverbal intelligence: intelligence as measured by performance on tasks requiring minimal use of verbal materials. Such tests are called *performance tests* and utilize incomplete forms, block designs, picture completion tests, and so forth. Psychologists do not believe there is one kind of intelligence that is nonverbal and another kind that is verbal. Rather, the nonverbal test is useful as a supplement to the verbal test, particularly in cases where verbal tests might be unfair, such as in testing recent immigrants or children with sensory defects.

nonverbal test: see NONLANGUAGE TEST.

noradrenaline; norepinephrine: a hormone believed to be the chemical transmitter in some sympathetic synapses. In most respects its action is similar to that of adrenaline or epinephrine.

norm: 1. a representative standard or value for a given group. A norm may be a single value or a range of values expressing the typical performance of a group against which any indvidual can be compared. Norms may be expressed in terms of age, percentile, or simple average. 2. any pattern, standard, or representative performance for a group. Thus, a social norm may represent the kind of behavior expected from a group. See also CULTURAL NORM.

normal: 1. that which does not deviate markedly from the usual, the average, or the norm. 2. in statistics, a distribution that does not deviate significantly from a bell-shaped, or Gaussian, curve. 3. regular or standard. The concept of normalcy as applied to behavior and personality causes great difficulty in definition. Some psychologists prefer the statistical definition. That is, the individual who does not differ widely from the norm or average is considered normal. Others insist that the quality of the individual's adjustment is equally important.

normal distribution: a frequency distribution in which the values or scores group around the mean, with the greatest number of cases near the mean and with the frequency of cases trailing off on either side of the mean. A perfectly normal distribution will give rise to the normal probability curve when plotted. Normal distributions arise when the variations in scores are due to a large number of random and independent factors.

normality: the state of being normal in respect to any criterion.

normalize: to adjust or alter a set of measures in such a way that they will conform to the normal frequency curve.

normal-probability curve: a curve representing the frequency with which a variable occurs when the occurrence of that variable is governed by the laws of chance. See illustration. *Syns.* normal frequency curve; normal curve; BELL-SHAPED CURVE; GAUSSIAN CURVE; PROBABILITY CURVE.

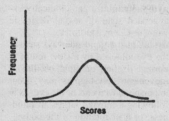

FIG. 22. *The normal probability curve.*

normative: pertaining to norms or standards.

normative science: any of those sciences, such as ethics, mental hygiene, logic, etc., that attempt to discover correct patterns of behavior.

norm line: a curve representing the mean (or median) scores of successive age groups. Such norm lines are often furnished with group tests for use in school systems.

nose: the structure containing the or-

gans for olfaction. The receptors are high up inside the nose, in the olfactory epithelium.

nosology: the branch of medicine dealing with the classification of diseases.

nosophobia: a fear of disease, especially of a specific disease.

notation: a system of representation using symbols.

noticeable: above threshold; sufficiently distinct to be perceived and reported.

notochord: analogue of the spinal cord and brain in primitive forms and in the embryonic stage in human beings.

nous: a Greek term for the intellect or highest faculty.

nuclear complex: in psychoanalysis and dynamic psychologies, the central or core problem in infancy. For the Freudians, the nuclear complex is the Oedipus complex, or the child's relation to the mother. In the Individual Psychology of Alfred Adler, it is the child's feelings of inferiority. *Syns.* ROOT CONFLICT; nuclear conflict.

nucleus: 1. the central, dark-staining portion of a cell often containing a nucleolus, or small, darkened mass. 2. the central portion, or mass, around which material is gathered. 3. a mass of cell bodies within the brain. 4. a cluster, such as a cluster of correlations in factor studies.

nucleus cuneatus: a nucleus in the medulla where fibers of *fasciculus gracilis* and *fasciculus cuneatus* terminate.

nucleus gracilis: a nucleus in the medulla where fibers of *fasciculus gracillis* and *fasciculus cuneatus* terminate.

nucleus tractus solitarius: a long narrow nucleus running the length of the medulla.

nucleolus: a small, spherical body within the nucleus of a cell.

null hypothesis: a statistical statement concerning a set of data to be obtained and formulated in such a way that the facts to be elicited by the experiment may disprove the statement. Thus, the null hypothesis is the contrary to the affirmative hypothesis of the experiment. The advantage of stating the hypothesis in a contradictory manner is that: (a) it can be subjected to tests of significance; and (b) since one exception can disprove a generalization, the null hypothesis is a more rigid procedure than attempting to prove the affirmative.

nulliplex inheritance: inheritance determined by two recessive factors.

number-completion test: a test in which the task is to complete a series of numbers by supplying a missing item. For example: 2, 4, 6, 8, —, 12.

number factor: in factor-analysis studies of intelligence, an ability revealed by competence at manipulating numbers and carrying out simple numerical operations. *Symbol* N.

number form: a vivid, imaginary representation of numbers in space. For example, the individual might imagine a number series to be a ladder with each rung representing a number in the series.

numerical value: any value expressed as an absolute number regardless of its sign.

nurturance: the provision of food, shelter, and care for the young.

nurturance need: (*Murray*) the need to protect, aid, and nourish a helpless organism.

nurture: environmental factors that influence the individual from the moment of conception onward. *Contr.* NATURE.

nutrient: any substance that can be taken into the body and converted into food for the tissues.

nyctalopia: 1. night blindness. 2. day blindness. The etymologically correct definition is night blindness.

nyctophobia: a pathological fear of darkness.

nymphomania: a pathologically exaggerated state of sexual desire in women. *Contr.* FRIGIDITY.

nystagmus: a rapid sideways snap of the eye followed by a slow return to normal fixation or rapid oscillatory movements. Nystagmus may occur in pursuit movements of the eye, as in following a moving target, in blindness, or after-rotation of the body.

O

object: 1. any part of the environment of which the individual is aware—a material thing, a person, or an abstraction. 2. an end or goal. 3. the person or thing eliciting an instinctive reaction.

object-assembly test: a test in which the subject is required to put together disassembled objects.

object assimilation: see ASSIMILATION 5.

object attitude: in structuralistic

psychology, the attitude in which the observer attends to the stimulus or object rather than to experience.

object blindness: a disorder in which one is unable to recognize visually presented objects because of brain injury in the visual association areas. *Syn.* VISUAL AGNOSIA.

object cathexis: (*Psychoan.*) the investment of the libido in a nonsexual object.

object choice: (*Psychoan.*) the selection of an object or person as the love object.

object color: color perceived as belonging to an object, that is, either to its surface or making up its volume.

object constancy: the tendency for objects to remain perceptually invariable regardless of wide variation in the conditions of observation. Thus, a chair remains a chair, regardless of the observer's position and in spite of the fact that under certain special conditions it may be no more than a disjointed collection of sticks. It must be noted that object constancy is not perfect. People appear "antlike" when viewed from the top of a building. However, object constancy holds over a remarkably wide range of conditions.

object finding: (*Psychoan.*) the process of directing the libido away from the body to objects or persons in the environment.

objectifying attitude: the quality or condition of reacting to the properties of an object while disregarding one's personal feelings toward it.

objectivation: (*Psychoan.*) the attributing of one's own feelings to another who, in fact, has such feelings. *Contr.* PROJECTION.

objective: 1. existing in fact or in physical reality. 2. independent of the observer, particularly independent of observer bias. 3. outside the body; in the environment. 4. pertaining to an object.

objective anxiety: anxiety for which there is an external and identifiable cause.

objective examination: tests of true-false or multiple-choice variety whose scoring standards permit no latitude of choice among examiners.

objective psychology: a point of view in psychology that would restrict psychological observation to behavioral processes open to public inspection and would exclude introspective or subjective data.

objective reference: the quality of perceptual experiences that assigns them to the environment.

objective scoring: scoring according to a formula, key, or rule so that the same score will be arrived at by a number of different scorers. Most multiple-choice tests are scored by means of an objective key. *Contr.* SUBJECTIVE SCORING.

objective set: perception whose frame of reference is directed toward the external world.

objective type: a class of individuals characterized by a tendency to view events and objects as things in themselves and not in relation to the viewer. *Contr.* SUBJECTIVE TYPE.

objectivity: freedom from bias or prejudice; freedom from subjective interpretation.

object libido: (*Psychoan.*) the libido as attached to persons or objects other than the self. *Contr.* EGO LIBIDO.

object loss: (*Psychoan.*) the loss of love from an individual who had at one time bestowed it.

object of instinct: the person, object, or situation eliciting instinctive action. For example, the mother duck elicits instinctive action in the duckling, the wild animal a fear reaction in the deer.

object permanence: (*Piaget*) the child's ability to recognize that objects continue to exist when hidden from view.

object size: the physical size of an object. In studies of constancy, the closer the perceived object is to its object size, the more perfect the constancy.

oblique: in factor analysis, characterizing the relationship between factors not at right angles to each other and which are therefore correlated. The more acute the angle formed by the axes, the higher the correlation.

oblique rotation: a rotation of the axes in a factor analysis in such a manner that the axes meet at acute angles. In such a case the factors will be correlated and a second- or third-order factor can then be extracted.

oblique solution: in factor analysis, a set of factors not at right angles and therefore correlated, in contrast to an *orthogonal solution*, in which the factors are not correlated.

obliviscence: 1. forgetfulness. 2. the tendency for ideas to gradually disappear with time. *Contr.* REMINISCENCE.

obscenity: gestures, language, printed material, or pictures that violate established codes of propriety. The precise definition of obscenity or the decision as to whether a given act or object is obscene is extremely difficult to render. Such decisions usually end up in the courts, which have shown a trend toward increasing liberalism over the years.

observation: 1. a purposive or intentional examination of something, particularly for the purpose of gathering facts. 2. a score of value. 3. a verbalization of what has been observed.

observational methods: techniques for increasing the accuracy of observation, such as stopwatches, checklists, etc.

observer: 1. the individual making an observation. 2. one engaged in introspective observation.

obsession: a persistent and often irrational idea that may be accompanied by a compulsion to carry out an act.

obsessional neurosis: a neurosis characterized primarily by the presence of obsessive ideas and compulsive actions.

obsessive-compulsive neurosis: a psychoneurosis characterized by persistent and often unwanted ideas (obsessions) and impulses to carry out compulsions, or irrational, stereotyped, and ritualistic acts. It is held that obsessive and compulsive behavior patterns are attempts to overcome anxiety or to assuage guilt feelings. The handwashing compulsion, for example, may reflect the individual's anxiety and guilt about masturbation.

obstacle sense: the ability of the blind to avoid objects in their path. The ability is primarily dependent upon echolocation, or hearing sounds bounced off such objects.

obstruction method: a technique for measuring the relative strength of animal drives by pitting one against another. For example, the animal may have to cross a charged grid in order to reach food. In this case the drive for food is pitted against the drive to avoid pain. Using the same technique, the thirst, sex, and maternal drives can then be studied and the number of crossings made to each within a given time period may be taken as indicative of the relative strength of the drives.

obtained mean: a mean calculated on the basis of actual observations. *Contr.* TRUE MEAN.

obtained score: a raw score; a score that has not yet been converted to other units.

Occam's razor: a principle of scientific interpretation according to which the simplest possible explanation for a phenomenon is to be preferred to complex explanations. *Syns.* principle of PARSIMONY; LLOYD MORGAN'S CANON; principle of economy.

occipital: pertaining to the back part of the brain, the occipital lobe.

occipital lobe: the rear portion of the cerebrum containing centers for vision.

occlusion: 1. the stopping of a passageway. 2. the manifestation of less than the expected number of motor unit responses, due to overlapping neuronal fields.

occupational ability: the individual's aptitude for a certain vocation or profession as measured by a standard test. Such abilities are typically reported in the form of a profile or pattern.

occupational analysis: see JOB ANALYSIS.

occupational family: a group of occupations or professions for which the requisite abilities are similar.

occupational hierarchy: 1. the arrangement of the various occupations according to the level of ability or competence required. 2. the serial arrangement of occupations according to their social status.

occupational-interest inventory: see INTEREST INVENTORY.

occupational level: 1. an occupational class as defined by the ability or skill required for success in that

occupation. 2. a classification of occupations as defined by the prestige associated with each.

occupational norm: the average or typical pattern of scores made by a given occupational group.

occupational stability: the characteristic of remaining in one occupation for a long period of time.

occupational test: a test designed to measure achievement or aptitude for a given occupation.

occupational therapy: the treatment of mental disorders by giving the individual useful work to do.

ochlophobia: a fear of crowds.

octave: an interval of pitch between two tones such that one has a frequency twice that of the other.

ocular: pertaining to the eye.

ocular dominance: preferential use of one eye in reading, sighting, etc. One of the manifestations of lateral dominance.

ocular pursuit: the following of a moving object by successive fixations of the eye.

oculogyral illusion: or **movement:** the illusory movement of a faint light in a darkened room following rotation of the body.

oculomotor: pertaining to eye movements.

oculomotor nerve: the third cranial nerve, which contains motor components innervating all the extrinsic eye muscles except the lateral rectus and superior oblique. It also contains afferent proprioceptive fibers from the muscles of innervation.

oculomotor nucleus: the nerve cells in the superior colliculus and third ventricle that give rise to the oculomotor nerves.

odd-even technique: a technique for obtaining an estimate of the reliability of a test by finding the correlation between the odd- and even-numbered items. *Syn.* SPLIT-HALF TECHNIQUE.

odor: 1. a sensory experience aroused by a gaseous substance. 2. any stimulus for the olfactory sense. *Syn.* SMELL.

odorimetry: the measurement of odors. *Syn.* olfactometry.

odorivector: any substance that emits particles which, in contact with olfactory receptors, stimulate olfactory sensations.

odor prism: a diagrammatic representation of the six primary odors according to Henning. See illustration.

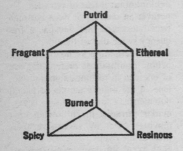

FIG. 23. *The odor prism.*

Oedipus complex; Edipus complex: (*Psychoan.*) the child's repressed desires for sexual intercourse with the parent of the opposite sex. Originally, Freud used the term *Oedipus complex* to refer to the boy's desire for the mother, and the term *Electra complex* to refer to the corresponding desire of the girl for the father. More recently, psychoanalysts use *Oedipus complex* to refer to both sexes. The Oedipus complex was named after a Greek tragedy by Sophocles in which the hero, Oedipus, unwittingly killed his father and married his mother. In his youth the hero had had his feet

pierced (*Oedipus* means "swollen feet") and was left to die on a mountain, but was saved by a shepherd and fulfilled his fate.

The Oedipal stage of development in early childhood is one manifestation of the early genital phase of development. Because the parents are presumed to be aware of the child's incestuous desires, and because they threaten retaliation, the child must suppress or repress his desires. As the libido continues to demand an outlet, this is found through identification with the parent of the same sex. Thus, the child obtains vicarious satisfaction in the sexual relations of that parent with the desired one. The Oedipus complex is also partly converted into the energy needed by the child for socialization through a process that Freud called *sublimation*.

off fibers: fibers in the optic nerve that respond to the cessation of stimulation.

ogive: a form of mathematical function that takes an S shape. For illustration, see LEARNING.

Ohm's law: 1. in audition, the principle that the ear analyzes a complex tone into simple tones whose frequencies are a series of sine waves. 2. in electricity, the generalization that the current flowing in a circuit is proportional to the electromotive force and inversely proportional to resistance in the circuit.

olfactie: a unit of smell intensity equal to the threshold strength of a stimulus as measured by the Zwaardemaker olfactometer.

olfaction: the sense of smell whose receptors are in the upper part of the nose and consist of hair cells in a specialized tissue called the olfactory epithelium. The stimulus for smell is a substance in gaseous state.

olfactometer: a device for regulating the amount and intensity of olfactory stimuli in threshold experiments.

olfactory: pertaining to olfaction, or the sense of smell.

olfactory brain: the rhinencephalon ($q.v.$).

olfactory bulb: two protuberances lying along the under part of the cerebrum and extending forward toward the eyes. The olfactory bulbs are actually an extension of the brain and mediate the sense of smell.

olfactory lobe: the region of the brain under the frontal lobe. It includes the olfactory bulbs and their associated structures. Many of the subcortical centers formerly believed to have an olfactory function are now considered to be a part of the limbic system.

oligergasia: intellectual deficiency; feeblemindedness.

oligoencephaly: mental deficiency caused by constitutional defects.

oligophrenia: mental deficiency.

oliogophrenic detail: (*Rorschach*) an extremely low-level response indicative of mental deficiency.

olivary nucleus: a mass of nerve cells shaped like an olive, a complex structure in the medulla.

omnibus test: a test in which the various types of tasks are randomly distributed instead of being grouped according to the nature of the task involved.

omnipotence of the id: (*Psychoan.*) the infantile conviction that wishes must and will be fulfilled.

onanism: 1. coitus interruptus; withdrawal on the part of the male prior to ejaculation. 2. masturbation.

oneiric: pertaining to dreamlike states.

one-trial learning: the complete mastery of a skill, or the mastery of an increment of learning, on a single trial. See GUTHRIE'S CONTIGUOUS CONDITIONING; SKINNER'S OPERANT CONDITIONING; and HULL'S MATHEMATICO-DEDUCTIVE THEORY OF LEARNING for discussion of the role of practice in learning and the possibility of one-trial learning.

one-way screen or **mirror:** a screen or mirror fashioned in such a way as to permit only one-way vision. It is frequently used in the observation of children.

onomatopoeic: pertaining to the formation of words that sound like their referents, as *buzz*, *crack*, *boom*. The ding-dong theory of language attributes the origin of language to onomatopoeia.

ontogenesis; ontogency: the origin of individual organisms. *Contr.* PHYLOGENESIS, the origin of species.

ontology: the branch of philosophy concerned with the nature of being.

open-cue situation: in learning, tasks in which all cues or means necessary to achieve the goal are presented to the animal.

open-ended question: in questionnaires or public-opinion polls, any question the subject is allowed to answer in his own way, in contrast to questions for which alternative answers are given.

open system: a biological system that, in contrast to physical systems, is not subject to the laws of thermodynamics, does not demonstrate constancy of energy relations, and is capable of growth. *Contr.* CLOSED SYSTEM.

operant: pertaining to a response defined in terms of its effects on the environment. The specific stimulus or pattern of stimuli need not be known in order to identify operant behavior.

Thus, an individual may reach into a drawer for his pen, which is not visible to him from the outside. We know only the consequence of the behavior, not the stimulus initiating the behavior. Operant behavior is also called type-R behavior, since the emphasis is on response, in contrast to type-S behavior, which is studied in classical conditioning and in which there is a specific stimulus with emphasis on the association between that stimulus and the response. See SKINNER'S OPERANT CONDITIONING for further discussion.

operant conditioning: see CONDITIONING 2.

operant learning: a learning situation in which the organism is reinforced for making a certain response in order to increase the probability of that response on the next trial. By progressively reinforcing responses that are in the direction of a desired pattern of responses, highly complicated behavior patterns can be learned.

operant level: 1. the rate of occurrence of an operant response before reinforcement. 2. the rate of an operant response following experimental extinction.

operant reserve: (*Skinner*) the number of responses made after reinforcement has been withdrawn in operant conditioning. The procedure measures the strength of conditioning. *Syn.* REFLEX RESERVE.

operating characteristic: in tests of significance, the probability of accepting the null hypothesis in a specific situation.

operation: (*Guilford*) one of three basic dimensions of intelligence, the other two being content and products. Operations involve how information or content is utilized. See also CON-

VERGENT THINKING, DIVERGENT THINKING.

operational operations research: the identification and study of factors in any system with the purpose of discovering how that system can be made to operate more effectively.

operationism: the generalization that the validity of a construct rests on the validity of the procedures used to establish it. Thus, the concept of intelligence has no other meaning than the procedures utilized on a specific test designed to measure intelligence—memory for sentences, vocabulary, reasoning problems, etc.—and is valid only to the extent that those procedures are valid. Thus, intelligence may be defined differently according to the test used.

The term *operationism* comes from the science of physics, where it was introduced by Percy Bridgman in order to divest physical concepts of spurious and surplus meanings. Thus, resistance has no meaning other than the procedures used to measure it. It is not an entity apart from those measures. Many psychologists believe that the concept of operationism is useful in psychology for divesting psychological terms of validity they do not, in fact, possess. *Syn.* operationalism.

operator: in statistical equations, the symbol indicates an operation to be performed on a number or other symbol.

ophidiphobia: fear of snakes.

opthalmia: an inflammation of the conjunctiva or other outer tissues of the eye.

opthalmic: pertaining to the eye.

opthalmology: the branch of medicine specializing in diseases of the eye and their correction.

opthalmotrope: a model for demonstrating the movement of the eyes through the action of the six extrinsic eye muscles.

opiate: 1. a drug of the opium class. 2. any agent that tends to quiet or soothe.

opinion: 1. a belief, particularly one that is tentative and still open to modification. Opinions lie somewhere between faith, which is belief that is intrinsically unverifiable, and knowledge, which has been verified and is no longer subject to individual interpretation. 2. an attitude; an enduring predisposition to behave in a certain manner toward objects, animals, or persons.

opinionaire: a questionnaire designed to measure opinions.

opinion poll: a survey of opinions obtained by questioning a sample of people. The results of such polls are reported in summary form, usually in terms of the percentage of the sample holding an opinion in question.

opium: a narcotic drug obtained from a species of poppy. The chief derivatives are morphine and codeine. Opium and its derivatives depress the higher nervous centers and induce a state of euphoria or extreme feelings of well-being.

opponent processes: in vision, systems composed of three types of cells, one of which is stimulated by green and inhibited by red; a second stimulated by yellow and inhibited by blue; and a third activated by achromatic stimuli. All color experiences are considered to be mediated by these processes singly or in combination.

opposites test: a test in which the subject's task is to give the opposite of the stimulus word.

opsin: a metabolic breakdown product of rhodopsin in rod vision.

optacon: a device for converting light intensities into vibratory patterns on the fingertips, enabling the blind to read.

optical or **optic:** 1. pertaining to the science of optics. 2. pertaining to the eye.

optical axis: the line passing through the center of vision.

optical defect: any condition that within the eye that prevents light rays from focusing properly or interferes with their passage to the retina. The most common defects are *myopia*, or nearsightedness; *hyperopia*, or farsightedness; *presbyopia*, or loss of accommodation with age; and *astigmatism*, in which the rays of light are focused unevenly.

optical illusion: any illusion mediated through the visual senses.

optical image: see RETINAL IMAGE.

optical projection: 1. the formation of an image by means of an optical instrument such as a projector. 2. the objective reference of sensation to the environment. 3. the localization of objects in space as projected on the retina by the refractive mechanism of the eye.

optic chiasm: the point at which the optic fibers from the eye join and diverge again at the base of the brain. In man and many animals fibers from the nasal halves of the two retinas cross over to the opposite side before continuing on to the cerebral cortex. The temporal fibers do not cross

optic disk: the area in the retina where the neurons are gathered just before leaving the eyeball. Because there are few sense cells in the area, it is nearly insensitive to light and is therefore blind under ordinary conditions. *Syn.* BLIND SPOT.

optic lobe: the superior of the two pairs of *corpora quadrigemina;* the superior colliculi.

optics: the branch of physics that studies light.

optimal stimulation, principle of: the generalization that organisms tend to learn those behaviors that result in optimal excitation or stimulation.

optimum: the most favorable or best value in a series for the case in hand.

optogram: the image of an object on the retina of the eye.

optokinetic reaction: movement of the eyes caused by visual stimulation. Optokinetic reaction may result in apparent motion.

oral: 1. pertaining to the mouth. 2. pertaining to the spoken word.

oral-aggressive: (*Psychoan.*) pertaining to a character type resulting from sublimation of the late oral stage of infantile development characterized by biting and chewing. The oral-aggressive adult attempts to exploit others and is envious and aggressive in social relationships.

oral cavity: the cavity extending from the lips to the pharynx.

oral character: (*Psychoan.*) 1. the fixation and carryover into adulthood of early infantile experiences at the oral stage. If sucking has been abundant, the individual will be overoptimistic and dependent; in the case of oral deprivation, he will be aggressive. 2. an individual whose satisfactions are derived primarily from oral eroticism.

oral dependence: (*Psychoan.*) the desire to return to the early oral stage of development.

oral dynamism: an enduring configuration of energy centered around oral activities.

oral eroticism: the derivation of pleasure from oral activities—sucking, biting, talking, chewing, smoking, etc.

oral incorporation: the tendency on the part of the young child to put things into the mouth, interpreted by analysts as a desire to incorporate the mother or other object of attachment into the self.

orality: the oral component in eroticism or neuroticism.

oral method: 1. lip reading by the deaf. 2. a method of study wherein the material is read aloud.

oral neurosis: (*Psychoan.*) stuttering, stammering, and speech defects as manifestations of psychic disorders associated with oral eroticism.

oral-passive type: see RECEPTIVE CHARACTER.

oral personality: see ORAL CHARACTER.

oral primacy: the attachment of the libido to the oral zone in infancy, with satisfaction obtained from sucking, biting, chewing, etc.

oral reading: the tendency of poor readers to move the lips while reading silently.

oral regression: (*Psychoan.*) the tendency to return to the oral stage of development.

oral sadism: (*Psychoan.*) the desire to hurt or destroy by biting or chewing.

oral stage: (*Psychoan.*) the stage of infantile development when the infant obtains satisfaction from nursing, biting, and chewing. The early oral phase is held by some psychoanalysts to be passive; the late phase to be active or aggressive.

oral test: a test administered and answered orally.

orbital: pertaining to the bony cavity surrounding the eye.

order: 1. a temporal and/or spatial arrangement. 2. in biology, a group of organisms above the family and below the class. 3. a position on a scale of merit or in a quantitative series.

order of magnitude: an arrangement of values in an array from the highest to the lowest degree.

order of merit: an arrangement of data, persons, etc., in the order of magnitude with respect of any specified trait. Thus, works of art might be put into an order of merit on the basis of the pooled judgment of critics.

ordinal: pertaining to or indicating order or succession of magnitude. *Contr.* cardinal.

ordinal position: rank according to ordinal numbers—first, second, third, etc.

ordinal scale: a scale that does not start from an absolute zero point and assigns values according to ordinal numbers—first, second, third, etc.

ordinate: 1. the vertical axis of a two-dimensional reference axis. 2. a line erected on the abscissa of a frequency curve that meets the line connecting the midpoint of the frequencies.

Orestes complex: (*Psychoan.*) the desire on the part of the son to kill his mother.

orexis: the affective and conative aspects of behavior in contrast to its cognitive aspect.

organ: a specialized structure within the body designed to carry out a particular function.

organ eroticism: (*Psychoan.*) sexual attachment for a particular organ; or sexual arousal associated with a particular organ.

organic: 1. pertaining to an organ or somatic tissues. 2. vital or biological in its properties, as opposed to mechanical. 3. somatic or bodily, as opposed to functional. See also FUNCTIONAL; FUNCTIONAL DISORDER.

organic deafness: a general category for deafness due to any structural defect or disease.

organic disorder: a disease that is the result of a known pathological condition of the tissues. *Contr.* FUNCTIONAL DEFECT; functional disorder.

organic evolution: the theory that the present species developed through modification of previous species. See also EVOLUTION.

organicism: 1. the philosophical point of view that life is the end product of organization. 2. the view that all disorders, whether physical or mental, are organic in origin.

organic psychosis: a psychosis caused by pathological changes in the brain, such as general paresis and alcoholic psychosis.

organic repression: see ANTEROGRADE AMNESIA.

organic sensations: sensations arising from within the body. *Syn.* visceral sensations.

organic set: a preparation on the part of the organism to receive stimuli. *Syn.* PREPARATORY SET.

organic variable or **O variable:** a condition or process within the organism that, along with stimuli, accounts for responses.

organ inferiority: (*Adler*) the hypothesis that real or imagined organ defects or deficiencies cause accentuated feelings of inferiority which, if severe enough, lead to neurosis.

organism: 1. any living being capable of carrying out life functions such as metabolism, respiration, digestion, excretion, and reproduction. The broadest general division of organisms is into plants and animals. When the term is used without specification in psychological writing, it refers to animals. 2. metaphorically, the social group.

organismic: 1. pertaining to organisms 2. pertaining to a point of view in psychology and biology emphasizing holistic attitudes in experimentation and interpretation. 3. interbehavioral.

organismic autonomy: (*Angyal*) the power of the organism to maintain itself because of the presence of intrinsic self-regulating mechanisms.

organismic psychology: the point of view held by psychologists such as A. Gelb, K. Goldstein, J. Kantor, and R. Wheeler, emphasizing that psychology is the study of the biological organism. Mind-body distinctions are typically rejected or ignored by organismic psychologists. The general approach resembles that of the Gestalt school, in that organismic psychologists do not favor reductionistic analysis but instead tend to study behavior as molar.

organization: 1. a structure or grouping composed of units that function in an interrelated manner so as to form a unified whole. 2. in Gestalt psychology, the process whereby excitations form a unified and stable field.

organize: 1. to arrange units or parts in such a manner that they will work together in a coordinated whole. 2. to arrange data in such a manner as to reveal relationships among the members.

organized play: directed play planned in advance, supervised and carried out with regard to rules.

organ libido: eroticism associated with a specific bodily organ.

organ of Corti: a spiral structure within the cochlea that contains the receptor cells for hearing.

organogenic: originating in a specific organ.

organ pleasure: (*Psychoan.*) pleasure associated with a particular organ. *Syn.* ORGAN LIBIDO.

orgasm: a pattern of involuntary movements of the genital organs and associated movements of the voluntary musculature, accompanied by intense pleasure and strong sexual feelings and culminating in the ejaculation of semen by the male. Orgasm normally is the climax of coitus, but it may be induced in other ways, as through masturbation.

orgastic impotence: the inability to achieve orgasm during the sex act.

orgone theory: the theory formulated by Wilhelm Reich that all space is filled with a specific form of energy called orgone energy, which accounts for life and living functions.

orientation: 1. knowledge of one's position in time and space. 2. the position that a cell, organ, or limb is in. 3. the active turning toward a source of stimulation, such as occurs in tropisms. 4. a point of view or frame of reference. 5. in personnel practice, assisting the individual to know his job and the regulations and rewards associated with it.

oriented: 1. pointed in a certain direction or lying along a certain axis. 2. having knowledge of where one is in space or time. 3. having knowledge of what is expected of one in a given situation.

orienting response: a response that alters the organism's position with respect to a source of stimulation.

origin: 1. the deference or starting point of an operation. 2. the beginning of a behavior pattern or disorder. 3. the intersection of the abscissa and ordinate.

original response: (*Rorschach*) an unusual response that does not occur more than once in 100 test sessions.

original score: a raw score.

orthogenic: (*Werner*) characterizing development from a nondifferentiated or global state to a differentiated and hierarchically integrated state.

orthogenesis: 1. the doctrine that evolution has a certain direction and that in successive generations an organism will follow a certain line irrespective of natural selection. 2. the theory that social evolution follows in the same direction and passes through the same stages in various social groups despite differences in culture.

orthogenital: pertaining to sexual patterns that are normal and, hence, closely related to sexual intercourse with members of the opposite sex.

orthogonal: rectilinear, or forming right angles.

orthogonal rotation: in factor analysis, a rotation of the axes in such a manner that the axes will be at right angles and therefore uncorrelated.

orthogonal solution: in factor analysis, a solution in which the axes representing the factors are at right angles to each other and are therefore uncorrelated. *Contr.* OBLIQUE SOLUTION.

orthogonal trait: any trait that has a zero correlation with other traits in a factor matrix.

orthopsychiatry: a branch of psychiatry emphasizing the early treatment and prevention of mental disorders. The discipline deals primarily with borderline cases and is closely allied to mental hygiene.

oscillation: any change characterized by a relatively steady reversal of direction.

oscillograph: a device for making graphic records of wavelike forms of electrical energy. See also OSCILLOSCOPE.

oscillometer: a device for measuring oscillation or vibratory motion.

oscilloscope: an electronic device, similar in principle to a television set, for making possible the visualization and measurement of electrical changes. Oscilloscopes are widely used in the study of nervous impulses

osmometric thirst: thirst produced by cellular dehydration due to increased osmotic pressure from the intracellular fluids.

osmoreceptor: a complex of cells in the hypothalamus that respond to changes in osmotic pressure in the blood. Osmoreceptors control the emission of antidiuretic hormones and stimulate thirst.

osmosis: the diffusion of fluids through a membrane.

osphresis: the sense of smell; olfaction.

osseous: pertaining to bones; bonelike.

ossification ratio: an anatomical index consisting of the ratio of the ossified area of the wrist bones as revealed by X-ray plates to a certain selected area of the wrist.

ossify: to harden and become bonelike.

Ostwald colors: a series of chromatic and achromatic sample colors based on a mixture of pigments, with black and white added for tints and shades.

OT data: objective test data.

O technique: see R CORRELATION.

otic: pertaining to receptor cells in the inner ear.

Otis-Lennon Mental Ability Tests: a group verbal IQ test of general ability useful for grades 1–12.

otocyst: see STATOCYST.

otogenic tone: a subjective tone, or tone arising from the auditory mechanism.

otoliths: small calcium deposits in the endolymph of the inner ear which, when the head moves, activate neuronal endings to aid in maintaing equilibrium. *Syn.* STATOLITH.

otology: the science of the ear—its anatomy, physiology, functions, and disorders.

otosclerosis: a progressive disease of the ear caused by hardening of the ossicles.

outbreeding: mating outside a designated social group. *Contr.* INBREEDING.

outgroup: any group of individuals other than the group to which the designator belongs; those who are not members of a specified group.

outlet: any activity associated with the satisfaction of a drive or need. The term is often used specifically to refer to techniques for achieving orgasm.

outpatient: a nonhospitalized patient who comes to a clinic or hospital for treatment.

output: 1. production; that which is produced over a given period of time. 2. signals emitted by transmitting equipment or amplifiers.

oval window: an oval opening in the wall of the bony labyrinth covered by a membrane against which the stirrup vibrates, communcating vibrations to the inner ear. See also EAR.

O variable: see ORGANIC VARIABLE.

ovary: a glandular organ in the female that produces the egg, or ovum, and the estrogens, or female sex hormones. The ovaries are paired bodies located in the abdominal cavity and are connected to the uterus by means of the Fallopian tubes.

overachievement: performance exceeding predictions made on the basis of aptitude tests.

overage: beyond the appropriate chronological age for any designated activity.

overcompensation: engaging in excessive efforts to counterbalance a deficiency. For example, a physically weak individual may go to extremes of muscular development by prolonged exercise.

overdetermined: having many causes, or being the result of many factors. The term is frequently used by psychoanalysts to characterize dream elements and neurotic symptoms as being the result of several converging factors.

overexclusion: a tendency to quickly and rigidly exclude responses, thus sacrificing flexibility of behavior. See also OVERINCLUSION.

overinclusion: a tendency to fail to eliminate inefficient and inappropriate responses. See OVEREXCLUSION.

overinhibited: excessively rigid in behavior.

overlapping factor: any factor common to two or more tests.

overlapping groups: two groups whose scores in part fall within the same limits or the same distribution.

overlapping responses: responses that occur with sufficient rapidity for the second to begin before the first has terminated.

overlearning: learning in which practice goes beyond the criterion of learning, usually two successive perfect repetitions. Thus, if it look ten trials to learn a list of nonsense syllables, practice for ten additional trials is defined as 100 percent over-learning, and practice for 5 additional trials 50 percent overlearning, etc.

overproduction: excessive reproduction of a given species so that there are too many individuals for the existing food supply.

overprotection: the tendency on the part of parents to shelter a child excessively, providing protection from physical and psychological harm to such a degree that the child fails to become independent.

overreaction: an excessive response or reaction, particularly said of emotional reactions.

overt: open to public observation; not concealed. *Contr.* COVERT.

overt behavior: behavior that is readily observable without the aid of instruments. *Contr.* covert behavior.

overtone: a partial tone created by partial vibrations of the sounding body.

ovum (plural **ova**): The female sex cell.

oxytocin: a hormone produced by the hypothalamus that is stored and released by the pituitary gland. It causes contractions of the uterus and the release of milk from the mammary glands.

P

Pacinian corpuscle: a specialized, encapsulated neuronal ending believed to mediate deep pressure and joint sensitivity.

pacing: 1. providing tasks that will lead the learner at a rate appropriate to his developmental speed. 2. forcing or controlling the speed with which an activity is carried out.

paederastia: see PEDERASTY.

pain: 1. unpleasantness; the opposite of pleasure. 2. the sensation resulting from damage to tissue. 3. the stimulation of the free nerve ending receptors on the skin.

pain principle: see DEATH INSTINCT.

pain sense: a sensory modality whose receptors are free nerve endings and is experienced both on the periphery and internal parts of the body.

pain spot: a point or spot on the skin particularly sensitive to pain. Such spots may be stimulated by sharp instruments or by electrical stimuli discharged from a condenser.

paired associates: in experimental investigation of learning, items (words, nonsense syllables, numbers, etc.) presented in pairs with one as the stimulus item, the other as the response item. The subject's task is to learn to give the appropriate response term when presented with the stimulus term.

paired-comparisons method: a psychophysical technique in which the stimuli are compared with each other, pair by pair, in all possible combinations; that is, A is compared with B, with C, with D, etc; then B is compared with C, and D, etc., and so on until all pairs have been compared.

palatable: 1. aggreeable to the taste.

2. acceptable in terms of measured intake. The *palatability* of a food is presumed to be dependent upon sensory stimuli from the head receptors.

paleopsychology: the investigation of primitive psychological processes believed to be vestigial carryovers from earlier evolutionary periods.

palingraphia: mirror writing.

palinphrasia: exaggerated or pathological repetition of words or phrases in speaking.

pallesthesia: sensitivity to vibration. *Syn.* PALMESTHESIS.

pallium: the cerebral cortex. The newer parts of the cortex are often referred to as the neopallium; the older as the archipallium.

palmar response: the hand-grasping response of the newborn.

palmesthesis: sensitivity to vibration. *Syn.* PALLESTHESIA.

palmistry: the pseudoscience of character and personality description by reading lines, prominences, shape, and other characteristics of the hand.

palp; palpate: 1. to touch. 2. to feel a sensation of touch.

palpebral: pertaining to the eyelid.

palpitation: rapid beating of the heart. Palpitations are characteristic of anxiety attacks.

palsy: paralysis accompanied by coarse tremor of the hands. See also CEREBRAL PALSY.

panic: an overwhelming fear often accompanied by reckless or ill-advised behavior.

panophobia: fear of everything.

panpsychism: the philosophic doctrine that the only ultimate reality is psychological in nature.

pansexualism: the point of view that everything in human behavior is to be explained in terms of the sex motive.

Pansexualism is ascribed to the Freudians by their critics and opponents.

pantophobia: see PANOPHOBIA.

panum phenomenon: the principle that if two lines close together are presented to one eye and a third line to the other eye, and either of the first two is combined with the third stereoscopically, then the resulting combination line will be seen as closer.

paper-and-pencil test: a test requiring written answers.

Papez circuit: the circuit of fibers interconnecting the nuclei of the limbic system (*q.v.*). Believed by Papez to mediate emotional tone.

papilla: a small, nipplelike prominence.

parabiosis: 1. a temporary loss of conductivity in a nerve. 2. the sharing of a common organ system, particularly the circulatory system.

parabiotic twins: two organisms whose bodily systems are joined together; for example, Siamese twins or animals so joined surgically for experimental purposes.

paracentral gyrus: a convolution in the middle of the cerebral hemisphere that surrounds the upper end of the central fissure and runs downward toward the caudal end of the *sulcus cinguli*.

paracentral vision: seeing by means of the area immediately surrounding the fovea.

parachromatopsia: partial color blindness.

paracontrast: forward visual masking where the mask is presented first on one visual area and the target second on another area.

paracusia: 1. relative deafness to deep tones. 2. increased ability to hear conversation among the partially deaf in the presence of background noises.

Probably an illusion due to the speaker's speaking more loudly to overcome the masking effect of deep tones, which cannot be heard in any case by the paracusic, thus giving him a relative advantage.

paradigm: 1. a model or pattern demonstrating all the possible functions of what it represents. 2. a plan of research based on specific concepts. 3. an experimental design.

paradoxical cold: the sensation of cold felt when a warm object, 43° C or over, stimulates a cold spot on the skin.

paradoxical sleep: a state of sleep characterized by an electroencephalographic pattern similar to that in light sleep. However, the individual is not easily awakened. Paradoxical sleep may be accompanied by rapid eye movements and dreaming.

paradoxical warmth: the sensation ⅜of warmth felt when a stimulus 29–31° C stimulates a receptor for cold.

paraesthesia: see PARESTHESIA.

paragenital: pertaining to coitus in which conception is prevented.

parageusia: a taste hallucination; a distorted taste senation.

paragraphia: the habitual insertion of incorrect and unintended words into speech due to a pathological condition of the nervous system.

paragraph-meaning test: a verbal test in which the subject must give the sense or essence of a paragraph.

paralanguage: the manner in which speech is uttered (inflection, volume, pacing) as opposed to its verbal content.

paralexia: the misreading of words and phrases, including transposition and substitution of letters and words.

paralinguistics: study of the nonlinguistic aspects of speech, such as stress, intonation, gestures.

parallax: the apparent movement of the two unequally distant objects in the field of vision as the eyes are moved from side to side. The nearer object seems to move in the direction opposite to the shift; those closer in the same direction.

parallel dream: (*Jung*) a dream whose latent content is the same as a consciously expressed attitude or wish.

parallel law: (*Fechner*) the psychophysical principle that where two stimuli of different intensities are presented to a sense modality, the absolute intensity diminishes, due to sensory adaptation and fatigue, but the ratio of the difference between them remains the same.

parallel play: independent play, or play side by side, without interaction between the participants.

parallel processing: in information processing, the categorizing and utilization of several incoming streams of information simultaneously

paralog: a two-syllable nonsense word.

paralysis: a partial or complete loss of function in the voluntary musculature. Paralyses may be of two fundamental types, *spastic* and *flaccid*. Spastic paralyses involve destruction of the upper motor neurons from the brain, while flaccid paralyses indicate involvement of the lower motor neurons that extend outward from the spinal cord to the muscle. Paralyses are also commonly classified in terms of the part of the spinal cord involved. *Paraplegia* results from complete sectioning of the cord, with paralysis of both lower limbs. *Hemiplegia*, or paralysis on one side, is the result of a destruction of one side of the cord; *diplegia* of both sides.

paralysis agitans: paralysis accompanied by tremor of the hands. In popular language, palsy. *Syn.* PARKINSON'S DISEASE.

paralytic dementia: see PARESIS.

parameter: 1. any constant that defines the curve of an equation representing some psychological function. The parameter may be based on empirical evidence or it may be based on a theory. 2. a variable that is constant during a particular experiment but may be varied from experiment to experiment.

paramimia: a disorder in which gestures fail to express the underlying feelings.

paramnesia: 1. false recognition; déjà vu. 2. a false memory, or distortion of memory.

paranoia: a psychotic disorder characterized by highly systematized delusions of persecution or grandeur with little deterioration. In either case, they are persistent, defended strongly by the patient, and incapacitating. See also PARANOID SCHIZOPHRENIA.

paranoic or **paranoiac:** 1. an individual who suffers from paranoia or paranoid schizophrenia.

paranoid: 1. pertaining to, or similar to, paranoia. 2. characterizing an individual whose behavior or whose attitudes resemble those of the paranoiac, particularly said of those who feel persecuted by others or by circumstances.

paranoid dementia: see PARANOID SCHIZOPHRENIA.

paranoid personality: a personality characterized by enviousness, suspiciousness, hostility, and oversensitivity, but without deterioration or delusions.

paranoid schizophrenia: a form of schiozphrenia in which the chief symptom is delusions of persecution or of grandeur. There are also disturbances of thinking, hallucinations, and deterioration.

paranormal: characterizing any phenomenon that cannot be accounted for according to accepted scientific laws.

paranosic: see ADVANTAGE BY ILLNESS.

parplegia: paralysis of the lower limbs due to injuries of the spinal cord.

parapraxis: a general term for minor errors—slips of the tongue, mistakes in writing, motor movements, forgetting things, and small accidents. Freud called such phenomena the "psychopathology of everyday life" and attributed them to unconscious motivational forces.

parapsychology: the field of psychology that investigates all psychological phenomena that apparently cannot be explained in terms of natural scientific laws or principles. Parapsychology includes the study of clairvoyance, dowsing, telekinesis, mediumistic trances, poltergeists, etc. *Syns.* PSYCHIC RESEARCH, PARAPSYCHICS, METAPSYCHICS.

parasagittal: parallel to the sagittal or longitudinal plane of an organ.

parasexuality: perversions or abnormal sexual behavior patterns.

parasocial speech: in a young child, talking to oneself.

parasympathetic: see AUTONOMIC NERVOUS SYSTEM.

parataxic: 1. characterized by abnormalities is emotional behavior. 2. characterized by the possession of aptitudes, ideas, or attitudes that are not integrated or exist in logic-tight comparments. 3. pertaining to distorted ideas.

parathyroid glands: four glands, each about the size of a pea, located in the neck in the region of the thyroid gland. The hormone secreted by the parathyroids is necessary in calcium metabolism.

paratypic: pertaining to influences arising from the environment.

paraventricular nucleus: the hypothalamic nucleus that produces oxyciticin (*q.v.*).

parent image: 1. a parent, in general or characteristic aspect, as remembered by an individual. Such images need not necessarily correspond to reality. 2. a parent surrogate or substitute.

paregastic reactions: schizophrenic reactions.

paresis: a psychosis accompanied by a progressive paralysis. Paresis is caused by syphilis of the nervous system. *Syns.* general paresis; DEMENTIA PARALYTICA; paretic psychosis; general paralysis of the insane.

paresthesia: abnormal or incorrectly localized cutaneous sensations, such as itching, pricking, or burning.

parietal: 1. pertaining to the middle region of the top of the skull between the frontal and occipital regions. 2. pertaining to the portion of the brain lying under the parietal bone of the skull.

parietal lobe: the division of the cerebral hemisphere lying under the parietal bone. The parietal lobe contains somesthetic centers.

Parkinson's disease: a neurological disorder characterized by rigidity, tremor, and difficulty in controlling movements. Believed to be caused by a dopamine deficiency in the nigrostriatal fibers.

parmia: (*R. B. Cattell*) the high score of a personality dimension characterized by venturesomeness, boldness, and insusceptibility to threat.

parorexia: a pathological desire to ingest unusual foods or other substances.

parosmia: 1. any disorder of the olfactory sense. 2. an olfactory hallucination.

parosphresia: 1. parosmia. 2. partial anosmia, or the inability to smell.

parotid gland: the salivary gland just below the ear and under the articulation of the jawbone.

paroxysm: 1. a spasm or convulsion. 2. a sudden intensification of a disorder or of an emotional state.

parsimony, principle of: a scientific canon or guide to thinking, stating that the simplest of alternative explanations for a phenomenon is to be preferred. *Syns.* principle of economy; LLOYD MORGAN'S CANON; OCCAM'S RAZOR.

parthenogenesis: the process of reproduction from an unfertilized ovum, such as occurs in the case of the male bee.

partial aim: (*Psychoan.*) the pregenital means of libidinal gratification, such as oral and anal eroticism.

partial color blindness: see COLOR BLINDNESS.

partial correlation: the net correlation between two variables when the influence of one or more additional variables that could either increase or decrease their relationship has been eliminated. The formula for a first-order partial correlation is:

$$r12.3 = \frac{r12 - r13\ r23}{\sqrt{(1-r^2 13)}\sqrt{(1-r^2 23)}}$$

partial instinct: (*Psychoan.*) a component instinct of the sex drive or the libidinal energies arising from the oral, anal, urethral, or genital part of the body.

partial love: (*Psychoan.*) love directed toward a part of a person instead of the person as a whole. See also PART OBJECT.

partial-regression equation: see MULTIPLE-REGRESSION EQUATION.

partial reinforcement: 1. intermittent reinforcement. 2. administration of only part of a reward.

partial sight: seriously defective vision but less than blindness.

partial tone; partial: any of the simple constituents that make up a tone. Any sounding body vibrates not only in its entirety but also in fractional parts (see illustration). The tone resulting from the first partial vibration of the body is called the fundamental tone. This is the loudest and lowest in pitch of all partials. The rest are called upper partials or overtones and become progressively weaker. Partial tones lend various instruments their characteristic sounds. *Syns.* HARMONIC; OVERTONE.

FIG. 24. *A figure to illustrate partials. The string vibrates as a whole, in halves, fourths, eighths, etc.*

participation: 1. the process of taking part in an activity. 2. (*Piaget*) the confusion of inner and outer events by children. Thus, the child may attribute reality to dreams or to his own thoughts.

particular complex: (*Psychoan.*) a complex based on a specific incident in an individual's life, as opposed to a universal complex, such as the Oedipus complex.

partile: one of a set of points that divides a distribution into a number of classes or divisions, each of which has an equal number of values or scores. The most common form of the partile is the *percentile*, which divides the distribution into 100 equal parts.

part instinct: see PARTIAL INSTINCT.

partition measure: any statistic or constant that separates parts of a distribution from one another.

part method of learning: learning in which the material to be learned is broken up into parts for separate mastery. For example, in learning a poem, the stanzas would be memorized one at a time.

partobject: (*Psychoan.*) an anatomical portion that is the object of love, such as the breast, the nipple, etc.

parturition: the process of giving birth.

passive: 1. characterizing behavior primarily initiated by outside forces. 2. the submissive role in sexual behavior.

passive-aggressive personality: a diagnostic category describing individuals who tend to resist demands on the part of others for competent performance; covert aggression is presumed to underlie their resistance. Other symptoms include procrastination, forgetfulness, inefficiency, complaining, and fault-finding.

passive analysis: (*Psychoan.*) psychoanalysis in which there is a minimum of direct interpretation and suggestion on the part of the analyst. *Contr.* ACTIVE ANALYSIS.

passive instinct: (*Psychoan.*) an instinct whose aim is the individual himself, in contrast to *active instinct*, whose aim is directed away from the self.

passive introversion: (*Jung*) involuntary introversion; inability to direct the psyche outward.

passive learning: learning in which there is little or no intent to learn. *Contr.* ACTIVE LEARNING.

passivism: a personality pattern characterized by submissiveness, particularly in sexual relations.

past-pointing: the tendency on the part of a subject who has been rotated to point past the spot indicated by the experimenter.

patella: the kneecap.

patellar reflex: SEE KNEE-JERK REFLEX.

paternalism: overprotection and control of the behavior of either children or adults by those in authority.

path: 1. a line of conduction along a nerve network. 2. an alleyway or line through a maze. 3. any route over which locomotion takes place.

path-choice coefficient: (*R. B. Cattell*) a factor-analysis design measuring a single individual on the same set of variables on a number of different occasions.

pathemia: (*R. B. Cattell*) one pole of a personality dimension characterized by emotional immaturity with poorly focused feelings rather than realistic and objective attitudes.

pathergasia: (*Meyer*) any bodily malfunction or defect that interferes with the individual's adjustment.

pathetic nerve: SEE TROCHLEAR NERVE.

pathic: pertaining to disease.

pathogenesis: the origin and developmental course of a disease or mental disorder.

pathognomy: 1. the capacity for recognizing feelings and emotions. 2.

the recognition and diagnosis of disease.

pathological fallacy: attributing abnormal or pathological characteristics to all mankind upon observing them in abnormal individuals. Essentially, the pathological fallacy is a case of overgeneralization.

pathological liar: one who habitually utters falsehoods or tells imaginary tales even though he can expect no benefit from concealing the truth.

pathology: 1. the science of diseases and disorders. 2. a condition of disease or disorder.

pathomimicry; pathomimesis: the feigning of a disease or disorder either deliberately or unconsciously.

pathoneurosis: (*Psychoan.*) a neurosis centered around a morbid preoccupation with a diseased organ.

patrilineal: pertaining to descent or kinship through the father's line.

pattern: 1. (*noun*) an organization of parts that form a design or work together harmoniously. 2. (*noun*) a model or sample to be copied or duplicated. 3. (*verb*) to integrate or organize a group of sensations.

pattern analysis: a technique for identifying test items that go together or measure a common variable. For example, interest test results are analyzed according to the patterning of answers on certain items, all of which theoretically indicate a common core of attitudes and personality traits likely to make for success in a given occupation. *Syn.* PROFILE ANALYSIS.

pattern, break-and-run: in fixed interval schedules of reinforcement, a response pattern in which very few responses occur until approximately two thirds of the way through the interval, when a high rate suddenly occurs until reinforcement is given.

pattern discrimination: a response made to the total pattern rather than to one or more of the components making up the pattern. For example, to react to a chord as opposed to its individual tones is pattern discrimination.

patterning: 1. imposition of an organization or pattern upon a set of stimulus data. 2. acquiring responses to organized patterns, or wholes, rather than to parts.

pattern-similarity coefficient: (*R. B. Cattell*) a statistic ranging between + 1.00 and − 1.00, expressing the degree of similarity or dissimilarity between two profiles of factor scores.

Pavlov, Ivan P.: Russian physiologist (1849–1936). Pavlov's undergraduate training was in the field of science, his graduate work in medicine. In 1884 he left a post in physiology at St. Petersburg (now Leningrad) to work in Germany. He returned to St. Petersburg in 1890 as director of the department of physiology in the Institute of Experimental Medicine. There he began his famous series of researches on the physiology of digestion, which won him the Nobel prize in 1904. In the course of his investigations, he noticed that dogs anticipate being fed by salivating at the sight of the keeper. Taking his finding into the laboratory, Pavlov began a systematic investigation of conditioned responses culminating in his famous studies of conflict, sleep, the psychic secretion of digestive juices, and abnormal states. His work in conditioning profoundly influenced the American behavioristic school of psychology started by John B. Watson. Pavlov's most important writings are *The Work of the Digestive Glands* (1902) and *Conditioned Reflexes*

(1927). He also published numerous scientific papers in the years 1900–1930.

Pavlovian conditioning: see CONDITIONING 1.

Pavlovianism: the point of view expressed by I. P. Pavlov to the effect that the psychic processes are identical with physiological processes in the brain and that these can be investigated experimentally by means of conditioning.

pavor: terror. *Pavor diurnus* is a fear reaction in children arising during the afternoon nap and consisting of hallucinations of strange people or animals, agitation, screaming, and running around. *Pavor nocturnus* is a similar reaction occurring during the night.

Peabody Picture Vocabulary Test, Revised: An individual vocabulary test frequently used as an abbreviated test of general ability. Ages 2½ to adult.

peak clipping: in transmitting speech, the elimination of the high-amplitude portion of the speech wave, with minimal loss of intelligibility. *Contr.* center clipping, or the elimination of the central portion of the wave, with severe loss in intelligibility.

peak experiences: (*Maslow*) moments of great awe, happiness, or rapture, during which the individual loses his self-consciousness and becomes one with the world. Some individuals report that during peak experiences they have penetrating insight into the mystery of life.

Pearson(ian) correlation: see PRODUCT-MOMENT CORRELATION.

peccatophobia: a pathological fear of sinning or committing a crime.

pecking order: the sequential hierarchy of dominance and privilege assumed by animals. The term originated from studies of chickens but applies to other animals as well.

pectoral: pertaining to the breast, particularly the breast muscle.

pederasty: anal sexual intercourse with a young male.

pederosis: the utilization of children as sexual objects by adults. *Syn.* PEDOPHILIA.

pediatrics: the specialized branch of medicine dealing with the diseases of children.

pedication: 1. pederasty. 2. sexual intercourse with animals.

pedophilia: sexual attraction for immature children.

peduncle: a stalklike bundle of fibers in the superficial layers of the brain.

peeping Tom: a voyeur.

peer: 1. an equal, legally or psychologically. 2. one of the same age

peer group: a group with which a child associates.

peer rating: a rating carried out by one's associates.

pegboard: a performance test consisting of a number of holes into which pegs are to be inserted as rapidly as possible. See PURDUE PEGBOARD.

pellet: a small piece of food used in animal experimentation. Pellets may be standard in size, nutritional elements, and weight.

penalty: 1. punishment or, more generally, any unpleasant consequence inflicted upon the individual for violation of a law or of a custom. 2. in learning, any form of deprivation or physical detainment inflicted as punishment for making an error.

penilingus: see FELLATIO.

penis: the male sex organ.

penis envy: (*Psychoan.*) the repressed wish on the part of a woman to possess a penis.

penology: the science of punitive and preventive treatment for criminal offenders.

Pentothal: a trademark name for thiopental, a drug used as a general anesthetic. See also NARCOANALYSIS.

peptic: pertaining to the digestive processes or the stomach.

perceive: to be aware of objects and events on the basis of the senses. See also PERCEPTION.

perceived self: the self as the individual experiences it; the totality of experiences included under the concept of "me" or "I."

percentile: 1. one of the points dividing an array of scores into parts or divisions, each of which contains one hundredth of the number of scores or individuals. Thus, a percentile score of 36 means that 36 percent of the group are below that value and 64 percent above that value. The 50th percentile is the median score, since it divides the distribution into two equal parts. It should be noted that percentiles may refer to scores, people, rats, grades etc. Percentiles do not indicate the number of items done correctly on a test. 2. a centile division or rank.

percentile curve or **graph:** an ogival, or S-shaped, curve in which percentages are cumulated.

percentile norm: a norm given in terms of the percentile standings of individuals on the test or measure in question. More commonly, norms are given in means or averages.

percentile score: a score representing the number of cases falling below a certain score. Thus, a score at the 90th percentile means that the individual in question falls below only 10 percent of the group and exceeds the performance of 90 percent of the group.

percept: 1. that which is perceived. 2. a perceptual act. The use of the term *percept* refers to the conscious experience and not to the physical object. Physical objects of perception are referred to as *stimuli*.

perception: 1. the process of knowing objects and objective events by means of the senses. 2. awareness of organic processes. 3. (*Titchener*) a group of sensations to which meaning is added from past experience. 4. an intervening variable inferred from the organism's ability to discriminate among stimuli. 5. an intuitive awareness of truth, or immediate belief about something.

In contemporary psychology perception is commonly treated as an intervening variable dependent upon stimulus factors, learning sets, moods, and emotional and motivational factors. Thus, the meaning of an object or objective event is determined both by stimulus conditions and by organism factors. For this reason, perception of the world by different persons is different, since each individual perceives in terms of those aspects of the situation that have special significance for him. In the decade following World War II, research emphasis in perception was on discovering the relationships between perception and the various O factors that influence the process. More recently, perceptual research has been heavily influenced by information processing theory (*q.v.*) with the result that the perceptual processes are conceptualized in terms of input-processing-output systems.

The perceptual process begins with attention, which is the process of selectively observing. The important stimulus factors in attending are change, intensity, repetition, contrast, and movement. Important organism factors are interests and learned habits of attention. Perception, which is the second stage in observing our world, involves understanding and knowing objects and events. Perceptions are organized into figure and ground. Figures are characterized by good shape, definite contour, and clarity in attention. The ground is fuzzy, not well contoured, and poorly localized. Perceptions may also be organized by such stimulus factors as similarity, proximity of stimuli, and continuity of lines. Highly important in perception are the perceptual constancies that refer to the tendency to see objects as invariable, regardless of wide variations in viewing conditions. The important constancies are color, size, shape, and brightness. Illusions are exceptions to the constancies and consist of distorted perceptions, which occur for a number of reasons, including complex stimulus patterns (see MÜLLER-LYER ILLUSION) and sets from past experience (see DISTORTED ROOM).

Depth perception is possible through the utilization of such physiological cues as accommodation convergence, retinal disparity of the eyes, and because of learned cues of linear and aerial perspective, interposition, relative size of objects in juxtaposition, shadows, and texture gradients. A great deal of research has been devoted to the question of whether our basic depth perceptions are learned, but the issue remains in doubt. Psychologists have found it difficult to design experiments where the relative roles of maturation and learned factors can be held constant. Studies of animals reared in darkness and of human patients who recover their sight as adults suggest that while primitive space perception may be inherent, complex interactions with objects in space are dependent upon learning.

perceptual anchoring: see ANCHORING POINT.

perceptual defense: selectivity of perception so that unpleasant or anxiety-producing stimuli are blocked from awareness. Experimentally, perceptual defense has been demonstrated where taboo words are presented rapidly and are misperceived. For example, *bitch* might be perceived as *ditch*.

perceptual distortion: a lack of correspondence between physical reality and psychological experience such as occurs in illusions, emotional excitement, pathological states, dreams, and hypnosis.

perceptual field: the conscious counterpart of a stimulus situation. The perceptual field may not contain all the elements of the stimulus situation, and there may be distorted and illusory elements present. For the influences that impinge on the perceptual field, see also PERCEPTION.

perceptual induction: see EMPATHY.

perceptual learning: learning in which the task is to achieve a new or modified perceptual response. Mirror drawing exemplifies perceptual learning, since the subject must overcome habitual perceptual responses.

perceptual-motor learning: learning in which both new and perceptual and motor relations are involved, such as in learning to throw darts at an underwater target.

perceptual restructuring: the process of changing a perception in accordance with new information. Thus, one's attitude toward a political party may change upon being given more information about the leading candidate's personal life.

perceptual schema: the cognitive map that provides a frame of reference for reacting to the environment.

perceptual segregation: the separation or differentiation of one part of a perceptual field from the field as a whole. The placement of boundaries, barriers, dividing lines, etc., is the usual means of effecting segregation.

perceptual sensitization: lowered recognition threshold for certain types of stimuli. Increased perceptual vigilance.

perceptual set: a readiness to perceive in a certain way or according to a certain frame of reference.

perceptual speed: in factor-analysis tests of ability, a primary mental ability consisting of rapid and effective dealing with perceptual forms.

perceptual structure: the organization of a percept or conscious experience in terms of the interrelationship of parts to one another and to the whole. The simplest perceptual structure is the figure-ground perception.

perceptual transformation: the change that can be induced in a percept by adding new elements, explanations, or insights to the situation. Perceptual transformation often occurs in problem solving when an object, perceived in a new light, leads to a solution.

percipient: 1. one who perceives. 2. in parapsychology or psychic research, one who receives messages.

performance: 1. any activity. 2. behavior that produces a result, particularly behavior that alters the environment in some manner. The two most common ways of measuring performance in psychology are by means of ability tests and learning situations.

performance test: a test utilizing

concrete, nonverbal materials, such as form boards, mazes, disassembled figures, and block designs.

perimacular vision: vision using the area of the retina surrounding the macula.

perimeter: a device for mapping the visual zones of the retina. The perimeter is typically used to determine the limits of achromatic and chromatic vision and also to define areas of visual defect. The instrument consists of a circular band mounted at eye level along which stimuli can be moved outward and inward from the center to the periphery. The subject fixates a point on the center of the band.

perimetry: the use and interpretation of data obtained from the perimeter.

period: 1. the time for one complete cycle of a wavelike phenomenon, such as sound, to occur. 2. the menstrual discharge.

periodic: that which occurs regularly in a cyclic manner, such as the wave form generated by a pure tone.

periodic reinforcement: reinforcement given regularly according to a predetermined time schedule. *Contr.* APERIODIC REINFORCEMENT.

peripheral: 1. pertaining to the surface or outside of a body or an organ. 2. pertaining to the sensory and motor neurons that travel to and from the spinal cord to the surface of the body. 3. pertaining to all psychological processes that occur in the sense organs and effectors, as opposed to *central* processes, which occur in the brain. 4. marginal; of questionable importance in an argument.

peripheralconstruct: (*Kelly*) a construct (*q.v.*) that is not fundamental or basic to a construct system and

therefore can be easily modified. *Contr.* CORE CONSTRUCT.

peripheral hallucination: a hallucination in which there is a clear relation to an outside stimulus.

peripheralism: a point of view emphasizing events taking place at the peripheral level. The strongest proponents of the peripheralist position are the behaviorists, who seek to avoid the mentalistic connotations associated with centralist psychology. Thus, Watson, the founder of behaviorism, attributed thinking to effector processes in the muscles, specifically the laryngeal muscles. Feeling, another stronghold of the centralists, he attributed to activity of the sex organs.

peripheral neuron or **nerve:** a nerve fiber or bundle of fibers mediating either sensory or motor processes on the surface of the body. See also NERVOUS SYSTEM.

peripheral nervous system: see NERVOUS SYSTEM.

peripheral theory of thinking: see PERIPHERALISM.

peripheral vision: seeing by means of the outer portions of the retina. Peripheral vision is rod vision and is therefore color-blind.

permeable: 1. having the capability of being permeated or penetrated, as in the case of a membrane that allows certain fluid substances to pass through. 2. having the capability of being penetrated by outside forces, as in the case of a boundary.

permeable construct: (*Kelly*) a construct (*q.v.*) that permits the assimilation of new elements. *Contr.* IMPERMEABLE CONSTRUCT.

permissiveness: an attitude on the part of those in authority that grants great latitude and freedom of choice to those subject to authority. *Contr.* AUTHORITARIANISM.

pernicious trend: a serious and significant regression away from mature modes of behavior.

perseveration: 1. a tendency to continue an ongoing activity even when it becomes inappropriate. 2. the tendency on the part of an idea to recur in the absence of a stimulus. 3. the pathological repetition of a word or phrase in speaking.

perseveration set: a set that carries over from one situation to another.

perseverative error: the persistent repetition of an error already made.

persistence of vision: the tendency for a visual sensation to remain after the removal of the stimulus. The phenomenon is caused by sensory lag.

persona: (from the Latin *persona*, a mask worn by actors in classical dramas) the personality, with reference to that aspect involved in playing a role.

personal construct: the individual's way of interpreting the world.

personal data sheet: a questionnaire inquiring about biographical and psychological information.

personal document: any record (such as a letter, diary, biographical sketch, etc.) that reveals useful psychological information about an individual. Gordon Allport advocates the use of personal documents as a method of studying personality.

personal equation: 1. specifically and historically, a difference in reaction time between two observers. 2. more generally, any difference in performance due to individual differences.

personal identity: 1. the sense of personal continuity over time. 2. the persistence of the personality despite environmental and structural changes with time.

personal idiom: individual idiosyncrasies and mannerisms that distinguish one individual from another.

personal image: (*Jung*) 1. an unconscious representation of a personal experience. 2. a part of the unconscious that arises from the individual's experience, as contrasted with the collective, or racial, unconscious.

personalism: the point of view that the individual personality must be the central subject matter of psychology. See also PERSONALISTIC PSYCHOLOGY.

personalistic psychology: 1. the psychology of personalism. 2. the point of view emphasizing the embeddedness of behavior in the individual personality. See also ALLPORT'S PSYCHOLOGY OF INDIVIDUALITY.

personality: 1. (*Allport*) "the dynamic organization within the individual of those psychophysical systems that determine his characteristic behavior and thought." 2. (*R. B. Cattell*) "that which permits a prediction of what a person will do in a given situation." 3. (*Murray*) "the continuity of functional forms and forces manifested through sequences of organized regnant processes and overt behaviors from birth to death." 4. (*Freud*) the integration of the id, the ego, and the superego. 5. (*Adler*) the individual's style of life, or characteristic manner of responding to life's problems, including life goals. 6. (*Jung*) the integration of the ego, the personal and collective unconscious, the complexes, the archetypes, the persona, and the anima.

As the definitions given above show, personality has been defined in a number of different ways by various theorists. Other theorists have emphasized temperament (Sheldon, Kretschmer) as the core of personality. In popular usage, the social-stimulus value of the individual is equated with personality. The psychotherapist is likely to emphasize the individual's characteristic patterns of adjustment. Regardless of differences in emphasis, there is a core of agreement in considering personality as an integration of traits that can be investigated and described in order to render an account of the unique quality of the individual. For further discussion see entries under the names of the personality theorists mentioned above.

personality disintegration: the breaking apart of the unified organization of traits that comprise personality. It may be accompanied by some degree of intellectual deterioration, demoralization, loss of motivation, and impaired judgment.

personality disorder: a difficulty in social adjustment that is not as serious as neurosis or psychosis but includes inadequacies in motivational and emotional processes and may include schizoid, paranoid, and clyclothymic tendencies as well as the sociopathic or societal disturbances.

personality dynamics: the study of the motivational and emotional components of personality.

personality integration: the organization of the various trait systems that constitute personality into a harmonious whole, resulting in effective adjustment.

personality inventory: a questionnaire-type device to be answered by the individual about himself. Typically, a series of statements is presented to which the individual responds with *Yes, No,* or *?.* Norms are provided for the purpose of comparing a given individual's performance with that of the standardization group.

personality organization: see PERSONALITY INTEGRATION.

personality problem: a persistent maladjustment without psychosis or neurosis that interferes with social relations and personal happiness. Feelings of inferiority and jealousy and excessive preoccupation with sex are examples of personality problems.

personality reorganization: a fundamental change in personality with redirection of goals and values brought about by extensive psychotherapy.

personality sphere: (*R. B. Cattell*) the range of measurable human personality.

personality structure: the integration of traits and systems constituting the personality.

personality syndrome: an acquired organization of traits in a given culture that resembles the personality organization of other individuals in that culture. The analogy is to a disease that, although it may vary from case to case, is a recognizable entity because of the common symptoms involved.

personality test: any instrument or technique used in the evaluation of personality or in the measurement of personality or character traits.

personality type: a classification of the individual into one or two or more categories on the basis of how closely his pattern of traits corresponds to the type category.

personal space: the area around an individual considered to belong to him and whose invasion is experienced as threatening or unpleasant.

personal unconscious: (*Jung*) that part of the unconscious unique to the individual and which develops as a result of the repression of individual experience. *Contr.* COLLECTIVE UN-CONSCIOUS.

personification: 1. attributing personal or human characteristics to abstractions, models, or objects. 2. attributing qualities to another that are missing in oneself.

personnel: 1 (*noun*) the total group of individuals employed in an organization. 2. (*adj.*) pertaining to human factors in industrial or business operation.

personnel psychology: the branch of applied psychology that investigates employment procedures, selection techniques, placement, transfer, promotion, rewards for work, and that in some cases may include limited guidance and therapy.

personology: 1. the study of personality. 2. the point of view that all behavior should be studied in relation to the central core of personality.

perspective: 1. the representation of the relative position, size, and distance of objects on a surface. 2. a point of view or frame of reference from which parts or elements of an object or a problem are seen to better advantage or form a better organization.

perspective size: the size of an object according to the geometric relations in perspective.

perversion: a socially unacceptable form of sexual conduct. Fetishism, exhibitionism, sadism, and masochism are the most common types of perversion.

perverted: engaging in perversion; misdirected.

petit mal: a form of epilepsy in which there is a momentary loss of consciousness and transitory compulsive behavior. See EPILEPSY

peyote: 1. a cactus, *Lophophora Williamsii*, from which mescaline is derived. 2. loosely, the drug mescaline.

PGO spike (wave): large encephalographic waves recorded from the pons, lateral geniculate nuclei, and occipital cortex during REM sleep.

phacoscope: a device for observing the accommodation of the lens by observing changes in the reflected images from its surfaces.

phallic: pertaining to the penis; representative of the penis.

phallic love: (*Psychoan.*) love for the penis, or its equivalent in the case of girls. Phallic love is demonstrated by pride in the penis and by masturbation.

phallic primacy: (*Psychoan.*) the fixation of erotic interest on the penis or the penis equivalent during the early genital phase of infantile development.

phallic stage or **phase:** (*Psychoan.*) the infantile period following the oral and anal periods in which the child discovers the pleasure-giving possibilities of the penis (or its symbolic equivalent in girls).

phallic symbol: any pointed or upright object, such as a pencil, telephone pole, or church spire, that may represent or suggest a penis. Phallic symbols are particularly evident in dreams, according to psychoanalysts.

phallic worship: religious or fertility rites associated with worship of the phallus, an artifact designed to represent the male organ. See PHALLUS.

phallus: a representation of the penis, often utilized as an object of veneration in ancient Greek cults, particularly the Dionysian.

phantasy: see FANTASY.

phantom limb: imagined sensations

arising from the stump of amputated limbs.

phantom sound: an unlocalized sound heard when sounds of slightly different phase or intensity are fed into two ears separately.

phase: 1. a recurrent state of anything that occurs in a cyclic manner, such as a sound wave or the changes in the moon. 2. a stage in the individual's life that is temporary and during which certain typical behavior patterns occur.

phase difference: any difference in the phase sequences of two sound waves so that trough and trough and crest and crest fail to correspond. Slight differences in phase cause beats, or alternating intensifications and diminution of loudness.

phase sequence: (*Hebb*) a number of assemblies of nerve cells joined together in a functional relationship for the mediation of learned behavior. See also HEBB'S THEORY OF PERCEPTUAL LEARNING.

phasic contraction: intermittent, but regular, muscular contraction.

phenobarbital: a narcotic drug used to induce sleep and hypnotic conditions.

phenomenal or **phenomenological field:** that which the individual experiences at any given moment.

phenomenalism: 1. the doctrine that we can know only appearances and not ultimate reality, a philosophical position taken by Schopenhauer and Kant. 2. phenomenology.

phenomenalistic introspection or **inspection:** a report in everyday language of what one sees or thinks about, in contrast to structuralistic introspection, which demanded a rigid and objective analysis of the content of consciousness.

phenomenal motion: apparent or illusory motion, as contrasted to real motion.

phenomenal regression: a shift away from perfect perceptual constancy toward true physical size. In perception, the size of objects one perceives lies between what would be expected from the physical stimulus size and what would be expected from object constancy. Seeing a man at 200 yards, according to physical expectation, would make him seem like a pygmy. Perfect object constancy would have him appear as tall as he would if he were only a few feet away. Perceived size lies between the extremes.

pheneomenal report: a verbal account of experience from the phenomenological point of view.

phenomenal report: a verbal account of experience from the phenomenological point of view.

phenomenal self: 1. the self as experienced in relation to the environment. 2. the self as known directly in self-perception, as opposed to the *inferred self* as given by tests, observations of others, etc.

phenomenistic causality: a type of thinking found in children in which contiguous phenomena are assumed to bear a causal relationship. Thus, the child may say that the moon stays in the sky because it is yellow.

phenomenological structure: the organization of the perceptual field in terms of figure-ground and other, more complex relationships.

phenomenology: 1. the study of phenomena or events as they occur immediatly in experience without interpretation. 2. the philosophic position that the transcendental subjective is immediate experience. According to Husserl, a phenomenological psychology is the study of the types of intentional psychology.

phenomenon: 1. that which occurs and is open to observation. 2. any datum. 3. a fact or proven event. 4. the appearance of events, in contrast with ultimate reality.

phenomotive: a motive that is accessible to introspective observation. *Contr.* GENOMOTIVE.

phenotype: the visible characteristics of a group as contrasted with the underlying hereditary characteristics. *Contr.* GENOTYPE.

phenylketonuria: an inherited form of mental retardation due to a disorder of amino-acid metabolism.

phenylpyruvic oligophrenia: a severe mental deficiency resulting from the lack of an enzyme necessary for the oxidization of phenylalanine.

pheromones: chemical products secreted by certain species for communicating information, particularly that associated with mating.

phi coefficient: a statistic for estimating the degree of relationship between variables divided into two discrete groups, such as men and women, short and tall, etc.

phi gamma function: the integration of the normal distribution of judgments obtained by the method of constant-stimulus differences and stated in terms of h, an index of precision that measures how closely data are centered around the mean.

phi gamma hypothesis: the assumption that data obtained by the method of constant stimuli will fit the phi gamma function.

phi phenomenon: 1. (*Wertheimer*) the perception of pure movement as an experience not analyzable into anything else. 2. the generation of apparent motion by the successive appear-

ance of two spatially separated stimuli, as the flashing of two lights. The impression is that the stimulus is moving from one position to the other. The device is frequently used in advertising as when a neon arrow seems to move into a restaurant when, in fact, it is a series of lighted arrows occurring in rapid succession.

phlegmatic: apathetic and sluggish; not easily aroused.

phobia: a strong, persistent, and irrational fear elicited by a specific stimulus or situation, such as a morbid fear of closed places. Some of the more common phobias are: *acrophobia*, fear of heights; *agoraphobia*, fear of open places; *claustrophobia*, fear of closed places; *hematophobia*, fear of blood; *nyctophobia*, fear of darkness, *xenophobia*, fear of strangers, *zoophobia*, fear of animals.

phobophobia: fear of fearing.

phon: a unit of loudness in which a sound is subjectively equated relative to the decibel level of a reference tone of 1000 Hz.

phonation: the production of speech sounds.

phone: an elementary speech sound or sound unit.

phoneme: a group of closely related speech sounds spelled with the same or equivalent letters and commonly regarded as the same sound. They may vary somewhat with differing phonetic conditions.

phonetic: 1. pertaining to phonetics. 2. pertaining to the systematic representation of speech sounds by means of symbols.

phonetic method: a technique for teaching foreign languages by means of phonetics.

phonetics: the study of the production of speech sounds, their physical, physiological, and psychological correlates.

phonic: pertaining to vocal sounds.

phonic method: the teaching of reading by immediately correlating the sounds with the letters that represent them.

phonogram: 1. a symbolic repesentation of a speech sound. 2. a diagrammatic representation of the vocal organs in the process of making speech sounds.

phonophobia: dread of one's own voice.

phonoscope: a general name for any device for making sound waves visible.

phon scale: a subjective scale of loudness developed by comparing various frequencies to a standard of 1000 Hz.

phoria: 1. the turning of the eyeballs in sighting an object. 2. the vertical or lateral balance of muscles of binocular vision.

phorometry: the measurement of the degree of imbalance existing in the external muscles of the eye.

phosphene: a phosphorescent glow of light seen in the dark when the eyeball is subjected to mechanical distortion, or that may be brought on by the process of accommodation.

phot: a unit of illumination equal to the illumination produced at a surface one centimeter from a point source of light or one candlepower strength. *Syn.* centimeter candle.

photerythrous: pertaining to the increased sensitivity of some individuals for wavelengths in the long end of the spectrum.

photic: pertaining to light.

photic driving: the rhythmic stimulation of the brain by applying a stroboscopic light to the eyes in order to accentuate brain waves. In photic driv-

ing the alpha rhythm may be brought into synchrony with the light.

photism: 1. a false perception of light that sometimes occurs in pathological conditions. 2. a form of synesthesia in which colors are attached to stimuli from other sense modalities. For example, seeing blue when presented with the number 4.

photochromatic interval: the range of stimulus intensity over which a chromatic or colored stimulus is perceived as light but not yet as hue or color.

photokinesis: the general activity of lower organisms in response to light.

photoma: a simple hallucination of flashing light, sparks, points of illumination, etc.

photometer: any optical device that allows for the measurement of candle-power illumination or brilliance by means of comparing standard and variable stimuli juxtaposed in the visual field.

photometric measure: any measure of light in photometric terms, such as candlepower, illumination, luminance, rather than in terms of physical energy or the magnitude of sensation.

photon: a measure of brightness defined as the retinal illumination that results when a surface brightness of one candle per square meter is seen through a pupillary area of one square millimeter. *Syn.* TROLAND.

photophobia: an extreme sensitivity to light, such as occurs in persons whose eyes lack pigmentation.

photopic adaptation: see BRIGHTNESS ADAPTATION.

photopic vision: daylight vision; vision in conditions of relatively strong illumination when the cones are functional; hence, color vision. *Contr.* SCOTOPIC VISION.

photoreceptor: a receptor for which the adequate or normal stimulus is light.

phototaxis: see PHOTOTROPISM.

phototropism: an orienting movement on the part of lower forms toward light. Phototropisms may be negative (away from light), or positive (toward light).

phrenasthenia: mental deficiency.

phrenology: the pseudoscience asserting that certain mental faculties are localized in parts of the brain and that the skull configuration reveals the best developed parts of the brain with consequent high development of the faculties.

phrictopathic sensations: sensations of irritation and tingling that are poorly localized.

phyletic: pertaining to a phylum.

phylogenesis: the origin and evolution of species. *Syn.* phylogeny.

phylogenetic: 1. pertaining to the origin and development of a species. 2. pertaining to traits or characteristics that are hereditary.

phylogenetic memory: a memory or idea presumably to be found in all races of contemporary man.

phylogenetic principle: the doctrine that *ontogeny* (individual) recapitulates *phylogeny* (species) in its development. That is, the individual goes through all the stages of primitive man in his development. Thus the child plays at being a savage, at cowboys and Indians, etc. *Syn.* RECAPITULATION THEORY.

phylogeny: see PHYLOGENESIS.

phylum: the most comprehensive of the divisions applied to biological forms.

physicalism: the point of view that undistorted propositions or meanings can be stated in the language of the

physical sciences. Physicalism would encourage the use of operational definitions.

physical stimulus: any stimulus that occurs as a result of external energy changes.

physiochemical: pertaining to the realm of physics and chemistry.

physiogenic: pertaining to disorders that originate in the bodily organs.

physiognomic: 1. pertaining to physiognomy (*q.v.*). 2. a type of empathetic reaction in which affective or conative elements are added to cognitive experiences. For example, a dilapidated car is said to look tired, a fine tree, proud.

physiognomy: 1. the art of judging personality or mental abilities and attitudes from the structure and expression of the face and other bodily organs. 2. the expression of the face.

physiological age: the individual's developmental level as estimated by the maturational status of his glands, muscles, nervous system, etc.

physiological gradient: a continuous diminution in physiological activity from an area of high metabolism to an area of low metabolism.

physiological limit: the theoretical limit beyond which further practice would be of no benefit. The physiological limit is rarely, if ever, reached in practice. Rather, it is approached in increasingly smaller increments of gain. *Syn.* psychological limit.

physiological motive: one of the motives based on a known bodily need or physiological rhythm, such as sex, hunger, or thirst.

physiological psychology: the branch of psychology concerned with the interrelationships of the nervous system, receptors, and endocrine glands, and of behavior and the mental processes.

physiological scotoma: the blind spot where the optic neurons leave the retina.

physiological zero: the temperature on the skin at which an object feels neutral—neither warm nor cold. The physiological zero point varies with the part of the body tested, but on the exposed surfaces of the hands and face in an ordinary room it is a little over 32° C.

physique: the overall structural organization and appearance of the individual.

Piaget, Jean: Swiss psychologist (1896-1980). Born in Neuchtal, Switzerland, Piaget was educated in Zurich and Paris. He was professor of child psychology at Geneva University. From 1929 until his death he was director of studies at the Jean Jacques Rousseau Institute at Geneva. Piaget's world-famous studies of children's thinking began in his teens and resulted in an important early publication, *The Language and Thought of the Child* (1923), which was followed by hundreds of additional publications on the child's conception of physical causality, the development of moral judgment, the growth of intelligence, and the development of logical and mathematical concepts. Piaget was noted for his original methods for studying children's thinking, for his conceptualization of the stages of cognitive development, and for his enormous body of research. His most important publications are *The Child's Conception of Physical Causality* (1927), *The Moral Judgment of the Child* (1932), *The Origins of Intelligence* (1952), and *Six Psychological Studies* (1967).

Piaget's theory of cognitive development: Piaget's theory of cognitive development is built around four fundamental stages during which the child acquires the ability to think in increasingly complex modes. However, basic to the stages of development are certain processes that form the matrix of cognitive change and growth. The first of these is assimilation or the process by means of which the brain adjusts to the object that is being assimilated. The schemata are cognitive structures forming a framework that grows and changes through assimilation and accomodation. Finally, equilibration refers to the process by means of which schemata change from one stage to another.

The four periods of development begin with the sensorimotor stage (birth to about 2 years), which is the period in which the child learns about objects and how to manipulate them. He also learns the significance of time and space but lacks the necessary conceptual equipment to think of objects, time, and space abstractly.

The second stage is that of preoperational thinking (2–7 years). During this period the child can think in terms of simple categories. He can represent objects symbolically and therefore can conceive of object permanence even in the absence of an object. However, his thinking lacks flexibility during this stage.

During the third or concrete stage (7–11 years), the child is closely tied to objects and events that are present but he can also master concepts of conservation (*q.v.*) of mass, length, and volume. His thinking during this stage is increasingly flexible and less egocentric than in earlier stages.

During the final stage of formal operations (11 years and after), adult capability in reasoning, abstracting, and thinking hypothetically gradually emerges.

pia mater: a very thin vascular membrane covering the brain and spinal cord. The pia mater is covered by two other tissues, the *arachnoid* and *dura mater*.

piano theory of hearing: see HEARING THEORIES.

pica: a strong craving to eat non-nutritive objects, bits of trash, pieces of plants, etc.

Pick's disease: progressive dementia characterized by circumscribed atrophy of the cerebral cortex. There is dulling of the emotions, stereotyped action and speech, and loss of moral judgment and memory.

picture-arrangement test: a series of cartoons that tell a story when arranged in proper sequence. A picture-arrangement test is used on the Wechsler-Bellevue Scale of Intelligence.

picture-completion test: a set of drawings of objects or animals with parts missing. The task for the subject is to identify the missing part.

Picture-Frustration Study: a projective technique in which a frustrating situation is portrayed and the subject is asked to indicate what he would probably say if he were in the situation. Responses are classified according to the type of aggression or other defensive reactions verbalized by the subject.

picture-interpretation test: a test in which the subject must make an interpretation of a pictorial scene. Picture interpretation is used on several levels of the Binet Scale.

Piderit drawings: a series of line drawings of the human face that show, in highly simplified form, various emotional expressions. Cut up into composite parts, the pictures have been used to determined how changes in one part of the face affect overall emotional expression.

piecemeal activity, law of: (*Thorndike*) the generalization that a part or aspect of a learning situation may become connected with a response so that an animal subject will give the response even though other parts of the situation are absent.

pigment layer: the layer next to the rods and cones, or the first retinal layer, which consists of pigmented cells.

pillars of Corti: see RODS OF CORTI.

pilomotor response: the erection of the hairs, as in shivering or in fright.

pilot study: a preliminary simplified version of a study to be carried out in detail. The pilot study is for the purpose of finding out whether the final study is feasible and likely to yield the information desired.

pineal gland or **body:** a small glandular outgrowth of the thalamic region near the center of the brain. Its function is unknown. The pineal gland was the site selected by Descartes for the interaction of mind and body. *Syn.* epiphysis cerebri.

pinna: the fleshy part of the external ear.

Piper's law: in a uniform portion of the retina, the threshold luminance is inversely proportional to the square root of the area stimulated.

pitch: the qualitative character of tones and sounds described as "high" or "low." On the physical side, pitch is primarily related to the frequency of vibration of a sounding body. In man the range of pitch appreciation is approximately 20–20,000 Hz.

pituitary gland: a highly complex endocrine gland about the size of a pea located at the base of the brain. In general, the gland is divided into the anterior and posterior lobes. The anterior lobe produces hormones that regulate growth and, in addition, a number of trophic hormones that regulate the functions of the other endocrine glands. The posterior lobe produces a hormone that regulates water metabolism and in addition has several other functions. Because of its regulating influence on the other endocrine glands, the pituitary is called the "master gland."

pity: an emotion aroused by the suffering or misfortune of another and characterized by strong feelings of sympathy and solicitude.

PKU: see phenylketonuria.

placebo: a preparation, often in pill form, used as a control in experiments requiring the administration of drugs. The placebo, which is made of sugar, acts as a control on possible suggestive effects from the knowledge that one is getting a drug.

place learning: (*Tolman*) learning the location of a goal in space. *Contr.* RESPONSE LEARNING. For a further discussion, see TOLMAN'S PURPOSIVE BEHAVIORISM.

placement: the assignment of workers to positions for which they are best suited on the basis of experience and aptitude tests.

placement test: a test used by schools and colleges to help place pupils in sections for which they are best suited according to ability and achievement.

placenta: the organ of attachment of the fetus to the mother's uterus. The organ is highly vascular and allows the osmotic transmission of food products and respiratory gasses to take place between the blood of the fetus and that of the mother.

plan: 1. a scheme of action. 2. a design for an experiment, taking into account the variables and how they will be administered, controlled, and how the data will be processed.

planchette: a small tripod one of whose legs is a pencil. The device is used in experiments on automatic writing. The operator's hand, hidden behind a screen, is allowed to rest lightly on the planchette, which, in turn, rests on a writing surface and records the subject's movements.

planophrasia: a flight of ideas, such as is observed in manic-depressive psychoses.

plantar reflex: the flexion of the toes when the sole of the foot is stroked.

plantigrade: characterizing locomotion in which the entire foot is placed on the ground.

plasticity: 1. flexibility of response. 2. the state of being teachable or docile. 3. adaptability.

plastic tonus: a kind of tonus in which the limb remains in the position in which it is placed. This disorder is characteristic of catatonia.

plateau: a period of several trials in the course of learning in which there is no change in the slope of the learning curve, indicating that learning has temporarily come to a halt. Plateaus may be due to fatigue, loss of motivation, or the consolidation of one level of skill before the next higher level is undertaken.

Plato: Greek philosopher and writer (c. 427–347 B.C.). Plato received the usual education of a well-born Athenian youth in the fields of music, literature, and gymnastics. When he was about twenty, he became a disciple of Socrates and remained with the master until he was about twenty-eight. After Socrates' death, Plato left Athens to study with Euclid and to travel extensively in what is now called Egypt, Italy, and Sicily. Shortly after his return, he established his famous academy in his own garden at Athens, where he taught by the methods of discussion and conversation for the next forty years. Some of his pupils were to become eminent men in their own right, including Aristotle, Demosthenes, and Lycurgus. Among his writings are the *Dialogues, The Republic, The Laws, Phaedrus, Symposium, Gorgias,* and the *Phaedo.* Plato is important in the history of psychology for his distinction between mind and body in his famous doctrine of dualism. He held that mind and body are two separate entities. In one form or another, dualism has come down through the ages in the doctrines of interactionism, psychophysical parallelism, and isomorphism. Plato is also known in psychology for the rationalistic method and for attributing motivation to three sources: desire, primarily sexual; emotion, whose source is the heat of the blood; and knowledge, which stems from the head.

Platonic love: love in which there is an absence of erotic or sexual elements.

Platonize: 1. to render a relationship nonerotic; to sublimate. 2. to idealize. 3. to consider an act without carrying it out.

platykurtic: characterizing a frequency curve that is flat. See also KURTOSIS.

play therapy: the utilization of play as a form of catharsis to enable the child to express feelings and emotions that, if allowed to build up, could cause maladjustment. Play therapy may also be a useful technique for diagnosing the source of a child's difficulty.

pleasantness: a positve feeling associated with the desire to prolong the exciting conditions. *Contr.* UNPLEASANTNESS.

pleasure-pain: a compound term used to characterize the antithetical poles of extreme pleasantness and unpleasantness.

pleasure principle; pleasure-pain principle: (*Psychoan.*) the doctrine that man is governed by the search for pleasure and the avoidance of pain. The pleasure principle is demonstrated in the demands originating out of the libido or the life instinct (Eros) and the desire on the part of the individual to reduce tensions.

plethysmograph: a device for measuring changes in the volume of a part of the body such as the finger or hand. The plethysmograph gives an indirect index of blood volume in that member.

plexus: a network, such as a network of nerves or blood vessels.

plot: 1. (*verb*) to enter scores on a scatter diagram. 2. (*noun*) a scatter diagram.

pluralism: 1. the philosphic position that ultimate reality consists of more than one kind of entity, as opposed to *monism*, which holds that all things are ultimately reducible to a final element. 2. the quality or state of being more than one.

pluralistic behavior: behavior engaged in universally or almost universally, such as wearing clothing.

pluralistic ignorance: a situation where members of a group believe that their private opinions differ from the group norm but, in fact, do not.

plus-minus conflict: see APPROACH-AVOIDANCE CONFLICT.

plus-plus conflict: see APPROACH-APPROACH CONFLICT.

pneumocardiograph: a pneumatic instrument for recording the heartbeat.

pneumogastric nerve: see VAGUS.

pneumograph: an instrument consisting of a closed tube placed around the chest and connected to a writing pen for recording the duration and strength of inspiration and expiration.

Poetzl phenomenon: dreaming about previously unreported parts of a tachistoscopically presented picture.

Poggendorf illusion: a geometrical illusion in which a straight line appears to become jagged as it passes through two parallel rectangles. See illustration.

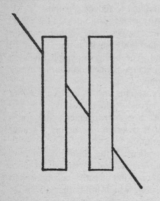

FIG. 25. *The Poggendorf illusion.*

point-biserial correlation: a correlation between a dichotomous and a continuous variable. For example, to correlate sex (dichotomous variable) with intelligence (continuous variable) would require a point-biserial correlation.

point-for-point correspondence: any spatial or logical relationship such that for every point in one variable there is a corresponding point in the other variable. Point-for-point correspondence is said to occur between the retina and the termination of optic neurons on the occipital lobe. It is also a part of the Gestalt doctrine of isomorphism.

point of regard: the fixation point or line along which an object is sighted so that it falls on the fovea of the retina.

point of subjective equality: 1. the value of the variable or comparison stimulus regarded as equal to the standard stimulus. 2. the point at which psychometric functions of greater or lesser judgments intersect; the point at which stimuli are just as likely to be judged greater as they are lesser. 3. the point halfway between upper and lower thresholds.

point ratio: a weighted index of grades in secondary schools and colleges in which letter grades are assigned numerical values according to a sliding scale such as the following: A = 4; B = 3; C = 2, etc. Each number is then multiplied by the hours of credit assigned to the course and the student's average is calculated by dividing the total of the point-ratio scores by the total number of credit hours involved.

point scale: a type of test in which each item is assigned a point value and the individual's performance is rated according to the total number of points earned.

point score: the raw score on a point scale.

point source: a source of light which, in comparison with its distance from the subject, may be regarded as a point.

polar continuum: a continuum or series whose end points are completely opposite, such as the personality-trait continuum of dominance and submission.

polarity: 1. the condition of having two poles or opposite ends. 2. the resting condition of a neuron that shows an equilibrium of positive and negative ions across the cell membrane. 3. the manifestation of opposite or conflicting behavior patterns or motives, such as love and hate. 4. a center of attractiveness or a focal point.

polarization: 1. the treatment of a light beam so that all waves oscillate in parallel to a single axis. 2. the state of concentration of electrical energy at one pole. 3. in neurons, an equilibrium of ions across the cell membrane.

polar opposites: two diametrically opposed items—as, for example, behavior patterns.

poll: 1. an opinion survey. 2. a counting of a group's votes or expressions of opinion

Pollyanna mechanism: the sweet lemon philosophy or reaction that all is well despite obvious evidence to the contrary.

polyandry: condition or custom of having more than one husband; the social system under which a woman may have several husbands at the same time.

polychromatic: many-colored; having several colors.

polydactylism: having more than five fingers.

polydipsia: a pathological condition characterized by excessive drinking.

polygraph: an instrument for the simultaneous recording of a number of physiological reactions. The lie detector is a form of polygraph.

polylogia: continuous and incoherent

talking characteristic of certain mental disorders.

polymorphous perverse: (*Psychoan.*) characteristic of the sexuality of the infant satisfied by oral, anal, and masturbatory forms of eroticism that would be considered perversions in adults.

polyneuritis: simultaneous inflammation of a number of nerves.

polyopia: a pathological irregularity in the refractive mechanism of the eye resulting in the formation of more than one image on the retina.

polyphrasia: incoherent and excessive speech. *Syn.* LOGORRHEA.

polyuria: excessive urination.

pons or **pons varolii:** a swelling at the base of the brain on the underside of the medulla formed by a transverse band of fibers connecting the cerebrum with the opposite side of the cerebellum.

pooling: combining values, scores, or results and treating the combination as a single variable. Some system of weighting may be necessary prior to pooling.

popular response: a response commonly given. For example, on the Rorschach Ink Blot Test some responses to particular cards occur with a high frequency among testees and are therefore classified as *popular*.

population: the totality of all organisms in a given geographical area. In statistical studies, the population is contrasted with the sample, which is a limited number of individuals drawn from the population and presumed to be representative of it. There are statistical checks to determine whether or not the sample is truly representative of the population.

poriomania: an unmotivated, aimless desire to wander.

porphyria: an inborn metabolic disturbance of the blood accompanied by psychological disturbance.

porropsia: a pathological condition in vision in which objects look more distant than they are.

Porter's law: the principle that the critical flicker-fusion frequency increases with the logarithm of stimulus brightness and is independent of stimulus wavelength. *Syn.* FERRY-PORTER LAW.

Porteus Maze Test: an individual performance test of intelligence useful from age three and over, consisting of a graded series of paper mazes, and leaning heavily on foresight and spatial judgment.

position: 1. the spatial location of an object in reference to an observer or to other objects. 2. the social standing of an individual in a group or the standing of an animal in a hierarchy of dominance. 3. a theoretical statement or attitude taken in regard to a problem. 4. a region of a life space in which an object or event takes place.

position factor: the influence of stimulus position upon the outcome of the response. Because animals tend to build up position habits, the spatial location of stimuli must be carefully controlled. See POSITION HABIT.

position habit: a tendency to go to a certain place or side in a discrimination apparatus.

position response: (*Rorschach*) a response determined by the position of a segment of the inkblot associated with a similar position of something in the environment. Thus, a feature at the top of the blot might be reported as a head because it is at the top.

positive: 1. in mathematics, a number or symbol having a plus (+) sign; not negative, and greater than zero. 2. confident; strongly affirmative. 3. unqualified, as a *positive statement*. 4. oriented in a certain way in space or having a certain attitudinal orientation. The phrase "the power of positive thinking" illustrates the latter usage; the moth's positive tropism toward light illustrates the former.

positive acceleration: an increasing rate of change in a function with time or practice.

positive afterimage: see AFTERIMAGE.

positive correlation: see CORRELATION COEFFICIENT.

positive feedback: a type of feedback in which more output is demanded as input increases. *Contr.* NEGATIVE FEEDBACK.

positive fixation: the preferential learning of a response or a mode of response because it is reinforced.

positive induction: a decrease in inhibition in a neural system due to the influence of preceding stimulation. *Contr.* negative induction.

positive-negative conflict: see APPROACH-AVOIDANCE CONFLICT.

positive-positive conflict: see APPROACH-APPROACH CONFLICT.

positive reward: a reward. The term *positive* is redundant except to emphasize that negative rewards are not employed.

positive transfer: see TRANSFER.

positive tropism: an orienting reaction that moves the organism toward the source of stimulation.

positivism: the philosophical and scientific position that knowledge is limited to experience and to observed facts and that metaphysical questions concerning the nature of ultimate reality are outside the scope of science or philosophy. Positivism in psychology is associated with a strongly behavioristic outlook with emphasis on environmentalism, reductionism, analysis, and rejection of mind and mentalistic concepts.

possessive instinct: (*Psychoan.*) the drive for power; the urge to dominate the love object. The earliest manifestations of the possessive instincts are in sucking and swallowing.

possessiveness: a tendency on the part of a parent or spouse to maintain an overprotective attitude and to exert excessive control.

postconventional stage of moral development: the stage in which the individual defines moral values in relation to their situational application rather than in terms of the dictates of social groups, institutions, or tradition.

posterior: at the rear of the body or to the rear of an organ. *Contr.* ANTERIOR.

posterior root: the rear or dorsal root of the spinal cord. The posterior roots are sensory in function. *Syn.* dorsal root; *Contr.* ventral root.

posthypnotic amnesia: the subject's inability to remember in the waking state what took place during the hypnotic state.

posthypnotic suggestion: a suggestion given to a subject while under hypnosis to the effect that he will behave in a certain way after awakening. The subject typically carries out the suggestion without knowing why and then attempts to rationalize his behavior.

postnatal: occurring after birth. *Contr.* PRENATAL.

post partum: after birth; a term used to characterize normal or pathological conditions following childbirth.

post partum depression (psychosis): a period of depression, usually of short duration, following the birth of a child.

postpubertal: the period immediately following puberty.

postremity principle: the principle that the last act carried out by an organism in a learning situation is the most probable thing that organism will do upon being presented with a repetition of the situation. See also GUTHRIE'S CONTIGUOUS CONDITIONING.

postrotational nystagmus: nystagmus induced after cessation of rapid rotation of the body.

postsynaptic inhibition: direct inhibition or the hyperpolarization of a neuron.

post traumatic amnesia: see ANTEROGRADE AMNESIA.

post traumatic disorders (syndrome): patterns of symptoms involving anxiety reactions, tensions, nightmares, and depression following a disaster such as a earthquake or tornado.

postulate: a fundamental principle or assumption that is taken to be true or is provisionally adopted as a link in a chain of reasoning. Postulates are to be distinguished from axioms and hypotheses. The axiom is held to be a self-evident truth. The hypothesis is a statement of a conclusion to be tested by experimental procedures. For an example of the use of postulates in psychology. See HULL'S MATHEMATICO-DEDUCTIVE THEORY OF LEARNING.

postural: pertaining to posture or the position of the body or the attitude of its members.

postural reflexes: the reflexes associated with the maintenance of posture.

postural set: a muscular adjustment that readies the individual to respond in a certain way. The runner's crouch at the starting line illustrates this type of set.

potency: 1. power, particularly latent power. 2. the power of reproduction in the male. 3. the capability of the male to perform the sex act and to achieve ejaculation.

potential: 1. characterized by potency. 2. having latent ability to perform or behave in some way, particularly in a way involving talent or intelligence. 3. in neurons a difference in electrical charge between a reference point and a point of measurement or recording.

potentiality: the characteristic of possessing a latent ability or power to behave in a certain manner in the future.

power: 1. in mathematics, the product of a number multiplied by itself one or more times; the superscript to show how many times a number is to be multiplied by itself. 2. muscular strength. 3. ability or the degree to which an individual possesses a trait. 4. the degree to which a lens magnifies objects. 5. ability or authority to control others; social power.

power factor: an intellectual factor that serves as an energizer or other intellectual factors.

power figure: an individual who represents a high degree of authority.

power function: in statistics, an index of whether or not a hypothesis should be rejected at a given level of risk.

power law: (*Stevens*) the relationship between stimulus magnitude and judged sensory magnitude where the magnitude of sensation varies as the intensity of the stimulus raised to a certain power, the exponent depending upon the sense modality in question.

power spectrum: in audition, a graphic representation of the mean square amplitude of a sound wave.

power test: a test designed to measure the level the individual can attain. On power tests the items are arranged in increasing order of difficulty and there is less emphasis on time limits than in speed tests.

practice: 1. the repetition of an act or behavior function for the purpose of improving the function. 2. that which is customary or typical. 3. that which is habitual.

practice curve: a graphic representation of the progress of learning where success or errors are plotted on the vertical axis and trials on the horizontal axis.

practice effect: any change following practice.

practice limit: the upper limit of improvement attainable by practice.

practice material: several items or problems given before a test or experimental run to allow the subject to become used to the nature of the task.

practice period: 1. an interval of time in which practice occurs. 2. a preliminary period in which the individual is given an opportunity to familiarize himself with the task.

practice theory of play: the theory that the child's play prepares him for an adult role.

pragmatic: practical or concrete; concerned with results rather than theory.

pragmatism: the doctrine that the meaning or truth of anything is found in its consequences in action. *Syn.* instrumentalism.

Prägnanz: (*Gestalt psychology*) tendency for forms to assume the best possible shape or figure. The figure tends toward meaningfulness, completeness, and simplicity.

prandial: characterizing drinking by

animals with lesions in the lateral hypothalamus whose water intake is confined to washing down dry food.

praxernia: (*R. B. Cattell*) a personality dimension associated with practical, conforming behavior. *Contr.* AUTIA.

preadolescence: a variable period typically considered to be the two years before the onset of puberty, or approximately the period 10–12 years of age.

precision alternative: (*Rorschach*) a second response to a blot offered by the subject as though it were intended to be a more precise interpretation.

precision, index of: a measure of the degree of closeness with which a series of measures clusters about the mean. *Sym. h.* The formula is:

$$h = \frac{l}{\sigma\sqrt{2}}$$

precision, law of: in Gestalt psychology, a general law of perception according to which percepts (and by extension memories and behavior in general) become organized into well-articulated, regular, and symmetrical forms. See also PRÄGNANZ.

precocity: unusually early development of a function.

precoding: the assigning of code symbols to data, particularly on questionnaires where numbers are often assigned for recording possible alternative answers. Precoding makes the tabulation of data much simpler than it otherwise would be.

precognition: in parapsychology, the knowledge of an event in the future that could not be known by any rational avenue.

preconception: a viewpoint, frame

of reference, or conclusion arrived at before the facts are in.

preconditioning: the repeated presentation of two arbitrary stimuli without reinforcement, following which the animal is conditioned to respond to one of the stimuli in the usual manner. If the animal shows conditioning to the second stimulus without reinforcement, preconditioning is said to have occurred.

preconscious: (*Psychoan.*) that which is not in consciousness but can be recalled without special techniques. *Syn.* foreconscious. *Contr.* UNCONSCIOUS. See also SUBCONSCIOUS.

predelay reinforcement: an experimental arrangement in which the animal is rewarded in a certain place and then made to delay before being released to see if he can return to the appropriate place.

predicate thinking: a type of thinking in which objects are considered identical only because they resemble each other in some way.

predication: 1. the association of one concept with another. 2. the attribution of certain characteristics to the subject of a proposition.

predictability: the state or quality of being predictable or subject to prediction. See PREDICTION.

prediction: a statement about an event with respect to its future outcome. Predicions are usually cast into quantitative form as probabilities with a certain degree of certainty. In test design, the predictive value of a test is directly related to its validity coefficient, which is a measure of its predictive value.

predictive efficiency: the actual measure or proportion of correct predictions that a test or other predictive device is capable of making.

predictive index: see FORECASTING EFFICIENCY, INDEX OF.

predictive validity: the degree to which a test measures what it was designed to measure, as determined by actually correlating it with an independent sample of behavior. For the test to be valid, those who succeed on the test must succeed on the behavior sample. An example of predictive validity would involve the design of a test to predict performance in school. If all or a representative group of the individuals who have taken a specific test are allowed to go on to school and have their grades correlated with their test standing, the validity of the test can be assessed directly by the magnitude of the correlation coefficient.

predictive value: the validity of a test or measure.

predisposing cause: any factor that although not the direct cause of an event, ensures that the event is more likely to occur in its presence than in its absence. The term is used primarily to refer to diseases or hereditary characteristics.

predisposition: any hereditary characteristic favoring the development of a certain trait.

preemptive construct: (*Kelly*) the "nothing but" type of construct (*q.v.*), which preempts its elements for exclusive use in its own realm.

preference: 1. a selection or choice of stimuli, pathways, modes of behavior, etc. 2. a liking for one thing above others.

preference method: a research technique in which two or more stimuli are presented for the subject to choose from. The method applies to choices of foods by animals, artistic preferences, and vocational preferences as measured by verbal tests.

preference test: see KUDER PREFERENCE RECORD; STRONG VOCATIONAL INTEREST BLANK.

preformism: the doctrine that the various characteristics of the individual are already present in the germ plasm and that development consists of the unfolding of these characteristics.

prefrontal: pertaining to that portion of the frontal lobes ahead of the precentral gyrus or primary motor area.

prefrontal leucotomy or **lobotomy:** the surgical transection of the fiber tracts connecting the frontal areas to the thalamus and hypothalamus. The operation has been used to alleviate psychotic symptoms but has now been superseded by tranquilizers.

prefrontal lobectomy: the surgical ablation of the prefrontal areas.

pregenital state or **phase:** (*Psychoan.*) the infantile period preceding the genital phase; the pregenital state is one during which the libido seeks satisfaction from the anal and oral regions.

pregnance: see PRÄGNANZ.

pregnant: 1. pertaining to the state of pregnancy. 2. pertaining to figures or Gestalts that show the characteristic of *Prägnanz*.

prehensile: having the requisite structure and ability for grasping objects.

prehension: 1. grasping, as in picking up an object. 2. grasping, in a mental sense; mental apprehension.

prejudice: 1. an attitude, either positive or negative, formulated in advance of sufficient evidence and held with emotional tenacity. 2. a belief or judgment, usually unfavorable, predisposing the individual to behave in a certain way or to think in a certain way toward others. *Syn.* BIAS.

preliterate: nonliterate, as in reference to a culture or society without a written or recorded language.

prelogical thinking: thinking that does not follow the rules of logic but may have a logic of its own. Sometimes observed in children and adult psychotics.

Premack principle: given two responses that differ in the probability of occurrence, the less probable can be reinforced by using the more probable as a reward.

premature: characteristic of an infant born weighing less than five pounds or that is less than 270 days of conceptual age at delivery.

premeditation: in forensic psychology and law, the deliberate planning of a crime, especially murder.

premise: a proposition from which a conclusion is drawn.

premsia: (*R. B. Cattell*) a personality dimension associated with emotional sensitivity, dependence, lack of aggressiveness, and tender-mindedness.

prenatal: prior to birth.

prenatal influence: any influence affecting the fetus prior to birth. For example, smoking on the part of the mother increases fetal heart rate. Prenatal influences are not to be confused with the discredited doctrine of *maternal impression*, which held that the mother could transmit the results of her experiences to the fetus.

prenubile: 1. before puberty. 2. nonmarriagable because of immaturity.

pre-Oedipal: pertaining to the stage of development before the onset of the Oedipus complex, or the child's

sexual attraction for the parent of the opposite sex.

preoperational stage: (*Piaget*) the stage in the child's development occurring from the second to the seventh year during which he learns to thing symbolically and can encounter reality on a representational level. See also CONCRETE OPERATIONAL STAGE; FORMAL OPERATIONAL STAGE; SENSORI-MOTOR STAGE.

preparation: 1. the first part of an act; a readiness. 2. the first stage in creative thinking in which the individual ''loads up,'' that is, obtains all the information he can and makes tentative attempts to solve the problem. 3. an animal that has been subjected to surgical procedures for experimental purposes. See also INCUBATION; ILLUMINATION; VERIFICATION.

preparatory interval: the time between a ready signal and the actual presentation of the stimulus.

preparatory response: any response not immediately goal-directed or that does not obtain a reward.

preparatory set: readiness to react or respond in a certain manner.

preperception: 1. the anticipatory state just prior to perception which may include imagery in anticipation of the oncoming stimulus. 2. perceptual set, or a readiness to perceive one's environment in a certain way.

prepotent reflex: a reflex, particularly a protective reflex, that takes precedence over other reflexes. The phrase is now little used. It was formerly substituted for the term *instinct* by strongly behavioristic psychologists.

prepotent response: any response that takes precedence over other responses.

prepotent stimulus: any stimulus tending to prevail over all other stimuli present.

prepsychotic: pertaining to states in which the individual is behaving in such a manner as to indicate the approach of a psychosis.

prepubertal: pertaining to the period before puberty, typically the one or two years before puberty is intended. *Syn.* PREADOLESCENT.

prepyriform area: the projection area for olfaction located at the base of the brain.

prerecognition hypothesis: an inferred and unverbalized expectancy of what is about to occur.

presbyophrenia: senile psychosis combined with serious memory defects but with a relatively high level of mental alertness.

presbyopia: a visual defect common in old age. There is failure of accommodation due to hardening of the lens, and near vision is affected more than distant vision. The condition is correctable with bifocal lenses.

preschool: 1. characterizing the period of the child's life prior to entrance into formal schooling. 2. designating a form of kindergarten.

presentation: 1. placing stimuli or tasks before the subject. 2. more specifically, the systematic placing of stimuli before a subject in a series of experimental trials in learning situations. 3. that which is used in an experiment; the stimuli.

press (plural **press** or **presses**): (*Murray*) an environmental object or event that has significance for the individual. A thunderstorm for an anxious child may constitute a press of significance.

press-need pattern: (*Murray*) the relationship between needs (motives) and environmental situations that lead to attempts to satisfy need conditions. Thus, the child may perceive the father as an authoritarian figure to be placated. The father is a press, the need is for affiliation with the father. The behavior of the child in attempting to win the father's approval by any and all means is the need-press pattern.

pressure: 1. pressure sensation (*q.v.*). 2. the proposing of significant considerations in an attempt to force an individual to act whether he wishes to or not.

pressure balance: 1. a device used in tests of pressure sensitivity for controlling the amount of pressure to the surface of the body. 2. an instrument for testing judgments of lifted weights.

pressure gradient: the gradual diminution of pressure from the point of stimulation outward when a stimulus object is placed against the skin.

pressure sensation: a sense modality aroused by relatively intense mechanical deformation of the skin and by tension in muscles, tendons, and joints. The receptors are believed to be Pacinian corpuscles. Distinctions are sometimes made between light pressure and deep pressure. It is likely that contact or touch may sometimes be confused in the literature with light pressure, whereas the terms *deep pressure* and simply *pressure* imply relatively intense stimulation.

pressure spot: any spot on the surface of the body with a relatively low threshold for pressure.

prestige: a condition of being held in high regard or esteem by one's colleagues or by the community in general.

prestige motive: the desire to attain prestige or position in the community of one's colleagues or in general.

prestige suggestion: the use of opinions from persons held in high regard in order to influence other individuals. Prestige suggestions are frequently used in advertising campaigns.

prestriate: parts of the brain that are anterior to the striate area located at the extreme rear of the occipital lobe.

presupposition: a postulate or assumption.

pretectal area: centers in the posterior part of the forebrain that control the iris and ciliary body.

pretend: to feign or sham, as in pretending to be ill. 2. to imagine vividly, as in children's play. *Syn.* make believe.

pretest: 1. a practice test to allow subjects to become familiar with the procedures to be used during an experiment. 2. a preliminary series of trials for the purpose of establishing a standard or baseline. The scores obtained after the experimental variable has been administered can then be subtracted from the results of the pretest and the difference is the result of the independent variable.

preverbal construct: 1. a concept, without a verbal symbol, which may have been developed before the ability to speak but is continued in use. 2. (*Kelly*) a construct (*q.v.*) that can be employed but not verbalized. *Contr.* VERBAL CONSTRUCT.

priapism: 1. persistent state of erection of the penis unaccompanied by sexual desire. 2. satyriasis.

primacy: the state or condition of being first in any respect.

primacy, law of: the principle that the first of a series of learned acts will be remembered better than others.

primal anxiety: (*Psychoan.*) the anxiety associated with the separation of the infant from the mother and with the flooding of the infant's immature nervous system with stimuli immedi-

ately after birth. According to Freud, primal anxiety is the basis of all other types of anxiety.

primal-horde stage: a hypothetical stage in human development when the group consisted of a dominant male, his females, and subordinate males.

primal scene: (*Psychoan.*) fragmentary recollections from early childhood based on real or imagined experiences of seduction or observation of parental intercourse. The recollections and fantasies make up the elements of the neurosis.

primal trauma: (*Psychoan.*) an event in the early life of the child that is extremely painful psychologically and impresses permanent harm on the individual. The birth trauma is an example. Witnessing the parents perform intercourse is another example.

primary: 1. first in time. 2. first in importance. 3. fundamental, such as a *primary* color or taste quality.

primary amentia: hereditary feeble-mindedness.

primary attention: attention without effort or strain, such as attending to strong or compelling stimuli; involuntary attention.

primary circular reaction: (*Piaget*) the early, repetitive actions of infancy.

primary color: see COLOR PRIMARY.

primary data: data as originally obtained or collected.

primary drive: a drive that is universal in any given species, unlearned in its arousal aspect, and for which there is an organic basis. *Contr.* ACQUIRED DRIVE.

primary emotion: the affective process associated with instincts.

primary factor: in centroid factor analysis, a factor that shows simple structure. See also SIMPLE STRUCTURE.

primary gain: a direct gain secured from being ill, such as an excuse from work. *Contr.* SECONDARY GAIN.

primary group: a face-to-face group in intimate association, such as the family or a small club. The primary group exerts an enduring influence on the individual.

primary hue: a primary color.

primary identification: (*Psychoan.*) the identification of the child with the parents, particularly with the parent of the same sex.

primary integration: (*Psychoan.*) the recognition by the child that his body is something distinct from the environment.

primary mental abilities: the fundamental or basic abilities that make up intelligence. The best-known list of primary abilities is that based on the factor analytic work of L. L. Thurstone. They are: Verbal (V); Word Fluency (WF); Numerical (N); Space (S); Memory (M); Perceptual (P); Reasoning (R). Each of these is defined under its appropriate entry.

primary mental deficiency: subnormality in intelligence resulting from genetic deficiencies.

primary motivation: motivation arising from unlearned bodily needs, such as the hunger, thirst, and sex needs. Primary motives are also defined as universal in the species and unlearned as to origin. However, they may be, and typically are, considerably modified by learning in respect to manner of satisfaction. *Contr.* SECONDARY MOTIVATION.

primary narcissism: (*Psychoan.*) in the early stage of development in which the infant's libido is directed toward his own body.

primary need: a basic, unlearned need that is biologically determined.

Hunger and thirst exemplify such needs. However, it is recognized by psychologists that primary needs and the drives to which they give rise may be modified by learning.

primary personality: the original personality as compared to the *secondary personality*, which is the split-off aspect of a multiple personality.

primary position: the position assumed by the eyes when the individual is standing with head erect and fixating on a point infinitely distant.

primary process: (*Psychoan.*) the process in the id by means of which direct satisfaction of libidinal or other instinctual wishes is obtained. *Contr.* SECONDARY PROCESS.

primary quality: a fundamental or basic property indispensable to the perceptual existence of an object. Thus, the moon's yellowness is not primary, since the moon can exist in perception without it; but the moon's spatiality is basic, since without it the moon could not exist. The philosopher John Locke was the first to distinguish between primary and secondary qualities in formulating his empirical theory of perception. *Contr.* SECONDARY QUALITY.

primary reinforcement: 1. any stimulus that increases the probability of a response without the necessity of learning the value of the reinforcer. Thus, food is a primary reinforcer. By way of contrast, a poker chip may serve as a secondary reinforcer but only if it is associated with the possibility of obtaining a reward (*primary reinforcer*) through learning. 2. the reduction of a primary-drive state; drive-stimulus reduction.

primary repression: (*Psychoan.*) the denial or re-entry into consciousness of any mental content that would arouse feelings of guilt and anxiety. *Contr*. SECONDARY REPRESSION.

primary reward: any reward, such as food, whose satisfying nature does not have to be learned.

primary zone: (*Psychoan*.) the zone at a given stage of development that gives greatest satisfaction to the libido.

primary stimulus generalization; see STIMULUS GENERALIZATION.

primate: the highest order of the mammals, including the monkey, the ape, and man.

primipara: a female who has borne offspring only once. *Contr*. multipara.

primitive: 1. pertaining to the earliest stages of development in a given species, particularly man. 2. characterizing peoples who have no written history or are not literate. 3. crude, undeveloped.

primitivization: regression; a return to levels of behavior more appropriate at an earlier age.

primordial; primary; first in order.

primordial image (*Jung*) an archetypal idea; an experience in the unconscious derived from the racial unconscious.

principal-component method: a factor-analysis method that locates one axis, called the major principal axis, in such a way that it defines a factor accounting for the maximum variance in the correlation matrix. Another factor, the minor principal axis, located at right angles, or orthogonal, to the first, accounts for the maximum possible portion of the remaining variance.

principal focus: the point in an optical system at which parallel rays converge after passing through the system.

principal plane: a plane at right angles to a lens or optical system.

principle: 1. a working hypothesis or

a maxim for conduct or for scientific investigation. 2. a fundamental law or uniformity of nature. 3. the active ingredient in a substance that causes its characteristic reaction.

principle of inertia: (*Psychoan*.) a fixation; a need to repeat something over and over again.

prior entry, law of: the displacement of simultaneous impressions in such a way that the stimulus that is actively attended will seem to have been presented sooner than the one not actively attended.

prism: a triangular lens with the property of refracting or bending light passing through it in such a way as to separate the various component wavelengths. The result is the spectrum, or band of colors.

prisoner's dilemma: a game situation in which the participants may cooperate or compete and whose outcome is dependent upon the choice made by the other party. The game is based on the classic detective situation in which two suspects are questioned separately and may either confess or not confess, thereby implicating or not implicating each other.

private: 1. pertaining to a single individual as contrasted with a group. 2. that which belongs to an individual, as opposed to a group or an institution. 3. subjective or open only to individual impression or inspection.

privation: condition of lacking a specific satisfaction or the means to satisfy needs.

privileged communication: a therapeutic, medical, or legal document or recorded statement not open to public inspection.

proactive: any stimulus, particularly verbal material, that affects the memory or learning of a subsequent process.

Contr. RETROACTIVE. Proactive is usually used jointly with the concept of inhibition to refer to learning situations where materials given to the subject prior to subsequent learning interfere with that learning.

proactive inhibition: the interference effect of earlier learning on retention of later learning. The experimental test model to measure proactive inhibition is as follows:

ing the expected frequency of occurrence of a variable. 2. the normal probability curve.

probability function: the mathematical function whose graph is represented in the normal probability curve.

probability integral: 1. the integral of the probability function. 2. the cases falling between two given abscissa values on the normal probability curve.

(Equated Groups)			
Group I	Learn A	Learn B	Recall B
Group II	Rest	Learn B	Recall B
		Difference in Recall of B = PI	

probabilism: the position that it is possible to make predictions on the basis of rational and empirical data. Probabilism does not assume a perfect determinism or one-to-one correspondence between cause and event, but rather assumes that within the limits of mathematical probability one may make valid predictions.

probabilistic functionalism: the theoretical point of view that behavior is best understood in terms of the probability of success in dealing with goals. Thus, our perceptual constancies depend on our having built up strong expectancies that objects have definite shapes, colors, sizes, etc.

probability: 1. in mathematics, the degree to which it is likely that an event will occur in a certain way as opposed to other possible ways. Thus, the likelihood of picking one specific playing card out of a deck is one in 52. 2. the quality or state of being probable or likely of occurrence. 3. the science of probability or probability theory.

probability curve: 1. any curve show-

probability of response: the frequency of occurrence of a response relative to the theoretical maximum frequency of occurrence of that response or class of responses under a given set of conditions.

probability ratio: the ratio obtained by dividing the number of ways an event could occur by the total number of possible events, assuming that all occurrences of the event have an equal chance of occurring.

probability table: a table giving the frequency with which a variable is likely to occur under certain specified conditions.

probability theory: that branch of mathematics dealing with probability. Probability theory is based on certain assumptions regarding the uniformity of nature, laws of change, equality of opportunity of occurrence of certain events, and complementary errors canceling each other out if sufficient observations occur.

probable error: an index of the reliability of an obtained measure in terms of the extent to which the obtained values deviate from the mean of the measure in question. *Abbr*. P.E. or PE. The probable error is equal to .6745 of the standard error. In a normal distribution, half of the deviations from the mean fall within ± 1 PE.

proband: see INDEX CASE.

probing technique: in short-term memory, the presentation of a series of items, one of which must be recalled. The subject does not know which item will be tested for recall when the initial presentation is made. *Contr*. DISTRACTOR TECHNIQUE.

problem: 1. a mathematical statement requiring the solution of an unknown. 2. any situation in which there is a novel or unknown characteristic to be ascertained.

problematic; problematical: pertaining to a problem or to a situation wherein the outcome is uncertain.

problem behavior: behavior that is perplexing, antisocial, maladjustive, or destructive.

problem box: a box that must be opened in order to obtain a reward. Problem boxes are typically fastened with intricate devices that require a good deal of trial and error to solve.

problem checklist: a list of problem situations in the area of personality and adjustment, with blank spaces in which the individual is required to check those situations that pertain to him.

problem child: a child whose behavior deviates so widely from acceptable standards that special techniques must be used in dealing with him.

problem solving: the process involved in discovering the correct sequence of alternatives leading to a goal or to an ideational solution.

proceeding: (*Murray*) a single or limited motivated pattern of behavior

involving a subject and object, or subject and another person. See also MURRAY'S PERSONOLOGY.

process: 1. any change in an object or organism, particularly a behavioral or physiological change. 2. the manner in which a change in an organism or a response is brought about. 3. (*Titchener*) a sensation or other conscious content without reference to its context or meaning. 4. a projection or outgrowth from an organ or cell.

process attitude: in introspective studies, an attitude in which the observer attends to the conscious processes—sensations, feelings, images—and describes them. *Contr*. OBJECT ATTITUDE.

processing error: an error that occurs during the recording or analysis of data.

process schizophrenia: chronic schizophrenia.

prodigy: an exceptionally gifted child, either intellectually or artistically.

prodrome: a preliminary or warning symptom of an oncoming disorder.

productive memory: a kind of creative memory wherein objects or events are put together although they did not originally occur together.

productive memory: a kind of creative memory wherein objects or events are put together although they did not originally occur together.

productiveness: the quality of being creative or of accomplishing a great deal in terms of research, publication, etc.

product matrix: the result obtained when factor loadings are multiplied.

product moment: in correlation technique, the deviations from the means of the variables raised to a power, multiplied, and summated.

product-moment correlation: the most common technique for the computation of the coefficient of correlation. *Sym.* r. The formula is:

$$rxy = \frac{\Sigma(xy)}{N\sigma x \sigma y \sigma}$$

products: (*Guilford*) one of three basic dimensions of intelligence. The other two are contents and operations. Products involve the result of operations on the content of problems.

product scale: a type of ordinal scale consisting of concrete products or performance samples against which an unknown is judged. For example, a series of pictures might be utilized as a scale against which to judge the artistic merit of an unknown work.

proficiency: an ability or skill of high degree. See also ABILITY.

profile: a graphic representation of scores by means of a curved line or a series of histograms or bars.

profile analysis: an appraisal of the individual in which his pattern of abilities or personality traits is reported in relation to a set of norms or standards.

profile chart: see PROFILE; PROFILE ANALYSIS.

progeria: dwarfism combined with premature senility.

prognosis: the prediction of the outcome of a disease or mental disorder. Some indication of its expected duration, severity, and probable final status is part of the prognosis.

prognostic test: a test designed to predict the outcome of training or education for a given skill.

programming: the preparation of tapes, cards or other devices to be fed into a computing machine. Typically, programming consists of supplying information relative to the kind of operation wanted, the actual data to be computed, and the sequence of operations, if the latter are complex. For many of the more frequently used statistical operations, prepared tapes are available to ''instruct'' the machine.

progression: 1. locomotion—walking, running, crawling. 2. a mathematical series in which each term bears a constant relation to the preceding. For example, 2, 4, 6, 8, 10, 12, etc., is a simple progression.

progression, law of: the principle that successive increments of sensation increase by arithmetical progression as the corresponding stimulus increments increase by geometric progression. It is a substitute for Weber's law (*q.v.*).

progressive relaxation: a psychotherapeutic technique that involves teaching the individual to achieve a state of relaxation and well-being by gradually allowing his muscles to relax.

progressive total: a cumulative total.

projection: 1. attributing one's own traits, attitudes, or faults to others. 2. in anatomy, a protuberance or jutting out. 3. a prediction beyond the given data. 4. perceiving one's personality traits, needs, desires, goals, etc. in unstructured stimuli, such as in inkblots. 5. in factor-analytic studies, the plotting of the factor loadings on a sphere. 6. in the cerebral cortex, the spatial spread of sensory fibers as they stream up from the spinal cord.

projection fibers: the neurons leading into the cortical areas that mediate sensory experiences.

projective play: play in which the child, with materials such as a set of dolls and a toy house, unconsciously exhibits attitudes and feelings that are helpful to the therapist in making a diagnosis. See also PLAY THERAPY.

projective technique: the utilization of vague, ambiguous, unstructured stimulus objects or situations in order to elicit the individual's characteristic modes of perceiving his world or of behaving in it. The most commonly used techniques are the Rorschach Ink Blot Test, consisting of ten ink-blots the subject must interpret; the Murray Thematic Apperception Test, which consists of a series of pictures about which the subject must tell a story; and various forms of play in which the child's behavior is observed as he plays with dolls, dollhouses, or other materials.

projective test: see PROJECTIVE TECHNIQUE.

prolactin: a pituitary hormone that stimulates the secretion of milk.

proliferation: a multiplication, particularly of cells or tissues.

Promethean will: (*R. B. Cattell*) a factor trait characterized by irreverence, aggressiveness, resourcefulness, determination, and egotism.

prompting method: in verbal learning, a procedure in which the rate of learning is measured by the number of prompts necessary to achieve perfect mastery of a list. As the lists are gone through, the experimenter prompts the subject whenever he cannot give the expected response.

pronation: a movement of the hand (or forelimb) so that the hand is oriented downward.

proof: evidence supporting belief. Proof may be of the inductive variety (reasoning from the specific to the general) or the deductive variety (reasoning from the general to the specific).

proofreader's illusion: an illusion of visual perception in which an omitted letter, transposition, or omission is not noticed because of the compelling effect of habit.

propaedeutic task: a task used as an aid in teaching the mentally retarded. For example, the child might be given the task of drawing lines before undertaking the drawing of a triangle.

propaganda: the organized attempt to influence the attitudes and opinions of others.

propaganda analysis: the investigation of the effectiveness of propaganda by the study of its techniques, materials, and appeals.

propagandize: to engage in a deliberate attempt to influence the attitudes and opinions of others.

propagation: 1. reproduction. 2. the transmission of a nervous impulse. 3. the dissemination of information.

propanediols: a group of antianxiety drugs.

propensity: a strong, persistent tendency toward a certain type of action. Propensities may arise from hereditary sources or from habit.

prophecy formula: any formula employed for the estimation of scores to be obtained on some future measurement.

proportion: 1. the ratio of one magnitude or value to another. 2. balance, especially pleasing or artistic balance.

proportionality: in factor analysis, the requirement that any two columns of correlation coefficients must be in direct proportion if a two-factor pattern is to be assumed for that series of tests.

proposition: a verbal or symbolic statement of a judgment that remains to be tested.

propositional construct: (*Kelly*) a

construct (*q.v.*) that does not prevent other constructs from applying to it.

propositional speech: speech in which new meaning is given by the relationship among the words and is not merely the effect of the additive position of the words.

propriate: (*Allport*) characterizing a form of striving that is self-directed and originates out of the self. Propriate striving does not wait upon favorable circumstances but attempts to forge its own circumstances.

proprioception: the sense of the position of the body and of the movement of the body and its limbs. See PROPRIOCEPTOR.

proprioceptive: pertaining to reflexes associated with the proprioceptors, particularly reflexes involved in the movement and placing of limbs.

proprioceptor: any receptor that mediates proprioception. The chief receptors of the proprioceptive sense are: (1) Pacinian corpuscles, responsive to deep pressure; (2) muscle spindles, responsive to muscle stretch; (3) Golgi tendon organs, responsive to muscle stretch; (4) the receptors of movement and balance in the nonauditory labyrinth.

proprium: (*Allport*) the aspects of personality forming the integrated unity that constitutes the individual's uniqueness and sense of individuality.

prosocial behavior: see ALTRUISM.

prostration: extreme exhaustion to the point where many reflexes are abolished.

protanomaly: a form of color vision in which there is diminished sensitivity to the red end of the spectrum.

protanopia: a form of red-green color-blindness in which reds are confused with blue-greens and the red end of the spectrum appears darkened (red appears as a very dark gray).

protective response or **reflex:** a movement designed to rid the organism of a painful or noxious stimulus.

protension: (*R. B. Cattell*) suspiciousness, jealousy, and rigidity in defense.

protensity: the attribute of a mental process characterized by its temporality or stretching forward in time.

prothetic continuum: a psychophysical scale involving the quantity of stimulation (brightness, loudness) involved.

protocol: the original notes or records of an experiment.

protopathic: (*Head*) pertaining to sensitivity, such as extreme temperature sensation and pain which, according to Head, are relatively cruder than epicritic sensitivity, which involves tactile discrimination, light touch, and warm and cool discrimination.

protoplasm: the fluidlike substance of which the interiors of cells are composed.

prototaxic: pertaining to modes of experience in which events are apprehended as unrelated and external events are only dimly perceived and are organized only in a primitive manner. Characteristic of the minds of infants and of deeply psychotic adults.

prototype: a primitive or early form of anything.

proverbs test: an item in which the testee is asked to explain the meaning of a proverb.

provisional try: the behavior of an animal seeking to find the route to a goal. The concept is similar to trial-and-error behavior.

proxemics: the investigation of spatial factors such as seating arrangements and distance in interpersonal interactions.

proximal: 1. near a point of reference or close to the central axis of the body. 2. contiguous; touching.

proximal response: an immediate muscular or glandular reaction. *Contr.* DISTAL RESPONSE.

proximal stimulus: a stimulus that impinges upon a receptor and makes it active. *Contr.* DISTAL STIMULUS.

proximity, principle of: the principle of Gestalt psychology that, other things being equal, those objects in perception that are close together will be perceived as a unity.

proximo-distal trend: a developmental trend in which functions close to the central axis of the body develop earlier than those farther out on the periphery.

prudery; prudishness: an exaggerated concern over conformity to the moral code, manifested as avoidance of bodily display, shrinking from sexual encounters, and an excessively moral attitude.

pseudesthesia: a false or illusory sensation, such as the illusion of irritation in an amputated limb.

pseudo angina: a functional attack of pain in the chest resembling a true heart attack.

pseudochromesthesia: the eliciting of a color sensation by a tone. *Syn.* CHROMESTHESIA.

pseudo conditioning: the elicitation of a response to a neutral stimulus by presenting that stimulus after a conditioning series involving a different conditioned stimulus. Apparently the conditioning series sensitizes the subject to respond. Some authorities consider it a process of reflex sensitization in cases where reflexes are involved.

pseudocyesis: false pregnancy; belief on the part of a woman that she is pregnant when she is not.

pseudomentia: an extreme condition of low motivation and apathy but without deterioration of judgment and intelligence.

pseudofovea: an area of maximal distinctness of vision that may develop in cases of blindness in one half of the visual field

pseudo-isochromatic charts: plates for testing color vision. The plates are composed of a series of dots of random saturation and brightness but with a pattern (number or letter) formed by contrasting hues. The color-blind cannot, of course, recognize hues, and therefore cannot see the figure, which is easily visible to the normal eye.

pseudolalia: meaningless speech sounds.

pseudomemory: a false memory.

pseudomnesia: a severe or pathological form of false memory.

pseudophone: a device developed by P. T. Young for transmitting sounds that normally arrive at the right ear into the left ear and vice versa. The device was formerly used for studying sound localization.

pseudopsychology: any unscientific system, such as graphology, palmistry, or phrenology, that pretends to discover psychological information but whose means are unscientific or deliberately fraudulent.

pseudoscope: an optical system for transposing the visual images to the eyes. The solidity of objects is also affected so that solid objects seem hollow and an incised figure appears to be a bas relief.

psi: in parapsychology, the mental processes involved in telepathy that cannot be accounted for on the basis of natural laws.

psilocybin: a hallucinogenic substance, extracted from a Mexican mushroom, which produces psychotic states.

psopholalia: unintelligible speech.

psychasthenia: (*Janet*) a type of neurosis characterized by anxiety reactions, obsessions, and fixed ideas. The term is now considered obsolete.

psyche: 1. the principle of life. 2. the mind, including both conscious and unconscious processes. 3. the self.

psychedelic: characterizing conscious states of intensified sensory experience, distorted perceptions, hallucinations, and feelings of euphoria or depression. See also DRUGS AND BEHAVIOR.

psychiatric social worker: an individual with special training in the fields of sociology and psychology who, in close collaboration with psychiatrists, works with mental patients and their families.

psychiatrist: a medical doctor with a specialty in abnormal psychology who is engaged in the diagnosis, treatment, and prevention of mental disorders.

psychiatry: the specialized branch of medicine dealing with the diagnosis, treatment, and prevention of mental disorders.

psychic: 1. pertaining to mind. 2. pertaining to spiritualism or the mediums who practice spiritualism. 3. pertaining to disorders that are psychogenic or psychological in origin.

psychic blindness: 1. an inability to see, because of functional or hysterical conditions. In this type of blindness the receptor system is normal. 2. inability to make simple discriminations, such as to discriminate food

from nuts and bolts, because of severe lesions in the temporal lobes.

psychic determinism: the assumption that behind every mental process, including errors, slips of the tongue, dreams, etc., there is a cause, either conscious or unconscious.

psychic impotence: 1. impotence due to psychological factors. 2. a temporary paralysis of the mental processes, resulting in an inability to perform acts ordinarily performed.

psychic isolation: (*Jung*) defense by withdrawal from social contacts. The individual is believed to be harboring a shameful or fearful secret he does not wish to reveal.

psychic research: investigation of psychological phenomena that apparently cannot be explained according to natural law.

psychic secretion: (*Pavlov*) conditioned salivation.

psychic trauma: any painful experience causing serious and lasting damage to the self or personality.

psychic vaginismus: a functional spasm of the vagina preventing coitus, caused by frigidity or fear of intercourse.

psychism: see METAPHYSICS; PARAPSYCHOLOGY.

psychoacoustics: a joint field of physics and psychology that deals with the phenomena of sound as related to audition.

psychoanalysis: a system of psychology directed toward the understanding, cure, and prevention of mental disorders. As conceived by Sigmund Freud, psychoanalysis is a dynamic system of psychology that seeks the roots of human behavior in unconscious motivation and conflict. It takes as its point of departure the concept of the *libido*, which is defined basically as sexual energy, both in its original form and as it is modified during development into all forms of love, affection, and the will to live. How sexual energy develops in the child—whether normal, or blocked and distorted into unhealthy channels—is of great significance in the individual's overall development and ability to adjust to life's problems.

In the earliest stage the libido is said to be *polymorphous perverse*, since it is fixated on several parts of the body in turn, attachments, that, if they occur in the adult, are considered perversions. The first source of satisfaction is the oral region, with pleasure being obtained from sucking, chewing, and biting. Weaning eventually interferes with this source of satisfaction, and the infant's libido is next directed toward the anal region, with satisfaction being obtained from the activities of the lower bowel and from playing with feces, a stage of infantile development known as the *anal erotic stage*. Anal eroticism is eventually frustrated by toilet training and the child progresses to the period of early *genital eroticism*, satisfaction being derived from masturbation. Fixations may occur during any of these stages, with a resulting weakly developed character structure. (See ORAL CHARACTER and ANAL CHARACTER.)

The child is also seeking an external object to satisfy his erotic desires and because of proximity and tenderness toward him, the parent of the opposite sex is chosen. In the boy, this complex of desires is called the *Oedipus complex;* in the girl it is called the *Electra complex*. Because the child fears retaliation on the part of the parent for his incestuous desires,

he eventually represses them, and a considerable portion of the libidinal energies is directed toward socialization. The beginning of this stage of development marks the end of the infantile period and the beginning of the latent period, which lasts until puberty. With the onset of puberty, the stage of adult genital sexuality is reached.

Freud's account of mind and personality follows a tripartite schema, which in the case of mind involves three levels of consciousness, respectively called the unconscious, the subconscious, and the conscious. The unconscious—the seat of the libido and of repressed memories— is considered by Freud to be the most important level of mind. Personality is considered to have developed out of the primitive, *id*, or the original, animalistic aspect of the self characteristic of the infant. From the id develops the *ego*, the part of personality that attempts to deal with reality at the same time as it strives to allow the id as many of its demands as possible. The ego is also under pressure from the *superego*—Freud's equivalent of the conscience—which originates from the internalization of parental prohibitions and restrictions and continues to be a kind of ideal aspect of the self that seeks to govern the id through its mediator, the ego. Thus, in Freudian theory, mind is a three-way battleground. Neuroses occur when the ego becomes weakened through severe conflict with the id or with the environment. Normally the ego can withstand great stress but, if its energies have been depleted by maintaining repressions, insufficient energy remains for dealing with reality.

Psychoanalysis as a therapy attempts to overcome repressions and thereby release energy for healthy, normal living. This is largely accomplished by means of free association and dream analysis conducted over long periods of time in order to overcome resistances and get at the sources of the unconscious impulses.

Psychoanalysts are not in agreement as to the mechanisms of development or the conduct of psychoanalysis as a form of therapy. The neo-Freudian psychoanalysts, like Karen Horney, Clara Thompson, and Harry Stack Sullivan, put much more emphasis on security and interpersonal relations in the development of personality and the causation of the neuroses than on sex. However, the technique of psychoanalysis has remained more or less unchanged since it was developed by Freud. See also JUNG'S ANALYTICAL PSYCHOLOGY and ADLER'S INDIVIDIDUAL PSYCHOLOGY.

psychoanalyst: one who practices psychoanalysis.

psychoasthenics: the investigation of mental deficiency.

psychobiology: the field of psychology from the biological point of view, stressing the investigation of the organism in relation to its adaptation to its environment as this is made possible by the nervous system, endocrine glands, receptors, etc.

psychodiagnosis: any technique for the study of personality that aims at discovering underlying traits, particularly as these dispose the individual toward mental disorders.

psychodiagnostics: the study of personality through the interpretation of behavioral signs, walking, gestures, facial expressions, voice, etc.

psychodrama: a diagnostic and therapeutic technique developed by J. L. Moreno that consists of having the individual act out on a stage his relations with others around whom conflicts center. The performance is carried out in the presence of a psychiatrist and others. Other actors may also take part in a session.

psychodynamic: 1. pertaining to the branch of psychology that investigates motivation and emotional processes. 2. pertaining to psychoanalytic and related depth psychologies. 3. pertaining to processes undergoing change or development.

psychogalvanic response or **reflex:** see GALVANIC SKIN RESPONSE.

psychogalvanometer: a highly sensitive galvanometer used for measuring electrical changes on the surface of the skin. See also GALVANIC SKIN RESPONSE.

psychogenesis: 1. the origin and developmental history of the mind or psyche. 2. the origin and development of any mental process or behavioral act.

psychogenic: pertaining to disorders that are functional in origin. See also PSYCHOGENIC DISORDER.

psychogenic disorder: a functional disorder that has no known organic basis and is therefore likely to be due to conflict or emotional stress.

psychogenetics: the investigation of the hereditary causation of psychological traits. See also BEHAVIORAL GENETICS.

psychognosis: 1. the study of the individual from anatomical signs. 2. the study of the individual by means of hypnosis.

psychogram: 1. a profile of the individual's relative standing on traits, test scores, etc.; a psychograph. 2. (*Murray*) representation of the thema, or manner in which needs and psychological press (events of significance for the individual) interact to produce behavior.

psychography: the art of writing a biography or character description relying heavily on a psychological analysis of the subject.

psychoid: 1. (*noun*) a hypothetical vital process found in human behavior. 2. (*adj.*) resembling the psychic.

psychokinesis: 1. in parapsychology, a hypothetical influence exerted by the individual on inanimate objects. *Abbr.* PK. A common form of psychokinetic experiment involves attempting to influence the fall of dice. 2. in psychiatric literature, violent or maniacal motor behavior.

psycholagny: sexual excitement confined to imagination.

psycholepsy: a sudden and dramatic decrease in the level of alertness or mental tension; a depressive state.

psycholinguistics: the study of language and communication as related to the individuals who use language.

Language serves several functions. First, it allows individuals to communicate with others who share the same language. Second, the concepts of language serve as tools of thought. Third, language serves an expressive function for feelings and emotions. Finally, language as literature is an important aesthetic medium.

Linguists analyze all languages into elementary sounds called *phonemes*. Phonemes approximate the manner in which vowels and consonants are pronounced. Each language has a different number of phonemes, some having as few as 15, others over 80. English utilizes approximately 45. The smallest meaningful linguistic units are *morphemes*. These include words,

prefixes, and suffixes. A word standing alone, such as *sad*, is a free morpheme. The suffix *ness* is a bound morpheme, since it cannot stand alone. Combined with *sad* into *sadness* we have a new term describing a quality or a state of being. The study of phonemes and morphemes is called *phonology*. The relationship between the sounds and meanings of a language is called its *morphology*.

The study of morphology and *syntax* (the term or structure of word order in sentences) emphasizes the *surface structure* of language. Formerly linguistics was primarily concerned with syntax, the rules of phrasing, sentence parsing, and correct grammatical usage. More recently, largely due to the impact of the work of Noam Chomsky (*q.v.*), psycholinguists are showing more interest in the *deep structure* of language, which is concerned with the real meaning of a sentence. The difference between surface and deep structure is illustrated by ambiguous sentences such as "Some workers are automatons," which may mean that some workingmen behave like machines or it may mean that some units in a production line are operated by manlike machines. Psycholinguists study the transformational rules that enable speakers to generate surface structures from deep structures.

The suggestion that children the world over may have a common language acquisition device (LAD) has generated considerable interest and controversy in recent years. Studies of language development reveal that regardless of their national or racial origin or the difficulty of their native tongue, children acquire a fully functional language in a surprisingly short time and in the process all go through similar stages. These studies also present evidence to show that children do not acquire language through passive imitation of their elders, but utilize a kind of "telegraphese" with its own rules, out of which they can generate new combinations of words. The characterization of the language of young children as telegraphese is intended to convey the fact that it utilizes mostly nouns and verbs, omitting adjectives and adverbs. Thus the child is likely to render the sentence "We are going for a ride in the car" as "Ride in car." Those who emphasize conditioning and learning in the developmental process take the position that language is learned through the reinforcement of those sounds, words, and combinations of words favored by the verbal community in which the child develops.

Among other recent interests of psycholinguists are the study of how language determines thought, whether language and thought can develop independently, and to what extent animals can utilize language. Some investigations have suggested that language determines thought (Whorfian hypothesis), while others (notably Piaget's) suggest that thinking and language develop separately through interaction with objects, in the case of thinking, and with people, in the case of language. Among the more popular developments in the study of animal communication are those concerned with the investigation of the complex sonar system of porpoises and the ability of the chimpanzee to acquire American Sign Language.

psychological: 1. pertaining to psychology. 2. characterizing any event as within the domain of psychology. 3. mental in origin.

psychological autopsy: an investigation to determine whether a death was suicide.

psychological environment: those aspects of the external world influencing the individual. The Gestalt psychologists and field theorists would include imagined or remembered aspects of the world under this category. See also LIFE SPACE.

psychological field: (*Lewin*) the environment as perceived by the individual; the individual's life space at any given moment.

psychological freedom: the awareness of the absence of external influence in making decisions; the feeling that one is able to make his own decisions without undue influence.

psychological limit: see PHYSIOLOGICAL LIMIT.

psychological me: the self or self-concept.

psychological primary: see COLOR PRIMARY.

psychological region: in topological psychology, any differentiated division of the life space.

psychological scale: a device for making measurements of psychological functions, such as attitudes, artistic judgments, or mental ability.

psychological space: see LIFE SPACE.

psychological statistics: see STATISTICS; PSYCHOMETRICS.

psychological test: a general concept including mental-ability scales, achievement tests, various kinds of special-aptitude tests, and tests of personality. For specific types, see TEST.

psychological time: time estimated subjectively, without the aid of a clock or the position of the sun. Such factors as the number of events that have occurred, their nature, and physiological rhythms are used in making such judgments.

psychological type: any scheme for classifying individuals according to a set of personality characteristics, such as *extrovert* and *introvert*.

psychological warfare: a general concept referring to all attempts to weaken the enemy's ability to wage war by weakening his morale, with corresponding attempts to strengthen one's own war potential.

psychological weaning: 1. the process of breaking away from dependence on the parents. 2. overcoming parental domination.

psychologism: 1. the point of view that psychology is the basic science among all those sciences that deal with man. 2. the point of view that the normative sciences (ethics, logic, and aesthetics) rest on empirical facts.

psychologist: an individual who, by means of a course of training at least through the level of the master's degree and in most cases through the doctorate, has made a specialized study of the science of psychology.

psychologist's fallacy: projecting into the mind or behavior of another individual what is actually in the mind of a psychologist or what he believes is logical and appropriate in the situation.

psychology as a science: the science of human and animal behavior; the study of the organism in all its variety and complexity as it responds to the flux and flow of the physical and social events that make up the environment.

Behavior is sometimes overt or public, as the maneuvers of an astronaut at the controls of a space vehicle. Sometimes behavior is covert, or

hidden, as exemplified by glandular secretions, muscular tensions, or stomach contractions. Some behavior is describable as logical, orderly, and constructive, like the behavior of a scientist engaged in a program of research, while other behavior—the behavior of the psychotic—appears irrational, strange, and occasionally bizarre. All types of behavior, whether overt or covert, simple or complex, rational or irrational, are studied by psychologists. By studying human behavior in its many manifestations, the psychologist ultimately hopes to understand the nature of man—his desires, hopes, fears, abilities, and limitations. The psychologist attempts to discover why people do the things they do. He would like to understand man's unrivaled ability to adapt to his environment, the nature of his intelligence, the sources of his inner conflicts, his behavior as a social animal—indeed, it might be said that psychology, broadly speaking, is a search for the answer to that age-old question, what is man?

Many sciences and disciplines study human behavior. Anthropologists, historians, sociologists, economists, political scientists, and others in related fields, seek to know the nature of man; and, in this sense, psychology is but one among many *behavioral sciences*. Each of these disciplines focuses on certain aspects of human behavior—the sociologist on man's institutional and group behavior, the anthropologist on primitive races and cultures, the economist on behavior leading to the production and consumption of goods. The psychologist emphasizes the study of the *individual*. This is not to say that psychologists never study people in groups or are uninterested in political or economic behavior. Rather, it means that for the psychologist *the individual is the unit of study*, whether that individual is alone or in a group. For the sociologist, the group or institution constitutes the unit; for the anthropologist, the primitive culture. However, there is considerable borrowing and cooperation among the behavioral sciences. They are neither rivals nor competitors, but all are engaged in unraveling the mystery of man, each in the light of its own special interest and point of view.

Behavior as Responding

The behavior of a child reciting a poem or of a policeman arresting a criminal is easily observable. Such behavior patterns are *responses* that can be observed without the aid of instruments. But many responses are not so readily observable. Some people feel anxious or frightened when they have to make a speech. Unless they are trembling, their distress may go unnoticed by their listeners. However, if such an individual is connected to a "lie detector" capable of measuring hidden emotional responses, the subtle bodily changes underlying his anxiety can be amplified by the apparatus and made publicly observable. From these bodily changes his state of anxiety can then be inferred by a psychologist.

Much of the same situation is true of most covert or hidden responses. Psychologists have discovered ways of detecting them by means of suitable instrumentation or by employing other experimental arrangements in which covert behavior can be made overt. For example, when an individual is angry, subtle changes occur in his digestive tract, his vascular system, and in his breathing. Indeed, the emotion of anger *is*, in part, these hidden bodily changes. In order to make them available for psychological study, special instruments must be employed.

Consciousness and Unconscious Processes

It is a fundamental fact of existence that we are consciously aware of our own mental activities. Everyone knows what it is like to feel pain, hunger, thirst, cold, anger, and fear, or to sense colors, odors, tastes, and sounds. We are conscious of our own opinions, aspirations, imaginings, regrets. This private world of experience is directly accessible only to the experiencing individual. But this does not mean that conscious experience must be totally inaccessible to psychological investigation. Traditionally, the *verbal-report* technique offers the possibility of studying another's conscious experience by having him verbalize his consciousness either as it is in progress or afterward. A subject might be asked to report an emotional experience, describe a dream, or tell how he solved a difficult problem in mathematics. Clearly, such a verbal report is liable to subjective errors and mistakes in interpretation and for these reasons is considered by most psychologists to be less reliable than the more objective technique of observing the subject's responses. However, most psychologists would agree that the study of conscious experience has a place in psychology; consequently the verbal report is accepted in lieu of more objective behavioral responses whenever experimental conditions make this necessary.

Mental activities of which the individual is unaware are called *unconscious processes*. A friend forgets a dental appointment; a child is unreasonably afraid of enclosed places; a student habitually excuses failures by blaming his instructors for including ambiguous questions on examinations. In all these instances the individual is unaware of the reasons for his behavior, and it is sometimes said that his "subconscious" or "unconscious" is responsible for his actions. Strictly speaking, any such description that implies there is a part or segment of the mind that serves as a reservoir for all sorts of undesirable patterns of behavior is misleading. That the individual in question has *behaved* in a certain way is all that can be observed. Because of the nature of his behavior, the psychologist *infers* that he is unaware of the reasons for his actions. The problem here is the same as that which arises whenever the psychologist tries to go beyond the observable. For example, he sees a person stop and drink at a fountain in a park on a hot summer's day. He may infer that the individual is thirsty. In this instance he is inferring a *motive*; as it happens, a motive of which the individual is aware. But whether conscious or unconscious, motives are inferred from observed behavior, and it must be remembered that these represent underlying *processes* within the individual and are not mysterious entities. In the case of thirst it is a changing of physiological conditions; in the rationalizing student, it may be feelings of inadequacy in the face of life's problems which he is unable to admit and for which he has devel-

oped a system of defenses, the basis of which he is unaware. But in no instance is it proper to assume that behavior is the result of "forces" or "the unconscious mind," since these have no independent existence apart from behavior.

More generally, it is wise to consider personal attributes in terms of action. To possess intelligence means that one behaves intelligently. To have an emotion means that one is experiencing certain feelings and bodily changes. To have a motive is a shorthand way of saying that one is undergoing physiological changes that arouse him to action or that learned habits are guiding his activities. By thinking of psychological concepts as *processes* rather than real *entities* we avoid the error of personification. It may be helpful to compare the psychologist's reasoning about his working concepts with that of a physicist. The latter speaks of a wire as having a certain "resistance." The physicist has no way of observing the wire's resistance apart from its behavior as a current is passed through it. In other words, resistance is a property inferred from the observed characteristics of wires in the same way that intelligence is an attribute inferred from a standard sample of a human subject's behavior called a *test*.

Varieties of Behavior

Just as psychologists can describe some behavioral processes as conscious and others as unconscious, behavior can be classified in many other ways. Some behavior is *voluntary*, such as getting up and opening a door, while other behavior is *involuntary*, like blinking one's eye to a puff of air. Some of the behavior patterns in lower forms we describe as *instincts*, such as the wasp's nest building. Thus, there are levels of complexity in behavior ranging from simple, involuntary reflexes, such as eye blinking, to highly complicated forms of behavior, as are found in creative writing or painting. Simpler reflex behavior patterns are sometimes called *molecular units*, while more complex behavior patterns are known as *molar units*. The analogy here is, of course, to gases. The chemist may study the molecules (molecular behavior) that comprise a gas, or he may investigate the behavior of the gas as a whole (molar behavior). Psychologists study behavior at all levels of complexity. However, most psychologists are more interested in molar than in molecular behavior, and even when they investigate behavior at the molecular level, it is usually in an attempt to cast light on more complex psychological processes.

Methods in Psychology

Methodology in the behavioral sciences is closely allied to the particular research interests of the scientist. To a lesser extent this is also true of the physical and biological sciences. The astronomer's star-gazing, which is naturalistic observation, is not the same as the chemist's active experimentation with chemical compounds. Both are observing nature, but one is taking a more active, manipulative role than the other. Similarly, the psychologist observing children playing in a nursery school is using a different method than if he were experimenting on the effect of rewards on learning, or striving to help an emo-

tionally disturbed child. In short, the nature of the psychologist's problem determines the method he will employ in a given instance.

Basically, the aim of psychology is the same as that of any other science—the ability to make accurate predictions about the phenomena with which it deals. Because the key to predicting behavior, the phenomena of psychology, lies in discovering the *antecedent conditions* that give rise to behavior, the psychologist attempts to discover those conditions by employing two basic methods: the experimental method and the method of naturalistic observation. Both of these procedures ultimately rely upon *observation*. In the first, the experimental method, the psychologist actively manipulates antecedent conditions and observes concomitant, or parallel, variations in behavior. In the second, the method of naturalistic observation, he observes differences in behavior as they exist in nature, as these are related to antecedent conditions. It must be emphasized that the psychologist's observations are not the casual, incidental observations of everyday life, but instead are carefully designed to provide specific and meaningful information. The psychologist, in contrast to the casual observer, is *ready* to observe and is a *trained* observer. His attitude is *objective*, and he is careful to *record* his observations as they occur so as not to become a victim of the errors of his own memory. Finally, he records *negative instances*, or failures, as well as positive instances, something a biased everyday observer often fails to do.

When he employs the experimental method, the psychologist assumes an active role in controlling the antecedent conditions, his subject's behavior, and the conditions of observation. To accomplish this, he must first identify the several variables with which he will be working. The antecedent condition that the psychologist believes may be the cause of the behavior he has under study is called the *independent* (or *experimental*) *variable*. The *controlled variables* are all those extraneous conditions that might influence the subject's reaction and which must, therefore, be held constant. If such conditions were allowed to influence the subject at the same time that the experimental variable is under investigation, the experimenter would not know which was responsible for the subject's reaction.

Psychological experiments are designed to assess the influence of stimuli in responses. However, because stimuli must act on something or someone, the formula for an experiment is often written "S–O–R" rather than "S–R." However, the only observables are the stimuli and the responses. The O-variables are, of course, inferred from the subject's reaction. Psychologists call these O-factors *intervening variables*, since they intervene between stimuli and responses. From this point of view, psychology is the study of intervening variables within the organism that mediate between stimuli and responses. They are analogous to such terms as *resistance, energy, gravity,* and the like, which physicists employ to account for the behavior of physical systems. None of these physical concepts has independent existence apart from the experimental operations employed in its measurement or demonstration. Precisely the same is

true of intervening variables in psychology. They must be operationally defined in terms of manipulable antecedent conditions. For example, intelligence has no independent existence apart from the tests used to measure it.

Psychologists, like other scientists, formulate their experimental questions about natural phenomena in the form of *hypotheses*. A hypothesis is a shrewd hunch about the outcome of an experiment and is based upon the psychologist's knowledge of the phenomenon under study. It is, therefore, not a wild guess, but an educated prediction. If the results of the experiment confirm his hunch, the hypothesis is proved and the investigator has achieved his aim of being able to predict behavior. He may then *generalize* his conclusions within reasonable limits and predict that whenever the same antecedent conditions occur the subject (or subjects) will react as predicted. Of course, if the results of the experiment fail to confirm his hypothesis, it must be discarded.

Naturalistic observation, another widely used method in psychology, is the oldest of the scientific methods. Essentially, it consists of the observation of natural phenomena under carefully controlled conditions. It differs from the experimental method in that the psychologist finds a situation in which he studies behavior without manipulating the subjects or the antecedent conditions that give rise to their behavior. Because the experimenter does not manipulate conditions, he has less control over them. Suppose, for example, that he is interested in discovering whether restricting infants' movements will significantly delay their walking. For ethical reasons he cannot restrain infants, since the experimental procedures involved might do permanent harm to the children. However, he can study Indian children who, as infants, are kept restricted by their mothers in cradle boards. Just as is true in the experimental method, the psychologist in this case needs a control group with which to compare the restricted group. Fortunately, some Indian mothers do not place their children in cradle boards, and the psychologist can select a control group similar in age, genetic makeup, and other relevant factors, with which he can compare the original group.

Naturalistic observation is useful whenever the psychologist may be unable for practical or ethical reasons to use the more active experimental method. It is particularly useful in situations where there is a danger that experimental work might interfere with the behavior under study, as is often true when young children are involved. Many studies of children, animals, social groups, and mentally disturbed individuals have been carried out with the aid of this technique.

The Individual in Psychology

The academic psychologist who carries out his research programs with the experimental method and the method of naturalistic observation is primarily concerned with establishing general laws and principles by means of which he can predict and, ultimately, understand human behavior. His aims are the aims of the "pure" as opposed to the "applied" scientist. He is interested in the individual not as a person but as a representative of people in general. From the study of many individuals, he hopes to discover the nature of the behavioral processes.

However, many psychologists focus their interests on the individual. This is particularly true of those who practice psychology as a profession, among whom we may include the clinical psychologist, the industrial psychologist, the vocational counselor, and the educational psychologist. Their aims are those of the applied scientist who seeks to bring the knowledge and tools of theoretical science to bear upon the solutions of practical problems. In doing so, the applied scientist often improves the tools of his trade, uncovers new problems of theoretical importance, and contributes in many other ways to the progress of pure science. Thus, in psychology, these two broad areas— pure and applied, or academic and professional—are neither mutually exclusive nor antagonistic but a cooperative endeavor whose various phases complement one another.

The largest single field of professional psychology is that of clinical psychology, whose primary concern is with the development and application of diagnostic and therapeutic techniques for the identification and treatment of behavioral disorders. Notable among these are the *psychological test* and the *clinical interview*, both of which are also widely employed in vocational, industrial, and educational applications.

Psychological tests, are, in effect, real-life situations into which the testee is placed in order to compare his intellectual abiility or his personality with that of others. Standardized tests must be developed under controlled conditions. The questions are chosen with care and are evaluated by special statistical tests. In their formative stages tests are administered to large, representative groups of subjects in order to establish standards of performance for future comparisons of any individual with the standardization group. The administration of the final form of the test to individual subjects for diagnostic purposes requires special training, as does the interpretation of the results. Tests are also used by psychologists as instruments of research in the areas of personality and intelligence. By analyzing the results of tests given to large samples of individuals the psychologist strives to arrive at a more complete understanding of the abilities that he is measuring.

The case history and interview have found wide usage in two main areas: vocational selection and clinical situations. A case history is a collection of developmental data including test scores, the results of interviews, and, if appropriate, a diagnosis of prognosis of the person under study. Today, psychologists and psychiatrists may be assisted in the development of case histories by social workers with the result that the case history becomes a multidimensional analysis of the individual's assets and liabilities. Interviews may be directive or nondirective. The typical, formal job interview is likely to be highly directive in that its primary purpose is to gather factual information about the applicant, such as a record of his education, job experience, and personal background. The nondirective interview is more frequently employed in clinical or therapeutic situations in which the therapist allows the interviewee to talk freely while he strives to create a warm, permissive atmosphere in which the subject can both express himself fully and arrive at a better understanding of his problems.

psychometric: 1. pertaining to any form of mental testing. 2. pertaining to a psychophysical function, such as the equation representing the probability of greater or lesser judgments in a differential-threshold experiment.

psychometric constant delta: a constant in the method of constant stimuli which is equal to h, and index of precision equal to

$$\frac{1}{\sigma\sqrt{2}} \times I$$

(the I being a constant for the individual observer).

psychometric function: a mathematical expression of relationship between quantitative variations in a series of stimuli and the observer's judgments of those stimuli according to a predetermined criterion. For example, in the method of limits as applied to the problem of obtaining an absolute threshold, a psychometric function may be plotted with the stimulus values on the base line and the proportion of judgments of presence or absence of a sensation as reported by the subject on the vertical axis.

psychometrician: 1. an individual who engages in the administration of mental tests. 2. a specialist in the statistical analysis of psychological data, particularly in the analysis of mental-test data. *Syn.* psychometrist.

psychometrics: 1. the specialized branch of psychology dealing with mental tests. 2. the branch of psychology dealing with the development and application of statistical and other mathematical procedures to psychology.

psychometrist: see PSYCHOMETRICIAN.

psychometry: mental measurements or mental testing.

psychomimetic: resembling or mimicking a natural psychological process. The term is usually applied to psychoses induced by drugs.

psychoneural parallelism: the principle that for every conscious event there is a corresponding neural event.

psychoneurosis: see NEUROSIS.

psychoneurotic inventory: a questionnaire about attitudes, symptoms, emotional reactions, and other behavior patterns indicative of the presence of neurosis.

psychonomic: 1. pertaining to factors that influence mental development. 2. pertaining to environmental factors in relation to psychological development.

psychopath: 1. an individual suffering from a mental disorder. 2. an individual with a personality disorder not psychotic in nature, which is lacking in manifest anxiety and involves inadequate social adjustment. The term is so all-inclusive that it has gone out of use in favor of more specific diagnostic categories.

psychopathic: pertaining to any mental disorder, particularly to an unspecified or not yet diagnosed disorder.

psychopathic inferior: see CONSTITUTIONAL INFERIOR.

psychopathic personality: see ANTISOCIAL PERSONALITY.

psychopathology: the branch of psychology concerned with the investigation of mental disorders and other abnormal phenomena.

psychopathy: a mental disorder that may be unspecified or given a qualifying diagnostic name.

psychopedics: the branch of psychology concerned with the guidance and clinical treatment of children.

psychopharmacology: the study of the effects of drugs on psychological processes. See also DRUGS AND BEHAVIOR.

psychophysical: 1. pertaining to psychophysics. 2. pertaining to processes that have both bodily or material and psychological or mental aspects.

psychophysical dualism: the doctrine that mental processes have both a bodily and a mental aspect, that neither is the cause of the other, and that there is no interaction, between them. See also DUALISM; PSYCHOPHYSICAL PARALLELISM.

psychophysical function: any mathematically expressed relationship between a stimulus and observed judgments about that stimulus. See also PSYCHOMETRIC FUNCTION.

psychophysical methods: the standard methods used in the investigation of psychophysical problems. Specifically, the *method of average error*, the *method of limits*, the *method of equal-appearing intervals*, and the *constant methods*.

psychophysical parallelism: the doctrine that for every event of consciousness there is a corresponding event in the nervous system. The doctrine of psychophysical parallelism is a form of dualism. Dualism was first promulgated by Plato and took the form of the separation of mind and body as two different and noninteracting entities. Descartes denied the separation, postulating interactionism as a modified dualism in which mind and body, though separate substances, interact at the site of the pineal gland. Wundt and Titchener subscribed to the doctrine of psychophysical parallelism, arguing that conscious events have their neural counterparts but that there are no causal relations between mind and body.

psychophysics: 1. the branch of psychology that investigates relationships between stimulus magnitudes, stimulus differences, and their corresponding sensory processes. 2 *(Fechner)* the science of the relation between mind and body.

psychophysiological: pertaining to processes in which psychological and physiological factors are present.

psychophysiology: see PHYSIOLOGICAL PSYCHOLOGY.

psychosensory: pertaining to experiences, such as imagined experiences, that do not originate in the sense organs.

psychosexual: 1. pertaining to sexuality in its broadest sense, including both mental and somantic aspects. 2. characterizing a mental process as originating in sexual development.

psychosis: a severe mental disorder characterized by disorganization of the thought processes, disturbances in emotionality, disorientation as to time, space, and person, and, in some cases, hallucinations and delusions. For discussions of specific types, see MANIC-DEPRESSIVE PSYCHOSIS; PARANOIA; SCHIZOPHRENIA; PARESIS; ALCOHOLIC PSYCHOSIS.

psychosocial: pertaining to social relationships involving psychological factors.

psychosomatic: 1. pertaining to processes that are both somatic (bodily) and psychic (mental) in nature. 2. pertaining to the relation of mind and body. See also DUALISM.

psychosomatic disorder: a disorder caused by a combination of organic

and psychological factors. In psychosomatic disorders there may be tissue changes, as with peptic ulcers. Some psychosomatic disorders, such as allergic reactions, are clearly triggered by the invasion of foreign proteins into the body. However, the victim's psychological state makes a great deal of difference as to how he will react to those substances. In other instances, such as migraine headache, there may be a hereditary predisposition, but the typical personality pattern of the hard-driving, rigid intellectual in the third or fourth decade of life is also clearly related to the frequency and severity of the attacks. Psychosomatic disorders should be distinguished from conversion reactions, a form of hysteria. In conversion reactions there is no tissue change, as there is in psychosomatic disorders. Moreover, the symptoms in psychosomatic disorders are not logically or symbolically related to the psychological conflict, nor do they relieve the anxiety and tension as they do in conversion reactions.

psychosomatic medicine: a medical specialty dealing with the diagnosis and treatment of psychosomatic disorders.

psychosurgery: any brain operation for the alleviation of a mental disorder. See also PREFRONTAL LEUCOTOMY.

psychotechnician: an individual not fully qualified to work independently as a psychologist but skilled in the administration and interpretation of tests and experiments under supervision.

psychotechnics: the practical application of psychological principles to the control and management of behavior.

psychotechnology: the body of general principles and empirical facts involved in the application of psychology to practical problems.

psychotherapeutic: 1. pertaining to psychotherapy. 2. having curative power.

psychotherapist: one who is professionally engaged in the practice of psychotherapy.

psychotherapy: the application of specialized techniques to the treatment of mental disorders or to the problems of everyday adjustment. In its strictest sense, the term includes only those techniques (psychoanalysis, nondirective or directive counseling, psychodrama, etc.) utilized by specialists. More loosely, psychotherapy can include informal talks with ministers, faith cures, and personal discussions with teachers or friends.

The major techniques employed by psychotherapists include depth interviews, conditioning, suggestion, and interpretation. Some authorities would also include under techniques of psychotherapy various medical techniques, such as psychosurgery, electroshock therapy, and chemotherapy. Regardless of their differences, all forms of psychotherapy utilizing psychological techniques have basic features in common. All involve close communication between therapist and patient, in which the patient is encouraged to discuss his anxieties and most intimate experiences without moral judgment or criticism on the part of the therapist. The therapist, in turn, exhibits a warm, understanding attitude toward the patient in order to encourage freedom of expression and to minimize embarrassment.

To some degree the goal of all psychotherapies is to encourage understanding of the problem on the part of the patient, whose lack of insight into the nature of the maladjustment arouses anxiety and makes it difficult for him to cope with the demands of everyday living. Systems of therapy that emphasize insight and understanding are often classified as depth therapies in order to distinguish them from systems that minimize understanding and insight and stress symptom modification, such as behavior therapy.

Ultimately the goal of all forms of psychotherapy is modification of the patient's behavior in such a way as to bring about a more effective adjustment to his environment.

Techniques such as psychoanalysis, client-centered therapy, and behavior therapy have proved most successful with milder forms of behavior disorders. Psychotic individuals are so disturbed or withdrawn that medical intervention in the form of electroshock treatments or chemotherapy is necessary before such patients are amenable to treatment by psychological techniques. See also BEHAVIOR THERAPY; CLIENT-CENTERED THERAPY; GESTALT THERAPY; GROUP THERAPY; PSYCHOANALYSIS; ELECTROSHOCK THERAPY; DRUGS AND BEHAVIOR.

psychotic: characterizing a state of psychosis or resembling the behavior of an individual who has a psychosis.

psychotic surrender: the failure to face reality, characteristic of some of the mental disorders.

psychotomimetic: characteristic of drugs that produce a state similar to or symptomatic of psychoses.

P technique: a technique for determining the degree of unity of a pattern of behaviors by studying how they vary together statistically on different occasions.

puberal or **pubertal:** pertaining to puberty.

puberty praecox: precocious or extremely rapid development of the secondary sexual characteristics and the initiation of function in the primary sex glands.

puberty: that period in life during which the maturation of the sex organs reaches a stage where they become functional. There is a considerable variation among different individuals, but in general the age for termination of the period is given as thirteen in girls and fourteen in boys.

puberty rites: initiation into adult status in preliterate cultures. The rites typically involve some indoctrination into tribal lore, dancing, ceremonials, and a formal initiation ceremony.

pubes: the hair or the hairy region of the lower abdomen and genital region.

pubescence: the period during which puberty is being attained.

pubic: pertaining to the genital region

pubic rites: ceremonies associated with puberty during which the genitals may be scarified or otherwise mutilated.

public: 1. open to inspection. 2. nonsubjective; objective. 3. pertaining to or belonging to the state or to the people of a state.

public opinion: the general trend of opinion or attitude of a major segment of the population on a specific issue or group of issues.

pudenda: the external genital organs.

puerperal: pertaining to the process of childbirth.

Pulfrich phenomenon or **effect:** the tendency for a pendulumlike object that is moving back and forth in a horizontal plane to appear to be oscillating in an ellipse when viewed through a filter.

pulmonary: pertaining to the lungs.

pulsation: a throbbing; a beating, or rhythmic rise and fall in the intensity of sound or other pressure system.

pulse: the rhythmic beating in the arteries due to the pressure exerted by the action of the heart muscle.

punctate: characterizing a point on the skin that responds to a stimulus, such as a cold stimulus or a touch stimulus.

punctiform: point-shaped; pointed.

punishment: 1. the infliction of pain or discomfort upon a subject for failure to conform to a predetermined course of action in an experiment. 2. a stimulus with negative valence or a stimulus capable of inflicting pain or discomfort. 3. the imposition of a period of incarceration on a legal offender. *Contr.* REWARD.

punishment fantasy: the wish to be punished, expressed in the form of an imagined situation or fantasy of punishment.

pupil: 1. the aperture in the iris of the eye. 2. a child attending a school or undergoing tutoring.

pupillary reflex: change in size of pupil in response to light or to changes in fixation point.

Purdue pegboard: a test of manual dexterity utilizing pegs, washers, and collars that must be assembled. The test measures gross movements of the arms, wrists, and fingers.

pure: 1. unadulterated or unmixed, as a *pure tone* or a *pure color*. 2. characterizing those who are morally upright, particularly in the sexual sphere.

pure-stimulus act: (*Hull*) any act that does not bring the organism nearer to the goal but activates proprioceptive cues initiating responses that modify the environmental conditions leading to the goal.

pure tone: a tone arising as a result of simple vibrations, such as those emitted by a tuning fork.

puritis: 1. itching as a result of sensory nerve irritation. 2. psychogenic or functional itching.

Purkinje afterimage: the second positive visual aftersensation that appears most plainly in the hue complementary to that of the primary sensation. *Syn.* BIDWELL'S GHOST.

Purkinje cell: a large multibranched cell found in the middle layer of the cerebellar cortex.

Purkinje effect or **phenomenon:** the decrease in brilliance of the red, or long-wave, end of the spectrum with decreasing illumination. The blue, or short-wave, end also loses brilliance, but more slowly.

Purkinje figures: the shadowy network on the retina caused by the layer of blood vessels that lie between the sensitive cells and the incoming rays of light. These shadows may be seen under special conditions.

Purkinje-Sanson images: the reflections of a fixated object that are formed on the surface of the cornea and on the front and back of the lens.

purple: a hue obtained by a mixture of the long- and short-wavelengths of the spectrum, that is, blue and red.

purpose: 1. an awareness of an end or goal that guides the individual's behavior in pursuit of that end or goal. 2. an inferred or intervening variable to account for the arousal, maintenance, and direction of behavior toward a goal.

purposive psychology: the point of view in psychology that behavior is characterized by purpose and is not the running-off of reflexes or machinelike physiological processes. See TOLMAN'S PURPOSIVE BEHAVIORISM.

purposivism: a system of psychology that holds that purposes interacting with stimulus conditions are the determiners of behavior.

pursuitmeter: a device designed to measure a subject's skill in manipulating a pointer as he follows a constantly moving and erratic target.

pursuit pendulum: a type of pursuitmeter in which the moving ojbect is a pendulum, the pointer of which the subject attempts to follow.

pursuit reaction: a response to a moving target, such as following the moving stimulus in a pursuitmeter.

puzzle box: a box in which an animal subject must manipulate a certain lever, pull a string, or take apart a complicated set of fastenings in order to achieve the goal, which may be a food reward or simply the intrinsic reward of "a job well done."

Pygmalion effect: see SELF-FULFILLING PROPHECY.

pyknic: characterizing a physique that shows roundness of contour, fat, and relative shortness to girth. Kretschmer believed the pyknic type was subject to manic-depressive psychoses.

pyramidal tract: the large group of motor neurons that originate in the precentral gyrus of the cerebral cortex, pass down through the medulla, where about 80 percent cross at the decussation of the pyramids and continue downward to terminate in the ventral horns of the spinal cord.

pyramids: the elevated areas on the front of the medulla on either side of the median fissure. The elevation is caused by the crossing of the pyramidal tracts.

pyromania: a chronic impulse to set fires.

pyrophobia: a pathological fear of fire.

Q

Q data: information, or *data*, obtained through questionnaires.

Q method: the use of questionnaires in collecting psychological data.

Q sort: a personality questionnaire in which the subject sorts a large number of statements into piles that represent the degrees to which he believes the statements apply to him.

Q technique: the correlation of the scores of two persons on a series of tests. Q techniques are used to obtain a measure of the relatedness of the two persons in regard to the traits measured by the tests.

quadrant: one of the four cells in a 2-by-2 table.

quadrigemina: see CORPORA QUADRIGEMINA.

quadriplegia: paralysis of all four limbs.

quale: a sensation considered as a simple bit of experience, without regard to its meaning or significance.

quality: 1. a basic aspect of a sensation by means of which it is distinguished from all other sensations. Quality as used in this sense implies a difference in kind and not in degree. 2. the relative level of goodness or excellence of anything.

quality scale: a scale in which the steps are represented by a series of items of increasing worth or value.

quantal hypothesis: the assumption that changes in sensation take place by discrete steps rather than along a continuum.

quantity: the characteristic of a phenomenon that permits it to be measured or counted. Quantity results in variations in degree rather than in kind.

quantum: 1. a specific or discrete amount of anything. 2. in physics, the elemental unit of energy, such as a quantum of light.

quartile: 1. one of the three points by which a serially ordered distribution of values can be divided into equal quarters. 2. the set of scores contained in a quartile division of a distribution. 3. the range that represents a quartile.

quartile deviation: a measure of variability equal to one half the difference between the 25th and 75th percentiles. In a normal distribution, the deviation quartile is equal to the probable error.

quasi need: a purpose that excites and directs behavior toward a goal but does not originate in changing physiological rhythms.

questionnaire or **questionary:** a set of questions dealing with a single topic or a set of related topics to be answered by the subject. Questionnaires have been developed for the purpose of measuring interests, personality problems and opinions, and for recording biographical information.

quota control: a technique for population sampling in which the elements chosen for the sample are proportionate in numbers to the number of elements in the population as a whole.

quota sampling: the selecting of a certain proportion of elements from a set of subgroups that make up the population from which the sample is drawn.

quotidian: daily; occurring from day to day as daily fluctuations in a function.

R

race: a large subdivision of man characterized by a common ancestry and a number of common characteristics, particularly visible or somatic characteristics. The term *race* has become highly controversial because of exceptions to the rule of what constitutes any given race, since there are so many variations in skin color, hair quality, physique, facial contour, etc., that it is very difficult to establish criteria with any degree of certainty.

race differences: physical or mental differences associated with race. It has been difficult to substantiate mental or intellectual differences between races, because of the lack of cross-cultural tests.

race prejudice: a prejudgment of an individual made on the basis of his race. Such attitudes are usually associated with the belief that the members of the race in question possess undesirable qualities.

racial memory: those structures, ideas, feelings, and memory traces presumed to be inherited. Carl Jung was the chief exponent of the theory that memories in the form of a racial unconscious could be inherited from one's ancestors. See also Jung's ANALYTICAL PSYCHOLOGY.

racial unconscious: see COLLECTIVE UNCONSCIOUS.

racism: the social and political belief that utilizes race as a basis for economic, political, and social segregation, denial of rights, and treatment of the disadvantaged group as inferior.

radiance: the rate of emission of radiant energy. See RADIANT ENERGY.

radiant energy: the electromagnetic disturbance of an oscillatory or wavelike nature commonly called light. The human retina is sensitive to wavelengths of approximately 400 to 760 nanometers.

radiant flux: the rate of emission of radiant energy as expressed in ergs per second.

radiation: 1. divergence or diffusion of anything from a source or center. 2. the spread of excitation from an active neural center to adjacent areas. 3. radiant energy.

radical: 1. characterizing persons or proposals that seek to bring about fundamental and extreme changes. 2. a mathematical sign ($\sqrt{}$) signifying a root.

radix: a bundle of nerve fibers at their point of entry into or departure from the central nervous system.

rage: intense anger accompanied by strong visceral reactions, bodily and facial contortions, and in some instances, an attack pattern.

ramus or **ramus communicans** (plural **rami** or **rami communicantes**): 1. a branch of a nerve or vein. 2. a bundle of neurons connecting the sympathetic ganglia to the spinal cord and to the visceral and peripheral organs. The white rami connect the cord and the ganglia, the gray rami connect the ganglia and ventral roots leading to the organs.

random: occurring by chance; in a haphazard manner.

random activity: behavior not guided or directed toward any goal or biological purpose. The movements of the infant exemplify random activity.

random error: a chance error. Such errors form a normal distribution around the mean of measurements.

random group: see RANDOM SAMPLE.

randomize: to select in such a way that all known selective or biasing factors have been eliminated; to select a random sample. See RANDOM SAMPLE.

random movement: see RANDOM ACTIVITY.

random noise: noise that is a mixture of a number of different frequencies that are not multiples or harmonics of each other.

random observation: any observation that has not been planned in advance and is not a part of a systematic series of observations.

random sample: a number of cases taken from the entire population of persons, values, scores, etc., in such a way as to ensure that any one selection has as much chance of being picked as any other and that the sample will be a valid representation of the entire population.

range: 1. the interval between the highest and lowest score. 2. the value obtained by substracting the lowest score from the highest. 3. the interval between the limits of dispersion of a biological species. 4. any interval, such as the range of audibility.

range effect: in pursuit tracking, the tendency on the part of the subject to make overly large movements when the movement of the target is small and overly small movements when the movement of the target is large.

range of attention: see SPAN OF ATTENTION.

range of audibility or **hearing:** the area between upper and lower limits of hearable tones. In the normal young adult this is usually given as 20–20,000 Hz.

range of convenience: (*Kelly*) those events or situations included in a construct or construct system (*q.v.*)

rank: (*noun*) ordinal position on a scale or in a series of values, or in a hierarchy of individuals, values, etc.; the number describing such position. 2. (*verb*) to put items, values, or individuals in an order from lowest to highest according to some criterion.

ranked distribution: an array of scores or values put in order from high to low according to some criterion.

rank order: the arrangement of a series of values, individuals, scores, etc., in the order of magnitude.

rank-order correlation: a technique for finding the correlation coefficient between two sets of magnitudes that have been ranked. The formula usually employed is:

$$\rho = \frac{6 \times \text{Sum of } d^2}{N(N^2-1)}$$

where d is the difference between

ranks and N is the number of cases ranked.

rank-order method: a technique in which individuals (or scores) are arranged according to the order of merit of the individual cases. Thus, a series of composers might be arranged in a rank order from greatest to least great by members of a symphony orchestra or music critics. *Syn.* ORDER OF MERIT.

rank-difference correlation: see RANK-ORDER CORRELATION.

raphe nucleus: a brain stem nucleus which, if destroyed, results in abolition of slow wave and paradoxical sleep.

rapid eye movements (REM): rapid horizontal or vertical movements of the eyes during sleep. Dreaming occurs during REM sleep.

rapport: 1. in mental-testing situations, a comfortable, warm atmosphere between tester and testee. 2. more generally, a warm, close relationship between any two individuals in a psychological situation.

rapture: a state of spiritual or emotional ecstasy; extreme joy or pleasure.

raptus: agitation.

rare detail: (*Rorschach*) a scoring category for details that are not often reported.

rate: 1. an ordinal position assigned to data or to an individual. 2. an expression of change in a variable found by dividing the variable for a given time period by the value of the variable before the change occurs. Thus, a change from 30 to 40 in the number of successful runs through a maze over a period of a week represents a rate of change of 30/40 or .75. 3. a numerical ratio.

ratee: the individual being rated.

rate score: a speed score developed in terms of the number of items completed per unit of time.

rating: 1. the assignment of a rank or score to an individual or to data. 2. the rank or score assigned to data or to an individual.

rating behavior: 1. recording the presence (or absence) of specified behaviors. 2. assigning a rating to certain specified behaviors.

ratio: a relationship between any two magnitudes expressed as a quotient or the product of a division. The IQ is a ratio of the mental age divided by the chronological age.

rational: 1. pertaining to reasoning, or characterized by ability to reason. 2. possessing the ability to reason. 3. influenced or guided by reason rather than emotion.

rationale: the reason for an opinion or hypothesis.

rational emotive therapy: (*Ellis*) a form of therapy that emphasizes the establishment of more realistic goals and the elimination of irrational beliefs.

rational equation: a mathematical equation based on assumptions as to the nature of the psychological process in question. Rational equations attempt to predict psychological phenomena by making careful assumptions as to the psychological nature of the parameters in the equation and the relationship between those parameters. *Contr.* EMPIRICAL EQUATION.

rationalism: the philosophical position first emphasized by Plato in which reason is extolled as a means of arriving at the truth.

rationality: the state or quality of being reasonable.

rationalization: 1. the process of explaining or interpreting the reason for a phenomenon. 2. the process of justifying one's conduct by offering plausible or socially acceptable reasons in place of real reasons.

rational learning: learning that is meaningful and includes an understanding of the material and the relations among the elements of the material.

rational problem solving: arriving at the solution to a problem on the basis of reasoning or logic rather than trial and error.

rational psychology: any system of psychology founded on philosophical or theological concepts. *Contr*. EMPIRICAL PSYCHOLOGY.

rational type: (*Jung*) an individual whose behavior is guided primarily by thinking and feeling in contrast to the irrational type, whose behavior is governed by intuition and sensation. See also Jung's ANALYTICAL PSYCHOLOGY.

ratio reinforcement: in operant conditioning, the administration of a reinforcement only after the animal has made a certain predetermined number of responses.

ratio scale: a type of scale on which the various increments are equal and can be added or divided. However, the scale does not have an absolute zero. The ratio scale is employed in psychophysical measurements and is obtained by taking a certain interval or fraction as a standard and constructing a scale of intervals by finding equal-appearing increments.

Raven's Progressive Matrices: A test of general ability consisting of designs with missing parts the examinee must supply from options presented. Claims to be culture-fair. Ages 5–adult.

raw score: a score that is presented in terms of the original test units.

Typically it is simply the number of items passed. *Syns*. ORIGINAL SCORE; OBTAINED SCORE.

ray: a line, either real or imaginary, that represents the direction of travel of a beam of light.

Rayleigh equation: a quantitative statement of the proportion of spectral red and green the normal human eye requires to match yellow. Persons who are red-green color-blind or red-green weak require more than the normal amount of either red or green, depending on the predominant weakness; the equation can therefore be used as a test for color-blindness or weakness.

R correlation: a method for discovering how two functions are related by correlating them for a large number of individuals. *Contr*. Q TECHNIQUE, which correlates persons rather than functions, and the P TECHNIQUE and O technique, which are factor-analysis techniques for the investigation of the relationships among functions.

RCRT test: see REP TEST.

reactance theory: the position that if opportunity to choose an object or activity is limited, its attractiveness will be increased.

reaction: 1. a response to a stimulus. 2. a behavioral patterning that constitutes a disease syndrome of a personality type. 3. an attitude or response, such as a popular vote indicating a *reaction* against a party in power.

reaction chain: see CHAIN BEHAVIOR.

reaction formation: (*Psychoan*.) the development of a personality trait that is the opposite of the original, unconscious, or repressed trait. Thus, an attractive young woman might show unusual solicitude for a crippled father for whom she must care when her real feelings express the unconscious wish that he would die so that she would be free to marry.

reaction key: a switch, similar in appearance to a telegraph key, used to interrupt circuits in reaction-time experiments.

reaction potential: (*Hull*) the probability of occurrence of a response as dependent upon the level of organismic drive and habit strength.

reaction time: the minimum time between a stimulus and a response. In the typical experiment for measuring simple-reaction time, the subject is confronted with a stimulus, such as a small light, and when it goes on, he is to release a reaction key which interrupts a highly sensitive timer that began running upon the presentation of the light. The reaction time is the elapsed time between the onset of the stimulus and the release of the switch. If more than one stimulus is employed, the experiment is then called a discrimination reaction-time experiment; if more than one response is required for alternative stimulus possibilities, the experiment is called a choice reaction-time experiment. For example, in a discrimination experiment, the subject might be required to react only if a red light comes on and not if a green light appears. In a choice reaction, he might have to react with the right hand to a red light and with the left hand when a green light appears. Variations of the experiment employ reaction time to words, called association reaction time, and to colors in which the subject's task is to name a series of color patches as rapidly as possible.

reaction type: 1. in reaction-time experiments, a phrase used to characterize a particular type of readiness or set—motor, sensory, or mixed. The subject is instructed to assume the desired set and to concentrate either on his musculature (motor set) or on the stimulus (sensory set). 2. a type of psychotic syndrome or symptom pattern, such as the paranoid reaction, schizophrenic reaction, or manic-depressive reaction.

reactive inhibition: (*Hull*) the tendency toward a lessened magnitude of response with increasing practice or fatigue. Reactive inhibition is dissipated by time and is independent of reinforcement. It is maximized in mass learning and minimized in distributed learning.

reactive measure: a measurement that is susceptible to change through the process of measuring it.

reactive psychosis: a psychosis that is the result of severe environmental pressure.

reactive reinforcement: (*Psychoan.*) the tendency for a conscious process to encourage its unconscious opposite. Thus, hate may generate love, or vice versa. See also REACTION FORMATION.

reactive schizophrenia: an acute attack of schizophrenia that comes on suddenly. The prognosis for such cases is ordinarily more favorable than for the more insidious varieties.

reactive type: an individual whose behavior is determined primarily by environmental conditions.

readiness: 1. preparedness to react or respond; a set. 2. a developmental level of maturity that makes practice profitable. For example, it has been held by many reading experts that a child must have a mental age of six to make instruction in reading profitable.

readiness, law of: (*Thorndike*) in learning theory, the generalization that "when a conduction unit is ready to conduct, conduction by it is satisfying."

reading: 1. the visual perception of words and their meaning. 2. the perception of Braille symbols. 3. the perception of musical symbols. 4. the perception of gestures or lip movements. 5. an interpretation given by a fortune-teller, palmist, or phrenologist.

reading age: 1. an age score on a standardized reading test. 2. the age at which reading can be initiated, approximately age six for the normal child.

reading disability: a marked retardation in level of reading ability in comparison with what is normal for the child's chronological age.

reading quotient: an index of the child's ability to read, as compared with the reading ability of other children of his age. It is obtained by dividing his reading age, as measured by a standardized reading test, by his chronological age.

reading readiness: the developmental stage at which the child can profit by instruction in reading. A specific age for reading readiness is difficult to define, since reading readiness depends upon both maturation and experiential factors. The traditional rule of thumb held that children were not ready to read until they had reached a mental age of six. Recent experimental reading programs have encouraged children of two to three years of age to read.

reading span: the number of words the subject can comprehend in a single fixation pause or the brief period of time when the eye is not moving.

reafference: changes in sensory input resulting from the subject's movements.

real: 1. having existence; not imaginary. 2. existing empirically, as opposed to theoretically. 3. existing physically, as opposed to mentally or psychologically.

real anxiety: see OBJECTIVE ANXIETY.

realism: 1. the philosophical point of view that the world has independent or objective existence apart from the perception of an observer. 2. the point of view that accepts things as they are, as opposed to an idealistic view. 3. (*Piaget*) a type of thinking in children in which the child confuses his perceptions of things with objective or physical reality.

reality: 1. existence of the universe in general. 2. the totality of conditions or contingencies that limit the freedom of the individual.

reality ego: (*Psychoan.*) the pleasurable objects of the external world that have been absorbed into the ego by introjection.

reality principles: (*Psychoan.*) the awareness of the demands of the environment and the necessity of conforming to those demands. *Contr.* PLEASURE PRINCIPLE.

reality testing: (*Psychoan.*) the fundamental function of the ego, which consists of the objective evaluation and judgment of the external world.

reason: 1. the totality of the intellectual processes involved in thinking and problem solving. 2. a cause for any event. 3. a motive for behavior. 4. a logical, well-ordered mind—as in "a man of reason."

reasoning: the process of thinking, especially of logical thinking or problem solving.

reassurance: in counseling and psychotherapy, the use of verbal techniques to make the patient believe in a favorable outcome for the course of therapy.

rebirth fantasy: (*Psychoan.*) an unconscious and symbolic fantasy of being born again, usually represented as being in or emerging from water.

recall: 1. the process of invoking in the memory something that has been learned. 2. the verbal reproduction of something once learned. The essay examination is an example of a recall test.

recall method: measuring retention by calculating the percentage of material once learned that can be correctly reproduced after an interval.

recall test: a test, such as an essay examination, in which the task is to reproduce items or material once learned.

recapitulation theory: the theory that in their individual development organisms pass through all the various stages of evolutionary development characteristic of the race.

receiver: 1. in communications theory, that which transforms a signal into a message. 2. any electronic device for picking up electrical signals from a transmitter.

receiver operating characteristics curve (ROC curve): the curve representing the relationship between correct stimuli detections (hits) and false alarms. *Syn.* relative operating characteristics.

receiving hospital: an institution designed specifically for the reception of individuals suffering from the onset of mental disorders. Diagnosis and preliminary treatment are carried out without commitment; further treatment may be recommended in other institutions.

recency, law of or **principle of:** the generalization that, other things being equal, the most recent items or experiences are remembered best.

recept: 1. a mental image formed by the repetition of percepts. 2. an afferent impulse or process in the nervous system.

receptive aphasia: a language disability in which the individual cannot understand spoken or written material; any type of sensory aphasia.

receptive character: an orientation in which the individual expects support from the outside—from parents, friends, authorities, and God.

receptive-expressive aphasia: a language disorder in which the individual cannot understand spoken or written material and, in addition, cannot communicate with others verbally.

receptive field: the region of a receptor surface where the response to a stimulus is effective. Particularly employed in reference to the retina.

receptivity: 1. openness or willingness to accept ideas or suggestions. 2. capable of being stimulated. 3. an attitude of passivity or dependency.

receptor: a specialized structure particularly sensitive to certain kinds of stimuli. In general, receptors may be divided into four classes: (1) photic, or receptors sensitive to light; (2) mechanical, or receptors sensitive to mechanical stimulation, such as the ear or skin; (3) chemical, such as receptors in the nose and tongue; and (4) thermal, or receptors sensitive to warm and cold.

receptor site: specialized region on neurons that receives and reacts to transmitters at synapses.

recessive: 1. pertaining to a gene that does not show its effects in the presence of a dominant gene. 2. the quality of holding back or not expressing the self. *Contr.* DOMINANT.

recessive trait: in genetics, a trait that does not show in the offspring in the presence of a dominant trait. If both parents have a recessive trait, the offspring will show the trait.

recidivism: the repetition of criminal or delinquent behavior. The term is usually applied only in the case of habitual criminals with two or more convictions.

reciprocal: 1. in mathematics, unity divided by any number. 2. characterizing a relationship that is opposite or reverse. such as reciprocal muscles, which work in antagonistic directions.

reciprocal inhibition: 1. the inhibition of one neuronal arc by the simultaneous activity of another. 2. a form of behavior therapy developed by Joseph Wolpe in which classical conditioning is used to condition responses incompatible with a response to be eliminated. *Syn.* COUNTER-CONDITIONING. 3. an inability to recall one of two associations because of mutual interference.

reciprocal innervation: the relationship between the members of any pair of neuronal arcs that mediate muscle reflexes such that when one is active, the other is inhibited. Reciprocal innervation makes possible the mutual working relationship between antagonistic muscle pairs.

reciprocity: 1. (*Piaget*) the child's belief that punishment should be logically related to an offense. 2. the principle or law that responses are the product of duration and intensity of stimulation. For example, a weak visual stimulus of infinite duration may equal a brief stimulus of higher intensity. The principle holds only over a narrow range. *Syn.* BUNSEN-ROSCOE LAW.

reciprocity norm: the belief that one should treat another as he has treated you. See also EQUITY THEORY.

recitation: 1. the oral recall of learned material. 2. in education, the instructional technique of question and answer between pupils and teacher.

recitation method: memorizing by giving a certain proportion of time to attempting to repeat orally (or silently) what has been learned, in contrast to spending all one's time reading silently.

recognition: 1. an awareness that an object, person, or event is familiar or has been learned in the past. 2. acknowledgment of accomplishment or merit.

recognition method: the use of recognition as a means of measuring the amount of material retained after a learning session.

recognition span: the reading span, or number of words that can be grasped in one fixation.

recognition test: a test in which the subject is required to choose an item previously learned from among several items not learned. A multiple-choice test is a recognition test.

recognition vocabulary: see PASSIVE VOCABULARY.

recollection: the process of remembering an event from the past.

reconditioning: reestablishing a conditioned response after extinction has set in by further repetition with reinforcement.

reconstruction: (*Psychoan.*) the interpretation of psychoanalytic data so as to illuminate the past development of personality and the present meaning of the material for the individual.

reconstruction method: a technique for the study of memory in which the individual is asked to restore to its original order a distorted series of items that were studied in the original sequence.

recovery: 1. a return to a condition of normalcy after a disease, mental disorder, or a lesion. 2. a return to a resting state following stimulation.

recovery time: the time needed for tissue to recover full irritability following a stimulus.

recruitment: the gradual increase in response units upon prolonged stimulation with a stimulus of constant intensity. The phenomenon is attributed to periodic fluctuations in irritability with some neural units gradually becoming excited as they increase in irritability.

recruitment of loudness: the principle that as intensity of a tone increases, the perceived loudness of the tone increases more for the partially deaf than for the normal. *Syn.* auditory regression.

rectilinear: characterized as being a straight-line function; capable of being represented as a straight-line function.

rectilinear distribution: a distribution of scores with approximately equal numbers of cases in all categories as opposed to a normal distribution, where the greatest number of cases falls close to the mean.

rectilinear regression: linear regression.

recurrent vision: a succession of positive and negative afterimages.

red: the hue or color evoked by a stimulation with light whose wavelength is around 650–750 nanometers.

red-green blindness: a form of partial color-blindness in which certain shades of red and green are confused. This is the most common form of color-blindness, affecting about 7 percent of the male population and 1–3 percent of females. It is presumed to be due to a weakness or absence of the necessary receptors in the retina.

redintegration: 1. the reinstatement of a memory upon the appearance of a stimulus element that was part of a stimulus complex that formerly aroused the event. Thus, a few notes of "Yankee Doodle" will arouse the total perception of the song. 2. the capability of any sensory stimulus associated with another stimulus of arousing the response learned to the first. This form of redintegration occurs in classical conditioning whenever stimulus generalization occurs.

red nucleus: nerve cells in the front part of the tegmentum in the midbrain. The red nucleus gives rise to the rubrospinal tract.

red-sighted: in some individuals, the tendency for the eye to display a heightened sensitivity to red. It may be the result of retinal or nervous pathology or due to overexposure to green, the complement of red.

reduced cue: the principle of learning stating that after repeated trials a smaller or incomplete part of the original stimulus situation is capable of arousing a response.

reduced eye: a schematic model of the unaccommodated human eye.

reduced score: a score from which a constant has been subtracted in order to facilitate computation.

reduction: a lessening or diminution of a function, such as need reduction following upon drive satisfaction.

reduction division: see MEIOSIS.

reductionism: the point of view that the correct method to employ in the understanding of phenomena is to analyze or reduce them to their component parts. The structuralistic and behavioristic psychologies are more reductionistic in their point of view than the functionalistic and Gestalt schools. The Gestalt psychologists

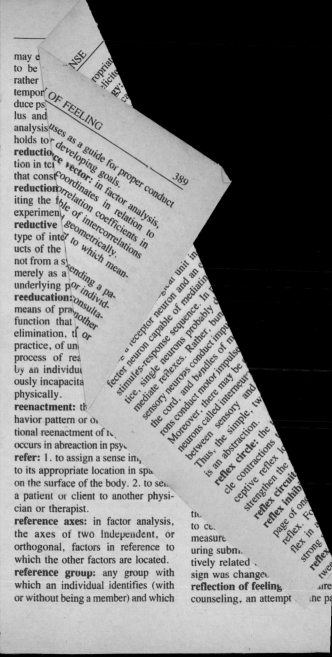

may e
to be
rather
tempor
duce ps
lus and
analysis
holds to
reductio
tion in te
that cons
reduction
iting the f
experimen
reductive
type of inte
ucts of the
not from a s
merely as a
underlying p
reeducation:
means of pra
function that
elimination, t
practice, of un
process of rea
by an individu
ously incapacit
physically.

reenactment: th
havior pattern or o
tional reenactment of r
occurs in abreaction in psy

refer: 1. to assign a sense im
to its appropriate location in spa
on the surface of the body. 2. to se
a patient or client to another physician or therapist.

reference axes: in factor analysis,
the axes of two independent, or
orthogonal, factors in reference to
which the other factors are located.

reference group: any group with
which an individual identifies (with
or without being a member) and which

ropriate
licite
gy:
ca

uses as a guide for proper conduct
developing goals.
ce vector: in factor analysis,
coordinates in relation to
correlation coefficients in
role of intercorrelations
geometrically.
to which mean-
ending a pa-
or individ-
consulta-
another
or

...al unit i
factor neuron and an e
factor neuron capable of mediatin
stimulus-response sequence. In
tice, single neurons probably d
mediate reflexes. Rather bun
sensory neurons conduct imp
the cord, and bundles of m
rons conduct motor impulse
Moreover, there may be
neurons called interneur
between sensory and
Thus, the simple, tw
is an abstraction.
reflex circle: the
cle contractions
ceptive reflex l
strengthen the
reflex circui
reflex inhib
page of on
reflex. Fo
flex in a
strong
reflex
twe

tie
to ce
measure
uring subm
tively related
sign was change
reflection of feeling
counseling, an attempt   the pa

stimulation, reflexes
d.

the point of view that all
ultimately be reducible

serve: a term formerly em-
by Skinner to characterize the
of responses that will be made
the reinforcement has been
drawn. *Syn.* OPERANT RESERVE.

lex sensitization principle: the
eneralization that once a response
as been well practiced with a certain
stimulus, the same response may then
be elicited by a previously neutral
stimulus.

reflex time: see REFLEX LATENCY.

refraction: the bending or change in
direction of a wave, such as a light
wave, by any medium.

refraction, index of: a number that
gives the degree to which a ray of
light is bent in passing through a
refracting medium.

refractory: 1. unresponsive (see
REFRACTORY PERIOD). 2. not docile;
resistant to discipline.

refractory period: a brief period of
time following stimulation of a neuron or muscle fiber when the tissue
either is completely unresponsive
(*absolute refractory period*) or requires a stronger than normal stimulus (*relative refractory period*). The
absolute refractory period is coexten-
sive with the passage of the nervous
impulse and lasts only a few tenths of
a millisecond, while the relative refractory period follows immediately
afterward and is much longer and
more variable than the absolute refractory period, depending upon the condition of the tissue.

regeneration: 1. the restoration of a
lost or damaged part by growth. 2.
rejuvenation or restoration of vitality.

f-
g a
rac-
o not
lles of
ses into
otor neu-
s outward.
ne or more
ns interposed
motor units.
-neuron reflex

endency for mus-
o activate proprio-
ops which, in turn,
uscular contraction.
REFLEX ARC.

tion: the reflexive stop-
reflex by an antagonistic
example, the scratch re-
dog can be inhibited by a
hock to the foot.

latency: the time interval be-
the application of a stimulus
e beginning of a reflex response.

ogenous zone: a specific area
e surface of the body where,

regimen: a systematic program regulating hours of rest, diet, exercise, etc., in order to improve health.

region: 1. a space or area. 2. in topological psychology, any part of the life space.

regnancy: (*Murray*) the shortest unit or aspect of experience.

regnant construct: (*Kelly*) a superordinate construct that assigns its elements on an all-or-nothing basis to other constructs.

regression: 1. a retreating; a moving backward. 2. a return to earlier levels of development; the manifestation in older individuals of more primitive levels of behavior. 3. in statistics, the relationships between two paired variables. The regression is expressed in the form of an equation such that for each value of x there is a given value of y, and vice versa. 4. in genetics, the tendency for individual organisms to revert to the typical form. Thus, the children of very tall men tend not to be as tall as their fathers. 5. in conditioning, the fact that a previously extinguished conditioned response may reappear after punishment. Compare with (2) above. Occasionally, previously acquired conditioned responses may reappear without punishment.

regression analysis: a statistical technique for predicting the value of a continuously quantitative variable from qualitative ratings. The technique is illustrated in industry when the worker's output is predicted on the basis of his foreman's ratings.

regression curve: a curve or line fitted to the means of a set of arrayed variables in a correlation table.

regression equation: the formula for computing the probable value of y, a paired, correlated variable from the other variable, x, or vice versa.

regression line: the line or curve representing the regression of one variable to another. Regression lines are drawn on the basis of the regression equation.

regression neurosis: a neurosis characterized by primitivization of behavior or returning to behavior patterns more appropriate for an earlier age.

regression time: in reading, the time spent to reexamine words already passed.

regression weight: a regression coefficient.

regressive substitute: see REGRESSION.

regulatory behavior: behavior that aids in maintaining a balance or steady state in the organism by fulfilling bodily needs.

rehabilitation: the restoration to normal, or to as satisfactory a status as possible, of an individual who has been injured or suffered a mental disorder.

rehearsal: 1. a practice performance of an act prior to a public appearance. 2. a review of already learned material.

reinforce: 1. to strengthen. 2. to increase the probability of a response. See also REINFORCEMENT.

reinforcement: 1. the strengthening of a response by adding an increment of habit strength. 2. increasing the probability of a response. 3. strengthening of one reflex activity by the stimulatenous elicitation of another. Thus, the knee jerk is strengthened by having the subject squeeze hard on the hand dynamometer. 4. the presentation or occurrence of the unconditioned stimulus (food, for example) with the conditioned stimulus (bell, for example). 5. a reward, such as food. 6. anything that reduces or partially reduces a need. 7. anything that reduces drive stimuli. 8. knowledge of results or self-recognition of the correctness of a response, such as occurs in the use of teaching machines.

reinforcement schedule: a program determining when the subject will be reinforced, either according to a time interval or to the number of responses he makes. See CONTINUOUS REINFORCEMENT; INTERMITTENT REINFORCEMENT; FIXED-INTERVAL REINFORCEMENT; VARIABLE-INTERVAL REINFORCEMENT; RATIO REINFORCEMENT.

reinforcing stimulus: the unconditioned stimulus or the reward administered after the subject has made the appropriate response.

reintegration: see REDINTEGRATION.

rejection: 1. the assumption of a negative or antagonistic attitude toward another individual. 2. in test development, the discarding of useless items.

relation: 1. any connection between two variables such that variation in one is accompanied by variation in the other. 2. a situation of dependency between two variables such that one is an antecedent condition for another.

relational concept: a concept defined in terms of relations between elements rather than in absolute terms.

relation learning: learning in which the tasks demand that the subject learn relationships among items.

relationship therapy: between client and therapist, a relationship in which the individual learns to modify his feelings and his behavior patterns and subsequently can transfer these newly acquired adjustments to situations outside the therapeutic situation.

relativism: the principle that no experience is intrinsically self-sufficient but is dependent upon other experiences for its meaning.

relaxation: 1. the return of a muscle to a resting state following contraction. 2. a state of low tension with an absence of strong emotions.

relaxation therapy: a form of therapy in which emphasis is put on teaching the patient how to relax, on the assumption that muscular relaxation will help bring about a lessening of psychological tensions.

relearning: 1. learning again what one originally learned but has forgotten. 2. a procedure for studying retention by having the individual learn a list and then having him relearn it after an interval. The amount of retention is measured as the savings in time or trials on the second learning. *Syn.* SAVINGS METHOD.

relative error: the absolute error (observed value minus the true value) divided by the true value.

relative pitch: 1. the pitch of a tone higher or lower than a given standard or as determined by its position on the musical scale. 2. the ability to recognize or reproduce pitch intervals.

releaser: a highly specific stimulus that initiates species-specific behavior. Thus, the sight of the mother duck releases imprinting behavior about thirteen hours after hatching.

release therapy: 1. a form of play therapy designed to permit the expression of deep-seated emotional conflicts. 2. more generally, any type of psychotherapy that enables the individual to release pent-up emotions, particularly hostile and destructive impulses.

reliability: 1. in characterizing personality, trustworthiness and dependability. 2. in mental measurements, the dependability of a test as reflected in the consistency of its scores upon repeated measurements of the same group. One common measure of reliability is the test-retest correlation-coefficient technique. The test is given twice to the same group with an interval of several months between testings to allow for forgetting of specific items. The results are then correlated. High correlations (+.90 or above) are taken as indices that the test is reliable. There are a number of other measures of internal consistency that give estimates of reliability. These may be found in any manual of psychological statistics.

reliability, index of: an estimate of the correlation between scores on a test and the corresponding theoretical true scores. The index is equal to $\sqrt{r}$.

reliability sampling: a measure of the agreement between two or more samples taken from the same population.

religious resignation: (R. B. Cattell) renunciation and lack of will. *Contr.* PROMETHEAN WILL.

remedial reading: specialized instruction designed to correct faulty reading habits.

remember: to reinstate a previous experience; to recall or reproduce what was learned previously. *Syn.* recollect.

reminiscence: 1. the recall of a previous experience, especially relatively complete recall in an attitude of enjoyment of the memories in question. 2. a temporary rise in retention without intervening practice.

remission: a temporary cessation in the symptoms of a disease or mental disorder.

remote: 1. distant, particularly of an

association between two remembered items far removed from each other. 2. characterizing kinesthetic sensations that arise from receptors not located in the member being moved. 3. characterizing percepts that arise through intermediaries rather than direct sensation. For example, a blindfolded individual may be asked to explore an object with a stick and report its characteristics.

remote association: in verbal learning, the connection between one item in a list and another item removed by more than one step from the first.

remote conditioning: see TRACE CONDITIONED RESPONSE.

REM sleep: sleep characterized by rapid eye movements that are picked up and recorded by electrodes strapped to the skin around the eyes. REM sleep is accompanied by dreaming.

renal: pertaining to the kidney.

renifleur: an individual who associates sexual excitement with odors.

Renshaw cells: Golgi type II neurons that release gamma-amino-butyric acid to inhibit other neurons.

renunciation: 1. a surrender of one's own will to a supernatural being. 2. refusing to obtain satisfaction for one's impulses. See REPRESSION.

reorganization principle: in Gestalt theory, the generalization that in new learning or in perception, there is an alteration of the entire structure of the remembered Gestalten. Presumably new elements added to old cognitive structures result in disequilibrium. The consequent reorganization seeks to achieve a new state of equilibrium with a minimum of distortion to the previous structure.

repetition: 1. practicing anything with a view to learning it. 2. a single trial or experiment. 3. a replica or duplication of something.

repetition compulsion: the pathological need to repeat a behavior pattern over and over again.

repetition, law of: see FREQUENCY, LAW OF; USE, LAW OF.

replicate: to duplicate an experiment in all detail.

replication: 1. the subdivision of an experiment into several parts, each containing all the essential parameters, in order to compare the several replicas for assessing possible extraneous or uncontrolled variables. 2. The repetition of an experiment.

replication therapy: in behavior therapy, a technique in which the therapist elicits and reinforces behavior patterns similar to those in the patient's everyday environment.

representation: act of taking the place of, or symbolizing, something. The term is used a great deal by psychologists of the psychoanalytic school, who believe that many of our memories, dreams, and perceptions really represent unconscious impulses or repressed experiences. The term is also employed in perceptual psychology to indicate the fact that psychological processes do not mirror the external world but are only representative of it. See ISOMORPHISM.

representative: characterizing samples considered true or valid indices of the characteristics of the entire population.

representative design: 1. combining experimental and statistical manipulation of variables in order to permit all relevant variables to influence the dependent variable. 2. the inclusion of a representative or stratified sample of subject in an experiment.

representative factors: verbal symbols and imagery that serve as mediators of ideational activity.

representative measure or **score:** a number, such as the mean or median, that best stands for all the scores collectively. Thus, if we say that a student's grade average is a C, this indicates that his work in all his courses is best characterized as C, or average, even though there may be individual exceptions in some courses.

representative sampling: selecting the respondents or items in a sample in such a manner that they are valid indices of the entire population from which the sample was drawn.

repress: 1. (*Psychoan.*) to forcefully eject from consciousness shameful or painful experiences or impulses the individual feels are incompatible with his evaluation of himself or which cause anxiety. 2. to suppress or reject consciously. This usage is common but technically incorrect. See also REPRESSION.

repressed complex: (*Psychoan.*) an emotional constellation centering around an individual or situation the individual inhibits from coming to a conscious level. For an example, see OEDIPUS COMPLEX.

repressed wish: a wish or impulse inhibited from reaching a conscious level.

repression: (*Psychoan.*) the forceful ejection from consciousness of impulses, memories, or experiences that are painful or shameful and generate a high level of anxiety. Repression, according to Freudian psychoanalysis, is a function of the ego. Impulses arising from the primitive, pleasure-seeking id attempt to gain consciousness so that they may force the ego or rational mind to seek satisfaction for them. The ego, however, dealing as it does with reality and the demands of the superego, attempts to repress such impulses. Repression can also arise through the necessity of ridding the consciousness of extremely painful experiences, such as the memory of a sexual assault. The mechanism is essentially the same; that is, the ego forces the experiences into the unconscious. Any repressed impulse or experience may gain entry to the upper levels of mind in a symbolic form in dreams, errors, slips of the tongue, and in the guise of neurotic symptoms. Repression should not be confused with *suppression* or *inhibition*. Both of the latter processes are voluntary. The essential mechanism of repression was held by Freud to be unconscious and involuntary.

reproduction: 1. in learning or memory, carrying out a task in the manner in which it was first learned. 2. in psychophysics, the method of average error.

reproductive facilitation: in learning, the increase in ability to reproduce previously learned material as a result of intervening activities, such as rest, reminiscence, etc.

reproductive function: 1. the totality of processes involved in the production of a new individual. 2. a specific activity, such as sexual intercourse, involved in bringing a new individual into the world.

reproductive interference: retroactive inhibition or the tendency for new learning to interfere with the retention and reproducibility of old learning.

reproductive strength: in learning, the summation of all factors favoring the probability that a response will be made on a given occasion.

reproof: a verbal reprimand. *Contr*. PRAISE.

REP test: (*Kelly*) role construction repertory test to determine the individual's constructs (*q.v.*) how they are applied and interrelated.

required behavior: behavior patterns that, in a given culture, are demanded of individuals.

rereading method: a procedure in which the individual's memory is tested following a prescribed number of readings of the material to be learned.

research: 1. a systematic attempt to discover by means of experimental investigation or naturalistic observation the laws or principles governing the operation of phenomena. 2. library investigation of documents, publications, etc., for the purpose of developing an historical perspective on a subject or discovering existing facts.

research system: in human engineering, the investigation of general principles applicable to the design and development of new machines in relation to their human operators.

resentment: an attitude of anger or antipathy.

reserve: 1. a tendency to avoid participation in social situations. 2. a reservoir of habit strength.

residual: 1. pertaining to that which remains after an accident or operation, as *residual vision* or *residual hearing*. 2. in factor analysis, the variance that remains after all factors have been extracted from the matrix.

residual matrix: the matrix that remains after the factor loadings have been extracted.

residual schizophrenia: a designation for patients no longer psychotic following a psychotic episode diagnosed as schizophrenic.

residuum: 1. the remainder. 2. an engram or trace left after an experience.

resinous: a quality of olfactory sensation; pine pitch, for example.

resistance: 1. the action of any body in opposition to a force. 2. the opposition of a circuit to the passage of an electric current. 3. (*Psychoan*). the attempt on the part of the patient to avoid having unconscious material come to consciousness. 4. social opposition or negativism in response to orders, rules, political policies, etc. 5. the first stage of the adaptation syndrome, in which the body mobilizes its resources in order to meet stress.

resocialization: the attainment, by a seriously maladjusted person, of skills that will enable him to integrate into the community.

resolution of anxiety: (*Psychoan*.) the process of discovering the cause and anxiety in the unconscious and thereby releasing it.

resolving power: the ability of the eye to see two distinct objects as distinct. An ancient test of resolving power consisted of determining whether the individual could see a double star in the handle of the Big Dipper as double.

resonance: 1. the vibration of any sounding body in response to an external sound. Thus, a violin will vibrate if a trumpet is sounded nearby. The eardrum resonates in sympathy with external sounds, thus enabling the sound to get into the internal ear. See also HEARING THEORIES. 2. a deep, rich vocal quality.

resonance-volley theory of hearing: see HEARING THEORIES.

resonator: a device used to intensify the sound of the tuning fork or other source of sound. A small box is usually employed to amplify the sound of a tuning fork.

respirograph: a graphic record of the breathing cycle.

respondent: 1. (*adj.*) pertaining to behavior, elicited by a specific, known stimulus. *Contr.* OPERANT. 2. (*noun*) the individual or organism that reacts to a stimulus. The term is frequently used to designate an individual who responds to a questionnaire.

response: 1. any muscular or glandular process elicited by a stimulus. 2. an answer, especially an answer to a test question or questionnaire. 3. any behavior, whether overt or covert. For further definitions of *response*, see PSYCHOLOGY. The term *response* is a very general one and one of the most widely used terms in psychology, usually with qualifiers.

response amplitude: the magnitude of a response as measured in terms of some predetermined dimension. For example, the response amplitude of the knee jerk would be the height of the jerk as measured in centimeters. See also RESPONSE MAGNITUDE.

response attitude: in reaction-time experiments, the set of the individual to respond as soon as the stimulus is given. The attention is concentrated on the musculature rather than on the stimulus. *Contr.* STIMULUS ATTITUDE.

response by analogy principle: (*Thorndike*) the generalization that an animal in an unfamiliar situation will respond in a similar manner to the way he responds in a similar but familiar situation. Thorndike's law of transfer.

response circuit: a neuronal chain or loop connecting receptors and effectors.

response class: a class of behavior patterns, all of which produce essentially the same change in an organism's environment.

response-cost contingencies: in operant conditioning, a technique in which stimuli from the subject's environment are removed in order to weaken preceding responses.

response detail: (*Rorschach*) a response involving less than the entire blot.

response dispersion: a random or scattered series of responses given by the organism when thwarted or frustrated in attempts to reach a goal.

response equivalance: a similar response made to a similar stimulus.

response generalization principle: the generalization that when a subject has been conditioned to a certain stimulus, that stimulus becomes effective in eliciting similar responses.

response hierarchy: a class of behavior patterns arranged in the serial order of probability of their occurrence.

response intensity: the dimension of magnitude or amplitude of a response. In a salivary conditioning experiment, the number of drops of saliva secreted by the animal would be the measure of the response intensity.

response latency: the duration of the interval between a stimulus and a response.

response learning: learning in which the goal is reached by making certain responses, as opposed to learning that is primarily cognitive or involves the learning of the location of the goal in space.

response magnitude: the strength of a response in terms of amplitude, duration, intensity, or frequency.

response-oriented theories or **systems:** all systems of psychology that place primary emphasis on responses.

For an example, see SKINNER'S OPERANT CONDITIONING.

response pattern: a grouping of responses into a distinct unit of activity.

response rate: the number of responses occurring per unit of time. Response rate is an important measure of learning in operant conditioning.

response reference: the position of a response on the dimensional continuum from distal responses to proximal responses.

response set: 1. in reaction-time experiments, a state of concentration on the muscular phase of the process in contrast to a *stimulus set*, in which the individual concentrates strongly on the stimulus. 2. more generally, a readiness to engage in a certain type of response.

response strength: 1. magnitude or intensity of a response. 2. the magnitude of a response as a function of the number of times it has been reinforced.

response system: 1. the muscular and glandular system. 2. the neural, muscular, and glandular systems involved in responses. 3. the totality of physiological, neural, and psychological processes involved in a response.

response threshold: the critical state of all relevant systems that will just produce a particular response.

response time: the time involved in making a response.

response variable: the subject's reaction in a psychological experiment.

responsive: 1. characterizing an organism that emits reactions to stimuli. 2. characterizing one whose answers or reactions are pertinent to the question under discussion.

rest: 1. the condition of an organism or of tissue that is not responding. 2. a period of recuperation or rehabilitation following recovery from a mental disorder or disease.

restructure: 1. to change a psychological field. 2. to bring about a fundamental change in a problem or percept.

retained-members method: a technique for measuring retention by recording the number of units of a whole that can be recalled at the time of testing.

retardation: 1. the slowing of any process. 2. the slowing of an individual's mental development. 3. a failure to progress normally in school.

retarded depression: a pathological slowing of motor activities, accompanied by dejection, self-depreciation, and delusions of worthlessness.

retention: the persistence of a learned act or experience during an interval of no practice. The most widely used measures of retention are: (a) recall, (b) recognition, (c) reproduction, (d) relearning (*q.q.v.*).

The course of forgetting has been studied in terms of both quantitative and qualitative changes. The quantitative decay of retention depends upon the conditions of original learning (conditions favoring efficient learning also favor good retention); the nature of the materials learned (materials that are meaningful and lend themselves to good organization are better remembered); and attitudinal and motivational factors (things we desire to remember are more easily remembered, while indifference or lack of interest may make for more rapid forgetting). Qualitative changes are revealed as distortions in memory, such as occur in rumors or in pictorial materials transmitted from person to person or recalled only at intervals by a single individual. Details are either

omitted or added, and sometimes the story or picture is made "better" than the original.

Theories of forgetting have been formulated in terms of retroactive and proactive inhibition effects, systematic distortions in memory, and motivational factors. *Retroactive inhibition* refers to a loss in retention as the result of new learning which acts back upon and inhibits the traces of older learning, whereas *proactive inhibition* refers to similar inhibitory effects that occur when the interpolated material is placed ahead of the material to be learned. *Systematic distortions* in memory are assumed to occur because of the selective dropping of details and the tendency to accentuate certain features of remembered events. In general, such effects are presumed to follow the same principles that account for good organization in original perceptions. *Motivational factors* include amnesia, which is the complete forgetting of one's personal past, and repression, which is the forgetting of material that is psychologically painful or inconsistent with the individual's evaluation of the self.

retention curve: a graphic representation of the course of retention over a period of time.

reticular formation or **reticular activating system:** a loosely defined network of cells extending from the upper part of the spinal cord through the medulla and pons to the brain stem. *Abbr.* RAS. The reticular activating system is believed to be an important center for regulation of attention, alertness, and sleep, and for selectivity of perception.

reticularis pontis oralis: a portion of the brain-stem reticular formation believed to be essential to arousal. Its destruction results in a comatose condition.

retina: the innermost layer of the eye, which contains the light-sensitive cells, or rods and cones. The rods function in scotopic, or twilight, vision, the cones in photopic, or daylight, vision.

retinal disparity: the difference between the image received by one eye and that received by the other, caused by the separation of the eyes. If the forefinger is held directly in front of the face and fixated alternately with the two eyes, more of the fingernail will be seen with one eye than the other. Retinal disparity is a cue to depth perception.

retinal elements: the rods and cones.

retinal field: the patterns of sensory cells on the retina upon which the image falls.

retinal horizon: the horizontal line across the retina, corresponding to the terrestrial horizon when the eye is at rest and fixating on a point in the infinite distance.

retinal image: the optical image of external objects formed on the retina of the eye by the lens and other refracting media.

retinal light: the idioretinal visual sensation of light that occurs in the absence of any kind of stimulation and is presumed to be due to the intrinsic activity of the retina and cortex. *Syn.* cortical gray.

retinal oscillations: the excitation effect of a momentary isolated stimulus resulting in a succession of alternating light and dark bands, as in Charpentier's bands, or in persistent afterimages.

retinal picture: the retinal image.

retinal rivalry: alternating sensations from one eye and the other under conditions where a unitary image is impossible, such as in looking at two different colors in a stereoscope. *Syn.* BINOCULAR RIVALRY. *Contr.* BINOCULAR FUSION.

retinal zones: see COLOR ZONES.

retinene: a pigment of the retina from which, in the presence of vitamin A and certain proteins, visual purple is formed. *Syn.* VISUAL YELLOW.

retinitis: inflammation of the retina.

retinitis pigmentosa: a pathological condition of the pigment layer of the retina resulting in diminished color sensitivity, particularly to blue. There is also a deficiency in color adaptation.

retinoscope: a mirror with a small aperture in the center for observing the interior of the eye as light is projected into it by reflection from the mirror, which is rocked back and forth.

retraction: the flexion of a limb.

retreat from reality: see FLIGHT FROM REALITY.

retrieval: the process of removing information from storage or from long-term memory.

retroactive: acting backward in time; affecting what has already taken place, such as present learning affecting the retention of previously learned material.

retroactive association: a learned connection between any item in a list and an item that precedes it.

retroactive facilitation: the strengthening of a learned association by an association learned earlier. *Syn.* positive retroaction.

retroactive inhibition: interference effect of subsequent learning on retention of material already learned. The experimental model for measuring the degree of retroactive inhibition is as follows:

(Equated Groups)			
Group I	Learn A	Rest	Recall A
Group II	Learn A	Learn B	Recall A
Difference in Recall of A = RI			

retrobulbar: 1. toward the posterior side of the medulla. 2. to the rear of the eyeball.

retrogenesis: the theory that new growth develops out of undifferentiated tissue rather than from fully developed structures.

retrograde: 1. going backward. 2. degenerating.

retrograde amnesia: loss of memory for events occurring before the onset of amnesia.

retrogression: a reaction to frustration by returning to satisfactions more appropriate at an earlier level of development. For example, for an older child to revert to thumbsucking when frustrated exemplifies retrogression. *Syn.* REGRESSION; PRIMITIVIZATION.

retrospection: an objective observation and report on a conscious experience that has already passed, in contrast to *introspection*, which is an observation and report on a present experience.

retrospective falsification: an unintentional memory error in a report of an event.

return sweep: the movement of the eyes in going from the end of one line to the beginning of another.

re-uptake: the return of a neurotransmitter to the cell that liberated it, thus terminating the postsynaptic potential.

reverberatory circuit: a system of neurons in the brain or in the autonomic nervous system, capable of maintaining activity after the initiating impulse has died out. Reverberatory circuits were first discovered in the autonomic nervous system but

have been hypothesized to exist in the central nervous system. They are employed to account for the persistence of attitudes, perceptual learning, and motivational states. It is not necessary to assume that such circuits must be continuously active. An outside stimulus could rearouse the circuit to activity just as a glance at piano music may stimulate a player to sit down and play a long-forgotten tune without further recourse to the music. See also HEBB'S THEORY OF PERCEPTUAL LEARNING.

reverie: a kind of ideational activity without aim or purpose, which tends to wander over a wide range of incidents or ideas. See also DAYDREAM.

reversal formation: see REACTION FORMATION.

reversible figure: a special form of ambiguous figure in which the perspective readily reverses. For an illustration, see AMBIGUOUS FIGURE.

reversible perspective: see ALTERNATING PERSPECTIVE.

reversion: 1. inheritance of a recessive trait. 2. regression, or a return to an earlier level of development. 3. atavism; reappearance of a hereditary character absent in immediately preceding generations.

review: a return to material already learned for the purpose of further study.

revival: the recall of an experience.

reward: any stimulus, situation, or verbal statement that produces satisfaction or increases the probability of a learned act. *Syn.* REINFORCEMENT.

In general, behavioristic psychologists prefer the term *reinforcement*, since *reward* has a somewhat mentalistic connotation and is associated with satisfaction, an inner, nonobservable state. Most psychologists, when referring to children, particularly in educational situations, use the term *reward*.

reward expectancy: (*Tolman*) a set or readiness that leads the animal to search for a goal. Reward expectancy is built up after a number of trials, associating a certain place or pathway with a reward. The animal then comes to expect the reward, the expectation being manifested by excited, searching behavior until it is found.

rhabdomancy: divining by means of rods; dowsing.

rhathymia: in factor-analysis studies of personality, a factor indicative of a carefree, happy-go-lucky attitude.

rheobase: a strength of current of infinitely long duration, just sufficient to excite tissue. See also CHRONAXIE.

rheotropism: an orienting response in which the organism in a stream of water turns toward the direction of flow.

Rhine, Joseph Banks: American parapsychologist (1895–1980). Rhine's professional education was at the University of Chicago, where he received the Ph.D. degree in biology in 1925. Within the next decade his interests turned toward the study of extrasensory perception and with William McDougall he founded the Parapsychology Laboratory at Duke University, where his world-famous experiments on ESP were carried out. He later served as director of its successor, the Foundation for Research on the Nature of Man, in Durham, North Carolina.

Rhine's contributions to psychology are many. He stimulated quantitative research in an area neglected by most experimental psychologists and popularized parapsychology through the *Journal of Parapsychology*, which he founded, and through his many articles, books, and lectures on the subject. His major publications include *Extrasensory Perception* (1935), coauthor of *Extrasensory Perception after 60 Years* (1940), *The Reaches of the Mind* (1947), and *Parapsychology: Frontier Science of the Mind* (1957).

rhinencephalon: the portion of the brain consisting of the olfactory bulbs, pyriform lobes, hippocampus, and fornix. *Syn.* OLFACTORY BRAIN. Many of what were formerly considered to be the olfactory functions of the rhinencephalon are now believed to be associated with emotional behavior.

rho (ρ): the rank-order correlation coefficient. Its formula is:

$$\rho = 1 - \frac{6 \Sigma D^2}{N (N^2 - 1)}$$

where D is a deviation in ranks and N is the number of cases ranked.

rhodopsin: visual purple, the pigmented material that stimulates the rods in the retina. It bleaches in strong light and recovers in darkness. *Syn.* VISUAL PURPLE.

rhombencephalon: the hindbrain, consisting of cerebellum, pons, and medulla.

rhythm: the serial recurrence of sounds or other phenomena marked off by time intervals.

ribonucleic acid (RNA): giant protein molecules in the cell nuclei believed to act as messengers and transfer agents in the genetic development of a new organism. Some investigators also believe that RNA may be involved in memory. See also DEOXY-RIBONUCLEIC ACID.

Ricco's law: the relationship between a constant visual threshold (C), and the area (A) and intensity (I) of retinal stimulation for small areas:

$$C = A \times I.$$

right-associates procedure: see PAIRED ASSOCIATES.

righting reflex: a reflexive act that functions to return an organism to an upright position when the organism has been thrown off balance or placed on its back.

rigid: 1. pedantic; logically precise. 2. inflexible in adjustmental behavior.

rigidity: 1. a condition of strong muscular contraction that strongly flexes or contracts the afflicted member. 2. a personality trait characterized by inability to change one's attitudes, opinions, or manner of adjustment.

risk level: the percentage of samples that may be expected to fall outside stated statistical limits, such as the 5 or 10 percent level. Thus, at the 10 percent level, the chances are 10 in 100 or 1 in 10, that with repeated samplings the statistic obtained will be significantly greater or less than chance fluctuations.

risky shift: the finding that a group decision is often less conservative than the average of the individual decisions taken prior to group discussion.

ritalin: a drug widely used in treating hyperactive children.

ritual: 1. a system of rites or ceremonies. 2. the irrational, compulsive behavior patterns of the compulsive-obsessive. 3. any rigid or stereotyped behavior.

rivalry: a competition between two groups or individuals.

RNA: see RIBONUCLEIC ACID.

robot: 1. a machine capable of carrying out certain human functions. 2. a person who is rigid in his behavior and performs like a machine.

ROC curve: see RECEIVER OPERATING CHARACTERISTIC CURVE.

rods: the elongated elements in the retina that function in scotopic, or twilight, vision.

rods of Corti: rodlike structures that form an arch in the organ of Corti in the inner ear. The organ of Corti is the receptor for hearing. *Syns.* PILLARS OF CORTI.

rod vision: scotopic, or twilight, vision in which only the rods function.

Rogers, Carl: American psychologist (1902–). Rogers was educated at the University of Wisconsin, Union Theological Seminary, and Teachers College, Columbia University, where he became interested in clinical psychology. His master's degree in psychology was awarded by Columbia in 1928 and his doctorate in 1931. His first important professional appointment was at the Rochester Guidance Center in Rochester, New York, where he developed the material for *The Clinical Treatment of the Problem Child* (1939). In 1940 he transferred to Ohio State University, where he wrote his influential *Counseling and Psychotherapy,* which was published in 1942. Three years later Rogers accepted an appointment at the University of Chicago, where he became director of the Counseling Center, and in 1946 he was elected president of the American Psychological Association. Rogers became professor of psychology and psychiatry at the University of Wisconsin in 1957, where he remained until 1963. He became a Resident Fellow at the Western Behavioral Science Institute at La Jolla, California, in 1968. Rogers's published works also include: *Client-Centered Therapy: Its Current Practice, Implication, and Theory* (1951), *On Becoming a Person* (1961), *Freedom to Learn* (1969), *Carl Rogers on encounter Groups* (1970), *Becoming Partners: Marriage and its Alternatives* (1972), and *A Way of Being* (1980).

Rogers' Self Theory of Personality: Rogers's theory of personality grew out of his work with client-centered, or nondirective, therapy, which he developed during the postwar years at the University of Chicago. The technique consists in allowing the maladjusted individual to talk to a counselor in much the same manner as that of a client talking to his lawyer—seated, face-to-face—with the therapist taking a minimal role in eliciting clinical material and attempting to develop a warm, permissive atmosphere in which the client will feel free to talk and, in talking, come to understand himself. The therapist occasionally attempts to clarify statements made by the client by repeating them with emphasis or modifying them to bring out significant points, but interpretation in the ordinary sense is kept to an absolute minimum. Thus, the patient, in a manner of speaking, is his own therapist.

The assumption that the individual can come to understand himself given the proper conditions to do so grows out of Rogers's conviction that distorted experiences and symbolizations of experiences are the cause of maladjustment. Ordinarily, we may ignore some experiences and make

others, which we believe to be of significance, part of the self. But some experiences are neither ignored nor fully integrated. Instead they are distorted or denied. Thus, the child who is constantly told he is a "bad boy" for teasing his little brother may eventually distort his true feelings into the form "I don't like to tease my brother" (whereas in reality he does), because he fears losing his parents' approval. Distorted or denied experiences result in states of conflict, feelings of anxiety, a divided self. The personality ceases to grow and to develop in a healthy manner until the conflict is resolved.

Rogers is strongly optimistic about human nature. He believes that the most basic drive is to actualize, to maintain, and to enhance the self. He believes that given a chance, the individual will develop in a forward-moving, adaptable manner. However, many values and attitudes are not the result of the individual's own direct experiences but have been introjected from parents, teachers, and associates, and have been given distorted symbolization with consequent improper integration into the self. Consequently, many individuals become divided, unhappy, and unable to realize fully their potentialities. The process of nondirective counseling enables the individual to discover his true feelings of positive self-regard and conditions of worth.

Rolandic fissure: see CENTRAL FISSURE.

role: 1. an individual's function or part in a group or institution. 2. the function or behavior expected of an individual or characteristic of him. 3. the function of any variable in a cause-and-effect relationship. 4. (*Kelly*) how the individual interprets the constructs of others with whom he is associated.

Role Constructs Repertory Test: a categorizing performance test measuring the subject's personal constructs and their organization into a system.

role-playing: taking on a role or acting out a role. Role-playing has been found useful in psychotherapy and in industry as an educational technique for leadership training.

Romberg sign or **symptom:** the swaying of an individual with locomotor ataxia when he attempts to stand quietly with feet together and eyes closed.

root: 1. a bundle of nerve fibers entering or leaving the central nervous system, particularly the spinal cord. 2. in mathematics, the factor that, taken an indicated number of times, produces another quantity. Thus, 2 is the square root of 4; 3, the cube root of 27, etc.

root conflict: see CONFLICT.

root mean square: the square root of the sum of the values squared. When the values are deviations from the mean and are divided by N, we have the standard deviation or sigma:

$$\sqrt{\frac{\Sigma d^2}{N}}$$

Rorschach: see RORSCHACH TEST.

Rorschach category: a classification of content according to which the subject's responses are evaluated for each of the 10 inkblots used on the Rorschach test.

Rorschach ranking test: a modification of the Rorschach test in which the subject is asked to rank each card according to 9 possible alternative responses from best to worst.

Rorschach test: a projective technique in which the subject is shown 10 plates or cards containing bisymmetrical inkblots. Five of the blots are in black and white with various shaded areas; 2 contain black, white, and colors in varying amounts; 3 are in various colors. The cards are presented to the subject in a prescribed sequence and he is asked "What does it look like? What could this be?" Responses are categorized and evaluated according to such factors as the amount of movement seen, the content of the blot, color responses, shading, form, and originality or popularity. Responses to color are indicative of the individual's impulsive and emotional life. Form and location are important indices of the individual's overall apperception or approach to his world. Movement is indicative of introversion. Original responses are indicative of intelligence, although bizarre responses may be indicators of mental disturbance. A number of ratios are also calculated and evaluated in scoring the Rorschach, and the final evaluation is a diagnostic of the personality as a whole.

Rorschach determinant: any one of several characteristics of the inkblot to which the subject responds. The more important objective determinants are the color, form, detail, and shading of the blots. Movement is an important subjective determinant. See also RORSCHACH TEST.

Rosenthal effect: the generalization that beliefs about what the individual expects to happen may lead him to behave in such a way that his expectations become self-fulfilling prophecies.

Rosenzweig Picture Frustration Study: a projective test in which the subject is shown pictures indicative of mildly frustrating situations and is asked to tell what the frustrated person would probably say. Responses are scored in terms of various ego-defense mechanisms, particularly Rosenzweig's indices of *intropunitive, extrapunitive,* and *impunitive (q.q.v.)* modes of aggression.

rostral: pertaining to the head end.

rotary pursuit test: a test in which the subject's task is to follow an irregularly moving target with a pointer.

rotation: 1. movement about the center of an axis. 2. in factor analysis, a stage in which the axes are moved in order to maximize the number of loadings that fall along the planes of the axes. See also OBLIQUE ROTATION; ORTHOGONAL ROTATION.

rotation perception: a quality of static sensitivity induced when the individual is rotated.

rote learning: memorizing in which little or no understanding of the material is required. Memorizing a list of nonsense syllables illustrates rote learning.

roughness: 1. sensation experienced when stimuli of contrasting intensity are presented to the skin, such as occurs when the finger is placed on sandpaper. 2. a quality of certain tones in which there is rapid and irregular vibrations, such as occurs in beats.

round window: a small membranous opening into the cochlea where the pressures set up by the vibration of the stirrup, or stapes, can be absorbed.

R–R conditioning: conditioning where one response is made a necessary condition or prerequisite for the occurrence of a second response.

R–R or **r–r laws:** laws formulated around responses. R–R laws refer to observable responses; r–r laws to subjectively experienced events. *Contr.* S–R laws.

R technique: see R CORRELATION.

Rubin's figure: an ambiguous figure that can be seen as a goblet or as two profiles.

rudiment: 1. that which is undeveloped or only beginning. 2. the essentials or elements, as the *rudiments of a language.* 3. an organ arrested at an early stage of development.

Ruffini corpuscle or **cylinder:** a specialized branched neuronal ending found in the subcutaneous tissues and believed by some to mediate warmth.

Ruffini papillary ending: any of the nerve endings in the papillary layer of the skin, believed to mediate pressure.

rumor: an unverified story or report circulated generally, typically by word of mouth.

run: 1. (*verb*) to give an animal trials in a maze or other apparatus. 2. (*noun*) the single presentation of an experimental condition or task.

runway: a pathway in a maze; a pathway leading from a starting box to the main part of an apparatus.

rut: the oestrus, or period of heat, in an animal.

S

saccadic movement: a jump of the eye from one fixation point to another.

saccule: the smaller of the two sac-like swellings of the vestibule of the inner ear.

sacral: pertaining to the sacrum or back of the pelvis.

sacral division: the lower part of the autonomic nervous system in the region of the sacrum. Sacral fibers, along with those arising out of the cranial division, are parasympathetic in function while thoracic-lumbar fibers are sympathetic in function. See AUTONOMIC NERVOUS SYSTEM.

sacrum: the triangular bone near the base of the spinal column which forms the dorsal part of the pelvis.

sadism: a sexual perversion in which sexual satisfaction is associated with the infliction of pain. *Contr.* MASOCHISM.

sado-masochism: the tendency toward both sadism and masochism.

safety motive: 1. the tendency to seek security. 2. the tendency to protect oneself from threat or possible failure by refusing to try, or by lowering the level of aspiration.

saggital: the line or plane passing through the long axis of the head.

sagittal axis: the line that runs from the center of the retina outward through the eye of the center of the object in view.

saggital fissure: the longitudinal fissure that separates the two cerebral hemispheres.

St. Vitus's dance: a form of chorea marked by irritability, restlessness, and sometimes delirium. *Syn.* Sydenham's chorea.

salience: 1. in sensation, the characteristic of standing out sharply, as a *salient odor*. 2. the relative prominence or distinctiveness of some parts of the cognitive field over others.

Salpetrière: a French asylum for the insane where Charcot practiced hypnotism and founded his so-called Salpetrière school of psychopathology based on hypnotic phenomena.

saltatory conduction: conduction characteristic of large myelinated neurons in which the nervous impulse jumps from one node of Ranvier (*q.v.*) to the next, resulting in high-speed conduction.

sample: a selected part representative of the whole—as a *sample of a population*.

sample bias: in the selection of a sample, any methodological variable that can cause the sample to be nonrepresentative. For example, the *Literary Digest*, a news magazine, sampled voters by telephone in the 1936 Roosevelt-Landon election campaign as to their voting intentions. On the basis of the sample, a London landslide was predicted. The error resulted from the fact that more Republicans than Democrats had telephones, Republicans during the Depression years typically being at a higher economic level than Democrats.

sample group: the group selected as the sample of a population.

sample interview: an interview with an individual who forms part of a sample.

sampling: the process of selecting a sample.

sampling error: an error caused by having a nonrepresentative sample or by generalizing the probable behavior of a population from a nonrepresentative sample.

sampling population: the population or entire universe of cases from which a sample is drawn.

sampling servo: a device for measuring errors in a process and applying corrections at predetermined intervals.

sampling stability: a state reached when successive samplings from a population give consistent results and are regarded as having reliability.

sampling theory: the principles involved in drawing representative and adequate samples. See SAMPLE; SAMPLING.

sampling validity: a determination of how well test items represent the range of behavior being measured by the test as a whole.

sampling variability: the degree to which a series of samples differs from a truly random sample as estimated from the standard deviation of the series.

sanction: 1. approval for an act. 2. (usually plural) a system of rewards and punishments designed to force a group to conform.

sanguine: optimistic; enthusiastic; free from anxiety. The term was derived from the theory that the predominance of blood (*sanguis*) was responsible for this type of temperament.

sanity: a condition of normalcy with respect to behavior.

Sanson images: See PURKINJE-SANSON IMAGES.

sapid: capable of being tasted.

Sapphism: homosexuality among women; Lesbianism.

satiation: 1. complete gratification. 2. insensitivity to stimulation because of fatigue induced by a series of immediately preceding stimulations.

satisfaction: 1. a state of pleasantness and well-being consequent upon having achieved a goal. 2. the feeling attendant upon having gratified an appetite or motive.

satisfier: a reward or any situation leading to satisfaction. *Contr.* ANNOYER.

SAT Test: See SCHOLASTIC APTITUDE TEST.

saturated test: in factor analysis, a test that has a high correlation with a factor.

saturation: 1. in colors, a state of purity and fullness of hue or color. 2. the degree to which a test is correlated with a factor.

satyriasis: pathologically strong sexual desire in men.

savings method: a technique for measuring retention by comparing the time or trials necessary for relearning something that has already been learned. The degree of retention is measured by the amount of savings in time or trials.

scalability: the characteristic of being represented in a quantitative series.

scala media: the cochlear canal, or tube in the inner ear, containing the organ of Corti.

scalar analysis: the process involved in discovering where an item falls on a scale. The term is usually applied to a motivational analysis, which seeks to determine the strength of a motive.

scala tympani: a tube in the cochlea filled with endolymph and which extends from the round window to the apex, where it connects with scala vestibuli.

scala vestibuli: one of the three cochlear tubes. It is filled with fluid, transmits sound waves from the stapes, and allows them to enter the cochlear canal, where they stimulate the organ of Corti.

scale: 1. any progressive series of values or magnitudes according to which a phenomenon can be quantified. 2. a physical representation of a series of qualified values, such as the yardstick, a thermometer, or a device for measuring blood pressure. 3. a test consisting of a series of items that have been assigned quantitative ranks or values according to their difficulty as ascertained with a standardization group. 4. in music, a succession of tones that differ from each other according to regular intervals of pitch. See also CHROMATIC SCALE; DIATONIC SCALE.

scaled test: 1. a test in which the items are arranged in increasing order of difficulty. 2. a test analyzed to ensure that the various items have been assigned a value according to a principle or working rule.

scale value: the number assigned to a point on a psychological scale.

scaling: 1. the process of constructing a psychological scale. 2. the assigning of an object or item to its proper place along a psychological scale.

scallop pattern: a response pattern characteristic of fixed interval schedules of reinforcement in which few responses occur at the beginning of the interval followed by increasingly larger numbers of responses just prior to the end of the interval.

scalogram: see CUMULATIVE SCALE.

scalogram board: a device to facilitate the selection of items for a cumulative scale.

scan: 1. to examine quickly or superficially. 2. to look over something for the presence of certain items. 3. to traverse any area with a device, such as a camera, for the purpose of recording what is present.

scanning speech: halting, drawling speech with poor inflection: *Syn.* ataxic speech.

scapegoat: an individual or group that is the object of blame or displaced aggression.

scatological: 1. characterized by interest in filth or excrement. 2. pertaining to obscene speech.

scatter: 1. the degree of dispersion or spread of values around one of the measures of central tendency. Scatter is most commonly measured by the standard deviation. 2. the degree to which an individual who has taken an intelligence test shows the tendency to succeed on items from widely different levels of difficulty.

scatter analysis: a type of analysis designed to discover relationships among various subtest scores.

scatter diagram: a correlation diagram; a plot of two variables against each other in such a way as to show their relationship. The score of one (X variable) are entered along horizontal rows and the scores for the other variable (Y variable) are entered along vertical columns. A tally mark is made at the point of intersection.

scattergram: 1. a scatter diagram. 2. the graphic representation of an individual's scores on subtests of a group of tests.

scatter plot: a scatter diagram.

scedasticity: the variability of the rows and columns of a scatter diagram. See also HOMOSCEDASTICITY and HETEROSCEDASTICITY.

schedule: 1. a plan for a series of operations. 2. a form or questionnaire. 3. a plan for an experiment, particularly with respect to the time of food deprivation and running.

schedule of reinforcement: see REINFORCEMENT SCHEDULE.

schema: 1. a cognitive framework consisting of a number of organized ideas. 2. a frame of reference for recording events or data. 3. a model or drawing. 4. (*Head*) a frame of reference consisting of preceding responses which serve as a standard against which subsequent responses are made. Thus, if one has just extended his right leg in ice skating, the most likely next response is the extension of the left. 5. (*Piaget*) cognitive framework that grows and differentiates with experience. See also PIAGET'S THEORY OF COGNITIVE DEVELOPMENT.

schematic: 1. pertaining to a schema. 2. a diagrammatic or sketchy outline or drawing.

schematic eye: see REDUCED EYE.

schematization: the reduction of a complex whole to its outline or to its most simplified form.

schizoid: 1. pertaining to schizophrenia. 2. pertaining to behavior resembling the schizophrenic's.

schizoid personality: a personality that is withdrawn from others, has difficulty expressing aggressive impulses in a direct manner, and engages in introverted, shut-in thinking.

schizokinesis: dissociation of visceral and motor functions under drugs.

schizophasia: word salad; scrambled speech, such as is found in schizophrenia.

schizophrenia: a general name for a group of psychotic reactions characterized by withdrawal, disturbances in emotional and affective life, and depending upon the type, the presence of hallucinations, delusions, negativistic behavior, and progressive deterioration.

In *disorganized schizophrenia* the symptoms are incoherence in speech and flat, incongrous, or silly emotional reactions with a tendency for social withdrawal and oddities of behavior. Systematized delusions and hallucinations are absent. In *catatonic schizophrenia* there is marked withdrawal or decreased reactivity, often to the point of prolonged stupor. Or the patient may exhibit an agitated or excited phase in which there is a marked increase in purposeless motor activity. In *paranoid schizophrenia* the prominent symptoms are delusions of grandeur and persecution with hallucinations. In *undifferentiated schizophrenia* there are pronounced delusions and hallucinations with disorganization of behavior. However, the symptom pattern does not meet the criteria for one of the other types or is a mixture of more than one.

The search for underlying causes of schizophrenia have centered on both functional and organic factors. Functional theories stress psychological maladjustment in parent-child relationships with the parents showing either marked psychopathology or immaturity in behavior, each vying with the other and using the child as an intermediary in the struggle to meet their needs. Genetic factor theories emphasize numerous studies that show a hereditary predisposition toward developing the disorder. Particularly striking is the finding that identical twins, even though reared apart, show a much higher incidence of schizophrenia than other children. Moreover, the relatives of schizophrenic individuals in general show a higher likelihood of developing the disorder than individuals from families without a history of the disorder.

In searching for possible biochemical factors in schizophrenia, investigators have searched for products in the blood of schizophrenics that is not found in normals and have attempted to analyze disorders in the neurotransmitter substances in the brain. Since the antipsychotic drugs have a marked effect on reducing the symptoms of the disorder, many investigators believe that further research in the biochemistry of the brain is promising.

It must be emphasized, however, that the cause or causes of schizophrenia are obscure and may turn out to be the result of the interaction of two or more factors. A better understanding of the complex disorder awaits the results of ongoing research.

schizophrenogenic: pertaining to a characteristic or factor that contributes to the development of schizophrenia.

schizothymia: a tendency to schizoid behavior within the limits of normalcy.

scholastic: 1. pertaining to a school. 2. pertaining to a system of philosophy popular among theologians during the Middle Ages.

scholastic acceleration: see EDUCATIONAL ACCELERATION.

scholastic aptitude: aptitude for academic subjects as measured by aptitude tests or by achievement in school.

Scholastic Aptitude Test (SAT): A widely used group test administered by the College Entrance Examination Board to high school students applying for college entrance. Separate scores are reported for the verbal and mathematical sections.

scholastic test: any test in a school subject.

school: 1. an educational institution. 2. a group of psychologists with common aims and interests who have joined together to promulgate their point of view. Often, but not necessarily, a school of psychology may be located in a certain geographical area. This was particularly true of the older schools. Functionalism, for example, was centered at the University of Chicago, structuralism at Cornell. This is no longer true, since formal schools as such have disappeared. Contemporary emphasis in systematic psychology centers around miniature systems or theories and not in the larger, more programmatic schools that flourished in the early part of the century. For specific definitions, see BEHAVIORISM; FUNCTIONALISM; STRUCTURALISM; GESTALT PSYCHOLOGY; PSYCHOANALYSIS.

school psychologist: a psychologist who specializes in the problems associated with elementary and secondary educational systems. Specifically, he may counsel or advise children, may help to plan curricular units, is alert to serious behavioral disorders, administers tests, and assists in the interpretation of test results to children and parents.

Schwann cell: a cell wrapped around peripheral neurons that forms the neurilemma, providing one layer of the myelin sheath.

sciascope: see SKIASCOPE.

science: 1. an organized and systematic body of knowledge. 2. the study of natural phenomena by experimental methods. 3. any particular body of knowledge. Broadly speaking, the sciences may be divided into the physical, biological, and social sciences. The physical sciences include physics, chemistry, and geology; the biological sciences include zoology, botany, and physiology; the social sciences include anthropology, economics, psychology, political science, and sociology. See also BEHAVIORAL SCIENCES.

scientific attitude: the attitude characteristic of the sciences—involving chiefly the search for objective facts by empirical methods. See also SCIENTIFIC METHOD.

scientific management: the application of scientific methods to improving worker efficiency and conditions of work.

scientific method: the techniques employed by scientists in the pursuit of knowledge. The scientist may utilize either naturalistic observation or experimentation. *Naturalistic observation* is the objective observing, recording, and interpreting of facts as they are found in nature. In *experimentation*, the scientist manipulates the environment in some way so as to better understand the antecedent conditions that give rise to phenomena. There are, of course, many special procedures utilized in special areas of science.

scientific psychology: any system of psychology or body of psychological facts based on the scientific method.

scintillating scotoma: the appearance of bright flashes before the eyes.

sclerosis: hardening. Used in many combinations, such as *lateral sclerosis*, a hardening of the motor nerve tracts in the cord.

sclerotic: pertaining to sclerosis.

sclerotic coat or **layer,** or **sclera:** the tough white outermost layer of the eye.

scopic: pertaining to systems of measurement in which the scores or data are directly observed, as opposed to graphic methods where they are recorded by instruments.

scopophilia; scoptophilia; scotophilia: sexual pleasure derived from looking at the naked human form or at sexual acts. *Syn.* voyeurism.

score: 1. quantitative value assigned to a test response, learned response, aesthetic judgment, attitude, etc. 2. the sum or total of a number of individual scores or passed items earned by an individual. *Syns.* VALUE; MEASURE; MAGNITUDE.

scoterythrous: possessing a type of color vision in which there is a loss on the red end of the spectrum so that reds appear darkened.

scotoma: a blind or partially blind area on the retina of the eye.

scotomization: development of "mental" blind spots; unwillingness to recognize that which is in conflict with the ego.

scotopic adaptation: dark adaptation; adjustment of the retina in darkness, resulting in greatly increased sensitivity to dim light.

scotopic vision: twilight vision; rod vision; vision under conditions of dim illumination. *Contr.* PHOTOPIC VISION.

scratch reflex: a scratching movement of an animal's hind limb, elicited by pinching or mildly shocking the animal's skin on the flank or back.

screen: a device for blacking out part of the visual field. The common form is a reduction screen, which is essentially a tube that limits vision to the central portion of the field, thus blocking out the background.

screening: 1. selecting test items for exclusion (or inclusion) in the final form of a test. 2. selecting individuals on a preliminary test for a more thorough evaluation.

screen memory: (*Psychoan.*) fragmentary childhood memories that have been able to overcome the repressive forces of the ego but which, like dreams, are condensed, symbolic, and reveal displacement from the real object of the memory.

scrying: crystal gazing.

☺-curve: an ogival curve resembling the letter *S*. The S-shaped curve is commonly found in learning where the items are at first difficult then become easier as the subject gets used to the task and then become difficult again as the limit of learning is approached.

Seashore Tests of Musical Talent: a series of recorded tests of pitch discrimination, tonal memory, loudness, discrimination, rhythm, time, and timbre, useful in identifying the relative standing of an individual on the components of musical aptitude.

seclusion need: (*Murray*) the need for privacy; the need to be alone.

seclusiveness: the tendency to cut oneself off from human companionship.

secondary: 1. of second rank; of second importance. *Contr.* PRIMARY. 2. dependent upon or derived from something else, such as the view that social motives are secondary motives derived from primary motives through learning.

secondary attention: voluntary, active attention, such as occurs in reading.

secondary circular reaction: (*Piaget*) actions that are repeated, have met with success, and are directed toward the manipulation of external objects.

secondary drive: see ACQUIRED DRIVE.

secondary elaboration: (*Psychoan.*) the tendency upon awakening to fill in gaps in a dream and make a better "story" out of the fragmentary, symbolic nature of the manifest content.

secondary extinction: the tendency of one conditioned response to weaken or extinguish as a result of the extinction of a similar response.

secondary gain: the gain or advantage a person experiences through being ill—the attention, relief from work, etc. *Contr.* PRIMARY GAIN.

secondary group: any group not having close or primary ties but with some goals in common. The members of a school class constitute a secondary group.

secondary identification: identifying with someone other than the parents, such as a teacher or hero figure.

secondary integration: (*Psychoan.*) the unification of the pregenital psychic components into an integrated psychosexual unity.

secondary mental deficiency: subnormality in intelligence due to brain injury or disease.

secondary motivation: learned motives that are not universal in a culture and for which the bodily basis is not known. *Contr.* PRIMARY MOTIVATION.

secondary narcissism: (*Psychoan.*) the withdrawal of the libido from the body and its investment in the ego.

secondary personality: the split-off aspect of a multiple personality.

secondary process: (*Psychoan.*) conscious activity, particularly conscious and rational activity directed toward the satisfaction of drives. *Contr.* PRIMARY PROCESS.

secondary quality: the properties of an object that are not necessary to the existence of the object as an object. Thus, the moon's yellowness is a secondary quality; the moon's mass is a primary quality.

secondary reinforcement: a learned reinforcer. For example, a monkey may learn the value of a poker chip as a reinforcer if he is trained to utilize it in a vending machine for a reward of grapes.

secondary repression: (*Psychoan.*) the repression of psychic contents associated with primary repression and which would thus remind the individual of the primary material.

secondary reward: a reward whose value to the subject must be learned. For example, apes can be trained to value poker chips if these can be "spent" in vending machines for grapes.

secondary sex character: a genetically determined characteristic typically found in one of the sexes. The male's beard and lower-pitched voice are such characters. The secondary sex characters are not vital for reproduction but lend the typical form and structure appropriate to the two sexes.

second-order factor: a factor common to the first-order factors; correlation among the first-order factors.

second-signal system: (*Pavlov*) man's ability to "signal" the external signal of the conditioned stimulus.

sect: a group of individuals who strongly adhere to a set of principles and beliefs.

section: 1. (*noun*) a slice through tissue. 2. (*verb*) to cut through or destroy tissue.

secular: 1. pertaining to the slow evolution of cultural change. 2. pertaining to nonreligious matters.

security: the state of feeling safe and nonapprehensive about the future satisfaction of one's needs.

segregation: 1. the isolation of mental processes into compartments with relatively little interaction between them. The popular term *logic-tight compartments* refers to such a segregation. 2. in genetics, the process of reduction division. 3. social isolation of a minority group by the provision of special schools, churches, living areas, etc.

seizure: a sudden attack of a convulsive disorder. *Syn.* FIT; CONVULSION.

selected group: any group drawn from a population according to certain criteria.

selection: 1. the choice of an individual, a test item, or an experimental stimulus for inclusion in a study, a test, or an experiment. 2. in genetics, the manner in which the genes change from generation to generation because of some biological advantage that favors change.

selection index: a formula for determining the discriminatory power of an item or a test.

selective-answer test: a test in which the problems or questions are presented along with several alternatives; the testee being required to select the correct alternative. The multiple-choice test is an example of a selective-answer test.

selective breeding: mating animals possessing desired characteristics. Usually followed by breeding the offspring for a number of generations according to the same criteria utilized in the original breeding. The objective is to obtain relatively purebred strains.

selective inattention: perceptual responses not guided by perceived aspects of the surroundings. See also PERCEPTUAL DEFENSE; SUBLIMINAL PERCEPTION.

selective response: a differential response; a response that has been differentiated out of a number of possible alternative responses.

selective retention: the preservation in memory of some types of material better than others.

selectivity: the perceptual characteristic that certain aspects of the environment are responded to while others are ignored.

self: 1. the individual as a conscious being. 2. the ego or I. 3. the personality or organization of traits. 4. (*Allport*) the proprium, or the body senses; the awareness on the part of the individual of his identity, continuity, striving, and image. See also SELF-COMBINATIONS.

self-abasement: depreciating oneself; submission or yielding to another.

self-abuse: masturbation or stimulation of one's own sexual organs to the point of orgasm. An absolescent term reflecting a moral judgment.

self-acceptance: the attitude of being essentially satisfied with oneself, one's qualities, and one's aptitudes, and of recognizing one's limitations.

self-actualization: the tendency to develop one's talents and capacities. *Syn.* SELF-REALIZATION.

self-alienation: 1. a condition in which the individual experiences the feeling that the self is unreal. 2. a condition in which the individual experiences a growing sense of distance from life, a feeling of hopelessness, and a sense of futility.

self-analysis: 1. the practice of psychoanalysis on oneself, advocated under certain conditions by Freud and Karen Horney. 2. more generally, an attempt on the part of the individual to understand himself—his motives, emotions, potentialities, and limitations.

self-administering test: a test in which the instructions have been formulated in such a manner that the testee can readily follow them without assistance.

self-appraisal: see SELF-CONCEPT.

self-assessment: see SELF-CONCEPT.

self-attitude: see SELF-CONCEPT.

self-awareness: insight into the reasons for one's own behavior; self-understanding.

self-comprehension: see SELF-AWARENESS.

self-concept: the individual's evaluation of himself; the appraisal of the self by the individual himself.

selfconsciousness: 1. oversensitivity about one's behavior. 2. awareness of one's own mental processes. 3. awareness of one's own existence as a unique individual.

self-consistency: 1. behavior that shows a high degree of interrelatedness with the self. 2. reliability of behavior. 3. the characteristic of a theory, system, or explanation that all its parts are compatible.

self-control: the ability to guide one's own behavior; the ability to repress or inhibit impulsive behavior or impulses.

self-correlation: the correlation or relationship of a measuring instrument with itself.

self-criticism: 1. the ability to recognize one's weaknesses or limitations. 2. the recognition that one's accomplishments do not measure up to social standards or to expectations set by the self.

self-deception: failure to recognize

one's own limitations or to recognize the reasons for one's behavior.

self-demand schedule or **feeding:** an arrangement in which the infant determines his own times of feeding. The mother presents food whenever the infant shows he is hungry. The procedure has been extended to animals under certain conditions.

self-denial: act or practice of forgoing satisfactions or desires.

self-desensitization: in behavior therapy, a technique in which the patient is instructed to carry out muscle relaxation when anxiety-arousing stimuli are present in the everyday environment.

self-determination: the regulation of one's own behavior by inner-directed controls rather than as a result of social pressure.

self-development: the growth of the individual's potentialities and abilities.

self-direction: see SELF-DETERMINATION.

self-discipline: 1. the regulation of one's own conduct. 2. the self-application of punishment.

self-dynamisms: the motivational processes underlying the self.

self-evaluation: a rating or judgment made by the individual about himself.

self-expression: 1. behavior engaged in for the satisfaction of exercising one's abilities. 2. behavior that reveals the self.

self-fulfilling prophecy: the finding that without being aware of doing so people behave as they believe others expect them to behave. More generally, any expectation that serves to bring about its own fulfillment.

self-gratification: the satisfaction of one's needs, particularly of needs associated with display, prestige, or excessive appetites.

Self-Ideal Q Sort: a personality test designed to measure the discrepancy between the self-concept and the self-ideal.

self-identification: admiring another because he strongly resembles the self.

self-image: the self as the individual pictures it or imagines it to be. The self-image may differ widely from the true self. See also IDEALIZED SELF.

self-inventory: a questionnaire on which the individual checks the traits or characteristics that he believes to be his own.

self-love: extreme self-regard; narcissism; the centering of love or erotic processes on one's own body.

self-marking test: a test designed in such a manner that the testee's response is immediately scored by one of several devices, such as a carbon backing sheet that transmits the subject's response to "right" or "wrong" spaces.

self-observation: 1. introspection; objective examination of one's own conscious processes. 2. observing one's own behavior, motives, traits, etc.

self-perception theory: the position that people often make inferences about their attitudes as a result of observing their own behavior.

self psychology: any system of psychology stating that the self should be the central fact of psychology and that all behavior must be interpreted in reference to the self.

self-rating: see SELF-EVALUATION.

self-realization: fulfillment of the individual's potentialities; the actualization of aptitudes, talents, etc.

self-recitation: a learning method in which the individual spends some part of the study time attempting to recite or recall the material.

self-regard: 1. consideration for one's own interests. 2. possession of a high evaluation of the self.

self-report: see SELF-EVALUATION.

self-report inventory: a questionnaire on which the individual marks items that describe traits he feels belong to him.

semantic conditioning: the conditioning of a word (conditional stimulus) to the object it symbolizes (unconditional stimulus).

semantic counseling: counseling based on the assumption that adjustmental problems are caused by difficulties in the interpretation of meanings.

semantic differential: a technique for utilizing rating scales in the study of the connotative meanings of words. Words are rated by the subject in terms of such dimensions as strength, action, or pleasantness-unpleasantness.

semantics: the science dealing with the meanings of words.

semantic therapy: a system of psychotherapy that attempts to readjust individuals by reinterpreting the distorted meanings that such individuals have associated with words.

semantogenic disorder: a mental disorder that has come about through the faulty interpretation of the meaning of emotionally charged words.

semasiology: the science of the development of meanings and their changes through history.

semeiology: 1. the science of signs and sign language. 2. the investigation of symptoms of diseases or the science of symptomology.

semen: the male sperm cells and the fluid vehicle secreted by the testes and prostate gland respectively.

semicircular canals: three semicircular tubes in the inner ear that are set at approximate right angles to each other in three planes and which contain the receptors sensitive to acceleration and deceleration of the body.

semi-interquartile range: the quartile deviation, or one half of the difference between the 75th and 25th percentiles. *Sym*. Q.

semilogarithmic: pertaining to graphs, graph paper, scales, etc., in which one axis is scaled logarithmically and the other according to another system, such as arithmetic.

semiology: see SEMEIOLOGY.

semiotics: see SEMEIOLOGY.

semitone: one half of a whole tone; the smallest musical interval used in Western music. *Syns*. half step; half tone.

senescence: the period during which the individual becomes old; the process of growing old.

senile: pertaining to old age; manifesting the behavior characteristic of old age.

senile dementia: a gradual deterioration in intellectual, judgmental, and particularly memory processes, found in some individuals in old age. *Syn*. old-age insanity.

senile psychosis: a disorder of old age characterized by deterioration of cerebral tissue with accompanying loss of memory, irritability, narrowing of outlook, and stubbornness.

senilism: the presence of symptoms of senility with or without old age.

senility: 1. old age. 2. the loss of intellectual, memory, and physical functions with advanced age.

senium: old age.

sensa: sense data.

sensate focus therapy: in treating sexual dysfunctions, the use of mutual touching and caressing in order to enhance pleasure and reduce anxiety.

sensation: 1. the elementary process or experience aroused when a stimulus has excited a receptor. 2. the process of sensing. 3. (*Titchener*) with images and feelings, one of the three elements of consciousness. 4. in psychophysics, a discriminable experience.

sensationalism: 1. the doctrine that all knowledge is derived from sensation. *Syn.* EMPIRICISM. 2. the doctrine that all experience consists of sensations and their derivatives.

sensation increment: in psychophysics, an increase in the intensity of a sensory experience.

sensation level: the intensity level of a sensation, such as the intensity level of a sound in decibels.

sensation threshold: the absolute threshold.

sensation type: (*Jung*) personality classification characterized by behavior that is primarily governed by sensing.

sensation unit: 1. a discriminable experience in any sensory modality. 2. the just-noticeable difference, or j.n.d. 3. in audition, the logarithmic unit of loudness corresponding to the energy unit, which is measured in decibels.

sense: 1. a classification of experiences; a sense modality. 2. the meaning of anything, especially in summary form. 3. a receptor, especially when qualified with a modality, such as the *sense organ for hearing*. 4. a special kind of awareness, such as a *sense of fair play* or a *sense of justice*. 5. intelligence or good judgment.

sense datum: 1. a sensation. 2. information given by receptor activity.

sensed difference: a perceived difference in two stimuli that have been presented either successively or simultaneously.

sense distance: the interval along any scale of sensation that separates two sensations from each other.

sense experience: the awareness resulting from sensory stimulation or receptor activity.

sense feeling: a complex of organic or kinesthetic sensations blended with feelings of pleasantness or unpleasantness.

sense illusion; sensory illusion: an error in perception that results from the characteristics of the stimulus complex. *Syn.* perceptual illusion.

sense impression: 1. a sensation. 2. a sense datum. 3. a reported sensory experience.

sense limen: the absolute threshold or point at which the subject experiences a sensation 50 percent of the time.

sense modality: a sense department. A sense category, such as warm, cold, pressure, pain, vision, hearing, and taste. *Syn.* sensory mode.

sense organ: 1. a receptor. 2. the specialized cells and their associated structures that are especially sensitive to a certain kind of stimulation. 3. a group of specialized often encapsulated, afferent, neurons located in the skin.

sense perception: the process of obtaining knowledge about objects and events on the basis of the sense organs.

sense quality: 1. the attribute of a sense experience that distinguishes it from all other sense experiences. 2. a sense datum or particular quality of experience.

sense-ratios method: a process of scaling sensory magnitudes which is based on selecting stimuli so as to form equal fractions along a scale. See EQUAL-APPEARING INTERVALS METHOD.

sensibilia: collectively, objects of qualities that can be apprehended by the senses.

sensibility: 1. the capacity or ability to sense. 2. a strong susceptibility for emotional reactions.

sensible: 1. pertaining to an object that can be apprehended through the senses. 2. above the threshold; capable of being experienced. 3. possessing good judgment or common sense.

sensing: the process of apprehending the activities of a receptor; being aware of sense data.

sensitive: 1. pertaining to sensitivity. 2. describing an individual whose threshold of emotionality is low and is therefore easily hurt. 3. in psychic research, capable of receiving supernormal information.

sensitive zone: a place on the body particularly receptive to stimulation.

sensitivity: 1. the condition or ability involved in being receptive to stimuli. 2. the degree of responsiveness on the part of an individual, animal, or instrument to changes of small magnitude. 3. a trait that makes the individual highly responsive to the feelings of others. 4. the tendency to be easily offended.

sensitization: the process of becoming sensitive to a stimulus.

sensor: a receptor or sense organ.

sensorial: pertaining to sensory areas in the brain.

sensorimotor: 1. pertaining to processes that involve afferent (*sensory*) nervous paths and efferent (*motor*) pathways. 2. characterizing any behavioral act dependent upon afferent and efferent neural chains.

sensorimotor stage: (*Piaget*) the stage from birth to two years of age, during which the child learns to deal with objects, time, and space on a concrete basis. He cannot conceptualize abstractly during this stage.

sensorium: 1. the sensory areas of the brain. 2. the entire sensory mechanism—receptors, the afferent nerves, and sensory areas in the brain.

sensory: pertaining to the sense organs, to sense data, or to the neurological mechanisms involved in the processes of sensation. *Contr*. MOTOR.

sensory acuity: 1. the ability to respond to stimuli of minimal intensity or duration. 2. the ability to discriminate minimal differences among stimuli. See also ABSOLUTE THRESHOLD; DIFFERENCE THRESHOLD.

sensory adaptation: 1. a general concept referring to any alteration in a receptor as a result of stimulation. Depending on the condition of the organ and the nature of the stimulus, the effect may be either an increase or a decrease in sensitivity. 2. a reduction in sensitivity of a receptor as a result of prolonged stimulation. 3. in dark adaptation, the increased sensitivity of the rods under conditions of low illumination.

sensory areas: the regions of the cerebral cortex that are the terminal points for the afferent tracts leading inward from the receptors.

sensory circle: see TACTILE CIRCLE.

sensory conditioning: a procedure in which two stimuli are paired over a number of trials until one of the two can be used as a substitute for the other in eliciting a response. For example, a light and a tone are sounded for a large number of trials. No reinforcement is given. Then either the light or the tone is reinforced until the desired response is elicited. If the other stimulus is effective in eliciting the response. *sensory conditioning* has taken place.

sensory cortex: those parts of the cerebral cortex that are the terminal points for incoming sensory neurons.

sensory deprivation: an experimental or natural situation wherein the intensity of stimulus patterns is much reduced, as in an isolation chamber.

sensory discrimination: the process of distinguishing between stimuli.

sensory drive: a drive for sensory stimuli, such as the desire for sweetness.

sensory field: the totality of stimuli that affect the receptors or the individual as a whole at any given time. See also PERCEPTUAL FIELD.

sensory gating: see GATING.

sensory habit: a learned performance in which the primary task has been to differentiate between stimuli, in contrast to motor habits, in which the primary task has been to learn new combinations of responses.

sensory interaction: the mutual interdependence between sensory processes, such as the response of finding a bird in a tree by a combination of listening to it and searching for it with the visual apparatus.

sensory modality: see SENSE MODALITY.

sensory nerve: a nerve, or bundle of neurons, leading from a receptor to the central nervous system.

sensory organization: the form supplied by the stimulus pattern which results in a coordinated and meaningful percept.

sensory process: 1. process that originates in the receptors. 2. process of sensing or apprehending sense data.

sensory projection area: specific area of the cerebral cortex where the afferent fibers originating in receptors terminate.

sensory quality: see SENSE QUALITY.

sensory root: any of the dorsal roots of the spinal cord that are sensory in function. *Contr.* MOTOR ROOT.

sensory spot: a place on the skin that is highly sensitive to the various stimuli that arouse the skin receptors.

sensory stimulus: a stimulus or change in energy that makes a receptor active.

sensory system: the receptors; the afferent, or sensory, neurons; and the sensory projection areas.

sensory transduction: see TRANSDUCTION.

sensual: pertaining to gratification, particularly excessive gratification, obtained from the senses.

sensum (plural sense): sense datum.

sentence-completion test: a test in which the subject must supply an appropriate word or phrase to complete a given sentence, or a test in which the subject completes a sentence item in any way that he sees fit. The first type is usually a test of ability, the second is often used as a projective technique.

sentence-repetition test: a test in which the subject must repeat a sentence correctly after hearing it read by the examiner.

sentience: 1. ability of a nervous system to receive stimuli. 2. the simplest form of cognition, in which there is bare sensing without associated meanings.

sentience need: (*Murray*) the need to experience sensuous pleasures.

sentiendum: a sensation; sense datum.

sentiment: 1. a disposition to act in a certain way toward another person or object. 2. a complex or combination of instincts constituting a propensity or persistent motivating condition. 3. (*R. B. Cattell*) acquired dynamic trait structure that causes its possessor to attend to certain objects and to react toward them in a characteristic manner.

sentimentality: 1. an exaggerated indulgence in emotion or sentiment. 2. a superficial or shallow emotion.

separation anxiety: (*Psychoan.*) the infant's fear of losing the mother.

septum: a partition or division in the brain or other organ.

sequela (plural **sequelae**): the lingering or more or less chronic aftermath of a disease.

sequence: 1. the following of one phenomenon by another. 2. a temporal series, or the order in which a series of events occurs. 3. a succession of quantities in which each is derived from the preceding by the same operation; a mathematical series.

sequence preference: the tendency on the part of an animal to make responses in a certain order, such as left-right-left-right, etc.

sequential analysis: an analysis carried out at each step or stage of a series of operations in order to determine whether the entire set of data may be accepted or if more cases must be added.

sequential test: a statistical test applied to determine whether the addition of cases would increase the significance of a finding.

serial-anticipation method: in learning, the technique of presenting stimulus-response combinations successively, with each stimulus being the cue for the following response. When the subject can correctly anticipate all responses upon being presented with the stimuli, the list is considered learned. *Syn.* PROMPTING METHOD.

serial association: in verbal learning, the learning of items in a list in the order in which they are presented.

serial behavior: behavior that takes a sequential form, or where the order of the responses is a significant factor.

serial discrimeter: a device that presents a stimulus for discrimination immediately following the subject's correct discrimination of the preceding stimulus.

serial-exploration method: a technique for determining how small a difference can just be perceived. *Syn.* JUST-NOTICEABLE-DIFFERENCES METHOD.

serialization: the tendency to arrange objects along a quantified dimension, such as size or weight.

serial or **serial-order learning:** the learning of items in a prescribed order. The serial-order method is frequently utilized in the rote learning of nonsense syllables.

serial memorization: memorizing a sequence of items in a predetermined order.

serial method: see SERIAL LEARNING.

serial-position effect: in learning, the influence of the position of an item on the speed and accuracy with which it is learned.

serial reinforcement: in a serial-learning problem, a series of reactions that reinforce or increase the probability of each choice. Thus, as the animal runs through the maze, each correct choice becomes a kind of reinforcement or confirming reaction and increases the probability of that choice being made again.

serial response: a response in a chain of responses that follow each other in a certain order.

seriatim: sequential; in a series.

seriation: the arrangement of data into a series.

serotonergic: characterizing neurons that employ serotonin as a transmitter.

serotonin: a compound found in the brain that is believed to act as a neural transmitter and to play a role in the regulation of sleep and emotion.

servomechanism: a control system for maintaining an operation according to a certain predetermined plan. The guided missile utilizes such a device. Simple examples are the thermostat or the governor on a steam engine.

set: 1. a temporary condition of the organism that makes it ready to respond in a certain manner. *Syn.* EINSTELLUNG; DETERMINING TENDENCY; PREPARATION; PROPENSITY. 2. in mathematics, a group or series, such as a set of data.

setpoint: in feedback systems, a point of reference exemplified by the setting on a home thermostat.

sex: 1. the characteristic distinction between the male and female, or between the organism that produces the egg and produces the sperm cells. 2. the process of reproduction. 3. the organic pleasure or satisfaction associated with stimulation of the genital organs.

sex anomaly: 1. a wide deviation from normal in the sexual organs. 2. a functional sexual deviation; a perversion.

sex character: any trait, structural or functional, that is typically found in one sex more than another.

sex chromosome: the chromosome, or dark staining body bearing the genes, responsible for determining the sex of the individual. In the human being sex is determined by a special pair called the XX chromosomes in the female and the XY in the male. The female chromosomes make a true pair,

whereas in the male the Y chromosome is smaller than the X chromosome.

sex determination: the genetic mechanism that determines the sex of the offspring.

sex differences: any significant differences between males and females on physical or mental traits.

sex differentiation: the interaction of those biological and environmental factors during development that jointly determine the differences between the sexes. Thus, the male's greater muscular strength is a joint function of inherent biological differences and of training.

sex distribution: the proportion of males and females in a given sample or in the population as a whole. *Syn.* sex ratio.

sex education: 1. instruction in the physiology of reproduction. 2. instruction in the physiology of reproduction and in attitudes promoting good sexual adjustment toward sexuality in general and marriage in particular.

sex feeling: the distinctive, pleasurable feeling or emotion associated with stimulation of the sexual organs or with sexual intercourse.

sex hygiene: the science of maintenance of health and prevention of disease, through proper conduct and sanitary techniques, in the area of sexual activity.

sex-influenced character: a trait transmitted as dominant in one sex but recessive in the other. Thus, baldness in men may be transmitted by either parent but must be transmitted by both if it is to appear in the offspring.

sex-limited character: a trait that can be suppressed by a sex hormone.

Thus, in birds the presence of estrogens, or female hormones, permits the growth of female feather patterns but not male patterns.

sex-linked character: a trait transmitted by the sex chromosomes, such as red-green color-blindness.

sex perversion: sexual behavior that differs widely from normal standards and is typically prohibited by law in most states; exhibitionism, fetishism, and rape are examples.

sex ratio: see SEX DISTRIBUTION.

sex reversal: a change in an adult hermaphrodite that occurs when the sex organs of one sex are surgically removed or degenerate and the others are encouraged to develop.

sex rivalry: 1. behavior that tends to exalt one sex as opposed to the other. 2. (*Psychoan.*) competition between the parent and child of the same sex for the affections of the parent of the opposite sex.

sex role: the behavioral patterns and attitudes characteristic of members of one sex.

sex sensations: the characteristic sensations initiated through tactile receptors in the genital organs and erogenous zones.

sexual: 1. pertaining to reproduction by the union of two different individuals who produce an egg and sperm respectively. 2. in general, pertaining to behavior, feelings, or emotions associated with stimulation of the genital organs, erogenous zones, or with the process of reproduction.

sexual aim: the goal of sexual satisfaction or pleasure; the release of sexual tension.

sexual anesthesia: the inability to enjoy sexual activities; a lack of sexual feeling. *Syn.* FRIGIDITY.

sexual anomaly: see SEX ANOMALY.

sexual congress: sexual intercourse; coition.

sexual deviation: any form of sexual behavior differing markedly from the standards set up by a given society. Child molestation, masochism, rape, and fetishism are examples of sexual deviations in our society.

sexual function: a physiological function performed by members of one sex.

sexual instinct: 1. (*Psychoan.*) the tendency toward pleasure seeking, particularly through achieving sexual aims and objects. 2. the tendency on the part of the mature organism to seek sexual union with a member of the opposite sex.

sexual intercourse: 1. the introduction of the penis or male sexual organ into the vagina of the female with accompanying rhythmic pelvic movements to the point of orgasm. 2. the introduction of the penis into the body of another male; technically, anal intercourse.

sexual inversion: see INVERSION.

sexuality: 1. the capacity to behave sexually or to engage in sexual intercourse. 2. the characteristic of being attractive from the sexual point of view. 3. a tendency toward excessive concern with sex.

sexual latency: see LATENCY PERIOD.

sexual maturation: the development of the reproductive organs to the level where sexual intercourse and reproduction are possible.

sexual object: an individual or an object toward which sexual desire and behavior are directed.

sexual reflex: the erection of sexual tissue.

sexual reproduction: the production of a new individual by the union of sex cells.

sexual selection: a mating preference favoring certain physical or behavioral traits and eventually resulting in the preponderance of those traits in the population.

sexual trauma: a highly disturbing or psychically harmful experience related to sex and likely to cause repression and subsequent anxiety.

s factor: a specific or special factor found in factor-analysis studies of ability tests. The specific factor is unique for each test and represents the kind of specialized ability needed to do well on that test. See also GENERAL FACTOR.

shade: pertaining to a darker color than median gray.

shading: one of the determinants of the responses to the Rorschach inkblots.

shading shock: the manifestation of an emotional reaction in response to shading on a Rorschach inkblot.

shadow: (*Jung*) the unconscious opposite of what the individual stresses in his consciousness.

shadowing: a procedure in studying attention in which the subject is required to repeat aloud a message presented to one ear while attempting to attend to a different message presented to the other ear.

shaman: 1. an Oriental magician. 2. a medicine man.

shame: an emotion characterized by feelings of guilt, embarrassment, and avoidance.

shame aversion therapy: in behavior therapy, an aversive technique primarily applied to sexual deviations in which the behavior to be eliminated is performed in front of a neutral audience. The embarrassment to the patient serves as aversive re-inforcement.

sham feeding: a type of feeding in experimental preparations in which everything that the animal swallows falls out of an opening in the esophagus before reaching the stomach.

shamming: faking, counterfeiting.

sham rage: an undirected, brief outburst of emotion that occurs in decorticate animals upon being stimulated with a noxious stimulus.

shape: 1. the spatial form of an object or figure. 2. a figure as it stands out from its surroundings.

shape constancy: the tendency to perceive objects as having the same shape regardless of wide variations in the conditions of viewing. Thus, plates on a table look round regardless of whether one is sitting or standing, although when one is sitting, plates on the far end of the table cast a sharply elliptical image on the retina.

shaping: (*Skinner*) teaching a desired response by reinforcing the series of successive steps that lead to the final response. *Syn.* method of SUCCESSIVE APPROXIMATIONS.

sharp: 1. pertaining to a note raised in pitch by one semitone. 2. pertaining to a tone slightly higher than it is intended to be.

sharpening: the process of accentuating certain details and dropping others in memory, so that objects and events become more sharply defined in the recall than they were in the original experience.

Sheldon's Constitutional Theory of Personality: theory that each individual possesses some degree of each of three primary temperamental components: *viscerotonia*, *somatatonia*, and *cerebrotonia*. *Viscerotonia* is revealed in such traits as relaxation in posture, love of physical comfort, enjoyment in companionship, eating, deep sleep, relaxation under alcohol, and orientation toward childhood and family relations. *Somatotonia* is characterized by assertiveness, love of adventure, need and enjoyment of exercise, love of risk, physical courage, indifference to pain, aggressiveness under alcohol, and orientation toward youth. *Cerebrotonia* is shown in such traits as restraint in posture, overly fast reactions, sensitivity, avoidance of social contacts, hypersensitivity to pain, and resistance to alcohol. Sheldon believes that he has found evidence that the three primary temperaments are related to three basic bodily builds: *ectomorphy, mesomorphy*, and *endomorphy*. The ectomorph tends toward a long, stringy, skinny body; the mesomorph toward stockiness and good muscular development; and the endomorph toward roundness, heaviness, and a preponderance of visceral development.

Each of the temperamental and bodily components is measured on a 7-point scale. An extreme ectomorph would be rated as a 7-1-1; an extreme viscerotonic, 1-7-1; an extreme endomorph, 1-1-7. The individual who is average is rated 4-4-4. Sheldon reports correlations of over .80 for relational studies among the following temperamental and bodily traits: Viscerotonia correlates highly with endomorphy; somatotonia with mesomorphy; and cerebrotinia with ectomorphy. However, independent studies of the relation between bodily build and temperament or personality have failed to confirm Sheldon's findings and the matter remains controversial.

shell shock: any of several situational neuroses associated with prolonged exposure to battle. The term was used in World War I; the corresponding term in World War II was *battle fatigue*.

sheltered workshop: a professionally designed and managed workshop in which retardates or handicapped persons can acquire useful skills.

shifting, law of: (*Thorndike*) the principle that responses learned to one set of stimuli may be learned to a new set of stimuli, provided that the situation is kept relatively intact during the substitutive learning.

shift of level, principle of: (*Lewin*) the generalization that when circumstances alter the position of two stimuli on a continuum, the two tend to keep their relative relation to each other. Thus, two musical notes transposed into a new key will maintain their relative separation of pitch.

shock: 1. a sudden, often fatal, depression of physiological processes induced by an accident, surgery, or a powerful emotion. 2. the condition resulting when a strong electric current is passed through the body. 3. a condition of depressed excitability in a nerve or in the spinal cord as a result of injury to the nervous system.

shock therapy: the treatment of mental disorders by passing an electric current through the brain or by the administration of drugs that induce convulsions. The technique is purely empirical; why it is beneficial in many cases is not known.

short-answer test: any test of the objective variety utilizing multiple choice, fill-in, matching alternatives, and the like, that do not require lengthy or complex answers.

short-circuit appeal: the attempt to arouse people to action by appealing to emotional rather than intellectual considerations.

short-circuiting: 1. the passage of a nervous impulse through a shorter path as a result of practice. Theoretically, the alternative path has always been present; practice lowered its threshold of excitability. 2. the elimination of certain nonvital aspects of an act as it becomes thoroughly habitual.

short-circuiting therapy: (*Wertheimer*) a hypothetical explanation of apparent motion on the surface of the skin or retina in terms of the spread of excitation from the two points alternately stimulated to intermediate receptors, thus giving the illusion of one continuous motion.

short-term memory (STM): memory that has short duration (typically a few seconds) and is of limited capacity (5–9 items).

shut-in personality: a withdrawn, schizoid personality.

shyness: a condition of discomfort, embarrassment, and inhibition in the presence of others.

sib; sibling: one of a brother-brother, sister-sister, or brother-sister pair.

sibling rivalry: a competition between siblings—brother and brother, sister and sister, or sister and brother.

side compromise: in psychophysical judgments, the influence of preceding comparisons on the comparison under consideration.

Sidman avoidance: avoidance conditioning without an external signal. For example, the animal must press a lever to avoid a shock delivered at regular intervals. Each bar press delays the shock for a certain period, and the animal can avoid shock altogether if the rate of pressing is sufficiently high.

sight: see VISION.

sighting line: the visual axis or a straight line from the point of fixation to the point of clearest vision on the retina.

sight method: a technique for teaching reading by training the pupils to recognize entire words rather than parts of words. *Contr.* PHONIC METHOD.

sigma: see STANDARD DEVIATION.

sigma measure; sigma score: see STANDARD SCORE.

sign: 1. an indicator that serves as a signal to action. 2. any object substituted for another object. Thus Σ is a sign for summation. 3. an event that has underlying significance, such as a symptom of a disorder.

signal: 1. a sign communicated from one individual to another. 2. a transmitted electromagnetic disturbance, such as radio or radar signal. 3. a stimulus pattern that serves as a basis for a response.

signal detection theory: an alternative to classical psychophysics in which the detection of signals based on stimulus and organism factors replaces the concept of sensory thresholds.

signal-to-noise ratio: the relative intensity of a target signal to other stimuli or "noises" that influence the observer.

signature: a local sign or an attribute of a sensation that enables the individual to discriminate its spatiality.

sign Gestalt: (*Tolman*) a cognitive process consisting of a learned relationship between environmental cues and an animal subject's expectations.

significant difference: see STATISTICAL SIGNIFICANCE.

significant figure: in mathematics, any figure that expresses a magnitude. Thus, 206 consists of three significant figures, but the number .0006 contains only one significant figure, since the zeros serve only to locate the decimal point.

significant others: persons in the immediate environment who exert psychological influence on the individual.

significate: (*Tolman*) a signified object; one of the three parts of a sign Gestalt. The other two parts are the *sign object*, or *sign*, and the *signified means–end relation* between sign and signified object.

signified object: (*Tolman*) See SIGNIFICATE.

sign learning: (*Tolman*) the animal's development of appreciation of the significance of signs or stimulus patterns that serve as cues for action leading toward a specific goal. See also TOLMAN'S PURPOSIVE BEHAVIORISM.

sign-significance relation: an expectancy.

sign test: a nonparametric test for significance of differences, useful where an experiment can be construed as a series of events following a binomial distribution.

similarities test: 1. a test in which the subject states the likenesses or similarities between two objects. 2. a test in which objects must be arranged in categories according to their similarities or resemblances.

similarity, law of: an associationistic principle according to which one thought tends to elicit another with like properties.

similarity paradox: as the similarity between interpolated material and the original material is reduced from near identity, retention falls away to a minimum and then increases again; however, with decreasing similarity it never reaches the level obtained with maximum similarity. *Syn.* Skaggs-Robinson hypothesis.

similarity pole: (*Kelly*) the manner in which two elements of a construct (*q.v.*) are perceived to be similar to each other.

simple cell: a cell in the visual cortex that responds to a line stimulus (bar of light or edge) presented in a specific orientation.

simple schizophrenia: an obsolete term found in the older literature. See SCHIZOPHRENIA.

simplest path, law of: in Gestalt psychology, a generalization to the effect that an animal will follow the path of least resistance.

simple structure: in factor analysis, the stage following factor rotation when such simplicity in the relation of test correlations with the factors has demonstrated that further mathematical manipulation is unwarranted. In simple structure the factors have been rotated in such a way that the number of zero correlations with the test factors is maximized and the intercorrelation matrix has been accounted for by the smallest number of factors.

simple tone: see PURE TONE.

simulator: a training device resembling the equipment to be used in the final performance. The Link Trainer is an example of a simulator.

simultaneous conditioning: conditioning where the conditioned stimulus and unconditioned stimulus are presented together, or where the onset of the conditioned stimulus precedes the unconditioned stimulus by several seconds and continues until the unconditioned stimulus is presented.

simultaneous contrast: see COLOR CONTRAST.

sine wave: a simple physical wave that rises to its crest and falls to its trough in a regular, rhythmic manner.

single variable, rule of: the general experimental rule that only one factor at a time should be treated as the experimental or independent variable.

sinistral: pertaining to the left side of the body.

sinistrality: a preference for using the left hand or left side of the body in motor activity.

sinusoid: any class of wavelike phenomena that resemble the sine wave.

sitophobia: a pathological fear of eating.

situation: 1. the stimulus pattern upon which a given perception is based. 2. a place or spatial position. 3. in topological psychology, a part of a life space at any given moment.

situational analysis: the technique of studying behavior in natural or lifelike settings, as opposed to artificial laboratory situations.

situationalism: the point of view that the situation or environmental conditions are of primary importance as behavioral determinants.

situational sampling: the observation and analysis of an individual's behavior in real-life situations believed to be representative and significant.

situational-stress test: a situation test (*q.v.*) to which stress has been added.

situation neurosis: (*Horney*) a neurosis induced by a situation that is highly traumatic, such as combat, as contrasted with a character neurosis resulting from severe personality disturbances in childhood.

situation set: a readiness to respond in an appropriate manner in a certain situation. For example, in looking out the window and observing snow on the ground, one would assume a readiness for cold weather.

situation test: a test involving a real-life sample of behavior (or a simulated real-life problem) that must be solved. For example, a squad of soldiers might be required to build a bridge while under stress.

situation psychosis: see REACTIVE PSYCHOSIS.

Sixteen D scale; 16-D scale: an intelligence-measuring score derived from a multiple of the standard deviation from the mean score at age sixteen on several standardized tests.

Sixteen Personality Factor Questionnaire: a questionnaire designed to yield scores on 16 first-order factors and 8 second-order factors according to Cattell's system of personality analysis.

size-age confusion: the tendency to judge age by size and consequently to assume that larger children should show more mature patterns of behavior than are, in fact, appropriate for their age.

size constancy: the tendency to perceive objects as the same size regardless of wide variations in the conditions of viewing.

size-weight illusion: the tendency to perceive a visually larger object as heavier than a small one.

Skaggs-Robinson hypothesis: see SIMILARITY PARADOX.

skeletal age: see CARPAL AGE.

skeletal muscle: the striated or striped muscles that are under voluntary control.

skelic index: the ratio of leg length to length of trunk.

skewed regression: curvilinear regression.

skewness: the extention of a frequency curve farther to one side than to another, with a consequent tendency to peak more on one side than on another.

skiascope: an instrument for measuring the refractive condition of the eye.

skill: an ability of a high order enabling the individual to perform a complex motor act smoothly and with precision. See also FUNDAMENTAL SKILL; HIGHER-LEVEL SKILLS.

skin: the external covering of animals. It consists of two distinct portions or layers, the epidermis (outer covering) and the dermis (deeper tissue).

skin eroticism: the obtaining of sexual or erotic pleasure from stroking or rubbing the skin.

Skinner, Burrhus F.: American psychologist (1904–   ). Skinner was educated at Hamilton College and at Harvard University, where he received a Ph.D. degree in 1931. He has held a Research Fellowship of the National Research Council, a junior fellowship of the Harvard Society of Fellows, and a Guggenheim Fellowship, and during the years 1942–1943 he served as a director of a wartime research project sponsored by General Mills. Skinner has held academic appointments at the University of Minnesota, at Indiana University, and at Harvard, where he delivered the William James Lectures in 1947, and was professor of psychology from 1948 to 1974, when he became professor emeritus. His books include: *The Behavior of Organisms* (1938), *Walden Two* (1948), *Science and Human Behavior* (1953), *Verbal Behavior* (1957), *Schedules of Reinforcement,* with C. B. Ferster (1957), *Cumulative Record* (1959; revised, 1961), *Beyond Freedom and Dignity* (1971), *Reflections on Behavior and Society* (1978), and *The Shaping of a Behaviorist* (1979). See also SKINNER'S OPERANT CONDITIONING.

Skinner's Operant Conditioning: Skinner's system of operant conditioning is a descriptive behaviorism that seeks to establish the laws of behavior through the study of operant learning. An *operant* is an emitted response, in contrast to *respondents,* a class of behavior studied by the technique of Pavlovian conditioning. By contrast, operants may be studied independently of the stimulus conditions that give rise to them—indeed, in the usual case the stimulus may be unknown. The experimental arrangement for studying operant behavior in the laboratory consists of what has come to be known as a Skinner box, an enclosure in which the animal is maintained free from distracting stimuli and in which he can receive a reinforcement upon emitting the proper operant. In the case of the rat, the operant is a bar press, and the reinforcement is a pellet of food. As many times as the rat presses the bar, a magazine will deliver a pellet and conditioning will proceed at a rapid rate. More recently the pigeon has come into extensive use in the Skinner box, and in this case the operant is pecking at a dot, the reinforcement a measured amount of grain.

The fundamental law of operant conditioning is that if the occurrence of an operant is followed by a reinforcing stimulus, the rate of responding will increase. Rate of responding is typically measured during a run to extinction, since the time-consuming process of eating during the reinforcing series obscures the rate of responding. Reinforcers may be both positive and negative. Stimuli such as food, water, or sexual contacts, which serve as positive reinforcers, directly increase the probability of a response. Negative reinforcers strengthen the probability of a response only when they are removed from the situation. Such reinforcers are exemplified by shocks, bright lights, loud noises, etc.

Perhaps the most important variable associated with reinforcement is the time schedule on which the reinforcing stimulus is delivered. Continuous reinforcement is the regular presentation of the reinforcement with each operant response. Intermittent reinforcement is irregular reinforcement delivered according to a predetermined time schedule. There are two important types of intermittent reinforcement, *interval* and *fixed-ratio*. In *interval reinforcement*, the reinforcement is given at certain fixed intervals of time, say every two minutes, regardless of how frequently the animal responds. Under such conditions of periodic reinforcement the shorter intervals yield the highest rates of responding. In *ratio reinforcement*, the animal is given reinforcement after a certain number of responses; for example, the pigeon might get a portion of grain only after pecking ten times. In ratio reinforcement very high rates of responding can be maintained with high ratios, provided these are approached gradually. Reinforcement schedules may also be arranged as *variable intervals* or *variable ratios* under special research conditions. Secondary reinforcement occurs when a stimulus not originally a reinforcer becomes reinforcing through association with a reinforcing stimulus. For example, if a weak light is flashed each time the reinforcement is delivered upon the animal's pressing the bar, the light will come to have reinforcing qualities and can be used to maintain bar pressing for long periods of time in the absence of any primary reinforcer.

Stimulus generalization or induction can be studied by a process of having the reinforcer delivered upon presentation of a positive stimulus and not delivered upon presentation of a neutral or negative stimulus. For example, a tone of 256 Hz may be followed by a delivery of food, while a tone of 100 Hz will not be followed by a delivery of food. The animal will learn to press the bar only in response to the positive tone. The limits of discrimination may be studied by gradually reducing the separation between the stimuli.

The learning of complex skills can be studied by a proccess called *shaping*. In shaping, a series of acts is gradually brought under control of the reinforcement by reinforcing each separate act in turn. Thus, through shaping, a seal can be taught to play "My Country 'Tis of Thee" on a calliope by first reinforcing the animal for approaching the instrument, then for pressing the first correct key, and so forth until the complete performance can be run off for a final single reinforcement.

Skinner's basic techniques of operant conditioning have been extended into the use of human teaching machines that operate on the principle of self-reinforcing learning. The use of reinforcement with speech sounds has made it possible to demonstrate that human symbolic behavior can be learned according to the same principles that apply to more elementary forms of learning. Finally, Skinner and his associates have attempted to extend their methods into the field of behavior therapy (*q.v.*)

Skinner box: an enclosed boxlike structure wherein the correct operation of a mechanism brings the animal a reward. With small animals, the operation requires the pressing of a bar; with birds, pecking at a spot. In some boxes elaborate controls on temperature, humidity, external sounds, lights, and odors are maintained.

skin potential: the electrical potential on the surface of the skin. See also GALVANIC SKIN RESPONSES.

sleep: a condition of the organism characterized by markedly reduced consciousness, inactivity, depressed metabolic processes, and relative insensitiveness to stimulation.

sleep center: a hypothalamic nucleus that, stimulated, causes the animal to go to sleep.

sleeper effect: the finding that the effects of a persuasive communication may be maximal only after a delay.

sleeping sickness: see ENCEPHALITIS.

sleep spindles: bursts of high voltage, 12–14 Hz waves on the electroencephalogram. Characteristic of light sleep.

sleepwalking: see SOMNAMBULISM.

slip of the tongue; slip of the pen: an inadvertent word or phrase inserted into speech or writing which is regarded by the psychoanalytic school and others as significant or as representing what the individual unconsciously wanted to say or write. *Syns. lapsus linguae; lapsus calami.*

slope of a curve: the inclination of a line tangenital to its base line. For illustrations of several common types of learning curves, see NEGATIVE ACCELERATION; POSITIVE ACCELERATION.

slow learner: a nontechnical term variously applied to children who are somewhat mentally retarded or developing at a slower than normal rate.

small-sample theory: a small number of related mathematical techniques from which inferences can be drawn.

smell: see OLFACTION.

smooth curve: a curve that does not change its slope in a sudden manner.

smoothed curve: a curve from which erratic or sudden changes in slope have been removed in order to more clearly reveal the fundamental shape and direction of the function.

smoothing: the process of removing sudden or erratic changes from a curve or of fitting a smooth line to a function in order to bring out its essential characteristics.

smooth muscle: muscle, such as found in the intestines and blood vessels, that shows no striations and is not under voluntary control. The action of smooth muscles is mediated by the autonomic nervous system.

smoothness: 1. a tactile quality characterized by an impression of uniformity and an absence of granularity. 2. a property of a succession of tones, each of which blends into the next, the entire succession forming a continuous, harmonious whole.

snake symbol: (*Psychoan.*) the male sex organ.

Snellen Chart: a card containing printed letters ranging from very large to very small, to be read by the subject at a specified distance as a test of visual acuity.

snow: 1. in American slang, cocaine. 2. in electronic jargon, the granular effect resembling a snowstorm caused by static, or ''noise,'' on a television or oscilloscope tube.

snow blindness: a temporary condition of marked visual impairment due to overexposure to intense white light such as may occur in skiing, watching electric welding, etc. The condition may range from a sensation that all objects are tinged with red to actual blackout of visual forms.

sociability: the tendency to seek out others; friendliness.

sociability rating: a comparative assessment of the degree to which a person is sociable.

social: pertaining to the relationship among two or more individuals. The term is a broad one and is used to characterize any function, habit, characteristic, trait, etc., acquired in a social context.

social action: a collective endeavor, particularly any effort to change social or political institutions.

social adaptiveness: 1. the characteristic integration of traits that enable the individual to get along harmoniously with others in social situations. 2. the condition of having accepted the customs, mores, and folkways of the society in which one is living.

social adjustment: 1. the establishment of a harmonious relationship with the social environment. 2. learning the necessary behavior patterns, or modifying existing habits, so as to fit into a social community.

social aggregate: all persons occupying a defined geographical area.

social anchoring: the individual's dependence on a group rather than on his own judgment in making a decision. For example, a voter's inability to decide which candidate he will vote for until the polls show a clear trend.

social anthropology: see CULTURAL ANTHROPOLOGY.

social assimilation: the process by means of which two or more cultures or subcultures are merged. Typically, the less dominant culture is submerged.

social atom: the psychological relations of the individual to the smallest social structure—for example, the child and the family.

social attitude: 1. a predisposition to behave in a certain way toward people. 2. a commonly held opinion. 3. an attitude directed to social as opposed to private ends.

social behavior: 1. behavior influenced by the presence of others. 2. group behavior. 3. behavior under the control of society.

social being: any organism dependent upon others for its survival.

social casework: see SOCIAL WORK.

social class: a grouping of people according to some combination of criteria, such as economic level, religion, education, family background.

social climate: 1. the totality of social stimulation influencing the individual or the group. 2. the folkways and mores of a society.

social climbing: an attempt to rise from a lower class to a higher class.

social code: any system of social regulations, whether formal or informal.

social cohesion: the tendency of a group to hold together, particularly under threat or attack from the outside.

social consciousness: 1. the awareness on the part of the individual that certain experiences involve other people. 2. the awareness that some experiences are shared by others. 3. the group mind. 4. awareness of the needs of others.

social control: the regulation of individual behavior by means of group or institutional decisions.

social convention: see CONVENTION.

social diad: see SOCIAL DYAD.

social disintegration: the disruption and fragmentation of a social group or nation. Loss of control, institutional and legal breakdowns, demoralization, and individual behavioral aberrations may be consequences of social disorganization.

social distance: 1. the degree to which an individual or group is willing to associate with other individuals or groups. 2. the degree to which two people or two groups show a difference along any variable. *Syn.* GROUP DIFFERENCE.

Social Distance Scale: a rating scale on which the individual indicates the degree of intimacy he would be willing to accept in association with a member of another social group.

social drive: the motive to seek personal relations with other individuals; the tendency toward gregariousness.

social dyad: 1. a group consisting of two persons. 2. a unit for the classification of the dynamic interaction of pairs of persons. For example, the possibilities of choice between two persons, A and B, involve six dynamic diads: A chooses B; B chooses A; A chooses B, B rejects A; A rejects B, B chooses A; A rejects B; B rejects A.

social dynamics: 1. the branches of social psychology and sociology that investigate the process of cultural change. 2. the processes underlying social change.

social exchange theory: the assumption that the individual's actions are determined by the rewards he thinks his actions will bring.

social facilitation: an augmentation in behavior due to the presence of other individuals. For example, if a nonhungry chicken is brought in among a number of hungry chickens, she will begin to eat. On the human level it has been found that production will increase if workers are in groups.

social factor: any behavioral determinant that can be attributed to a relationship among persons.

social fission: the splitting or division of a social group.

social group: a collection of individuals who have some characteristic in common or who are pursuing a common goal. Two or more persons who interact in any way constitute a group. It is not necessary, however, for the members of a group to interact directly or in a face-to-face manner. See also PRIMARY GROUP; REFERENCE GROUP; SECONDARY GROUP.

social habit: a consistent and relatively automatic form of behavior utilized in social situations.

social heritage: the institutions, folkways, mores, and cultural patterns transmitted from one generation to the next.

social immobility: a condition of rigid social systems in which individuals of one class find it difficult or impossible to move to another class.

social increment: an increase in a behavioral variable that can be attributed to the presence of other persons.

social inhibition: social restraint on conduct.

social instinct: the tendency for individuals to form groups; gregariousness.

social integration: 1. the process by which the individual fits into a social group. 2. the unification of diverse elements in a society.

social intelligence: the ability to function effectively in one's relations with others.

social interaction: the interpersonal

processes between two or more individuals.

sociality: 1. the characteristic of being cooperative, of adapting to social demands. 2. gregariousness or the tendency to form groups.

socialization: 1. the process of learning the customs, habits, folkways, and mores of a given culture. 2. the control of industries by a government.

socialize: 1. to render the individual social. 2. to mingle or play freely with others. 3. to encourage social behavior or interaction.

socialized drive: a primary drive that has been modified by learning in such a way as to make its satisfaction conform to socially acceptable ways of behaving.

social lag: a failure on the part of institutions to keep up technological and scientific advances.

social learning: learning involving social standards, folkways, mores, customs, etc.

social learning theory: Social learning theory grew out of the work of John Dollard (1900–1980) and Neal Miller (1909–   ) at Yale in the 1940s and more recently of Albert Bandura (*q.v.*), the leading contemporary exponent of this point of view.

Social learning theory is a modified form of behaviorism that stresses the importance of cognitive processes as causal agents in behavior. In their early work Dollard and Miller emphasized the theoretical importance of imitation in the development of behavior. Bandura confirmed their hypothesis in a series of well-known experiments on modeling and observational learning conducted on children. Among these studies were experiments showing that children can learn aggression by watching adults model aggressive behavior, an important finding in support of the position that aggression in human beings is not necessarily inherent but may be the result of environmental influences. Modeling has also been shown to be a useful therapeutic technique, as exemplified by subjects who fear objects or situations, are desensitized and taught skills useful in coping with their fears by observing others, then behave toward the same situations without fear.

Bandura has also stressed beliefs, expectation, choice, and self-reinforcement as important determiners of behavior, in contrast to the radical behaviorists, who assert that reinforcement acts on behavior without regard to conscious or cognitive processes. In part Bandura's emphasis on cognitive processes in the causation of behavior is a reflection of his extensive use of human subjects as opposed to the traditional use of animals by other behaviorists. His work has received wide critical acclaim and been an important influence in the recent trend toward a cognitive psychology and the development of behavior therapy.

social locomotion: see SOCIAL MOBILITY.

social maladjustment: a lack of the requisite skills necessary for success in social living.

social maturity: an individual's development of the skills and customs characteristic of the group.

social mind: 1. the group mind, a hypothetical construct (*q.v.*) invoked to explain behavior that cannot be explained in terms of the sum total of the characteristics of the individuals who make up the group. 2. the typical or average level of opinion in a given community.

social-mindedness: the tendency to be concerned with social problems.

social mobility: the movement of an individual or a group from one class to another within a given society.

social motive: a learned motive as opposed to a physiological drive. The social motives are learned, are not vital for survival, and are not universally found in all cultures, but are dependent upon a given culture.

social need: see SOCIAL MOTIVE.

social norm: 1. social behavior typical of a particular group and sanctioned by that group. 2. a standard of reference based on sanctioned behavior by which an individual or subgroup is judged.

social object: an individual or a group of individuals.

social organism: the social group from the viewpoint that the group functions as a living organism.

social organization: 1. the pattern of relationships found in a society or in a social group. 2. a group of individuals who have formally united their efforts, under a common set of rules, for the achievement of a common purpose.

social perception: 1. awareness of behavior on the part of another which reveals his attitudes, sets, and intentions. 2. awareness of social objects or events.

social phenomenon: any process, object, or event that depends upon the interaction of two or more individuals.

social pressure: any type of coercion exerted by an institution or a group of individuals.

social process: 1. any social change. 2. the interaction between two or more individuals.

social psychiatry: a viewpoint in psychiatry that emphasizes social factors in the causation of the mental disorders.

social psychology: the branch of psychology concerned with psychological processes that occur in groups. It deals with the behavioral interaction of individuals within groups and the interaction between groups. The social psychologist emphasizes those concepts that are derived from the study of individual behavior, whereas the sociologist tends to emphasize concepts derived from the study of institutions and groups. There is free borrowing of problems and concepts among sociologists, psychologists, and anthropologists.

social reality: the individual's perception of a situation based on his shared beliefs with others. Does not necessarily conform to physical reality. *Syn.* DEFINITION OF THE SITUATION.

social role: the individual's role in the group.

social sanction: social approval of an act.

social scale: the social classes and the criteria for assigning individuals to those classes.

social sciences: those sciences concerned primarily with man as living in relation to his fellowmen, including anthropology, psychology, sociology, economics, history, political science, and economic geography.

social selection: biological selection by social means, giving certain individuals a better chance of survival in the struggle for existence.

social self: 1. those aspects of the self determined by social influences. 2. those aspects of the self important in social relations. 3. those aspects of the self perceived by others in social situations.

social sensitivity: the characteristic of being aware of how another feels.

social situation: the environment as it consists of other persons who may influence the individual.

social status: see SOCIOECONOMIC STATUS.

social stimulus: a person or group that serves as a stimulus.

social stratification: the division of a society into social classes.

social structure: 1. the characteristics and interpersonal relationships that distinguish a group from any other group. 2. the organization of any group—its interpersonal relationships, stratification of personnel, institutional objectives, etc.

social transmission: the passing on, from one generation to another, of the folkways, mores, language, customs, and so forth, that make a culture distinct.

social type: 1. a class of individuals who, in respect of their relation to their social environment, possess a common character or manifest a common pattern of behavior. 2. one whose goals are primarily socially determined.

social work: the field of social service that attempts to improve social conditions in a given community.

societal: pertaining to a society or social group.

society: 1. the group of individuals of a given species, particularly the human species, who live together. 2. mankind as a whole. 3. any formally organized social group.

sociocenter: the individual most frequently chosen in a sociometric test. For example, the most popular person in a group as revealed by a balloting procedure in which each member votes for his choice.

sociocentrism: the tendency to take one's own social group as a standard.

sociodrama: the use of dramatization and role-playing to teach social skills.

socioeconomic status: the individual's relative position in the community. Some of the factors contributing to socioeconomic status are profession, income, place, and cost of residence and relatives.

socioempathy: awareness of one's own and another's status.

sociogenesis: the origination of social behavior.

sociogenetic: 1. pertaining to the origin of society. 2. pertaining to behavior as determined by social experience.

sociogram: a diagram showing the

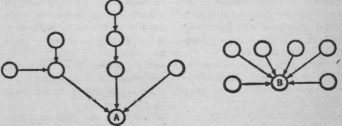

FIG. 26. *The sociograms of a powerful person (A) and a popular person (B). A is powerful since, although only three persons report to him directly, seven persons report to him indirectly. B is less powerful than A but is more popular.*

interactions between members of a group. The two accompanying illustrations show the social interactions of (a) a powerful person and (b) a popular person.

sociology: the science dealing with the organization and functions of groups and institutions.

sociometry: a technique for mapping the relationships of attraction and rejection among members of a group. Typically, each individual expresses his choices either for or against other members of the group. The social map or sociogram is constructed on the basis of these choices.

socionomics: the study of nonsocial influences, such as the effects of weather, on the group or society as a whole.

sociopathic personality: see ANTI-SOCIAL PERSONALITY.

sociotype: see STEREOTYPE.

socius: the individual as a member of society.

sodium amytal: see AMYTAL.

sodium-potassium pump: the mechanism in the neuronal membrane that moves sodium from the inside to the outside of the membrane and potassium from the outside to the inside.

sodomy: 1. sexual intercourse between males by way of the anus. 2. sexual intercourse with animals. 3. any kind of illegal or socially disapproved sexual behavior.

soft colors: the blue-green tints.

softening of the brain: destruction of brain tissue by syphilis of the central nervous system.

softness: 1. the tactile quality characterized by the feeling of objects that yield to pressure readily. 2. characteristic of colors that do not possess a high degree of brightness and glare.

3. property of tones, played at low intensity.

soldier's heart: a group of functional symptoms consisting of rapid heart, rapid and shallow breathing, easy fatigability in the absence of any detectable organic pathology.

solipsism: the philosophical position that only one's own experience can be known.

solution: 1. the resolution of a problem; the discovery of an answer to a dilemma or problem. 2. a mathematical resolution of a problem by the discovery of the constants that satisfy the demands of an equation or problem.

soma: the body or all cells of the body with the exception of the germ or sex cells.

somaesthesia: see SOMESTHESIA.

somatic: 1. pertaining to the body. 2. bodily, as opposed to *mental* or *psychological* in origin.

somatic disorder: 1. a disorder of the body, excluding disorders of the nervous system. 2. an organic disorder, as distinguished from a functional disorder; any disorder having a recognized basis in diseases of the tissues, as opposed to psychogenic disorders.

somatic nervous system: the voluntary nervous system; the nervous system controlling the striated or voluntary muscles.

somatic nerves: the nerves serving the striated or skeletal muscles, in contrast to *visceral nerves*, which serve the internal organs.

somatist: one who attributes all mental disorders to organic causes.

somatogenesis: 1. the development of behavioral patterns as a result of changes in the tissues. 2. the transformation of the germ cell material into bodily cells through cell division.

somatogenic need: a primary or internal need.

somatoplasm: the bodily cells exclusive of the germ cells.

somatopsychic: 1. psychosomatic (*q.v.*). 2. characterizing psychological symptoms or disorders whose origin is physical or organic.

somatopsychosis: a mental disorder in which the delusional symptoms are primarily centered around the individual's own body.

somatosexuality: sexuality expressed in bodily activity.

somatotonia: see SHELDON'S CONSTITUTIONAL THEORY OF PERSONALITY.

somatotype: the individual's body type.

somatotypology: the classification of individuals on the basis of their bodily build. For example, see SHELDON'S CONSTITUTIONAL THEORY OF PERSONALITY.

somesthesia; somesthesis; somaesthesis: the body sense including tactile, kinesthetic, and internal sensitivity.

somnambulism: sleepwalking; performance of complex acts while asleep.

somniferous: inducing sleep; a soporific.

somnolence: 1. drowsiness or sleepiness. 2. a pathological condition of prolonged drowsiness.

sonant: a voiced speech sound.

sone: a unit on the ratio scale of loudness. The standard is a loudness of 40 decibels above the mean threshold at a frequency level of 1,000 Hz.

sonometer: an instrument consisting of one or more strings stretched over a resonating box. It is used in auditory research and demonstrations.

sophism: a false argument; typically, a subtly or intentionally false argument.

soporific: a sleep-inducing agent.

sorting test: a test involving the classification of objects, colors, etc., into certain categories. Such tests are utilized to measure the individual's ability to conceptualize, abstract, or generalize.

soul: 1. in theology, an entity hypothesized to have real and permanent existence beyond mortal life. 2. historically, the mind. 3. emotional qualities as opposed to intellectual or rational qualities. 4. pertaining to or characteristic of Negroes.

soul-image: (*Jung*) a deeply unconscious portion of the psyche made up of the animus and the anima, or male and female components respectively.

sound: 1. physically, a mechanical disturbance in the atmosphere or other sounding medium. 2. an auditory sensation. 3. a mode of sensation dependent upon the interaction of sound waves with the mechanism of the inner ear.

sound cage: a device for measuring how well sounds can be localized.

sound energy flux: the energy in ergs per second for a full cycle of the rate at which an acoustic stimulus is transmitted through a given area.

sound flutter: see AUDITORY FLICKER.

sound intensity: 1. physically, the sound energy flux (*q.v.*) over a given area. 2. loudness, or quantitative attribute of a sound, which is dependent primarily upon the waves amplitude of the stimulus.

sound perimetry: process of measuring the subject's ability to localize sounds in space.

sound-pressure level: the intensity of a sound in decibels.

sound-sensation level: the intensity

of a sound as expressed in decibels above the absolute threshold level.

sound shadow: the area from which a sound is blocked by a nontransmitting object. The head creates a sound shadow for sounds originating tangentially to the side of the body.

sound spectograph: a device for indicating change in intensity and frequency of sounds as a function of time.

sound substitution: the use of one speech sound in place of another.

sound wave: the periodic alternation in rarefaction and condensation of an elastic medium. The average human ear in sensitive to vibrations of 20–20,000 Hz. Sound waves have three dimensions: wavelength, wave amplitude, and wave complexity. Associated with wavelength is pitch, with wave amplitude loudness, and wave complexity timbre, or resonance.

sour: one of the fundamental or elementary taste qualities. The others are usually given as sweet, salty, and bitter.

source: any system that emits a sound wave, a light, or any type of electronic signal.

source trait: 1. a fundamental trait postulated to account for behavior patterns. 2. (*R. B. Cattell*) a factor identified in a factor-analysis study of personality measures.

sour-grapes mechanism: a common defense reaction consisting of a verbal statement to the effect that the individual did not really want to reach a goal or obtain satisfaction of a need for which he has been striving but has given up. The term comes from the Aesop fable in which the fox, unable to reach the grapes, said that they were probably sour anyway.

space: 1. any system of position, magnitudes, and direction. 2. that which can be characterized by extension in all directions. 3. any interval between two points or objects.

spaced practice: practice during which relatively lengthy time intervals are allowed between practice periods. *Contr.* MASSED PRACTICE.

space error: a tendency to deviate in one direction or other because of bias induced by the spatial position of stimuli in relation to the subject.

space factor: the factor ability revealed in the aptitude for dealing with objects, diagrams, etc., in space.

space orientation: 1. the ability to locate oneself in space. 2. a position in space. 3. the adjustment of the position of the body in space.

space perception: awareness, on the basis of the senses, of the spatial properties, dimensions, distances, etc., of objects and object relations in the environment.

span of attention: 1. the amount of material that can be grasped after a single brief exposure. The material used is typically random digits or letters. 2. in popular terminology, the duration of an individual's attention to a single object or event. *Syn.* APPREHENSION SPAN.

span of consciousness: historically, the number of objects of which the individual can be simultaneously aware. The term is now obsolete.

spasm: a localized, involuntary muscular contraction.

spasmoarthria: the speech characteristic of those suffering from spastic paralysis.

spasticity: 1. an increased tone in the voluntary muscles, heightened resistance to movement of a joint, and a drawn-up appearance of a limb. 2. spastic paralysis.

spastic paralysis: a paralysis characterized by increased tension in the muscles due to loss of upper motor neuron control. A limb affected is drawn up and the movements are spasmodic and jerky.

spastic speech: the labored, difficult speech characteristic of the spastic.

spatial: pertaining to space.

spatial summation: the addition of two or more volleys to result in a motor response. Volleys of nervous impulses may summate, provided that these arrive at a synapse within a few milliseconds.

spatial threshold: the two-point threshold, or point of stimulus separation, at which two stimuli are just perceived as two, rather than as one.

spay: to remove the ovaries or sex glands of a female animal.

Spearman-Brown prophecy formula: a formula for estimating the reliability of an entire test from the reliability of the two halves of the tests. The appropriate formulas is:

$$r_{AA} = \frac{^{Ar}11}{1 + (A-1) \quad ^r 11}$$

where $^{Ar}11$ is the reliability of the single length and A is the number of times the test is lengthened.

Spearman footrule: see FOOTRULE CORRELATION.

special ability: see SPECIFIC ABILITY.

special aptitude: see SPECIFIC ABILITY.

special case: 1. an atypical instance of anything. 2. a case so deviant from its class as to be unrepresentative and to require special treatment.

special senses: the four senses—vision, audition, taste, olfaction—whose receptors are in the head.

species: 1. the biological subdivision immediately below genus and above

variety. 2. any special class or subdivision.

species-specific: characteristic of behavior that is the same or nearly the same in all members of a species. Because of its universality and relative lack of variability, it is assumed to be unlearned. *Syn.* INSTINCTIVE.

specific: 1. pertaining to a species. 2. distinctive or set apart in some way. 3. in factor studies of mental ability, uncorrelated.

specific ability: an ability revealed by the fact that it does not correlate with other factors, in contrast to a *general ability*, which shows moderate to high correlations with other abilities. Spearman's theory of mental abilities postulates that every test requires a certain amount of general ability and a certain amount of specific ability. The general ability is the same ability used in all cognitive tests; the specific ability is specific or special to that test.

specific-energies doctrine: (*Müller*) the principle that every nerve has its special form of energy to which it gives rise regardless of how it is stimulated. Thus, if it were possible to cross the optic and auditory nerves, as James once suggested, we could see the thunder and hear the lightning. In fact, it is not nerves that possess specific energies as Müller thought, but it is the receptors and sensory centers in the brain that are responsible for discriminating among stimuli.

specific factor: a factor found in only one test or in a very limited range of tests. (*Abbr. s.*) *Contr.* GENERAL FACTOR.

specific hunger: a hunger for a special food or class of foods, such as carbohydrates, fats, and proteins. *Contr.* general hunger.

specificity: 1. the quality of being unique or limited to one phenomenon. 2. in factor-analysis studies, that part of the correlation or variance not correlated with other factors.

specific thalamic projection system: the anatomically distinct and direct sensory pathways for vision, hearing, and somesthesis.

spectral: pertaining to the spectrum; produced by the spectrum.

spectral color: one of the colors that lie along the spectrum, or band, produced when white light is refracted by a prism.

spectral hue: a hue or color that is in the spectrum, such as red, green, yellow, blue, and violet.

spectral line: any of the fine lines found on the spectrum which represent lights of certain wavelengths. These lines are characteristic of substances in a gaseous state and appear bright with emission and dark with absorption and are thus useful for analytic work.

spectrometer: a device used for the measurement of wavelengths in the spectrum.

spectrophobia: 1. fear of seeing oneself in a mirror. 2. fear of specters or phantoms.

spectrophotometer: an instrument that is a combined spectrometer and photometer, permitting the measurement of the relative intensities of light at approximately one wavelength.

spectroscope: a device for making the spectrum visible.

spectrum: 1. the band of radiant energy that can be projected after being passed through a prism. 2. the series of colors spread out in a band after white light is refracted by a prism.

speculation: thinking in the absence of significant or convincing evidence.

speech block: a temporary inability to produce sounds; speech blocks are a form of stuttering.

speech center: the third frontal convolution in the brain. Broadmann's area 44–45, which controls speech. The speech center is also called Broca's area after its discoverer, Paul Broca. More recent evidence has established that there are many areas of the brain associated with speech functions, not one.

speech disorder: any functional or organic difficulty sufficiently serious to cause significant difficulty in communications.

speech impediment: a nontechnical term meaning any interruption to the smooth flow of speech.

speech therapy: therapy directed to the correction of speech disorders.

speed: the rate of change per unit of time in any function.

speed test: a test whose primary emphasis is on the number of problems the subject can do in a given time period. *Contr.* POWER TEST.

sperm: 1. the male sex cells. 2. the semen.

spermatozoon: a mature sperm cell or male sex cell.

spherical aberration: the failure of light rays to converge at an identical focal point, because of the curvature of the lens. Rays reflected by the outer surface are bent more than those refracted by the inner surface.

sphincter: a muscle that closes an opening by drawing together like a purse string.

sphincter morality: (*Psychoan.*) attitudes of prudishness, pettiness, overconcern with detail, and other attributes of the anal character, presumed to be induced by overly harsh toilet training.

sphygmograph: an instrument for recording the pulse beat.

sphygmomanometer: an instrument for measuring arterial blood pressure.

spike: the large, conspicuous potential change associated with the onset of the nervous impulse.

spike potential: the state of strong negative potentially correlated with the absolute refractory period.

spinal: pertaining to the backbone or the spinal cord.

spinal animal: a laboratory preparation in which the animal's spinal cord is cut in such a way that all control from the brain is abolished.

spinal canal: the small tube that runs down the center of the spinal cord and which contains cerebrospinal fluid.

spinal column: the backbone.

spinal cord: the large bundle of neurons that runs through the spinal column.

spinal fluid: the cerebrospinal fluid.

spinal ganglia: the clusters of nerve cell bodies of the sensory neurons that form the dorsal roots of the spinal cord.

spinal induction: the elicitation of the response by the summation of two afferent impulses arriving from two simultaneously stimulated receptors. Stimulation of either receptor alone would be insufficient to elicit the response. The summation effect occurs at the synapse due to overlapping fields.

spinal meningitis: an acute inflammation of the meninges, or covering layers of the spinal cord.

spinal nerves: the 31 pairs of nerves that leave the cord at each vertebral level—8 cervical, 12 thoracic, 5 lumbar, 5 sacral, and 1 coccygeal pair.

spinal reflex: a reflex mediated entirely at the spinal level. At a bare minimum a spinal reflex would require the action of a sensory (afferent) neuron and a motor (efferent) neuron. In practice, hundreds of neurons grouped in bundles mediate reflexes.

spinal root: the portion of the spinal nerve that joins the cord. The ventral roots are motor in function, the dorsal roots sensory. This generalization is known as the Bell-Magendie Law.

spinal tonus: the tonus, or constant degree of contractility, maintained by the spinal cord after all connections to the brain have been severed.

spindle tendon: see GOLGI TENDON ORGAN.

spiral test: a test in which items in various categories keep repeating at higher and higher levels of difficulty. Thus, the test might contain a vocabulary item, followed by an arithmetic reasoning problem and a perceptual task. The entire cycle would then be repeated with each item in the sequence being more difficult.

spirit: 1. an immaterial being, usually of divine origin, to which is attributed many of the characteristics of human beings. 2. a ghost or disembodied human being appearing after death. 3. vigor; vitality; energy; disposition. 4. morals or motivation. 5. the unwritten or unvoiced intention of a proposal, law, etc.

spiritism: 1. a belief in the possibility of communication with deceased individuals; spiritualism. 3. a philosophical or metaphysical position that all living creatures are possessed of a nonphysical organizing property or vital principle.

spiritual: 1. having to do with spirit. 2. religious; concerned with transcendental values. 3. mental as opposed to physical or material.

spiritualism: see SPIRITISM.

spirograph: a device to measure the rate and magnitude of breathing.

split-brain technique: the separation of the brain at the corpus callosum and, in some cases, at the optic chiasma, in order to study the different functions of the two cerebral hemispheres.

split-half correlation: a technique for determining the reliability of a test by correlating the two halves of the test, usually the odd-numbered versus the even-numbered items. In such cases it is necessary to apply the Spearman-Brown prophecy formula to the coefficient of correlation in order to correct for the attenuation of the test caused by splitting it.

split-half reliability: a technique for estimating reliability by correlating the odd and even scores on a test given to a large sample of people. The theory is that the test must be internally consistent in order to be reliable..

split-off consciousness: (*James*) a partly organized group of experiences that are maintained independently of consciousness. See also MULTIPLE PERSONALITY.

spontaneity: state or quality of being self-initiated; the property of behavior that occurs without the necessity of external stimulation.

spontaneity test: part of the general process of psychodrama where the individual is placed in a real-life situation in which he acts out his feelings and typical behavior patterns toward other individuals.

spontaneity therapy or **training:** psychodrama, or role-playing, directed toward acting out one's problems with a view toward discovering more adaptive modes of behavior.

spontaneous: possessing spontaneity; descriptive of behavior not elicited by an external stimulus.

spontaneous discharge: a burst of neural impulses or rhythmic discharges of spike potentials that are not directly dependent upon external stimuli.

spontaneous recovery: the reappearance of a conditioned response following a period of rest after experimental extinction. In spontaneous recovery, the response strength is usually greatly diminished, and it will quickly extinguish again if no reinforcement is given.

spontaneous regression: in hypnosis, the spontaneous reliving of a specific episode that occurred at an earlier age. When the hypnotist suggests that the subject is younger, the subject often exhibits behavior appropriate to the age suggested and may speak of incidents from that age.

spontaneous remission: the cessation of disease symptoms or of a mental disorder without intervening therapy.

s population: see STIMULUS POPULATION.

sport: an organism that differs radically from its parents on biological characteristics because of genetic mutations.

spread of effect: (*Thorndike*) the hypothesis that the satisfaction or dissatisfaction associated with a response will spread to temporally and spatially adjacent responses or bonds.

spurious: not genuine; invalid.

spurious correlation: a correlation partly or wholly the result of factors other than those to which it is attributed. For example, the Binet test can be shown to correlate highly with the length of children's feet in grade school. This would be a spurious correlation, since both foot length and mental growth are related in turn to physical growth.

spurt: 1. a sharp increase in the rate at which production or learning occurs, due to a sudden increase in motivation. One common form of spurt is the end spurt that occurs near the end of the workday. 2. a sudden increase in the rate of growth. Growth spurts are common in adolescence.

squint: see STRABISMUS.

SRA mechanical-aptitude test: a test of mechanical aptitude involving three subtests designed to measure mechanical information involved in the names and uses of tools, form perception and spatial visualization, and the solution of problems in shop arithmetic.

SRA Primary Mental Abilities, Revised: A battery of general intelligence tests including verbal, number, reasoning, space, for grades 1–12.

stabilimeter: a device for measuring the degree of bodily sway under conditions where the subject stands erect, blindfolded or with eyes closed, and attempts to remain immobile.

stability: 1. physically, the absence of motion in a body in relation to its surroundings. 2. biologically, invariance in genetically determined characteristics from generation to generation. 3. the personality characteristic of being relatively free from radical changes in mood. 4. reliability (as regards experimental results, for example).

stability coefficient: the reliability coefficient.

stabilized retinal image: a retinal image produced by an experimental technique, such as etching a stimulus on a contact lens, which negates the effect of normal eye movements.

stage: a natural or common division of the developmental process, characterized by types of behavior or by biological properties or manifestations.

staircase illusion: a reversible figure in the form of a staircase in which the steps can be seen as from above or below.

staircase phenomenon: a steplike increase in a muscle's response to stimulation due to a warm-up effect. *Syn.* TREPPE.

stammering: see STUTTERING.

standard: 1. a model, average, or guide against which a performance is evaluated. 2. a fixed unit of comparison, such as the standard meter or candle.

standard deviation: (SD; σ; σ_{dist}) a measure of scatter or dispersion of a distribution. The standard deviation is found by the following formula:

$$SD = \sqrt{\frac{\Sigma x^2}{N}}$$

where X = an individual score minus the mean, N = the number of cases, and Σ = the sum of.

In normal distributions, 68.2 percent of the cases fall between ± 1SD from the mean; 95.4 percent of the cases fall between ± 2SD from the mean, and 99.7 percent of the cases fall between ± 3SD from the mean.

standard difference: the difference between two means divided by the standard error of that difference.

standard error: an estimate of sampling errors that affect a statistic. The standard error measures the degree to which the statistic will differ from its true value by chance. *Abbr.* SE. It is equal to the standard deviation of the distribution of the statistic in question. In practice the standard error is estimated, not actually obtained. The most common use of the standard error is in evaluating the significance of the difference between two means according to the formula:

$$CR = \frac{M_1 - M_2}{\sqrt{\sigma M_1 + \sigma^2 M_2}}$$

where *CR* is the *critical ratio* (a critical ratio of 2.0 can be obtained on 5 in 100 times) and is therefore used as a criterion for evaluating the significance of a difference; σ is the obtained standard deviation of the distribution of scores; and *M* is the mean.

standard error of estimate: the standard deviation of the difference between the actual values of a dependent variable and those estimated from a regression equation. Its formula is:

$$\sigma_{est} = \sigma \sqrt{1 - r^2}$$

standard error of the mean: an estimate of the amount that an obtained mean may be expected to differ from the true mean by chance. *Sym.* SD_M. The formula is:

$$SD_M = \frac{SD_{dist}}{\sqrt{N - 1}}$$

standardization: the process of establishing norms for a test by administering it to a large and representative sample. At the same time, the establishment of directions, time limits, and permissible variations in procedure are determined.

standardization group: a group presumed to be representative of a population and is used for the purpose of establishing test norms.

standardize: 1. to establish the procedures and scoring standards to be used in the administration of a test or

other quantitative device. 2. to establish standards of performance. 3. to bring a group of data into relation with each other according to a standard.

standardized test: a test subjected to thorough empirical tryout and analysis and which provides time limits, instructions, scoring standards, reliability and validity coefficients, and norms.

standard measure: the standard score. Standard score =

$$\frac{X - M}{\sigma_{dist}}$$

standard observer: an individual whose receptors are normal.

standard pitch: a tone of fixed vibration rate used for tuning musical instruments. Standard orchestra and band pitch is $a' = 440$ dvb.

standard ratio: see STANDARD DIFFERENCE.

standard score: 1. a derived score that uses as its unit the standard deviation of the population upon which the test was standardized. 2. a *z score* (*q.v.*).

standard stimulus: in psychophysical experiments, the stimulus used as a basis of comparison. For example, a series of weights might be compared to a single standard weight.

Stanford Achievement Test: a test designed to measure a pupil's progress in paragraph meaning, word meaning, and grammatical usage.

Stanford-Binet Scale: the revision (1916) of the original scale developed by Binet and Simon in 1905 to fit American conditions. The test was revised again in 1937 with the establishment of new norms and in 1960, when the L and M forms were combined on the basis of a statistical revision.

stanine: a statistical measure representing one ninth of the range of the standard scores of a distribution. The statistic was the United States Air Force during World War II and was used in their testing program.

stapes: one of the three auditory ossicles. The stapes is attached to the oval window of the cochlea. *Syn.* STIRRUP.

startle reflex or **pattern** or **response:** a complex response to a loud and unexpected sound. It consists of a general flexion of the muscles of the body accompanied by visceral changes. It is regarded as a kind of primitive emotional response.

static: unchanging, unmoving. *Contr.* DYNAMIC.

static equilibrium: a system in which the forces are so well balanced with respect to each other that no change is taking place.

static response or **reflex:** a postural or orienting movement of the body in response to the effect of gravity or any other force.

static sense: the sense of head orientation and body movement. The sense organs consist of hair cells in the vestibule of the inner ear and in the semicircular canals. *Syn.* vestibular sense, labyrinthine sense, sense of equilibrium.

stationary state: see HOMEOSTASIS.

statistic: 1. any term of a statistical series. 2. the result of a series of mathematical operations representing a population or sample.

statistical constant: a representative value, such as the mean or standard deviation.

statistical control: the utilization of statistical techniques to eliminate the effect of identified and measurable factors that could not be eliminated or controlled during the experiment.

statistical error: any inaccuracy of measurement, of sampling or treatment of data that makes it impossible to draw a valid conclusion from the results.

statistical psychology: the branch of psychology that utilizes statistical models and techniques to derive explanatory constructs. An early example of such a technique was Ebbinghaus' use of the formula $R = k \log t$—or retention is the function of the logarithm of time.

statistical significance: the degree to which an obtained value will not occur by chance and can therefore be attributed to another factor. The degree of significance is typically stated in terms of some level. Thus, that the difference between two means is significant at the 0.01 level means that out of 100 samplings, the obtained difference could occur only once by chance alone.

statistical universe: the entire basis upon which statistical assumptions or inferences are made; the entire population from which samples are drawn.

statistics: that branch of mathematics dealing with data either *descriptively*, in terms of summaries, such as the measures of central tendency, dispersion, and relationship, or *inferentially*, in terms of sampling the significance of data and errors of observation.

statoacoustic nerve: the eighth cranial nerve. An efferent nerve from the inner ear mediating hearing and balance.

statocyst: the sense organ that detects changes in response to motion and position of the body. *Syn*. OTO-CYST.

statokinetic responses: postural reflexes and adjustments that serve to maintain stability and good orientation while the body is in motion.

statolith: a bony structure in the statocyst that responds to gravity and linear bodily motion. *Syn*. OTOLITH.

statue of Condillac: a hypothetical account of the importance of sensation in mental life, utilizing the parable of a statue endowed with one sensation after another until it was fully conscious. The parable was used by the philosoper Condillac and a number of early writers in support of sensationalism.

status: 1. the state of affairs or condition of any thing or any individual. 2. the position of an individual in a social group in terms of his relative standing in the class structure, the honor or awards accorded to him, and the formal or informal power accorded to his position.

status epilepticus: a series of epileptic seizures without periods of intervening consciousness.

status grouping: grouping according to social level.

status need: the need for achieving a high level of social superiority as revealed by striving for prestige, power, and popularity.

status validity: see CONCURRENT VALIDITY.

staves scale: a scale exactly like the sten scale (*q.v.*) except that the units are fives.

steady state: see HOMEOSTASIS.

stencil: a perforated form placed over an answer sheet so that the perforations identify the correct answers.

sten scale: a standard scale of 10 units or scores, each step being one-half of a standard deviation.

step interval: a class interval in a frequency distribution; the range of values in a given class or category.

stepwise phenomena: any series of stimuli consisting of finite steps which are nevertheless perceived as a smooth configuration. The musical scale illustrates the nature of stepwise phenomena.

stereochemical theory: in olfaction, the position that odors can be classified into seven primary groups on the basis of their molecular shape.

stereognosis: perception of objects or forms through the modality of touch.

stereogram: a picture that is placed in a stereoscope to give striking depth effects.

stereopsis: 1. the three-dimensional visual perception of objects. 2. the displacement of two objects in the third dimension. 3. the acuity with which an individual can make visual discriminations in the third dimension.

stereoscope: a device for viewing stereograms or two-dimensional pictures taken with a double-lens camera whose openings are set apart the same distance as the eyes. When the images are brought together in the stereoscope, the effect is one of depth.

stereoscopic vision: depth perception based on the fusion of two somewhat disparate images, such as those obtained with a stereoscope.

stereotaxic instrument: an apparatus for positioning accurately the tip of an electrode in an animal's brain by utilizing skull landmarks and a three-dimensional atlas of the brain.

stereotropism: a positive orienting response manifested as a tendency to crawl into corners or openings. Thus, the cockroach, if presented with a box, will tend to crawl into a corner.

stereotype: 1. a rigid, biased perception of an object, animal, individual, or group. The conception of the capitalist as a huge, bloated individual with avaricious, piglike eyes is a stereotype. 2. a uniform, inflexible mode of behavior.

stereotype accuracy: the ability to judge correctly the group mean or norm for any given trait.

stereotyped response: an inflexible, uniform mood of behavior.

stereotyped movement: a pathological movement, posture, verbal utterance, etc., that is relatively meaningless and recurs persistently without regard to its appropriateness.

stereotypy: the pathological condition in which the individual manifests mannerisms, irrational and delusional forms of thinking, and inflexibility in behavior patterns. Some degree of stereotypy is characteristic of most of the neuroses and psychoses.

sterility: the inability, because of physiological or psychological deficiencies, to reproduce.

sterilization: the process of rendering the individual incapable of reproduction by castration or vasectomy in the male or by salpingectomy or ovariectomy in the female.

Stern variator: see TONE VARIATOR.

Stevens' power law: see POWER LAW.

sthenia: strength.

stigma (plural **stigmata** or **stigmas**): 1. a marking on the body. Popularly, stigmata have been associated with either degeneracy or extreme sanctity, in which case the marks are said to resemble Christ's wounds at the crucifixion. 2. a blemish on one's character.

Stiles-Crawford effect: the general-

ization that light rays passing through the periphery of the pupil have less stimulating effect than those that pass through the center of the pupil.

Stilling test: a test consisting of a chart with numerous colored dots of various hues, saturations, and intensities, for the detection of color weakness. Some of the dots are arranged to form numbers visible to the normal eye but invisible to the color-blind or color-weak eye.

stimulant: 1. a drug that accelerates physiological or psychological functions. 2. more generally, any agent that increases physiological or psychological activity.

stimulation: 1. the application of any form of energy (stimulus) to a receptor. 2. more generally, the arousal of an organism by any change in energy, whether external or internal.

stimulus: 1. any change in physical energy that activates a receptor. 2. more generally, any change in external or internal energy that alerts or activates an organism. 3. a sign or a signal for action.

stimulus attitude: 1. in reaction-time experiments, the subject's set to observe the stimulus as quickly as possible, allowing the response to follow more or less automatically. 2. an attitude in which the observer attends to the stimulus as an object.

stimulus-bound: 1. designating perception that is almost totally dependent upon the qualities of the stimulus. 2. characteristic of an individual whose perceptions tend to be inflexible and determined wholly by the nature of the stimulating conditions.

stimulus continuum: any series of stimuli, such as a series of grays, which form a smooth, unbroken hierarchy from top to bottom.

stimulus differentiation: 1. the process by means of which the individual learns to discriminate between similar stimuli. 2. in Gestalt psychology, the process by means of which the visual field comes to be perceived as composed of various patterns or different parts.

stimulus equivalence: a condition in which one stimulus may substitute for another in eliciting a response. Stimulus equivalence is a form of transfer in learning.

stimulus error: (*Titchener*) in giving an introspective report, the tendency to report in terms of the meaning of the properties, attributes, and characteristics of the stimulus. For example, to say that an apple presented for an introspective report is an apple is to commit the stimulus error. To describe its shape, color, odor, etc., is to report in terms of the stimulus properties and avoid the stimulus error.

stimulus generalization: the principle that when a subject has been conditioned to make a response to a stimulus, similar stimuli will also evoke that response.

stimulus-induced maturation: a developmental function that is released by a stimulus but whose fundamental nature and direction is controlled by intrinsic processes.

stimulus object: an object or an individual that serves as a stimulus.

stimulus pattern: a grouping of stimuli into an organized configuration that serves as a stimulus. A piece of music is a stimulus pattern made up of an organized group of stimuli.

stimulus population: a finite number of independent environmental events of which only one sample is effective at any given time. The concept is used primarily in statistical

models of behavior. See ESTES' STATISTICAL MODEL OF LEARNING.

stimulus-response psychology: the point of view that the task of the psychologist is to discover the functional relationships between stimuli and responses. The stimulus-response view is not necessarily behavioristic or objective, but it tends to be associated with behavioristic and peripheralistic models.

stimulus set: in reaction-time experiments, a strong concentration on the stimulus, in contrast to a *response set*, in which the subject's readiness is directed toward his muscles.

stimulus situation: the complex of conditions that surround an organism and collectively act as a stimulus eliciting behavioral patterns from that organism. The concept of stimulus situation is intended to emphasize that most responses are not elicited by a single stimulus but are the consequence of a stimulus pattern.

stimulus trace: (*Hull*) the afferent, or sensory, aftereffects of a stimulus in the central nervous system. Stimulus traces are postulated by Hull to allow for the afferent interaction of stimuli.

stimulus value: the quantitative extent or intensity of a stimulus.

stimulus variable: the stimulus as a variable among a group of variables.

stimulus word: in word-association or reaction-time tests, a word presented to the subject that is intended to elicit a response in the form of an associated word.

stirrup: one of the auditory ossicles. The stirrup articulates with the incus or anvil and is attached to the oval window. *Syn.* STAPES.

stochastic: pertaining to systems of events for which the probability of a given outcome approaches the true probability as the number of events increases.

stocking anesthesia: an hysterical or functional absence of sensation in the leg. The term comes from the fact that the extent of the anesthesia is the same as the area covered by a stocking—a neurological impossibility and a sign that the difficulty is functional. See also GLOVE ANESTHESIA.

storm-and-stress period: a period of early adolescence characterized by a great deal of emotional turmoil.

story-recall test: any test that makes use of the subject's ability to recall details of a story.

strabismus: a condition in which one or both of the eyes fails to fixate properly. The appearance may be that of cross-eyedness or divergence of the eyes. *Syn.* HETEROTROPIA.

straight line sensory system: the main nervous pathway over which sensory impulses travel from sense organs to brain.

strain: 1. muscular tension. 2. a condition of extreme and prolonged psychological tension. 3. the sensation resulting from the activation of the kinesthetic receptors. 4. a pathological condition in a muscle or joint resulting from overuse or injury.

stratification: a series of horizontal divisions of a social group or society.

stratified sample: a population divided into a number of nonoverlapping classes to be surveyed. All cases are then taken at random from within the categories, the number from each category being proportional to the total number in the category.

Stratton's experiment: a classic experiment in which the retinal image was inverted by the use of a special lens.

stream of action: the ongoing activities of the organism. The concept of the stream of action was suggested as a substitute for the functionalistic concept of the stream of consciousness.

stream of consciousness: (*James*) the processes of consciousness conceived of as a flowing, ongoing stream of images and ideas, analogous to a stream of water.

strephosymbolia: the reversal of right and left in perception, particularly in the letter order in words. Thus, *top* would be read as *pot*.

stress: 1. (*noun*) a state of strain, whether physical or psychological. 2. (*verb*) to emphasize in speaking or writing.

stress interview: an interview conducted while the interviewee is deliberately put under an emotional strain.

stress test: a real-life situation in which the individual is put under pressure while his ability to carry out a task is measured. For example, he might be required to build a bridge over a stream during a simulated attack by enemy forces.

striate body: see CORPUS STRIATUM.

striated muscle: muscle of the voluntary system, so called because of its striped appearance. *Syn.* striped muscle.

stridor dentum: grinding of the teeth.

striped muscle: see STRIATED MUSCLE.

strip key: a scoring key arranged on a long strip to permit aligning the key with the testee's responses.

stroboscope: a device for exposing a series of related visual stimuli rapidly. Under such conditions the stimuli give rise to an illusion of continuous movement. See STROBOSCOPIC ILLUSION.

stroboscopic illusion or **effect:** 1. the apparent motion of two stimuli presented in close succession. Motion pictures are common examples of the stroboscopic effect. 2. the perceptual effect of illuminating a moving object with an intermittent light with the result that it may be made to stand still, reverse itself, or move forward at any desired speed. Thus, if a stroboscopic light is directed on a rotating fan, the blades can be seen as if they were motionless, made to reverse, etc.

stroke: a sudden cerebral accident caused by the rupture of a blood vessel in the brain. If the damage is extensive, the individual will suffer paralysis on the side opposite that on which the rupture occurred.

Strong-Campbell Interest Inventory: An interest inventory consisting of 325 items referring to occupations, activities, school subjects, amusements, etc., for which the examinee expresses like, dislike or indifference. Scores are reported for the degree to which the examinee's interests are similar to those for men and women in some 50 different occupations.

Strong Vocational Interest Blank, Revised (for men and women): See STRONG-CAMPBELL INTEREST INVENTORY.

Stroop effect: the finding that subjects have difficulty in eliminating irrelevant information from a task.

structural: pertaining to, or having the characteristics of, a structure—that is, a relatively stable, permanent organization. *Contr.* FUNCTIONAL. See also STRUCTURE.

structuralism; structural psychology: a system of psychology associated with the teachings of Wilhelm

Wundt (*q.v.*) and Edward Bradford Titchener (*q.v.*). Structuralism held that psychology is human experience studied from the point of view of the experiencing person. The method of psychology is introspection, or self-inspection. The aim of psychology, according to the structuralists, was to investigate the *what,* the *how,* and the *why* of experience or consciousness. Under *what* are included the results of introspective analysis of the mental processes. In short, the question of *what* deals with the *content* of experience and the problem of its analysis. *How* is concerned with the manner in which the various mental processes are related to each other—that is, with the problem of synthesis. *Why* is concerned with the cause-and-effect relationships between the mental processes and between experience and underlying physiological processes in the nervous system.

The structuralists resolved the problem of the relation of consciousness to brain or body by invoking the principle of *psychophysical parallelism,* a form of dualism in which mind and body are considered to be separate substances without interaction between them but parallel to each other in such a way that for every event in consciousness there is a corresponding event in body. However, mind does not *cause* bodily events nor do bodily events *cause* states of consciousness. The two are strictly parallel, never interactive. Wundt and Titchener's position on the mind-body problem was made necessary by their separation of mental events from the totality of behavior. It is not possible to use a nonmaterial mind to explain a physical body nor a physical body to explain a nonphysical mind.

The analysis of consciousness into its elements resulted in three irreducibles: sensations, images, and affective states (states of feeling and emotion). Each of these is an element in the sense that it cannot be further broken down by introspective analysis. But each can be described in terms of its attributes. All elements have the attributes of quality, intensity, and duration. Quality is the most fundamental attribute, which enables the individual to distinguish one experience from another; thus, in the sense of taste, sweet is clearly distinct from sour, and in vision, blue from yellow. The attribute of intensity is the quantitative aspect of experience; loudness-softness, brightness-dullness, weakness-strength are some of the descriptive terms we utilize to characterize this attribute. The attribute of duration characterizes how long a sensation, image, or affective state persists in time.

For some years (approximately 1890–1920) structuralism was the dominant school of psychology in the United States and Germany; thereafter it was successfully attacked by rival systems. In the United States, functionalism and behaviorism became the favorite system; in Germany, Gestalt psychology. Structuralism failed because it was too narrow. It provided excellent subjective reports of sensory, imaginal, and affective states of consciousness, but it could not successfully extend the method to include the behavior of children, or animals, or to provide for mental tests and behavioral studies of learning.

structure: 1 (noun) an enduring organization, pattern, or aggregate of elements. In this usage, structure is contrasted with function, the latter referring to a process that is transitory and does not lend itself to description in terms of elements or organization of parts. However, many psychologists employ structure in referring to processes that have stability. Freud, for example, spoke of the structure of the mind in terms of ego, id, and superego, referring thereby to processes rather than entities. The difficulty arises when these structurally described processes are given the status of entities or are personified, as frequently happens. 2. (noun) regular patterns of behavior in a group, including status, role, norms, use of communication, space, and time. 3. (verb) to impose an organization on anything. For example, to structure an interview is to impose a certain form and purpose on it, in contrast to a nondirective interview, which may take any form or direction.

structured interview: an interview whose direction is predetermined and in which the questions asked revolve around a single subject.

structured stimulus: a clearly organized stimulus in which the various parts are delineated and defined. Contr. unstructured stimulus, exemplified by a Rorschach inkblot.

stimulus structure: the organization or patterning of individual stimuli to form a complex stimulus.

Student's test: see T TEST.

study: a research investigation, typically not as formal as an experiment in that a study usually does not involve the manipulation of independent and dependent variables.

Study of Values: An inventory designed to reveal the relative strength of interest in the following areas: theoretical, religious, social, aesthetic, economic, and political.

study skill: a technique utilized in studying, such as outlining, underscoring, silent recitation, etc.

stupor: 1. a severely retarded condition in which the individual is inaccessible to stimuli, shows loss of orientation, and makes few or no motor responses. 2. inability to speak. *Syn.* MUTISM.

stuttering: a pathological condition of speech in which the flow of words is interrupted by hesitations, blocking, repetitions, muscular spasms, and difficulty in breathing, depending upon the severity of the case. Some writers reserve the term *stammering* for blocking and the term *stuttering* for repetitions or partial repetitions, but the two have become virtually interchangeable.

style: in aesthetics, a distinctive mode of presentation in literary compositions, music, painting, sculpture, etc.

style of life: (*Adler*) a person's individual and characteristic way of coping with his environment and his needs or aspirations. The concept embraces the totality of the individual's motivations and behavior patterns in the course of his living. One aspect of the individual's style of life, for example, would be his way of overcoming feelings of inferiority.

stylus: 1. a pointed device used for recording on smoked drums, graphic recording paper, etc. 2. a pen-shaped instrument for use in a human maze whose pathways are sunken into a surface.

stylus maze: a modification of the finger maze (see MAZE) in which the individual traces the path by means of a stylus.

subception: the ability to react to an emotion-provoking stimulus that is not perceived to the point of being reported correctly, although it may be detected by means of the psychogalvanometer or from reaction time to such stimuli as compared with reaction time to neutral stimuli. See also PERCEPTUAL DEFENSE; SUBLIMINAL.

subconscious: 1. (*noun*) in Freudian nomenclature, a transition zone through which any repressed material must pass on its way from the unconscious to consciousness. *Syn.* PRECONSCIOUS. 2. (*adj.*) descriptive of processes of which the individual is not aware but that can be brought to consciousness. Many memories would fall into this class. 3. (*adj.*) pertaining to what is in the margin of attention; pertaining to that of which one is only dimly aware.

subcortical: pertaining to nervous structures or functions below the level of the cortex. There are a great many nuclei below the level of the cortex embedded in the white matter of the cerebrum and associated structures. Many of these are capable of mediating functions not directly controlled by the cortex.

subculture: a division of a total culture set apart by special folkways and mores from the culture as a whole yet sharing its major characteristics.

subcutaneous: 1. below the surface of the skin. 2. pertaining to receptors located beneath the surface of the skin.

subject: 1. the individual who participates in the psychological experiment. 2. an individual who is reporting his experiences. 3. a topic for a course of study.

subjection: the condition of being

under the domination or control of another.

subjective: 1. pertaining to or dependent upon a subject (sense 1). 2. dependent upon individual interpretation, or accessible only to private experience, as opposed to *objective*, or accessible to public observation. 3. pertaining to systems or points of view in psychology that make the subject the central fact in psychology. 4. pertaining to sensory information originating within the individual, such as pain, fatigue, and organic sensations. 5. originating in hallucinatory or illusory processes. 6. untrustworthy, biased, or unreliable because of the influence of individual differences, prejudices, etc. 7. pertaining to judgments made without the aid of instruments.

subjective accent or rhythm: rhythm read into a series of objective stimuli, such as the beating of a metronome.

subjective attributes: the characteristics of a perception that are dependent upon the experiencer or subject. Color is such an attribute.

subjective colors: pastel colors in various patterns that may be seen when interleaved black and white disks are rotated slowly on a color wheel. *Syn.* FECHNER'S COLORS.

subjective error: an error due to prejudice, bias, or individual differences in the ability to make estimations.

subjective examination: an essay-type examination whose scoring standards depend upon the discretion of the examiner.

subjective psychology: any system of psychology utilizing the method of introspection or phenomenological reporting.

subjective rhythm: see SUBJECTIVE ACCENT.

subjective scoring: scoring according to expert opinions, as in the evaluation of essay examinations. *Contr.* OBJECTIVE SCORING.

subjective sensation: 1. a sensation, such as ringing in the ears, that does not arise as a result of external stimulation. 2. any sensory information not referring to the external world.

subjective test: a test that does not have objective scoring standards, as an essay examination made up and used by a teacher in a school.

subjective tone: see OTOGENIC TONE.

subjective type: a class of individuals characterized by a tendency to judge others and events in terms of one's own needs and aspirations. *Contr.* OBJECTIVE TYPE.

subjectivism: 1. the tendency to think and perceive in terms of one's own past experiences, needs, motives. 2. the doctrine that the only true test of reality must be subjective or personal.

sublimation: 1. (*Freud*) an unconscious process whereby the libido, or sex instinct, is directed or transformed into a more acceptable form of outlet. Freud accounted for artistic creation as a manifestation of sublimation. 2. loosely, any redirection of socially unacceptable impulses into acceptable channels.

subliminal: 1. below the absolute threshold of awareness. 2. pertaining to stimuli of insufficient strength to be perceived consciously but which can nevertheless influence behavior. See also SUBCEPTION.

subliminal consciousness: the result of stimulation too weak to reach the threshold of consciousness but which may nevertheless affect behavior. See also SUBLIMINAL PERCEPTION.

subliminal learning: learning that cannot be directly recalled because it is not sufficiently advanced or because it is a habit of which the individual is not aware.

subliminal perception: a state of being influenced by stimuli too weak to be apprehended consciously. See also PERCEPTUAL DEFENSE.

subliminal stimulus: a stimulus below the threshold of a receptor.

submission: a state of conforming to the wishes of another; submissiveness.

submissiveness: a trait that leads one to seek and accept the domination of others.

subnormal: less than normal; inferior in any degree.

subordinate construct: (*Kelly*) a construct (*q.v.*) that is one element of a superordinate construct.

subordination: 1. the placing of an object, datum, or individual in a lower category. 2. a state of accepting the domination of others.

subshock therapy: a mild degree of shock therapy.

subsidiation: 1. the relationship of a means to a goal and the goal itself. 2. (*R. B. Cattell*) the interrelationships between attitudes, sentiments, and ergs.

substance abuse: the use of any drug or chemical to modify mood or behavior that results in impairment. See also DRUGS AND BEHAVIOR.

substantia nigra: a pigmented layer of gray matter separating the dorsal and ventral portions of the cerebral péduncles.

substitute formation: (*Psychoan.*) a complex of ideas to which a feeling or affect becomes attached after repression banishes the original complex of ideas to which it was attached.

substitution: 1. the replacing of one goal with another, when the individual's route to the first has been blocked. 2. in reading or writing, replacement of one letter, word, or syllable with another. 3. a defense mechanism in which the individual replaces socially disapproved activities or goals with socially acceptable goals.

substitution test: a test in which the subject's task is to substitute one set of symbols for another. The code test is a substitution test and on a simple level may consist of the substitution of numbers for letters according to a prearranged plan.

subtest: a part or division of a test battery.

subtraction method: in reaction time, the calculation of a value by subtracting one observation from another. For example, if the simple sensory and motor time is known, then subtracting it from the total time for a complex reaction theoretically gives the association time, or time involved in making a choice.

subvocal speech: slight, inaudible movements of the lips, tongue, larynx, etc., similar to those made in speaking.

successive-approximations method: see APPROXIMATION CONDITIONING.

successive contrast: see COLOR CONTRAST.

successive-intervals method: a modification of the method of equal-appearing intervals in which the intervals are defined verbally or by presenting the subject with samples.

successive-practice method: a technique for measuring the extent of transfer of training by measuring the experimental group's saving of time or trials in Y as a result of having learned X, while a control group learns Y without having learned X.

successive-reproductions method: a technique for studying changes in long-term memory by having the individual reproduce material at relatively long intervals of time.

succorance need: (*Murray*) the need to receive aid, protection, support, love, consolation, and guidance from another. One of the several "psychological needs" listed by Murray (*q.v.*) In his enumeration of basic motivation underlying human behavior.

suckling: 1. the reflex chain involved in grasping the nipple, drawing, and swallowing milk. 2. the act of presenting the breast to the infant. 3. an infant during the nursing stage.

sudoriferous glands: the sweat glands.

sufficient reason, law of: the principle that given sufficient information it is possible to determine how and why an event occurs.

suggestibility: the state of being open to suggestion; a more or less permanent state of susceptibility to suggestion.

suggestion: 1. the process of inducing another to behave according to one's wishes or uncritically to accept one's ideas without the use of force or coercion. 2. the verbal communication constituting a stimulus for inducing a state of suggestibility.

sulcus: a shallow groove on the surface of the brain.

summation: 1. the total of any set or aggregation. 2. in sensation, the increase in experienced intensity when two stimuli are presented to a receptor in rapid succession. 3. in neurology, the arousal of an impulse by two or more stimuli in rapid succession when any one of the stimuli is insufficient to arouse an impulse. For summation to take place, events must occur very rapidly in time,

within milliseconds, and the excitatory fields of the neurons must overlap. When stimulating impulses arrive over the same sensory neuron, the effect is called *temporal summation;* when the arrival route is over separate sensory neurons, the effect is known as *spatial summation.*

summation model: the position that people form overall evaluations of others that are a simple sum of individual evaluations.

summation tone: one of the combination tones heard when two tones of more than 50 Hz apart are sounded simultaneously. The summation tone is the sum of the frequencies. *Contr.* DIFFERENCE TONE, which is equal to the difference between the frequencies.

superego: (*Freud*) that part of the psyche or personality that develops from the incorporation of moral standards and prohibitions from the parents, particularly the father. The superego is roughly equivalent to conscience.

superficial: 1. on the surface; pertaining to the surface. 2. descriptive of psychological processes that are not fundamental, primary, or of central importance. *Contr.* CENTRAL.

superficial reflex: a contraction of muscles elicited by scratching the skin.

superior: 1. higher; more advanced. 2. anatomically, above or anterior.

superior colliculi: the anterior pair of the *corpora quadrigemina* believed to function in optic reflexes.

superior intelligence: a level of general mental ability exceeded by only 15 percent of the population. On the Stanford-Binet Scale, an IQ equivalent of 120 or better.

superiority feelings: a complex of attitudes invading exaggerated estimates of the individual's mental

ability, physical traits, or personality. *Contr.* INFERIORITY COMPLEX; INFERIORITY FEELINGS.

superior oblique: one of the extrinsic eye muscles. The superior oblique rotates the eyeball downward.

supernatural: 1. belonging to a transcendent order. 2. beyond the natural order or natural law.

supernormal: 1. significantly beyond the normal range yet within the scope of natural law. 2. pertaining to extremely high intellectual ability.

supernormal period: a brief stage in the recovery of a neuron following the passage of an impulse when the threshold of excitation is lower.

superordinate construct: (*Kelly*) a construct (*q.v.*) high in a system of constructs that includes other subordinate constructs within it.

superordination: placing something in a higher category.

superstition: 1. tendency to ascribe events to supernatural causes. 2. tendency to assign cause-and-effect relationships to events because of temporal association or connections that are supposed to exist between them. For example, if a subject is reinforced after making some arbitrary movement that has no connection with the reinforcement, he will tend to repeat that movement. Thus, a pigeon that stretches out a wing, if reinforced immediately afterward, will tend to stretch the wing again. The pigeon has acquired a superstition.

supervalent thought: see OBSESSION.

supination: a movement of the hand (or forelimb) that brings the palm upward.

support: 1. to provide for the needs of another. 2. to provide encouragement and advice to another in a decision-making situation.

supportive therapy: a form of therapy in which the therapist gives advice and encouragement and otherwise assists the individual, especially during painful periods in the course of therapy.

suppression: 1. a stoppage of any neurological or physiological activity. 2. voluntary inhibition of activities on the part of an individual. 3. (*Psychoan.*) a conscious inhibition of impulses or ideas that are incompatible with the individual's evaluation of himself according to his ego ideal. *Contr.* REPRESSION.

suppressor area: a cortical area whose activation leads to inhibition in other areas.

suppressor variable: in a battery of tests, a test that has a zero correlation with the criterion, but a high correlation with one of the test predictors in the battery. Such tests can be used to eliminate spurious relationships between certain tests and the criteria. Thus, a certain clerical test might correlate highly with success in clerical work, but it might allow the selection of clerks who are merely good in general verbal ability and have no aptitude for clerical work. If a test of general verbal ability correlated highly with the clerical test but not with the criterion, it can then be used to eliminate those whose ability is based on "pure" verbal ability.

superaliminal: above the threshold.

superaliminal difference: any difference between stimuli above the difference threshold.

suprarenal glands: see ADRENAL GLANDS.

surdimutism: see DEAF MUTE.

surdity: deafness.

surface color: any color perceived

as lying on the surface of an object. For example, the color of a wall is defined as a surface color.

surface structure: in psycholinguistics, the stated form of a sentence. *Contr.* DEEP STRUCTURE.

surface trait: 1. a pattern of behavior manifested consistently over a wide range of situations. 2. (*R. B. Cattell*) a trait identified by correlation clusters. A surface trait is postulated to account for the correlations observed among tests of personality. Factor analysis of those correlations reveals source traits.

surgency: a personality trait characterized by cheerfulness, sociability, trustworthiness, and social responsiveness. *Contr.* DESURGENCY.

surrogate: 1. one who functions in the place of another's parent. Surrogates may take the form of real individuals (a child's teacher may become a parental surrogate), or surrogates may be imaginary (part of the fantasy life, as in the case of dreams where powerful figures may represent the father). 2. (*Harlow*) a mother substitute consisting of cloth or wire used in studies of infant monkeys' attachments to real and substitute mothers.

sursumvergence: a deviation of one eye in the upward direction in relation to the other eye.

survey: 1. an inspection or examination. 2. an extensive and widespread study designed to yield specific information.

survey research: the measurement of public opinion by the use of sampling and questionnaire techniques.

survey tests: tests designed to provide knowledge about the level of an entire class or group. *Contr.* INDIVIDUAL TEST.

survival value: usefulness of some quality (a mental or physical trait) in the prolonging of life of an individual or a species.

suspicion: 1. an attitude of doubt concerning the sincerity of others. 2. a trait characterized by the presence of doubt concerning the sincerity of others, feelings of hostility, fear of being injured by others, and unwillingness to trust people.

S variable: a stimulus variable.

sweet: one of the fundamental taste qualities with salty, sour, and bitter.

Swindel's ghost: a prolonged positive afterimage.

Sydenham's chorea: see CHOREA.

syllogism: a form of reasoning in which a statement is given followed by a second statement, the two together leading to a conclusion in the form of a third statement. The problem is to determine the truth or falsity of the third. The two preliminary statements are known as the major and minor premise, respectively; the third as the conclusion. For example:

Major premise: All men are mortal.
Minor premise: Socrates is a man.
Conclusion: Socrates is mortal.

Sylvian fissure: the lateral fissure separating the temporal from the parietal lobe.

symbiosis: 1. a biological relationship in which two species cannot survive without each other. Many flowers, for example, are dependent upon bees for pollination, and the bees are dependent upon the flowers for food material. 2. (*Psychoan.*) the incorporation of a symptom into the ego and therefore into the personality. For example, a delusion of persecution. 3. a close, sometimes neurotic, attachment of one individual for another.

symbol: 1. any object that represents another object. 2. in writing, printing, or musical notation, any mark, character, or diagram that takes the place of words or is used to indicate an operation. 3. (*Psychoan.*) a disguised representation of a repressed wish or impulse. Symbols are most commonly found in dreams, where they take two fundamental forms: universal symbols and individual symbols. For examples, see DREAM INTERPRETATION. 4. (*Psychoan.*) an act, such as slip of the tongue or pen, that represents an unconscious wish. 5. (*Psychoan.*) a symptom. According to psychoanalysts, symptoms represent desires that have been repressed.

symbol-digit test: see CODE TEST.

symbolic process: behavior involved in using symbols; thinking or problem solving.

symbolism: 1. the use of symbols, as in communications, religious rites, etc. 2. (*Psychoan.*) the psychological processes involved in disguised or repressed wishes and experiences. According to Jung, the world's art, religion, and myths are heavily involved with symbolism.

symbol-substitution test: see CODE TEST.

symmetry: the characteristic of being balanced, in good proportion, or aesthetically pleasing.

Symonds' Picture Study Test: a projective technique consisting of a set of twenty pictures depicting various interpersonal situations. The subject is asked to tell a story about each. The stories are analyzed in terms of

the psychological force that gave rise to them. Designed for use with adolescents.

sympathectomy: the sectioning of the sympathetic division of the autonomic nervous system in order to prevent its influence or to study its effects in experimental animals.

sympathetic ganglion: any one of the nerve centers of the sympathetic division of the autonomic nervous system. The ganglia lie on either side of the spinal column in a beadlike chain.

sympathetic induction: the arousal in one individual of emotions or feelings being expressed by another individual.

sympathetic nerve: see VAGUS.

sympathetic nervous system: see NERVOUS SYSTEM.

sympathetic vibration: resonance, or the induction of vibrations, in one sounding body by another sounding body.

sympathin: an adrenalinelike hormone secreted by the nerve endings of the sympathetic division of the autonomic nervous system.

sympathomimetic: having the same general effects as those characteristic of the sympathetic nervous system.

sympathy: an emotional attitude characterized by feeling with another person who is undergoing an emotional experience.

symptom: 1. in medical and psychological pathology, an indicator of the presence of a disease or disorder. 2. in general, any event indicating the presence of another event. Thus, inflation may be symptomatic of a coming economic recession.

symptomatic act: (*Psychoan.*) any behavior that represents an unconscious process, such as a slip of the tongue, or a compulsion.

symptomatic epilepsy: a condition in which epileptoid convulsions represent a symptom of underlying organic disease.

symptom cluster: a syndrome, or group of related symptoms, that typically appear together.

symptom formation: (*Psychoan.*) the process by means of which a substitute in the form of a bodily or behavioral symptom replaces an unconscious wish or repressed conflict.

Synanon: a private organization founded by former drug addicts to rehabilitate addicts through a controlled environment and group encounters.

synapse: the junction between two neurons. It is believed that the junction takes the form of a close contact between the fibrils of the end brush of one neuron and the dendrites and cell body of the next. The contact is not an anatomical connection, but a functional connection, allowing the nervous impulse to pass from one to another.

synaptic cleft: the space between pre- and postsynaptic cell membranes at the synapse.

synaptic conduction: the transmission of the nervous impulse across the terminal endings of one neuron to the dendrites of another.

synaptic junction: a synapse.

synaptic knob: a bulblike thickening in the termination of the end brush of an axon that comes into contact with the dendrites or cell body of the following neuron at the synapse. *Syns.* END BUTTON, end foot, bouton terminal, terminal button.

synaptic resistance: the tendency for the synapse to offer resistance or op-

position to the passage of an impulse. It is believed that most impulses that do pass are the result of spatial or temporal summation effects that overcome synaptic resistance.

synaptic vesicle: small globular-shaped structures in presynaptic endings that contain the neurotransmitter. The contents of the vesicle are released into the synaptic cleft when the nervous impulse arrives at the presynaptic ending.

synchronicity: (*Jung*) events that occur at the same time or are coincidental but bear no known causal relationship to each other. Used by Jung to account for clairvoyance, psychic phenomena, and strange coincidences such as the death of a person following a dream of that person's death.

syncope: a temporary cessation of consciousness; a fainting spell.

syncretism: 1. an attempt to combine unresolved elements of a group of propositions or doctrines into a system without regard for contradictions. 2. a form of children's thinking in which things thought of together are assumed to belong together or to bear a cause-and-effect relationship to each other.

syndrome: 1. a collection of related symptoms. The syndrome for influenza consists of the separate symptoms of sore throat, cough, high fever, and muscular aches. 2. a cluster or organization of personality traits or other behavior patterns.

synergic: exerting a force together, as synergic muscles work together to move a limb.

synergism: the theory that responses or ideas tend to consist of combinations of factors, simultaneously aroused and working in a coordinated fashion.

synesthesia: a condition in which stimulation in one sensory modality arouses imagery in a different modality. Colored hearing is an example of synesthesia that has sometimes been reported. A more common example occurs when we remark that "it looks cold outside."

synonym-antonym test: a test in which pairs of words are presented and the subject must indicate whether they are the same or opposite. *Syn.* same-opposites test.

synoptic: 1. pertaining to synopsia, or colored hearing, a form of synesthesia. 2. very brief; sketchy.

syntactical aphasia: see ACATAPHASIA.

syntality: the characteristic nature of a social group as revealed by its consistent behavior.

syntaxic: (*Sullivan*) pertaining to those experiences that can be communicated by means of concepts having definite objective referents.

synthesis: a whole that has been put together from discrete elements.

synthetic: 1. pertaining to synthesis. 2. artificial, as opposed to natural.

synthetic speech: speechlike sounds that can be produced by machines.

synthetic trainer: a device for providing practice under conditions that closely simulate actual operating conditions.

syntone: one whose personality is in harmony with the environment.

syntonia: a personality trait manifested as a high degree of emotional responsiveness and harmonious relationship with the environment.

syntrophy: a state of wholesome relations with others.

syringomyelia: a disease of the spinal cord that starts in the central canal and works its way outward, with involvement of the pain and temperature tracts, resulting in loss of pain and temperature sensibility.

system: 1. a set of data, propositions, or other entities related to each other in an orderly manner. 2. a set of concepts that serve as a framework for ordering the facts of a science. For examples, see BEHAVIORISM; GESTALT PSYCHOLOGY; FUNCTIONALISM; STRUCTURALISM; PSYCHOANALYSTS.

systematic: 1. pertaining to a system. 2. having the characteristic of a system.

systematic desensitization: in behavior therapy, a technique developed by Joseph Wolpe in which the patient imagines a hierarchy of anxiety-producing situations under conditions of physical relaxation with the goal of weakening the anxiety responses. *Syn.* COUNTERCONDITIONING, DESENSITIZATION, RECIPROCAL INHIBITION.

systematic distortion: a concept applied to memory traces that show gradual and progressive changes with time. Usually the changes are in an orderly and consistent direction. For specific ways in which memory traces may be distorted, see LEVELING; SHARPENING; ASSIMILATION.

systematic error: 1. a regular or consistent deviation in measurement due to a persistent experimental inadequacy. 2. a constant error.

systematized delusions: a set of false beliefs that are internally consistent.

systemic: pertaining to the organs of the body as an interrelated whole.

systemic sense: the interoceptive sense whose receptors are in the internal organs.

systole: the phase of the cardiac contraction cycle during which the heart is in contraction.

Szondi test: a projective test in which the subject must choose from among pictures of psychiatric patients those he likes best and those he likes least.

T

tabes; tabes dorsalis: a degeneration of the posterior columns of the spinal cord (*fasciculus gracilis* and *fasciculus cuneatus*) resulting in severe locomotor disturbances.

table: a systematic arrangement of scores, statistics, constants, or other information.

taboo: a traditional social ban on a certain act.

tabula rasa: a blank tablet. The concept was popularized by John Locke in an effort to emphasize that the mind of the infant is totally without ideational content until exposed to experiences.

tachistoscope: an instrument for exposing material for very brief durations of time. The general principle of operation is similar to that of a camera shutter.

tachycardia: a rapid pulse.

tact function: (*Skinner*) a vocal utterance of naming something.

tactile: pertaining to touch; tactual.

tactile circle: an area on the surface of the skin within which two points presented simultaneously are sensed as one.

tactual: pertaining to the sense of touch; tactile.

tail: the portions of the frequency curve beyond any given ordinate. The two ends of the curve "tail off" toward the base line.

tail assumption: in psychophysics, the assumption that the class intervals beyond the stimulus value last presented at each end of a series of measurements involved in determining the absolute threshold contain all the remaining frequencies.

Talbot-Plateau law: the principle that if the retina is stimulated by a flickering light set at a flicker frequency above the threshold, the brilliance of the continuous light will be the same as if the total amount of light had been uniformly distributed and continuously applied.

talent: a special form of ability, such as musical ability, which is inherited and enables the individual to profit from a high degree of training.

talking out: in counseling or psychotherapy, the spontaneous and complete discussion of a problem.

tambour: any type of membrane used on recording devices. Typically, the tambour is a thin rubber membrane that is stretched over a closed system and upon which rests a writing stylus. As pressure changes are communicated to the tambour, it moves the writing stylus, which can be made to record on a smoked drum or other device.

tandem reinforcement: a type of single reinforcement contingent upon the successful completion of two units of behavior, each of which would ordinarily have been separately reinforced.

tantrum: an outburst of strong emotion accompanied by anger, aggressive attack, crying, striking the feet and hands on the ground or floor. *Syn.* temper tantrum.

taphophilia: a morbid attraction for graves and cemeteries.

tapping test: a test in which the task is to make as many taps as possible within a prescribed area and time limit.

tarantism: a pathological desire to dance.

taraxein: a protein fraction found in the blood of schizophrenics.

Tarchanoff phenomenon: the production by the body of a weak current on the surface of the skin. See also GALVANIC SKIN RESPONSE.

tardive dyskinesia: involuntary movements, especially of the facial muscles, which occurs as a side effect of prolonged use of antipsychotic drugs.

target behavior: behavior designated as requring modification by a behavior therapist.

Tartini's tone: a difference tone.

taste: 1. the sensory modality whose receptors are taste buds on the tongue and in the oral cavity and whose stimuli are substances in solution. There is general agreement that there are four primary taste qualities—sweet, salty, sour, and bitter—and that these are mediated by specialized sensory neurons and receptors. 2. the individual's characteristic aesthetic judgments, particularly as these apply to the selection of clothing, reading material, furniture for the home, music, and artistic products.

taste buds: see TASTE.

taste tetrahedron: a schematic figure showing the relationships of the four primary tastes.

tau effect: the finding that the greater the separation in time between two events, the greater their perceived spatial distance. *Contr.* KAPPA EFFECT.

tautophone: a projective device in the form of a phonograph that emits indistinct sounds the subject is asked to describe in terms of what they suggest to him.

taxis: 1. a tropism. 2. a simple adaptive response elicited by a stimulus, such as catching a falling object.

Taylorism; Taylor system: the first formally developed system of scientific management of workers.

T data: (*R. B. Cattell*) information obtained by means of tests (also known as OT data).

t distribution: see T TEST.

tele: (*Moreno*) 1. a feeling or an attitude projected outward toward others. Teles may be positive or negative. 2. the unit of measurement of the sociometric technique.

telebinocular: a kind of stereoscope used in testing vision.

teleceptor: a distance receptor, such as the eye or ear.

telegnosis: in psychic research and parapsychology, the knowledge of distant events by unknown means.

telegraphic speech: the speech of young children who tend to omit articles, adjectives, and other auxiliaries, using mostly nouns and verbs.

telekinesis: in parapsychology, the movement of objects by other than physical means.

telencephalon: the anterior end of the embryonic brain that develops into the cerebral hemispheres endbrain.

teleological: 1. pertaining to ends or purposes. 2. pertaining to the doctrine of teleology, which holds that behavior should be studied from the point of view of its purpose. *Syn.* hormic. See also HORMIC PSYCHOLOGY.

teleonomic: pertaining to behaviors that are a function of inferred purposes.

teleoreceptor: a distance receptor, such as the eye or ear.

telepathy: knowledge conveyed from one individual to another by means other than the senses. Telepathic communication is presumed to be direct communication from one mind to the other without the intervention of any known physical form of energy transmission.

telephone theory of hearing: see HEARING THEORIES.

telesis: the assumption of certain values as goals to be attained by conscious striving toward those ends.

telestereoscope: a stereoscope that gives exaggerated depth effects.

telesthesia: in psychic research, the perception of objects and events beyond the normal range for perception by ordinary means.

teletractor: a device for amplifying sound waves and transmitting them to the skin, where they can be sensed as mechanical vibrations by the blind.

telic: pertaining to that which has an end or purpose.

telic continuum: a curve representing the frequency with which a custom or law is carried out by individuals. The general form of such conformity curves is a J-shaped curve.

telodendrion: a terminal filament of the end brush of an axon.

temper: 1. a display of anger. 2. in historical writings, a synonym for the temperament or disposition. 3. the overall manner in which the individual behaves as dependent upon metabolic changes going on in his bodily tissues.

temperament: 1. the individual's reactive disposition. 2. a system of tuning a musical instrument according to a tempered scale.

temperamental ardor: inflexibility and intensity in motivational demands.

temperature sense: the senses of warmth and coolness. The receptors for the temperature sense are not yet agreed upon. The feeling of warmth is a reaction to stimuli of a temperature between that of the skin (aproximately 33 degrees C.) and 50 degrees C. The sensation of coolness is aroused by stimuli of a temperature between that of the skin and 12 degrees C.

temperature spots: regions on the skin that are particularly sensitive to warm and cool stimuli.

temper tantrum: see TANTRUM.

template: a pattern or model.

temporal lobe: the portion of the brain lying below the lateral fissure between the occipital and frontal lobes. For illustration, see BRAIN.

temporal maze: a maze in which the subject is required to traverse certain pathways in a predetermined sequence. The ability measured is that of being able to appreciate temporal order rather than spatial sequences. See illustration.

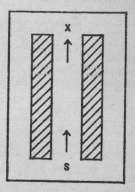

FIG. 27. *The temporal maze. The subject starts at S. At point X he must go either to the right or to the left, as predetermined by the experimenter. A simple pattern might consist of RR or LL. More complex patterns would involve multiple turns of the order RLRLRL.*

temporal summation: see SUMMATION.

tendency: a set or disposition to behave in a certain way.

tendentious apperception: (*Adler*) the perception of the world as shaped by the individual's will to power.

tender-minded: in a formulation by William James, one of two categories into which people can be placed, the other being the *tough-minded*. The tender-minded are idealistic, optimistic, and religious, believe in free will, and are rationalistic in their thinking. The tough-minded are realistic, materialistic, pessimistic, irreligious, and fatalistic.

tendon reflex: the contraction of a muscle elicited by stretching a tendon. A common example of the tendon reflex occurs in the knee jerk.

tendon sensation: kinesthetic sensations or tension aroused by the stretch of a tendon.

tension: 1. in physiology, the strain under which a muscle, tendon, or other tissue is maintained by muscular contraction. 2. the kinesthetic sensation associated with muscular contraction. 3. a condition of anxiety, unrest, and restlessness accompanied by feelings of muscular strain.

tension reduction: the decrease in strain or tension associated with the attainment of a goal in an act of adjustment.

tension-relaxation dimension: (*Wundt*) one of the three dimensions of feelings, the other two being pleasantness-unpleasantness and excitement-depression.

tensor tympani: a muscle attached to the malleus (hammer) and the eardrum. Its function is to exert pressure on the eardrum.

Terman, Lewis M.: American psychologist (1877–1956). Born in Johnson County, Indiana, Terman received his professional education at Indiana University and at Clark University, where he was granted the Ph.D. in 1905. His professional career was spent at Stanford University, where he carried out his work on intelligence testing and the study of gifted children. In 1916 he published an American revision of the Binet-Simon test, which became a leading instrument for the measurement of intelligence. In 1921 he and his associates began the studies of 1500 gifted children (IQ 140 and above), which were followed by several subsequent reevaluations of the group. His best-known works as author or coauthor are: *The Measurement of Intelligence* (1916), *Genetic Studies of Genius* (1925), and *The Gifted Child Grows Up* (1947).

terminal bulb: a synaptic knob.

terminal reinforcement: a reward obtained at a goal.

terminal sensitivity: the highest degree of sensitivity of which an organ is capable.

terminal stimulus: the maximal stimulus to which an organism is capable of responding.

terminal threshold: the maximal stimulus intensity that will produce a sensation.

territoriality: the drive displayed by some species of animals to defend their habitats against encroachment by others of the same species.

terror: extreme fear.

tertiary circular reaction: (*Piaget*) actions similar to secondary circular reactions (*q.v.*) but which involve novel reactions in handling new situations.

test: 1. a set of standardized questions administered to an individual for the purpose of measuring his aptitude or achievement in a given field. 2. more generally, any measurement that yields quantitative data, such as an unstandardized test administered in a schoolroom. 3. in logic, any operation applied to reasoning in order to assess its validity. 4. a statistical operation designed to assess the significance of a statistic.

The standardization of an intelligence or other type of aptitude test used in psychological clinics or schools involves five steps. First, items must be written or selected. Second, a preliminary tryout of the items arranged in test form is held with a large sample of testees. Poor items are weeded out and approximate time limits and scoring standards are determined. Third, the standardization administration is conducted on a representative sample of testees from all parts of the country. This process may involve years of work by trained specialists and may cost millions of dollars. Fourth, on the basis of the standardization administration, norms or standards are developed. In the case of individual verbal tests these may be given in mental age units or in IQ units. In the case of group tests they may be in percentile units. Fifth, the validity and reliability of the test are determined. Validity measures the extent to which the test measures what it was designed to measure. Reliability measures the degree to which the test gives consistent results from time to time.

Psychologists employ many different types of tests for the measurement of intelligence and special aptitudes. There are also specialized aptitude and achievement tests for industrial, military, and educational use. Broadly speaking, aptitude and achievement tests may be divided into: (a) *individual tests* and *group tests;* (b) *verbal tests* and *performance tests*. Individual tests are given to a single testee by a trained psychologist. Group tests are given to large numbers of testees simultaneously. Verbal tests require the understanding and use of language in either oral or written form. Performance tests make minimal use of language, utilizing instead concrete nonverbal materials.

test age: the score obtained on a test that has been standardized in age units.

test battery: a group of tests whose results are combined into a single score.

testis: one of a pair of organs contained in the scrotum that constitute the male sex glands. *Syn.* testicle. *Contr.* OVARY, the female sex gland.

test item: an element or question in a test

testosterone: one of the male sex hormones.

test profile: a chart showing the subject's relative standing on several tests.

test-retest coefficient: the coefficient of correlation obtained from two administrations of the same test. The test-retest coefficient is used as an index of reliability.

test scaling: the process of assigning values to test items by administering the preliminary scale to a sample group of individuals.

test score: a numerical value assigned to the performance of a subject on a test.

test vector: the representation of a test by a vector, or directed straight line. The use of vectors to represent tests is found in factor analysis. In factor representations, the angle between two vectors represents the correlation coefficient, a right angle being a zero correlation, and the correlation approaching 100 as the angle of the vectors becomes more and more acute.

test-wise: characterizing an individual who has taken many tests and is therefore likely to have an advantage over an entirely naive subject.

tetanic contraction: continuous or sustained muscular contraction.

tetartanopia: a form of partial color-blindness involving confusion of blue and yellow.

tetrachoric correlation: a correlation of two continuous variables expressed as two classes. For example, *tallness-shortness* correlated with *brightness-dullness* would be expressed as a tetrachoric correlation.

tetrachromatism: color vision characterized by the ability to see four primary colors. See COLOR THEORIES.

tetrad difference criterion: a now obsolete method for determining whether more than one factor is present in a set of intercorrelations. Spearman's G-and-s theory of cognitive abilities was based on the use of tetrad differences. The method has now been superceded by factor analysis.

tetrahydrocannabinol (THC): the psychoactive principle in marijuana and hashish.

texture gradient: the apparent increase in density and loss of separateness of the elements in a perceptual field, with increasing distance. The effect is very striking in looking at a plowed field; the clods in the foreground are well separated and appear less dense than those in the distance.

texture response: (*Rorschach*) a scoring category for responses based on the texture of the inkblot.

t function: see T TEST.

T group: see ENCOUNTER GROUP.

thalamic theory of the emotions: a theory postulated by Cannon and Bard that stresses the role of the hypothalamus as the center of the emotions. It is assumed that emotion-provoking stimuli gives rise to impulses that stimulate the hypothalamus, which, in turn, activates the cortex and the visceral process. The cortical activation arouses the emotional experience; the visceral stimulation readies the individual for an emergency. *Contr.* JAMES- LANGE THEORY.

thalamus: a mass of gray matter near the base of the cerebrum, bounding and projecting into the third ventricle. The thalamus consists of a number of distinct nuclei, many of which serve as relay stations for incoming sensory impulses.

Thanatos: (*Freud*) the Greek name for a mythical personification of death, borrowed by Freud to represent the death instinct. See also DEATH INSTINCT.

thema: (*Murray*) the interaction of the individual and the environment in a behavior episode. The thema is essentially a description of how a need and a press interact to bring satisfaction. Murray's Thematic Apperception Test was designed to investigate themas and through them to reveal personality.

Thematic Apperception Test: (*Murray*) a projective technique in which the subject is asked to tell a story suggested by each of a series of 19 pictures that are relatively unstructured and thus suitable material into which the subject can project his own needs, emotions, conflicts, etc.

theorem of escape: the generalization that the self tends not to be influenced by experiences incongruent with its present state of functioning.

theoretical explanation: a tentative explanation based in part on whatever facts are available, supplemented with hypotheses that fill any gaps in knowledge of the phenomenon under consideration.

theoretical mode: an estimate of the true mode obtained by fitting a theoretical frequency curve to a set of observations and erecting an abscissa. The mode is at the point of the abscissa.

theory: a general principle formulated to explain a group of related phenomena.

theory-begging: a scientific fallacy in which a theoretical assumption is given the name of an established fact, thereby seeming to prove the correctness of the theory.

therapeutic: pertaining to that which is curative in function.

therapeutics: the branch of any science dealing with the treatment of diseases or disorders.

therapist: an individual trained in the treatment of diseases and disorders.

therapy: treatment directed toward the cure of a pathological condition.

therapy puppet: see PLAY THERAPY.

therblig: a unit of work activity used in time and motion studies.

theriomorphism: attributing animal qualities to human beings. *Syn.* ZOO-MORPHISM.

thermal; 1. pertaining to heat. 2. pertaining to sensitivity to heat or cold.

thermalgesia: a pathological condition in which stimulation by warmth causes pain.

thermalgia: a sensation of burning pain. *Syn.* CAUSALGIA.

thermal sensitivity: the temperature sense; the sense of warmth and coolness.

thermanesthesia: insensitivity to warm and cool stimuli.

thermocouple: an instrument to measure differences in temperature.

thermoreceptor: a receptor for the temperature sense.

thermotropism: an orienting response to warm or cold stimulation.

thesis: 1. a formal proposition offered for proof or disproof. 2. a systematic treatise, particularly one offered by a candidate for an advanced degree.

thinking: 1. a symbolic process. 2. problem solving involving ideational activity. 3. a train of ideas. 4. (*Watson*) subvocal speech.

thinking type: (*Jung*) a category for individuals whose actions and reactions are dominated by thinking.

thirst: 1. a desire for water. 2. by analogy, a strong desire for anything. 3. (*Cannon*) a state of tissue dehydration resulting in dryness in the oral cavity, the latter condition giving rise to the conscious aspect of thirst. 4. a hypothetical drive state caused by cellular dehydration.

thobbing: emotional thinking; thinking distorted by emotional factors, attitudes, and beliefs.

thorax: that part of the body between the neck and the abdomen.

Thorndike, Edward L.: American psychologist (1874–1949). Thorndike studied at Wesleyan University in Connecticut, at Harvard, and at Columbia. His entire professional career was spent at Teachers College, Columbia, except for a year (1898–1899) at Western Reserve. He is best known for his early work in animal learning and for his pioneer work in the area of educational psychology. His early interest in animal learning culminated in the development of his famous theory of trial-and-error learning. He is also known as a pioneer in the development of mental measurements, for his compilation of words that occur most frequently in the English language, and for his three-volume *Educational Psychology* (1913–1914), in which he applied his broad knowledge of the principles of learning to problems in educational psychology. Among his other important publications are *Animal Intelligence* (1911), *The Psychology of Learning* (1914), *The Measurement of Intelligence* (1926), and *Human Nature and the Social Order* (1940).

Thorndike Handwriting Scale: a scale consisting of samples of handwriting arranged in classes that differ on the basis of general merit.

Thorndike's Trial-and-Error Learning: Thorndike's system of trial-and-error learning takes as its fundamental principles the laws of effect and exercise developed from the results of his early studies of animal learning typified by his famous experiments on cats in puzzle boxes. Thorndike announced the generalization that the correct response in a puzzle box was only gradually stamped in (imprinted) during a slow process in which the animal proceeded blindly, the correct response selected out of a number of irrelevant responses by the operation of the law of effect. The law of effect holds that, other

things being equal, those bonds or associations that lead to a satisfying state of affairs are stamped in and those that lead to a dissatisfying or annoying state of affairs are stamped out. The law of exercise—also operative in trial-and-error learning—states that, other things being equal, those associations or bonds that are practiced or exercised are stamped in and those not used fade out. Thorndike found that practice per se was not effective in stamping in learning. Practice must be accompanied by a reward or by knowledge of results in order to promote learning. Moreover, he discovered in his early research on the law of effect that only the first half of it was correct. Punishment does not stamp out learning; it only inhibits the performance of learning, and when the punishment is removed, the response will reappear.

Thorndike's research in the role of rewards and knowledge of results in learning led to the discovery of the spread of effect, or the carryover of the benefits of reward to adjacent responses in close proximity to the correct one. But he also had to admit—largely as a result of the findings of the Gestalt school of psychology—that the role of reward was not entirely mechanical or blind. Belongingness is also an important factor in facilitating learning, and items that naturally go together are therefore more easily learned than those merely juxtaposed without regard to their relationship to each other. Many of the details of Thorndike's theory of trial-and-error learning have been brought into question by subsequent research, but contemporary authorities in the field of learning rank him as one of the greatest figures in this important area of psychology.

thought: 1. a single idea. 2. a symbolic process. 3. (*Watson*) covert or subvocal speech. 4. problem solving involving ideational activity.

thought impulses: (*Psychoan.*) elements of the dream that are not generated by id or instinctual processes but arise out of the tensions of everyday life.

thought stopping: in behavior therapy, a technique in which the therapist stops undesirable thought sequences by shouting "Stop!" The patient is then instructed to apply the technique to himself.

threat: (*Kelly*) the individual's awareness of an imminent, widespread change in a construct system (*q.v.*).

threcia: (*R. B. Cattell*) a personality factor characterized by timidity and withdrawal. *Contr.* PARMIA.

three-color theory; three-component theory: see TRICHROMATIC THEORY.

threshold: 1. a statistically determined point on a stimulus continuum at which there is a transition in a series of sensations or judgments. 2. in neurophysiology, the minimal stimulus necessary to excite a neuron.

THS: see THYROTROPIC HORMONE.

Thurstone, Louis L.: American psychologist (1887–1955). Thurstone was educated at Cornell and the University of Chicago, which was to be his academic home for the rest of his active professional career, except for eight years spent at the Carnegie Institute of Technology. Thurstone is best noted for his pioneer work in the area of intelligence-test development through the use of multiple factor analysis. He is also recognized for his early work in attitude-scale construction, the development of

rational-learning curves, and the law of comparative judgment in psychophysics.

Thurstone's major publications, beginning with *The Nature of Intelligence* (1924) and ending with *Multiple Factor Analysis* (1947), reflect his interests in developing a quantitative approach to the investigation of mental abilities. His other important publications include *Measurements of Attitudes* (1929), *Primary Mental Abilities* (1938), coauthored with Thelma Gwynne Thurstone, his wife and professional colleague, and *Factoral Studies of Intelligence* (1941).

Thurstone Attitude Scale: an attitude scale derived from a modification of the psychophysical method of equal-appearing intervals. A series of statements is assigned a scale value on the basis of the pooled judgment of a large number of raters, and the final scale is made up of statements representing the entire range of opinion on the variable in question. The subject's score on the final form is the means of the items with which he expressed agreement.

Thurstone's Theory of Primary Mental Abilities: Thurstone's theory of mental abilities is based on his discoveries of the interrelationships among tests of ability utilizing the technique of multiple factor analysis. Thurstone found that all tests correlate positively, indicating that there must be a common factor or factors among them. His factor analysis of tests given to large numbers of individuals indicate that there are at least seven primary mental abilities:

1. Verbal ability (V): the ability to understand and use verbal concepts effectively.

2. Number (N): the ability to carry out fundamental arithmetic operations quickly and correctly.

3. Spatial (S): the ability to deal with objects in space and to utilize spatial relationships.

4. Perceptual (P): the ability to identify objects quickly and accurately.

5. Memory (M): the ability to learn and retain information.

6. Reasoning (R): the ability to perceive and use abstract relationships in the solution of problems.

7. Word Fluency (WF): the ability to think of words rapidly.

Thurstone's findings are in opposition to the position taken by those who, like Binet, conceive of intelligence as a unitary ability and who measure it by means of a test yielding a single score or IQ. Thurstone favored the use of a number of tests specifically designed to assess the individual's standing on the various special types of ability tests. In his practical application of his theory of mental abilities, he used percentile ratings reflecting the individual's standing on each of the primary ability tests.

thymergastic behavior: a pathological condition of the emotional and affective processes.

thymus: a ductless gland, located in the lower neck region. Its function is uncertain. It reaches its maximum size about the time of puberty and then atrophies.

thyroid: an endocrine gland, located in the neck, whose function is the regulation of general metabolism. See also HYPOTHYROIDISM; HYPERTHYROIDISM; CRETINISM.

thyroid stimulating hormone (THS): see THYROTROPIC HORMONE.

thyrotropic hormone: a hormone produced by the anterior pituitary gland that stimulates the thyroid gland.

tic: 1. an uncontrollable muscle twitch sometimes accompanied by a vocalization. 2. more generally, any compulsive nervous habit.

tic douloureux: a type of facial neuralgia characterized by paroxysmal bursts of excruciating pain.

tickle: a complex cutaneous quality elicited by stroking the skin lightly, especially in sensitive regions. Tickling involves a strong feeling tone, attempts to escape the source of stimulation, and uncontrollable laughter.

tied image: an image correlated with an ongoing perceptual experience. For example, the imagined taste of a watermelon that one is examining.

tight construct: (*Kelly*) a construct (*q.v.*) that permits invariable predictions irrespective of circumstances. *Contr.* LOOSE CONSTRUCT.

timbre: tonal quality, or the subjective experience whose physical correlate is the pattern of overtones or harmonics emphasized by a particular instrument.

time: see PSYCHOLOGICAL TIME.

time-and-motion study: an investigation of the time involved in carrying out certain units of an industrial operation with an analysis of the motions involved.

timed test: a test for which time limits have been established and are imposed on the testee.

time error: a tendency to be influenced in judging objects by the relative temporal position in which they are experienced. For example, in judging the weight of two stimuli the second stimulus will tend to be judged heavier than the first. More generally, if the first of two stimuli is judged to be greater than the second, the error is said to be positive; if the second is judged greater, negative.

time out from reinforcement: in behavior therapy, the weakening of undesirable behavior patterns by removing the individual to a nonreinforcing area.

time perception: the ability to judge or apprehend the passage of time by the order of occurrence of experiences, physiological rhythms, etc.

time sample: a sample selected according to the number of cases that fall within a given time period. For example, the number of finished products on a production line that must be rejected because of spoilage between 4 and 5 P.M.

time score: the duration of time required to perform an act, such as the time involved in running a maze from beginning to end.

time sense: the ability to judge intervals of time; time perception.

timidity: the tendency to experience anxiety in new situations; hesitancy in becoming involved in new situations or in meeting new people.

tinnitus: a ringing in the ears caused by pathological conditions in the receptor mechanism.

tint: see COLOR TINT.

tissue: any organismic structure composed of similar cells with a common function.

tissue need: a primary need of the tissues for food products, water, oxygen, etc.

Titchener, Edward Bradford: American psychologist (1867–1927). Titchener was educated at Oxford and at Leipzig, where he studied under Wilhelm Wundt, the founder of the structuralistic point of view in psychology. In 1892 he accepted an appointment at Cornell University, where he spent his long and productive career as professor of psychology and head of the department. Titchener was thoroughly German in outlook. He considered Wundt's works of greatest importance and spent a large portion of his time translating them into English. His unwillingness to show flexibility in his attitude toward new developments in psychology tended to limit the growth of structuralism and eventually resulted in its collapse as a school.

Titchener's most important work was his two-volume *Experimental Psychology* (1901–1905), in which he described the technique of introspective analysis—the fundamental technique of the structuralists—and the results obtained employing this method. His *Textbook of Psychology* (1909–1910) is also regarded as a definitive statement of his position. Among his other important books are *Lectures on the Elementary Psychology* (1908) and *A Beginner's Psychology* (1915). See also STRUCTURALISM.

titillate: 1. to tickle. 2. to excite sexually.

toilet training: teaching the child the place and manner in which defecation and urination are performed.

token economy: the utilization of secondary reinforcement to shape behavior. In the hospital setting the individual may earn tokens that can be utilized for television time, in exchange for passes, special foods, and the like.

token reward: any object that has

no intrinsic reward value but whose value depends upon learning that it can be exchanged for a primary reinforcer. Thus a poker chip may be a token reward if a monkey learns that he can exchange it for food.

tolerance: 1. an attitude of liberality or noninterference in the behavior and beliefs of others. 2. the ability to endure strain, drugs, or other procedures without undue psychological or physiological harm.

Tolman, Edward Chace: American psychologist (1866–1959). Tolman's undergraduate work was done at the Massachusetts Institute of Technology and his graduate work at Harvard, where he was awarded the Ph.D. degree in 1915. His professional appointments included Northwestern University and the University of California, where he spent most of his academic career. Tolman is best known for his systematic theory of learning, which is a blend of Gestalt psychology and behaviorism. Among his many publications are his *Purposive Behavior in Animals and Men* (1932), and *Drives toward War* (1942). See also TOLMAN'S PURPOSIVE BEHAVIORISM.

Tolman's Purposive Behaviorism: Tolman's Purposive Behaviorism is a systematic treatment of the data of psychology from the point of view of a molar behaviorism. The systematic framework is a careful blending of the Gestalt point of view with the scientific methodology of the behaviorists. It strongly emphasizes learning, particularly animal learning and more specifically maze learning in rats, a research topic to which its author was devoted. Tolman's fundamental law of acquisition holds that animal maze learning consists in the

building up of sign Gestalts or cognitive processes consisting of learned relationships between environmental cues and the animal's expectations. A pattern of sign Gestalts is called a cognitive map, and it is the animal's cognitive map of the maze that enables him to run it correctly.

The evidence for cognitive processes in animals comes from three types of experiments: place learning, reward expectancy, and latent learning. *Place learning* involves a situation wherein the animal learns a maze whose cues favor going to the same place whether or not the response remains the same. That is, if started from a different direction, the animal may have to learn first to go to a certain place by making a right turn, then to the same place by making a left turn. Such learning, Tolman and his associates claimed, was easier for animals than *response learning*, in which the animal learned to go to different places but always by making the same directional turn. *Reward-expectancy* experiments involve having animals learn to go through a maze for a certain type of reward, whereupon the reward is suddenly switched to a less favored type of food. The animals' evident disturbance, Tolman holds, indicates the expectancy for a certain type of reward. *Latent learning*, the third type of evidence in favor of cognitive processes, involves having nonhungry animals wander through a maze unrewarded for a number of trials. Upon being made hungry and given a reward, their very rapid catching up to regularly rewarded animals shows that they had been learning incidentally, even though not making the specific responses that led through the maze.

Transfer and forgetting, important topics in other systems of learning, do not occupy an important place in Tolman's system because of his use of animals and mazes—instruments of research that do not lend themselves to high levels of transfer in learning. Tolman formulated a large number of additional laws of learning that are beyond the scope of a brief treatment. In general, they deal with (1) factors involving the animals' capacity for learning; (2) laws relating to stimulus factors; and (3) laws relating to the manner in which the stimulus material is presented.

tonal: pertaining to tones.

tonal attribute: any measurable characteristic of a tone. The generally agreed-upon attributes are pitch, loudness, timbre, and volume.

tonal bell: a bell-shaped model designed to illustrate the interrelations among the various tonal attributes.

tonal brightness: an attribute of tones characterized by the relative density of the sound. A piccolo has a dense, solid tone; an organ a diffuse tone. *Syn.* tonal density.

tonal character: see TIMBRE.

tonal chroma: tonality.

tonal fusion: the blending of two or more tones into a unitary experience.

tonal gap: a certain range of pitches to which the individual is insensitive due to a pathological condition of the auditory mechanism.

tonal interaction: the combining of two simultaneously sounded tones into beats or combination tones. Beats are alternate amplifications and cancellations of two tones less than 50 Hz apart. Combination tones may be additive or subtractive. The additive tone is the sum of the frequencies of two originals more than 50 Hz apart; the subtractive is equal to their difference.

tonal intermittence: see AUDITORY FLICKER.

tonal island: a region of normal acuity for pitch or frequency surrounded by areas of insensitivity.

tonality: a characteristic of musical tones that arises through their relationship to other tones, specifically, each tone and its octave are considered equivalent in regard to tonality. The term is sometimes employed to characterize all musical sounds as opposed to noises.

tonal pencil: a diagrammatic scheme for portraying the relationship between pitch and volume.

tonal scale: the range of vibrations perceptible to the normal human ear—20 to 20,000 Hz in the young adult.

tonal volume: the extensity or space-filling attribute of a tone. A flute or piccolo produces what seems to be localized sounds; an organ fills all space. Tonal volume is distinguished from pitch and loudness by virtue of the fact that their thresholds are different.

tone: 1. a sound whose source is a periodic vibration or sound wave. 2. a measure of the musical interval. In Western music, one sixth of an octave. 3. muscular tonus. 4. a general level of background emotionality or feeling.

tone color: the timbre or quality of a sound, particularly as determined by the pattern of harmonics produced by the sounding instrument.

tone deafness: less than the normal ability to discriminate differences in pitch.

tone tint: see TIMBRE.

tone variator: a device for producing pure tones of variable pitch.

tonic: 1. (*adj.*) pertaining to muscular tonus. 2. (*noun*) the keynote of any scale or a chord having this note as its root.

tonic contraction: the contraction of those groups of muscle fibers that maintain muscular tonus.

tonic immobility: a condition of complete immobility that occurs in some animals as a result of certain stimuli. *Syn.* death feigning.

tonicity: 1. tonality. 2. a state of tonus.

tonic reflex: a state of maintained extensor thrust an animal displays when placed on its back.

tonometer: a device for measuring the pitch of tones or for producing tones of known pitch.

tonotopic organization: the approximate topographic projection of the basilar membrane to the auditory cortex.

tonus: a slight stretching of the muscle maintained by proprioceptive reflexes and whose function is to keep the muscles in a state of readiness and good physiological condition.

topectomy: the destruction of the superficial layers of the brain in the frontal region in an attempt to alleviate psychotic symptoms.

topographic: pertaining to the spatial or mental organization of phenomena or processes.

topography: 1. any system for mapping or localizing mental processes according to the region of mind in which they are found. The psychoanalysts, for example, located the id, ego, and superego along three levels of consciousness—unconscious, preconscious, and conscious. See PSYCHO

ANALYSIS. 2. the patterning of a response.

topological psychology: (*Lewin*) a descriptive system of psychology used to describe behavior in the life space. See also FIELD THEORY.

topology: a branch of mathematics dealing with transformations in space. Kurt Lewin adopted some of the principles of topology for his field theory.

torsion or **torsional movement:** the slight rotation of the eyeballs around their long axis as a component of the normal, coordinated movements of the eyes.

totem: among primitive or nonliterate peoples, an animal, plant, or inanimate object held in veneration, symbolic of the group, and acting as the group's protector.

touch: 1. contact of an individual with another person or an object. 2. the experience aroused by contact with another person or object. The "sense of touch" is a popular, not a scientific, concept. Properly, the sense of light touch or contact is part of the cutaneous senses.

touch spot: a small area on the surface of the skin that is especially sensitive to light contact.

tough-minded: in a formulation by William James, one of two types or categories into which people can be placed. The tough-minded are empirical, materialistic, skeptical, pessimistic, and fatalistic in their thinking. *Contr.* TENDER-MINDED.

toxic psychosis: a psychotic condition brought on by drugs or poisons.

trace: a hypothetical structural modification of the nervous system as a result of learning or experience.

trace conditioned response: when a conditioned stimulus is presented and followed by a blank interval, then by reinforcement, the resulting response is called a trace conditioned response.

trace perseverative: (*Hull*) a neural impulse that persists for a brief period of time after the cessation of the stimulus. Postulated by Hull to account for the possibility of sensory or afferent interaction.

tracking: following a target by continuous or intermittent adjustment of the following instrument. Radar tracking is commonly used in following the flight of space vehicles.

tract: a bundle of nerve fibers.

trade test: a test designed to measure levels of competence in a trade. The trade test may be of the aptitude or of the achievement type or a mixture of both.

tradition: a body of practices or social customs that has been handed down from previous generations.

train: to guide or direct the behavior of an animal or person for the purpose of inducing a certain pattern of predeterminded responses, particularly habitual responses.

trainability: the capacity for training; teachableness.

training: 1. the systematic series of activities—instruction, practice, review, examinations, etc.—to which the individual being trained is subjected. 2. a program of physical exercise designed to improve physical fitness. 3. the care and instruction of the young. In common speech and informal writing, toilet training may be intended by the concept.

training analysis: see DIDACTIC ANALYSIS.

trait: 1. a relatively persistent and consistent behavior pattern manifested in a wide range of circumstances. 2. a biological characteristic.

trait organization: the interrelationship among the various traits that make up the individual's personality.

trait profile: a chart or diagram on which are shown the relative standings of the individual's traits as measured by tests or other instruments.

trait variability: the spread or dispersion shown by the individual on trait measures.

trance: 1. a sleeplike state of dissociation in which there is a marked reduction in responsiveness to stimuli. 2. the hypnotic state.

transaction: behavior from the point of view of the individual in interaction with the physical and social environment.

transactional theory of perception: the functionalistic theory of perception that our fundamental perceptions are learned reactions on the basis of our transactions or interactions with the environment. The transactional functionalists hold that we build up probabilities of what to expect perceptually on the basis of our experiences and that we bring these probabilities to each new situation. The most striking instance of this effect is seen when the individual brings his expectation of rooms as being rectilinear to a distorted room. He will distort the people in it in order to make the room seem perceptually normal.

transactional therapy: a form of therapy in which the games family members engage in with each other are analyzed and replaced with more adaptive modes of behavior.

transcendental meditation: the type of meditation involving a mantra as taught by the Maharishi Mahesh Yogi.

transcortical: across the cortex; or more properly, from one part of the cortex to another by way of connecting tracts.

transduction: the process of converting one type of energy into another.

transection: cutting across a nerve fiber or tract.

transexual: an individual who is physically one sex but psychologically the opposite. A number of such individuals elect to have surgical and hormonal treatments to alter their physical appearance and gender.

transfer: learning in one situation carrying over to another situation. In general, there are two broad types of transfer, positive and negative. In positive transfer, learning in one situation facilitates learning in another. Positive transfer is illustrated by learning to drive in one car and then driving in another. There is almost 100 percent positive transfer. Negative transfer occurs when learning in one situation has a detrimental effect on learning in another situation. Negative transfer is illustrated when the individual attempts to draw in a mirror. Because mirrors reverse right and left, he has considerable difficulty since he must build up a new eye-hand coordination that contradicts all his past experience.

transfer by generalization: the transfer of general principles from one situation to another rather than the transfer of specific behavior patterns.

transference: (*Psychoan.*) 1. in general, any displacement of an affect from one object to another. 2. specifically, the displacement of affect toward the parent to the analyst.

transference neurosis: (*Psychoan.*) a neurosis in which libidinal satisfaction is obtained by substitutive mechanisms or substitutive attachments, as when the patient becomes attached to the analyst as a parent substitute.

transference resistance: (*Psychoan.*) the attempt on the part of the individual being analyzed to maintain repression over affects or impulses during the process of transference. Thus, the patient may have strong sexual feelings toward the analyst, but these are kept buried, just as similar feelings toward the parent were repressed.

transfer of principles: see TRANSFER BY GENERALIZATION.

transfer of training: see TRANSFER.

transfer RNA: ribonucleic acid that has been patterned by messenger RNA that assembles amino acids into the enzymes necessary for cell specialization or repair.

transformation: (*Psychoan.*) a change in feelings or impulses so as to disguise them for the purpose of gaining admittance to consciousness.

transformism or **transformation theory:** the assumption that one biological form or species becomes changed into another over a long period of time.

transitional cortex: that part of the cerebral cortex intermediate in cytoarchitectural and functional features between the phylogenetically old and new areas of the cortex.

transmission: 1. the sequential firing of one neuron in response to the firing of another. 2. the genetic passing of a trait to the offspring. 3. the sending of a message by a transmitter to a receiver. 4. the handing down of customs, mores, and folkways, from generation to generation.

transmission unit: a logarithmic unit of sound intensity, such as the decibel.

transmitter: 1. any instrument for sending a message in the form of a signal to a receiver. 2. a substance released at the synaptic junction that either depolarizes or hyperpolarizes the adjacent neuron.

transmutation of measures: the process of changing raw scores into some type of derived scores, such as standard scores.

transmuted scores: a set of scores transformed into a different scale.

transparency: the property of being able to transmit light without significantly diffusing it.

transparent surface color: a color with the property of transparency, such as that possessed by a colored glass or plastic sheet, which allows objects to be seen through it.

transpersonal psychology: a cross-cultural approach to psychology blending Eastern and Western conceptions of human nature.

transposition: 1. any interchange of position between two or more elements in a system. The change may be temporal, spatial, or psychological. 2. in music, the changing of a tune or composition from one key to another. 3. in learning situations, the subject's reacting to the relationship among the elements of the problem instead of to the elements themselves. Thus, if a hen is taught to peck a grain from the darker of two shades of gray paper, A and B (B being the darker), and is then presented with B and C where C is the darker, the hen will peck at C without difficulty. Reinforcement theory, however, would predict that she would continue to peck at B, since this was the reinforced response. The Gestalt psychologists use transposition experiments to support their theory of transfer of training as based on a transfer of relationships.

transposition of affect: the displacement of an affect or feeling from one person or object to another.

transvestism: the wearing of clothes of the opposite sex, particularly if this tendency is associated with sexual excitement or an attempt to function psychologically or sexually in the manner of the opposite sex.

trapezoid body: a tract of transverse fibers in the lower pons that arise from the cells of the cochlear nucleus.

trauma (plural **traumata**): an injury, either physical or psychological.

traumatic delirium: a state of delirium resulting from brain injury.

traumatic neurosis: a neurosis brought on by an extremely painful experience; a situation neurosis.

traumatic psychosis: a psychotic state brought on by injury to the brain.

traumatophilic diathesis: accident-proneness.

treatment: 1. the application of measures designed to alleviate a pathological condition. 2. the systematic working-over of data. 3. the manner in which a subject or person is subjected to experimental procedures.

treatment variable: see EXPERIMENTAL VARIABLE.

tremograph: a device for measuring the tremor of a bodily member or of the body as a whole.

tremor: a shaking or trembling of the limbs of the entire body. The *tremor of rest* occurs more or less constantly; the *tremor of intention* only when the individual attempts to carry out voluntary movements, such as threading a needle.

trend: 1. a systematic direction or variation in a variable. 2. a tendency or inclination to behave in a certain manner.

trend analysis: a statistical analysis carried out at several different points in time in order to establish whether or not a trend is in evidence.

trephine: a small drill, usually hollow inside, used to cut plugs out of the skull.

trial: 1. a single performance, such as an animal's run through a maze or a human subject's repetition of a list of nonsense syllables correctly. 2. a tryout or test of anything.

trial-and-error learning: learning in which the primary task is the acquisition of a new stimulus-response relationship, but in which there is a minimum of understanding and the new relationship is only gradually acquired after the elimination of incorrect responses.

trichesthesia: the sensation resulting when a hair is touched.

trichotillomania: an uncontrollable impulse to pull out one's hair.

trichotomy: a division into three parts.

trichromatic theory: a theory of color vision based on three primary hues and their corresponding receptor organs. The primaries most frequently chosen are red, green, and violet, since mixtures of these three will yield all other colors, including white. See also COLOR THEORIES.

trichromatism: normal color vision, so-called on the basis of trichromatic theory. *Contr.* ACHROMATISM; DICHROMATISM.

trick: (*Indiv. Psychol.*) self-deception; a psychological mechanism by means of which the individual conceals his own weaknesses. *Syn.* DEFENSE MECHANISM.

tridimensional theory of feeling: (*Wundt*) the generalization that each feeling moves through three dimensions: pleasantness-unpleasantness, excitement-depression, and tension-relaxation.

trigeminal nerve: the fifth cranial nerve, which has afferent branches to the face and scalp mediating general sensation, afferent branches from the mucosa of the nose and tongue, and efferent branches to the tear glands.

trigeminal nucleus: a mass of nerve cells in the pons and medulla from whence the trigeminal nerve arises.

trigger action: action of muscles, receptors, and neurons, in which the stimulus releases energy in these organs in an all-or-nothing fashion, just as the trigger of a gun releases all available energy in the bullet.

trigram: a three-letter nonsense syllable.

triceptor theory: a color theory stating that there are three types of cones or receptors in the retina of the eye.

trip: an occasion or period of time during which the individual is under the influence of a hallucinogenic drug, particularly LSD.

triskaidekaphobia: fear of the number 13.

tristimulus value: the hue of a given sample color stated in terms of the percentage of the three primaries (red, green, and blue) needed to match it in a mixture.

tritanopia: a rare form of color blindness in which the spectrum is shortened at the violet end and in which reddish-blue and greenish-yellow may be confused.

trochlear nerve: the fourth cranial nerve, which sends afferent impulses to the superior oblique muscles of the eye. It also has a proprioceptive component from the same muscles.

trochlear nucleus: a mass of nerve cells in the ventral portion of the gray matter that surrounds the aqueduct. The trochlear nucleus gives rise to the trochlear nerve.

troland: a unit of visual stimulation defined as the illuminance of the retina equal to that produced by viewing a surface whose luminance is one candle per square meter when seen through an artificial pupil of one square millimeter. *Syn.* PHOTON.

trophic: pertaining to nutrition and nutritive functions.

tropism: an unlearned orienting movement of the organism as a whole toward a stimulus. Some of the common tropisms are *phototropism* (turning toward light), *heliotropism* (turning toward the sun), *geotropism* (turning toward the earth), and *chemotropism* (orientation toward a chemical).

true age: see CONCEPTIONAL AGE.

true measure: see TRUE SCORE.

true mean: the hypothetic mean or average that would result if all scores or values in the universe could be measured with perfect reliability. The obtained mean is an estimate of the true mean and is based on a sample or population from the entire universe of items under consideration. The best estimate of the true mean is the mean of a number of repeated samplings.

true mode: the mode of the universe of observations from which a given sample was drawn.

true score: the value of a measure or magnitude completely free from error. Because the true value of measures or scores cannot be obtained in practice, the mean of a large number of observations is taken as the best estimate of the true value.

true value: see TRUE SCORE.

true variance: differences in test scores that are attributable to true differences among individuals in the characteristics under consideration.

truncated distribution: a distribution cut off at the ends through a failure to obtain a sufficient number of cases on one or both of the extreme ends of the distribution of values.

T scale: a scale based on standard scores of the distribution of unselected 12-year-old children for any specified test.

t test: the ratio of a statistic to its standard error. The statistical significance of *t* is dependent upon its size and the number of degrees of freedom, or the number of observations minus the number of independent restrictions on the sample. A common use of *t* is in the determination of the significance of differences between two means. The *t* test is then stated in terms of the probability, or *p* value, with which it may be expected that additional samples of data would yield by chance differences just as large as those obtained. For differences to be significantly greater than chance, *p* values of .01 to .05 are conventionally accepted as highly significant.

T type: a class of individuals who have a constitutional tendency toward tetany and whose eidetic imagery is of a photographic quality.

tuitional analysis: a training or didactic analysis.

tumescence: the swelling of tissue, particularly of genital tissues.

tuning fork: a double-pronged, or two-tined, instrument made of highly tempered steel and tuned to emit a sound wave of specific pitch.

tunnel vision: a condition in which peripheral vision is lacking or severely limited.

Turner's syndrome: an abnormal genetic condition in which a female possesses one X chromosome instead of the usual XX pair. Girls with the syndrome fail to develop sexually at puberty.

twilight attacks: an epileptic condition in which the individual experiences sudden changes in consciousness with motor automatisms and jumbled speech.

twilight vision: see SCOTOPIC VISION.

twitch: a small, localized, convulsive muscular contraction.

two-factor theory: see FACTOR THEORY.

two-point threshold: the minimal stimulus separation of two points placed on the skin simultaneously that are perceived as two.

two-tailed test: a test of the significance of a difference when it is assumed that the difference might occur in either direction. The experimental conditions might permit M_1 to be greater than M_2, or vice versa; if the difference can be only in one direction, then the one-tailed test is used.

two-way table: a scatter diagram.

tympanic: pertaining to the eardrum.

tympanum or **tympanic membrane:** the eardrum.

type: 1. a grouping of individuals distinguished from all others by the possession of a specified attribute. 2. an individual who possesses all or most of the characteristics of a group. 3. a pattern of characteristics that serves as a guide for placing individuals in categories. 4. the extremes of a continuum or distribution, such as implied in *aggressive type*, or *social type*.

type fallacy: the assumption that individuals fall into distinct groups when the evidence shows they form a continuum on the characteristics in question. For example, many people believe that the bright and the dull form distinct groups when, in fact, intelligence is distributed over a continuum with most people falling at the average.

Type R conditioning: see CONDITIONING.

Type S conditioning: see CONDITIONING.

typing: the process of placing an individual into a category.

typological: pertaining to the use of types or to psychological systems based on type concepts.

typology: 1. the study of types. 2. a system used for classification of individuals according to certain criteria.

U

U fibers: short fibers connecting adjacent gyri in the cerebral cortex.

ultrasonic: (literally, *beyond sound*) pertaining to sound waves of frequencies beyond the range of human hearing —that is, greater than 20,000 Hz.

ultraviolet: pertaining to light waves beyond the violet end of the spectrum.

umbilical cord: the cord connecting the fetus to the placenta.

Umklammerungs response: the startle response in an infant.

Umweg behavior: detour behavior or roundabout behavior.

Umwelt: 1. the environment that is meaningful and effective for a given species. 2. in existential literature, nature in relation to man. *Cf.* EIGEN-WELT; MITWELT.

unambivalent: (*Psychoan.*) not opposite in kind or nature—commonly applied to two motives or affects existing in the same person, as love and respect. In contrast, love and hate for a single object, person, or group are considered *ambivalent*. See also AMBIVALENCE.

unbiased estimate: an estimate based on an adequate and representative sample.

uncertainty interval: see INTERVAL OF UNCERTAINTY.

unconditioned response or **reflex:** a response evoked by a stimulus without the necessity of learning. Thus, salivation to food is a natural, un-learned response that occurs at the beginning of a conditioning series, before learning trials have been initiated. Salivation to the sound of the bell, by contrast, is a *conditioned response*, dependent upon learning.

unconditioned stimulus: a stimulus that evokes a response without the necessity of learning or conditioning. *Abbr.* US. See also UNCONDITIONED RESPONSE. In the example provided by Pavlov's dog-food-bell experiment, the food is the unconditioned stimulus, whereas the bell is the conditioned stimulus.

unconscious: 1. (*adj.*) characterizing an activity for which the individual does not know the reason or motive for the act. 2. (*adj.*) pertaining to the state of an individual who has suffered a loss of consciousness, such as a person in a faint or coma.

3. (*adj.*) pertaining to all psychic processes that cannot be brought to awareness by ordinary means. 4. (*Psychoan.*) (*noun*) the region of the mind that is the seat of the id and of repressions.

unconscious cerebration: thinking that occurs without awareness. See also INCUBATION.

unconscious inference: a judgment that is not verbalized but is acted upon without awareness.

unconscious memory: (*Psychoan.*) repressions; memories that have been forced out of the conscious level of mind into the unconscious.

unconscious motivation: motivation of which the individual is unaware. For example, the individual may forget an unpleasant appointment, convinced that it was a mere accident. The depth psychologist believes that it is revealing of a wish to forget.

uncontrolled: pertaining to variables not regulated or held constant by the experimenter.

underachievement: performance that does not measure up to the individual's level of aptitude.

underachiever: a person who does not perform at the level indicated by his aptitude.

underproductive: (*Rorschach*) pertaining to unusually poor responses to the inkblots.

understanding. 1. the process of apprehending meaning. 2. in historical writings, the faculty by means of which the individual apprehends meaning. 3. sympathy; feeling for another's point of view.

undifferentiated: pertaining to tissues that have not yet developed into characteristic forms and structures according to their hereditary potential.

undoing: a kind of defense mechanism whereby the individual engages is a ritual intended to abolish the effect of an act previously completed.

unfinished business: uncompleted tasks that have not been terminated with a desired degree of finality from the subject's point of view, and which become objects of continuing unpleasant concern or tension.

ungrouped scores: scores not yet tabulated into classes.

uniaural: see MONAURAL.

unicellular: consisting of only one cell.

unidextrality: the use of one hand or limb in preference to the other.

unimodal: having only one dimension. *Contr.* multidimensional.

uniform density: see COMMON FATE.

unilateral: pertaining to one side only.

unimodal: having only one peak or mode. *Contr.* bimodal; MULTIMODAL.

uniocular: monocular.

unique factor: a factor found in only one test of correlation matrix. *Syn.* SPECIFIC FACTOR.

unique trait: 1. a personality trait found only in a single individual. 2. a trait that shows a zero correlation with all other traits being measured.

unitary trait: a pattern of behavior that functions as a whole.

unitary type: an individual whose afterimages, memory images, and eidetic images are similar in type.

unit character: in genetics, a biological characteristic that if transmitted to an offspring, appears as a whole, not partially.

unity: 1. the state of consisting of one element, without parts or divisions. 2. harmony or concord in literary or artistic works. 3. a totality or whole.

univariate: composed of a single variable.

universal complex: (*Psychoan.*) any complex derived from an instinct.

universality: 1. the characteristic or quality of being universal. 2. a criterion or test of validity that consists of finding acceptance (of an idea or proposition) by everyone, everywhere.

universal symbol: (*Psychoan*). an object or idea that represents the same thing for people everywhere. For example, dreaming of water represents the desire to return to the womb. Dreams of pointed objects are phallic symbols. *Contr.* individual symbol.

univeral trait: a trait common to all members of a culture. *Syn.* COMMON TRAIT.

univocal: referring to only one object or class of objects. *Syn.* UNEQUIVOCAL.

unlearned: pertaining to behavior that does not depend upon practice or experience for its appearance. However, all behavior is modified by learning and is dependent upon environmental conditions; hence, the term *unlearned* is somewhat misleading.

unlearning: a deliberate attempt to overcome the effect of previous learning—usually attempted in the case of undesirable habits.

unnatural: contrary to nature. The term is popular rather than scientific.

unpleasant: characterizing experiences that are disagreeable and which the subject would like to avoid.

unpleasantness: (*Titchener*) with pleasantness, one of two poles of feeling or affective tone. Unpleasantness is characterized by dislike and ambient behavior; pleasantness by adient behavior.

unreadiness, principle of: (*Thorn-*

dike) the generalization that, if a conduction unit is not ready to conduct, conduction by it is unsatisfying. *Contr.* READINESS.

unreasonable: 1. characterizing a hypothesis or conclusion as being contrary to logic or reason. 2. describing an individual whose behavior is such that it makes unjustified demands upon others. 3. describing an individual who refuses to accept evidence ordinarily accepted by others.

unreasoning: pertaining to an individual or behavior not guided by logical thinking.

unreliable: not consistent; unable to meet a criterion of reliability. In the use of the correlation coefficient between split halves of tests or for test-retest, psychologists usually demand coefficients of .90 or above.

unselected: pertaining to samples not chosen according to any criterion or to avoid bias.

unsocial or **unsociable:** 1. characterizing one who avoids the company of others or does not seek others out. 2. characterizing one who does not fit into the social system.

unspaced learning: see UNSPACED PRACTICE.

unspaced practice: pertaining to learning situations in which no rest periods are given between trials. *Syn.* MASSED PRACTICE.

unspaced trials: see UNSPACED PRACTICE.

unstable: 1. unpredictable in behavior, particularly in moods, attitudes, or emotional behavior. 2. suffering from intermittent periods of mental disorder. 3. unreliable.

unstriped muscle: muscle lacking striations; smooth muscle.

unstructured: pertaining to stimulus situations whose patterning is not definite or is vague, ambiguous, or otherwise capable of being interpreted in different ways by different individuals. The materials used on projective techniques are said to be unstructured.

unweighted: pertaining to scores that have not been multiplied by a constant before being combined with other scores.

upper category: in the method of single stimuli in psychophysical experiments, a class of reports that will outnumber other reports as the stimulus magnitude is increased.

uranism: male homosexuality.

Urban's constant process: see CONSTANT STIMULUS METHOD.

Urban's weights: see MÜLLER-URBAN WEIGHTS.

urethra: the duct leading from the bladder to the exterior, for the discharge of urine.

urethral eroticism: (*Psychoan.*) the centering of sexual feeling in the urethra.

urning: a male homosexual who takes the role of a woman toward other males.

urolagnia: the association of sexual excitement with urination or urine.

use, law of: the generalization that, all other factors being equal, an association that is practiced will be strengthened.

uterus: the saclike, muscular organ in which the embryo develops.

U test: a nonparametric test for the significance of differences between means and unmatched groups.

utility: 1. the fitness of an organ or of a genetic modification in terms of biological survival value. 2. in general, the practical usefulness of a test or discovery.

utricle: the saclike structure of the inner ear containing the receptors that react to changes in head position.

V

vacuum activity: behavior that occurs in the absence of appropriate stimuli and believed by ethologists to be the result of a high drive state.

vagina: the passage leading from the uterus to the exterior of the body.

vaginismus or **vaginism:** a painful and involuntary contraction of the muscles associated with the vagina. The disorder may prevent coitus and is believed to be the result of psychological factors.

vagotomy: sectioning or cutting of the vagus nerve for medical or experimental reasons.

vagus: the tenth cranial nerve. The vagus sends fibers to the heart, lungs, thorax, larynx, pharynx, external ear, and abdominal viscera. Both motor and sensory fibers are included.

valence: (*Lewin*) psychological attractiveness of objects. Positive valence signifies attractiveness; negative valence, unattractiveness.

validation: 1. process of determining whether a measuring instrument measures what it was designed to measure. 2. more generally, the process of establishing the objective proof of a proposition, process, measuring instrument, etc.

validity: 1. the characteristic of a proposition, logical argument, etc., that it is founded on truth or is consistent with law or fact. 2. the property of a measuring device that it measures in fact what it is intended to measure. Validity is established by correlating the results of the test with an outside criterion or independent measure. If the test is designed to measure aptitude for medical school, then it should correlate highly with grades earned in medical school.

validity coefficient: the correlation coefficient between a measuring instrument and an outside or independent measure of the function that the test was designed to measure. If those who stand high on the test stand high on the outside criterion, and those who stand low on the test are low on the outside criterion, the test is valid. Most investigators believe that a coefficient of .70 or higher is necessary for a single test to show validity. If a battery of tests is being used, a multiple correlation of .50 may be worthwhile as a predictor, particularly if large numbers of cases are involved.

validity criterion: an outside or independent measure of what a test is designed to measure. The correlation between the test and the criterion is taken as an index of the test's validity.

Valium: a trade name for diazepam, a tranquilizer.

value: 1. a quantitative measure or score. 2. the worth or excellence of anything. 3. a social end or goal considered desirable of achievement. 4. in color descriptions, brilliance.

value analysis: a type of content analysis in which the proportion of expressions referring to a certain value are tabulated.

value judgment: a reaction to persons, objects, aesthetic products, etc., in terms of their value or worth, as opposed to their objective characteristics.

value system: the set of values accepted by an individual or by society. See VALUE 3.

variability: the characteristic of being subject to change whether continuous or discontinuous. In descriptive statistics, the common measures of variability are the standard deviation, average deviation, and the range.

variability coefficient: see VARIATION COEFFICIENT.

variable: 1. a quantity that may increase or decrease. 2. a factor dependent upon other factors. See independent variable; dependent variable.

variable error: the deviation of a measure from the mean. Variable errors occur on either side of the mean. Their extent may be predicted by the measures of dispersion, but they cannot be corrected. *Syn.* CHANCE ERROR. *Contr.* CONSTANT ERROR.

variable interval reinforcement: reinforcement delivered according to a random sequence of time intervals. Typically the intervals lie between prearranged arbitrary values with a fixed mean. *Contr.* FIXED INTERVAL REINFORCEMENT.

variable ratio reinforcement: a type of intermittent reinforcement in which the animal is given reinforcement, such as a pellet of food, after a certain number of responses, the number of responses varying from trial to trial but lying between arbitrary values with a fixed average.

variable stumulus: in psychological experiments, any one of the set of stimuli that are systematically compared with a constant stimulus.

variance: the square of the standard-deviation employed as a measure of the extent to which individual scores in a set of scores differ from each other. *Syns.* mean-square deviation; MEAN-SQUARE ERROR

variate: the value of a variable.

variation: 1. change in condition. 2. a difference. 3. biological differences between organisms. 4. differences among statistical constants.

variation coefficient: a measure of relative variability given by the formula $V = \dfrac{100\sigma}{M}$.

variation tone: the tone heard when the source of sound is interrupted rapidly.

vas: a duct.

vascular: 1. pertaining to blood vessels. 2. characterizing tissue richly endowed with blood vessels.

vascular theory of thermal sensitivity: (*Nafe*) the theory that thermal sensations are correlated with changes in the constriction and dilation of arterioles and veinules.

vasoconstriction: the constriction or closing of the diameter of a blood vessel.

vasodilation: the opening or enlargement of the diameter of a blood vessel.

vasomotor: pertaining to vasoconstriction and vasodilation.

vasopressin: a hormone produced by the posterior pituitary gland that increases blood pressure and decreases the production of urine.

vector: 1. a directed line or magnitude. 2. in field theory, a symbol of motivation or a representation of a force that causes locomotion toward or away from an incentive. 3. in statistics, the representation of a score by means of a line having direction and length.

vector field: (*Lewin*) a field in which there is direction and magnitude of all forces (vectors). Vectors, or directed lines, represent motivational forces in field theory.

vector psychology: (*Lewin*) an analysis of motivation or dynamic psychology with the use of vectors. Vector theory is a part of topology or field theory.

veg: a psychophysical unit of measurement in a scale for perceived weight constructed by the method of equal-appearing intervals.

vegetative: 1. pertaining to plants or the growth of plants. 2. pertaining to physiological activities such as respiration, digestion, growth, etc.

vegetative nervous system: the autonomic nervous system.

vegetative neurosis: (*Psychoan.*) a neurosis expressed as a disturbance of the vegetative functions.

Veith-Müller circle: a circle centered at the visual origin for a set of points at a constant visual distance.

velocity: the rate of motion in a given direction.

ventral: pertaining to the anterior or abdominal side of the body. *Contr.* DORSAL.

ventricle: 1. any one of the cavities within the brain that form a continuous channel for the flow of the cerebrospinal fluids. 2. one of the chambers within the heart. 3. more generally, any cavity within an organ of the body.

verbal: pertaining to words in any form—oral, written, printed, etc.

verbal generalization: 1. a universal or widely held principle. 2. in verbal conditioning, stimulus generalization; that is, responding in the same way to words with the same general meaning.

verbal image: a representation in verbal terms of a memory or remembered object.

verbal intelligence: the ability to deal effectively with words and symbols; the ability to solve problems utilizing verbal symbols. *Contr.* CONCRETE INTELLIGENCE.

verbalism: 1. undue reliance on words in thinking, without reference to what lies behind the words. 2. uncritical acceptance of definitions in place of explanations.

verbalization: 1. a statement or expression in the form of words. 2. expressing oneself in words instead of action. 3. wordiness; verbosity.

verbal learning: the learning of lists or words, nonsense syllables, etc. Verbal learning is often contrasted with conditioning, maze learning, and perceptual-motor learning.

verbal scale test: a scale that utilizes words in the administration and taking of the test. *Contr.* PERFORMANCE TEST.

verbal summator: a projective technique in which an instrument produces low-intensity vowel sounds in response to which the subject is asked to tell what words he hears.

verbigeration: a pathological condition characterized by meaningless and stereotyped repetition of words.

verbomania: pathological volubility that is typically incoherent. *Syn.* LOGORRHEA.

verbone: (*Murray*) a verbal action pattern.

vergence: any turning movement of the eyeballs.

veridical: corresponding to objective reality.

verification: 1. the collecting of empirical data for the purpose of testing a hypothesis. 2. one of the states of creative or artistic thinking in which the thinker evaluates the results of illumination or a sudden solution of the problem.

vermis: the median lobe of the cerebellum lying between the cerebellar hemispheres.

vernier: a finely calibrated scale, usually subsidiary to a scale with larger calibrations.

vertebra: any one of the series of bones making up the spinal column.

Vertebrata: the large division of the animal kingdom consisting of all animals with a backbone.

vertex: 1. the uppermost point of a geometrical figure. 2. the meeting point of two angular lines. 3. the top of the head.

vertical: 1. pertaining to direction of the force of gravity; up and down. 2. pertaining to the head-to-tail (or head-to-foot) axis of the animal body.

vertical group: a group that draws upon two or more social classes. *Contr.* HORIZONTAL GROUP.

vertical mobility: movement from one social class to another.

vertigo: dizziness.

vesania: a psychosis of the functional variety.

vesicle: 1. any saclike structure containing fluid. 2. invaginated saccules at the synapse containing transmitter substance.

vestibular: pertaining to the vestibule or sensations mediated by the utricle and saccule.

vestibule: a bony cavity in the labyrinth of the inner ear consisting of two sacs, the utricle and the saccule, which contain hair cells that are affected by acceleration and deceleration of the body and by changes in head position. The sense (more accurately a perception) is called the *vestibular sense.*

vestibule school: an industrial-train-

ing program that must be successfully completed by beginners.

vestige: a rudimentary organ more highly developed in ancestral forms.

V factor: verbal comprehension. See THURSTONE'S THEORY OF PRIMARY MENTAL ABILITIES.

vibration: a regular or periodic motion of a body, such as the vibration of a string on a musical instrument. Vibrations are conventionally measured in cycles per second (cps), or in the older literature, in double vibrations per second.

vibration sense: see VIBRATORY SENSITIVITY.

vibratory sensitivity: the bodily sense of being in contact with a vibrating stimulus.

vicarious: pertaining to a substitute. May be used in the sense of a mother attempting to obtain substitutive satisfaction from her daughter's social activities, or in connection with brain mechanisms where one part of the brain may function in place of another that has been injured.

vicarious function: the substitution of one psychological process for another.

vicarious trial and error: the substitution of mental performance for overt performance. The average chess player engages in a good deal of vicarious trial and error before making a move.

Viennese School: Freud's followers in the theory and practice of psychoanalysis.

Vierordt's law: the principle that the more mobile the part of the body, the lower the two-point threshold.

viewing angle: the angle formed by the line of regard from the eye to an observed surface.

viewing conditions: stimulus, retinal,

and surrounding factors at the time of making a visual observation.

vigilance function: SEE AROUSAL.

Vigotsky test: a concept-formation test that requires the subject to sort out blocks of various shapes, colors, and sizes.

Vincent curve: a group curve constructed by a technique for making comparable the learning curves of different subjects by dividing the individual curves into equal fractions (such as fifths or sixths) and averaging the results, on the assumption that an equal fraction of the total time or trials is equivalent from one individual to another.

Vineland Social Maturity Scale: a rating scale of maturity, based on samples of behavior characteristic of individuals at specified ages.

violet: the visual sensation aroused by wavelengths of about 433 nm and shorter.

viraginity: the characteristic in a woman of being like a man.

virile: having the qualities of the mature male; manly.

virile reflex: the erection of the penis in the male.

virilism: the development in a woman of the secondary sexual characteristics of the male.

virtue: the habit of conforming to the moral code, particularly in regard to sexual matters.

virulent: 1. pertaining to the olfactory sensation represented by the odor of morphine. 2. deadly or poisonous; destructive.

viscera: the organs enclosed in the abdominal and thoracic cavities.

visceral: 1. pertaining to the viscera. 2. pertaining to the functioning of the organs that make up the viscera.

visceral drive: a drive originating in a physiological need.

visceral sense: the organic sense; a sensation arising from the viscera.

visceroreceptor: a receptor of the visceral organs.

viscerogenic: having its origin in the viscera.

viscerotonia: SEE SHELDON'S CONSTITUTIONAL THEORY OF PERSONALITY.

visibility: 1. in a short range of electromagnetic or radiant energy, the property of being capable of exciting the retinal receptors. 2. the property of being easily seen.

visibility coefficient: a numerical designation of the relative visibility of radiant energy, especially of a certain spectral wavelength. The relative visibility coefficient has as its standard the maximum visibility of a wavelength of approximately 554 nm.

visibility curve: a graphic representation of the relative visibility of radiant energy plotted in relation to wavelength.

visible speech: the representation of units of spoken sound by means of patterns of black, white, and gray. Sound waves are transformed into visible light and then photographed for the purpose of making speech visible.

visile: an individual or class of individuals whose imagery is primarily visual.

vision: 1. the sense of sight whose receptor is the eye and whose stimulus is radiant energy ranging from approximately 400 to 760 nm. 2. that which is seen. 3. a visual hallucination.

vision theory: SEE COLOR THEORIES; DUPLICITY THEORY.

vista response: (*Rorschach*) a response to the inkblot in which shading is interpreted as depth.

visual: pertaining to vision.

visual acuity: the ability of the retina to separate or discriminate stimuli. Acuity may be measured by acuity gratings or, more commonly, by means of the Snellen Chart, which employs letters of graded size. If the individual can discriminate letters that can just be discriminated by the normal eye at the standard distance of 20 feet, he is said to have 20/20, or normal, vision. A rating of 20/200 signifies that at 20 feet the individual is able to discriminate only what the normal person can discriminate at 200 feet. Correspondingly, 15/20 signifies that the individual can discriminate at 20 feet what the normal eye cannot discriminate at more than 15 feet.

visual adaptation: the tendency for the retina to adjust to conditions of continued stimulation or lack of stimulation. For specific types of adaptation, see DARK ADAPTATION; BRIGHTNESS ADAPTATION; CHROMATIC ADAPTATION.

visual agnosia: inability to interpret visual stimuli, resulting from injuries to the visual association areas (parastriate; peristriate).

visual angle: the angle formed by lines from opposite extreme points of an object to the nodal point of the eye.

visual axis: a straight line passing through the external point of fixation and the nodal point of the eye to the fovea.

visual cliff: an instrument for testing whether depth perception is inherent by presenting the infant or baby animal with a situation in which he must crawl toward the experimenter over a heavy sheet of glass that bridges a sharp drop-off or cliff. If depth perception is inherent, the subject should refuse to cross the glass; if not, he should unhesitatingly go over the "cliff."

visual displacement: the angles at which the eyes deviate either vertically or horizontally from the primary position when viewing objects.

visual field: 1. the totality of all objects available to the unmoving eye at any given time. 2. the subjective, three-dimensional space in which objects are perceived.

visual fixation: the turning of the eyes so that images fall on the foveas.

visual induction: the influence of stimulation of one part of the retina on another part. Thus, a small yellow square will make a surrounding gray field take on a bluish tinge.

visualization: the ability to perceive things in terms of visual imagery.

visual motor Gestalt test: see BENDER GESTALT TEST.

visual organization: in Gestalt psychology, the fact that the perceived visual field appears organized and meaningful.

visual process: 1. the operation of seeing. 2. any function—receptor, nervous, cortical—involved in the process of seeing.

visual projection: the process of attributing objective location to a visually perceived object.

visual purple: see RHODOPSIN.

visual-righting reflexes: reflexes associated with the orientation of the head according to the fixation of objects in the visual field.

visual space: the visual field or the three-dimensional subjective space in which objects are perceived.

visual type: an individual whose imagery is primarily visual.

visual yellow: SEE RETINENE.

vitalism: the theory that living substances contain a nonmaterial entity crucial to their existence.

vitality: 1. the property of being alive or of being able to stay alive. 2. vigor; energy; power of endurance.

vital statistics: data about the rate of birth and death of human beings.

vitreous humor: the transparent, jellylike material that fills the eyeball between the retina and the lens. *Contr.* AQUEOUS HUMOR.

vocabulary: 1. any list of words. 2. the totality of words employed in a language. 3. the individual's stock of words as measured by a test.

vocabulary test: a test designed to assess the number of words that a person can use or understand. Vocabulary tests may be either part of an aptitude test or part of a language achievement test.

vocal: 1. pertaining to the voice. 2. a propensity for giving verbal expression to one's feelings or opinions.

vocal cords: the ligaments in the larynx concerned with the production of sounds.

vocalization: the utterance of sounds, as in speaking, babbling, screaming, etc.

vocal organs: the totality of the organs involved in speech.

vocal register: the tonal range, or compass of pitch, of an individual's voice.

vocation: 1. the manner in which one earns his living. 2. in religious writing, a call to the religious life.

vocational adjustment: the degree to which the individual is suited to his job or profession.

vocational aptitude: potential or predicted achievement in a particular job or profession.

vocational-aptitude test: a test designed to evaluate, through measurement of ability, personality traits, interests, and potential achievement or success in a specific occupation or profession.

vocational counseling: counseling as applied to the problems of vocational adjustment. Theoretically, vocational counseling involves only problems connected with employment, but vocational counselors find that personal problems and home conditions play an important role in job satisfaction.

vocational education: training designed to fit a person for a particular job or profession.

vocational guidance: the process of assisting an individual to choose a vocation. Vocational guidance involves interviews, the use of aptitude and personality tests, and interest blanks.

vocational interest blank: see STRONG-CAMPBELL INTEREST INVENTORY.

vocational maladjustment: a condition resulting from an individual's attempting to work in a job or profession for which he is unsuited.

Vocational Preference Inventory: An interest inventory for grades 12–16 and adults. The examinee indicates like or dislike for 160 occupational titles. There are also built-in personality scales.

vocational selection: a choice made among applicants for a job or profession in terms of the individual most likely to succeed.

voice key: a switch, used in reaction time experiments, that automatically activates a clock when the subject speaks.

volar: pertaining to the palm of the hand or the sole of the foot.

volition: 1. will; the process of deciding upon a course of action. 2. any voluntary activity. 3. in structuralistic psychology, a complex experience consisting of kinesthetic sensations of effort and ideational images of a goal or end.

volley: a synchronous discharge of nervous impulses.

volley theory: see HEARING THEORIES.

volume: an attribute or dimension of sensory experience, particularly of sounds.

volume color: any color perceived as occupying three-dimensional space. For example, a glass sphere filled with colored liquid, when viewed, results in the experience of volume color.

voluntarism: the doctrine that will or volition is the fundamental psychological process to which all others are related. *Contr.* DETERMINISM.

voluntary: 1. pertaining to volition. 2. pertaining to psychological or muscular processes under the direct control of the cerebral cortex.

voluntary movement: 1. movement originating as a result of an intention to move. 2. movement made by the striped or straited muscles under the control of the central nervous system.

voluntary muscle: a muscle that can be contracted voluntarily. *Contr.* SMOOTH MUSCLE.

voyeur: one who obtains sexual gratification by watching others undress or engage in sexual activity. *Syn.* PEEPING TOM.

V test: a modification of the *t test*, used when the samples are large and the variance is unequal.

vulva: the external genitalia of the female.

W

wakefulness of choice: the wakefulness of a sleep cycle that results from learning; normally a single waking period each day.

wakefulness of necessity: wakefulness that results from bodily need or discomfort.

waking center: a brain center in the posterior hypothalamus presumed to regulate sleeping and waking. Defined by some neurologists as a part of the reticular activating system.

Wallerian degeneration: in peripheral sensory and motor neurons, the deterioration of the myelin sheath and axis cylinder from the point of an injury toward the periphery. If the neuralemma is left intact, regeneration will occur.

walleye: see EXOTROPIA.

warming-up period: in learning and motor tasks, an initial stage in which the individual starts out slowly and is inexact in his responses even though familiar with the tasks but then rapidly regains his efficiency.

warm spot: a spot on the skin that is particularly sensitive to warm stimuli.

warmth: a sensory modality whose stimulus is warmer than the tissue to which it is applied. On the skin this temperature is normally about 33° C. There is no general agreement upon the receptors for thermal sensitivity.

Wassermann test: a test made of a blood sample or of a sample of cerebrospinal fluid for the presence of the syphilis spirochete.

wat: (*Hull*) a unit of measurement of the reaction potential.

watch test: a rough test of auditory acuity carried out by moving a ticking watch toward and away from the subject until the threshold is ascertained.

Watson, John Broadus: American psychologist (1878–1958). Watson, who began his educational career in a one-room schoolhouse, earned his M.A. degree at Furman University and his Ph.D. at the University of Chicago, where he remained as an instructor and came under the influence of Angell and Dewey. However, he rejected the teachings of the functionalist school, and after transferring to Johns Hopkins University in 1908, he espoused a militant behaviorism. He remained at Johns Hopkins until 1920 and achieved a reputation as a brilliant young teacher and writer. His important works during this period began with an article, "Psychology as the Behaviorist Views It," in the *Psychological Review* in 1913; in it he announced the program of his behavioristic psychology. In 1920 he left the field of academic psychology and entered the advertising business. Watson's books include: *Behavior: An Introduction to Comparative Psychology* (1914), *Psychology from the Standpoint of a Behaviorist* (1919), *Behaviorism* (1925),

and *Psychological Care of the Infant and Child* (1928).

Watson's Behaviorism: Watson defines psychology as the science of behavior. The aim of behaviorism is to be able to predict responses from a knowledge of stimulus conditions and, conversely, knowing responses, to be able to predict the antecedent stimulus conditions. Watson lists four characteristic methods to be utilized by behaviorists in their investigations: (1) observation, with and without instrumental controls; (2) method of conditioned reflexes developed by Pavlov; (3) verbal report method; (4) testing methods. The verbal-report method is of special interest, since, by introducing it, Watson hoped to be able to deal with such mentalistic phenomena as thinking, feeling, imagery, etc., which had been in the stronghold of the structuralistic psychologists.

Watson's objective methods favored the study of animals and children—two areas of psychology neglected by the then dominant structuralists and functionalists. His studies on the conditioning of children's fears are now regarded as classics in the field, and his pioneer work in emphasizing the desirability of using animals gave great impetus to the development of comparative psychology. Perhaps the most famous and most controversial of Watson's theories was his account of the thought processes, in which he took and strongly defended a peripheralistic stand, arguing that thought was identifiable with laryngeal movements or subvocal speech. This was a deliberate attempt to develop a behavioral theory of thinking to remove it from the camp of the structuralists. A similarly peripheral theory of feelings and emotion is less well-known but was also an attempt to translate conscious experience into objectively observable processes.

Watson's system of behaviorism, although it remained largely programmatic, had a profound influence on American psychology, which is today strongly behavioristic in its methods, although its aims and spirit are functionalistic.

wave: a periodic to-and-fro motion of particles in such a manner that the motion continuously advances.

wave amplitude: the height of a wave as measured from trough to crest.

wave frequency: the number of times a complete waveform passes a given point per second.

wavelength: the distance from two adjacent crests (or troughs) of a wave. Wavelength is inversely related to frequency, the longer waves being slower and the shorter waves faster.

wave of excitation: 1. a nervous impulse. 2. any electrochemical change propagated through tissue, such as the electrical impulses associated with the heartbeat.

waxy flexibility: see FLEXIBILITAS CEREA.

W-A-Y technique: a projective technique in which the subject is asked to write three short answers to the question, Who are you?

W compulsion: (*Rorschach*) the tendency to utilize all of the card for a content description.

weaning: the process of accustoming the child to loss of the mother's milk or its substitute. See also PSYCHOLOGICAL WEANING.

Weber-Fechner law: see WEBER'S LAW; FECHNER'S LAW.

Weber's law: the principle that the just-perceptible difference between two stimulus magnitudes is a certain constant fraction of the total magnitude. In mathematical form the law reads:

$$\frac{\triangle R}{R} = K$$

Where $\triangle R$ is the change in the stimulus; R is a stimulus; and K is a constant.

Wechsler Adult Intelligence Scale (WAIS): An individual general intelligence test similar to the Stanford-Binet but which yields both verbal and performance IQ's as well as a total IQ. The test is also believed to have diagnostic significance for certain psychiatric problems.

Wechsler Intelligence Scale for Children (WISC): An individual intelligence test for children 6–16 years of age similar in nature to the Wechsler Adult Intelligence Scale. A preschool test is also available.

we group: the group to which the individual who expresses similar ideas, goals, and feelings belongs. *Contr.* THEY GROUP; OUT GROUP.

weight: 1. a multiplicative factor designed to give more or less relative importance to a score. 2. the relative contribution of a factor toward the final result.

weight-lifting experiment: a psychophysical experiment in which subjects judge the differences in magnitude between small weights.

weighting: the process of determining the relative influence each item or score in a series should have in determining the total score.

Weigl-Goldstein-Scheerer Test: a concept-formation test that requires the subject to sort blocks according to color and shape. Goldstein has used this and similar tests in his studies of brain-injured people.

well-adjusted: a state of harmonious relationship with one's social and physical environments.

Weltanschauung: (literally, *world view*) one's total outlook or philosophy of life. Freud's latter period is often called his *Weltanschauung* period.

Weltschmerz: (literally, *world sorrow*) a sentimental type of sorrow over the state of the world.

Wernicke's area: a cerebral area comprising parts of the first and second temporal gyri and the supramarginal angular gyrus, formerly considered to be the area for understanding spoken language.

Wertheimer, Max: founder of the Gestalt school of psychology (1880–1943). After his graduation from the *Gymnasium* in Prague, Wertheimer studied law for two years, but abandoned it in favor of philosophy and studied at the universities in Prague, Berlin, and Würzburg, where he earned his Ph.D. He held appointments at Frankfurt and Berlin, but left Germany in 1934 because of the political situation. He became associated with the New School for Social Research in New York City. It was in 1910 that Wertheimer made the discovery that led to the founding of the Gestalt school of psychology. Having noticed a stroboscope in the window of a toy shop, he bought it, experimented with it, and convinced himself that the apparent motion generated by successively viewing a series of still pictures could not be explained on a structuralistic basis. In association with Köhler and Koffka he developed and formulated the Gestalt system. After coming to the

United States Wertheimer developed a strong interest in the area of thinking, and this led to the publication of his classic, *Productive Thinking* (1945). In this work he deplores the rigid, associationistic type of drill, which, he argues, leads to blind, unproductive thinking and offers evidence that children can be taught to think by insightful means.

wet dream: a nocturnal emission.

Wetzel grid: a device for plotting height, weight, and age, with norms for development based on the interrelationships among these factors.

Wever-Bray effect: electrical activity generated in the cochlea in response to an external stimulus, also known as aural microphonics. It is not identical with the nervous impulse that goes out over the auditory nerve, but instead appears to be associated with the conversion of the mechanical energy of sound into the electrical energy of the nervous impulse.

w factor: see WILL FACTOR.

Wherry-Doolittle method: a shortcut for selecting a small number of tests that will yield a correlation with a criterion only slightly smaller than the multiple correlation obtained with a large number of tests.

whisper test: a crude hearing test in which the subject, with one ear plugged, stands 20 feet away from the examiner, who pronounces test words in a distinct whisper. The subject is not allowed to watch the examiner's lips during the test.

white: the visual sensations evoked by a mixture of radiant wavelengths approximating those whose physiological action is equivalent to that stimulated by natural daylight; the extreme of the bright end of the series comprising the black-gray-white dimension of visual experience.

white matter: the parts of the brain and spinal cord made up of axons and dendrites that have a pale-gray or white color. Gray matter indicates the presence of cell bodies.

whiteness constancy: the perception of objects as having the same brightness under widely differing conditions of illumination.

white noise: (analogous to *white light*—blending light waves of all lengths) sound effect of a number of random sound waves presented simultaneously.

whiteout: a temporary loss of visual perception due to intense stimulation.

white-space response: (*Rorschach*) a category for responses made to the unblotted portions of the cards.

whole method of learning: learning in which the material is practiced in its entirety. For example, in learning a poem, the poem as a whole would be repeated until memorized. *Contr.* PART METHOD OF LEARNING, in which the poem in the foregoing example would be learned stanza by stanza.

whole object: (*Psychoan.*) a person as an object of love. *Contr.* PART OBJECT.

whole response: (*Rorschach*) a scoring category for responses that make use of the blots as wholes.

wholism: see HOLISM.

Whorf's hypothesis: the assumption that differences in linguistic habits cause differences in nonlinguistic behavior.

Wiggly Block Test: a test of manual dexterity in which the task is to reassemble 9 blocks cut from rectangular blocks in wavy lines.

Wild boy of Aveyron: an allegedly wild boy studied by the French physician, Itard. Considerable doubt has been cast on all reported cases on "wild" children. The most likely explanation is that such children were subnormal to begin with and had been taken out and abandoned by the parents.

will: 1. the function involved in conscious action. 2. the totality of impulses, conscious and unconscious. The term is little used in contemporary psychology because of the long history of conflict between those who uphold the concept of free will and those who insist on a strict determinism in accounting for behavior. The contemporary psychologist is more likely to search for antecedent conditions in heredity and environment as casual factors than to postulate will.

will factor: in factor-analysis studies of personality, the factor correlated with purpose, striving, or persistence.

Will-Temperament Tests: a test of temperamental differences based on samples of handwriting taken in controlled situations.

will to power: the drive to be superior to others and to dominate them. Adler used the notion of the will to power in his theory of superiority and inferiority feelings. See also INDIVIDUAL PSYCHOLOGY.

will therapy: a form of therapy, developed by Otto Rank, based on the theory of the birth trauma, in which the patient is encouraged to assert himself as in separating from the womb and achieving independence.

windmill illusion: an intermittent change in the apparent direction of rotation of a wheel or wheel-like figure. See also STROBOSCOPIC ILLUSION.

wish: a desire or longing, either conscious or unconscious, often without an overt attempt to obtain the object of desire.

wish fulfillment: (*Psychoan.*) the striving of the psyche for freedom from tension. According to Freud, wish fulfillment is most clearly seen in dreams, slips of the tongue, and in certain neurotic symptoms.

wishful thinking: thinking directed more by personal wishes than by objective or rational factors.

witches' milk: a milklike secretion sometimes excreted by the mammary glands of newborn infants.

withdrawal: 1. a pattern of behavior that removes the individual from thwarting or frustration. Withdrawal may become a habitual defense mechanism involving serious symptoms of retreat from reality, drug addiction, alcoholism, etc. 2. removal of the penis during sexual intercourse in order to prevent conception. *Syn.* COITUS INTERRUPTUS.

withdrawal symptoms: a number of physical and mental symptoms, including anxiety, profuse perspiration, cramps, etc., associated with the loss of dependence on narcotics.

within-group variance: the variance that occurs within an experimental condition as contrasted with the variance occurring as a result of different experimental conditions.

wolf child: see FERAL CHILD.

Wolffian duct system: a primitive duct system in all embryos that develops into male sexual organs (epididymides, vas deferens, and seminal vesicles) when testes are present in the embryo. *Contr.* MÜLLERIAN DUCT SYSTEM.

Woodworth-Matthews Personal Data Sheet: a neurotic inventory used largely for screening children or adolescents in educational institutions.

word-association test: see ASSOCIATION TEST.

word blindness: see ALEXIA.

word-building test: a test in which the subject is asked to construct as many words as possible out of a limited number of letters.

word configuration: the pattern of a word—its overall features, length, typography, etc.

word count: a study of the frequency with which certain words occur in written or spoken speech.

word deafness: see AUDITORY APHASIA.

word salad: a meaningless jumble of words. Word salad is a characteristic of certain schizophrenic disorders.

work: 1. physically, the action of a force acting against a resistance. 2. physiologically, the expenditure of energy during bodily activity. 3. psychologically, the completion of a task.

work decrement: a drop in output per unit of time.

working mean: the assumed mean.

working through: (*Psychoan.*) the process of having the patient thoroughly explore and master the conflicts that brought him to therapy.

work-limit test: a test in which each subject performs the same task and the subjects are evaluated on the length of time required to complete the tasks.

work sample: a selected operation taken as representative of an individual's job. Work samples may be used to select new employees or as criteria for the purpose of validating other tests.

worry: an emotional attitude characterized by anxiety about the outcome of future events.

W response: (*Rorschach*) a whole response.

Wundt, Wilhelm: the founder of modern psychology and the leader of the school of structuralism (1832–1920). Wundt, the son of a Lutheran pastor, attended the local schools in Baden, Germany, and later was tutored by one of his father's assistants. After completing one year at the University of Tübingen, he entered Heidelberg, where he took a degree in medicine. But his interests turned toward research in physiology and, because of his deep interest in sensory processes, eventually led him into the field of psychology. In 1875, after one year at Zurich, he went to Leipzig, where he spent the next 46 years. It was at Leipzig that he founded the first experimental laboratory of psychology and trained many of the world's leading psychologists. Wundt was a prolific writer, having published during his career the equivalent of about 54,000 printed pages. He wrote books in the areas of physiological psychology, social psychology, experimental psychology, and philosophy. Most of his important work in psychology was translated by E. B. Titchener, the leading exponent of the structuralistic school in the United States.

Würzburg school: a group of psychologists from Würzburg, Germany, who believed that their introspective studies revealed evidence for imageless thought.

X

xanthocyanopsia: yellow vision; red-green color-blindness in which things are seen as yellow or blue.

xanthopsia: yellow-sightedness; a heightened sensitivity to yellow.

X axis: see AXIS.

X chromosome: see CHROMOSOME.

X coordinate: the abscissa or horizontal axis.

xenoglossophilia: the use of strange, foreign, or pretentious words.

xenoglossophobia: a pathological fear of foreign languages.

xenophobia: a pathological fear of strangers.

xi: see POINT OF SUBJECTIVE EQUALITY.

X-O test: (*Pressey*) a test of attitudes and interests in which the individual either crosses out or circles certain preferences.

x value: see AXIS.

XYZ pattern: a gentic abnormality believed to be related to criminal or aggressive behavior.

Y

yantra: a visual pattern used in meditation.

Y axis: the ordinate.

Y chromosomes: see CHROMOSOME.

year scale: see AGE-EQUIVALENT SCALE.

yellow: the visual experience aroused by radiant energy of a wavelength of approximately 582 nanometers.

yellow-sighted: pertaining to a pathological condition in which there is a heightened sensitivity to yellow.

yellow spot: see MACULA LUTEA.

Yerkes-Bridges Point Scale: an early adaptation of the Binet Scale utilizing points instead of months of mental age.

Yerkes-Dodson law: the generalization that moderate levels of arousal or motivation yield optimal performance.

Young-Helmholtz Theory: see COLOR THEORIES.

y value: see AXIS.

Z

Zeigarnik effect: the finding that interrupted tasks are remembered better than completed tasks, provided that the subject is ego-involved in the uncompleted tasks.

Zeitgeist: (literally, *time spirit*) the spirit of the times.

zeppia: (*R. B. Cattell*) a factor trait identified as a flexible superego.

zero-order: pertaining to correlation coefficients computed from data in which neither variable has been held constant. The typical product-moment correlation coefficient is a *zero-order correlation. Contr.* PARTIAL CORRELATION.

zeta (ζ): the difference between the squares of the correlation ratio and the correlation coefficient. In terms of a formula:

$$\xi = (\eta^2 - r^2)$$

where η = the correlation ratio, or the degree to which the correlation is nonlinear.

r = the correlation coefficient.

zoanthropy: see LYCANTHROPY.

zoetrope: see STROBOSCOPE.

Zöllner illusion: an illusion of visual space perception in which parallel lines intersected by numerous short diagonal lines slanting in the opposite direction seem to diverge. See illustration.

FIG. 28. *The Zöllner illusion.*

zoöerasty: sexual intercourse with an animal.

zoomorphism: the interpretation of human behavior in animal terms.

zoophilia: a strong love or attraction for animals.

zoophobia: fear of animals.

z score: a standard score consisting of the difference between the obtained score and the mean divided by the standard deviation of the distribution—

$$z = \frac{X-M}{SD}$$

Zurich School: the name given to the followers of Carl Jung, who founded his system in Zurich, Switzerland. See ANALYTICAL PSYCHOLOGY.

zygote: a cell formed by the union of two gametes or sex cells.

For those who have strong spiritual needs— even in today's modern world

The cloud of unknowing

Ira Progoff, translator

This extraordinary 14th-century work, about contemplative devotion and the soul's union with God, is astonishingly timely for the pressing spiritual needs of modern man. Written by an English monk, it is a classic of Christian mystical thought. $3.95